NIXON

*The Education
of a Politician
1913-1962*

STEPHEN E. AMBROSE

A TOUCHSTONE BOOK
PUBLISHED BY SIMON & SCHUSTER INC.
NEW YORK | LONDON | TORONTO | SYDNEY | TOKYO

Copyright © 1987 by Stephen E. Ambrose
All rights reserved
including the right of reproduction
in whole or in part in any form
First Touchstone Edition, 1988
Published by Simon and Schuster Inc.
Simon & Schuster Building
Rockefeller Center
1230 Avenue of the Americas
New York, New York 10020
TOUCHSTONE and colophon are
registered trademarks of Simon & Schuster Inc.
Designed by Edith Fowler
Manufactured in the United States of America

10 9 8 7 6 5 4 3 2
10 9 8 7 6 5 4 3 2 1 Pbk.

Library of Congress Cataloging in Publication Data

Ambrose, Stephen E.
    Nixon: the education of a politician, 1913–1962.

    Bibliography: p.
    Includes index.
    1. Nixon, Richard M. (Richard Milhous), 1913–
2. Presidents—United States—Biography. I. Title.
E856.A72 1987 973.924'092'4 [B] 86-26126
ISBN 0-671-52836-X
ISBN 0-671-65722-4 Pbk.

For my brothers Harry and Bill,
who always ensured a two-to-one vote for Nixon
from the Ambrose boys.

CONTENTS

CHAPTER ONE

FRANK AND HANNAH
1878–1912

RICHARD NIXON had no famous ancestors, nor any who were rich. There was not a political leader among them. He came from humble folk and was born in the turn-of-the-century California equivalent of a log cabin.

On his father's side, his progenitors were generally loud, boisterous, emotional, and Methodist. On his mother's side, they were generally quiet, restrained, unemotional, and Quaker. What they had in common was a penchant for taking risks. They were men and women unafraid to move on west with the frontier.

Nixon's maternal ancestors were Germans who came to England to fight for Cromwell, and who received as their pay an estate in Timahoe, Ireland. Their name was anglicized from Melhausen to Milhous. In Ireland, the Milhouses became Quaker converts of William Penn, and in 1729 Thomas Milhous and his family migrated to Chester County, Pennsylvania. A century later, his descendants were living in a Quaker colony in Ohio. In 1854, when Richard's grandfather, Franklin Milhous, was six years old, the family moved west again, to Jennings County, Indiana. The family was abolitionist, and the farm was a way station on the Underground Railroad. In 1879 Franklin Milhous, a widower at age twenty-eight, married Almira Burdg. Together they raised two sons and seven daughters; the daughters included Richard Nixon's mother, Hannah, born in 1885.

The Milhouses were gentle Quaker folk, living an unpretentious and frugal life. Almira was a schoolteacher; Franklin, a farmer. Ordinary though their occupations were, they shared an

9

urge to migrate. California beckoned, for all its usual reasons—the agreeable climate, the orange groves, the space, the low price of land—and because in 1887, just east of Los Angeles, the Society of Friends had founded a Quaker community, Whittier, named for the famous Quaker poet, John Greenleaf Whittier. The founders chose a site away from the railroad line, a site suitable for the peaceful, conservative Quakers, who wanted to grow their crops and live their lives away from the city and the hurly-burly of modern life. The lure proved irresistible to many Indiana Quakers, including nearly the whole of the large Milhous clan. Whittier soon became the largest Quaker colony in the United States.

In 1897 Franklin, his mother, his wife Almira, and his nine children made the move. They brought with them the doors, window frames, and much of the lumber from the farmhouse in Indiana. Franklin loaded it on a freight car, along with his livestock. On the outskirts of Whittier he planted orange groves and a nursery. A good husbandman, he was successful enough to become a prominent member of the community, well known for his honesty. His children helped him graft the plants; he guaranteed the pedigree and hardiness of each plant, and if it sickened and died, or did not grow true, he would replace it. He also traded actively in real estate. He saved enough money to establish a trust fund at Whittier College for his grandchildren's education.

While Franklin tended the crops, Almira made their home into a center for social and religious activities, with her dining room as the focus of events. She loved gathering the constantly growing Milhous family around her; in time her family reunions ran to forty and fifty people. They used "thee" and "thou" and other Quaker expressions in their ordinary speech. Religion, work, and family were the center and almost the circumference of their existence. The religion was neither overbearing nor overpowering, rather peaceful and comforting, but it was always there—in speech, in dress, in mannerisms, in daily prayers and Bible readings. It was a religion without doctrines, one that put a great stress on individual conscience and responsibility.[1]

Franklin was a jovial man, liked by everyone and adored by his family. He took Almira and the children on trips, to San Francisco and Yosemite. "Father loved music," Hannah later told reporter Bela Kornitzer. "He sang in the church choir and played the organ. Later on, he took up the accordion. Evenings, he used to sing hymns and then read aloud to us. His favorite tale was James Whitcomb Riley's *Bear Story*." Hannah said her mother Almira "was even more appreciative of the pleasures of life. . . . She loved social contacts and special events, whether in our home, picnics at the park, at the beach, the mountains, or at church. She loved to work in the yard, tending her plants or caring for her chickens." As parents, Hannah recalled, "Father and Mother were full of love, faith and optimism. I don't recall ever seeing them in despair. . . . [They] never talked loud—never yelled orders."[2]

Richard Nixon had vivid memories of his grandmother Almira. "My grandmother set the standards for the whole family. Honesty, hard work, do your best at all times—humanitarian ideals. She was always taking care of every tramp that came along the road. . . . She had strong feelings about pacifism and very strong feelings on civil liberties. She probably affected me in that respect. At her house no servant ever ate at a separate table. They always ate with the family. There were Negroes, Indians and people from Mexico—she was always taking somebody in."

Most of all, Almira held the family together. "Every year at Christmas and usually once during the summer we had a family reunion. . . . She was a prolific letter writer. On birthdays she composed rhymes and couplets and sent them to us." She used the plain speech, "thee" and "thou," exclusively, but her daughters did not use it with their children.[3]

Almira was a staunch Republican, as were most Quakers with their abolitionist backgrounds and dedication to hard work and thrift. "She virtually worshipped Lincoln," Richard Nixon later recalled. "On my thirteenth birthday she gave me, in addition to a very welcome five-dollar bill, a picture of her idol. Underneath, written in her own hand, was the last part of Longfellow's *Psalm of Life*. I can remember part of it even now:

> *Lives of great men oft' remind us,*
> *We can make our lives sublime,*
> *And departing, leave behind us,*
> *Footprints on the sands of time."*[4]

Almira and Franklin Milhous' emphasis on religion, family, and duty dominated Hannah's youth, and left her with lifelong values. To an outsider her life may have seemed dull and dispiriting, her boundaries limited by the backwater town where nothing ever happened, but she found Whittier a source of strength and comfort. Her father gave her security; her mother, inspiration and guidance; her sisters and brothers and the entire Quaker community provided playmates aplenty, while church, school, and work were outlets for her energy.

Discipline in the family was done verbally rather than physically, and the words of criticism were spoken softly rather than shouted. "Father never paddled us," Hannah recalled in her old age. "Mother switched my ankles once with an apple twig."[5] By high-school age, she had a dark, brooding look. Of medium height, she was exceedingly slender, bony in her shoulders and face. She usually did up her long black hair in a knot. Her eyes were dark and deep-set. Her lips were narrow and pursed, her mouth a bit too wide for her narrow face. Her nose was deep and broad at the nostrils, narrow and pinched at the top. The line of the curve looked a bit like a ski jump, a trait her son Richard inherited. All the photographs taken of her during her adolescence show a serious, almost forbidding face, and the testimony of her childhood friends and family agrees that she was indeed a serious young lady.

She was no great beauty, and she had no talent that set her apart from the community, aside from her devotion to her religion, which even in Quaker Whittier went beyond the norm. One of her brothers-in-law thought she was too gentle, too soft-willed, and called her "the angel unaware." But an acquaintance found her to be "cranky and Puritanical" and a family friend dismissed her as a "colorless little thing."[6] She did not appeal to the boys—one of her sisters said, "Hannah sometimes went out with a group but she never had a single date. . . . "[7]

After graduating from Whittier High School, Hannah entered Whittier College, which she attended for two years before dropping out to teach school. On February 15, 1908, at a social gathering at the Friends Church in East Whittier, she met Frank Nixon. Whatever impression she made on the other young men in the community, she swept Frank off his feet. He walked her home that night, and as he later testified, "I immediately stopped going with the five other girls I was dating, and I saw Hannah every night."[8]

FRANK NIXON had arrived in California a year earlier, marking the end of a westward migration of Nixons that had begun in the seventeenth century, when Frank's ancestors had moved over to County Wexford, in Ireland, from Scotland. The name, in Celtic, was variously spelled Nicholl, Nicholson, Nicholas, Nickson, and Nickerson, all meaning, roughly, "he wins" or "he faileth not." In the 1730s the Nixons became part of that great wave of emigration of Scotch-Irish to America. Later critics of Richard Nixon, referring to him as a "black Irishman," missed the truth. Whatever the cause of the adult Nixon's dark moods, introspection, and depression, it was not Irish blood, at least not such as any Catholic citizen of the Irish Republic would recognize.

James Nixon was the first to come to America. He settled in New Castle County, Delaware, within twenty miles of Hannah Milhous' ancestor Thomas. James became a substantial, if not prominent, citizen; his will, dated May 16, 1773, included a sixty-pound bequest to his wife, Mary, forty-five pounds to his daughters, a hundred-acre farm to his son George, and two slaves to his other son, James, Jr. Both sons fought in the Revolution, George crossing the Delaware with Washington to fight in the Battle of Trenton, and both moved west after independence, following the frontier to Ohio. George Nixon III enlisted with Company B, 73rd Ohio, in 1861, and fought and died in the Battle of Gettysburg. He is buried in the national cemetery. He left behind eight children, including a son, Samuel Brady Nixon.

On April 10, 1873, Samuel, then aged twenty-six, married a twenty-year-old schoolteacher, Sarah Ann Wadsworth. They had five children, three boys and two girls. The second-oldest, Francis Anthony Nixon, was always called Frank. He was born on December 3, 1878, in Vinton County, Ohio; he became Richard Nixon's father.[9]

Shortly after Frank's birth, Sarah contracted tuberculosis, the most dreaded disease of the nineteenth century, thought erroneously to be inherited. Samuel sold his farm, piled the children into a covered wagon, and headed south for Georgia and the Carolinas, where he hoped Sarah might recover in the warmer climate. But her condition worsened, then became acute. In despair Samuel returned to Ohio, where, in January 1886, Sarah died in her father's home.[10]

Frank went to live with an uncle, while his father, Samuel, tried to overcome his grief and poverty. Samuel worked in a pottery factory, taught school in Vinton, and carried the mail. He eventually saved enough money to buy a forty-acre farm and bring Frank home. "When we moved there," Frank's younger brother, Ernest, remembered, "Dad's only assets were a five-dollar bill and a hen setting on a nest of eggs. He gave those last dollars to the man who helped us move. Still, we never begged, nor did we let on we were next to destitute. He said: 'Here we are and it's root, hog, or die.' "[11]

In 1890, when Frank was eleven years old, Samuel remarried. Frank's stepmother was harsh, demanding, even cruel. "She was hard and beat Frank," a relative recalled.[12]

He had other problems. "Frank and I attended a one-room country school, known as Ebenezer, miles from home," Ernest later reported. "We were newcomers; poor, strange, and badly dressed. The big boys would follow us home through the woods to pick a fight. Frank was the more aggressive of us, slow to anger but a wild bull if things went too far."

Frank could not put up with this stepmother, school, or poverty. At fourteen, only past the fourth grade, a consequence of all the disruptions in his life, he quit school and ran away from home. He took a job as a hired hand with a local farmer at $13 per month, plus the right to put a calf he had bought on the pasture. In the fall he sold the fatted calf. He had promised to send his earnings home to his family, but, as Ernest related, instead he used the profit from the sale on his wardrobe. "He seemed to take keen delight in showing his former classmates that he was dressed just a bit better and was more mannerly. He acquired a pride that became the armor of his body and soul." [13]

Life as a farmhand, however, had little appeal. "We usually had milk and bread for dinner," Frank recalled. "Fifty to seventy-five cents a day was just about tops in wages for a farmhand in those days." [14] Restless by nature, skilled with his hands, he was willing to work. "The dignity of labor was . . . my brother's philosophy," Ernest declared. "He liked to quote the Scripture: 'In the sweat of thy face shalt thou eat bread.' " He became a jack-of-all-trades, and something of a rolling stone, as he journeyed across Ohio, taking jobs as a glass worker, potter, house painter ("I even painted Pullmans at one time"), potato farmer, telephone linesman, motorman, and carpenter. (Ernest stayed in school, eventually earned a Ph.D., and became a professor at Penn State.)

Frank did not prosper, he did not starve, he did not improve his station in life. He knew a great deal about machines and tools, little about people. He was argumentative, cantankerous, opinionated; he shouted a great deal; he was critical of his bosses; small wonder that every spring found him working at a new job.

Like Hannah Milhous, Frank was deeply religious. Unlike her, he was demonstrative about it. He came from a long line of frontier, fundamentalist, Bible-thumping Methodists, which placed him in a tradition about as different from that of the Quakers as one Protestant sect can be from another. The Methodists were loud, in their sermons, in their hymns, in their greetings, in everything. They had a set of strict rules for folks to live by and were dogmatic about them. These precepts both fit and helped shape Frank's personality. Hannah's Quakerism led her to love God; Frank's Methodist faith led him to fear God.

Neither Hannah nor Frank ever smoked or drank. In Hannah's case, no one around her did either, but in Frank's case abstaining was far more difficult. He lived in many a rough environment, working beside roustabouts of all types, men who tempted him with their tobacco, whiskey, and tales of amorous adventures. He never gave in, a mark of both the depth of his religion and the strength of his willpower. Nor did he abstain through avoidance— he led a hectic social life, with many dates and parties.

He was a handsome young devil, of average height but big in the shoulders and hands, as befit a workingman. When dressed for a social event, he wore his dark hair slicked down and precisely parted. He had a fine full face, a strong but not oversized nose and jaw, deep, penetrating eyes, and a firm mouth. He wore stiffly starched high collars, precisely tied bow ties, double-breasted suits, always with a watch chain hanging down the front and a handkerchief hanging out of the breast pocket. In short, he cut quite a figure. His good looks, careful grooming, and animated ways drew people to him, but unfortunately his loud and aggressive personality drove many of them away.

Even in the hard times of 1896, when he was seventeen, Frank worked hard enough and long enough to save some money. ("I never missed a day's work in my life," Frank later boasted to an interviewer.) He spent his money on his wardrobe, but still had enough left over for a magnificent four-year-old sorrel horse, plus all kinds of accouterments, such as trimming on the reins, gold cloth for the saddle, and ribbons everywhere.

Along with his Methodist faith, Frank had inherited Democratic politics. Thomas Jefferson and Andrew Jackson, not Lincoln and Grant, were the heroes of his youth. But Frank was a boy with a questioning, not an accepting, mind. Whatever his inheritance in politics, by age seventeen he had lost faith in the Democrats. He blamed President Grover Cleveland for the Depression. In 1952, he explained that he had learned the value of a dollar the hard way, and that he was thus "all for" the Republicans' sound money policy.

An incident in the 1896 presidential campaign completed Frank's conversion. William McKinley was coming to town, for a parade and other hoopla; McKinley himself would ride in a carriage at the head of the parade. Frank got his colt brushed, put on all its finest gear, dressed himself to the teeth, and rode out to join the tag end of the parade. The parade marshal came riding along and spotted him. Much impressed, the marshal called out, "Come on, son. Ride up to the front of the line with me."

Frank galloped to the front and soon was at the side of McKinley's carriage, in the place of honor. When the parade ended, McKinley got out of the carriage and walked over to Frank. He patted the colt and said, "Mighty fine horse you have there, son. Finest I ever saw." Turning to leave, he called out, "How are you going to vote, son?" Frank replied loud enough for the surrounding crowd to hear, "Republican, of course!"

"Naturally," he later explained, "I was elated. I was too young to vote in that election, but in 1900 I voted for McKinley. I've been voting Republican ever since." [15]

In 1904 Frank decided to give the West a try, and spent eighteen months in Colorado, but he discovered that for all Colorado's beauty and appeal, it was a tough place to find a good-paying job. He returned to Ohio, where he went to work for the Columbus Railway and Light Company. He became a motorman on the street-car line. It gave him an opportunity to wear a fancy uniform, with a bandmaster's headpiece, covered with braid, a double-breasted suit with bright buttons, and a gold watch chain across the coat.

Unfortunately, the working conditions were not so pleasing. He operated the streetcar from an open vestibule, and in the wintertime his feet froze. One particularly cold day, he organized the motormen of Columbus to demand better conditions. Together with another delegate, Frank went to a young lawyer with political ambitions. "If you'll help us get legislation against the open vestibules," Frank told the lawyer, "we motormen will help you get elected to the state senate." The lawyer agreed, got elected, introduced the necessary legislation, and, against the opposition of the company, got it passed.[16]

It was Frank's sole excursion into either politics or labor organizing. Rather than use his victory as a base for advancement in Columbus, he indulged his rootless, restless nature and headed west again, this time for California, the land of perpetual summer. He carried with him an enthusiastic letter of recommendation from his employer, an indication that his organizing efforts had not been held against him.[17]

He arrived in Los Angeles in January 1907, and immediately got a job with the Pacific Electric Railway Company as a motorman, his letter of recommendation stating specifically that he was "an experienced streetcar man." For eighteen cents per hour he ran old red cars along the narrow streets between Whittier and the sprawling town of Los Angeles. His good start came to a crashing halt when he hit an automobile and forthwith lost his job.

He found work on a ranch east of Whittier—back to being a farmhand again. He also discovered that the Quakers so dominated the area that there was no social life outside the church. He began to attend the meetings and the socials. Day laborer or not, he still cut a fine figure in the evening. He made a good enough impression to be invited to the Milhous home following a Valentine Day's party at the church. That night he walked with Hannah and lost his heart. He saw her every night thereafter, through the winter and spring.

WHY HANNAH kept seeing him, her sisters could not understand. For one thing, Frank was always free and open with physical embraces, which made them uncomfortable. As Richard Nixon's cousin the novelist Jessamyn West relates, "There was not much hugging or kissing or daughters sitting on their fathers' knees in Quaker families."[18] West, with her novelist's insight, describes Frank as "temperamentally . . . a Democrat and a Methodist" who converted to Republican and Quaker. "He was very unlike my birthright relatives," she continued, "who were quiet, subdued, inclined to see both sides of every question. Frank saw one side: his; and he was not bashful about letting you know what was wrong with your side."[19]

Not only was Frank boisterous, argumentative, and much too loud to suit the Milhous girls, he was also just a common laborer, far beneath Hannah's station as the daughter of a leader in the community. Hannah's youngest sister, Olive, so thoroughly disapproved of Hannah's continuing to go on dates with Frank that she climbed into a tree, took out her tablet, and wrote, "Hannah is a bad girl."[20] After Hannah married Frank, Jessamyn West recalled, "Every Milhous daughter was convinced that she had married beneath her."[21] Hannah's younger sister Jane remembers her father taking her aside some years after the wedding and saying that he hoped she would marry a Quaker, "someone who has been raised our way. It is best for people to marry those of like faith."[22]

In the face of this opposition, Frank persisted, not surprising considering his bullheadedness and considering how badly he had been smitten by the fair Quaker maid. What is surprising is Hannah's persistence. Everyone she valued urged her to end the relationship. Frank had no education, no culture, no particular skill, no prospects. Their personalities, traditions, and experiences were at opposite poles. In spite of all, Hannah was drawn to Frank as much as he to her, and she had the strength of character to ignore the gibes of her sisters and friends, the disapproval of her parents, and the differences in temperament between her and Frank. On June 25, 1908, four months after they met, Frank and Hannah were married.

IT WAS a union of opposites that was hugely successful. Hannah's calm ways, her compassion for others, and her peaceful thoughts were a nice balance to Frank's excitability, his inability to see someone else's point of view, and his aggressive nature. He softened under her gentle guidance, made a formal conversion to the Quaker faith, toned down a bit.

As a married man, Frank had to give up dancing. Quaker disapproval was one factor, but the other stemmed from his self-knowledge and his self-discipline. Frank explained his reason to

Jessamyn West's father: "When his arms went around a woman, his amorous propensities were instantly aroused." He avoided temptation and embarrassment by not dancing, but he did not completely suppress his exuberance and appreciation for the opposite sex. "He never saw my mother, a plain woman," West wrote, "without exclaiming, 'Grace, I swear you get prettier every time I see you. How do you do it? I want your recipe. Come here and let me give you a hug.' " Grace would always protest afterward that Frank had embarrassed her, but as West commented, "She was also secretly pleased." [23]

Frank was even more expansive in his compliments to Hannah. He was aware of the value of her love. In 1952, in his first interview as the father of a famous son, he told Richard Gardner, "I knew I had picked the very best. And I haven't changed my mind in the forty-four years since then." [24]

In the first months of their marriage Frank continued working at the citrus ranch. When Hannah got pregnant, her father invited the couple to live in his house and gave Frank a job as a foreman on his ranch. The first son, Harold, was born in 1909. Within a year Frank pulled up and moved his family to Lindsay, north of Bakersfield, to work at yet another ranch that Frank Milhous had bought on speculation. In 1912 he had saved enough money to return to Southern California and buy—with his father-in-law's money—a small lemon ranch at a place called Yorba Linda. He had either bad luck or poor judgment—the land he picked had a clay subsoil, did not drain well, and produced inferior lemons. Frank supported his family by doing odd jobs of whatever kind. He found enough time to build a two-story frame house, and build it well enough so that it still stood and was occupied three-quarters of a century later.

His commitment to his religion deepened, and he began to teach Sunday school for the Quakers of Yorba Linda. He used the opportunity to let out a bit of his frontier Methodist upbringing, even among the staid Quakers, and as Jessamyn West remembered, he was popular with his pupils. "I doubt that Frank Nixon could do anything halfheartedly," she wrote, "and this trait is appealing to young people. . . . Frank was certainly ardent in his Sunday-school teaching. His cheeks flamed, and his voice trembled."

Frank would express his strong political convictions in his teaching; he was, West declared, "the first person to make me understand that there was a great lack of practicing Christianity in civic affairs." He may have voted Republican, but "what Frank had to say about probity in politics pointed . . . straight to Norman Thomas," at least so far as West was concerned. "All of us who had been in Frank's class had been convinced that Christians should be political, and that politics, if not Christian, should at least be ethical."[25]

Hannah was pregnant again while Frank was building the new home. She cared for her son, Harold, and worked endless hours in the lemon grove, planting, irrigating, pruning. Although she had her family only ten miles away in Whittier, and her church activities, essentially she led the lonely life of a farmer's wife before the age of telephone, television, and the automobile.

WHEN CECIL PICKERING moved to Yorba Linda on August 1, 1910, his was the third white family to arrive. Frank Nixon's family was fifth or sixth. Pickering described the place: "It wasn't a town. It was turkey mullein, cactus, rattlesnakes, tumbleweeds and tracks." Yorba Linda was on the edge of the desert. There were terrible dust winds, with no trees to offer protection. But overall the climate was ideal, and if the soil was good and if you could get water to it, the land grew marvelous citrus crops. Frank's venture was only one of many—between 1910 and 1913 the entire area was planted to citrus orchards, and Yorba Linda began to turn into a town. Frank helped build it—he worked on the first warehouse in town, plus most of the new homes. The water, source of Yorba Linda's life, came from the Anaheim Union Water Company canal that ran through the town, smack in front of Frank's house.[26]

The people coming into Yorba Linda were mainly young couples, and nearly all Quaker. They imposed a Puritan streak on the town; there were no liquor stores, no bars, no dance halls, no theaters, nothing at all to do—except church activities. Soon an elementary school went up. Mary Skidmore, who taught in the first grade, said that the teachers were informed by the school board that they were forbidden to dance, or talk to men on the streets. The teachers felt spied upon and knew for a fact that they were gossiped about.[27]

In short, for all its idyllic location, its booming economy, and its Quaker domination, Yorba Linda was like every small town "back east," a place where everyone knew everyone else and talked about each other's activities without embarrassment or hesitation. It did not urge, but rather insisted upon, conformity; it also insisted that the church have a monopoly on leisure time and entertainment activity. That suited Frank and Hannah. Frank livened things up by arguing politics, but people tolerated his harsh manner because he gave so much of himself to the church.

They were known as people who paid their bills on time, which was good for their reputation but harmful to Frank's fortunes. He would not go into debt, not even to improve his land.

Friends told him he could sweeten up that clay soil of his with loads of manure, but Frank always replied, "I won't buy fertilizer until I raise enough lemons to pay for it." But he couldn't raise the lemons.[28]

So through the first years of their marriage, as their sons were born and began to grow, Frank and Hannah lived on the edge of poverty. "Many days I had nothing to serve but corn meal," Hannah confessed years later. "I'd bring it to the table and exclaim, 'See what we have tonight—wonderful corn meal!' "[29] Frank could not afford to indulge his sartorial proclivities—one shirt and one pair of pants had to do, along with a suit for church.

He always found work, and in 1912 earned enough to hire help of his own in the lemon grove. But as soon as Frank was able to buy a tractor he dispensed with the hired help. He hated to spend money. "Uncle Frank wouldn't spend a nickel for a firecracker," his niece said. "He was . . . too tight with money. He didn't have to be as tight as he was."[30] Hannah too dressed plainly, and didn't indulge herself in any extravagance. "She was a great saver," a relative said.[31] Although the Nixons lived on a farm, and in due course had a family of growing boys, they never had a dog or cat or any other pet. They did not take vacations. They worked.

YORBA LINDA
1913–1922

ON JANUARY 9, 1913, Hannah Nixon was ready to deliver her second child. There had been a record-breaking cold snap the previous two days, and although it had moderated a bit, Frank had brought an extra wood stove into the house and kept both stoves going full blast through the day and night. When contractions began, he feared that the doctor from Whittier would not arrive in time, so he went down the road to the neighbors to ask for help. Ella Furnas, a young widow with two small children of her own, accompanied the increasingly nervous Frank back to his house, where she did what she could for Hannah. Although she had borne two children, "I didn't know anything about delivery" and she was frightened. The doctor, with nurse Henrietta Shockney, arrived just in time for the birth, which came at 9:35 P.M. The baby boy weighed eleven pounds, was dark-haired and brown-eyed, and— nurse Shockney recalled—had a "powerful ringing voice." [1]

Hannah named him Richard, after Richard the Lion-Hearted, with Milhous for a middle name. The next morning, a neighbor reported, Frank "threw his hands in the air and danced around the yard," shouting "I've got another boy." Hannah's recovery was long and difficult, as had been the case after Harold's birth. When Richard was nine months old, she went to the hospital for a mastoid operation. After leaving the hospital, she went to Whittier to live with her parents while she recuperated.

At that time, the infant Richard became his grandmother Almira's favorite. Hannah was breast-feeding, and when the baby was full, Almira would walk, cuddle, and burp him. Almira was impressed by the strength of his voice: "Seems like when Richard cries he makes such a *loud* noise," she said. But although others in the family complained about "such a squall and noise," Almira was pleased with that good set of lungs. Her mother had been a Quaker preacher, and she announced that with his voice, her grandson Richard would make a good preacher or a good teacher.[2]

Hannah recovered, and soon was back in Yorba Linda, caring for Frank and her children, working in the lemon grove, and nursing a second child. Her sister Elizabeth Harrison had a son six months younger than Richard, but was too ill to nurse the baby. So Hannah took him to her breast, along with her own son.[3]

By the time of his first birthday, Richard had quieted down considerably. When he was almost two years old, Hannah had another son, Donald. With three boys to support, Frank worked harder than ever. He had a hired hand, Ollie Burdge, to help him. Burdge ate at the family table. He remembered Hannah as "the quietest woman." She "would hardly ever sit down and eat with us," and was "generally cooking and bringing stuff to the table . . . and then she'd feed herself." Richard, Burdge said, "got along with his dad; he always sat with his dad at the table, and his dad always fed him."[4]

Frank sometimes would take the boy along with him when he went to work. By the time he was three years old, Richard was riding around with the groceryman, making deliveries in his buggy. Richard liked seeing new things, new places, new people. He had a lively imagination. Ollie Burdge brought his fiancée to the house, he recalled, and she sat Richard on her lap. "He was quite a talker. He was telling her about how, when he got big, he was going to kill wild animals, and elephants, and lions and tigers."[5]

He also liked to be read to. In 1918, when Hannah was pregnant again, Frank got a hired girl to help her around the house. The girl, Elizabeth Guptill Rez, later recorded that at night she would tuck in the boys in a little back bedroom. Then she would read poetry to them. Richard especially liked James W. Riley's poems, and asked to have them read over and over. Then there were prayers: "He'd clasp his little hands and close his eyes, and you could just feel it," Elizabeth recalled. "He was really praying instead of just saying his prayers."[6]

Richard was fearless, in a little boy's way. He would not sit down in a wagon, for example, no matter how hard Hannah tried to force him to do so. One day in 1916, Hannah asked an eleven-year-old neighbor girl, Elizabeth Eidson, to ride with her to a friend's house in order to watch Richard while she held Donald in

her lap and drove the horse. But Richard refused to sit, the horse went around a short corner, the boy toppled over, and a wheel ran over his head, cutting his scalp badly. Elizabeth ran to pick him up: "His scalp was hanging down . . . I held the scalp edges together while walking him back to the buggy . . . it was awful." Hannah drove to Dr. Marshburn's, where the wound was stitched together.[7]

The Anaheim canal ran across the front of the Nixon homestead. Its slippery dirt banks made it dangerous for small boys, but its two or three feet of flowing water on a hot day made it irresistible. Frank forbade his children to play near the ditch, or to swim in it, but Harold was an irrepressible youth, eager for fun and adventure, and he swam often. Once Frank caught him, Merle West (Jessamyn's brother) related: "I still remember Uncle Frank pulling Harold out by the scruff of the neck [and] beating him so hard his hollering could be heard all up and down the ditch." Another time Jessamyn saw Frank haul Richard and Harold out of the ditch, then fling them back in again, shouting, "Do you like water? Have some more of it!" An aunt who was with Jessamyn began screaming, "You'll kill them, Frank! You'll kill them!"[8] Frank's reaction and punishment may have seemed extreme to the witnesses, but small children had drowned in the ditch and Frank could never break his children from swimming in it no matter what the punishment.

In 1918, when Richard was five, Hannah was pregnant again. Twelve years later, in a college essay, Richard described the birth of his third brother from his own point of view, in the process revealing some keen powers of perception: "Mother was away on a visit. [Father] came over to where we boys were quarreling over some toys and told us that there was a little doll over at the hospital for us, a real, live doll! Naturally we then began to quarrel over whose doll it would be, although each of us wished to have it merely to keep one of the others from getting it." But Frank assured his sons that they would all have equal rights to the doll.

A few days later, Grandmother Almira "scrubbed us all up, especially gouging into the depths of our ears, and helped us to dress, for we were going to see our 'doll,' which we had learned by this time was a baby. At least, that was what brother Harold, who had reached the all-knowing age of nine, had said it was. He had told us secretly that it wasn't a doll but a baby. He warned us, though, not to let on he'd told us so."

Richard was disappointed when the baby came home—his mother named him Arthur, after yet another English king—because, as he wrote when he was seventeen years old, "a tiny baby is not as pretty as a doll." Busy growing up himself, Richard paid little attention to Arthur, but he was observant enough to note "how his eyes changed from their original baby-blue to an almost black shade; how his hair, blond at first, became dark brown; how his mouth, toothless for five months, was filled with tiny, white teeth . . . how he learned to roll over, then to crawl, and finally to walk."[9]

THAT SAME YEAR, 1918, there was another addition to the household. Frank made a trip to Ohio for the funeral of a brother-in-law. He brought the widow and her two sons home with him. The Wildermuths moved in and stayed for a year, until the widow found a place over in Fullerton. Her son Floyd was just the age of his cousin Harold.

Six-year-old Richard looked up to his ten-year-old brother and cousin, and was always trying to hang around them when they wished to be left alone. They took advantage of his eagerness to please them by sending him off on errands. In the process, they also took advantage of a characteristic he was beginning to show, competitiveness. So, Floyd relates, "We would bet him that he couldn't get up to the house and bring those cookies or a bottle of milk or something and get back to us before we could count to a hundred. He'd take off on the run, we'd sit there and visit until we saw him coming. Then we'd pick up the count somewhere in the nineties . . . and we'd just get him under the wire at about ninety-seven. He'd get there all puffing, but he'd always win."[10]

In an outburst of anger Frank would apply physical punishment, using a strap on his boys. It was quick and soon forgotten. Hannah's methods were different. In 1968, Richard recalled, "My mother used to say later on that she never gave us a spanking. I'm not so sure. She might have. But I do know that we dreaded far more than my father's hand, her tongue. It was never sharp, but she would just sit you down and she would talk very quietly and then when you got through you had been through an emotional experience." So, Nixon declared, "In our family, we would always prefer spanking." He recalled that when five-year-old Arthur was caught smoking a cigarette, he had pleaded, "Tell her to give me a spanking. Don't let her talk to me. I just can't stand it, to have her talk to me."[11]

When Richard was five or six, he came home with his hands and mouth full of grapes. Hannah asked where he got them. He said he had picked them from the neighbor's large grape arbor.

"You go right in the house and get the pennies you've been saving," Hannah ordered. "Then you go back where you got the grapes and pay the lady for them." Richard objected—pennies were hard to come by. Hannah insisted, Richard did as told, and the neighbor lady was embarrassed and sad, but Richard made her take the pennies.[12]

Hannah was serious about life. Innumerable oral reminiscences about her stress her dedication, her physical energy and capacity for hard work, her calmness, the depth of her religious convictions, and her service to others. Long before her son called her a saint, in his last speech as President, people around Yorba Linda and Whittier had habitually used the word "saint" to characterize her. None mentioned much joy in her life, there are no funny stories, no memory of pranks or laughter. She allowed no extravagances, nor any frivolous pursuits; it stung and embarrassed the boys, for example, that their parents would not give them even a quarter for some firecrackers on the Fourth of July. The family never ate at a restaurant, nor took even the briefest of vacations.

Hannah's tightfistedness had a purpose. If she was not ambitious for herself, or even for Frank, she was for the boys. She insisted that they have a college education; she achieved her goal. One relative recalled, "She instilled in the family this seriousness about growing up and being somebody."[13]

Frank too encouraged his boys to think big. "There was a drive to succeed," Nixon told columnist Stewart Alsop. "My mother and father instilled in us the desire to get going to be good not just at one single thing but at everything."[14]

Frank argued with everyone, including his small sons. At the dinner table he and they would get so carried away that Hannah would cry out, "Now hush, all of you." Frank would snap back, "You make them hush, and I'll hush."[15]

Merle West ate many an evening meal with the Nixons. He recalled, "Don would try to outshout Frank. He would just stand up and bellow at him right back, like two bulls. . . . Sometimes, just to get a word in edgewise you had to holler to do it." West said there were "tempestuous arguments" between Frank and his sons Don and Harold, when "their shouting could be heard all through the neighborhood."[16]

How Hannah put up with all that shouting, none of her friends and relatives could ever understand. She was, one friend said of her, "born to endure."[17]

Hannah dealt with Frank's big mouth and terrible temper by keeping quiet and never crossing him when he was angry. Her son Richard, already showing signs of being an acute observer, deliberately followed her example. "I used to tell my brothers not to argue with him," Nixon recalled. "I learned early that the only way to deal with him was to abide by the rules he laid down. Otherwise, I would probably have felt the touch of a ruler or the strap as my brothers did." [18]

So there was a lot of noise and violence in the Nixon home, with Richard and his mother trying to keep the peace between Frank and his other two sons, and seldom succeeding. In his memoirs, written after his Presidency, Nixon provided a psychological self-analysis of the effect on him of the daily dinnertime confrontations around the table: "Perhaps my own aversion to personal confrontations dates back to these early recollections." [19]

The easiest way to avoid the tension was to avoid his father. "When he was a small boy he wanted his mother to do things for him," Hannah's youngest sister, Mrs. Olive Marshburn, remembered. "He asked her rather than his father." Other forms of escape included daydreaming and reading. "I can still see him lying on the lawn, sky-viewing and daydreaming," Mrs. Marshburn said.[20] Floyd Wildermuth added, "I can recall that when we'd want Dick to do something, we could never find him. He was always gone. Dick would hide out. We got so we'd hunt him." Once Floyd and Harold found him in the pump house, reading. Hannah had taught him to read when he was five years old. Floyd noted that he read avidly, "everything he could get his hands on. He would disappear with a book. We were always wondering where he was and trying to get him in on his share of the work." [21]

The daydreaming and reading allowed him to escape not only Frank and his shouting matches but the dullness and routine of Yorba Linda life. At night, lying in his bed, Donald and Arthur and Harold sleeping beside him, he would listen to the train whistle. Hearing it, he wrote in his memoirs, "I dreamed of the far-off places I wanted to visit someday." [22]

It is a moment worth pausing over. The seven- or eight-year-old boy, crowded into one small bedroom with three brothers, out there on the last frontier, in a clapboard house built by his father that was the California equivalent of a log cabin, listening to the train whistle in the night and dreaming of the wonderful places he was going to and the great things he would do. The romance of that whistle, its promise of opportunity and adventure, had appealed to American boys since before the Civil War. Richard's response to the sound of the whistle was similar to that of large numbers of Americans. It was, he said as an adult, "the sweetest music I ever heard." [23]

But in his case, the direction the sound moved in was reversed. Instead of imagining himself hurtling westward on the train, he had to imagine himself hurtling east. Back to the city, back to civilization, not away from it.

As a child, he hardly traveled at all. The short hop to Whittier to see his grandparents and join the numerous family reunions was about all. He never went up to the mountains that he saw around him, and only once or twice to the ocean. He had no hobbies, not even those two most common forms of recreation for rural boys, hunting and fishing. Instead, he traveled in his mind. From his grandmother, from Aunt Olive, and from other relatives he borrowed books and magazines. The Marshburns subscribed to the *National Geographic*. "Nearly every time I visited them I borrowed a copy," Nixon wrote in his memoirs. "It was my favorite magazine."[24]

His ambition was to be a railroad engineer, a job with prestige that would allow him to travel. The one toy the boys possessed was a small electric train set; whenever they played with it, Richard insisted on being the engineer. His hero was a Santa Fe Railroad engineer who lived in Yorba Linda.[25]

WHEN HE BEGAN grade school, in 1918, he participated actively in the school-yard baseball and football games, but his coordination was poor, he was slow of foot and below average in size, so in no way did he stand out. His talent was for music. "He had a natural ear," Hannah recalled. "Before he was seven years old, he could play the piano without discord. At seven, he started piano and violin lessons with my brother Griffith."[26] The music lessons continued, and Richard stuck to them without complaining, although he was never wildly enthusiastic.

He was not a boy who enjoyed pranks and mischief. "He was very mature even when he was five or six years old," his mother said. "He was interested in things way beyond the usual grasp of a boy his age. He was thoughtful and serious. 'He always carried such a weight.' That's an expression we Quakers use for a person who doesn't take his responsibilities lightly."[27]

"He wasn't a little boy that you wanted to pick up and hug," Jessamyn West said. "It didn't strike me that he wanted to be hugged. He had a fastidiousness about him." It was a trait that intensified; as a high-school student, one of his cousins remembered, "He once said he didn't like to ride the school bus because the other children didn't smell good." He went to great pains to brush his teeth. He would ask his mother to smell his breath to make sure he would not offend anyone on the bus. He insisted on a clean, starched shirt each morning.[28]

But it was his seriousness and his mental ability that most impressed his contemporaries. Virginia Shaw, a neighbor child who was in the third grade in 1918 when Richard began school, was astonished when his teacher brought him in to recite a long poem. "I remember all of us were very, very envious that this little five-year-old could come in and recite this long poem." [29]

California-style, he came to school barefoot, as did his classmates. Mary Skidmore, his teacher in first grade, said that he came to school every day in "a freshly starched white shirt with a big black bow tie and knee pants. He always looked like his mother had scrubbed him from head to toe. The funny thing is, I can never remember him ever getting dirty." Skidmore also recalled that Hannah came to her in the first week of school to insist that he be called Richard, not Dick.

He sat at the back of the room in class, because he gave his teacher no trouble and did not have to be watched. "He absorbed knowledge of every kind like a blotter," she said. "In that year I think he read no less than thirty or forty books, maybe more, besides doing all of his other work." On Mary's recommendation, he skipped second grade altogether and moved into third grade in 1919.[30]

He liked books, he enjoyed reciting and was good at it, and he responded to an audience, speaking with confidence and talent. Virginia Shaw recalled a contest held at the Quaker church. The children stood on a small platform and recited poems. "So we all learned poems. Harold learned one, and I learned one, and my brother Gerald learned one, and Richard was in on it. So was Mildred Dorsey and her older sister. We got up on the platform and said these pieces. Of course, Harold and I were confident we were going to win. But Richard won it and we were so jealous. We just really thought it was because he was so little and had such a long piece. We were really quite disappointed that he won." [31]

His excellent memory helped him to store up grievances. Don Nixon related: "He wouldn't argue much with me . . . but once, when he had had just about as much of me as he could take, he cut loose and kept at it for a half to three quarters of an hour. He went back a year or two listing things I had done. He didn't leave out a thing. I was only eight, and he was ten, but I've had a lot of respect ever since for the way he can keep things in his mind." [32]

The most influential teacher in Richard's life was his father. Frank taught Sunday school; at the age of five Richard began attending regularly. Jessamyn West described Frank as "ardent" in his teaching. His theme was contemporary politics, and the need for practicing Christianity in civic affairs.[33] Richard, at six or seven years old, participated actively. "He took serious part in the discussions," a classmate recalled. "He expressed opinions. He had a remarkable memory for things that he had learned." [34]

Frank's politics were more intense than consistent. He had

chided Hannah for voting for Wilson in 1916, and boasted that he was a lifelong Republican, but by the early twenties he had become disenchanted with the Republicans and in 1924 voted for Bob La Follette's Progressives. In 1928 he returned to the Republican Party, voting for Hoover, but in 1936 he voted for Roosevelt.[35] But whoever his candidate, Frank was ardent about him, and politics in general. The other boys were not much interested, but Richard was fascinated. By age six he was reading the newspapers, the front page, not the comics, and discussing public events with his father. At age seven, Jessamyn West next remembered, Richard explained to his classmates on the way to school "the merits of some upcoming candidate and the issues he represented."

Merle West, who was present, later told Jessamyn, "I didn't understand a word he said."

"Where did a boy of seven pick up such ideas?" she asked.

"Frank, of course."[36]

When the Teapot Dome scandal broke in 1924, Frank denounced the corrupt politicians and the high-priced lawyers who defended them. Richard read the newspapers for more details. "When I get big," the eleven-year-old boy told his mother one day after reading the paper, "I'll be a lawyer they can't bribe."[37]

In 1919, there was an oil boom in Yorba Linda and Frank made a major financial error. A speculator offered him $45,000 for his property. Frank turned it down. "If there's oil on it, I'll hang on to it," he said. It turned out to be no better for oil than it was for lemons, and when Frank did sell, he got less than 10 percent of what had been offered. Worse luck followed. On the next move he chose Whittier, rejecting his wife's advocacy for a place in Santa Fe Springs. Two years later a big gusher came in on the Santa Fe property.[38]

In later family legend the story blurred and the two events ran together, so that in 1960 Hannah told a reporter, "After we moved [from Yorba Linda], oil was found under the lemon grove—oil that would have made us millionaires if we had remained—but while we were there the lemon grove only kept us poor." Richard Nixon repeated the we-might-have-been-millionaires story in his farewell address to his Cabinet and staff on his last morning as President.[39] But in fact oil was never found on the Yorba Linda property.

By 1922, Frank was having more trouble with his lemon grove. The trees were mature, but not producing. He decided to seek security for his family, so he sold the Yorba Linda place and moved to Whittier, where an oil boom had started. There he built a house and found work in the oil fields. Richard was nine years old when his family left Yorba Linda. It was not exactly leaving the farm for the city—Yorba Linda had become a small town, and Whittier was hardly Los Angeles—but, nevertheless, for a boy Richard's age, it was a move that meant expanding horizons.

RICHARD WAS a boy who attacked with words, rather than his fists. His talents were mental, not physical. He could never beat Harold, or his cousin Floyd, or almost anyone else in sports competition, but he beat them all as a speaker and as a student. People were amazed by his ability to memorize, by the interest he took in national politics, and by his knowledge about and understanding of public issues. Nearly everyone who knew him remarked on his serious nature, his competitiveness, and his ambition.

He grew up in an atmosphere of security, surrounded by love. He turned instinctively to his mother; he liked to have her sit with him while he read, and otherwise be with her. His father frightened him sometimes, and appalled him at others, but he never had cause to doubt Frank's love or protection. No one in Yorba Linda ever would have dared to touch one of Frank Nixon's boys.

He worked hard, not only in his studies but in the lemon grove as well. He had to hoe weeds for his father, and help with the irrigation. Although small for his age, he developed a strong set of shoulders and a tough physique. His hair was dark, long, and obviously home-cut, a great swath of it falling down nearly to his eyes, but neatly parted. He had a full share of baby fat in his cheeks, with dimples when he smiled. Dark, deep-set eyes and dark eyebrows, a nose that was thin at the top and wide at the base, and a hard-set, determined mouth were the features that stood out on his face. His movements were generally awkward, except at the piano.

He was an intimate part of a larger family, the huge Milhous clan spread all across the landscape. The get-togethers at his grandmother's house gave him a sense of belonging. Beyond the family, however, his circle of acquaintances was small, limited to the few dozen neighbors and fellow students at the small schoolhouse. He did meet Mexican-American children at school, but for the most part his contacts were exclusively with people like his parents, hardworking, deeply religious, strongly conservative Quakers.

Religion, family, and school were the center of his life. There were daily prayers, and church services of one kind or another four times every Sunday. There he learned tolerance, and the Quaker distaste for showing emotion or expressing feelings physically. He learned to love poetry, and to recite it before an audience. He learned modesty in all things. Most of all, he learned that God helps those who help themselves, and that it was by the sweat of his brow that man earned his bread.

Shyness and reserve with an individual or in a small group, complete confidence when speaking to a large audience—these were characteristics that Richard Nixon displayed throughout his life. In part, they were simply natural to him. That was just the way he was. But some of it came from his culture and his heritage. Many Quakers are shy and reserved in their personal relations but confident and successful in dealing with large affairs. Perhaps the style of Quaker meetings, the kind Richard Nixon attended, contributed to this blending of private reserve and public confidence. Sitting silently together, trusting to an Inward Light to lead him to his own experience of God, without intermediary rites, church, creed, or priesthood, was a personal and powerful experience. Everything was directed inward; there was no release of emotion through prayers recited together, or hymns sung together. The system could give to some who went through it a great inner strength, but it could also lead to a suppression not only of an outburst of religious feeling but of personal emotions generally. Coupled with the Quakers' traditional customs of plainness in dress and aversion to touching, the result could be extreme shyness.

The other side of Quaker meetings could be an equally powerful experience. The boy Nixon was encouraged to stand up and speak out, or pray, before the congregation. It was an individual decision, done only when the spirit moved him. What he said was usually more or less devoid of emotion, often more rational than religious. It was more a public speech than it was a personal disclosure.

All this is not meant to claim that the Quaker experience was the elusive key to Richard Nixon's character. That would be much too pat in so complex a case. It is meant to suggest that the impact of his Quaker heritage on his personality has been underestimated. Nixon spent his adult life giving public speeches; he learned how to do it as a small boy, in a plain Quaker meeting, expressing his convictions on nonpersonal matters to an audience of his elders. Throughout his adult life, he bottled up his emotions, in direct contrast to his father, who loudly expressed his personal feelings on every possible occasion, but in direct conformity to his mother's ways.

Many of his attitudes came from Frank's dual role as father and Sunday-school teacher. What Frank preached was a simple doctrine; as his son later summed it up, it was "that in America, with hard work and determination a man can achieve anything." [40] At the time he moved to Whittier, in 1922, most of Frank's life seemed to prove the opposite. Few men worked harder, or were more determined, than Frank, but he had achieved little. Still he had faith, which, it turned out, was not misplaced.

And anyway he was not doing all that badly. He always had a job and an income. His family ate well, all four boys had suits for church, he was a solid and respected member of the community ("It was considered quite a loss to this little town when he moved," a Yorba Linda neighbor recalled).

As an adult, Richard Nixon remembered it differently. "We were poor," he declared in a 1968 campaign film. "We had very little. We all used hand-me-down clothes. I wore my brother's shoes and my brother below me wore mine and other clothes of that sort. . . . "[41] "We never had any vacations. . . . We never ate out —never. We certainly had to learn the value of money." But he was able to put it all into perspective: "We had a pretty good time, with it all."[42] "I think [of] that wonderful statement that General Eisenhower made. . . . He was talking about his early days in Abilene and he said, 'I suppose that we were poor, but the glory of it was that we never knew it.' And that was what we were then."[43]

Jessamyn West echoed that remark. She said that as a candidate Nixon may have found it politically expedient "to put on . . . log cabin clothes," and that his contests with Jack Kennedy and Nelson Rockefeller may have made him feel that he had an underprivileged youth. "I only know that I, living in the same neighborhood, in the same kind of house, with more or less the same money or lack of it, wearing hand-me-downs, working every summer, did not then feel poor—and now feel that those years were a Midastime in my life." She was certain that no one in Yorba Linda ever thought of the Nixon family as poor.[44]

What the townspeople did think of Richard was more admiring. Although "he wasn't a boy that you wanted to hug," he was one people enjoyed listening to as he recited poetry. They were impressed by his powers of memory, and by his intelligent and active interest in politics at an astonishingly young age. But no one outside his family was close to him. He was not the sort who made deep, lifelong relationships as a boy. Except for his mother, Harold, and Don, there was no one he confided in.

The inability to trust anyone is one of the principal personality traits of Nixon as an adult, a theme he returned to again and again in interviews, private conversations, and his writings about himself. He insisted that "in my job [he was then Vice-President] you can't enjoy the luxury of intimate personal friendships. You can't confide absolutely in anyone."[45] What was the source of this trait? Nixon claimed that it went with the territory, that all professional politicians felt as he did, but that simply was not true. But then there is nothing in his inheritance or in his environment to explain his inability to trust. As a youth, he was surrounded by trusting people whom he had every reason to trust completely. In this regard, his childhood was so normal as to be dull. No one abused him; there were no traumas, no betrayals, only love and trust.

There is another mystery. Although he was shy and reserved by nature, embarrassed by his father's slap-on-the-back approach to people, and although he feared ridicule, he was at his best when he stood before a group, the center of attention, reciting a poem, or playing the piano or violin. All his life he was sensitive to criticism, yet all his life he put himself into positions and places in which criticism was inevitable. He had to force himself to so expose himself. In the process he developed a tremendous willpower, an ability to make himself do things, no matter how distasteful or frightening.

CHAPTER THREE

WHITTIER
1922–1930

WHITTIER, IN 1922, was an integral part of the great Southern California boom, but in its own special way. Like other towns in the area, Whittier almost doubled in population during those boom years, as did the level of business activity. But unlike most boom-towns—nearby Los Angeles, for example—Whittier had no bars or saloons, no brothels or speakeasies, no gambling dens, nothing that was raucous. For purposes of social life or entertainment, it was little more than a larger version of Yorba Linda.

Business was good, however, and kept getting better. Whittier offered unlimited opportunity, not for big business—Whittier had no factories and served as headquarters for no great corporations—but for the small entrepreneur. With a minimum monetary investment and a maximum of hard work, combined with a little imagination, a man could make himself into a substantial small businessman and a respected citizen, as an auto dealer, a drugstore owner, a service-station operator, a clothing or grocery-store owner, real-estate agent, or almost anything else. Richard Nixon lived there through his formative years, from nine to twenty-one, and the atmosphere that he absorbed from daily life in Whittier became as much a part of him as his education, his religion, and his physical growth. It was an atmosphere of success, with the rewards going to those who worked the hardest and were the smartest.

He saw it all around him, and most of all he saw it at home, literally, because his home was also his father's grocery store and the center of the family's life. To that store Frank Nixon, a quintessential small-business man, devoted his life; from it he drew his livelihood; with it he became, finally, a success.

"My father had a deep belief in the 'little man' in America," Nixon wrote in his memoirs. "He opposed the vested interests and the political machines that exercised so much control over American life at the beginning of the century." Frank regarded Standard Oil as a blight and chose to be supplied by the less well-known Richfield Oil company when he opened his service station. Later, as the Nixon Market grew, he became "a vociferous opponent of chain stores," which he feared would crush the independent operator.[1] To stave them off, Frank worked that much harder, and his business prospered. In the process, he proved to himself, to his son, to his neighbors, that America really was a country in which hard work and determination would be rewarded with success.

WHEN FRANK MOVED to Whittier, there was frantic oil drilling going on in the area. After building a frame clapboard house on South Painter Street, Frank went to work in the oil fields. After two years as a roustabout, he decided the only way to get ahead was to own his own business. With some savings and some borrowed money, he bought a place in East Whittier and opened a gasoline station between La Habra and Whittier, the only one on the boulevard. Business was good—by 1925 he was selling $5,000 worth of tires alone in a month. He expanded, adding small boxes of fruits and vegetables. When the Friends built a new church, he bought the old one, had it moved to his lot, and opened it as a general store. Eventually he leased the gasoline station to a neighbor and concentrated on the store.

Frank and Hannah spent virtually all their waking hours in the store, except on Sunday—and Frank managed to keep it open then, as well as attend church. And when their sons were not in school or church, they were in the store. "He worked us kids to death," Don Nixon said of his father, but Don also noted that because they worked together, they had "more of a real family life than anyone in the country."[2]

One of the features of the Nixon Market was Hannah's homemade pies. She sold them for thirty-five cents each, "and they were the most delicious pies you ever ate in your life," one customer declared. To produce them, Hannah got up at three or four in the morning to bake the day's pies. Then she worked in the store all day. "I've sometimes wondered how she survived," a friend said.[3]

Everyone in the family worked so hard that they seldom had time to eat their evening meal together. Hannah would put on a pot of stew, and Frank and the boys would help themselves when they could snatch a few minutes away from the store. Or they would take a steak from the meat counter and throw it in a frying pan.

Frank continued to bluster his way through life. He had a "nasty, loud way," a niece who worked part-time in the store remembered. "I was always frightened of Uncle Frank."[4] When something went wrong, "you could hear him bellowing clear uptown." He would yell at Hannah too, "but he loved her dearly." He could not stand it when she was gone five minutes out of his sight. "Hannah up there?" he would holler out when she was in the kitchen, out of the store.[5] And he would yell at the customers. Don Nixon recalled that his father "would argue politics with anybody who came in . . . and he couldn't stand Democrats. . . . My mother used to cringe during some of these arguments."[6] All the boys would conspire with their mother to keep Frank away from the customers; eventually Frank began spending his time exclusively preparing the meat, leaving waiting on the customers to his wife and children.

Many of the customers were Mexicans, from the nearby Leffingwell Ranch. Frank carried them on credit, not so much out of kindness as out of necessity. When the Depression began in 1930, and tramps started showing up in Whittier, Hannah would feed them. "She never turned a tramp away from the door," her son Richard remembered. Frank would object. "My father thought they ought to be made to work before helping them out. But Mother ran the house like a charitable operation. . . . Looking back, I think we had more people who did less, working for us, than any other house."[7]

HAROLD WAS an outgoing, easygoing, good-looking boy, popular with the other children, always on the lookout for a game or a bit of fun. Donald too was irrepressible, the only one of the boys who could give back to his father as good as he got. Arthur was spoiled —his parents, Frank especially, had wanted a girl, and until he was old enough to protest effectively, Arthur was dressed in girl's clothes and wore a girl's hairdo.* But Dick, as he was now called by everyone save his mother, was nicknamed "Gloomy Gus." His nose, it seemed, was always stuck in a book. Frank "could holler all he wanted," Floyd Wildermuth recalled, "but Dick would have a book and be out reading in the corner or behind the shed or anywhere he could go where Frank couldn't find him."[8]

One of Dick's favorite books was *Tom Sawyer*. He liked the episode where Tom tricks Ben Rogers into whitewashing his fence so much that he learned it all by heart. Nearly fifty years later,

---

* The same indignity was visited upon Milton Eisenhower, Ike's youngest brother, for the same reason.

when one of Mark Twain's relatives, Cyril Clemens, visited him in the White House, Nixon recited the episode without a mistake. He told Clemens he had first recited the piece in a grammar-school Tom Sawyer play.[9]

Dick had a vivid imagination, and an impressive ability as a writer. In November 1923, when he was ten years old, he wrote a "letter" that read:

> MY DEAR MASTER:
> The two boys that you left me with are very bad to me. Their dog, Jim, is very old and he will never talk or play with me.
> One Saturday the boys went hunting. Jim and myself went with them. While going through the woods one of the boys triped and fell on me. I lost my temper and bit him. He kiked me in the side and we started on. While we were walking I saw a black round thing in a tree. I hit it with my paw. A swarm of black thing came out of it. I felt a pain all over. I started to run and as both of my eys were swelled shut I fell into a pond. When I got home I was very sore. I wish you would come home right now.

He signed off "Your good dog, Richard."

Whether this strange document was a school assignment or a flight of fancy, or what, is not known. Nixon's numerous psychobiographers have assumed that it was a genuine letter to his mother, and consequently go to great lengths to analyze its hidden meanings, but all that is positively known about the document is that it exists, and that when Hannah gave it to Bela Kornitzer, who was interviewing her for a biography of her son, she presented it as "just another sign of her son's intelligence."[10]

Shortly after his eleventh birthday, Dick wrote another document, a job application. It was perfectly lined up on both sides, with small, neat penmanship, free of crossed-out words, and it showed not only his promise as a writer but also his eagerness to get out of the grocery store and away from Frank's voice. The document responded to an ad in the Los Angeles *Times*.

> DEAR SIR:
> Please consider me for the position of office boy mentioned in the Times paper. I am eleven years of age and I am in the Sixth grade of the East Whittier grammar school.
> I am very willing to work and would like the money for a vacation trip. I am willing to come to your office at any time and I will accept any pay offered. My address is Whittier boulavard and Leffingwell road. The phone num-

ber is 5274. For reference you can see, Miss Flowers prin-
caple of the East Whittier School. Hoping that you will
accept me for service, I am

> Yours truly,
> RICHARD M. NIXON [11]

Despite the businesslike presentation, he did not get the job.

He was conscientious about his schoolwork. Classmate Raymond Burbank remembered that even on Saturday afternoons,
"Dick very seldom came out and played. He was usually studying,
and there were remarks and cracks made about it." As a consequence of his bookworm habits, the long hours he spent at work,
and his shyness and sense of unease when with a friend or a small
group, he was not popular. "He was a little different from the rest
of us," another classmate recalled. "He was a kid you respected.
He knew everyone, he was very good in class, and when you talked
to him you always had his full attention. He was friendly, but not a
guy you'd put on a backpack and go fishing with." [12]

One characteristic that bothered his classmates was his love of
argument. Like Frank, he enjoyed it for its own sake, although he
was more inclined to use logic and reason than the strength of his
voice to make his points. "He liked to argue about anything," a
classmate said. "No matter what was discussed, he would take the
opposite side just for the sake of argument." She recalled the day
they returned from a picnic and Dick started an argument over
which would be more useful to take with you into the wilds, a goat
or a mule. First Dick argued for the goat, then the mule. [13] Another
time he was walking with Merle West and posed the question,
"Would you think it would be wiser to marry a pretty girl or a smart
girl?"

West thought to himself, "Oh, of all things," and walked
away. [14]

Dick's lack of popularity bothered him; he compensated with
aggressiveness. "Oh, he used to dislike us girls so!" Harriet Palmer
Hudspeth declared. "He would make horrible faces at us. As a
debater, his main theme in grammar school . . . was why he hated
girls. One thing was strange, though. He said he didn't like us, but
he didn't seem to mind arguing with us."

He was terribly stuffy. Harriet recalled going on a seventh-
grade outing to an amusement park at Long Beach with Dick. "My
mother made me promise not to go on the roller-coaster. All the
others went but . . . Dick made me stay on the ground. True to
form, he wouldn't let me disobey my mother. Then, when the others came back, he went for a ride alone." [15]

Clearly, he needed all the help he could get from Dale Carnegie's *How to Win Friends and Influence People*, which he would read aloud at night with his family, discussing passages together.[16] It did not help much, at least initially—he just was not lovable, not like his brothers.

That he knew it, that he resented it, he made clear a half century later, when shortly after his retirement he told an aide, Kenneth Clawson, "What starts the process, really, are laughs and slights and snubs when you are a kid." But, he added, "if you are reasonably intelligent and if your anger is deep enough and strong enough, you learn that you can change those attitudes by excellence, personal gut performance while those who have everything are sitting on their fat butts."[17]

He did earn his classmates' respect, if not their love. He brought home As, mostly, to Frank's delight. He was the valedictorian for his grammar school. And, to no one's surprise, he was the champion debater.

His first debate, in seventh grade, put him on the affirmative on the proposition "It is more economical to rent a house than to own one." He came to his father for help. Frank believed the opposite of the proposition, but he drilled his son in the arguments against owning. Dick won the debate. Later that year, Dick was a member of a two-boy team opposing a girls' team on the subject "*Resolved*, that insects are more beneficial than harmful." Dick spent several days in the library, gathering facts, and he consulted his uncle Ernest, a horticulturist, who provided him with additional arguments in favor of bugs. He won that debate too.

DICK'S RECREATION was playing the piano, at which he showed some talent. At Christmas 1924, at Grandmother Almira's house, he played for the family. His aunt Jane Milhous Beeson had studied music back East and was an accomplished performer and teacher. She suggested that Dick could develop his skills by coming to Lindsay, a Quaker enclave in central California, to live with her and take lessons. Hannah agreed, so Dick spent the first half of his twelfth year with Aunt Jane, Uncle Harold, and his cousins Alden and Sheldon in Lindsay.

He took daily piano lessons, and violin lessons from another teacher. His cousin Sheldon Beeson was also taking lessons. "I tried to encourage them to have a little competition," Jane Beeson remembered. "I told them that the one who would get in the most practice would get a prize. Of course, Richard got it. Any kind of a game, why, he would just go all out to win. He was just that nature."[18]

Memorizing came easily to him. Nor did he lose what he memorized. Fifty years later, he could still sit down and play through "Rustle of Spring," which he learned from Aunt Jane. Whether he had a great talent or not cannot be known, because he did not pursue a musical career. Mrs. Beeson thought he did. At his 1969 inaugural, she sat in the President's box with him during a concert. André Watts was playing. She leaned over and whispered to the President, "Now, Richard. If thee had practiced more on the piano, thee could have been down there instead of up here!"[19]

He loved music all his life. In his memoirs he said he had two great unfulfilled ambitions, to direct a symphony orchestra and to play an organ in a cathedral.[20] But much as he loved music, it did not provide the challenge he was looking for.

Aunt Jane told Dick, "You can do anything you want to do if you want to do it badly enough. The reason people don't accomplish their ideals is because they just don't have the try and the tenacity and the ambition to see it through." The principles sounded good to him; the thing was that he wanted to put them to use in a wider field than piano practice. Sunday school, for example, where he not only played the piano but participated actively in discussions. Aunt Jane recalled that "he was encouraged to get up on his feet, speak, and witness and give his testimony and lead meetings and that sort of thing."[21]

The six months in Lindsay included a semester of school. Dick was in the second half of seventh grade. He had his first course in American history; his teacher, Aunt Jane said, was "inspired. Dick became fascinated with the Constitution and the lives of the people who helped to formulate it." Dick read biographies of Washington, Jefferson, Lincoln, and others, children's biographies designed to teach and inspire, and he did learn, and he was inspired. He continued to read the newspapers avidly, and once repeated to Aunt Jane a remark he had made earlier to his mother: "When I grow up, I'm going to be an honest lawyer so things like that [the Teapot Dome scandal] can't happen."

One day he was helping his cousins cut corn for Uncle Harold. The boys started throwing the corn at each other instead of into the wagon. Mr. Beeson gave his two sons a solid whacking. Dick walked over to him. "Uncle Harold," he said, "I was throwing the corn too. I'm just as guilty as they are, so you must also punish me." Mr. Beeson grumbled that he should not do it again and stomped off.[22]

IN JUNE 1925, Dick returned to Whittier, the store, and his own family. Arthur greeted him with a solemn kiss on the cheek; Dick later learned that he had asked their mother if it would be proper to greet Dick with a kiss, since he had been away so long.

Most people did not much like Arthur—one neighbor said he was "terribly spoiled" and that no one wanted to be around him—but Dick did. In an English composition he wrote when he was a freshman in college, Dick related fond anecdotes about Arthur, including the time Arthur got caught at age five showing "the world that he was a man by getting some cigarettes out of our store and secretly smoking them back of the house." A gossipy neighbor saw him and told Hannah. Dick commented, "I have disliked that neighbor from that time." [23]

In his freshman composition about Arthur, Dick wrote that in the summer of 1925 "Arthur . . . became slightly ill; just a case of indigestion, we thought. But a week went by and his condition became worse instead of better. He began to become sleepy; he did not want to eat; he wanted to rest and sleep." Doctors were summoned; they shook their heads. One took a spinal tap; Dick recalled his father coming downstairs after the test. It was the first time he had seen his father cry. "The doctors are afraid that the little darling is going to die," Frank said.

The parents sent Dick and Don to live with an aunt, so that they could give full-time care to Arthur. A few days later, on August 11, the aunt woke them at midnight and drove them home. Arthur was dead. The doctor listed the cause as "encephalitis or tubercular meningitis." [24]

Dick took it hard. "He sank into a deep, impenetrable silence," his mother said. In his memoirs, Nixon wrote, "For weeks after Arthur's funeral there was not a day that I did not think about him and cry." [25]

Frank too was hard hit. He half believed that the tragedy was a judgment from God, and thereafter refused to open his market or service station on Sundays. He became, one member of his church thought, "extremely religious, almost to the point of being fanatic." Another recalled that he would get up to testify in church and shout, "We must have a reawakening! We've got to have a revival! We have got to get the people back to God!" [26] He began driving his family to Los Angeles to revival meetings, where they heard such evangelists as Paul Rader and Aimee Semple McPherson. At one of the Paul Rader revivals, Nixon told Billy Graham in 1962, "We joined hundreds of others . . . in making our personal commitments to Christ and to Christian service." [27]

Frank's reaction to Arthur's death was typically flamboyant; Dick's was deeper and lasted longer. It made him determined to do even better, to make up the loss to his parents. Five years after the funeral, Dick wrote, "And so when I am tired and worried, and am almost ready to quit trying to live as I should, I look up and see the picture of a little boy with sparkling eyes, and curly hair."[28] The image was enough to make him work harder, try harder.

The effect of Arthur's death on Richard Nixon has been speculated on by Nixon's psychobiographers in greater detail than any other incident of his childhood. The assumption is that the event had to have had a major impact on Nixon's developing character, because the death of a sibling *always* has a great impact on young children—guilt feelings leading to various kinds of neurotic behavior being the most common. But this is an assertion that is not proved. There is no evidence whatsoever that Nixon's reaction to his brother's death was in any way pathological. Death is always difficult for young children to deal with, but deal with it they must. Incurable child illnesses brought childhood death to many American households in the first half of this century. Tens of thousands of American children went through the experience of losing a sibling. Just because it was common, however, does not necessarily mean that Nixon was unaffected by it; it does remind us that he had seen other children die and could not have felt that God had singled out the Nixon family for special punishment. Whatever factors and experiences made Richard Nixon the man that he became, the death of Arthur was not one of the major ones.

Except in this sense, that he used Arthur's death as a spur to work harder and to try harder. Frank interpreted the tragedy as God's wrath, and reacted to it by promising God that he would rest and praise God on Sundays. Richard rejected his father's interpretation. He turned the tragedy around and made it work for him, as yet another reason to strive for more.

ONE DAY months after Arthur's funeral, Dick saw a customer shoplifting. She was a regular, with a large family, respected, and—in Hannah's words—"one of our best accounts." After Dick's report, Hannah watched the woman the next time she came in, and sure enough the customer slipped a roast beef under her coat. It happened three days in a row. Hannah went to the police; the officer in charge said he would arrest the woman next time.

"Well," Hannah said, "you wouldn't have to publish anything in the papers if she were arrested, would you?" The policeman said he had no control over the papers.

Hannah talked the problem over with the family. Frank wanted an immediate arrest. But the woman's sons were Dick's classmates, and he disagreed. "Let's drop the whole thing," he suggested. "You can't let them arrest her. You know what it will do to those boys to learn that their mother is a thief. Work it out some other way."

The next day, Hannah followed the woman out to her car. "Is there something bothering you?" Hannah asked. No, the customer replied, nothing.

"Look under your coat," Hannah said, before blushing, then turning and running back into the store.

The following morning the shoplifter came to Hannah. Tearfully, she confessed, then offered to pay a little each month until she had made up for what she had stolen. She begged Hannah not to let her husband know. Hannah agreed. "My husband thought the woman would never pay us back," Hannah recalled, "but Richard was sure that I had done the right thing. It took months and months, but eventually she paid us every cent. Richard *was* right."[29]

The store was a family operation. Everyone had specific responsibilities. When Dick was old enough to drive, his parents put him in charge of the vegetable counter. Over the next six years, he would get up each morning at 4 A.M. to drive the pickup truck to Los Angeles, where he would select produce from the farmer's market, then return to Whittier, where he set up the vegetables for the day. Merle West noted how well he did the job: "Boy, I mean, old Dick could peel those grimed-up leaves off the lettuce and tomatoes and make them look like new again. He would set them up and fluff them and get the good ones on top."[30] Years later, Nixon told an interviewer, "Never again will I go by a vegetable stand without feeling sorry for the guy who has to pick the rotten apples out of it."[31]

Despite his artistry with the lettuce, despite his skill on the piano and with the violin, and despite the long hours he spent in that old truck, Dick had no mechanical ability whatsoever. Gadgets that required any manual dexterity at all simply baffled him. One day he ran out of gas. He walked to the nearest station, bought a gallon, went back, and poured it into the tank. But the truck would not start. Dick ground away until the battery was exhausted. The problem was that the truck had a vacuum tank. There was no gas pump, and the gasoline had to be sucked into the carburetor through the vacuum tank.

Giving up, Dick hitched a ride back to Whittier. Harold filled a small can with gasoline, then drove Dick back to the truck in his Model T Ford. At the truck, Harold took the plug out of the vacuum, filled the vacuum tank, gave the truck a push, and it started.

Cleaning up, Harold turned to his brother. "Dick," he said, "in your studies, you've studied about a vacuum tank, haven't you?"

"Sure."

"What's the principle of the vacuum tank?"

Dick explained the principle, concisely and accurately.

"That's the trouble," Harold snorted. "You know it all, but you're not practical. You don't know how to use it." [32]

For his part, Harold was a marvel with gadgets. He was especially good with electronics. He set up a radio in the store, with a microphone back in the house connected to it, so that when a radio station was switched on he could broadcast directly through it. Dick was best at putting on fake programs. He would introduce a song, then play it over the radio. When a salesman came into the store, Dick would do an "advertisement" about the man's product, then say it was featured that day in the Nixon Market. He found he liked pretending, and was good at it—the radio gag was never discovered by any of the awestruck salesmen. [33]

IN THE FALL of 1926, Dick entered high school. Living in East Whittier, he was about halfway between Whittier High and Fullerton High, but the bus service went only to Fullerton, so he chose it. For Dick, coming from the small East Whittier grammar school, Fullerton High must have seemed monstrous. It had a thousand or so students and a representative cross section of Southern California population—rich kids, poor kids, middle-class kids, Quakers, Catholics, Mexicans, others. Alma Chapman, who made the move to Fullerton with Dick, felt "apart" from the other students, a hick. So did Dick, which reinforced his natural shyness and reserve.

The competition of high-school sports appealed to him, even though he was a boy who did not enjoy fighting. Don once recalled that "Dick used his tongue more than his fists." Whenever tempers flared, Dick would talk his antagonist out of a fight. "I remember we used to have plenty of fights," Don said, "but they were mostly verbal—and I think I lost them all." [34]

Sports were ways for Dick to be one of the boys, something he had always found difficult. Furthermore, organized violent activity —football especially—was pure fun for him. The greatest of fun, in fact, the one thing in his life he could throw himself completely into purely for its own sake. In all other things, winning, not enjoyment, was his goal. But in football he could hurl all of his 140 pounds at his opponent knowing that he was going to lose the contest and not mind a bit.

He had a reputation not only for doggedness but also for fair play. In his arguments and debates, according to one of his classmates, he would often twist the truth, and otherwise act unfairly in order to win. But not in football. There was a motto stuck up in the locker room that quoted Teddy Roosevelt: "Don't flinch, don't foul, but hit the line hard!" Dick adopted it as his own, and his team-mates and coach agreed that it fit.[35]

In grade school, he had played on the soccer team. In high school, at his father's urging, he went out for football, basketball, and track. There were long hours of practice involved, much hard work, and much frustration. "Dick just didn't seem to have the feel for it," a teammate said of his athletic abilities, but he would appear faithfully for practice every day. Frank encouraged him by coming to watch the practice sessions, and although Dick never made the starting team, he stuck it out.[36]

That he did so was little short of amazing, considering his lack of success and considering his overcrowded schedule. Between sports, schoolwork, study, the store, and church, he hardly had time to sleep. In fact, he slept far less than normal. A classmate said, "I often worried about his health, because on my way home from my dates, I'd see him at his dining-room table, poring over the books at one-thirty in the morning. Then he would get up at four and go to Los Angeles and get the vegetables." Dick kept to that brutal schedule through his high-school years and on into college.[37]

In class, he took the usual courses, English, history, math, science, and his favorite, public speaking. In it he learned the techniques of gestures, speech, enunciation, and vocabulary. He continued his debating activities.

In the fall of 1928, regular school-bus service to Whittier High began, and Dick transferred. Many teen-agers find a transfer midway in their high-school careers to be disconcerting, but not Dick. He already knew a number of the students, and anyway, as his Whittier principal, O. C. Albertson, put it, "He was a self-starter. He wasn't shy at Whittier." But, Albertson added, "He was just interested in being left alone enough to do the work he felt was important. He was too busy to be the center of any clique." A friend put it a bit differently: Tom Bewley said that "his mind was always much too busy for him to keep his attention on small talk."[38]

His inability to participate in casual conversation, a handicap that he never overcame, was also noted by his family. His aunt Olive said that "in his teens he would . . . grow weary of the small talk which went on in gatherings, and he would go away by himself to a secluded place, to read or just to be by himself. I always felt that he had a longing to be in educated company, where he could learn."[39]

At Whittier High he signed up for prelaw, telling classmate Richard Heffern that he thought he would study law, then go into politics.[40] Knowing that successful politicians are joiners of clubs, he signed up for as many as he could—the Latin Club, the debate team, the school newspaper, the school orchestra, and the athletic teams.

Like many teen-age boys, he was greatly concerned about his appearance, but as in athletics, he somehow could never get it quite right. Heffern recalled that "Dick either had pants too long, or they were too short." He usually wore a necktie, and still insisted on having a clean, starched shirt every morning. "Give me anything to iron but Richard's shirts," one of the girls who helped Hannah declared. "He's too fussy." [41]

Although most of his fellow students thought of him as a grind, a goody-goody, and an overachiever, he was not above having a bit of fun. He and his cousin Merle pooled their resources and, for $300, bought a Model A Ford. On one of their first outings they drove into Los Angeles to attend a burlesque show, something quite daring for two Quaker boys to do. They double-dated together. "He wasn't all that serious," Merle commented years later; in the privacy of the backseat of the car with his girl, Merle said, "he was very normal!" [42]

He was no movie star for looks, but he did his best with what he had. His eyebrows were getting darker and more pronounced, his ears stuck out, and the incline on his ski-jump nose was increasing. He was losing the baby fat from his cheeks, but it was settling into his jowls, which were rapidly becoming his most prominent feature. He had dark, curly hair, cut precisely at the line of the top of his ears, but grown to considerable length. Heffern, who played violin from a position directly behind Dick in the orchestra, enjoyed "running my fiddle bow through his hair, thus throwing his hair down in front of his face." When a piece was completed, Dick would warn through clenched teeth, "Don't do that again," but as soon as they began another number, "Down would go my bow again, and muss his hair." [43]

DEBATE WAS the activity into which Dick threw himself totally. Before a debate, he would get so tense he could not eat. When he was not studying for the next contest, he would drive over to Fullerton or Los Angeles to hear other debate teams. [44] His coach, Mrs. Clifford Vincent, said, "He was so good it kind of disturbed me. He had this ability to kind of slide round an argument instead of meeting it head on, and he could take any side of a debate." [45]

In the spring of 1929, Dick entered an area-wide oratorical contest sponsored by the Kiwanis Club. The subject was the Constitution. Some fifty students at Whittier entered. The favorite was Merton Wray. "But lo and behold," Wray recalled, "a young boy by the name of Richard Nixon transferred in from Fullerton and entered the contest."

Wray spoke first. He took the position that the principles of the Constitution should be extended around the world, that there should be a worldwide Bill of Rights and a world government to guarantee it. Nixon came next, and his theme was far more welcome to the Kiwanis Club judges. As Wray said, "He had a tremendous empathy with his audience. He had a way of reaching out and getting hold of them." [46]

Nixon called his speech "Our Privileges Under the Constitution." Wray's theme had been to extend those privileges; Dick's was to limit them to those Americans who were responsible citizens and thus entitled to them.

After a brief reference to mankind's centuries-long struggle for freedom, with a passing glance at the Magna Charta, Dick asserted that "the chief desire of man is that his life and personal liberty may be well protected." He then praised the Constitution for its protection of the citizen from arbitrary arrest, and on that right he placed no qualification whatsoever. Other rights did not fare so well.

On freedom of worship, Dick said that Americans were "truly fortunate to have this privilege," but he immediately warned against the danger that "persons may indulge in religious practices which are debasing to mind and character." Who such persons were, he did not say, but he insisted that "their practices are in direct contrast to the spirit of the Constitution."

With regard to freedom of speech and freedom of the press, Dick again saw dangers that others seemed to ignore. "There are," he said, "some who use these privileges as a cloak for covering libelous, indecent and injurious statements. . . . There are those who, under the pretense of freedom of speech . . . have incited riots, assailed our patriotism, and denounced the Constitution."

One struggles to imagine who "some" and "those" were. The year was 1929, conservative Republicanism was at its zenith, and there certainly were no labor agitators in Whittier, much less people going around denouncing the Constitution. Yet he delivered the lines with an intensity and sincerity that impressed the judges, who in any event heartily agreed with him. So did they approve of Dick's praise for "laws . . . for punishing those who abuse their Constitutional privileges," and of his statement, "We must obey the laws for they have been passed for our own welfare."

The greatest of the constitutional privileges, Dick continued, was the sovereignty of the people, expressed in every citizen's right to vote and in his right to hold office. He chastised those who failed to exercise the suffrage with a stirring passage: "To use the ballot is the citizen's duty to himself, to his fellowmen, and to his country. It is his debt to those innumerable patriots whose sacrifices have made possbile his present day privileges."

He went on to discuss the responsibility that devolved on those citizens who became officeholders, stressing their duty to give service willingly, to perform to the best of their abilities, and "to defend, maintain, and uphold the Constitution." Then another good point, also well made: "By these two political privileges, of suffrage and of holding office, the American citizen is a ruler more powerful than any king."

Dick's peroration was appropriately grand and sweeping, as befit the subject: "The rule of the Constitution has been built upon the very rock of freedom. . . . It is our duty to protect this previous document, to obey its laws, to hold sacred its mighty principles, that our descendants may have those priceless heritages—Our Privileges under the Constitution." [47]

It was a bravura performance, beginning to end, especially coming from a high-school junior. He won the contest. With the same speech, Dick went on to win at the district level. Wray, the idealist who was more concerned with extending human rights, was bitter, not only at this loss but also others he suffered in debates with Dick. In Wray's view, "Since high school Nixon has had an uncommon ability to take advantage of a situation. . . . His success is due to knowing what to do and when to do it, perfect timing in everything." [48]

The following year the contest was extemporaneous. Dick memorized his speech, which he called "America's Progress—Its Dependence Upon the Constitution." In it he used all his debating tricks. After a description of the growth of the United States since 1776, he posed his question: "What have been the causes for such stupendous progress, the forces which have made possible our present day world-wide power?" Then he offered what he called the three main theories commonly used to explain America's progress: race ("the people who settled in this country were of a superior type"); luck ("the tremendous natural resources of the land were especially fitted for the development of a nation"); and political acumen ("this nation owes its present position to . . . the Constitution").

According to Dick, there was force to each theory, but he pointed out that "surely we cannot say that the people who have settled in the southern countries are of an inferior type, for the Latin race once ruled the known world." As to natural resources, everyone knew that those of South America "are inestimable in extent," yet the continent was poverty-stricken.

This brought him to the heart of the question—what was unique to the United States? He then asserted as fact a proposition he had not proved, that "without question the Constitution has been the underlying force in America's progress."

If the logic was weak, the sentiment was strong. Once again, Dick saw enemies to the Constitution lurking about: "At the present time, a great wave of indifference to the Constitution's authority, disrespect of its law, and opposition to its basic principles threatens its very foundations." The source of these dangers he did not name, but he warned that "this wave of indifference to the laws of the Constitution must cease." He won again, this time receiving a $10 prize from the school and a $20 award from the Los Angeles *Times*. In the district competition at Monrovia High School, he placed second—almost his only loss as a debater or orator.[49]

HIS POPULARITY with the small-business men who served as judges for the Kiwanis Club did not extend to the student body. In his senior year he ran for student-body president. He lost to a candidate whom he described disparagingly as an "athlete and personality boy." As consolation he was appointed general manager of the student government.[50]

He was a consistent A or B-plus student, serious about his work, eager to learn. The marks did not come easily. He seldom relaxed, or engaged in comradery, or told small jokes. When a classmate commented, "You are lucky, Dick, to get such good grades so easily," he did not respond with a quip, or a shrug, or any other casual retort. Instead, he replied solemnly, "It isn't luck. You've got to dig for them."[51]

AT THE END of Dick's senior year, the Latin Club held its annual Roman banquet. The students wore togas, ate with their hands, and generally did their best to simulate a Roman atmosphere. After the meal, the seniors put on a three-act play in Latin, based on Vergil's *Aeneid*. Dick played Aeneas and Ola Florence Welsh played Dido. It was his first venture as an actor, and he was not very good at it (the nature of the play hardly helped; Vergil did not have American teen-agers in mind when he wrote it). Dick was stiff and wooden, especially in the romantic scenes. When he threw himself on Queen Dido's bier at the climax, there was—he later confessed— an embarrassing outburst of "catcalls, whistles, and laughter." At the play's end, the audience managed a round of polite applause. Determined to please, Dick rushed over to the teacher, June Steck, and volunteered to play the piano. "I'll do anything to make the party a success," he told her.[52]

Despite the relative failure of the play, he found that he enjoyed pretending to be someone else and felt that, given a decent role, he could be good at it. That he even tried acting came as a surprise to his classmates. It was a side of himself he had not shown, perhaps did not even know himself was there. Helen Letts remarked that "I couldn't imagine him going into acting. With him, everything was factual, all cut and dried."[53] But Alma Chapman saw the link that her friend Helen missed. Dick, she said, was "strong as a debater" because debating was "partly acting. He could get worked up on a point in debating and sometimes give the appearance of anger, but it was all showmanship." She said she never knew him to be genuinely angry; she felt he had complete control of his emotions and that his apparent outbursts of anger were just acting for effect.[54]

After the play, Dick and Ola Florence began dating, but it was an uneasy courtship. One of her friends commented that Dick "did not know how to be personable or sexy with girls. He didn't seem to have a sense of fun." Ola Florence probed a bit deeper: "He was smart and set apart," she said of Dick, but she added, "I think he felt unsure of himself deep down."[55]

Most high-school seniors are unsure of themselves, usually with good reason, certainly better reason than Dick Nixon had. He was a champion debater, had the lead role in the Latin play, was an honor student, and—upon graduation—was given the Harvard Club award as "best all-around student." With the award came a scholarship to Harvard. There was also the possibility of a tuition scholarship to Yale. But although Dick had "dreamed of going to college in the East," he had to turn down the offers, because the traveling and living expenses involved were too great. Instead, he settled on Whittier College. There he could live at home, and tuition was paid by his grandfather Milhous' scholarship fund. "I was not disappointed," Dick claimed in his memoirs, "because the idea of college was so exciting that nothing could have dimmed it for me."[56]

THE REASON the family did not have the money to take advantage of such an unmatchable opportunity as Harvard or Yale was Harold's long bout with tuberculosis. For the Nixon family, the tragedy of Harold's illness hit harder than anything they had ever gone through, including Arthur's death. Harold's struggle with tuberculosis was expensive, it created tension and anxiety in the family, and it brought out the best in each of them, as they all made genuine sacrifices for Harold's sake. Most of all, it brought them together.

Harold contracted tuberculosis in 1927. It was a disease already all too well known to members of both the Milhous and Nixon families. More than a half dozen had died as a result of TB over the past hundred years. Nor was the current generation spared: Jessamyn West contracted TB shortly after Harold did.

There were public facilities available for treatment, but Frank's pride stood in the way. "My father refused to let him go to the county tuberculosis hospital, one of the best in the country," Nixon wrote in his memoirs, "on the ground that going there would be taking charity." [57]

Instead, one Sunday morning Frank went over to his neighbor's house. "Harry," he said to Mr. Schuyler, "I want you to come across the street with me." Schuyler followed, and Frank pointed to the land behind his store. "Harry, I own this lot. I want you to buy it and pay me $85 per month so that I can put Harold in an institution in Arizona." Schuyler agreed, and Harold went to an expensive private sanatorium, then to another in the Antelope Valley in California. [58]

Harold improved enough to come home in 1928, but then he began to slip again. He was not a good patient. His therapy was absolute rest, but Harold loved life too much to spend his waking hours flat on his back. Merle West was helping at the service station at the time and recalled that "the poor guy would come from the house, a hundred feet away, to sit and talk. He would come up that little incline and it would take him ten minutes to come that fifty or sixty feet up. He would just go a little bit, just gasping for breath and sit there. He had a bad case."

Hannah hired a nurse to keep him on his back. "But old Harold did everything he shouldn't do. I mean he never slowed down. He couldn't stay down like he was supposed to. Now, Jessamyn, she practically died and this is what started her writing. She was on her back so long, flat on her back, couldn't do anything so she started writing lying in bed." [59]

Frank and Hannah drove to Prescott, Arizona, to find a place for Harold, but the treatment facilities were too expensive. Frank had no more lots to sell and could not raise the money for another private sanatorium. But Hannah insisted that Harold had to live in the high, dry Arizona mountains, widely believed to be the proper climate for TB cases, and that she be with him. She insisted that she alone could keep him quiet. She rented a cabin, at $25 per month, and took in three other tubercular patients to manage the expenses. The patients all slept on a screened porch, even in winter—a part of the recommended treatment. Hannah did everything for them, the cooking, cleaning, changing sheets, collecting and disposing of their sputum cups, scrubbing their bedpans.

Back in Whittier, Dick was in high school. Frank had to run the store alone during the day, when the boys were at school. They ate when they could, whatever was available. Occasionally Frank would drive the eight-hundred-mile round trip through the desert to Prescott for a weekend. "In our old car it took us fifteen or sixteen hours to get there," Dick said. "It was no joyride." Except for those few weekends, Frank, Dick, and Don were on their own.

In a 1968 campaign film, Nixon assessed the results of the separation: "It was a rather difficult time actually from the standpoint of the family being pulled apart. But looking back I don't think that we were any the worse off for it. You shared the adversity and you grew stronger and took care of yourself. Not having your mother to lean on we all grew up rather fast in those years." [60]

But, he also admitted later, "it was, from a financial standpoint, a disaster." During the five years of Harold's illness, he said, "my mother never bought a new dress." [61]

IN THE SUMMERS of 1928 and 1929, Dick lived in Prescott. He stayed in the lunger cabin with his mother and the four TB patients, who were coughing blood. But he did little more than sleep there, because he was working every possible hour. He did stoop labor in the fields for twenty-five cents an hour; he got a job as a janitor in the local country club; he hustled various jobs at the Slippery Gulch carnival during the weeklong Frontier Days' festival; he plucked and dressed chickens for a butcher shop. The job he liked best, and made the most money at, was as a barker at the carnival. In 1929, Dick's Wheel of Fortune made the most money of any of the concessions. [62]

In 1930 a most improbable event brought Hannah home to Whittier. A doctor said that Hannah, then aged forty-five, was pregnant. Frank was thunderstruck. "The doctor doesn't know what he is talking about," he shouted. But the doctor was right.

It was unthinkable that Hannah continue to nurse TB patients, much less have her baby, in a lunger cabin. She came home, while Harold stayed in Arizona. The baby, a boy, Edward, was born in May 1930 in the Whittier Hospital.

A month later, Richard Nixon graduated from high school. That summer he worked in the store, and did a lot of reading to get ready for college.

SEVENTEEN-YEAR-OLD Richard Nixon was a mass of contradictions. He was sympathetic and solicitous to the woman who was stealing from the family store, but outraged and eager to punish those who spoke against the Constitution. He knew everyone in Whittier High, but had no real friends. He was a student leader, often in the spotlight, whether in plays or at debates, but shy around people and nearly petrified around girls, with whom he managed to be simultaneously awkward and aggressive. We may assume that he suffered from an inferiority complex, the price everyone has to pay for the glorious experience of being seventeen years old, but he managed to hide his self-doubts and appear confident and contented.

His ability to deny what others regarded as obvious became his way of dealing with things beyond his control. He denied, at seventeen and later in his life as well, that having to go to Whittier rather than Harvard disappointed him. He insisted that Whittier was plenty good enough. But could it possibly have been true? Could a young man as bright as he was, and as ambitious, really not care whether he went to Harvard or Whittier? Still, denial that it hurt was much the most effective way to deal with the hurt. It could not be helped; the reality was that he could not go to Harvard, so it was realistic on Nixon's part to deny that he felt discriminated against or disappointed. Once again, he turned a negative into a positive.

CHAPTER FOUR

WHITTIER COLLEGE
1930–1934

In September 1930, Nixon entered college. He was seventeen years old, a year younger than his classmates. Harold had just come home from Arizona—he refused to stay there without his mother, and anyway insisted that he was well enough to work and carry his share of the load. For his part, Richard got up at 4 A.M., drove to Los Angeles, haggled over his purchases, drove back to the store, set up the vegetables, and then began his day. Afternoons and weekends he kept up the books for the store. He usually studied until past midnight.

At the end of his freshman year, he had one A (French), seven Bs, and one C (journalism). The 1931 college yearbook, the *Acropolis*, recorded some of his other freshman-year accomplishments— president of his class, member of the Joint Council of Control, president of the newly formed men's club, member of the debate team, featured performer in two plays, reporter for the campus newspaper, and sweater winner on the freshman football team.

As will be seen, he was just getting started.

Henry Adams once described Teddy Roosevelt as "pure act." The characterization fit Nixon's college career perfectly. Whittier College provided him with an ideal setting for learning, for exercising and expanding his talents, for growing. It was small enough that he could be the unquestioned BMOC; it was good enough that he had no easy time reaching that position.

Whittier College had about four hundred students. It began in 1887 as a Quaker Academy, and although by 1930 it was nonsectar-

ian, it was "devoted to higher education with a constant overtone
of Quaker responsibility in the social order" with the chief purpose
being "to educate for Christian Democracy." [1] Most students came
from the immediate area, about half from Whittier High. The majority of graduates went into teaching, the church, social work, or
the YMCA, usually in Southern California. Of the eighty-five graduates of Nixon's class of 1934, only twelve settled out of state, and
twenty-two lived their lives within walking distance of the college.[2] When Nixon entered the school, it could boast that the First
Lady, Mrs. Herbert Hoover, was a graduate and a member of the
board; President Hoover often sent the library a large consignment
of books.[3]

The college needed the free books, because like so many small
liberal arts schools, it was constantly on the brink of bankruptcy.
Ola Florence Welsh worked in the office of the college treasurer
while she was a student. "My instructions were first thing in the
morning to open the mail and deposit any money right away. It was
that close!" Faculty were often paid with real estate instead of
cash, and the administration would take groceries in lieu of tuition.
The football coach recalled hitching a ride to school in a truck
filled with manure. The driver said he was delivering it to the
school gardener as part payment of his son's $125 per semester
tuition. "Said he was just trading one type of B.S. for another type
of B.S."[4]

The school nestled in the shade of the tall eucalyptus trees on
the side of College Hill, back away from busy Whittier Boulevard.
Chapel was mandatory three times a week; smoking on campus
was taboo. Everyone knew everyone else. Classes were small, students pitched horseshoes with the faculty, and social events involved the entire community. The faculty was young, idealistic,
dedicated, and more concerned with teaching the students than
researching and writing scholarly monographs. They had good degrees from good schools—Dr. Paul Smith, Nixon's history teacher,
was a recent Ph.D. from Wisconsin, where he had studied in the
great Progressive tradition of Frederick Jackson Turner. Maxwell
Anderson had taught at Whittier. Most members of the faculty were
Quakers, but as Professor Smith pointed out, they were "far more
liberal" than most Quakers.

The faculty encouraged the students to think for themselves,
to question the received wisdom, to be independent. Dogma was
anathema. Not even pacifism, that bedrock of Quaker belief, was
sacrosanct. Smith noted that students "walked through the foyer of
the administration building and saw two service flags hanging in
that hall recording the names of those students and grads who

served in World War I. Alongside was another flag with the names of those who were conscientious objectors. The flags hung there side by side."[5]

Nixon characterized his English teacher, Dr. Albert Upton, as "an iconoclast. Nothing was sacred to him, and he stimulated us by his outspoken unorthodoxy." At the end of Nixon's junior year, Dr. Upton told him that his education would not be complete until he read the great Russian novelists. Nixon spent his reading time that summer poring through Tolstoy. He reacted with schoolboy enthusiasm and intensity to Tolstoy's program for peaceful revolution, his passionate opposition to war, and his emphasis on the spiritual elements in life, to the point that he wrote in his memoirs, "At that time in my life I became a Tolstoyan."[6]

THROUGH THE FIRST two and one-half years of Nixon's college career, Harold's condition worsened. In the family's view, the reason was that he just would not rest.[7] He insisted on working, and took a job fumigating the citrus groves. "Very dangerous work," a friend said. "People died." Harold hung around the local airport, ignoring the exhaust fumes and his father's wrath when Frank found out he had gone flying. But "flying airplanes was his passion," and the next week he would indulge himself again.

He became sicker. In 1932 his mother took him back to Prescott, where she once again took in other patients to pay the bills. He improved, and they came home again, Harold promising to be a good patient.

Instead, he threw himself into his last chance at enjoying life. Jessamyn West described one part of it: "Harold got himself engaged to a girl. He told Merle that if he was going to die he might as well have a fling." "He was headstrong; devil-may-care," a friend said of Harold. "At every turn [he] did the opposite of what his doctor and parents told him to do."[8]

Richard, Don, Frank and Hannah, the doctors, everyone tried to talk Harold into going back to Prescott. Floyd Wildermuth remembered, "I tried my best to get him to go back to Arizona. He told me that he wouldn't go back. He knew that he was going to die, but he would not go. I can remember begging him to go."[9]

The pain was intense for all those involved. There was not a person who knew Harold who did not like him, and he was wasting away, almost visibly, with every cup of sputum he coughed up.

Richard loved his older brother. He looked up to him, competed with him as younger brothers will do, learned from him, admired him. Their differences in character were great, but they were bonded together as brothers in a happy family, sharing not only a heritage and a bloodline but innumerable experiences, a love for their parents, and a love for each other.

In February 1933, the second semester of Nixon's junior year, Harold told his father he would like to see the desert. Frank dropped everything to make the trip, but three days after they left, they returned—Harold had had a hemorrhage. Harold told Richard that even so, he was glad he went. "I can still remember his voice," Nixon wrote in his memoirs, "when he described the beauty of the wild flowers in the foothills and the striking sight of snow in the mountains."

On March 6, Harold asked Richard to drive him downtown. They went to a hardware store, where Harold bought an electric mixer as a birthday present for Hannah. Richard had to support him on the walk from the car to the store. Back home, they hid the present.

The next morning, Harold said he needed to rest and that he would give his mother the mixer that evening. At noon Nixon was studying in the college library. He got a message to come home. When he arrived, there was a hearse parked in front of the house. Hannah told Dick that when he left for school, Harold had asked her to hug him close, then looked at her and said, "This is the last time I will see you, until we meet in heaven." One hour later he was dead. That evening, Richard got out the cake mixer and explained to Hannah that it was Harold's birthday present to her.[10]

Nixon was twenty years old at the time. Hannah said that when Harold died "he sank into a deep, impenetrable silence." But she also noted that his already fierce determination was intensified. "From that time on, it seemed that Richard was trying to be *three* sons in one, striving even harder than before to make up to his father and me for our loss. . . . Unconsciously, too, I think that Richard may have felt a kind of guilt that Harold and Arthur were dead and that he was alive."[11]

IN HIS senior year, Nixon took "The Philosophy of Christian Reconstruction" from Dr. J. Herschel Coffin. The students called the course "What Can I Believe?" At the beginning of the course, on October 9, 1933, Nixon wrote an essay on his personal religious beliefs, always a subject of immense importance to college students and especially so to Nixon, because he had had such a strict Quaker upbringing and because he had lost two brothers to death in the past few years.

Nixon's Quakerism had been shaken in this Quaker school. In his essay, Nixon sketched out his personal reconciliation of the Bible and modern science. The writing and the theme were not original, but for a college senior struggling with that most difficult and important of questions—What do I believe?—it was excellent. He wrote with feeling and verve, logic and confidence.

He was a birthright Quaker, he began, raised to accept the "infallibility and literal correctness of the Bible." He had been warned by his parents "not to be misled by college professors. . . ." Warned or not, he could no longer accept a literal interpretation of the Bible.

But, he added, "I still believe that God is the creator." As to Jesus Christ, Nixon could not accept that He was the Son of God in any physical sense; rather, he argued, Jesus "reached the highest conception of God. . . . His life was so perfect that he 'mingled' his soul with God's." He could not accept the resurrection story, and criticized "orthodox teachers" for insisting that the physical resurrection of Jesus was the cornerstone of Christian religion. "I believe that the modern world will find a real resurrection in the life and teachings of Jesus." [12]

From that point on, religion was no longer important to him. He continued his church activities, playing the piano and teaching Sunday school, but the church was not the center of his life. Hannah asked him about this time whether he would like to be a minister—he was such a powerful speaker, it seemed to her the perfect calling—but he dismissed the question casually, and never gave the ministry any serious thought. He had found a balance between what he had learned in his church and what he learned in school that satisfied him. Thereafter, there was nothing approaching a crisis of conscience or belief for Richard Nixon.

As a STUDENT, even in his junior year when Harold died, Nixon was close to ideal. He was extremely intelligent, quick to learn, polite, a hard worker who did his homework and then some, with an impressive ability to absorb and remember facts. If he had a shortcoming, it was a lack of originality in his thinking, but he could follow the most intricate arguments or difficult texts, and he was excellent at summarizing what others had written or thought. He was not interested in originality, rather he wanted good grades. "I realized that, if I were to go on to law school, I would probably have to have a scholarship," he later remarked. So "there was an urge to get the best possible marks . . . at Whittier."

The teacher whom Nixon called "the greatest intellectual inspiration of my early years" was Dr. Paul Smith, from whom he took four courses. Smith eventually became president of Whittier College after a distinguished career as a teacher there. In his American history course, he played a record, obtained at great expense and quite rare—it was William Jennings Bryan delivering the Cross of Gold speech at the 1896 Democratic Convention. "A magnificent speech!" Smith declared. "Talk about a thrill in the spine, that's it." [13] His text was the classic Morison and Commager *Growth of the American Republic*, Progressive in tone, magisterial in its judgments, sometimes critical, but at its heart a celebration of the American achievement.

Merton Wray remembered what a shock Professor Smith was to some of the more conservative Quakers. "The first thing this fellow did to these poor students was to introduce them to Beard's economic interpretation of the Constitution." [14] Smith was a Republican Progressive whose heroes included Lincoln, and he had Nixon read through the ten-volume Nicolay and Hay biography of Lincoln. As a result, Lincoln became one of Nixon's heroes; others, more contemporary, included Woodrow Wilson and Bob La Follette.

A student who took classes with Smith said that the professor "tried desperately to get people to think of entering a public office. Paul Smith wanted leadership in government, and this was all you heard. I can remember one time seeing inspiration come over Richard Nixon in Paul Smith's class. You just could almost feel him dreaming." [15]

Nixon's examination papers, Smith said, "nettled me because they were always so terribly brief. He had an analytical mind rather than a philosophical mind. He had no addenda at all on the sidelines of the paper. He went to the heart of the thing. So far as the question, nothing was left out. He gave all of what was asked but he didn't vouchsafe much beyond that." Smith gave him straight As. He did almost as well in his other courses. He continued, in his own words, to "plug away." [16]

As NOTED, Nixon not only kept up with his schoolwork, and work for the store, but in addition he carried an enormous load of extracurricular activities. He began practically the first day he walked on campus; within a month he had been elected president of his class and had organized a new men's society on the campus.

The idea of a new society was not original with Nixon, but he was the one who implemented it. Shortly after the semester began, and after Nixon's victory in the class presidency race, a sophomore named Dean Triggs approached him. Triggs said that there was only one men's society on the campus (fraternities were forbidden), called the Franklins. "They seem to be pretty powerful and kind of snobbish," Triggs said. "I think they need a little competition." The idea appealed to Nixon partly because he was always looking for something else to do, partly because he resented the Franklins, who were alleged to be blue-blooded, wealthy young men who wore tuxedoes at their social functions. Nixon later denied that there were any class distinctions involved, although he did admit that his society was composed of men who "had to work their way through college." [17] But Paul Smith believed that there were sharp class differences on the Whittier campus, noted by everyone. "Dick could see this and he had to be part of it. His family wasn't looked down upon, but the Frank Nixon family was in no way regarded at the social level of the Milhouses in Whittier." [18]

In any event, the new organization was composed primarily of athletes, who were Nixon's friends because he played on the freshman football team. Nixon put together a charter, gave the society a name (Orthogonians), a symbol (the square, standing for the well-rounded life of "beans, brawn, brain and bowels"), an insignia (a boar's head), and a motto (*Écrasons l'infâme,* translated as "stamp out evil"). Nixon also wrote the Orthogonian song: [19]

> *All hail the mighty boar*
> *Our patron beast is he*
> *Our aims forevermore*
> *In all our deeds must be*
> *To emulate his might*
> *His bravery and his fight*
> *Brothers together we'll travel on and on*
> *Worthy of the name of Orthogonian*

Naturally, he became the first president. The charter presented the society as a service club whose aim was to "develop campus spirit," but its real function was as a social club. Once a month the Orthogonians held a ritual feast—spaghetti and beans—and sponsored dances and other events. They deliberately set out to be as different from the Franklins as possible, having their pictures taken for the *Acropolis*, for example, in open-necked shirts instead of the tuxedoes the Franklins wore. For their part, the Franklins called the Orthogonians "the big pigs."

Nixon asked Dr. Upton, the English professor known as the Owl because of his thick glasses, to be the faculty sponsor. Upton agreed. If the Orthogonians wanted to be square, Upton said, that was all right by him—he was a sports fan and liked the players. But he warned them that they had to set the right tone. The Orthogonians, Upton later said, "recognized Nixon as a person they needed to compete with the Franklins. He was very trustworthy and he could outtalk any of them."

Nixon's first project in the late fall was to have the Orthogonians sponsor a dance in Wardman Gym. President Walter Dexter granted permission, although it was highly unusual to hold a dance on campus. "I don't think he got an hour's sleep that night," a student said of Dexter, "for Quakers waking him up saying he was leading the students down the road to Hell." Nixon attended the affair with Ola Florence, even though he hated dancing, because he was hopelessly awkward at it, but he took Ola anyway, for the principle of the thing.[20]

EVEN WITH the Orthogonians, his classes, football, and work, Nixon found time for a multitude of additional activities. He was a human dynamo in student government, the man everyone counted on. "If Dick Nixon took on a job," one student said, "you could depend on it, it would get done." Another said that "his interest and enthusiasm was just almost contagious." He continued, "Dick did a lot of the menial tasks. He completed them and you'd say, 'Who did that?' And the reply would be, 'Dick did it.'"[21]

He was a great booster of Whittier College, and quite in demand. He spoke before such groups as the First Methodist Church of Redondo or the Women's Civic Club of Los Angeles so often that in his senior year the *Quaker Campus* reported that "Dick spends half his life speaking to various organizations on behalf of the school; let's give him a hand. (He needs one. Has he shown you the four blisters, two bruises and one cut he received while helping to make the new path?)"[22] In October 1933, the *Quaker Campus* announced a picnic in Woodland Park and informed the students, "Free transportation is being provided by Dick Nixon."[23] If he was not a thinker, he was certainly a doer, the type without whom student governments could not exist. Nixon's big outlet, Ed Wunder remembered, was in "the fun of being in things, planning things."[24]

In his sophomore year, Nixon was elected to the honorary Society of Knights, a newly formed service group of campus leaders. He ran for vice-president of the student government on a platform that promised, "My policy will be one of impartial cooperation with the president and executive committee in solving student problems." He came in first in the primary, then won the final election over Norma Allen, 267 to 73.[25] A classmate recalled Nixon's elation and commented, "He wanted to win all the time; no matter what he was doing, he wanted to be a winner."[26]

To do so, and to meet all his other obligations, he practically had to stay in perpetual motion. Charles Kendle remarked, "He could be here one minute and the next minute he would be in the library." "He was always in a hurry to get to the next whatever-it-was," Professor Smith said.[27]

Already he had developed that politician's habit of being late.

"There was only one thing wrong with Dick as a debater," his debating manager said. "I had a lot of trouble getting him to be on time. He was never very good at punctuality. . . . But, once on the speaker's platform, he displayed a sense of timing that was amazing."[28]

At the beginning of his junior year, Nixon was the subject of a new *Quaker Campus* feature called "Impressions." The text listed his many accomplishments and was accompanied by the first of what would eventually become tens of thousands of cartoons of Nixon. Done by student Richard Harris, it captured the qualities of Nixon's face that Herblock, among others, relied upon—the dark, bushy hair, the heavy, straight-line eyebrows, the jutting ears, the bulging jowls, and of course the nose line.[29] Nixon organized six dances that year, although they had to be held off campus, at the Whittier Women's Club. He joined the History Society, and remained active in student government, football, debate, and was the lead in the junior-class play.[30]

In May 1933, he announced his candidacy for student-body president. His opponent was Dick Thomson of the Franklins. "Heavy campaigning is being carried on," the *Quaker Campus* reported. Nixon's platform was simple: "If elected president, I shall work for strict economy on the executive committee, student body dances on the campus, a more systematic use of the facilities within the student body for publicity in high schools and junior colleges, and better relations between alumni and the student body."[31]

The issue he concentrated on was to allow dancing on campus. Thomson's pledge was to work for a new student union building. Nixon won the election. Thomson analyzed the contest: "His issue had student appeal and I guess mine was a little too practical. I knew damn well I didn't have a Chinaman's chance. It was the silver-tongued orator up against a babbling idiot. Even if he didn't say anything it sounded good."[32]

Merton Wray, who had been opposing Nixon since high school and who supported Thomson, later said that the campaign "showed the tremendous ability that Nixon had to see a situation and take advantage of it."

His campaign manager, Bill Hornaday, was impressed by Nixon's abilities, not only as a politician but also as a student. "Nixon always knew what he was doing and was a planner with special goals. If he had certain things to do, they were well organized and he planned ahead what time would be given to them." Hornaday admitted that he had to cram, but Nixon never did. "I'd stay up all night writing a thesis at the end, while his was always in ahead of time."[33]

As president in his senior year, Nixon delivered on each one of his campaign pledges. At the beginning of the semester, he organized a reception for the entering freshmen, gave the welcoming address, and arranged for the entertainment.[34] Then he took charge of homecoming weekend—"President Nixon has literally worked his head off lately," the *Quaker Campus* reported.[35] He turned to Professor Upton for help in fulfilling his pledge to improve relations with the alumni and townspeople; Upton suggested an "all-college weekend," and Nixon eagerly took the idea and made it a reality. He brought in dance bands, arranged picnics, helped stage one-act comedies, planned games, made it possible for parents and alumni to spend a night in the dormitory, and gave a speech.[36]

During his year as president, he not only spoke to various clubs and civic groups on the virtues of Whittier College but also to numerous high-school classes on the joy of playing football for Whittier. His standard speech began, "You know the reason I play football for Whittier College is so I can make this speech." According to one observer, "It just laid the kids in the aisle. Then he went on with a good pep talk for Whittier."[37]

His high visibility engendered some resentment and hostility. "He was not generally liked by the girls whom I knew best," a coed reported, "one of whom detested his admitted cockiness." Another recalled that she "thought Dick Nixon was too stuck-up." A classmate, Helen S. Larson, said of Nixon, "He had an almost ruthless cocksureness, which perhaps was the reason some students disliked him."[38]

But more liked and admired him. A coed who took four classes with Nixon said he was a "brilliant student. His high scholarship ratings put him in a class by himself. So much higher, in my particular case, that I became one of hundreds who secretly admired and envied him more than he realized."[39] After Nixon returned to campus following a week-long trip with the Men's Glee Club, the *Quaker Campus* gossip columnist wrote: "Nixon, Nicky to those who know him best and the idol of those who would like to know him better, silent for an interim in his otherwise voluble life. Glad you're back, Nicky. Executive meetings weren't the same without you."[40]

The "Nicky" nickname, incidentally, never stuck. Although it seemingly was a natural, he hated it, and froze up whenever anyone called him Nicky. "Nothing is funnier than to call Richard Nixon 'Nicky' and watch him bristle," the gossip columnist wrote. "I did it once and he was too surprised to speak, if you can imagine Nixon inarticulate."[41]

His go-go spirit, his enthusiasm for everything, seemed to some of his classmates to be a put-on. One claimed that other students "would think of him as false. They just couldn't believe that a human being could be that sincere and feel that strong about things, because most people would have to act to do this." [42] Another classmate said of Nixon's enthusiasm, "I used to wonder if it was wholly genuine . . . how much was simulated for the benefit of all present." [43]

One reason for the feeling of falseness was the well-known fact that Nixon hated dancing, but had run for the presidency as an advocate of on-campus dances and then, once in office, went all out to fulfill the pledge. He appealed to President Dexter, unsuccessfully—Dexter had been burned badly enough when he allowed the Orthogonians to have a dance on campus three years earlier. Nixon next went to the trustees. He pointed out that, like it or not, the students were going to dance. He argued that it would be better for them to dance on campus, under supervision, than to frequent the smoke-filled dives of Los Angeles. The trustees relented, and through Nixon's senior year monthly dances were held in the gym, with bands brought in from Los Angeles.

"It was almost as if he had once upon a time taken a vow always to do his utmost," a classmate said of Nixon as president. He fulfilled all his campaign promises, and then some. In the spring of 1934, as he prepared for his own final exams, he devised a plan to bring in the newly elected student-body officers and train them in their jobs before the end of the school year, instead of letting them come in green, as he had. [44]

No wonder that the 1934 *Acropolis* featured Nixon in the front of the yearbook. The story concluded, "After one of the most successful years the college has ever witnessed we stop to reminisce, and come to the realization that much of the success was due to the efforts of this very gentleman. Always progressive, and with a liberal attitude, he has led us through the year with flying colors." [45]

His ONLY physical passion, and almost his only recreation, was football. To it he devoted huge chunks of his time and energy, from it he drew great pleasure.

"He loved to win," a teammate recalled, but in football he never did. The highest he rose was to third-string guard on a thirty-three-man team. And yet, the teammate continued, "I think that he got more out of the game than we did." [46]

When he entered college he had no plans to try to play football —after his experiences at Whittier High he had no illusions about his abilities. But only eleven men went out for the freshman football team in September 1930, so the coach came to Nixon and asked him to please come out so there would be one substitute available for the games. Nixon did his duty, and got to participate in every game. The next year he went out for the varsity, not out of a sense of duty, but because he liked hanging around with the athletes, enjoyed the prestige of being on the team, and most of all because he loved playing the game.

Every weekday at 3 P.M., all through the fall semester, he would put on the pads and go out to the practice field. The coach often kept them on the field until after dark, turning on the lights and using a white ball. On Saturdays, when Whittier was playing at home, Nixon would suit up for the games (he did not get to make the road trips). He seldom got into the games—nevertheless he got so nervous before they began that he could not eat. A teammate said he always tried to grab the seat next to Nixon at the training table "so I could eat my steak and his too." [47] When the coach did put him into the game, only in the last minutes after it was already won or lost, he was overeager. A classmate who was a linesman said, "When Dick went in, I always got out the five-yard penalty marker. . . . I knew he'd be offside just about every play." [48]

In scrimmages during practice sessions, when the first team would ride roughshod over the third team, Nixon amazed his teammates with his tenacity and spirit. "Let's get fired up," he would yell before digging in for the next play. Again, he would get run over.

"He wasn't cut out to play the sport," Clint Harris declared. Clint played tackle, across the line from Nixon. "He weighed 155 pounds and was 5 feet 11 and just 17 when he entered school. I was 20, 6 feet 4 and 211 pounds." Gail Jobe, also on the third team, recalled, "Nixon and I were cannon fodder. We used to get back there and make up our minds we'd smash some of them and we did. Guts. I'll say that for Nixon. He had guts."

Coach Wallace Newman agreed. "We used Nixon as a punching bag. If he'd had the physical ability he'd have been a terror." Harris remembered the time Newman kept the first team running the same play over and over again, to get it right. Nixon was the point of attack. Harris liked Nixon, but he knew that Newman was watching him and he dare not let up. "I remember now the sound of the impact of leather, canvas, and muscle; the heavy breathing of the players," Harris said. "I remember thinking, 'Dick Nixon, I don't know why you do this, but I admire your red-blooded intestinal fortitude. . . .' " [49]

"When a player got hurt," teammate Charles Kendle recalled, "the first guy that talked to him would be Dick. Dick would be over giving him a pep talk: 'You won't be out long, you'll be back in a couple of weeks.' " Kendle also sat on the bench; he remembered Nixon as a keen student of the game. As the game proceeded, "Dick would analyze and tell you what the tackle was doing or what the guard was doing." At halftime Nixon would go around the locker room telling each player what a great job he was doing. On a number of occasions, the coach would ask him to give the pep talk before sending the team out on the field.[50]

Nixon admired Coach Newman "more . . . than . . . any man I have ever known aside from my father."[51] Newman, called "Chief" by everyone because of his Indian blood, was a former All-American from USC and longtime Whittier coach. Invariably, observers compared him as a coach to Vince Lombardi. "With him 'good enough' wasn't good enough," Kendle said. "Show me a good loser," Newman told his players, "and I'll show you a loser." He said it was all a question of "being willing to pay the price." After a loss, he would say, "Now look here. I don't believe in this business about being a good loser. You've got to hate to lose, and that means that once you lose, then you fight back."

In his memoirs, Nixon flatly declared, "There is no way I can adequately describe Chief Newman's influence on me." He credited Newman with drilling into him "a competitive spirit and the determination to come back after you have been knocked down or after you lose."[52]

"HE TRIED [football] and it made him unanimously popular on and off the campus," one student wrote of Nixon. "I shall never forget the tremendous roar which went up from the rooting section when Dick got into the line-up."[53] But he was a long way from being an athletic hero, and he had no girls hanging on him as he went about campus.

In fact, he had a hard time with the girls in general. "Let's face it," one coed said, "he was stuffy!" He was also shy and not much interested besides. "All of us would have to needle Dick a little bit to be sure that he came up with a date," one Orthogonian said. "I don't believe that girls were as important to Dick as they were to some of the rest of us."[54]

Nevertheless, he was the steady beau of the most popular girl on campus, Ola Florence Welsh. Their high-school romance continued through the full four college years, although not without some problems along the way. "He'd go out with other girls but would not tell me," Ola said, "and I'd find out about it. I'd go out, but he always knew" and always complained.[55]

Ola was a small girl, with brown hair, a pert nose, a ready smile, and a trim figure. She was nearly as active as Nixon, in student government, in plays, and in her women's society. Their classmates considered them an odd couple nevertheless, because Ola had such a good sense of humor, and Nixon had none, and because Ola moved easily in any company and was much sought after as a date—thirty years later men were still boasting that they had once dated Ola Florence—while Nixon had no social graces at all, and was popular only as a leader, not as a person. "Why do you go out with him?" Ola's girl friends would ask her.

"I just thought he was the smartest man that ever was," she once gave as her answer. "We'd have marvelous arguments and talks. We used to argue politics constantly. He was a Republican. I thought Roosevelt was wonderful and he detested him."[56] At another time, she remarked, "I don't know why in retrospect I found Richard Nixon so fascinating. I am not counting out sex appeal, which as a subject, believe me, we didn't discuss in those days. . . . I considered myself provincial and him worldly." She told one Nixon psychobiographer that she considered him "a shy boy friend," and told Fawn Brodie, "We were very puritanical. There was no hanky-panky."[57]

He sometimes treated her shabbily. Gail Jobe said, "I remember the night of one of the dances. He came in 10 yards ahead of her and didn't act like she was with him." Jobe saw his chance and moved in on Ola, much to Nixon's displeasure. But at the next prom, Nixon got mad at Ola and drove off alone. She had to call her mother for a ride home.

Mrs. Welsh did not approve of Nixon anyway, and she detested his habit of honking his horn at the curb instead of coming to the door to meet her daughter. Ola enjoyed parties and gatherings, but she said of Nixon, "He didn't know how to mix. He would never double date. He had no real boy friends. And he didn't like my girl friends. He would stalk out of the room where they were, his head high."[58]

He just did not have time for an intimate relationship, nor did he have any idea how to go about it. He was "nervous on dates," Kenn Ball remembered. "He was no lady's man. I think he went on dates because he thought it was the thing to do."[59] And Ola Florence herself said, "He seemed lonely, and so solemn at school. . . . Sometimes I think I never really knew him, and I was as close to him as anyone. I still feel some of that—he was a mystery."[60]

The relationship grew weaker rather than stronger. At first it was only an occasional tiff: "He'd be harsh and I'd cry," Ola said. "Then we'd make up."[61] By their senior year, the fights—really, the temperamental differences—grew worse. Ola wanted to be "free and swinging." Nixon was hardly the beau for that. In addition, "For the first time I began to feel that I wasn't good enough for him."[62] One night they disagreed, over the telephone, on plans for the weekend. Nixon got furious and slammed down the phone, saying, "When I see you again, it'll be too soon."[63] People had assumed that they would get married after graduation, but by the time it came, the relationship between them was barely alive.

IF HE COULD NOT shine in personal relations, he could in public, most of all in his own favorite extracurricular activity, debate. It was in his debate experience, more than the classroom or the student government, that he got his real education. The debaters had to be prepared to argue either side of difficult questions, such as repayment of the war loans, or free trade, or the powers of the President, and other current issues. They studied hard—one room in the library was set aside for them, its contents changed for the various topics. Thanks to debate, in other words, Nixon was rapidly becoming an expert on the subject that fascinated him above all others, contemporary politics. As he noted in his memoirs, debate was "a healthy antidote to certainty, and a good lesson in seeing the other person's point of view."[64]

On most issues, he remained neutral so far as his personal beliefs were concerned, although he became a convinced free trader from his debates. On the question of whether a free economy was more efficient than a managed economy, he also had strong views, warning that "absolute control would destroy the benefits of the individualistic system, such as individual initiative, moral responsibility, and competition."[65]

He was on the four-man varsity debating team all four years. Together the students drove around the West, tens of thousands of miles, debating some of the top teams in the country. They won more than they lost, and one year beat the national champions from Redlands University.

The team manager, Kenn Ball, said that Nixon was a successful debater because he was never afraid of a challenge. "Another big attribute was his ability to get his opponent off-balance. He would so fluster the other speaker with his steady attack of irrefutable facts, that his opposition would become emotional and stop thinking clearly." A team member, William Hornaday, recalled Nixon as a debater: "He was very astute and serious, no humor, it was all to the point. . . . He would always have a surprise, but he never left himself unguarded."[66]

Nixon was an active analyst of his own emotions, and like an actor knew how to use them effectively. He was free with his advice too. "To be a good debater," he told his teammates, "you've got to be able to get mad on your feet without losing your head."[67]

"Pour it on at this point," he would tell them, or "Save your ammunition," or "Play to the judges: they're the ones who decide."

Nixon once almost lost his temper, Ball reported, after losing a debate. "Both of us became upset. We thought we should have won. His first inclination was just to walk out. But then he controlled himself and turned around to talk to the judge and see what he did wrong. The judge said we had not clearly defined the issue. The next time we did it right."[68]

The story illustrates how well Nixon had learned to control his temper, indeed to use his anger as a spur, transforming it into an internal challenge to do better next time. He had a way of turning negative emotions into positive assets. He may have been Chief Newman's worst football player, but he was the coach's best student. "You must get angry," Newman told him, "terribly angry about losing. But the mark of a good loser is that he takes his anger out on himself and not on his victorious opponents or on his teammates."[69]

Nixon's powers of memorization were a great help to him in preparing for the debates. How good those powers were he demonstrated when he entered the *Reader's Digest* Southern California Extemporaneous Speaking Contest. The contestants were required to read each article in the *Digest* stretching back some months. When they appeared for the contest, they were told to speak extemporaneously on a randomly selected article. Nixon was given "Youth of 1933," and he won hands down.[70]

NIXON ENJOYED acting on the stage almost as much as he did debating from behind the podium. The students put on a major production each year, and Nixon was an actor in every play put on during his college career. Twice he was the lead—in *Bird in Hand* and in *The Price of Coal*. *Bird in Hand* came in his junior year. The *Quaker Campus* critic pronounced it "the finest dramatic performance yet witnessed at Whittier College." Nixon, the critic continued, "gave an outstanding performance as Thomas Greenleaf, a middle class English inn keeper. He carried his part with exceptional skill. His interpretation of a difficult character was accomplished with a finesse seldom displayed by amateurs."[71]

Professor Upton was the drama coach. "Dick loved the stage . . . " Upton said of his pupil. "He was one of our first successful actors. . . . I wouldn't have been surprised if, after college, he had gone on to New York or Hollywood looking for a job as an actor." In *Bird in Hand*, Nixon played the part of an old man whose daughter, played by Ola Florence, eloped with a scoundrel. "My first problem was to teach him to walk across the stage as if he were at least forty years older," Upton said. "He had to express profound grief over the elopement. . . . "

In rehearsal Nixon got the walk down pretty good, but he could not summon real tears. Upton feared he would never make it. "Now, there are tricks to this," he told Nixon. "If you just concentrate real hard on getting a big lump in your throat, I think you can cry real tears." Then, to Upton's delight, "on the night of the performance, Dick sat in his chair as a man of sixty-five, and the tears rolled down and dropped off his nose as he told the pitiful story of losing his daughter. Buckets of tears. I was amazed at his perfection."[72]

Forty-five years later, Nixon told interviewer David Frost that he never cried except in public before an audience. When, in 1952, Eisenhower kept him on the ticket after the Checkers speech, Nixon put his head on Senator William Knowland's shoulder and wept. Upton, watching on television, exclaimed, "That's my boy! That's my actor!"[73]

IN JUNE 1934, Nixon graduated from Whittier College. He was on the honor society for the fourth straight year, and was second in his class. That spring he had seen a notice on the bulletin board announcing scholarships at a newly created law school at Duke University, in North Carolina, and had applied. He asked Professors Smith and Upton to write letters of recommendation.

Smith wrote: "I do not wish to badger professional schools on behalf of our students and it is only when I feel that we have an unusually well qualified one that I feel free to write to you as I do."

Upton wrote: "During the four years in which I have observed his rather prominent career at Whittier College he has displayed human understanding, personal eloquence and a marked ability to lead. He is intellectually honest, modest and youthfully enthusiastic. If he has any handicap, it is his lack of sophistication."[74]

In late May 1934, Nixon got the good news—he had won a scholarship to Duke's Law School. "The night he found out," Ola remembered, "oh, we had fun that night. He was not only fun, he was joyous, abandoned—the only time I remember him that way. He said it was the best thing that ever happened to him. We rode around in his car and just celebrated."[75]

If Nixon had spent more such evenings with Ola, he could have won and held her love. But if he had spent more such evenings, he might well have failed to win his scholarship. The choice was his, he made it, and he never regretted it, although he did regret losing Ola. But it could not be helped—she had to be sacrificed to his ambitions. Wooing and winning Ola would have involved the strong possibility of marriage, and children, with Nixon remaining in his father's grocery store to support his family. Much as he liked Ola, he did not love her enough to give up his ambitions, which extended far beyond the confines of the grocery.

"His ambition was a little engine that never quit." Billy Herndon said that of Abraham Lincoln. The statement fit Nixon as well. "We just always assumed he was going to law school," Ola said. This was in sharp contrast to his fellow graduates, nearly every one of whom went to work immediately in that Depression year.[76] None, however, were surprised at Nixon's decision. In bull sessions with the Orthogonians, he had often said that he was going to study law and then go into politics.

That he had a talent for it was obvious to all his classmates. One of them said of Nixon, "Whatever he became involved in, he had to be the leader. When he sees a need for something, he not only tries to do it himself, he tries to get everybody else involved in helping to do this and getting it going the way he thinks it should go."[77]

Nixon's various triumphs at Whittier College almost demanded prophecy, and his fellow students were ready to make their own. Ola Florence thought he would go on to the Supreme Court. The Orthogonians thought he would go even farther. "If this fellow keeps it up the way he is going," they said to each other, "someday he will be President."[78]

ALMOST THREE DECADES later, after he had lost the 1960 presidential election, Nixon described what he called "the Great American Legend as to how presidential candidates are born and made." The legend, he said, had a mother taking her child on her knee, looking into his eyes, sensing that there was something truly extraordinary about the baby, and saying to herself, "You, son, are going to be President some day." From that time on, Nixon continued, "he is tapped for greatness. He talks before he walks. He reads a thousand words a minute. He is bored by school because he is so much smarter than his teachers. He prepares himself for leadership by taking courses in public speaking and political science. He drives ever upward, calculating every step of the way until he reaches his and—less importantly—the nation's destiny by becoming President. . . . "[79]

Nixon denied that his legend had anything to do with him, but by that stage of his career, denial of what seemed obvious to everyone else had become second nature to him.

NIXON GAVE MUCH to Whittier College, and got a great deal in return, but one thing he never found there was friendship. He had a close student-teacher relationship with Chief Newman, and a good social relationship with the Orthogonians. He was widely admired and respected and had few enemies. But he had no real friends either. Bill Hornaday was his campaign manager, sat with him in class and beside him on the football bench, was a fellow Orthogonian and a fellow debater. They were together for many hours on almost every day for four years. Yet Hornaday felt he did not know Nixon. "I wouldn't say he was highly loved," Hornaday said, "because there was always this barrier. Always. You didn't feel like going and putting your arm around him."[80]

Nixon placed this barrier between his classmates and himself. He was a mystery to his steady girl friend. He was always lonely, even though his frenetic life-style meant that he was almost never alone. Harold's death played an important role in his loneliness, because Harold was his best chance at establishing an open, trusting, honest, loving, adult relationship with another human being. Harold could have thrown an arm around him, given him a hug, penetrated his mysteries, told him to stop being such a stuffed shirt, taught him to laugh and see the funny side of life, in general made him loosen up and enjoy himself. Harold was the kind of boy people did want to hug, or go backpacking with, and he might have brought out such qualities in his younger brother had he been healthy and had he lived. But Harold was not well enough to do these things for Dick before he died, and no one else could take his place.

Hannah thought that Dick might have felt guilty about surviving Arthur's and Harold's deaths. It seems just as likely that he felt cheated, deprived, abandoned, that he was sorry for himself, not for Harold. It also appears that his reaction was to never again give his love and admiration, as he had to Harold, for fear of the pain of separation.

In any event, as a college student Nixon was not trying to be loved. He was trying to get ahead, and he was successful. His recommendations to Duke were glowing. Along with those from Smith and Upton, there was one from Whittier's president, Walter Dexter, who wrote the Duke Law School dean, "I cannot recommend him too highly because I believe that Nixon will become one of America's important, if not great leaders."[81]

CHAPTER FIVE

DUKE LAW SCHOOL
1934–1937

DUKE'S LAW SCHOOL in 1934 was brand-new, but it had almost unlimited financial resources, a magnificent campus, and a determination to become the best law school in the South. The money came from James Buchanan Duke, who had made a fortune in tobacco and left a huge endowment to Trinity College in Durham, North Carolina. The austere little Methodist college took the money, and its benefactor's name, and almost overnight became a modern, comprehensive university. To attract gifted students to the Law School, in 1934 Duke offered twenty-five scholarships to an incoming class of forty-four. There were twelve professors; Duke kept the student-teacher ratio low to raise the school's reputation.

Nixon's letter from Dean Justin Miller, informing him that he had won a scholarship (a $250 full-tuition grant), also warned him that to retain the award in his second and third years he would have to maintain a B average or better.[1] When the letter arrived, Hannah said in 1960, it was "the proudest day of my life—yes, even prouder than the day Richard became Vice President. I was in the kitchen, baking pies. . . . The door swung open. Richard had an open letter in his hand. He waved it excitedly. 'Mother, guess what!' he exclaimed. 'I have a scholarship for Duke!' "[2]

He arrived in Durham in September, and was almost immediately beset by a crisis of confidence. For all its virtues, Whittier College was a small, backwater place. Going there from Whittier High was not a big step up—in fact, Nixon did little more than cross the street. Many of his college classmates had also attended Whittier High, and the remainder came from nearby high schools that were also competent but hardly outstanding. The competition had not changed, and Nixon's impressive success at the college had come with relative ease.

All that changed at Duke. Whittier College could have fit into one small corner of the Duke campus. There were beautiful gardens, lovely walks, spires and towers and stained glass everywhere. To Nixon, "Duke was like a medieval cathedral town."[3] He was three thousand miles from home, clear across the North American continent, the first time he had ever been east of the Rocky Mountains. He was meeting more new people in a day than he met in a year at Whittier, and from all over—the forty-four students in his class came from thirty-seven states. And he was challenged as Whittier could never challenge him. On his first day, he learned that his fellow students called the scholarship program "the meat grinder," because of the twenty-five awarded scholarships in 1934 only twelve would be renewed in 1935. A B average, it turned out, would not be enough by itself to stay on scholarship.

The competition was intense, far more so than at Whittier. One night in October, studying in the library, Nixon began to doubt that he could ever make it at Duke. He was homesick, overwhelmed by the material thrown at him in the seven courses he was taking, and worried that if he failed to hold his scholarship he would never be able to finish law school. He was so clearly upset that William Adelson, an upperclassman who happened by, asked him, "What's wrong?"

"I'm scared," Nixon replied. "I counted thirty-two Phi Beta Kappa keys in my class. I don't believe I can stay up top in that group."

"Listen, Nixon," Adelson rejoined, "you needn't worry. The fact that you are studying so late yourself shows you don't mind hard work. You've got an iron butt, and that's the secret of becoming a lawyer."[4]

Adelson was right on the mark. Duke used the case-study method—students were required to commit innumerable cases to memory, were expected to be able to give the details and the judgments in litigation of all types. The secrets to success were a strong memory and a willingness to sit in the library for endless hours. Nixon had both.

But it took more than one casual remark, indeed even more than outstanding grades in his first semester, for him to realize that he was capable of competing with the best on a national level. He wrote regularly to Ola Florence. They were "sad letters," she recalled. "He sounded like he was close to quitting two or three times."[5]

His financial situation added greatly to his anxiety. His scholarship was precarious, and he knew that his parents could not pay his tuition. Frank was loaning him $35 per month for his living expenses, and he made another $30 or so per month working in the library—the money came from the National Youth Administration, a New Deal agency. As will be seen, he lived as close to the bone as he possibly could, which was much closer than other poor students, indeed as close as most monks get. In fact, he could have lived more comfortably, had he wished, but he was saving money for a special purpose.

Money just did not matter to him. Had he wanted to make money, he could have stayed in Whittier and expanded the family business. Nor did he care very much about what money could buy —he would just as soon have a five-cent candy bar for breakfast as a fifteen-cent platter of eggs, he was indifferent as to his clothes, could not have cared less about his living accommodations, and could get along very well without the relaxation of an expensive date. He wanted only one thing out of Duke, a good law degree, and he got it.

As a law student, Nixon's chief characteristic was his willingness to work. A classmate recorded, "Some of us might fudge on the hours we worked at the library. Nixon never would. He was a copybook kind of guy without being obnoxious about it." Bill Perdue, who roomed with Nixon from January 1935 until they graduated, said, "Nixon had a quality of intensity in him, worked hard, pretty intense guy—he had a sense of privacy and not terribly strong on humor." Professor Lon Fuller said Nixon was competent, "though not terribly imaginative or profound. And he was what today we'd call uptight—there was the suggestion of an intellectual inferiority complex."[6] Whatever the cause, a classmate put it bluntly when he called Nixon "the hardest-working man I ever met."[7]

Anxiety and pessimism drove him to work ever harder, but sometimes, nevertheless, he was close to despair. "I'll never learn the law," he complained. "There is too much of it."[8] The challenge seemed too great. "I had never been faced with such an overwhelming mass of material." He complained enough, and looked sufficiently downcast, to earn the nickname "Gloomy Gus."

The name had another meaning, classmate Lyman Brownfield recalled. "There was a comic strip character by that name who was always puncturing people's fanciful balloons, bringing them down to earth. That was Nixon."[9] Another student remembered Nixon as "a very studious individual—almost fearfully so. I can see him sitting in the law library hunched over a book, seldom even looking up. He never smiled. . . . Even on Saturday nights, he was in the library, studying.[10]

"He never smiled." What an extraordinary thing for a young man who actually had a very nice smile and a great deal to smile about. When he allowed himself to smile, he could light up a room. He had good, straight, gleaming white teeth, with nice crinkles around his eyes. In repose, his heavy jowls sagged and added years to his appearance, but when he smiled, the jowls lifted up, dimples appeared, and what had been a slightly sinister appearance became a glowing one. But so seldom did he allow himself to feel good about himself that "he never smiled," and his classmates at Duke, like those back in Whittier, nicknamed him "Gloomy Gus." The art of studying is the art of applying the seat of the pants to the seat of a chair, and Nixon had not traveled across the continent to indulge himself in feeling good or counting his blessings. He stayed in his chair, his head down, eyes riveted on the printed page. He did not have time to look up and flash a grin of acknowledgment at a fellow student passing by.

The work paid off. At the Christmas break in 1934, he was maintaining an A average and stood near the top of the class. For the holiday, he joined his younger brother Don—who was attending Guilford Preparatory School in North Carolina—to drive to New York, their first visit to the city. They had saved money for the vacation, which was primarily a shopping expedition. As Hannah told the story, "The two boys . . . pooled their money, and they bought something for which they had also saved a long time—a fur piece for me. It was my first." [11]

Nixon had not only saved, he had sacrificed for that gift. For living quarters, he had moved into an abandoned toolshed in the woods near campus. A maintenance man found him there, studying, in an eight-by-twelve-foot shed, lined with corrugated cardboard. There was a bed but no stove. Amazed, the maintenance man asked, "You mean you're going to school and can't afford a room? You'll freeze to death."

"I'll manage all right if you don't run me out," Nixon replied. Thinking to himself, "This boy must want an education real bad," the maintenance man decided not to report him.[12]

To Nixon, there was no sacrifice involved in this Spartan style of life. He was indifferent to creature comforts. He really did not care what he ate, so long as it would sustain life, nor where he slept, so long as he could get enough sleep to be alert in class and the library, nor what he wore, so long as it did not excite comment. He did not regard student poverty as either romantic or crushing;

he did not particularly like it, but he did not particularly mind it either.

Following Christmas vacation, Nixon took a room at $5 per month, which he shared with Bill Perdue. He got up each day at 5 A.M., studied until classes began, worked afternoons in the library at menial jobs paying thirty-five cents an hour, and studied again in the evening until midnight or later.

Classmate Brownfield had a 1926 Packard, into which Nixon and eight other students would pile each day for a drive to a board-inghouse where they could eat all they could hold for twenty-five cents. That little trip provided the students with a major outlet for their physical energy. "Every time we collected in the car," Brownfield remembered, "the group climbed on someone's back and didn't let up until we reached the boardinghouse. Sometimes it was Nixon, sometimes it was someone else. . . . Nixon was thoroughly at home in the horseplay and joined in both as subject and tormentor. . . . "[13] He also tried to get in an hour of handball each afternoon, which provided him with an opportunity to take a shower in the locker room.[14] Another major form of release from tension came at the Duke football games, where Nixon cheered so loudly he came away hoarse.

NIXON'S CONSISTENT high marks brought attention to him, as did his willingness and ability to speak up in class. For all his private doubts and "Gloomy Gus" fears, he still had that old confidence he had felt as a debater for Whittier when he rose before a group.

One of his professors, Douglas B. Maggs, would deliberately press the students when he called on them to recite. Believing that a lawyer should be able to think under stress, he would raise his voice, pound his desk, ask questions bluntly or even insultingly, and generally try to create tension. Standing up to Maggs was "not easy," Brownfield remembered. "For the first couple of months I think all who did so felt a little like Christian martyrs facing the lions. Maggs would reduce you to a shambles in class. He'd make you look like an idiot."

But for Nixon, Maggs's classroom confrontations were mother's milk. He would be nervous before the bell rang, Brownfield said, but once he got on his feet to make a point, "I never saw him back down. I remember Nixon standing Maggs off in our freshman torts class."[15] Another student reported that "Dick was obviously just as nervous as anyone else, but, from the first time he recited in any class, I never saw him back down. . . . "[16]

IN THE SUMMER of 1935, Nixon and Don drove back across the continent to California to spend the summer working in their father's store. Nixon also tried to rekindle the romance with Ola, but was as inept as always. Although they had exchanged correspondence through the year, she had been dating Gail Jobe regularly (and would marry him shortly thereafter), and by no means considered herself to be Nixon's betrothed. But he thought of her as his girl, and even assumed that they would someday get married. He was not, however, willing to go to parties with her friends, or otherwise be the kind of person who appealed to her.

"He came home one time," she later said of that summer, "and was talking about torts. I said that's something you cook, and he said, 'You're going to have to learn something about the law terms now.' " [17] Instead of learning law, Ola got rid of Nixon.

Ola's rejection was Nixon's only contact with women during his years in law school. He never had a single date at Duke. "There were a few girls I liked and would have enjoyed dating," he later said, "but I didn't have the money." Time was another problem, as was an absence of social graces. A classmate said that Nixon was "stiff and stilted when talking to girls, informal and relaxed with male students." He seldom joined in the occasional social gatherings. Ethel Farley Hunter found him "dour and aloof, not given to fellowship." In addition, she said she "found his value system unattractive. . . . He was not unmoral, just amoral. He had no particular ethical system, no strong convictions." But she also recognized that "he was there to learn skills and advance himself personally." [18]

To those ends he continued to devote himself with his monklike dedication through his second year. Beyond the football games and his handball workouts, the only diversion he allowed himself was politics. In the spring of 1936, he ran for president of the Duke Student Bar Association. His opponent was Hale McCown, a popular campus figure who went on to become a member of the Supreme Court of Nebraska. Nixon won easily, according to his classmates because his scholastic ability was superior to McCown's.

Nixon also found time to serve on the law review, *Law and Contemporary Problems*, for which he wrote articles including "Changing Rules of Liability in Automobile Accident Litigation." He continued his job for the NYA in the library. His boss, a Miss Covington, was "a woman with set notions" and no student wanted to work for her—but Nixon had to. Brownfield recalled that "Dick was . . . subjected to a lot of ribbing because of his boss, but during my three years with him I never heard him complain about her. I am always reminded of his school job when I see his self-control and reserve in the face of severe abuses in politics." [19]

The work in the library, the research and writing for the *Law *and Contemporary Problems*, and the time taken to campaign for office, all took a toll in Nixon's second year. His average began to slip. At the end of his first year, he stood third in the class, behind Perdue and Brownfield. But toward the end of his second year, he felt he was in real trouble with his class standing.

Late that spring of 1936, Nixon, Perdue, and Frederick Albrink were walking past the dean's office. The grades and class standings were due to be posted, but for some reason there had been a delay. Restless and anxious, the students decided on action. There was a narrow transom above the dean's door, and although the door was locked, the transom was open. Nixon was the thinnest of the three, so Perdue and Albrink gave him a boost. Once inside, he opened the door; together the students found the key to the dean's desk drawer and located the records. Nixon learned that he had fallen below third place, that his average was B-plus. They replaced everything and left.

The incident remained unknown until Nixon told it to Bela Kornitzer in 1959.[20] In the mid-seventies, after Watergate, it was revived and re-examined—"Nixon's first breaking and entering"— and a great fuss was made over it. Fawn Brodie, who was full of moral indignation, interviewed Albrink and Perdue about it, but both denied that it had any special significance. "We found the files . . . and looked at them," Albrink related matter-of-factly. "Didn't take any . . . didn't change any. This was night; there was nobody in the building. What the heck!"[21]

THAT SUMMER, Nixon took the train back to Whittier, where he again worked in the store. In the fall, he moved into a shack in the woods with Albrink, Brownfield, and Perdue. They gave the cabin a fanciful name, Whippoorwill Manor. They had a single room, no electricity, no plumbing, only a sheet-metal stove and an outhouse. There was also a water pump outside. There were two double beds; Albrink and Brownfield shared one, Perdue and Nixon the other. "The first guy up would usually light the paper we kept in the stove," Albrink recalled. "We'd have heat for about five minutes and then the stove would be too hot to touch for an hour. You had to get dressed and out fast."

Nixon was up first, often rising an hour before the others so that he could get in the extra study time. "He was always thoughtful," Brownfield said. "When he'd get up early he'd dress in the cold, so we could use the stove when we got up." Nixon kept his shaving gear tucked behind some books in the stacks of the law-school library. He shaved in the men's room. His showers were in the gym, after handball. The roommates bought secondhand textbooks and shared them.[22]

Nixon's roommates were southerners who shared their region's prejudices and outlook. Back at Whittier, Nixon had been responsible for bringing William Brock into the Orthogonians—Brock was a star halfback and the only Negro on campus.[23] Segregation in the South, in the years before World War II, was total, unquestioned, observed by all, and none of Nixon's roommates could understand how on earth he could ever sit down at the same table with a Negro. When he said he had done it often, in his home as well as with the Orthogonians, they were doubly shocked.

For his part, Nixon began to learn, and to some extent to appreciate, the southern point of view, not only on race relations but also on the Civil War. When he came to Duke, Nixon said years later, "I was utterly convinced that Ulysses S. Grant was the best general produced on either side in the Civil War." But after rooming with Perdue for two years, "I was almost convinced by [his] constant hammering on it that Ulysses S. Grant would be lucky to be about fourth behind Robert E. Lee, Joseph Johnson, and Stonewall Jackson." He learned from Perdue to call the conflict the War Between the States.[24] Nixon also said that although he could not agree with his southern friends on the question of race relations, "I learned in these years to understand and respect them for their patriotism, their pride, and their enormous interest in national issues."[25]

He remained adamant on the race question. "He was shocked and disturbed at the prevalent North Carolina treatment of the Negro population as an inferior group," one classmate recalled. Another remembered his "very strong moral convictions." Nixon "never let many opportunities go by to express himself on those convictions with a great deal of feeling and finality." Specifically, he objected to the mistreatment of Negroes. "He looked upon the issue . . . as a moral issue and condemned it very strongly as such, but did not realize the problems that confronted the people of the South in regard to the negro."[26]

ALTHOUGH NIXON was president of the Student Bar Association, his position was more honorary than demanding. His responsibilities were to preside over the monthly meeting, which consisted of little more than introducing the speaker. He joined the Iredell fraternity, and did extracurricular work in the local legal clinic, primarily legwork on cases coming up for the district prosecuting attorney. That work was for free, but he added to his income by doing some research for Dean Horack under the auspices of the NYA. Horack and his wife took such a liking to Nixon that they frequently had him over for dinner, usually spaghetti, his favorite meal.[27]

A free meal was an event worthy of note, as Nixon continued to deny himself all but the bare essentials. Five weeks before graduation he wrote his folks, "The budget for the remainder of the year says that I will need $25. That, I am happy to say will be the last check I'll be asking for—for good—I hope." [28]

NIXON'S MATERNAL grandmother, Almira Milhous, helped out from time to time, with a $5 or $10 bill, or a package of food. She sent her grandson a pair of badly needed glasses. In return, he wrote her in early December of 1936 a letter that would melt the heart of any grandmother anywhere.

"At this Christmas season," he began, "I should like to be sending you a gift which would really express my love for you— but it will probably be several years before I reach such a high financial level—if ever." So, he explained, he was sending "this Christmas note" in lieu of a present. "You will never know how much I've appreciated your rememberances," he continued. Even more, however, he said he appreciated being a part of her extended family. "Sometimes—in our spare moments, some of us indulge in reminiscing sessions here at school—and the boys are amazed at the remarkable person I describe as my Quaker Grandmother. I myself share their respect." He signed off, "Your Loving Grandson, Richard Milhous Nixon." [29]

FOR CHRISTMAS vacation, Nixon used his savings for a trip to New York City. Bill Perdue went along, as did Harlan Leathers. They were job hunting, and they made the rounds of all the top law firms in the city. Wild Bill Donovan, who later commanded the OSS, was head of one; Herbert Brownell, Jr., who became Eisenhower's Attorney General, was a member of another; Thomas Dewey was associated with a third. Nixon was most impressed by Sullivan and Cromwell, of which John Foster Dulles was senior partner.

Perdue and Leathers, ranking first and second, got good jobs, but Nixon—ranking third in a small class from an unproved law school—did not. In 1959 Nixon declared, "If they had given me a job I'm sure I would have been there today, a corporation lawyer instead of Vice-President." [30]

That is where most of his classmates thought he would end up. "It just never entered our minds," Albrink said, "that he would make a career in politics." Another classmate said he thought of Nixon "as the man least likely to succeed in politics." [31] Basil Whitener, who later became a congressman from North Carolina, declared, "Nixon was not outward, but seemed shy. He was friendly in a quiet way. He was no smiler then; quite the contrary. Like most others, I figured he would wind up doing a wonderful job in a big law firm, handling securities or other matters that need the attention of a scholar, not a politician." [32]

It was a mark of how completely Nixon had suppressed himself that his classmates could not envision a political future for him. But in truth his ambition to be a leader was stronger than ever; to it he sacrificed his chances with Ola, his own physical comfort, and his recreation and entertainment for three years. He was interested in prestige, power, a leadership role, not the big money a top law firm could give him.

He was so uninterested, in fact, that he almost did not make the job-hunting trip, and only agreed to go at the last minute. Nor did he find New York attractive. To save money, they stayed at the YMCA. Perdue recalled that "in our naïveté we went into a saloon and ordered a sandwich. We waited interminably and found out later they had to send out for the sandwiches." Small wonder that, in Perdue's words, "Nixon was not charmed by New York . . . he had a West Coast prejudice."[33]

About a month after they returned to Durham, Nixon got a letter from Donovan, Leisure, Newton and Lombard asking if he would return to New York for another interview. "By that time," Nixon wrote in his memoirs, "I was no longer so keen on the idea of starting out in that cold and expensive city."[34]

Instead, he went to his professors for advice. Lon Fuller recalled, "He said he thought he might go back to Whittier and practice law. I sort of said ho-hum about that. I thought he could do better than that." Nixon said he had also been thinking of the FBI. "I said I thought he was too good a man for that, too."[35]

The FBI was recruiting at Duke, and as Nixon later remarked, "The FBI looked very good to a young lawyer wanting work that year." He submitted an application and had an interview. He also had Dean Horack write the director, J. Edgar Hoover. Horack went all out. Nixon, he wrote, is "one of the finest young men, both in character and ability, that I have ever had the opportunity of having in my classes. He is a superior student, alert, aggressive, a fine speaker and one who can do an exceptionally good piece of research when called upon to do so."[36]

Like Professor Fuller, however, Horack thought Nixon was rather too good for the FBI. But he knew Nixon better than Fuller did, had spent time with him discussing his future, and had a better sense of where Nixon was going, and how to get there. When no job offer from the FBI came through,* Horack called the discouraged Nixon into his office.

---

* Years later Hoover explained to Vice-President Nixon that he had been accepted, but the FBI appropriation was cut before the job could be offered.

"Dick," he said, "if you're going to go into politics, go back to your hometown and establish yourself in a law firm." Nixon decided to do just that.

GRADUATION WAS glorious. Nixon was third in his class and therefore a member of the Order of the Coif, an honorary society. At the Senior Beer Bust, an outdoor party in which the senior class played the faculty at softball, Nixon astonished his classmates when he caught a softball in one hand while holding his beer in the other.

He was not accustomed to drinking—he had never touched alcohol at Whittier and had been to only a couple of beer parties at Duke. After three or four beers, he mounted a picnic table and delivered a speech that convulsed his audience, in the process showing a side of himself he had completely suppressed throughout his years at Duke—his acting ability and, of all things, a genuine talent as a humorist.

Brownfield had a vivid memory of the speech. He recalled, "With a completely serious expression, [Nixon] titled his talk 'Insecurity,' and he managed to get everything about Social Security so tangled up and backwards that he sounded like Red Skelton."

Throughout graduation week, Brownfield continued, "every time a group of students found him near a convenient table, they tried to get him to make a funny speech. But . . . he seldom responded." [37] His mother, father, little brother Edward, and Grandmother Milhous—then eighty-eight years old—drove across the country to attend the ceremonies, and he concentrated on showing them around campus, not entertaining. "I'm fundamentally relatively shy," he explained in 1959 to Stewart Alsop. "It doesn't come natural to me to be a buddy-buddy boy." He added, "I can't really let my hair down with anyone."

Not even old friends? Alsop asked. "Not even with my family," Nixon responded. But, he quickly added, there was "one thing people are wrong about—I can have as good a time as anybody." [38] His performance at the Senior Beer Bust proved the point, but it also illustrated how tight a control Nixon kept on himself, how infrequently he would indulge his ability to relax and have fun.

NIXON DROVE BACK to Whittier with his family. He was surprised to learn that the special "prep" course given at USC for law graduates who were scheduled to take the California bar examination had been under way for three months. Despairing of catching up, but determined to try, Nixon went to work. He wrote Horack that he was working harder even than he had at Duke. He caught influenza. "I didn't miss a day of school due to illness at Duke," he told

Horack, "and the first thing when I get back to Southern California, I catch the flu."

When Horack wrote him to point out that he had the honor of being the first Duke graduate to take the California bar exam, Nixon replied, "The first graduate to take it has a darn good chance to fail it." Horack shot back, "They'll have to flunk them all if they don't let you by." In the event, he passed easily. On November 9, 1937, he was sworn in as a practicing attorney before the California Supreme Court.[39]

HE WAS two months short of his twenty-fifth birthday. His life to date had been an unbroken record of achievement and success. If he was unloved outside his family, he was widely respected. His peers had turned to him for leadership, from his grade-school days through law school, and he had always responded, indeed encouraged them to turn to him. His honesty and sincerity were known and appreciated, to the point that had he been in the used-car business his peers would have flocked to him to buy their vehicles. He had a strong sense of priorities, and never hesitated to put his own career ahead of everything else, but he also had a strong sense of duty. When he sought a job, or had one thrust upon him, he met the responsibilities of the post, without fail and without complaint.

To his southern classmates, he appeared to be "a true liberal." Brownfield made that judgment, but evidently he had race relations in mind, because he went on to describe a classic middle-of-the-road philosophical stance. Nixon, Brownfield said, "was strongly sympathetic of the rights of the individual, particularly when the individual found himself opposed by the unequal and artificially created force of big government, big society, or big business. However, Dick never felt that an individual could transfer his responsibilities to the government and at the same time keep his freedom."[40]

Nixon thought of himself as a conservative Republican; he was strongly anti-FDR. Not for Nixon the armchair socialism that was so popular with many highly educated, highly intelligent young men in the mid-thirties. His views were decidedly conventional; never in any way was he a rebel.

There were large vacuums in his life. He could memorize and summarize with the best anywhere, but there was little originality of thought. He was almost twenty-five years old, but had no women friends, much less the love of a woman he loved. In fact, he had no close friends at all, not even Perdue, with whom he shared a bed for a year and a room for two and one-half years. They hardly saw each other after graduation day and barely corresponded.[41]

NIXON'S UNWILLINGNESS to let anyone get close to him, and his apparent inability to get close to anyone, has been characteristic of Nixon throughout his life. From grade school to high school to college to law school and then out into the world, he left behind his old associates. His associations came to an end when Nixon no longer had an organizational connection with a person, whether as classmate, or teacher, or associate. When an acquaintance could only be called "a friend from the old days," Nixon lost interest in him. He had no friends from the old days. By limiting his friendships to men with whom he had a current working relationship, Nixon created a situation in which his friendships were never probing, open, inquisitive. He did not share emotions or spin fantasies, or indulge in the other intimacies of true friendship. Rather, his friendships were more like business meetings or staff seminars or study groups. Nixon used people, rather than responding to them; he hid himself from people, rather than opening himself to friends.

Nixon was twenty-four years old when he left Duke. He knew lots of intelligent people. Yet there was not one person in the world, save his mother, who would have claimed to know him well. He was as much a mystery to his roommates, despite a setting (Whippoorwill Manor) that could not have been more conducive to the spawning of lifelong friendships, as he was to Ola Florence. Moreover, not one of his acquaintances, including his roommates and Ola Florence, ever wanted to know him better. From the woman's point of view, he was not a person you wanted to hug; from a man's point of view, he was not the kind of guy you would ask on a backpacking trip.

He had a limited though real capacity to love and be loved, to trust and be trusting, as his relationships with his mother and his grandmother showed. He also had a capacity to joke and have fun and get people to laugh, as his graduation celebration demonstrated. But he suppressed this side of himself, to the point that it almost seemed he had taken a vow to ruthlessly spurn any characteristic that might keep him from achieving his ambitions. He denied himself the pleasure of simple fun and the joy of simple friendship. The time and energy saved he put into his work and career.

But although the young Nixon was not a man people wanted to get close to individually, he was someone with a magnetic appeal for people in groups. Crowds did not frighten him. Perhaps this was because crowds could not expect him to bare his soul before them, nor embarrass him by telling him innermost secrets. Instead, with people in groups he could concentrate on some action that needed to be carried out, an action requiring people to work together to achieve a common objective, whether it be a homecoming dance or arranging for a speaker or a graduation party, and in such activity he was superb. No one was a better organizer or had more energy or got more done than Dick Nixon.

He was a man most comfortable before an audience, most uncomfortable with individuals or a small group. He was a man of obvious leadership ability despite his lack of easy warmth and his loneliness of spirit. He was a man with first-rate mental equipment. Most of all, he was a man with a fierce drive, an eagerness to win, and an insatiable hunger for success.

He had learned all he could at Whittier and Duke. He was ready to launch his career and realize his ambitions, on which he placed no limits whatsoever.

CHAPTER SIX

WHITTIER:
LAW AND MARRIAGE
1937–1941

WHEN NIXON returned to Whittier, the town had grown to a population of about twenty-five thousand and was rapidly becoming a suburb of Los Angeles. It was still small enough, however, for family connections to count heavily, and Nixon used his to obtain his first job. His grandfather, Franklin Milhous, had been partners back in Indiana with Thomas Bewley's grandfather; Tom Bewley was a partner in the firm of Wingert and Bewley. Hannah Nixon heard that Wingert would be retiring soon, and while her son was still at Duke she asked Bewley if he would consider taking Nixon into his office. Bewley asked Professor Smith, "Paul, do you think we'd be making a mistake to take Dick into the firm?" Smith assured him that Nixon was one of his favorite pupils and should become a first-rate lawyer. Bewley told Hannah to have Nixon stop by. After passing the bar exam, he did so. Bewley later said, "When I interviewed Dick I was impressed with his mature looks, actions, and thinking. He was decisive; he knew what he wanted; he was direct and to the point. It took us no more than fifteen or twenty minutes to discuss our partnership." [1]

It really was less a job, more an opportunity. Bewley said he would give Nixon the responsibility for collecting bills, plus accident and divorce cases, all on a percentage basis. But at least Nixon had an office, access to the law firm's library, and a chance to make some money.

"I remember him coming into the office that first day," said Mrs. Evlyn Dorn, the firm's secretary. "He wore a navy blue suit and was a serious young man." Sitting around the office, waiting for some work to come his way, was hardly Nixon's style—on that first day, he went after the years of accumulated dust in the firm's library. He not only dusted the volumes, Mrs. Dorn recalled, but he rearranged them. "He took every one of them out, cleaned up all the shelves, and I think he even used some varnish on them."[2]

At the end of his first week, Nixon got his first assignment. It was a complex civil case in which Marie Schee was suing her uncle to pay back a $2,000 loan. The uncle owned a house; Nixon got a court order to pay Schee back by selling the house in an execution sale. The house was said to be worth $6,500. That was in November 1937. The execution sale took place on June 29, 1938. Tom Bewley was ill that day, so Nixon went alone. Waiting for the proceedings to begin, he made an egregious error; he innocently asked the opposition lawyer, David Schwartz, "Could you be of a little assistance to me when this comes up for sale?" Schwartz advised him to bid the entire sum due his client, which Nixon did, without consulting his client. It then turned out that there were two liens on the house. Countersuits were filed, the complexities deepened, and the net result was that Marie Schee lost everything. Enraged, she instituted a malpractice suit against Wingert and Bewley, who settled out of court for $4,800. It was an expensive blunder on Nixon's part—to the point that he took a short trip to Cuba to investigate the possibilities of going into legal practice there—but fortunately for Nixon, Bewley (who shouldered the blame) forgave him and forgot the incident. (Bewley later said, "I don't remember that he ever lost a case."[3])

THINGS HAD to improve, and they did, but it took time. Bewley put him to work on divorce cases, but Nixon found them distasteful. "I remember when I'd just started law practice," Nixon recalled in 1959. "I had a divorce case to handle, and this good-looking girl, beautiful really, began talking to me about her intimate marriage problems. . . . I turned fifteen colors of the rainbow. I suppose I came from a family too unmodern, really."[4] Accident cases were not so embarrassing to him, but there was not much profit in them. He did prove to be helpful at tax work, and became proficient in setting up small corporations.

"He worked hard," Bewley asserted. "He was always a terrific worker, sometimes putting in sixteen hours a day for days on end. I remember often, as I was returning late at night from some engagement or other, seeing Dick through the window of our office, hard at work. With his shoulders hunched over in his characteristic fashion, he would be pacing up and down the room. This was his habit when he was mulling over a problem, or dictating to a secretary."[5]

Nevertheless, business was slow, putting Nixon in the unfamiliar position of having to kill time. He had extended conversations with Bewley. "Like any young lawyer fresh out of law school," Bewley later said, "Dick was anxious to learn all he could and, at the same time, test out a few of the theories he had learned at the University." The talk often branched out to include politics. "Dick would argue that we needed more businessmen in government, and then we could cut down on the wasteful bureaucracy and run the nation's affairs with the same efficiency that one would run a business."

Even when killing time, Nixon could not relax and simply shoot the breeze. "Dick never joked," Bewley said, "or told stories, or talked about the usual things—women and such. He wasn't profane, but he wasn't a prude. He was just vitally interested in his work and had little time for anything else."[6]

That simply was not true—he had time for many activities, but with the single exception of going to the Whittier College football games on Saturday afternoons, he chose only those activities that would lead to either self-improvement or career success. He even had time to try his hand as a small-business man. It was a get-rich-quick scheme, based on an unusually heavy crop of oranges. A group of young businessmen asked Nixon to draw up incorporation papers for the Citra-Frost Company, and got him to make a small investment of his own. The total capitalization was $10,000. The group asked him to serve as president of the corporation. As he had been president of every organization he had belonged to all his life, Nixon readily agreed. The company set out to freeze orange juice and ship it back East.[7]

Nixon had made another egregious error. The technology was not capable of producing the product. Nixon got a contract with the Owl Drug Company, but the first shipment spoiled—Citra-Frost was trying to freeze the whole juice instead of concentrating it first. To save on costs, Nixon went to a do-it-yourself labor force. "He worked like a dog," Bewley recalled. "He was out there cutting oranges and squeezing oranges day and night after he'd do the work here, and he just couldn't realize that they couldn't make a success of it." He tried various kinds of packages—glass, cellophane, and cardboard—but nothing worked. After a year and a half Citra-Frost went belly up. "He lost all the money he had saved," Bewley said in 1976. "We're still carrying on the books some of the costs we extended in that venture. . . . You'll find people here who hate his guts because of that, people who put money in."[8]

A FAILURE as a businessman, Nixon was not much of a success as a lawyer either. At Bewley's urging, he opened an office in La Habra.

The town was growing, was up to a population of three thousand, had only two lawyers, and the Nixon name was known in the area. Bewley hoped Nixon could drum up some business. One of the La Habra lawyers laughed about it: "So they sent Dick out here, and he was in an old abandoned hardware store. He had a desk in the back end of it. He stayed out there for days on end waiting for business."[9]

Despite these setbacks, Nixon's dogged perseverance began to pay off. "We had a few drunks, some parking problems, traffic stuff," Bewley said. "That was the type of case Dick handled. He also worked with members of the council, drafting ordinances and the like." Slowly, Bewley began to appreciate Nixon's talents. Although the firm was not primarily a trial firm—"We tried to practice preventive medicine," Bewley explained—from time to time he needed a good trial lawyer. He discovered that Nixon was excellent.

"He always seemed to be way ahead of the witness, and could anticipate what answers the witness would make." Further, "he bored right into the heart of a question. And he had courtroom psychology. He could talk so that butter wouldn't melt in his mouth, or he could take hold of a cantankerous witness and shake him like a dog." He dressed with care before going into court, and when he spoke, Bewley said, "he had the right stance, and he used the right voice, which was low, but which he built up gradually with dramatic force." The courtroom gave Nixon an opportunity to use his acting and debating skills.[10] In 1939, Jeff Wingert and Bewley took him in as a partner, with primary responsibility for cross-examination in trials. When he wrote his memoirs, Nixon still recalled the pride he felt: "Now for the first time I was no longer Frank and Hannah Nixon's son—I was Mr. Nixon, the new partner in Wingert and Bewley."[11]

The new partner, according to Jeff Wingert, "was a better politician than he was a lawyer."[12] The dullness of a small-town law practice, coupled with the lack of enough work, could not begin to satisfy Nixon's yearning for success, nor his need to be constantly improving himself and his position. Consequently, he threw himself into civic affairs, his stated reason being that "young lawyers trying to get business for their firms are expected to join local clubs."[13]

He did it with a vengeance. It was almost impossible to hold a meeting anywhere in the area without Nixon attending and taking a prominent role. In his first three years as a lawyer, he served as president of four organizations (plus Citra-Frost) and as the youngest member of the Whittier College board of trustees. There was a movement afoot to make him president of Whittier College.[14]

The 20–30 Club consisted of young businessmen and professionals under thirty years of age. The Whittier local had about fifty members; there were other 20–30 Clubs scattered across the West. Nixon became the Whittier president. In 1939, he attended the national convention in San Francisco, advocating the election of a man from Inglewood for the national presidency. Although he himself did not drink, Nixon obtained a truckload of brandy and champagne and opened a hospitality suite, serving French 75s. He buttonholed delegates and made trade-offs for their votes—he promised the Long Beach club delegates that he would support their bid for the 1940 convention, and so on. It was playing at politics, rather than the real thing, but he found he liked it and was good at it—his candidate won.[15]

In addition to the 20–30 Club, Nixon was president of the Duke University Alumni of California, president of the Orange County Association of Cities, and president of the Whittier College Alumni Association.[16]

Even more amazing was that he got these leadership positions without engaging in any of the usual backslapping, rough-joking world of the small-town businessman and professional. He played no golf. He did not drink. He would not play cards. He told few jokes. He did not smoke. He just was not one of the boys, and never would be—nevertheless, the boys turned to him when they had a job that needed doing.

Older men saw his potential and began to groom him for bigger things. As a start, Bewley, who was the city attorney, made him the assistant attorney and gave him most of the work. Mr. Herman Perry, a local banker, brought him into the Young Republicans (naturally, Nixon became president). Through Perry, another Republican recalled, "Dick was given a pretty good education in local politics."[17] Perry's influence extended far beyond the district. He liked Nixon, liked the way he talked, the things he said he stood for (as did most other businessmen in Orange County), and therefore put him on the banquet circuit.

Nixon developed a speech—"Nine Old Men," an attack on FDR's court-packing plan—and in the first two years he was back in Whittier, according to Harold Stone, "he had given this talk to practically every service club in Southern California." He would drive to San Clemente and give it to the Kiwanis Club there, or to Long Beach to talk to the Lions.[18] Jeff Wingert, watching all this activity from his semiretirement, commented, "That boy will be President of the United States someday if he wants to."[19]

He suffered some setbacks. He tried to talk the La Habra council into making him the city attorney, but failed because the council was satisfied with the man it had. In 1939 he thought about running for the state assembly and discussed the possibility with Perry and others. They thought it was too soon, that he needed more time to establish himself, and he reluctantly accepted their judgment. He made speeches for Wendell Willkie, which proved to be another losing cause.[20]

Try as he might, Nixon could not find enough service clubs to keep him busy. Shortly after his return to Whittier, therefore, he joined the local little theater group. His purpose, he told one acquaintance, was not to have fun, but rather to meet people and perhaps pick up some "added contacts."[21] The group put on six plays per year; Nixon began by helping with the lighting and the sets.

In late 1937, the director, Mrs. Louise Baldwin, decided to produce a play with a famous jury trial, *The Night of January 16th*. She approached Wallace Black, a Whittier lawyer, and asked him to play the role of District Attorney Flint. Black could not accept, but on his way to lunch that day he ran into Nixon in the elevator in the Bank of America building, and it occurred to him that Nixon would be perfect for the part. Nixon hesitated, until Black said, "Well, if you get up there on the stage and make a good lawyer, it might bring you some business."[22]

Nixon read for the role, got it, and put on a convincing performance. He had "above-average acting ability," Mrs. Baldwin said, but "I wouldn't have put any money on his becoming a successful actor, unless he had gone into the movies. He was very handsome."[23]

Hortense Behrens played opposite Nixon. Because she did not know how to drive a car, he would take her home after rehearsals in his Model A Ford. She tried to tell jokes and otherwise get him to relax, "but I have never heard him *really*, honest-to-goodness laugh out loud." Shaking her head at the memory, Mrs. Behrens added, "I don't think he does."[24]

In January 1938, Mrs. Baldwin began the tryouts for *The Dark Tower*. Nixon was reading for the role of Barry Jones. Elizabeth Cloes, a local schoolteacher and member of the Whittier Community Players, encouraged a friend and fellow teacher, Pat Ryan, to try for the part of Daphne Martin. "I wasn't too anxious," Ryan recalled. The part called for her to sing a little song, and she was no singer. But "I was a new teacher in Whittier, and they encouraged teachers to take part in all the local events in town, including the Little Theater, which was quite thriving at the time." After the reading, Mrs. Baldwin offered her the role. She accepted, although she admitted afterward that "I was sort of pressured into it."[25]

A tall, slender woman in her mid-twenties, Ryan caught Nixon's eye immediately, and held it through the evening. Her cheeks, a friend said, were "like apricots, with just that little bit of freckling on them that looked so fresh." She had brownish-red hair, which she wore mid-length and neatly done, as befit a beginning teacher. Her eyes were dark and flashing; her nose, straight and thin. Her lips were small but curled up in a smile, even when at rest. She had high cheekbones. She moved with an easy grace that was the envy of her many friends. It was not just Nixon whose eye she caught—everyone felt drawn to this most attractive and pleasant young woman.[26]

Nixon was attentive all evening long. When the tryout ended, he offered to drive her and Elizabeth Cloes home in his Model A. They accepted, but then to his chagrin Cloes sat in the middle, next to him. Undaunted, he leaned across Cloes and said to Ryan, "I'd like to have a date with you."

"Oh, I'm too busy," she said, laughing.

At the next meeting of the little theater group, Nixon drove Cloes and Ryan to the rehearsal, then home again afterward. Again he asked for a date, only to be rebuffed.

As they were preparing to go home after the third meeting, Cloes said to Ryan, "Pat, you sit next to him." She refused. On the way home, Nixon leaned across Cloes again and asked, "When are you going to give me that date?" Again Ryan laughed and shook her head.

"Don't laugh," Nixon said, pointing his finger at her. "Someday I'm going to marry you."

This time, Cloes reported, "did she laugh!" Later, Ryan said, "I thought he was nuts or something. I guess I just looked at him. I couldn't imagine anyone ever saying anything like that so suddenly."[27] It was very out of character for Nixon, who never did anything on impulse. He himself put it best in his memoirs: "For me it was a case of love at first sight."[28]

THELMA CATHERINE RYAN was born on March 16, 1912, in Ely, Nevada, so she was ten months older than Nixon. Her father, William Ryan, was an Irishman who spent most of his life chasing the pot of gold at the end of the rainbow. Born in Connecticut in 1866, by the time he was forty-four he had been a deckhand on a whaling ship, a surveyor in the Philippines, and a gold miner in the Klondike and in the Black Hills of South Dakota.

While in the Hills he met a young widow with two children, Kate Halberstadt Bender, whose husband had died in a mining accident. Kate had been born in Hesse, Germany. They were married in 1909 and shortly afterward went chasing again, this time to

Ely, where Ryan set up his family in a tent city outside the mines
and got a job as a silver miner. Eventually the family moved into a
real house, where three children were born to the union—sons
William, Jr., and Thomas, and daughter Thelma. The proximity of
Thelma's birth to St. Patrick's Day led to her nickname, "Pat"—
but only her father called her that. To her mother, her brothers,
and her friends, she was Thelma, or—when they wanted to use a
nickname—"Buddy."

Kate understandably hated the mines, the daily fear that
her husband might get trapped below the surface. She pleaded
with Ryan to find safer employment. In 1914, when Thelma
was two, Ryan moved his family to Southern California, where he
bought an eleven-acre truck garden in Artesia, (since 1967
called Cerritos), about twenty miles southeast of Los Angeles.
He called the place a "ranch," himself a "rancher," but the truth
was that it was almost as bad as the tent city in Ely. The Artesia
house had no electricity or plumbing and only five small rooms
for a family of six. "It was very primitive," Thelma Ryan said
later. "It was a hard life, that's true. I didn't know what it was not
to work hard." [29]

But, to her at least, truck farming was not drudgery. "I loved to
be out of doors, so I worked right along with my brothers in the
field, really, which was lots of fun. We picked potatoes; we picked
tomatoes; we picked peppers and cauliflower. When I was real tiny
I just tagged along. But when I got older I was able to do more. I
drove the team of horses and things like that." For fun, the children
would ride the big draft horses bareback.

If her father was a relatively typical Irishman—a late marriage,
a footloose nature, a hard worker—her mother was a solid German
hausfrau. "My mother baked a lot," Thelma told Mazo. "She was
very good. She baked bread and cinnamon rolls and all sorts of
things like that. . . . We used to eat up the whole baking." [30] Thelma
walked a mile to the local grammar school, which was similar to
the one Nixon was then attending in Yorba Linda. Tragedy struck
when she was fourteen years old—her mother died of stomach
cancer.

Thelma took over the household chores. She rose at dawn to
prepare breakfast for her father and brothers, caught the bus to high
school, returned after classes to cook, sew, iron, wash, and clean,
and still found time to do chores in the fields. In addition, she was
nearly as active in high school as Nixon. She was a member of the
debating team, of the Filibuster Club, and (her favorite) the dra-
matics club. She was secretary of the student body in her senior
year and vice-president of her class. Her grades were good enough

that she just missed being valedictorian. The school yearbook described her thus:

Pseudonym:		Buddy
Intention	—	To run a boarding house
Liability	—	My two brothers
Occupation	—	Watching (brother) Tom
Talent	—	Watching (brother) Bill [31]

Pat graduated from high school in 1929. She had hoped to go straight to college as a full-time student, but her father contracted tuberculosis and she had to nurse him, plus work to provide income for the family. She got a job in an Artesia bank and signed up for morning classes at Fullerton Junior College. Her days were endless. In the morning, after making breakfast and seeing to her father, she rushed off to the bank, where she cleaned the lobby floor. Then classes. At 1 P.M. she was back at the bank, where she worked as a teller—and was once held up at gunpoint. Then home to cook the evening meal and care for her father.

She was eighteen when he died. On the day of his death, she decided to change her name to the one he preferred, Patricia.[32] Pat continued to work and to attend school and find time to play the lead in a school play, *Broken Dishes.*

She had an immense capacity for work, for denial of feelings, for self-restraint. After her mother's funeral, her friends had been waiting for fourteen-year-old Pat to come out of the funeral parlor, wondering what to do or say. Pat emerged smiling. "Didn't she look beautiful?" she said.[33]

"As a youngster life was sort of sad," Pat explained years later, "so I had to cheer everybody up. I learned to be that kind of person."[34] Suppression of her own feelings carried a price with it, however; as she told Jessamyn West, "I don't like to think back to that time."

Her ability to keep going, no matter what, eventually became legendary. Jessamyn West interviewed her in 1970 during an airplane flight following a hectic three days in three countries, with endless ceremonies featuring kings and queens, prime ministers and parliaments. On the day of the evening West did the interview, Pat had been to so many functions she had not eaten, save for one banana gulped down on the run.

"It's a pity to trouble you now when you must be so tired," West said in opening the interview.

"I'm never tired."

West could scarcely believe her, although Pat said it "quietly and matter-of-factly." Pointing out that only gods and machines never get tired, West went on to speculate on the claim: "That statement and Pat Nixon's belief in it probably grew out of her experiences as a girl; began in those days when, motherless, her father ill, she, a student, housekeeper and breadwinner all in one, no doubt told herself, 'You cannot be tired. You dare not be tired. Everything depends on you. You are *not* tired.' "[35]

PAT HAD her full share of her father's wanderlust, but no chance to indulge it. In 1931, she seized an opportunity. An elderly couple, visiting friends in California, wanted to return to Connecticut, but having just made the three-thousand-mile drive across country in their old Packard, they did not feel up to that grind again. They told Pat that if she would drive them to New York, they would buy her a bus ticket home. She accepted at once.

The switchbacks up and down the mountains on narrow roads, the desert heat, the endless monotony of the Great Plains, the heavy traffic on the two-lane highways of Pennsylvania and New Jersey—Pat endured it all without complaint. "Weren't you afraid to start out alone on such a trip?" Jessamyn West asked her.

"I am never afraid."

"What would you have done if you had become ill?"

"I don't get ill. And don't look so astounded. I just don't."

Then, forty years after the event, she confessed that she had suppressed a great anger. "Do you know what I remember most about it? Not fear or worry, but just plain exasperation. . . . The wife, who was not well, sat bundled up in the backseat. Her husband sat beside me up front. For three thousand miles, he made a clicking sound with his teeth. Flat tires, mud, rain—I could take them all, but that day-long sound of clicking stays with me yet."[36]

She liked New York and decided to stay. Others had great difficulty finding a job in that worst year of the Depression, but not Pat. She became a secretary at Seton Hospital in the Bronx. It treated tuberculosis patients. She enrolled at Columbia University for an intensive course in radiology. When she got her certificate as a technician, she moved up to a post in the X-ray department at Seton.

She worked with the patients. "They were so young, most of them, so eager to live," she told West. "And most of them were doomed to die young. My six months there were perhaps the most haunting of my life. They weren't supposed to do it, but some of the young patients would sneak away to go bobsledding, and I went with them. It gave them a lift to have someone who was well with them, not looking after them, not avoiding them."

"Weren't you afraid you might contract tuberculosis?"

"I never had the least fear of that. And it almost seemed that they believed they might contract health from me. . . . My being with them made them feel less separated from the real world. And that is what gives me the deepest pleasure in the world. Helping someone." [37]

In 1933 she took a bus back to California, stopping off at Niagara Falls on the way. She moved in with her brothers in a tiny apartment in Los Angeles, near USC. Her brothers were working their way through the university, where Pat also enrolled, as a major in merchandising. Naturally, she found work, a whole series of part-time jobs—in the student cafeteria, in the library, as a switchboard girl, as saleslady in a department store, as a dental assistant, and as a movie extra. She got $7 per day for appearing in mob scenes, and twice had bit parts that paid $25 per day. She had a walk-on part in *Small Town Girl*, starring Janet Gaynor and Robert Taylor, and developed a crush on Taylor: "I really eyed him." Two different directors asked her if she would like to try for bigger roles, but "I never thought of movies as a career because it seemed so very boring." Standing around all day, even for $7, was not her style. She watched the actors at work. "It was those retakes and retakes . . . going over and over and over about three words until you almost went mad." [38]

As a student, she made excellent grades. Her Shakespeare teacher, Professor Frank Baxter, remembered her as "a quiet girl, and pretty. And it always used to disturb me how tired her face was in repose." There was good reason, he knew, for it seemed to him every time he went into the cafeteria, there was Pat serving. When he went into the library, there was Pat checking out books. "Yet with it all, she was a good student, alert and interested. She stood out from the empty-headed, overdressed little sorority girls of that era like a good piece of literature on a shelf of cheap paperbacks." [39]

In 1937, the year Nixon graduated from law school, Pat graduated *cum laude* from USC. She wanted to become a buyer for a large department store, but when a higher-paying job came along, she grabbed it. The job was teaching business education in Whittier High School; the pay was $190 per month, which was "fabulous in 1937," as Pat put it. (Nixon, in his law practice, was making $50 per month.) Along with the money, Pat was attracted by that feature of education that every teacher knows is the most valuable: "I had great visions of those free summers when I could do what I wanted to. I really dreamed about those summer months." [40]

As a teacher, she was immediately and immensely popular. "She looked so young to us," Ellen Holt Waer, then sixteen, said. "She was very attractive, red hair, a very slim face. We were fascinated with her. She was soft-spoken, firm, and quite a good teacher."[41] "She treated us warmly," said Jean Lippiatt, greeting each student at the door by name, "but she insisted on results. . . . She expected clockwork punctuality from us and we absorbed the gentle hint that questions to her should be prefaced by her name." She forbade chewing gum or sloppy dress. "We found ourselves being very careful to comb our hair, to tie our shoelaces, and to straighten our skirts before greeting her at the door. We even adopted her very proper way of sitting and her erect posture during assemblies."[42]

Robert C. Pierpoint, who went on to become the White House correspondent for CBS, was a student in Whittier High at the time. "She was approachable, friendly, and outgoing," he recalled. "She was happy, enthusiastic, sprightly. Her disposition was sunny, not intermittently but all the time. . . . We liked her enormously because she never talked down to the students, always meeting them on an adult level, never intimidating them. Nor was she, as some teachers are, intimidated *by* them. She enjoyed her life and her work."[43]

At Whittier, Pat met a young teacher of English and history, Helene Colesie, who became—and remained—her closest friend. The two were inseparable. Helene worried about Pat's future at Whittier High. "You take a woman as young and beautiful as Pat was then, put her in with a faculty of older women, and you've got almost certain trouble," Helene said. Pat solved the problem easily. At PTA functions, for example, when the older faculty members were running the program, "Pat would be serving the coffee or out in the kitchen doing the dishes."[44]

Whittier fancied itself as a little gem of democracy. Residents took pride in their lack of prejudice toward Mexicans and Negroes. They bragged about their openness (they also bragged about the absence of any bars, taverns, or dance halls in town). But it was very much a class-conscious society. Pat was a young, self-made, ambitious career woman who was clearly on her way, a woman of talent, beauty, and tact, with a large capacity for work and self-sacrifice. She was so obviously a superior person that one would have thought any young man's family would regard her as quite a catch.

Nixon, meanwhile, was the son of a grocer who was still making his son pay back the money he had loaned him to go to law school. But after they began dating, Jeff Wingert's daughter remembered, "I have the feeling that perhaps some people felt that Dick should have been going with a girl from, you know, a better family. Whittier was very much like this."[45]

PAT'S LACK of a solid and respectable Quaker background did not deter Nixon. All through the rehearsals for *The Dark Tower* he pestered her for dates. Nor was he deterred by her stubborn refusals, or by her stubbornness in general, which she demonstrated at rehearsals. In one scene, Barry Jones, played by Nixon, sat at a piano and began playing "Stormy Weather." Daphne Martin, played by Pat, was supposed to begin to hum the tune, then sing it. But although she would hum, she refused to sing. "Pat," director Louise Baldwin exhorted, "sing, sing!" But she would not, although she promised she would sing on the two nights of the performance. In the event, she still refused to sing. [46]

She did, however, agree to a date with Nixon, after the first performance. "Richard insisted that his father and I should come to the opening," Hannah Nixon said. "We didn't suspect Richard of any motive other than his wanting us to see him act. But he also wanted us to see Pat." [47] Following the play, Nixon took Pat to his parents' home to introduce her. After driving Pat to her apartment, Nixon returned and asked Hannah what she thought of her. Hannah gave a careful mother's reply: "I told him she did her part nicely."

Nixon himself was far more positive. "He chased her," one of Pat's friends said, "but she was a little rat. She had Dick dating her roommate and all he did when he took the roommate out was talk about Pat." Years later, Pat explained, "I thought so much of him that I got him a date with my best friend." She herself had many old beaux from her USC days, and continued to go on dates with them. Nixon would not allow her to take the long trolley ride to Los Angeles; instead he drove her to her dates himself. He would hang around, going to a movie or reading in a hotel lobby, until it was time to drive her back home. [48]

Nixon had learned from his experiences with Ola something about how to court a young woman, primarily that to win her hand he would have to participate in the activities she enjoyed doing, and with her friends, not alone. "We had a young group, mostly my friends from college. He became part of that group when we dated." To please Pat, he took up ice skating at a newly opened artificial ice rink. "It was awful for Dick," Pat said. "He almost broke his head two or three times, but he still kept going." He had sense enough to keep away from heavy subjects. "There was no talk of politics or anything of that type. I didn't even think in terms of that." [49]

Nixon wanted to get married, but Pat hesitated. "I admired Dick from the very beginning," she later said, but "I was having a very good time and wasn't anxious to settle down. I had all these visions of doing all sorts of things, including travel. I always wanted to travel." [50] It must be said that, in the end, she certainly married the right man for that.

Pat gradually yielded to the intense young man who worked so hard to please her, to the point that—in Hannah Nixon's obviously prejudiced view—"Pat was chasing Dick." [51] To support her contention, Hannah cited Pat's increasing involvement with the family. "I can just as well come down in the early morning and help you get the pies ready," Pat told her, and from then on she would stop by on her way to school to prepare the baked pies for sale. Hannah admitted, "It touched me." [52]

Finally, after a courtship that lasted more than two years, Pat consented to marry Nixon. Whether it was love or a careful calculation of her prospects, only she knew. She was twenty-eight years old, possibly felt in peril of becoming an old-maid schoolteacher, and what Nixon was offering looked good. "He was making $50 a month," she acknowledged, but "I knew he was going to get places, though. He was vital, and ambitious—not ambitious for anything in particular, and certainly not for money—but he had drive." [53]

The elated Nixon set to work researching rings. "He was always serious about everything he did," Nixon's brother Don said. One evening Nixon told Don, "A man only buys a ring once in his lifetime, and that should be a ring his wife would always be proud to wear." They discussed rings "into the wee hours and I learned that Dick was an expert. He evidently had cross-examined a jeweler friend of his in 20–30, and he really knew a lot about stones and settings." [54]

He had knowledge, but no money. Pat, who did have savings, chipped in to buy her own ring. Nixon presented it to her inside a May Day flower basket. She agreed to a Quaker ceremony, and to adopt the Quaker faith, which naturally made Hannah happy. Before the wedding, Nixon decided to get a new car. Again he researched the subject, and concluded that it was cheaper for him to take a bus to Michigan and drive a new car home than it was to buy the car locally and pay the delivery costs. He bought an Oldsmobile, with more of Pat's money. [55]

THEY WERE MARRIED on June 21, 1940, at the Mission Inn in Riverside. The hotel was a garish, only-in-California kind of place, with bell towers, altars, balconies, fountains, stained-glass windows, a large rotunda with a spiral staircase, colonnades of arches, wrought-iron grilles, and other extravagant items. Nixon chose the Presidential Suite for the wedding room (careful as always, he rented it only for the afternoon). The immediate families and a handful of friends were the guests. He wore a dark new suit; Pat wore a light-blue dress with fitted bodice and a full-gathered skirt that extended to her ankles. By 5 P.M. that afternoon, they were off for their honeymoon in the new Olds, headed for Mexico. Nixon had $200 in his pocket, half of it Pat's money.[56]

"We just took off in our car," Pat remembered, "heading, generally, for Mexico City, but without any particular destination. We didn't have a trip outlined. We just went. We felt really splurgy."[57] They filled the trunk with canned food, only to discover that their friends, as a joke, had removed all the labels. Every meal was a game of chance; sometimes they had cold pork and beans for breakfast and grapefruit slices for dinner. They would drive all night to save the cost of a hotel. "I think we saw every temple, every church in old Mexico," Nixon said years later. And he bragged, "It all cost us only $178."[58]

After two weeks, they returned to Whittier and set up house in a duplex apartment. Nixon continued his law practice; Pat, her teaching. Pat's friend Helene had married Jack Drown, then a law student. They became a foursome. "We would go out to dinner," Drown recalled, "and Dick would take over the menu, and order for everyone." Despite the tightness of money, when Hannah's birthday came, Pat gave her a party and a birthday present of a pearl necklace.[59] Nixon was twenty-seven years old and, for an honors graduate of every school he had ever attended, not getting very far very fast. He seemed headed for a quiet, dull life as a small-town attorney and family man.

In 1941, Nixon decided to move to Washington. Later, he claimed that he and Pat simply pulled up and left Whittier after Pearl Harbor, to join the war effort in whatever capacity they could best serve. In fact, he had a job waiting for him before he left, with the Office of Price Administration (OPA). The pay was $3,200 per year, far more than he was making as a lawyer. One of his Duke professors, David Cavers, was a high-ranking official in the OPA, and offered him a position with the bureaucracy. When asked why Nixon did it, Wallace Black, another Whittier lawyer, was blunt: "It was a matter of economics. He could get a salary." Patriotism and a desire to serve evidently were not, despite Nixon's later claim, primary or even secondary motives.[60]

But he was not dodging the draft—as a birthright Quaker, he was entitled to an exemption from service. As a potential politician, however, he certainly knew that it would be disastrous to his ambitions if he did nothing to help win the war. The OPA offered a nice opportunity to serve and to make more money than he had ever seen before. There was another plus for a man with politics in his future; in Nixon's own words, the OPA allowed him "to go to Washington and observe the working of the government first-hand."[61]

The OPA was a new agency, but nevertheless it had a decided New Deal flavor to it. It was, at least in theory, the champion of the consumer, defending the common man from price gouging and wartime profiteers. Liberal lawyers flocked to it. Nixon joined the tire-rationing section, and there he had his first contact with left-wing activists.[62]

Professor Thomas Emerson was head of Nixon's section. He was a prominent New Dealer who subsequently became president of the National Lawyers Guild, and he became a leader in Henry Wallace's 1948 Progressive Party. Emerson liked Nixon. "He was a nice-looking boy," Emerson said, who "seemed intelligent and had an excellent record at Duke. He was obviously a person we could use."[63]

Their initial compatibility was based in part on Nixon's self-image. Although he was a registered Republican who had campaigned for Willkie, Nixon thought of himself as a liberal. "I came out of college more liberal than I am today," he said in 1958, "more liberal in the sense that I thought it was possible for government to do more than I later found it was practical to do."[64]

Washington, D.C., in January 1942, was the nerve center of the Allied war effort and to most people who worked there the most exciting place in the world. But not to Nixon. His office was in one of those awful temporary buildings on Independence Avenue; his job was to enforce tire rationing. In 1969 Nixon remarked that it "seemed very boring to me and I am sure to my secretary. The mission that I had was to develop the form letters and to write to thousands of people . . . to tell them why we could not give them an exception as far as their tire-rationing requests were concerned." He did admit that "what made it mean something was that we felt that we were part of a bigger cause."

He put in long hours, often working until midnight and all day Saturday. His immediate supervisor was Thomas E. Harris, later one of George Meany's top lawyers at the AFL.-CIO. Harris praised Nixon as "hard-working and diligent, a real plugger." But, according to Harris, "Nixon was uncomfortable among the liberals, the Eastern law-school graduates, the Jews he rubbed shoulders with on the job. No one thought of him as a right-winger in those days, but in style if not in politics he was thought of as a conservative. Because he lacked sophistication and the big-city graces, he never quite fit in."[65]

In his long political career, Nixon often referred back to his OPA days. He said that he learned from his experience. "I became more conservative. . . . I also became greatly disillusioned about bureaucracy and about what the government could do because I saw the terrible paper work that people had to go through. I also saw the mediocrity of so many civil servants."

There were other lessons. The OPA, he said, made him realize, for the first time, "that there were people in government who were not satisfied merely with interpreting the regulations, enforcing the law that Congress passed, but who actually had a passion to GET business and used their government jobs to that end. These were of course some of the remnants of the old, violent New Deal crowd. They set me to thinking a lot at that point."[66] J. Paull Marshall, the only other Republican on the staff, said, "We both believed in the capitalistic system, but the other lawyers were using rationing and price control as a means of controlling profits."[67]

Nixon discovered that some of his fellow bureaucrats, men with "lesser academic records and not as much legal experience" as he had, were a step or two higher on the ladder—and in salary —than he was. He protested to his supervisor, who told him, "Build a little staff. Request two or three people to assist you, and then we can raise you. . . ."

"But I don't need a staff," Nixon protested.

"Then you won't get a promotion."[68]

Nixon later said that in OPA he learned firsthand how "political appointees at the top feathered their nests with all kinds of overlapping and empire building."[69]

Nixon often said that another lesson he learned in the OPA was that price controls do not work. At a press conference in July 1971, for example, he declared with some sarcasm, "I was in the O.P.A. . . . You cannot have wage and price controls without rationing. . . . I just checked and found we had 47,000 in the O.P.A. in World War II enforcing all the regulations in wage and price controls over the country. It was not working because it will not. . . ."[70] Nixon looked back on his OPA days as almost a Road to Damascus experience. In his memoirs, he wrote that it had an "enormous effect" on his thinking.[71]

That he had to work for OPA to discover that he did not like bureaucracy or government interference in the private sector seems to stretch things a bit—it can be assumed that his friends in the 20–30 Club back in Whittier did not much like bureaucracy or government controls either, and that they did not need to work for OPA to discover that fact. That he was embarrassed, when he became a politician, by his association with OPA seems clear enough. When he first entered Congress, in 1947, he had to write a *Who's*

Who–type biography for the *Congressional Directory*. He listed as his employer for the period from January to August 1942 the Office of Emergency Management. He did not mention the OPA. It was true that OEM was an umbrella organization of which the OPA was one part, but as Milton Viorst points out, Nixon's listing of OEM as his employer "would be like an F.B.I. agent's saying he worked for the Justice Department." After Nixon became President, John Kenneth Galbraith—who was highly placed in OPA early in the war—enjoyed teasing him by sending him invitations to OPA reunions. Nixon never responded.[72]

NIXON COULD have stayed in the OPA. Had he done so, one would imagine that he would have risen in the civil service, given his abilities and his willingness to work. He also would have avoided a separation from Pat and the inherent dangers of a combat zone. But he was bored and dissatisfied, despite two raises in rank and pay in six months. In June 1942, after a long talk with Pat, he decided to join the Navy, which had put out a call for lawyers and offered a direct commission. He had already written Dean Horack at Duke, telling him that "if the Navy finds it can use me, I should like the opportunity to serve." [73]

By no means did he have to enlist and put on a uniform. His job with OPA gave him a draft deferment, and his religion protected him from conscription. But despite his Quaker faith, he was no pacifist, and although there was some soul-searching, he had no crisis of conscience over his decision. In his memoirs he said bluntly that he "never considered" taking a deferment as a conscientious objector.[74]

Pat later admitted, "I would have felt mighty uncomfortable if Dick hadn't done his part. Sure, I was unhappy, but so were thousands of other young wives. Because of Richard's upbringing he did much soul-searching before he made his decision. But, once it was made, I knew it was all for the best." [75]

He was hardly alone. Many young lawyers were leaving the civil service, after a half year or so, to join the military. Those who were harboring political ambitions felt, to a man, that military service was an absolute must.

In late August 1942, Nixon reported for his indoctrination school at Quonset Point, Rhode Island. Pat stayed in their Washington apartment—there were no accommodations for her at Quonset. She took a job, as an assistant business analyst earning $200 per month, with the OPA.[76]

CHAPTER SEVEN

U.S. NAVY
1942–1945

"I GREW UP in the Navy," President Richard Nixon told reporters in 1971. He explained that it was in the Navy that he learned to drink coffee—"because I had to." [1]

Caffeine was indeed the fuel that got the Navy through World War II, taken in the form of black coffee, scalding hot, always available, whether at training stations in the States, or on islands in the Pacific, or on the bridge of ships at sea. It was consumed in enormous quantities by virtually every sailor. Few indeed got through the war without becoming addicted to it.

But Nixon learned a great deal more in the Navy than how to drink coffee. He was twenty-nine years old when he enlisted, thirty-three when he got out. Until he put on his uniform, he had led a life that was sheltered from the ways of the world, a life that was remarkably free of small sins. He did not play cards, he did not drink, he did not swear, he did not gamble, he did not smoke. In his first twenty-one years, in Yorba Linda and in Whittier, he knew no one who indulged in such pleasures.

At Duke Law School he led such a monastic existence that he was only barely aware of the activities of his classmates, and seldom if ever participated with them in bull sessions, and only once in a drinking spree. As a lawyer in Whittier, his associates were, like him, strongly influenced by the Quaker traditions of the town, hardly the kind of men to tell off-color jokes or open a bottle of booze in their offices in the middle of the day for a quick snort and a long conversation. In the OPA his work load was almost as heavy as it had been at Duke, and in addition he did not get along well enough with his fellow employees to go out on the town with them. But in the Navy, all that changed.

He was not alone. Thousands of young men, from every continent, from every walk of life, had their lives permanently changed by their experiences in the war. They traveled to the far corners of the world, to places they had never even heard of before. They became buddies with fellow soldiers and sailors from economic and social classes far beyond anything in their previous experience. In combat zones, they lived in constant fear of death. They had no control over their own lives—they went where they were told to go, no questions asked. In combat or out, they had to endure long periods of total boredom, when there was absolutely nothing to do. They lived, most of them, without women, without the soft touch or civilizing graces of a mother, wife, sweetheart. It brought out the best in some of them, the worst in others. For Nixon, the war was above all a learning experience.

AFTER LEARNING how to salute, wear his uniform, distinguish a captain from a commander, and the barest rudiments of navigation, Lieutenant (J.G.) Nixon became one of those "instant wonders" of the World War II U.S. Navy, a full-fledged officer. The course at Quonset Point lasted only two months. Upon graduation, Nixon put in for sea duty.

But officer or not, Nixon had hardly been on a ship in his life, and the Navy knew better than to throw him into the middle of the battle then raging in the Pacific. Instead of sea duty, when he opened his orders he was astonished to find that he was going to Ottumwa, Iowa, which is about as far away from blue water as it is possible to get. The Navy was building an airfield in the middle of the cornfields, for initial pilot training. Nixon's job was to serve as aide to the executive officer.

He called Pat, who quit her job with OPA and took a bus to Iowa to join him there. Her philosophy was that "a woman must first and foremost be a homemaker," and she set to work in the tiny apartment he found in Ottumwa. She brought her sewing machine along. Her first purchase was material for new slipcovers for the battered furniture, and for drapes and curtains. Then she got a job as a teller in the local bank.[2]

Naval Air Station, Ottumwa, was a small base, with only twenty-five officers and fewer than two hundred enlisted men. The winter months were cold, the daily routine, dull. At the end of 1942, when Nixon saw a notice that applications for sea duty would be accepted from officers aged twenty-nine or younger, the twenty-nine-year-old Nixon seized the chance. What he got by way of assignment was not so glamorous as line officer on one of the new carriers but at least it took him to the South Pacific—he was ordered to join the South Pacific Combat Air Transport Command (SCAT) on the island of New Caledonia.

The Nixons drove to California for his embarkation. In Whittier, they had a last meal with his family before he took the train to San Francisco. His mother and grandmother were "deeply troubled" by the event. Seeing their Quaker boy in uniform, knowing that he was going to a war zone, violated their beliefs. But Nixon had decided that "in the face of Hitler and Tojo, pacifism not only failed to stop violence—it actually played into the hands of a barbarous foe. . . . " Hannah and Almira respected his decision and withheld their objections, but nevertheless "it was a painful meal, full of sad silences."[3]

Pat took the train with him, and after his ship sailed she found an apartment and a job in San Francisco, working for the Office of Civilian Defense as a secretary. In July, she left that post to become a secretary for the OPA in San Francisco. She stayed with the OPA until February of 1945, rising to the position of price economist and increasing her salary from $180 per month to $280 per month.[4] She lived in a boardinghouse, saving every dollar she could.

NIXON SAILED westward across the Pacific on the USS *President Monroe*. He shared a small cabin with eight other officers. Aside from daily exercises on the deck and a refresher course or two, there was little to do. For most of the junior officers it was a first sea voyage, and many of them became seasick—but not Nixon. "I was seasick most of the time," Lieutenant James Udall recalled with some chagrin. "Every day Nixon brought me crackers and soup." Those who were capable spent a great deal of time shooting the breeze. Lieutenant Lester Wroble remembered "Nick" as "quiet and considerate, more a listener than a talker. He didn't make inane remarks like we did, but he wasn't offended by ours."[5]

It was on this voyage, or shortly after his arrival on New Caledonia, that Nixon learned the rudiments of poker playing. "One day I noticed Nick lost in his thoughts," Lieutenant James Stewart recalled. "Finally he asked: 'Is there any sure way to win at poker?' " Stewart had a theory—not to stay in a pot unless he was sure he held a winning hand. "Nick liked what I said. I gave him his first lessons. We played two-handed poker without money for four or five days, until he learned the various plays. Soon his playing became tops. He never raised unless he was convinced he had the best hand."[6]

On New Caledonia, his duties were dull and routine. The

SCAT unit was responsible for preparing manifests and flight plans for the big C-47 cargo planes as they flew in and out, bringing in supplies and taking out wounded. Nixon supervised the loading and the unloading. The war was moving north, and New Caledonia had become a backwater.

In January 1944, Nixon's small SCAT detachment moved forward, to Bougainville, in the Solomon Islands. The airfield on the Island had fallen to American forces only two months earlier, and was within striking distance of the great Japanese base at Rabaul. Japanese bombers attacked regularly—in his first month on the island, Nixon's unit was bombed twenty-eight nights out of thirty. "Shortly after I arrived," he wrote in his memoirs, "the Japanese staged an assault. When it was over, we counted thirty-five shell holes within a hundred feet of the air raid bunker six of us shared. Our tent had been completely destroyed."[7]

Later, friendly campaign biographers exaggerated his combat experiences, for obvious reasons (it was just at this time that John F. Kennedy became an authentic hero), and Nixon himself would occasionally claim something more than the facts warranted, but at the time he was matter-of-fact about the experience. To his anxious mother, he wrote, "The only things that really bother me are lack of sleep and the centipedes," and in 1970, he told a reporter, "I didn't get hit or hit anyone. All I got was a case of fungus."[8]

Nixon did an outstanding job in what was essentially a quartermaster's role. He did it without complaint. It was a job lacking even the slightest hint of glory; it was often boring to the point of madness, but when the big cargo planes came in, there were hours of frantic activity. As the CO of his little group, Nixon showed a surprising ability to run the show with just the right touch. He kept his enlisted men happy and won their loyalty; he did his job without fanfare but with excellent efficiency; he did a great deal more than he had to do, and without hope of any reward for the extra effort.

When they were interviewed after Nixon became famous, the men who served with and under him spontaneously told different reporters that the comparison that came to their minds was with Mr. Roberts, the hero of the play, and later a movie, both starring Henry Fonda, about the World War II Navy, and one of the most likable characters imaginable.

This was a new Nixon. No one in Whittier or Durham had ever thought to compare Nixon to the laid-back, easygoing, wonderfully efficient Mr. Roberts, and no one who knew him after the war ever had such a comparison spring to mind. But Nixon responded strongly to the structured situation in which he found himself. He was not going to make a career out of the Navy, and as a reserve junior officer at an out-of-the-way supply depot he certainly was not going to have an opportunity for any heroics. There was no way he could satisfy any ambition in the Navy, so he just decided to do the best job he could. His place was fixed in the Navy's rigid hierarchy, which meant that no one below him was a threat and no one above him a block to his advancement. He could deal with enlisted men and officers alike as fellow workers for a common goal with a proscribed role to fill, and in that circumstance he was, for the only time in his life, genuinely popular with those around him. In the Southwest Pacific, Nixon could relax, suppressing his ambitions rather than himself.

ON THE MORNING of January 24, 1944, shortly after his arrival, the airstrip received thirty cargo planes carrying 135,000 pounds of rocket bombs. Nixon and his nine-man crew had to unload the C-47s, then load the bombs onto fighter planes that were going to bomb Rabaul, all in six hours. Before the cargo planes landed, Nixon briefed his men, telling each one what needed to be done but leaving the details of how to do it to the individual. Nixon took off his shirt and worked beside the crew. Together they completed the task in five and a half hours. Then they loaded wounded men onto the cargo planes.

That night Nixon managed to scrounge enough ham to give the men a ham dinner. The next day, censoring their mail, he was delighted to note that each man mentioned the ham dinner, but not one complained about the hard work.[9]

Nixon's assistant, James Stewart, recalled that in the weeks that followed, when the cargo planes came in, 'everyone was running around like mad. But Nick was sort of a calm island in a storm. He picked a base and directed the operations, comprised of supplying fresh food to the pilots and taking food back to the wounded, without fanfare. It all took place rather calmly, as if we were sitting in Washington.'[10] Nixon was "shy, competent, never lost his cool," according to another officer. "His men liked him."[11]

As a CO, Nixon was also admired. "He made an awful lot of sense," a junior officer recalled. "He had no more rank than most of us, he was our age generally speaking, but he commanded a lot of respect from the guys with whom he came in contact. When things got a bit hectic, he never lost his head. No matter how badly things got fouled up, Dick got his part of the operation straightened out and he did it without a lot of hullaballoo."[12]

On February 15, 1944, Nixon participated in the invasion of Green Island, but there were no heroics possible—he landed in a bay in a PBY seaplane, and the Japanese had already retreated. Nixon noted laconically in his memoirs, "The only danger came from a few straggling snipers and the ever-present giant centipedes." [13]

Although Green Island was not a combat zone, Nixon did see violent death. The Seabees were constructing an airfield. Before it was completed, and while bulldozers were still standing on it, a B-29 had to make a crash landing. It was nearly dark. Nixon and his men cheered as the plane made it down safely on its belly, then watched horrified as it crashed head-on into a bulldozer. Nixon helped carry the bodies away. [14]

On Green Island, Nixon found an outlet for his energy and his need to serve his community in some fashion. A good quartermaster, he was a first-rate scrounger. Utilizing his talents, he set up Nick's Snack Shack, where he served free hamburgers and Australian beer to grateful flight crews who had eaten little besides lamb for weeks.

A fellow officer, Edward J. McCaffrey, described Nixon's method: "Nick was able to wheedle the supplies for his Snack Shack from other outfits that were better stocked. Some of the stuff was, shall we say, 'liberated'—but Nick would swap anything. Just a small trade would set in motion a series of bigger trades. . . . Some of the items on the menu were not on the government issue list; an occasional bottle of whiskey for example—a rare treat which he doled out among the men without regard to their rank." [15]

There was an immense amount of material coming into and going out from Green Island. Most of it was stored in a navy supply depot. Nixon, in the time-honored tradition of the quartermaster, would trade "everything from captured Japanese rifles to introductions to the Army nurses who arrived to take care of the casualties." [16]

Nixon set up an informal school for his men, where he gave lectures on business law. He explained how to set up a small-business corporation, how to draw up a lease, how to prepare tax returns, and so on. For years afterward, he would get letters from his "pupils," telling him how much his lectures had helped them get started in their own business. [17]

Lieutenant Stewart said that "Nixon shared whatever he had. . . . And I never saw an enlisted man who didn't like him." When his orders came, the men decided to throw a farewell party. "Liquor was prohibited to enlisted men," Lieutenant Stewart explained. "Luckily, however, there was always some to be found if one knew where to look for it. The enlisted men in our outfit went on a search party, 'borrowed' all of the liquor they could find, and gave him a big party. All of them were strong for him, and hated to see him go."[18]

Nixon's superiors, too, were impressed by his performance. When he left the theater, Vice-Admiral J. H. Newton, Commander, South Pacific Area, sent him a Letter of Commendation praising him for "meritorious and efficient performance of duty as Officer in Charge of the South Pacific Combat Air Transport Command" on Green Island. Admiral Newton continued, "He displayed sound judgment and initiative in organizing the . . . Command at both Bougainville and Green Island. He established the efficient liaison which made possible the immediate supply by air of vital material and key personnel, and the prompt evacuation of battle casualties from these stations to rear areas."[19]

It was not exactly the equal of Jack Kennedy's heroism citation, to be sure, but that was not Nixon's fault. He had done the best he could, and the best that could be done, in a demanding and important job. He had earned his "well done."

IT WAS a "lonely war" for the men in the South Pacific, Nixon wrote in his memoirs, filled with "interminable periods" of waiting for some action. The "oppressive monotony," not the Japanese, was the enemy. To fill in his time, Nixon wrote Pat every day. He read the Bible through again and again, and old copies of *Life* magazine. He learned to drink, and smoke cigars, and to engage in bull sessions. But mainly, he killed time by playing poker.

The game became an obsession with him. It was "an irresistible diversion . . . instructive . . . entertaining and profitable." He played nightly, no matter what. Charles Lindbergh came to Green Island on an inspection trip. Nixon's CO invited him to a small dinner in Lindbergh's honor. Nixon declined—he had a poker game that night.[20] The innocent Quaker boy was coming into his manhood.

Nixon was at least as good a poker player as he was a CO. The mark of just how good he was came in the form of the conflicting memories of his fellow players. One, Lester Wroble, said, "Dick never lost, but he was never a big winner. He seemed always to end up a game somewhere between $30 and $60 ahead. That didn't look like showy winnings, but when you multiplied it day after day, I'd say he did all right." Another player declared, "There are a hundred Navy officers who will tell you that Nick never lost a cent at poker."[21] Others insisted that he never raised unless he knew he was holding the winning hand, and in general played a conservative game. When players got drunk and began throwing their money around in hopeless bluffs, Nixon was there to gather in the pot.

But at the right psychological moment, he himself would bluff. Lieutenant James Udall said, "Nixon was as good a poker player as, if not better than, anyone we had ever seen. He played a quiet game, but was not afraid of taking chances. He wasn't afraid of running a bluff. Sometimes the stakes were pretty big, but Nick had daring and a flair for knowing what to do." [22]

POKER IS the quintessential man's game, and in the Navy, in wartime, it reaches its highest form as a test of will and nerve. In its classic setting, it is played under a single unshielded light bulb, the table covered with overflowing ashtrays, cigar smoke thick enough to cut throughout the room, a drink in front of every player, one or two big and three or four little piles of chips or money beside the drinks, the pot in the center of the table containing the bets.

The players are a mixture of men who are bored to tears all day, every day, and will do anything for excitement, and men who have just returned from or are going on a combat mission. They do not need any more excitement in their lives, but they will do anything for some diversion. In either case, money has little meaning to them, because there is nothing for them to spend it on. To most of the men Nixon played poker with, the psychological pleasure of winning, the excitement and comradery, and the diversion from danger and tension were all more important than the money. But to the successful bluffer, it is the money that matters.

The talk is rough, whether about women or that day's experiences or whatever. "Goddamn it" and "son of a bitch" and "sweet Jesus" serve as exclamation points and are not considered swearing; to swear is to use sexual or anatomical terms, which are hurled back and forth with gusto.

Bluffing is poker's great art form. It requires an ability to act that goes far beyond the commonly used term "poker face." The bluffer has to vary his act for each audience, because in poker the audience is a single individual, the player who holds the best hand. The bluffer has to make quick judgments about the personality, mood, level of drunkenness, financial position, and other characteristics of the man he is trying to bluff. What cards the opponent actually holds is more or less irrelevant to the bluffer; what matters is what he can make his opponent think that he has.

Bluffing has nothing to do with gambling. The gambler puts his money into the pot on the basis of his belief (his gamble) that he has the best hand at the table. The bluffer *knows* that his hand is inferior, that if his bet is called he will lose. He is not gambling —he is making a psychological attack on his opponent.

To the bluffer, timing is everything. Early in the evening, before the alcohol has begun to do its work and the play is still cautious, the pots are not big enough to justify a bluff. Late in the evening, a bluff against a big winner who is going on a combat mission in the morning, and who has been drinking all night, can be a dreadful mistake.

But the timing problem in bluffing is even more complex than that. The successful poker player *wants* to get caught bluffing occasionally, so that when he really does have the best hand, the other players will call his bet, suspecting another bluff, thus building the pot. In addition, only one or two hands in an evening really lend themselves to a bluff. The bluffer, in short, must have great patience, plus a tiger's sense of the exact moment to strike.

The great bluffers are not only great actors with a superb sense of timing, but men with a nervous system that responds best to tension, the higher, the better. Throwing large sums of money into a pot when one holds the worst hand at the table takes guts and nerves that cannot be shattered, and an intense amount of concentration. The bluffer must be acutely aware of the effect his appearance and demeanor are having on his audience.

In *Six Crises*, written in 1962, Nixon wrote of the lessons he had learned from the political crises in his life. His analysis can be applied to his poker experiences equally well.

"When a man has been through even a minor crisis," Nixon wrote, "he learns not to worry when his muscles tense up, his breathing comes faster, his nerves tingle, his stomach churns. . . . He recognizes such symptoms as the natural and healthy signs that his system is keyed up for battle." He also learns to hide those symptoms.

"One man may have opportunities that others do not," Nixon admitted. "But what counts is whether the individual used what chances he had. Did he risk all when the stakes were such that he might win or lose all?" To be in that position, Nixon said, was to experience "exquisite agony."[23]

The total amount of Nixon's winnings in the South Pacific poker games is a matter of some dispute. Estimates range from $3,000 to $10,000. In 1950, McCaffery wrote him a chatty letter about the doings of their fellow officers. "Your prowess at stud poker is the thing I remember with very good reason," McCaffery confessed. "I'll never forget the apparent concern that troubled you because of your winnings and your expressed wish that I call Pat in 'Frisco and break the ice."

To win or lose all, not on a turn of the cards—all the cards had been dealt—but on an opponent's reaction to a bluff, is a character-testing experience requiring the nerves of a burglar. Nixon had that experience on at least one occasion. Udall related, "I once saw him bluff a lieutenant commander out of $1,500 with a pair of deuces."[24]

Poker gave Nixon the financial stake he needed to launch his political career. It also gave him invaluable lessons that were crucial to his political career. He learned how to take the measure of his opponents, to recognize the exact moment to strike, to realize when he could bluff the man with the strongest hand into an ignominious retreat, to know when to fold his own hand and quietly withdraw from the game.

THERE WERE other lessons to be learned in the Navy by a young man with political ambitions. As Nixon pointed out in letters home, he was thrown in overseas with men he never would have met otherwise, or mingled with by choice. Yet his experiences taught him to respect the men, and he developed a genuine affection for them. In 1951, when he was interviewed about his crew, Nixon remembered all their names and was eloquent in his descriptions of them—the farm boy from Nebraska, the son of a railroad engineer from New York, and so on.

Nixon described "Red" Hussey, from Texas: "Red was a boy who had quit school because his father died, and Red had to go to work and help support his four brothers and sisters. He worked in a foundry, entered the service, and displayed a remarkable sense of ingenuity as to getting a job done and in keeping up the morale of the other men. . . . It was this type of boy on which the hopes of America rests."[25]

No son of Frank Nixon, no husband of Pat Ryan, could fail to respond to Red's story. It was here, in the Navy, that Nixon discovered he had a real rapport with working-class Americans. He and they understood each other, shared common values, liked pretty much the same things. Despite the petit bourgeois pretensions of his father's grocery, Nixon knew what it was to work, and to struggle. So did his wife. He knew what Red was talking about, because he had been there himself. That Red, and the others, responded to him is obvious. And he discovered another strength in himself.

There were limits to the rapport with the enlisted men, however, the same limits that Nixon applied to his relationship with the officers. A wartime experience often brings men together into lifelong intimate friendships, but not for Nixon. According to one officer, Nixon "was a solitary type, a loner. . . . He was afraid of becoming involved with anyone, even as a friend because then he would have to reveal something of himself."[26]

There is no record that Nixon discussed politics in the South

Pacific, but the thought of his own future was present on at least one occasion. Harold Stassen, the "Boy Governor of Minnesota and a rapidly rising star in the Republican Party, came to Bougainville in February 1944 on an inspection tour. Nixon talked to him about politics. Stassen responded with a promise—if Nixon did decide to run for Congress, he would come to California to help campaign.[27]

BY JULY 1944, the South Pacific had become a rear area in the war, and the Navy was winding down its bases there. Nixon was ordered to Alameda, California, where he worked for Fleet Air Wing 8 on transportation problems. Pat joined him there and continued to work for the OPA.

While in Alameda, Nixon gave a speech to the local Rotary club. His subject was his own experience setting up SCAT in the Solomons, but he evidently managed to get in a couple of remarks that particularly pleased one member of his audience, Admiral Raymond Spruance, the hero of Midway and other Pacific battles. When Nixon finished, Spruance came up to shake his hand. "Young man," the admiral told the lieutenant, "that's the stuff. You're the kind we want down in Washington!"[28]

After four months in Alameda, Nixon was ordered to the East Coast. Pat quit her job and went with him. They lived and worked in Philadelphia, New York, and Middle River, Maryland. His assignment was winding up contracts with Glenn L. Martin and Bell Aircraft, and he did his customary outstanding job. He was credited with saving millions of dollars and received a citation from the Secretary of the Navy for "meritorious service, tireless effort, and devotion to duty."[29]

On the surface, it had been a dull and meaningless war for Nixon. He had neither a chance at heroics nor an opportunity to hobnob with the rich and powerful as an admiral's aide. He had apparently missed a big chance. There was nothing in his war record—nor, it appeared, in his experiences—that could be the slightest help to a man with political ambitions.

Yet in many ways the navy years were more important to Nixon than the years in Whittier or at Duke. He learned the ways of the world, and a great deal more about his own potentials, as a leader, poker player, and —perhaps—politician.

"He was one guy who knew where he was going," Lieutenant Lester Wroble said of Lieutenant Richard Nixon. "His plans were concise, concrete and specific."[30]

What was sad was the repeated pattern of Nixon's inability or unwillingness to keep a friendship alive after the original reason for it came to an end. He would not carry any excess baggage into his postwar career; in his world, he had time only for men who could help him get ahead. Trapped in the Navy, with no opportunity for advancement, he could afford to be Mr. Roberts, but back in the real world he suppressed that side of himself. He could talk eloquently about Red, but he never wrote him, never looked him up, never tried to contact him in any way. It is noteworthy that in his spectacularly successful postwar career, no one from the Navy, nor from Duke Law School, none of his classmates from Whittier High School or Whittier College, not even any member of his family, save only Pat, played a significant role, in public or private.

CHAPTER EIGHT

THE FIRST CAMPAIGN 1946

As THE WAR wound down, Nixon continued to work on navy contracts. In the evenings, he and Pat discussed their postdischarge future. He gave some thought to staying in the Navy, but quickly dismissed the idea.[1] Pat wanted to return to Whittier and pick up where they had left off, and Nixon could think of nothing better. Pat was four months' pregnant and he would soon have a child to support.

In September, shortly after the Japanese surrender, Nixon received a letter from Herman Perry containing an offer that made Whittier far more attractive. Perry asked "if you would like to be a candidate for Congress on the Republican ticket in 1946." He said that Jerry Voorhis, the Democratic incumbent, would run again. Although Voorhis had won five straight elections in the 12th Congressional District (the area east of Los Angeles), Perry pointed out that "registration is about 50–50" and "the Republicans are gaining." He asked for an airmail reply if Nixon was interested.[2]

Herman Perry was an old family friend and, as the leading banker, the most influential man in Whittier. Harry Schuyler, a past president of the Whittier Rotary, and one of the big ranchers in the area, gave a description of Perry's methods. Perry, he said, "was the kind of man that if something needed doing in the Republican Party, would call you up on the telephone and would say, 'Harry, this should be done and I want you to see that it's done.' And no one ever dared to turn him down. You just didn't turn him down, because of your connections with the bank and your respect for his ability. *He was a leader.*"[3]

Perry's letter to Nixon, then, was more a summons, less an inquiry. Before the war, Nixon had turned to Perry when he wanted to run for the state assembly, but Perry had vetoed the idea on the grounds that Nixon was too young. Now, his letter indicated, he thought Nixon was ready, and for a much bigger job than the assembly.

It was exactly the opportunity toward which Nixon had pointed his whole life, but he nevertheless went through the motions of discussing the pros and cons of Perry's offer with Pat. Pat pointed out that a campaign would cost money, both in cash outlay and in lost income. Nixon replied that instead of using the whole of their $10,000 in savings (from their salaries and his poker winnings) for the house they wanted to buy, they could put $5,000 down on the house and gamble the other $5,000 on the campaign.

Pat remained dubious, but her husband's eagerness overrode all her objections. She did get him to agree to two ground rules: that on no account would she ever be called upon to make a political speech, and that their home would be a quiet refuge where she could raise a normal family. She later explained, "I didn't feel strongly about it either way. . . . I felt that a man had to make up his mind what he wanted to do, then after he made it up, the only thing that I could do was to help him." Then she admitted, "But it would not have been a life that I would have chosen." To her biographer, Lester David, she put it bluntly: "I told him that it was his decision and I would do what he liked."[4]

His first hurdle crossed, Nixon charged ahead. He called Perry on the telephone—no airmail letter for him—and said he was honored and delighted and that he would be discharged in time to begin campaigning in January. When Perry finally got a chance to respond to Nixon's flow of words, he deflated Nixon by saying that the nomination was not his to offer. He explained that the Republicans in the district had created a search committee, called the Committee of 100, to find a candidate who could defeat Voorhis. He personally had suggested Nixon, but the Committee of 100 would interview several candidates before making its choice.

That slowed Nixon down, but only a bit. The next morning he wrote Perry to confirm his interest. He pledged his resolve and determination in a paragraph that said exactly what the committee wanted to hear: "I feel very strongly that Jerry Voorhis can be beaten, and I'd welcome the opportunity to take a crack at him. An aggressive, vigorous campaign on a platform of *practical* liberalism should be the antidote the people have been looking for to take the place of Voorhis' particular brand of New Deal idealism. My brief experience in Washington with the bureaucrats and my three and a half years in the Navy have given me a pretty good idea of what a mess things are in Washington."[5]

The Committee of 100, composed of small-business men, professional men, ranchers, and bankers, had been created by Roy Day. Day, a forty-six-year-old native Californian, was an advertising salesman for the Pomona *Progress Bulletin*. Far from being a front man for large corporate interests, Day was an authentic— albeit exceptionally talented and energetic—representative of the dissatisfied small-business men and ranchers of the 12th District.

Like their counterparts throughout Southern California, and indeed through the nation, these middle-class Old Guard Republicans were in a mood close to desperation. They hated FDR, but had never been able to beat him, and now they were stuck with Harry Truman for three more years. They groaned under the weight of New Deal regulations, but had been unable to lift them, and now Truman was talking about extending the New Deal. They cursed what they regarded as the coddling of labor unions by the New Deal, but union-led strikes continued to increase, to the point that there were more man-hours lost to strikes in 1946 than in any other year in American history. They feared for the future of democracy, as they convinced themselves through their own rhetoric that the New Deal really was going to turn their country over to socialism.

The men who formed the Committee of 100, like their counterparts throughout the nation, found a target for all their feelings of frustration, and simultaneously an inspiration for action of their own, in the CIO's Political Action Committee (PAC). Founded in the summer of 1943 under the chairmanship of Sidney Hillman, a Socialist and president of the Amalgamated Clothing Workers, PAC's function was to campaign for FDR's fourth term, using union funds. In July of 1944, a National Citizens PAC (NC-PAC), with Hillman as chairman, also began campaigning for FDR. The CIO-PAC had as its executive board CIO union leaders; the NC-PAC featured literary, academic, and entertainment figures, along with churchmen, politicians, and bureaucrats.

To Roy Day and his friends, the distinction between CIO-PAC and NC-PAC was inconsequential and even phony, given that Hillman headed both groups. As far as they were concerned, PAC was running the show for the New Deal. The ultimate proof of this belief came from FDR himself, who reportedly told his chieftains before the vice-presidential nomination at the 1944 convention to "clear it with Sidney." The phrase, widely quoted by conservatives, became their particular *bête noire*. They insisted that it showed the enormous and sinister power of the CIO in the Democratic Party.

Day created a conservative PAC of his own. He traveled to the small towns in the district, signing up volunteers—political amateurs all—for a citizens' committee to select a candidate. After the group organized itself, with Day as chairman, it put an advertisement in the local papers, asking potential candidates for Voorhis' seat to step forward. The results were disappointing. Frank Jorgensen, who had an insurance agency in San Marino, recalled thinking after the candidates presented themselves, "My God, if this is all we can get to run for Congress, let's don't waste our time." [6]

It was at this point, at the beginning of fall 1945, that Perry recommended Nixon to the committee. Day was sufficiently interested to get some of his fellows to buy plane tickets for Nixon and Pat to come to California. On November 2, they flew out. Pat went off to a lunch in San Marino, where she made a poor impression on the Republican ladies, one of whom remarked, "Why, this girl doesn't even know what color nail polish to wear!" [7] Nixon meanwhile met with the committee, where he made the best possible impression. Wearing his navy uniform, the only suit he had, he appeared eager, fit, intelligent, and as anxious to get rid of Voorhis as any man there. Five other candidates for the nomination talked before his turn came; he wisely decided to be brief.

He was marvelously effective. He had served on various civic organizations, and therefore he knew these men or men like them, knew what they wanted to hear, and how to say it. It was his first political speech in behalf of his own candidacy, and he rose to the occasion brilliantly.

He began by saying there were two conflicting views on the nature of the American system. "One advocated by the New Deal is government control in regulating our lives. The other calls for individual freedom and all that initiative can produce." Pausing, Nixon declared, "I hold with the latter viewpoint." He explained, "I believe the returning veterans, and I have talked to many of them in the foxholes, will not be satisfied with a dole or a government handout. They want a respectable job in private industry where they will be recognized for what they produce, or they want the opportunity to start their own business."

No member of the committee could have expressed his own feelings half so well. Nor could any member have matched Nixon's concluding pledge: that if selected, "I will be prepared to put on an aggressive and vigorous campaign . . . and with your help I feel very strongly that the present incumbent can be defeated." [8]

When Nixon finished, Day knew that he had a candidate. "This

man is salable merchandise," he told Jorgensen.[9] The Nixons returned to Baltimore. On November 28, Day polled the committee.
Nixon got sixty-three votes; his closest competitor, twelve. A second ballot made it unanimous. Day was delighted. "We felt we had
something we could really take out and sell to the people," he
recalled three decades later. "We didn't have to apologize for our
product in any way, shape, or form." He telephoned Nixon—it was
2 A.M. in Baltimore—and shouted, "Dick, the nomination's
yours!"[10]

NIXON BEGAN his campaign that morning. He wrote the minority
leader in the House of Representatives, Joseph Martin of Massachusetts, asking for an interview, which Martin granted. Martin
promised him, "We will do everything we can to bring about the
election of a Republican in your district."[11] Nixon talked with other
Republicans in the House about the campaign, concentrating on
their evaluations of Voorhis. He studied the *Congressional Digest*.
From the Republican Campaign Committee he obtained Voorhis'
complete voting record. "By the time of my discharge and return
to California in January," Nixon wrote in his memoirs, "I was confident that I knew Voorhis's record as well as he did himself. As it
turned out, I knew it even better."[12]

In December he wrote Day, saying that he was getting the
goods on Voorhis from Republican congressmen. "His 'conservative' reputation must be blasted." In addition, he urged Day to
"bring in the liberal fringe Republicans. We need *every* Republican and a few Democrats to win. I'm really hopped up over this
deal, and I believe I can win."[13]

He flew to California, leaving the seven-and-a-half-month-
pregnant Pat behind to do the packing and oversee the moving.
"Uncle Herman" Perry, as his friends and debtors called him, set
Nixon up in a small house in Whittier; despite its smallness, when
Pat arrived a couple of weeks later with the furniture, she discovered they did not have enough pieces to fill the rooms, and he had
no income. The members of the Committee of 100 were willing to
donate their time and energy to his campaign, but not their money,
and the central committee would not give him support until he had
won the primary nomination (Day's committee had only endorsed
him—it had no authority to offer the nomination).

Nixon began drawing on his savings for his personal expenses,
and for the cost of running his campaign. He paid the rent on a
storefront office; his mother contributed an old leather sofa; his
brother Don gave him the use of a truck. Pat was the entire full-
time office staff. Some of her friends came in from time to time to

help out, but she typed nearly all the campaign literature, took it to the printer, and then lugged the stuffed envelopes to the post office or distributed them by hand.[14]

She worked like a horse, as did her husband. Nixon's first task was to establish some name recognition. He was well known in Whittier and Yorba Linda, unknown everywhere else in the district. He hit the service-club circuit with a vengeance. The Optimists of Whittier, the Women's Republican Study Club of San Gabriel and Alhambra, the Rotary of San Gabriel, the Lions of Pasadena, the Two-in-One Class of the Methodist Church of Whittier, veterans' organizations throughout the 12th District, and many others heard him speak in January.

His standard speech, delivered over and over, told the story of his experiences behind the lines at Bougainville. His crew, he said, was a "typical melting pot." He described the men as ordinary guys from all over America. There was not a hero among them, yet they were men who "won the war." And they were the ones who would win the peace, if only the government would get out of the way and let them work. "The GI's are mighty good kids," he concluded, "and it is up to us to help them and give them the opportunities they deserve."[15]

Day and his committee members guided Nixon around the district, making arrangements and introductions. As Frank Jorgensen explained, "We were businessmen and we knew how to sell. We took the position that a political campaign was nothing more than selling a product—you got a candidate; if that's your product, how're you going to sell it?"[16]

In his initial speech, Nixon appeared in uniform. Day took him aside and informed him that there were a great many more enlisted men than officers among the district's veterans, and that to a man the enlisted disliked the officers. Together they went to Johnny Evans' store in Pomona, where Day talked Evans out of a new suit for Nixon. Like many veterans, Nixon's reaction to the drab uniform he had worn for almost four years was to pick the loudest ties he could find. After Nixon appeared in a really awful red tie, Day took him aside again. "Dick," he said, "these women are going to remember the tie you wore, and they won't know a word you said."[17]

The coffee hours were a standard technique, used extensively by Day and Nixon. The trouble was that neither Nixon nor his wife made a good initial impression. Pat was big as a barn, of course, and plainly dressed. She met the ladies with a tight little smile and a whispered, "Hello, I'm so pleased to meet you." Day remembered that she was "nervous, uptight, and tense."[18] Nixon was not much better. Day noticed that he was shy around women, would not look them in the eyes, but would drop or turn his head when talking to them.

Day delivered another lecture. "You have to look these people in the face," he told Nixon, "or they won't think you're telling the truth." But Nixon had one technique that even the critical Day had to admire. As Day himself explained it, "Dick would sit down and ask people what kind of government they wanted, what did they expect from the government. Then he'd reason with them. Rather than make a direct contradiction he would lead them around until he had them over in his corner. He has terrific ability in that regard." [19]

On Lincoln's Birthday, in Pomona, Nixon opened his formal campaign. He promised a "rocking, socking campaign." [20] In the days and weeks that followed, he was on the go for as many as twenty hours a day, every day, making speeches, writing leaflets, attending coffee klatches. Pat continued to work until February 17. On the twenty-first, she went into Murphy Memorial Hospital and gave birth to a girl. Pat called her Patricia, quickly shortened to "Tricia." Nixon was not present—he was out on the circuit, campaigning. Helene Drown was there to comfort Pat, and Jack Drown paced the waiting-room floor. [21]

Tricia's birth was fortunately timed. It gave Nixon free and extensive publicity. Nearly every newspaper in the district carried a photograph of the beaming parents, along with an interview with the proud father. He made the most of the opportunity. "Patricia is a lucky girl," he said. "She will grow up in the finest state in the union, in the greatest country on earth. She will grow up, go to schools and when the time comes she will register and vote Republican." When a reporter remarked that those were pretty heavy responsibilities for such a young lady, Nixon scowled. "That's just the way it is," he explained. "The task ahead is one of grave responsibilities for all of us." [22]

Pat cared for Tricia while Nixon sought support. He went to Norman Chandler, publisher of the Los Angeles *Times*, the leading Republican paper in Southern California. Nixon later admitted that he was "awed" by Chandler, that just being in his office "made a great impression on me." The meeting was brief, but Nixon had a longer conversation with Kyle Palmer, the political editor.

Palmer recalled, "My first impression of Nixon was that here was a serious, determined, somewhat gawky young fellow who was out on a sort of a giant-killer operation." Voorhis was widely popular, and most Republicans, including Palmer, thought it was a forlorn effort, "particularly when it was being made by a youngster who seemed to have none of the attributes of a rabblerouser who can go out and project himself before a crowd." But, Palmer added, "it wasn't too long after he settled down that we began to realize we had an extraordinary man on our hands."

Palmer brought Nixon back for another visit, and took him into Chandler's office for a twenty-minute talk. "His forthrightness, and the way he spoke, made a deep impression upon me," Chandler later said, "and so—after Nixon departed—I told Mr. Palmer: 'This young fellow makes sense. He looks like a comer. He has a lot of fight and fire. Let's support him.' "[23]

Murray Chotiner joined the Nixon team at this time. Chotiner had masterminded Earl Warren's campaign for governor, and was currently running William Knowland's senatorial campaign. He had a public-relations firm in Beverly Hills. Like Day, he had no use for losers; also like Day, he believed in attacking to win. He later became one of America's best-known political operators, some seeing him as the toughest, others as the most unscrupulous.

Throughout their long relationship, Nixon was ambiguous about Chotiner. It showed in their first contact. Chotiner put out a press release—Day had hired him at $500 per month for three months; he was the only paid Nixon supporter—under a letterhead reading "Murray M. Chotiner and Associates." Nixon scratched out the letterhead with blue ink and noted in the margin, "Do not use —R.N."[24] Still he would turn to Chotiner for advice, and for help with the press. But Nixon wrote his own handouts and speeches, and made his own decisions.

Chotiner was a sallow-skinned, fat, obsequious man, whose reputation far outstripped his actual influence. Variously described as the Machiavelli of California politics or as a master smear artist, he later became an important adviser to Nixon, and indispensable as a manager, but in this first campaign his role was minimal, partly because he was putting full time into the Knowland campaign, mainly because Nixon insisted on making the decisions himself. In addition, there were basic personality differences. Chotiner had a sense of humor; if Nixon had one, he seldom showed it. Tom Dixon, a radio announcer who worked for Nixon, said that Chotiner "for all his evil twists and turns was nevertheless a warm person, warmer than Nixon. He'd make jokes. I can't remember Nixon laughing at anything."[25]

One member of the committee recalled that "it didn't take Nixon long to get ahold of the reins, and once he had them he drove the horses."[26] And Roy Day, who was in the best position to know, told an interviewer, "Nixon knew what he wanted to say. He didn't need help with his speeches. We'd throw in some ideas. . . . Nixon was a brain. He knows what he's doing."[27]

Nevertheless, the legend grew. In the eyes of Nixon's critics, as a candidate he was merely a front man for Chotiner's evil manipulations. But it simply was not so.[28]

Chotiner was a heavyweight in California politics, but he was the only one in Nixon's camp. For the rest, prominent Republicans —and Republican money—were noticeable only by their absence. Most of them reasoned that Voorhis was unbeatable in a district composed of strongly New Deal farm laborers, and they concentrated their time and money on investments that had some prospect of showing a profit. The Committee of 100, as noted, was long on enthusiasm but short on money. So, during the primary season, from January to June 4, Nixon invested his own (and Pat's) money in the biggest gamble of his life to date.

In mid-March, three weeks after Tricia's birth, Pat went back to work for her husband. Each morning she would take Tricia over to Hannah's house and leave her for the day. In the evenings, exhausted, she would care for her child, holding Tricia on her lap and feeding her. "I'm glad now that I resisted the temptation to prop up the bottle," she said later.

She worked at a broken-down desk on a borrowed typewriter. The tension was as heavy as the work load. On at least one occasion it broke even her indomitable will. She spent a day typing and running off campaign literature only to discover late in the afternoon that there was no money to buy stamps to mail the material. She burst into tears and sobbed uncontrollably.

On another occasion she went into a rage when she discovered that she had fallen victim to one of the oldest tricks in politics. A group of "volunteers" showed up at headquarters and took a pile of handouts, promising to distribute them throughout the district. But the "volunteers" were all Democrats, and once out the door they tore up and threw away the literature.[29]

Nixon, too, showed the strain. One afternoon he was preparing a radio broadcast. Pat walked into the studio. "Nixon flared at her like a prima donna," an observer related. He ordered her out "with as little ceremony as he would have a dog, saying, 'You know I never want to be interrupted when I'm working!' " Tom Dixon, who was present, later said, "It gave me insight into the man. If he had been doing a brand-new speech, I could have understood it, but this speech he knew by heart."[30]

Despite this and other reported slights, Pat was steadfast. Dixon's wife recalled that Pat "had only two interests, her daughter and her husband, and that she talked incessantly about what a great man her husband was." When Roy Day got discouraged, Pat told him, "Don't worry about Dick. The tougher the going the better he gets."[31]

Nixon needed special handling, and he got it from his wife. He could gear himself up for a speech, but then fall into a dark depression afterward, full of self-doubt and criticism. Pat would bolster his sense of self-worth, assure him that things were going well and that the effort was worthwhile. Then she would launch into a criticism of what he had said—she would take shorthand notes while he talked, and tell him afterward what he had done wrong. As she often admitted, it was not a life she would have chosen for herself, not at all what she had envisioned during the war. But it was what her man wanted, and she threw her full energy into the effort. A close friend put it succinctly: "She gritted her teeth and did it because she felt it was her duty to do it." [32]

Jorgensen, who served as head of the finance committee, recalled that "Uncle Herman raised some money over in Whittier. There was some money raised in Pomona. But the money wasn't coming in as fast as it should, and it wasn't coming in as I was to know in later campaigns. When we got a $10 or $20 contribution we thought we were doing very well." [33] Pat recalled that "Dick couldn't even buy a suit. . . . He finally got a gray number, the one Johnny Evans gave him, much too small, to replace his uniform, but it was weeks before a friend in Los Angeles could get him a blue suit that fitted. The day it arrived we sold the gray for enough to buy another batch of office stationery." [34]

DESPITE THE OBVIOUS shoestring and amateur nature of Nixon's initial campaign, Nixon's critics later planted the story that he got into politics as a tool of big-business interests. Drew Pearson was not the first, but he was the most prominent, to make the charge. In his column of November 7, 1950, Pearson wrote: "The people who first promoted Nixon for the House of Representatives were Harry March, vice president of Signal Oil, and Sam Mosher, president of Signal. They . . . helped sell Nixon on the idea of running for Congress several years ago. . . . " [35]

Voorhis made a similar charge, but with different culprits. According to Voorhis, in October 1945, a major New York banker came to Southern California, where he met with local bankers and "bawled them out" for allowing Voorhis to represent them in Congress. Voorhis, he said, was "one of the most dangerous men in Washington," because Voorhis advocated a nationalized banking system. Voorhis charged that Nixon's campaign funds came from New York and Los Angeles bankers. [36]

The truth is that the Nixon campaign was a revolt of small-business men, not a plot by the oilmen and New York bankers. Perry was the only banker involved before the primary. As for

Harry March and Signal Oil, the story is more complex. Back in December 1945, when he was still in Baltimore, Nixon talked to his old navy acquaintance Paull Marshall. Marshall was on the staff of the Republican National Committee. He promised Nixon support if he won the primary.

On February 20, 1946, Marshall wrote Nixon. "I have had a good talk with Harry March about you," he began. March was on his way to California, Marshall continued, "and has suggested to me that I tell you to arrange an appointment to see him. I think he can do a lot for you if you get him interested."

Marshall next explained that March was "vitally interested in the Tidelands Oil question." President Truman was advocating national control over offshore oil, while the oil companies wanted to retain the present state control, for fear of tighter regulations and higher taxes under federal rule. Marshall added that March "might well be interested in your opinion on the subject." [37]

Whether this was a brazen attempt at influence peddling, or an honest effort by a man of affairs to protect his stockholders' interests, depends on one's point of view. What matters, for Nixon, is the date. Marshall wrote eight days after Nixon launched his formal campaign; clearly March had no input into his decision to run. Further, Nixon replied a month later, to report that he had not yet seen March. By April 23, when Marshall wrote back to Nixon, no meeting had yet taken place. [38] Evidently Nixon never did meet March.

HIS ORIGINAL supporters were small-business men and ranchers, professional men, successful men with large ambitions, who felt hampered by the New Deal, restricted in their opportunities by its regulations, punished by its taxes, destroyed by its prounion policies. These were the men who really hated FDR, far more than the corporate heads, who after all cut their own deals with "That Man in the White House" and learned to live with him.

The small-business man never did learn to live with FDR, and they were, of course, far more numerous and—collectively—worth far more than all the big businesses combined. Their hatred of Roosevelt was so intense it was almost a palpable thing, and so intense that it was still burning bright when transferred to Jerry Voorhis.

To the small-business man of the 12th District, Voorhis was the essence of the New Deal—a Socialist at heart (and by party affiliation in the 1920s), he was a dangerous man, just as the banker from New York supposedly said. But it was the Committee of 100, not outside corporate interests, that led the revolt against Voorhis.

It was this group that launched Nixon's political career—and it was this same group that stuck by him, faithfully, through the next thirty years of continuous controversy. Nixon's roots were planted in soil prepared and nurtured by the small-business men of Southern California, acting in behalf of their counterparts across the nation.

Nixon campaigned hard, using standard Republican rhetoric. "It is government's responsibility to see that opportunities for small business and new enterprise are not choked off by monopolistic practice in restraint of trade," Nixon said on May 14 at a women's club meeting in Claremont.[39] On April 18, he declared, "We must get rid of all unnecessary federal controls that are slowly choking to death the businessmen of this country."[40] On May 9, in San Marino, he told a mass meeting that there were now four branches of government, the fourth being the swollen federal bureaucracy.[41]

To UNDERSTAND the 1946 campaign, one must begin by recognizing the depth of Republican desperation. Sixteen years of minority-party status, years in which America underwent great change, had led Republicans to regard the 1946 election as almost Armageddon. Republicans felt that the New Deal had launched an attack on private property and free enterprise that threatened the existence of the American Republic. As Republicans saw it, union coddling by the Democrats was on the verge of destroying the economy, and all but the most partisan Democrats had to admit that Communist infiltration into the CIO in particular and big labor in general was a major problem.

Viewed from the podium of the Rotary Club, if the present was a near-disaster, the future looked like a total catastrophe. FDR's death had thrown the Democratic Party into confusion, which opened the party to control by the CIO and other radicals. Since the Democrats seemed unbeatable, the stroll down the path to socialism would quickly become a dash. And those leading the way would be Jerry Voorhis and his fellow liberals. Thus in the Republican analysis, men like Voorhis were more dangerous than the Communists themselves. It did not matter if Voorhis and his friends were well-meaning dupes or conscious agents of a Communist conspiracy, the effect was the same.

Republicans all across America felt in 1946 that if there ever was a time when the end justified the means, this was it. What they aimed to do, and to some extent managed to accomplish, was to re-create the Red Scare of 1919 (which, not incidentally, was led by a Democratic Attorney General, A. Mitchell Palmer). Republicans did not hesitate to charge, in 1946, that the New Deal Democrats, if not actually Communists themselves, were leading the country to socialism at home and surrender abroad. In Wisconsin, Judge Joseph R. McCarthy, running for the Senate as a Republican, charged that his opponent, Bob La Follette, Jr., was "playing into the hands of the Communists." This theme was played by Republicans everywhere, not just in the 12th Congressional District in California. Anything to win was the Republican attitude. Among other things, the 1946 campaign demonstrated that it is dangerous in a two-party democracy for one party to hold power for too long a time, if only because of the desperation it breeds in the party out of power.

As will be seen, Nixon's campaign came to center on a charge that Voorhis was a Communist sympathizer who had Communist support. This was absolutely untrue, as Nixon knew perfectly well, but it no more deterred him than it did Joe McCarthy, who made similar charges about La Follette. In point of fact, both Voorhis and La Follette had become anathema to the Communist Party, because both had denounced Russian aggression in Eastern Europe. But the truth mattered not one bit to either McCarthy or Nixon, or indeed to other Republican candidates across the country.

The point being a simple one—Richard Nixon did not invent anti-Communism, nor was he unique in his use, or misuse, of the issue. And it should be added that he was egged on by older and presumably wiser men—not that he needed much encouraging.

CROSS-FILING was the order of the day in California, and consequently in primary elections it was common practice for the leading candidates to run in both the Democratic and Republican primaries. Nixon and Voorhis did so in 1946. Nixon concentrated on general denunciations of big government, rather than his Republican opponents, none really serious candidates. He campaigned actively, while Voorhis stayed in Washington (where his colleagues in the House voted him the "hardest working" congressman).

ON APRIL 23, Nixon had Roy Crocker of the Committee of 100 release a statement that read: "Now that the Political Action Committee has publicly endorsed the candidacy of Jerry Voorhis for Congress, one of the real issues of the campaign is out in the open. . . . There can be no mistake. The choice now is: Shall it be the people represented by Nixon, or the PAC by Voorhis?"[42]

On May 18 the Alhambra *Post-Advocate's* news editor, Herbert Klein, ran an editorial criticizing Voorhis for accepting the "radical PAC endorsements." On May 24, the South Pasadena *Review* published a bitter personal attack on Voorhis, citing above all his endorsement by PAC.[43]

As this became the central issue in the campaign, some details are necessary. Although Voorhis had been endorsed by PAC in 1944, by 1946 he was out of favor with the CIO, and especially with the Communists in the organization (there was a bitter fight going on for control of PAC between the Communists and the liberals). Because Voorhis had criticized Russian moves in Eastern Europe, the Communists had refused to endorse him in 1946.

As for the Southern California branch of the National Citizens PAC, in that group the Communists led an attack on Voorhis, arguing that foreign policy was the key issue and anti-Russian "hysteria" should never be rewarded. Liberals in the group never-theless pushed for an endorsement of Voorhis, and one committee circulated a mimeographed bulletin within the organization rec-ommending an endorsement of Voorhis. But NC-PAC itself never endorsed him.[44]

Crocker's charge was false. Without question, Nixon was be-hind it. Where did he get the idea? Not from Chotiner—in fact, it was not a new idea at all. The Republican candidate in 1944 had tried to raise a storm about the PAC endorsement of Voorhis (which was real), but in the wartime atmosphere, when the Com-munists in the CIO were cooperating handsomely in turning out war goods, the charges fell flat. But Nixon had studied the cam-paign closely, and concluded correctly that the problem was not the issue but the timing. A combination of the huge number of strikes in 1946 and Russian aggression in Eastern Europe made voters far more responsive to charges that Voorhis had Communist support.

The only trouble was, he did not. Nixon decided that it did not matter. What mattered was that Voorhis was vulnerable on the issue of CIO domination—his voting record entitled him to a CIO endorsement, whether offered or not. To Nixon, the distinction between a 1944 endorsement and the absence of one in 1946 was a distinction without a difference, just as was the case with NC-PAC and CIO-PAC.

Nixon did not raise issues himself during the primary, although he orchestrated others who did. He was holding his fire until after the primary, in which he easily won the Republican nomination. But he was badly outpolled overall by Voorhis, who had seven thousand more votes than he did.

Nixon was a bit shaken and depressed by the vote, but he brightened up considerably when a Los Angeles *Times* reporter pointed out to him that Voorhis' total percentage of the primary vote was only 53.5 percent, and it had been 60 percent in 1944. This marked the beginning of what would become a lifelong obses-sion with the percentages.

Excited, Nixon scribbled a note to Roy Day. He cited the figures, then asserted, "All we need is a win complex and we'll take him in November." He told Day to write a "breezy" letter to all the campaign workers, informing them that "we had no machine politics (all volunteers and much new blood) and were opposed by a PAC backed candidate." He said "I'd be darned sure" copies went to his three defeated Republican opponents in order to "spike the sniping."

Finally, he wanted the workers made aware "that we used none of our big guns—purposely (suggesting we really are holding back some stuff—as we are)."[45]

THE "STUFF" was a combination of the supposed PAC endorsement and Voorhis' voting record in Congress. Through the summer months, while Voorhis stayed in Washington, Nixon worked these themes. "It's time to clean house in Washington," Nixon told the Woman's club at Puente on July 28. "I have no personal criticism of my opponent as a man," he said, but he did point out that Voorhis had a PAC endorsement and was associated with the left-wing Democrats. In mid-August, he repeated the speech in South Pasadena.[46] On August 29, he told a Whittier audience, "There are no strings attached to me. I have no support from any special interest or pressure group. I welcome the opposition of the PAC with its Communist principles and its huge slush fund."[47]

On September 11, Voorhis—who had just returned to campaign—made his first response. In both a paid advertisement and a news release, he flatly denied that he had a PAC endorsement. As one proof, he cited an editorial in *People's World*, the official Communist paper, dated July 3, 1946, which attacked him and concluded, "Voorhis is against unity with Communists on any issue under any circumstances." He admitted that the CIO in California had fallen under Communist influence, but argued that the "one effective enemy of the Communist or Fascist is . . . the earnest progressive."[48]

There were thirty newspapers in the district; twenty-six were for Nixon, three were neutral, and one supported Voorhis. These astonishing figures (half the voters were registered as Democrats) reflected the composition of the Committee of 100—they were the men who placed the advertisements in the small-town papers.

The editors did more than support Nixon; in many cases they actively helped. When Voorhis ran his advertisement denying a PAC endorsement, for example, editors gave Nixon an advance copy. So Nixon headquarters was able to respond on the same day the ad appeared—many papers put the two items side by side. The response promised that "we are prepared to offer proof of the present congressman's endorsement by the PAC." [49]

The opportunity came in mid-September, when the Independent Voters of South Pasadena, a liberal New Deal group struggling to maintain itself in the most conservative community in the district, invited Nixon and Voorhis to a "debate," really a joint appearance, with an opportunity to question each other afterward. Both accepted. [50]

Voorhis, the winner of five previous elections, with ten years' experience in congressional debate, then proceeded to make one major mistake after another, while Nixon, in his first campaign, made one right decision after another. On the excuse of a previous commitment, Nixon got Voorhis to agree to allow him to speak last —timing his entrance to perfection, he showed up onstage just as Voorhis reached his conclusion.

Voorhis had accepted another Nixon condition—that there be no set topic. That freed Nixon to make a campaign speech, which he did, hammering at the federal bureaucracy, calling for the abolition of the OPA and price ceilings. He stated his undying opposition to government ownership of the Federal Reserve Banks. It was his standard speech, well given and well received.

The real test came in the question period. Nixon had prepared himself by going over with Roy Day possible questions Voorhis would ask, and trying to anticipate his answers to Nixon's questions. Thus when Voorhis asked him to produce the promised "proof" of a PAC endorsement, Nixon was ready.

It was a moment toward which he had been pointing his life. The occasion let him use many of his hard-earned skills, and display some of his considerable natural talent. In response to Voorhis' question, Nixon grabbed a piece of paper, held it dramatically aloft, and began striding across the stage toward Voorhis. He was simultaneously Richard the actor, the debater, the courtroom lawyer, the clean-cut Quaker kid seething with righteous indignation over Teapot Dome, the poker player who could bet more than a year's salary on a bluff. Chin thrust forward, a deep scowl on his face, he thrust his paper at Voorhis. Here, he said, is the proof.

He took Voorhis completely by surprise. Nixon's confidence and dramatic presentation of the document threw him off balance, and from that moment on he never recovered.

The "proof," as proof, was not much. It consisted of the internal recommendation of a liberal group in the Southern California NC-PAC that Voorhis get an endorsement. Voorhis read it in some bemusement.

Nixon had laid a trap, but Voorhis had an easy way out. He

could have pointed out that the document was nothing more than a recommendation, which was in fact rejected by NC-PAC anyway, and then called Nixon a knowing liar. But Nixon had judged his man rightly in this face-to-face, winner-take-all encounter, and he carried out his role so well that he left Voorhis in complete confusion.

Glancing up from the paper, Voorhis mumbled that this was an NC-PAC document, not from the CIO-PAC. Nixon could not have hoped for a better answer. Scornfully, he read to the audience the names of those people who served in both organizations, charged that the two groups were in fact one and the same, and triumphantly proclaimed that Voorhis did indeed have the PAC endorsement.[51] Voorhis dug himself deeper, repeating that NC-PAC and CIO-PAC were different organizations.

Nixon kept up the pressure. At the end of the week, he put an advertisement in the district newspapers that would be hard to match for brazenness, boldness, or the depth of contempt it showed Nixon held for Voorhis. "THE TRUTH COMES OUT," the ad declared. "VOORHIS ADMITS PAC ENDORSEMENT." It cited a May 31 issue of *People's World* as proof of the endorsement. In fact that issue had specifically said of Voorhis, "No CIO Endorsement." Then Nixon brought out more of his "stuff." Voorhis, he charged, "HAS CONSISTENTLY VOTED THE PAC LINE IN CONGRESS," and claimed that of forty bills supported by PAC over the past four years, Voorhis voted for thirty-six of them.[52]

Voorhis, meanwhile, went from blunder to blunder. As Nixon's outrageously false ad was appearing, Voorhis fired off a telegram to NC-PAC headquarters in New York asking that the "qualified endorsement" be withdrawn on grounds of basic foreign policy disagreements. Making things even worse for himself, he distributed copies of the telegram to the newspapers, all of which gleefully printed it as proof positive that Voorhis *had* been endorsed by PAC, just as Nixon had charged, and now was weaseling.[53]

Nixon's supporters, including Murray Chotiner, urged him to challenge the by-now hapless Voorhis to more debates. "You must run a high-risk campaign," Chotiner told him.[54] Nixon did not need to be told—he immediately made the challenge, and Voorhis accepted. A week later, in the first of four debates, Nixon initiated another heated discussion about PAC. He again waved his document, and again got a reply from Voorhis that was ideal for his purposes. Voorhis said he had asked the organization to withdraw its endorsement, and muttered that he could not be responsible "for the action of any group."[55]

The next day, Nixon headquarters issued a statement saying

that the truth had caught up with Voorhis, and had the effrontery to demand that Voorhis apologize to Nixon for accusing him of not having evidence.[56]

And so it went, through the four debates, which attracted increasingly larger audiences, and which newspaper reporters who did not know much history compared to the Lincoln-Douglas debates. At the last debate, held in the Monrovia High School gym before an audience of twelve hundred, Voorhis showed that he still had not quite caught on to what was happening when he asserted once again that he had asked that any PAC endorsement be withdrawn.

Nixon leaped on that one. He announced to the audience that Voorhis' voting record "earned him the endorsement, whether he wanted it or not."[57]

On the matter of Voorhis' record, as on the question of a PAC endorsement, Nixon put Voorhis on the defensive and kept him there, primarily through vague charges that could only be answered with detailed refutations, which by the time they were prepared would be out-of-date, because Nixon would by then bring up new ones. Thus in October, a Nixon ad charged that Voorhis had voted against the "Communist dominated PAC" line only three times out of forty-six. Voorhis had not yet caught up with the original charge, that on forty occasions he had voted against CIO wishes only four times.

When Voorhis demanded to know what votes Nixon was referring to, Nixon produced a list compiled by the CIO of test votes. To Voorhis' amazement, the votes Nixon was criticizing included those for a school-lunch program, for abolishing the poll tax, and for the postwar loan to Great Britain (which bill the Communists bitterly opposed). In a number of instances, Voorhis' vote had been counted twice.

According to Voorhis, the distortion of his voting record "cut me pretty deeply." He and his advisers stayed up all night going over the votes Nixon had cited, then prepared a refutation. But they got it out only a week before the election, and it was so detailed few voters bothered to read it.[58]

IN THAT SAME October advertisement, Nixon asked the voters: "DO YOU KNOW THAT YOUR PRESENT CONGRESSMAN INTRODUCED 132 PUBLIC BILLS IN THE LAST FOUR YEARS: AND ONLY ONE OF THEM WAS PASSED? THAT THE ONE BILL ADOPTED TRANSFERRED ACTIVITIES CONCERNING RABBITS FROM ONE FEDERAL DEPARTMENT TO ANOTHER? A VOTE FOR NIXON IS A VOTE FOR CHANGE.[59] During the question period at the last debate, Nixon pounced on those rabbits; to the delight of his supporters in the audience, he suggested that one had to be a rabbit to get effective representation in the 12th District, because the only bill passed in the last four years with Voorhis' name on it was the rabbit bill.

Nixon's contempt for Voorhis was complete. As he later told Stewart Alsop, "Voorhis was a Don Quixote, an idealist . . . who never accomplished anything very much." [60] Actually he had accomplished a great deal, and Nixon's rabbit charge opened a marvelous opportunity for Voorhis. But he failed to seize it, because he allowed Nixon to pick the battleground. He could have replied, "Look, I'm the author of the Voorhis Act of 1940, requiring the registration of Communists, which is one reason the Communists hate me so, and why Nixon's charge of a PAC endorsement is as phony as this 'rabbit representative' business."

Instead, inexplicably, Voorhis stuck to the four-year period Nixon had chosen, and tried to explain that very few congressmen got their names on bills. He insisted that he had been involved in passing new legislation on atomic energy, school lunches, the various amendments to the Social Security Act, credit-union matters, and congressional reorganization, although none carried his name. In explaining congressional procedure to the audience, he pointed out that it was pure accident that his name was on the rabbit bill, which had been introduced by a colleague. All Voorhis did was add an amendment.

Ah ha, Nixon responded. Once again you admit the truth of my charges (citing Voorhis' alleged turnnabout on the PAC endorsement issue), and it turns out that you did not even sponsor the one bill that we generously gave you credit for. The whole thing was designed to make Voorhis look ridiculous, and it worked. [61]

Voorhis had never run into anyone like Nixon, and he was quite out of his league. For example, Nixon did his research and was never caught by surprise; Voorhis was almost always in a state of shock, disbelief, and surprise at Nixon's charges. In the last debate, Voorhis asserted that he did too have a bill carrying his name, the law that created the national "Employ the Physically Handicapped" week. Nixon was once again presented with an answer that was too good to be true. Once again he waved a "document" triumphantly above his head and smilingly told the audience that he had the "bill" in hand, and that it was a resolution, not a law. Voorhis stood there speechless. [62]

Not until a quarter century later, in 1972, did Voorhis think of the right answer. He was being interviewed about the campaign by Paul Bullock. "What I should have done," he told Bullock, "in a calm and calculated way, was to say, 'Well, Mr. Nixon just isn't informed about these matters in Congress, and the fact is that a joint resolution has the force of law.' "[63]

IN THE STRETCH DRIVE, Nixon was a whirlwind of activity, making speeches and radio talks, supervising his headquarters operation, taking out large and expensive and frequent advertisements in the newspapers. All this cost money, far more than Nixon's $5,000 personal investment.

But he did not have to worry. After his primary victory, and especially after the first debate, the money came pouring in. Harrison McCall, the treasurer of the campaign committee, estimated the total at $35,000. Given Voorhis' advocacy of a nationalized bank system, it was inevitable that the local bankers would get behind Nixon. The newspapers gave him cut rates for advertising, and assumed the expense of layout themselves. And there may have been some oil money behind Nixon, but no documentation exists on that point.

What is clear is that Nixon recovered his investment even before the election. However much of his own money he had put into the campaign up front—estimates range from $3,000 to $5,000—he got it all back. When he went to Washington, in January 1947, he took with him $10,000, his furniture, a new Ford, and $14,000 worth of life insurance.[64] As $10,000 was all he had at the beginning of the campaign, it seems obvious that whatever amount he spent on his own behalf, he later covered by reimbursing himself from campaign contributions.

IN THE FINAL WEEKS of the campaign, Nixon concentrated on rabbits and radicals. He projected the image of an embattled patriot, almost single-handedly resisting the Red tide. On October 18, he told the American Legion that Communists and fellow travelers were "gaining positions of importance in virtually every federal department and bureau," and that this was part of a conspiracy "calculated to gradually give the American people a Communist form of government." Citing his experiences in 1942 in the bureaucracy, he asserted, "I know what I am talking about. OPA is shot through with extreme left-wingers. They are boring from within, striving to force private enterprise into bankruptcy, and thus bring about the socialization of America's basic institutions and industries."[65]

In a mid-October advertisement that appeared in every paper in the district, Nixon proclaimed in bold type that "PAC looks after the interests of Russia." He brought in the rabbits. And he concluded, "REMEMBER, Voorhis is a former registered Socialist and his voting record in Congress is more Socialistic and Communistic than Democratic." [66]

"There is one point I should like to make very clear," Nixon told an El Monte audience in early October. "I do not question the motives of my opponent in voting the PAC line in Congress. I respect his right to believe in and to support that type of legislation." Then he proceeded to do exactly what he had said he would not do, question Voorhis' motives. He said he would "serve all the people impartially," that—unlike Voorhis—he would "not be obligated to any special interest or pressure group." [67]

As noted, Nixon was not unique in raising the Communist issue. Most California observers thought that Murray Chotiner's campaign for Knowland against Will Rogers, Jr., was more scurrilous than Nixon's against Voorhis. Americans have come to believe a great myth—that the anti-Communist crusade started with a Lincoln speech in 1950, when Wisconsin Senator Joe McCarthy waved some papers over his head and asserted that he had documentary proof that large numbers of Communists had infiltrated the State Department. But there was McCarthyism long before anyone outside Wisconsin had ever heard of Joe, and it lasted long after he disappeared. Nixon anticipated almost all of McCarthy's charges, including a statement in Pomona that charged "there are those walking in high official places . . . who would lead us into a disastrous foreign policy whereby we will be guilty of . . . depriving the people of smaller nations of their freedoms." [68]

WHILE NIXON concentrated on rabbits and radicals, he did not omit the issue that Republicans throughout the country were relying on for victory. It was succinctly expressed in the campaign slogan, "Had enough?"

After the binge of the V-J Day celebration, America went into a long hangover. Throughout the nation, people had eagerly anticipated the coming of peace. It would mean jobs, houses, new cars, new refrigerators, electric toasters, plentiful supplies of meat and liquor, the good life they had fought to preserve and expand. But a year after the Japanese surrender, all these items remained in short supply. The economic dislocations of the war could not be set straight overnight. Inevitably, if unfairly, people blamed the Democrats. The inflation rate—at 20 percent, the highest of the century—and the rash of strikes added to people's discontent. So did the widespread black market.

Nixon's proposed solution was to abolish the OPA and free private industry to meet the people's needs. The OPA price ceilings, he said—and to a large extent he was right—were not holding down prices, but were forcing them ever upward. Competition, not wage and price controls, was the way to progress. He explained that the ceilings on beef, for example, led to two things—higher prices for such substitutes as chicken and fish, and the withholding of cattle from the market by ranchers who would not accept the controlled low price for their product.[69]

In the eve-of-election speech, in Whittier, Nixon demanded protection of small-business men against the tyrannies of "big government, big business and big labor."[70]

BUT COMMUNISM was the big issue. In one of the last issues before the election, Herb Klein's Alhambra paper carried an editorial stating that Voorhis voted "the Communist party line. Jerry is not a Communist, but not many members of the House voted against more measures that Communists vigorously oppose than he."

In the next issue, Klein published a long editorial titled, "How Jerry and Vito Voted," which alleged that Voorhis had voted the same way as Democratic Congressman Vito Marcantonio of New York. Marcantonio, usually referred to as the "notorious fellow traveler," was a godsend to the Republican Party in general, and to Nixon in particular, who would clash with him frequently in Congress and who would use his name and voting record again, with devastating effectiveness, in the 1950 senatorial campaign.[71]

According to Voorhis' supporters, in the final days of the campaign Nixon used his most dastardly tactic. Democratic voters throughout the district began receiving phone calls. "This is a friend of yours," the call began, "but I can't tell you who I am. Did you know that Jerry Voorhis is a Communist?" Click.

The story is widely believed, and it does seem certain that at least a few such calls were made, but no firsthand evidence has ever been produced to prove that they came from Nixon's headquarters. Nixon supporters point out, quite rightly, that such techniques backfire as often as they work, and hint that the Democrats might have made the calls, hoping Nixon would get blamed. A Voorhis leader, on the other hand, is insistent that her niece worked for two days in a Nixon boiler room, with phones going all the time, and that she was paid $9 a day for calling Jerry a Communist.[72]

Whether or not Nixon initiated the telephone calls, his campaign as a whole was characterized by a vicious, snarling approach that was full of half-truths, full lies, and innuendos, hurled at such a pace that Voorhis could never catch up with them. Nixon had promised a "rocking, socking campaign," but what he gave the people of the 12th District was a dirty one.

And that puzzled many of those who had known him all their

lives. To them, this was a "new Nixon." One close friend of Nixon's from high school and college remembered, "There was never anything ruthless about Dick when we were growing up. If it was a fair fight, anything went . . . but not anything dirty. That's why I could never understand the positions he took in campaigns." He had decided that it was all due to Murray Chotiner's influence, "because Dick knew that a lot of us who are liberal are not Communists, in fact we are anti-Communists."

Another classmate of Nixon's revealed the depth of his resentment of Nixon's actions in the 1946 campaign when he said, "Real Quakers look at men with a level eye. Dick Nixon doesn't."

Nixon found it difficult to look people in the eye, a trait that grew more pronounced the older he grew. His eyes would dart from person to person, as he judged the effect of what he was saying or doing; they almost never came to rest on one individual. It was as if he had something to hide.

Enough Whittier residents were shocked by this new Nixon that after he became Vice-President and the City Council tried to name a street after him, they formed a citizens' group to block the council's initiative.[73]

Nevertheless, Nixon carried Whittier easily, 5,727 to 2,678. The majority liked what he said and the way that he said it. His original backers could not have been more delighted with their candidate and with his campaign. He had hit Voorhis exactly where the Committee of 100 wanted him to get hit, on his liberalism, his softness on Communism, his support for the New Deal bureaucracy and especially the hated OPA, his threats to the private banking system. As to the methods, these hardheaded businessmen took the practical view that it was up to Voorhis to defend himself. Just as one got away with whatever one could in a business deal, so too in politics. It was the morality of the marketplace. It was not Nixon's fault, they reasoned, that Voorhis was so dumb he let Nixon get away with barefaced lies.

As for Nixon himself, he appears to have made the transition from nice Quaker boy to ruthless politician without even noticing. Certainly there is no evidence that there was any soul-searching involved. To him it was all of a piece—you did whatever you could to win. That had been his way throughout his childhood, in his debates, in student government, in sports, in classroom work. That was the way of the young lawyer and of the poker-playing navy officer.

Nor was Nixon ever embarrassed by his campaign against Voorhis. In the decades that followed, newspapers would occasionally print stories claiming that Nixon had apologized for, or felt sorry about, the Voorhis campaign. Nixon always furiously denied the stories.[74]

In 1955, Nixon told a reporter that "Communism was not the issue at any time in the '46 campaign. Few people knew about Communism then, and even fewer cared." That was a breathtaking assertion, reckless in its disregard of the truth, outrageous in its denial of the facts, as was Nixon's further claim that he had never implied that Voorhis was a Communist or raised the issue of Communism in the campaign.[75]

When a Voorhis aide, Stanley Long, later accused Nixon to his face of lying during the campaign, Nixon replied, "Of course I knew Jerry Voorhis wasn't a Communist." On the rabbits, Nixon said, "You know I know better than that: I know the processes of the legislature and the Congress better than that. But it's a good political campaign fire to use. I had to win. That's the thing you don't understand. The important thing is to win. You're just being naïve."[76]

NIXON'S WIN was a big one. He had a margin of more than 15,000 votes, 56 percent of the total. In his concession statement, Voorhis wished Nixon well, but pointedly did not congratulate him on his victory. On December 7, back in Washington, he wrote Nixon. After a four-paragraph essay on the importance of Congress, Voorhis wrote, "I have refrained, for reasons which I am sure you will understand, from making any references in this letter to the circumstances of the campaign recently conducted in our District. It would only have spoiled the letter." He concluded with an offer to be of any assistance he could in helping Nixon get started.

Two weeks later Nixon walked into Voorhis' office. They smiled and shook hands. The office was bleak and bare; Voorhis' term was about to end. Nixon thanked Voorhis for his offer to help, then asked him for his mailing lists. Voorhis was enraged at what he regarded as Nixon's effrontery. He refused, but kept his temper, and later told reporters he hoped they had parted "as personal friends."[77]

For Nixon, as he put it in his memoirs, "nothing could equal the excitement and jubilation of winning the first campaign. Pat and I were happier on November 6, 1946, than we were ever to be again in my political career."[78]

For Whittier and the 12th District, Nixon's first campaign produced the first Nixon haters and the first group of Nixon supporters. This was a consequence of his campaigning style and his penchant for polarizing his constituents over basic issues. The numbers of both groups would grow in the years ahead, until virtually everyone in the nation belonged to either one or the other.

CHAPTER NINE

FRESHMAN CONGRESSMAN
1947–1948

JANUARY OF 1947 was an ideal time for Nixon to enter Congress. The Republicans were in control, for the only session from 1931 through 1952, and they were determined to act dramatically to prepare the way for the restoration, in the upcoming 1948 presidential election, of America's rightful rulers to the White House. If the New Deal had been a revolution, American-style, the newly elected Republicans wanted to use the Eightieth Congress to begin the counterrevolution.

The Chicago *Tribune* called the results of the election of 1946 "the greatest victory for the Republic since Appomattox," and Representative Daniel Reed of New York crowed, "What a glorious victory for the freedom loving citizens of this Republic!" *U.S. News* predicted "a new cycle in American political history."[1]

The Republicans had indeed won an overwhelming victory, gaining fifty-six seats in the House and thirteen in the Senate, which gave them decisive majorities in both. The "class of 1946" in the Senate was dominated by some of the most conservative members of the Republican Party, usually designated the "Old Guard": John Bricker of Ohio, William Jenner of Indiana, William Knowland of California, George Malone of Nevada, Joseph McCarthy of Wisconsin, Arthur Watkins of Utah, John Williams of Delaware, and others. In the House, there were Richard Nixon of California, Karl Mundt of South Dakota, Charles Kersten of Wisconsin, and many others.

In general, these members of the Old Guard were united in their opposition to the New Deal and all its manifestations, but especially the coddling of the labor unions, high income and corporate taxes, deficit financing, foreign interventionism and foreign aid in Europe, and the New Deal's apparently casual attitude toward internal security and evident indifference toward China.

Freshmen congressmen are supposed to be seen and not heard, but the unique circumstances of the Eightieth Congress gave Nixon an opportunity to play a leading role in three major areas—labor reform, subversive control, and foreign aid. He seized his opportunity so effectively that by the end of the session he was widely recognized as a comer. He could not have had such an impact in any other session, not the one that went before nor the one that followed, because then he would have been not only a freshman but a minority one to boot, and he could not have chaired important subcommittees, nor helped guide critical legislation through the House. Nor would he have been so in tune with majority sentiment in the House.

THE REPUBLICANS' first priority was to amend, if they could not kill outright, the National Labor Relations Act of 1935, which they regarded as practically the birth certificate of the CIO. Generally called the Wagner Act, it had given the unions the right to collective bargaining, in effect creating the closed shop, and other privileges. Nixon wanted to be in on the attack, at the heart of the action, and immediately after his election he had set about getting a place for himself on the Education and Labor Committee. He told Paull Marshall that what he wanted, above all else, was "a spot on the labor committee."[2] He talked to Herman Perry, who at his urging wrote Minority Leader (soon to be Speaker) Joe Martin, asking Martin to look after the young man. "I trust that you will personally take an interest in him," Perry wrote, "as he has a promising future and considerable drive and ability."

Martin's reply was prompt and encouraging, if predictable: "You can rest assured that I want to see that he gets every opportunity here and we shall give him a full chance to make good, so that his re-election will come as a matter of course."[3]

The Nixons moved to Washington right after the holidays. On January 3, 1947, he went to the Capitol for his swearing-in ceremony. In the Republican cloakroom, where the new members were milling about, meeting one another and waiting to take the oath, a reporter asked Nixon if he had any bill he planned to introduce, or pet project. "No, nothing in particular," Nixon replied, and then contradicted himself: "I was elected to smash the labor bosses." He vowed that "my one principle is to accept no dictation from the CIO-PAC," a vow that, in view of his campaign against Voorhis, hardly seemed necessary.[4] In fact, Nixon had made his hostility toward the CIO such a major feature of his successful campaign that it was almost automatic for Martin to grant his request for a seat on the Education and Labor Committee.

Nixon's second committee assignment was also a choice one. Martin put him on the House Committee on Un-American Activities (universally, if wrongly, known by the acronym HUAC, as it shall be called here). This put Nixon at the point position on the two most important issues on the Republican agenda, curbing the unions and rooting out the subversives. How Nixon got this second desirable appointment is not so clear.

According to Nixon, Martin asked him, as a personal favor, to sit on HUAC. "We need a young lawyer on that committee to smarten it up," Nixon quoted Martin as saying. In the office of fellow freshman Donald Jackson, also of California, Nixon weighed the pros and cons of accepting. "He felt the moral obligation to accept," Jackson said, "but he asked himself repeatedly, sometimes aloud, if the condemnation of the committee by the liberals was sound, if there were the injustices and the irresponsibilities complained of, if the committee could be brought to do a sound job." Nixon himself later told reporters, "Politically, it could have been the kiss of death, but I figured it was an opportunity as well as a risk, so I took it."[5]

Perhaps Nixon was surprised by the assignment, as he claimed, and perhaps he was reluctant to take it, as Jackson recalled. HUAC did have a reputation for witch-hunting, racism, and irresponsibility. But it should be noted that there were more Republican applicants for HUAC than there were seats available. The testimony of William Arnold, who was then serving as Nixon's administrative assistant and press secretary, also should be noted. Arnold wrote in his memoirs that at the end of December 1946 Nixon, "with characteristic prescience, sought and obtained positions on the House Education and Labor Committee and the Un-American Activities Committee."[6]

NIXON IS "the greenest congressman in town," said the Washington *Post*. Nixon himself said, "I had the same lost feeling I'd had when I went into military service."[7]

But he did not act like a lost young man. He was an astute, even brilliant, player of the political game. He was in the big leagues now, for sure, but it hardly gave him pause as he exerted his leadership with congressmen just as he had with the officers and men in the Navy.

His biggest weakness was his freshman status, but he managed to convert it into a strength. He joined fourteen other junior Republicans in the Chowder and Marching Club. The group met every Wednesday for strategy conferences and to pass along information. Its creation immediately made Nixon a member of a bloc, one big enough to command more attention than he could ever receive as an individual, yet not so big as to excite hostility. It was neither Old Guard nor liberal Republican, but rather a cross section. Charter members included Kenneth Keating of New York, J. Caleb Boggs of Delaware, Norris Cotton of New Hampshire, and Thruston B. Morton of Kentucky, all of whom went on to the Senate.[8] In 1949 Congressman Gerald Ford of Michigan became a member.[9]

During that first week of the session, Nixon also met John F. Kennedy, Democrat of Massachusetts. They met at the organizational meeting of the Labor Committee, where each drew the shortest straw and thus ended up as the most junior member for their respective parties. They were from opposite ends of the continent; one was fabulously rich, the other barely getting by; one had a Harvard degree, the other a degree from Whittier College. But as Nixon noted, they had a lot in common—the Navy, their youth (Kennedy was twenty-nine years old, Nixon about to turn thirty-four), and freshman status.[10]

In April 1947, at the request of the congressman from the area, Nixon and Kennedy went to McKeesport, Pennsylvania, to debate the Taft-Hartley bill. Each made his case, clearly and carefully, without saying anything new and with neither man able to claim a win. Afterward, they took the *Capital Limited* back to Washington, again drawing straws—to see who would get the lower Pullman berth. They did not become friends but they did respect each other.

ANOTHER ACQUAINTANCE Nixon made at that first meeting of the Labor Committee was Charles Kersten, freshman Republican from Wisconsin. Kersten had been investigating Communist influence in an Allis-Chalmers strike, and Nixon asked him to recommend an authority on Communism. Kersten arranged for Nixon to meet with Father John Cronin, a Maryknoll seminary teacher in Baltimore. On at least four occasions in late January and early February, Nixon and Kersten drove to Baltimore for briefings from Cronin.

Father Cronin was no Red-baiter. He had devoted his life to social causes and served as a CIO organizer in the early forties. But in his CIO experiences, he had become disturbed by the attempted Communist take-overs. He began collecting data on Communist involvement in the labor movement, in the process exchanging information with William Sullivan, an FBI agent.

In 1944, Cronin had circulated a series of reports on his findings to the Catholic bishops, who had been so impressed that they had asked Cronin to devote an entire year to preparing a study of Communism in America. He had completed it at the end of 1945 and had circulated one copy to each bishop. On one of Nixon's visits to Baltimore, Cronin let him read a copy.

The report, entitled "The Problem of American Communism," concentrated on Communist infiltration tactics in labor unions and in government. Cronin cited material given him by Sullivan from the voluntary testimony before the FBI of ex-Communist and current senior editor of *Time* magazine Whittaker Chambers. Chambers had named names. He said that John Abt, Lee Pressman, and Alger Hiss formed a Communist cell within the government. Cronin named Hiss four times in the report. The report stated that Chambers vowed to expose Hiss if he were named Secretary-General of the United Nations, an idea that was in the rumor mill, because Hiss had been the chief organizer of the San Francisco Conference that set up the United Nations. What Cronin did not know was that the Soviet Ambassador to the U.N., Andrei Gromyko, had urged Secretary of State Edward Stettinius to name Alger Hiss as the first U.N. Secretary-General.[11]

In his early meetings with Nixon, Cronin not only gave him some names to think about but also a great deal of practical advice on how to deal with the Communist Party (USA). He explained Communist tactics, put Nixon onto other ex-Communists who might be willing to talk, and in general gave Nixon a crash course on the subject. He emphasized the presence of "certain Communists . . . in the State Department" and urged Nixon to go after them.[12]

JUST AS NIXON was learning from Cronin that Communism was a bigger problem than simple infiltration of the CIO, he had the lesson reinforced by his initial experience on HUAC. On February 6, HUAC held its first meeting of the session under the chairmanship of J. Parnell Thomas, Republican of New Jersey. Robert Stripling, the committee's chief investigator, called out, "Mr. Gerhard Eisler, take the stand."

Eisler was an Austrian-born Communist who had been under investigation by Stripling and the FBI for some time. They believed, based on the testimony of ex-Communists, that Eisler was principal liaison man between the Comintern and the CP-USA. He had come into the United States from China in 1933, under the guise of being an anti-Fascist refugee. He was currently being detained on Ellis Island, where on February 4 he had been arrested on order from the Attorney General on charges of passport fraud.

"I am not going to take the stand," Eisler replied to Stripling.

He said he would not be sworn in until he was permitted to deliver a three-minute remark. Chairman Thomas promised him that privilege, but said he would first have to be sworn and questioned.

"That is where you are mistaken," Eisler replied. "I have to do nothing. A political prisoner has to do nothing." For fifteen minutes, he and Thomas yelled at each other. He was cited for contempt on the spot and taken back to Ellis Island.

This was Nixon's first view of a real Communist, and confirmation of what Father Cronin had told him about Communist tactics. Nixon's education broadened as he listened to the next witness, a friendly one, Eisler's sister, Ruth Fischer.

Fischer had been a founder of the CP in Austria, a leader of the party in Germany, and reportedly once a member of the Presidium in Moscow. In 1926 she had broken with Stalin and been expelled from the party. She came to the States, where she became a scholar and writer (Harvard University Press later published her book, *Stalin and German Communism*). She denounced her brother, with details. She charged he was not only an agent but a spy, not only a spy but "a dangerous terrorist." She accused him of murdering many Chinese Communists thought to be hostile to Moscow and of informing against his own friends to Stalin.

Nixon asked her if she was still sympathetic to the Communist cause or if her objections to Stalin were only to his methods. She indicated that Stalin was the chief terrorist in the world, and must be stopped. Nixon wanted to know if she had specific information on any murders Eisler was guilty of committing, but she could respond only with an account of his GPU training in Moscow, and with hearsay evidence of his involvement in purges in China and Moscow.[13] "This was really the first time I had brought home to me the character of the Communist Party and the threat which it presented to the country," Nixon later said. "[It] was the beginning of my education in this field."[14]

On February 18, Nixon used the Eisler contempt citation as the occasion for his maiden speech in Congress. Along with a number of others, he rose to demand that the full House find Eisler guilty of contempt of Congress. He began by describing Eisler as "a seasoned agent of the Communist International, who had been shuttling back and forth between Moscow and the United States from as early as 1933, to direct and mastermind the political and espionage activities of the Communist Party in the United States." Eisler came to the United States, Nixon said, not as a grateful refugee thankful for his opportunity, but "as an arrogant, defiant enemy of our government."

After citing instances of Eisler's lying to immigration authorities, Nixon said that "there is a tendency in some quarters to treat this case as one of a political prisoner, a harmless refugee whom this committee is persecuting because of his political belief[s]." But he cited Attorney General Tom Clark, who on the occasion of Eisler's arrest had spoken of the necessity of rooting out Communists. Eisler's story, Nixon said, was "replete with criminal acts against the United States, forged documents, perjury, failure to register as an alien."

The case was so clear, in fact, that Nixon said he was shocked by the laxity of the Immigration Service, which had given Eisler the complete run of the country. "It would certainly seem that an investigation should be made of . . . the personnel responsible for granting such privileges to dangerous aliens of this type."

No one would answer for the Democrats except Congressman Vito Marcantonio. He deplored the "hysteria," denounced the "innuendos," and damned the "propaganda." He said he found it ironic that "the anti-Fascist is on trial while pro-Fascists are at liberty to applaud and demand his persecution." When Marcantonio finished, the House cited Eisler for contempt, unanimously except for Marcantonio's single dissenting vote.

Newsweek described Nixon as "youthful and intensely sincere," "deeply impressive," with "a quality of steel behind the voice," yet all delivered in "calm, measured tones." He could hardly have dreamed of a better start.[15]

Eisler jumped bail, stowed away on a Polish steamer, and fled to East Germany. There he was given a professorship at the University of Leipzig. When he died in 1968 in the Soviet Union, *The New York Times* described him as "a man who had guided revolutions in four countries."[16] Eisler's actions after Nixon's attack on him, and his subsequent reception behind the Iron Curtain, convinced many previous doubters that Nixon had been right on the mark when he accused the man of being a hard-core Communist revolutionary.

THE AFTERNOON of the day he delivered his maiden speech, Nixon entered the White House for the first time, the occasion being a reception for the new members of Congress.

Less than a month later, President Truman went before a joint session of the Congress to announce the Truman Doctrine and to call for military and economic assistance to Greece and Turkey.

It was one of the most dramatic moments in American history, and could not have failed to make a deep impression on every member of the audience, including the young Nixon. Truman described the situation in Greece and Turkey as if there had been another Pearl Harbor. The President, in his turn, was responding to advice from Republican Senator Arthur Vandenberg of Michigan, who had told him that if he wanted support for a policy of intervention in the eastern Mediterranean he would have to "scare hell out of the American people." Truman did. He painted in dark hues the "totalitarian regimes" that threatened to snuff out freedom everywhere. The time had come, he said, when "nearly every nation must choose between alternative ways of life." Truman declared that "it must be the policy of the United States to support free peoples."

It was an all-encompassing doctrine of containment, anywhere and everywhere, promising American support to any anti-Communist government, whatever its nature. Walter Lippmann, the dean of the newspaper columnists, objected to its open-ended nature and promises to reactionary governments; Republican Senator Robert Taft objected to its potential costs; and a British diplomat was surprised at the "enormous hullaballoo" Truman created, saying that he found it shocking that Truman made "the policy of aid to Greece . . . seem hardly less than a declaration of war on the Soviet Union." [17]

But to Richard Nixon, and many others, what Truman said was just plain common sense. Never mind that the Truman Doctrine meant that for the first time in its history the United States was preparing to intervene in Europe and the Middle East during a period of general peace—the Communist threat had to be met. Still, Truman's request put many Republicans, especially those from the Midwest and the West, in a tight place. While they thought the President was right, many if not most of their constituents were dubious at best. And the potential cost, as Taft was warning, was enormous. To sell his program, Truman called small groups of Republicans into the Oval Office, where he explained world realities. Nixon's turn came at the beginning of July, when he, his friend Kersten, and two others attended a private meeting with the President. Nixon was duly impressed by the Oval Office, which he described, in notes made later that day, as a "big pleasant room." He also noted that Truman had "no gadgets" in it. Truman delivered his standard talk on the urgent need for European rehabilitation and the equally urgent need for a bipartisan foreign policy.[18]

AT THIS STAGE in the session, Nixon was more concerned with exposing Communists at home than he was with fighting them abroad. In addition, he—and the other members of HUAC— wanted to keep the momentum going. Three days after Nixon's Eisler speech, HUAC had created a subcommittee, under Nixon's chairmanship, to go to New York to investigate further the people who had helped Eisler obtain his forged passports. On March 5, 1947, in Room 2301 of the U.S. Courthouse in Foley Square, New York City, Nixon had chaired his first investigation. The witnesses, mainly CP officials, were unfriendly, and neither Nixon, nor Stripling, nor the other members could get much out of them.

On March 12, undaunted by this lack of success in New York, HUAC announced that it was going to hold hearings on a bill designed to outlaw the Communist Party. This was the first time in its history that HUAC had actually undertaken to write a piece of legislation, which is perhaps some excuse for how bad the proposed bill was. It outlawed the CP altogether, and provided a ten-year jail term for sending through the mails any publication "any part of which expresses or conveys the impression of sympathy with or approval of Communism." [19]

The committee was encouraged, indeed egged on, by the Administration. The Truman Doctrine speech created a climate of near-hysteria throughout the country. In addition, that same week at a meeting attended by Nixon, Secretary of Labor Lewis Schwellenbach told the Labor Committee that Communists should be barred from public office. Also that week, Attorney General Clark issued a statement saying that he favored "outlawing any party that has for its aim the destruction and overthrow of our form of government." [20]

On March 24, the HUAC hearings on "bills to curb or outlaw the Communist Party of the United States" began. From the outset, Nixon was openly dubious about the wisdom of the proposed legislation. To the American Legion representative, Nixon said, "You do believe that this committee must exercise judgment and are in determining, first, what a Communist is, and, second, what the front organizations are, so that we will know who the people are who are disloyal, as distinguished from those who may not be disloyal, but who may have a different political viewpoint from, say, the members of this committee." [21]

Nixon was putting words into the Legionnaire's mouth, words the man would not have used himself, but with which he could hardly disagree. It was a tactic Nixon was perfecting, and would use often. Nearly half his questions to witnesses, in both committees, began, "In other words. . . ." The main theme he pursued was the commonsense one that outlawing the Communist Party would be futile and counterproductive. He got powerful support from prestigious witnesses, including William C. Bullitt, former ambassador to Russia and to France, J. Edgar Hoover, and William Green, president of the AFL.

A typical exchange:

NIXON: In fact, you think there is a good chance that if we
. . . outlaw the CP, we might help the cause of communism
rather than crush it, by doing that?
GREEN: Yes, I fear very much that would be the result.
NIXON: By making martyrs of the Communists and by driving them underground?
GREEN: Yes.[22]

Eric Johnston, head of the Motion Picture Producers Association, was one witness, and Nixon used his presence to raise
an issue that would give HUAC its biggest headlines ever. Nixon
told Johnston he recalled all the wonderful anti-Nazi and anti-
Japanese movies Hollywood had turned out during the war.
"Can you tell me today the names of any pictures which Hollywood has made in the last five years showing the evils of totalitarian communism?"

Johnston could think of none.

"Do you not feel," Nixon continued, that Hollywood has an
obligation to inform the people of "the evils of totalitarian communism, [just] as the motion picture industry told them the evils of
totalitarian fascism?"

Johnston said the industry would certainly do so.

Nixon was not satisfied. He asked, "Is the motion picture industry doing anything to stop the infiltration of the Communist
influence in Hollywood, or to root out any of those who are . . .
sympathizers and use their positions in some subtle manner to
affect the film?"

Nixon's reference was to the Screen Writers Guild, reportedly
shot through with Communists. Johnston pleaded that the producers had contracts with the union and could not simply fire a writer
because of his politics. Thus was the groundwork laid for HUAC's
Hollywood Ten hearings.[23]

After five days of hearings, the committee voted 5 to 3 against
recommending the bill. Nixon was in the majority, and in fact had
led the others. He had decided against outright suppression of the
CP, and was beginning to think of possible legislation that could
lead to exposure of the Communists and their front organizations.

Nixon was less worried about real live Communists than he
was about fellow travelers, left-wing Democrats, and socialists.
Nixon saw early on what Chairman Thomas and other HUAC members missed—that the CP members were no threat to the Republic,
that outlawing their party would do no good and would not work
in any case, and that the real danger was with the dupes, whether
witting or not. And the leading dupes, as Nixon saw it, were the
New Dealers.

WHILE THE HEARINGS were going on, Truman stole the headlines from HUAC when he issued a sweeping executive order that made membership in or affiliation with any group judged subversive by the Attorney General to be grounds for dismissal from government service. HUAC's files were designated as one source of information on suspect employees.

A major justification for Truman's stringent action was the war scare that accompanied the Truman Doctrine. It was perfectly clear that if a war broke out between Russia and the West, the Communists within the United States would actively support Russia. Everyone recalled that during the Hitler–Stalin pact period, CIO unions that were Communist-dominated had called strikes for the purely political purpose of disrupting American aid to Britain. And most people also knew, although the Democrats were naturally reluctant to broadcast it, that the federal bureaucracy had taken on large numbers of Communists in its great expansion during the New Deal and the war.

Nixon had raised the issue of possible sabotage when he questioned J. Edgar Hoover. In a prepared report to the committee, Hoover had written that in 1917 there was only one Communist for every 2,777 people in Russia, whereas in 1947 there was one Communist for every 1,814 people in the United States. Nixon said he found the figures astounding, and asked Hoover to certify them. Hoover did, but only on his own assertion, without citing any sources. This exchange has been widely quoted by Nixon's critics ever since, with the implication that Nixon was so naïve that he actually believed the United States was in danger of take-over by the CP.

In fact he believed nothing of the kind, as he indicated in his next question. Obviously, he said, the American government was far stronger than that of the Czar in 1917, but he asked Hoover to comment on this point: "Having in mind infiltration of Communists . . . without doing anything to expose them, to drive them out of labor unions, out of Government . . . do you see a real present danger [of sabotage] to this country in the event of a conflict?" Hoover said he most certainly did.[24]

EXCEPT FOR the CP itself, and its fellow travelers, everyone in politics joined in the ensuing anti-Communist crusades. The President led the way, with his fire-breathing Truman Doctrine speech and his questionable executive order dismissing federal employees thought to be sympathetic to Communism. If the President himself thought the threat was that great, who was a freshman congressman to argue with him?

Nixon hardly invented anti-Communism, but he was one of the earliest leaders of the crusade. From the time of the Voorhis campaign and the Eisler speech through subsequent hearings, he stayed with the issue longer than anyone else. He could almost be said to have devoted his life to exposing and destroying Communists within the United States, and to halting and turning back Communist expansion overseas. He dedicated himself to that cause because he believed that the Communist challenge was the most critical threat democracy had ever been forced to face.

The anti-Communist crusade was also personally profitable to him. In his memoirs, Nixon wrote that "in the years 1946 to 1948 domestic communism was a peripheral issue." [25] That was laying it on a bit thick for a man who had just won an election on exactly that issue. Still it was true that anti-Communism ruined careers as well as made them. Republicans and Democrats alike clamored to get on the committee, especially after Nixon used it in the Hiss case as a springboard to overnight national fame and importance. But although many tried to use the committee to advance their own careers, the historic fact is that the only member of HUAC to ever profit from his association with it was Richard Nixon.

IN THE Labor Committee, Nixon was a member of a subcommittee holding hearings on the Taft-Hartley bill. That piece of legislation, denounced by most organized-labor leaders as a "slave labor bill," was the one bill the Republicans were most insistent upon passing. To them, it was overwhelmingly necessary to correct the imbalance that the Wagner Act of 1935 had created. The bill gave the states the option to pass "right to work" legislation, banned secondary boycotts and the closed shop, required a cooling-off period before a strike, and otherwise reacted against labor's gains in the New Deal. In the hearings, Nixon supported Taft-Hartley enthusiastically, and he worked hard at it, attending meetings every day, including Saturdays, from the beginning of February to the end of March.[26] The Republican leadership pushed it through the hearings as fast as possible, although scarcely fast enough to satisfy Republican constituents, who were clamoring for it.

On April 16, when Taft-Hartley was having its final debate on the House floor, the Republican leadership gave Nixon ten minutes to speak for the bill. It was a signal honor for so rank a freshman, and he made the most of it. He began by deploring the name-calling attacks on the bill, refuting the suggestions that it had been drawn up "because a few greedy monopolists in the National Association of Manufacturers . . . decided that they wanted more money and ordered a bill which would allow them to wring the last dollar out of the laboring men of this country." The fact was, Nixon said, the bill was a response to the $6 billion lost to industrial strife in 1946, a response to the "unprecedented force and violence" in labor disputes, a response to abuses by labor bosses, a response to complaints from the rank-and-file union members themselves about the lack of democracy in their organizations.

The bill did not attack the interests of American workers, Nixon asserted, but rather protected those workers. "Do they object to the fact that the bill gives them the right to speak freely in their union meetings? Do they object to the fact that the bill gives them the right to vote freely in democratic elections for their officers and to organize and bargain collectively? Do they object to the fact that the bill protects their right to strike over fundamental issues? . . . Do they object to the fact that we have attempted to control violence, mass picketing and other abuses which all good union leaders have decried?

"I submit to this House that the man who goes out on strike and who serves to lose most by going out should make the determination as to whether he should go out."

In his peroration, Nixon recalled King John at Runnymede. "In 1935 the New Deal Congress enacted the National Labor Relations Act [the Wagner Act]," he said, "which granted unrestricted sovereign power to the barons of union labor. Now, I submit it is the responsibility and the opportunity of this Congress to grant to American workers their bill of rights."[27]

The following day, the House passed the bill, 308 to 107. It went through the Senate almost as easily, and there were votes to spare to override President Truman's veto. Nixon's role in writing the bill, and in steering its passage through the House, had been minor but significant. As a defender of the bill, he took a large role. He circulated an analysis entitled "The Truth About the New Labor Law" among his constituents and his fellow Republican congressmen. It was a skillful essay, one that emphasized the points his small-business supporters on the Committee of 100, and his colleagues, wanted to hear. There would be no more secondary boycotts, no more jurisdictional strikes, no more violence on the picket line, no more mass picketing, no more closed shops, no more Communists in top positions (union leaders had to swear that they were not Communists). Nixon's essay was so well done that other Republicans ordered thousands of reprints as the best answer to organized labor's criticisms.[28]

THROUGHOUT THE SESSION, Nixon kept in close touch with his constituents, letting them know what he was doing and listening to their complaints and suggestions. He wrote a weekly column for the 12th District newspapers, and supplemented it with a weekly radio show and a regular newsletter.[29] In May he made a trip home, where he was able to make the headlines when he handed out HUAC subpoenas to some thirty Hollywood actors, writers, and producers. He also made a speech to the Sales Executives Club in Los Angeles on "Selling American Business." His theme was that "the only effective way to combat Communism is through the dynamic demonstration of the strength of our free American institutions."[30] And he carried on an extensive correspondence with the home folks, on subjects ranging from rent control to post-office services. He worked without letup. He had no private life to speak of—certainly Pat and Tricia hardly ever saw him—nor any social life. His reputation, deserved, was of a hardworking, not a hard-playing, congressman.

Already, in the summer of his first session, Nixon was assuming a role that would grow and expand in the future, that of liaison between the moderate center of the Republican Party and the right wing. When Speaker Martin put Nixon on HUAC, he was not necessarily doing the young man a favor, but Nixon managed to make himself into exactly what Martin had hoped he would become, a relative moderate on HUAC whose credentials as a conservative were unimpeachable. His earnest defense of Taft-Hartley impressed right-wingers as well as liberal Republicans. He was particularly good at explaining realities to the red-hots, who thought the 1946 election meant the time of the counterrevolution had come, and wanted to get on with it.

Most notable in this regard was Nixon's support of the Marshall Plan, for which he worked hard and effectively and at considerable risk to his own career. Once again, as with Taft-Hartley and HUAC, he found himself in center ring on a great issue of the day. On July 30, Nixon learned that Martin had appointed him one of nineteen members of a select committee, headed by Congressman Christian Herter of Massachusetts, to go to Europe to prepare a report on the aid plan Secretary of State George Marshall had recommended at the Harvard commencement in June. Martin needed a young man, and a westerner, to give balance to the committee (which the press universally praised as distinguished), and Nixon fit. But Martin also wanted someone who was intelligent, hardworking, rational, and persuasive, and Nixon had proved that he fit those categories too.

Again, Martin was not necessarily doing Nixon a favor. Nixon had been having a hard enough time persuading his constituents that his support for aid to Greece and Turkey was wise,[31] and it was going to be even harder to get them to accept a "giveaway" program for all Western Europe. What his constituents wanted were lower taxes, less government, a balanced budget—not a deep and expensive involvement in Europe.

Just before sailing for Europe in August, Nixon received a letter signed by six of his original supporters from the Committee of 100. It warned him that he was about to be subjected to "a skillful orientation program by the State Department and later, to no less skillfully prepared European propaganda." The letter also reminded him that 1948 was the Republican opportunity to sweep the Democrats out of office, to finish the job begun in 1946. "This can be done provided the Republican members of Congress are wise enough to refuse to be drawn into support of a dangerously unworkable and profoundly inflationary foreign policy and, provided further, that the Democrats do not succeed in so dividing our party by bipartisan internationalism that there no longer is any way to tell who is a Republican." [32]

These were not just the voices of California reactionaries; the Republican Party as a whole was having trouble swallowing the Marshall Plan. Senator Taft proclaimed that American money should not be poured into a "European T.V.A." Like many Republicans, Taft was disturbed at postwar steps in Western Europe to achieve democratic socialism, and he feared that the Europeans would use Marshall Plan money to nationalize basic industries, including American-owned plants. [33]

But despite the pressure from his constituents and from his party leaders, Nixon made up his own mind on the basis of what he saw and learned, showed that he could free himself from Republican dogma, and then, to top it off, convinced his constituents that he was right.

He sailed on the *Queen Mary* and landed in Southampton. From the moment they docked, he wrote later, "it was clear that we had come to a continent tottering on the brink of starvation and chaos." He realized immediately that without American food, millions would starve, and without long-term aid, "Europe would be plunged into anarchy, revolution, and, ultimately, communism."

He saw bombed-out London, attended tea at 10 Downing Street with Prime Minister Clement Attlee and his Foreign Secretary, Ernest Bevin. He inspected destroyed Berlin. He went to Greece, where he flew to the front lines for a personal inspection. He was in Trieste when a Communist-led mob started a riot. He watched Communists parade in Paris.

At his insistence, over the objections of the State Department people, he met with CP leaders in each country he visited. He said he was curious about how their minds worked, and wanted to assess their relations with the Soviet Union. This led to his first debate with a foreign Communist leader—there would be many others to follow—when he met with Giuseppe Di Vittorio, the Italian Communist leader.

In debating Communist leaders, Nixon liked to set little traps for them, as he had done back in high-school and college debates. He got Di Vittorio to say that he wanted labor unions in Italy to be free to strike. Then came the pounce: "From your answer, I assume that you favor the kind of government we have in the United States, where labor is striking at this very moment, rather than the kind of government they have in Russia, where labor . . . hasn't had a strike in the last twenty years."

But the mouse would not stay caught. Di Vittorio patiently explained to Nixon that because of capitalist reactionaries, workers in America had to strike to obtain their rights, but in Russia the workers ruled and thus there was no need to strike. This response, and others, gave Nixon the practical proof of something he had already read and accepted; as he put it in notes at that time, "This indicates definitely then that the Communists throughout the world owe their loyalty not to the countries in which they live but to Russia."[34]

When Nixon returned to the United States in October, he was solidly behind the Marshall Plan. But he took a poll in the 12th District (a device he used frequently), and 75 percent of his constituents were resolutely opposed to the program. Nixon nevertheless decided, "after what I had seen and learned in Europe," that "I had no choice but to vote my conscience and then try my hardest to convince my constituents." He discussed the Marshall Plan, and his reasons for supporting it, in his newspaper column, on the radio, and in his newsletter. He undertook an active round of speeches in the district, explaining what he had seen and why it was in America's interest to prevent starvation and Communism in Europe.[35]

Nixon spent nearly a month in California selling the Marshall Plan. At a press conference on October 25, in Los Angeles, he declared, "Unless the United States provides sufficient emergency aid to France and Italy over the winter and spring months to permit them to maintain their present bread ration, they surely will go Communistic." He continued, "Even if we do provide sufficient emergency aid, there is still no certainty that the Communists won't win in Europe—but if we don't there is no doubt about the outcome."[36]

When an El Monte businessman wrote to predict, "If the Marshall Plan is carried out, we will not have to go to Europe to find starvation; we will find it right here in this country," Nixon replied immediately. He reiterated that "I am unequivocally in favor" of the aid package, and declared, "This is a gamble I believe we must take, otherwise we will be faced with the almost certain prospect of a United States standing virtually alone." [37]

In his arguments for the Marshall Plan, Nixon emphasized what it would do for America. He knew, as he told one correspondent, "that there are still too many people who think that the way to solve our international difficulties is to isolate ourselves from the rest of the world and to become completely self-sufficient." But that was impossible. America had to export to live, and to sell exports, America had to import. "If we place proper emphasis upon importing from those countries to which we export, our own wealth will be increased rather than depleted in the end." [38]

One of the virtues of the Marshall Plan was that it had something in it for everyone. Nixon's constituents in the agricultural business quickly figured that out, and began pressing him to make certain that their produce—usually oranges—was included in the shipments of food to Europe. Nixon did all he could to help them. [39]

The only partisan note Nixon interjected into the great debate on the Marshall Plan was his insistence that businessmen, not Democratic party leaders, be put in charge of the administration of the program. For the rest, he was foursquare and out front in his support, and so convincing that in the end his position enhanced his popularity in his district. It was altogether an impressive performance from a freshman congressman who had no previous experience in foreign affairs. Nixon showed himself to be broadgauged, intelligent, and sensitive to world trends in his first involvement in foreign policy.

ON OCTOBER 20, in a jam-packed Caucus Room in the Old House Office Building, HUAC began its investigation of Communist infiltration in Hollywood. Nixon attended the opening session, then wisely absented himself from subsequent hearings, which were characterized by a lot of show biz, name-calling, shouting, threats, and defiance, and no light cast on any subject, least of all the amount of Communist influence in Hollywood. The details need not detain us here, except to note that almost no one—witnesses, prosecutors, or accused—did his own reputation any good. An exception was a trio of actors, Robert Montgomery, George Murphy, and Ronald Reagan. They had all been active in the Screen Actors Guild, and they agreed that the Communists had not taken over their guild.

Another exception was Nixon. He questioned Jack Warner of

Warner Brothers. He was not above throwing Warner some convoluted, marshmallow questions, for example: "Then so far as you are concerned, with your vital interest in the free press and the free screen, and in maintaining that in America, you believe it would be essential that we not have in the United States a form of government, totalitarian form of government, be it Nazi, Fascist, or Communist, which would when it came into power immediately deny a free press, free speech, and a free screen?" Warner could hardly register his agreement fast enough.

In his opening statement, Warner had extolled his own patriotism. Nixon led him on. He praised Warner for producing anti-Nazi movies, and for doing it "because you wanted to protect free speech and the free press in America," not for profit.

"Well," Jack replied modestly, "not only in America but in other civilized portions of the world where men can be free men."

Nixon then asked a 150-word one-sentence question that almost defied comprehension, but which seemed to ask if Warner thought he had a patriotic duty to oppose any kind of totalitarian infiltration into his industry.

WARNER: I am for everything you said.
NIXON: You agree with that statement?
WARNER: I agree wholeheartedly.
NIXON: The statement was a little long.
WARNER: It was a very good statement; it was the statement of a real American, and I am proud of it.

And so it went, Warner skipping gaily down the primrose path, holding Nixon's hand, quite pleased with himself, and having not the least idea of where they were going to end up.

Nixon congratulated Warner on *Confessions of a Nazi Spy*, a prewar release. Warner beamed. Nixon said the Warner Brothers studio had been the first and best at pointing out totalitarian methods, "the way they deny free speech and free press, so that Americans would be able to watch for that sort of thing in our own country and be able to resist it."

Warner triumphantly produced a list of forty-three anti-Nazi films he had produced, which Nixon solemnly ordered entered into the record. So too with the next list, thirty-nine pro-American short subjects turned out by the studio. Jack got in a plug for one of them, which he modestly refused to name but which he said was playing just across the street, "and it is worth seeing. Every American should see it. So should every foreigner." Nixon replied, "I think I can see why you have been so successful in selling your pictures to the American public. . . . You have indicated here in your statement that you are willing to establish a fund to ship to Russia the people who do not like our system of government. . . . " Warner acknowledged it.

Then Nixon pounced: "I would like to know whether or not Warner Brothers has made, or is making at the present time, any pictures pointing out the methods and the evils of totalitarian communism, as you so effectively have pointed out the evils of the totalitarian Nazis."

Warner began to deflate. Well, he said, we are working on one, but it is a delicate subject, and "we have been criticized. . . . I am sure we will come to it a little later." Nixon asked if Warner meant he feared opposition from within the industry to an anti-Communist film. Oh, not at all, Warner replied, then tried to turn the subject back to his pro-American films and how important they were as "a great counter to the Communist and Fascist way of life."

Nixon agreed absolutely, but then lectured Warner on his "positive duty" to produce films that exposed Communist methods. Always unspoken in Nixon's remarks, but always there, was the implication that the Jewish studio owners and the Communist movie writers were involved in a conspiracy. They were willing, in fact eager, to attack Nazis, but hesitant, not to say unwilling, to go after the Communists. Nixon practically committed the studio to a major production when he concluded, "This Committee is glad to hear that Warner Brothers is contemplating for the first time now making a motion picture in which they point out to the American people the dangers of totalitarian communism as well as fascism."

Warner replied by pledging himself and his brothers to "aid this great country with every ounce of energy we possess," then entering into the record a list of twenty-three additional pro-American short subjects his studio had produced.[40]

After that one foray, Nixon left the Hollywood hearings. He returned to the subject in November, at a special session called by Truman to appropriate funds for European aid. HUAC used the occasion to present contempt of Congress citations against the Hollywood Ten, scriptwriters who had refused to answer questions at the hearings on Fifth Amendment grounds.

Only a few representatives openly opposed the citations, primarily on the grounds of misconduct by HUAC—among the critics were Jacob Javits of New York and Helen Gahagan Douglas of California. Marcantonio objected on the grounds that it was another capitalist plot. John Rankin of Mississippi, a notorious anti-Semite, pointed out that HUAC had discovered that Danny Kaye's real name was David Kaminsky, that Edward G. Robinson's was Emanuel Goldenberg, that Melvyn Douglas' was Melvyn Hesselberg, and so on. The Jews were the people, Rankin said, who were critical of HUAC, and with that he rested his case.

HUAC Chairman Thomas, in some desperation, turned to Nixon, granting him all the remaining time. Nixon began by apologizing to the House for HUAC's "tendency to indulge in emotionalism and to get off on collateral issues which have nothing to do with the issue at hand." The problem before the House, he said, was simple, with only two parts. The first, a matter of fact: Had the witnesses refused to answer the committee's questions? The second, a matter of law: Did the committee have the power to ask those questions? As to self-incrimination, he pointed out that "it is not a crime to be a member of the Communist Party and consequently the guarantee against self-incrimination has no application whatever." He concluded, "The Committee was pursuing a legitimate legislative function and it was asking questions which it had a right to ask." [41] What he did not say, but what was perfectly clear, was that simply by questioning Hollywood figures, he and his HUAC friends guaranteed headlines for themselves.

Nixon continued his climb toward the position of the dominant member of HUAC. In late December he won an appointment as chairman of a special legislative subcommittee. Legislation was not HUAC's strong point, and Nixon's colleagues were glad to turn over to him a function they had never assumed.

Through January, Nixon worked closely with Republican Karl Mundt of South Dakota in preparation of a bill. On February 3, 1948, he announced in the House that his subcommittee would soon hold hearings on it, and others that had been submitted. In informing the House, Nixon presented his colleagues with certain conclusions he had incorporated in the Mundt-Nixon bill. The first was that the CP-USA "is the agent of a foreign government. The Communists of the United States owe their first and last loyalty to the Soviet Union." The CP was therefore "not a party at all and has no resemblance to a political party. It is a revolutionary conspiracy, Moscow-inspired and Moscow-directed." It was a potential source of sabotage and subversion in the event of war. It operated "secretly and deviously." "Freedom of speech is one thing and freedom of revolution is another."

Were present laws adequate to cope with the danger? Some thought so, and Nixon promised that they would be heard by the subcommittee. Nixon knew that others wanted new laws to outlaw the party altogether, and said they too would be heard. But he injected a doubt: "Outlawing the party is not the complete answer to the Communist question." He pointed out that when the CP seized power in Russia, it was a completely illegal party.

What needed to be done, Nixon continued, was to expose the Communists "for what they are—to get them and their front organizations out in the open, label them as Communists, and let the good sense of our people take care of them." But whatever was done, he concluded, "we want it to be in the democratic tradition, we want it to be clear-cut, and we want it to be effective."[42]

The two bills immediately before the subcommittee were one that outlawed the party and the Mundt-Nixon bill, which emphasized exposure. It required registration of all CP members, publication of the source of all printed and broadcast material issued by Communist-front organizations, denial of passports to party members, and creation of a Subversive Activities Control Board, which would determine whether an organization was a Communist front or not.

Nixon kept a tight control over the hearings, which he conducted in a fair and workmanlike manner but nevertheless managed to steer in the direction he wanted to go. "In other words," he said to almost every witness (in this case Attorney General Clark), "you think we are on the right track in working toward disclosure?" Clark agreed. So did a long string of prominent attorneys from various bar associations.[43]

The one day that Nixon did not chair the hearings (he had broken an elbow falling on ice while holding Tricia in his arms), the orderly procedure disintegrated. Rankin, whom Nixon had successfully suppressed, put Adolf Berle through a long lecture on how the white people of Mississippi were being slandered by the Justice Department, which kept accusing them of mistreatment of their Negroes.[44]

Nixon himself got into trouble with his penchant for putting words into people's mouths. He had his worst time with Arthur Garfield Hays, a liberal lawyer and leader in the American Civil Liberties Union (ACLU). Hays warned that it was impossible to legislate against dangerous thoughts, and said that the Smith Act of 1940 was sufficient to meet the Communist threat. He added that the CP-USA occasionally did some good, as, for example, in the case of the Scottsboro boys.

Nixon leaped on Hays: "And so by implication, you would like to leave with the committee the thought that the Communist Party in your opinion has been an influence for good in the United States." Hays corrected him; he said it had "done some good." After more disagreement, Nixon asked if Hays considered the CP of the late forties to be as dangerous as the Socialist Party of the twenties.

HAYS: I do, because I do not think either of them are at all dangerous.

NIXON: In other words, the Socialists and the Communists are just as dangerous.

HAYS: No; I do not say anything of the kind.

NIXON: Then what do you say?

HAYS: I said that since I regard neither of them as at all dangerous, I think one is as dangerous as the other.

NIXON: Then you do say that one is as dangerous as the other.

HAYS: Like zero is as to zero.[45]

In April, HUAC voted to endorse the Mundt-Nixon bill. In May, before the full House, Nixon served as floor manager for the bill, while Marcantonio took on leadership of the opposition for the Democrats (no one else on the Democratic side would touch it). The debate lasted three full days; throughout Nixon handled the bill like a veteran of many decades in Congress. He followed the exchange closely, interjected a word of interpretation here, of explanation there. He clearly knew the bill better than any other HUAC member. He treated Marcantonio courteously, even allowing him some extra time. He avoided the acrimonious exchanges that were so characteristic of HUAC. Overall, he impressed even his opponents with his serious and thoughtful approach.[46]

He spoke forcefully for his own bill. Noting that "member after member has expressed the fear that this bill strikes at all progressive organizations," he declared, "That is exactly the trouble in the country today. There is too much loose talk and confusion on the Communist issue. By passing this bill the Congress will go on record as to just what is subversive about communism in the United States." He predicted an overwhelming vote for the bill, "not because the bill happens to be against communism and this is a political year—I am not going to ask any Member of the House to vote for the bill on that basis. . . ." This was a Nixon technique that already was beginning to drive his opponents to distraction—denying that he had said what he had just said. But it served as an effective warning to Democrats—if they did not support the bill, the Republicans would use it against them in the election.[47]

In his summation, Nixon insisted that "this bill, far from being a police-state bill, is a bill which will prevent the creation of a police state. . . . No American liberal need have any fear of the denial or restriction of his civil, political or religious rights . . . who is not dominated or under the control of a foreign power." He quoted John Stuart Mill on the need for a people to fight to protect a free government, and said of the Communists, "We want to expose them, reveal them as enemies of the United States, and deal with them accordingly." He insisted that HUAC was aware that a much tougher bill, one that would "without doubt infringe upon the rights of others than those against whom it should be directed," could have been passed overwhelmingly in the House, because "this happens to be an election year and communism happens to be an issue." Finally, he thanked the members for their cooperation and indulgence: "As a new Member handling a measure on the floor for the first time, I was most gratified to find the Members of the House so considerate and thoughtful."[48]

Altogether, it was another bravura performance, and a winning one. The Mundt-Nixon bill passed the House by a vote of 319 to 58. But the satisfaction did not last. The Senate held hearings in late May, but there never was a chance of passage of such a controversial measure so late in the session. The entire left in American politics vigorously opposed the bill, led by the ADA, the CIO, the Socialist Party, the CP, and Henry Wallace's Progressive Party. Most major newspapers also were in opposition. More damaging to Nixon's cause was the opposition of liberal Republicans from the Northeast, led by Governor Tom Dewey of New York.

On May 17, even as the debate was going on, Dewey and Harold Stassen discussed the bill in a radio forum that attracted the largest audience in history to date, some 30 million listeners. The two men were full-time candidates for the Republican nomination for the Presidency, terribly busy. They completely confused everything. Stassen warned about the Communist danger, said the CP had to be outlawed, then claimed that it was exactly what the Mundt-Nixon bill would do. (Nixon had spent the entire day assuring the House that outlawing the CP was exactly what the bill would *not* do.)

Dewey opposed Mundt-Nixon on the spurious grounds that it would outlaw the CP and that such action would do no good—he cited Canada as an example of a nation that had outlawed the party, only to find itself host to an international espionage ring. The debate did give Dewey an opportunity to indulge in some good old-fashioned oratory: "I am unalterably, wholeheartedly, and unswervingly against any scheme to write laws outlawing people because of their . . . ideas. . . . I am against it because it is immoral and nothing but totalitarianism itself. . . . Stripped to its naked essentials, this is nothing but the method of Hitler and Stalin. It is thought control. . . . It is an attempt to beat down ideas with a club."[49]

With such conspicious opposition, not to mention such misunderstanding, Mundt-Nixon never got out of committee in the Senate, although some of its provisions were incorporated in the McCarran Act of 1950. That act, almost constantly tied up in the courts in the decade that followed, neither destroyed civil liberties in the United States, as its critics said it would do, nor exposed any Communists or front organizations, much less destroyed the CP, as its authors claimed it would do. At the Republican Convention that summer, Nixon supported Stassen, but pronounced himself happy with the ultimate ticket of Tom Dewey and Earl Warren.[50]

JULY 1948 was almost the only time off Nixon took during his first term in Congress. Most of his colleagues were back home campaigning, but he had swept both the Democratic and Republican primaries in June in the 12th District, against almost no opposition, and thus was guaranteed re-election.

It was a dazzling display of political strength. The Democrats had carried the 12th District in five straight elections through 1944. Now, four years later, they could not even beat Nixon in their own primary. This was voter approval with a vengeance.

Nixon had something else to celebrate. In a letter to Daisy Sherwood, a supporter in Alhambra, he explained: "As you have probably read in your paper by now, July 5 was a big day for the Nixon family. Our little girl, Patricia, now has a baby sister, Julie, to hand her clothes down to! Pat and I, of course, are really thrilled about the event. The baby just missed being born on the 4th of July by three hours. Incidentally, this means, of course, that I will not be able to come to the district as soon as I had planned because I shall want to remain here in Washington with Pat for at least a month or so. We are certainly glad that our friends at home went to bat for us so that I did not have to return for a tough final campaign!"[51]

Not a word about how the delivery went for Pat, or how she was recovering. With Nixon, it was first things first; when he wrote his old college professor Paul Smith, also the day after the birth, he did not even mention Julie. He went into analysis of how the campaign would go ("Although Dewey is an excellent administrator and fine speaker, he lacks the warmth that is essential to a really effective national campaigner.").[52]

A few days after Julie's birth, he was on a national radio program, *"Town Meeting of the Air."* "It was a pretty exciting evening for me going up against an array of big shots," he told a San Francisco friend. They debated Mundt-Nixon, and he did well.[53]

He planned to stay in Washington through the end of August. There would be some HUAC hearings, but he told Paul Smith he expected to be in California about September 1. He wanted to get together to discuss "some constructive legislation during the next session," based on the supposition of a Dewey-Warren victory in November.[54]

As THE SESSION wound down, Nixon could reflect on his political career to date with satisfaction. In just eighteen months, he had made himself into a national figure, albeit still a relatively minor one, on the three most publicized issues of the session; labor, Communism, and the Marshall Plan.

In Congress he had been as careful and exact with the facts in his statements and positions as he had been reckless and untruthful as a campaigner against Voorhis. In each case, as Nixon assessed the results, the tactics were appropriate and successful.

CHAPTER TEN

THE HISS CASE
August–December 1948

BECAUSE OF THE complexity of the Alger Hiss case, the emotions it aroused, the personalities of the principal characters involved, and its importance, entire shelves in the stacks of large libraries are filled with books on the subject. Small details have become the subject of big books. Four decades after the case, monographs continue to appear, "proving" this case or that, about Hiss's typewriter, or his car, or his CP involvement. It is almost the American Dreyfus affair. It stamped forever and obsessed the lives of those most directly involved—both the accused, Alger Hiss, and the accuser, Whittaker Chambers. Nixon used it more positively, as a springboard to the Senate and then the Vice-Presidency. But as the Watergate tapes indicate, there were elements of obsession even in his reaction. In the conversations the tapes recorded, President Nixon referred again and again to the Hiss case, which by then was a quarter century in the past.[1]

Summer 1948. President Harry S. Truman had been renominated, reluctantly, by the Democrats; Governor Thomas E. Dewey of New York was the Republican nominee. Although active campaigning would not begin until Labor Day, both parties were intent on using the last days of the congressional session—a special session, called by Truman to embarrass the Republicans (he dared them to pass the legislation they had called for in their party platform)—to create favorable campaign issues.

HUAC, for its part, wanted to raise the issue of Communist infiltration into the government. The Truman Administration let it be known that in the event of a Democratic victory in November it would abolish the committee. Thus the hearings that began on July 31 were the most crucial in HUAC's long and controversial career, because the very existence of the committee was at stake. What HUAC knew, thanks to Nixon's contacts with Father Cronin and to Robert Stripling's investigations, and what the Administration wanted to downplay or ignore, was that a number of ex-Communists, including Elizabeth Bentley (dubbed the "Red Spy Queen" by the press) and Whittaker Chambers, had told the FBI and other authorities of the existence of a Communist cell inside the government, but nothing had been done about it. To Nixon this inaction proved that either the Truman Administration was criminally lax in its security procedures or was shot through with traitors. To prove that thesis, however, he first had to prove that the cell actually existed.

In that summer of 1948, Americans lived in fear. It was a fear engendered by a series of events that had begun three years earlier, when the atomic bombs were used against Japan, with repercussions that were felt all over the world and in every area of human life, but all seeming to come down to one inescapable fact—a single bomb could now destroy a city. War had therefore taken on an entirely new meaning, especially for Americans, previously immune to foreign threat. With the bomb, and with the German development of ballistic missiles, suddenly America itself was potentially vulnerable. People tried to convince themselves that their government and their scientists possessed a "secret" that insured an American monopoly of the bomb, but to any thinking person it was perfectly obvious that if Americans could build a bomb, so could others, and that if Germans could build a rocket, so could others. Anyone who wished to inform himself knew that a scientific race was on, as the United States and the Soviet Union scrambled to get German scientists into their respective laboratories, and that the future of the world depended on the outcome.

Only the most optimistic still clung to hopes of postwar cooperation between Washington and Moscow. Attempts in the United Nations to achieve international control of atomic energy had failed. Attempts in the Council of Foreign Ministers to achieve agreement over divided Germany and other European and Asian problems had failed. The Truman Doctrine, as noted, had been practically a declaration of war against the Soviet Union.

Events in 1948 had fed the fears. There was, first of all, a series of atomic tests at Eniwetok Atoll that revealed new and more powerful and more frightening bombs. There was the Soviet take-over of Czechoslovakia, almost exactly ten years after Hitler had overrun the country as his first step on the road to world conquest. There was the Soviet blockade of West Berlin, which led the National Security Council (NSC), on July 15, 1948, to send two groups of B-29s to Britain—these were the bombers that carried the atomic weapons. All this created a major war scare, more frightening even than that of 1938 because of the existence of the new weapons.

A crisis was at hand, exacerbated by the upcoming presidential elections. The two parties were badly split, as far apart in their views as they had ever been, which meant that the tendency of the politicians was to feed the fears for their own benefit, rather than allay them for the benefit of the country. There was an air of desperation about their efforts to keep the other side out of the White House. The Democrats, in this struggle, had the great advantage in that they controlled the executive branch, which gave them control of the government's files and secrets. The Republicans' advantage was that they controlled the legislative branch, which gave them control of congressional probes and investigations. A further Republican advantage was that they knew the Democrats had let all kinds of liberals, socialists, fellow travelers, and even Communists into the government during the New Deal and the war years, and they suspected that Communist spies had also managed to infiltrate the Manhattan Project during the war. The Republican problem was to prove it.

The process began with Elizabeth Bentley's July 31 testimony before HUAC. It was sensational. She said she had been a courier for a Communist spy ring back in the late thirties and early forties, and she named names. But Bentley offered no supporting documents, and admitted that much of her information was hearsay, as a consequence of her having been only a courier, and because of the conspiratorial nature of the CP.

Nixon sat quietly through the hearing, raising only one question (to which he already knew the answer): Had Bentley taken her charges to the Justice Department? She certainly had, she replied, in January of 1946. "In other words," Nixon continued, "it is quite apparent . . . that this information has been available as to these Government employees for a period of almost two years." Nixon's friend Mundt commented, "It is also quite apparent that we need a new Attorney General." Nixon then praised Bentley for her courage in coming before the committee.[2]

HUAC needed corroboration. Nixon suggested to Stripling that he send committee investigators to question Whittaker Chambers. Nixon knew from Father Cronin that Chambers had named many of the same people Bentley had named, and that Chambers was much higher up in the CP than she had been, and therefore should know a great deal more.

Chambers told the investigators that he did indeed know more than Bentley and that he had told his story to the authorities as early as 1939. Stripling issued a subpoena on Chambers. On August 3, 1948, Chambers began his HUAC testimony. His immediate audience was the committee, composed of three Democrats (all southerners, all opposed to Truman because of his civil rights stand) and three Republicans. The former group consisted of John Rankin of Mississippi, J. Hardin Peterson of Florida, and F. Edward Hébert of Louisiana. The latter group was composed of Karl Mundt, the acting chairman, John McDowell of New Jersey, and Nixon. HUAC's chairman, J. Parnell Thomas of New Jersey, was not present—he had troubles of his own, which soon led to his indictment and conviction on charges of receiving kickbacks from his employees.

Chambers' larger audience was as broad as the nation as a whole, as the free world, as history itself. But neither his appearance nor his demeanor were appropriate to his subject. "He was short and pudgy," Nixon later wrote. "His clothes were unpressed. His shirt collar was curled up over his jacket. He spoke in a rather bored monotone."[3] But he had prepared his opening statement with great skill.

He explained that he had defected from the CP in 1938, and that in 1939, two days after the Hitler-Stalin pact, he told authorities in the United States government what he knew about Communist infiltration. He quoted himself as saying to his wife, shortly after his defection, that it was "better to die on the losing side than to live under Communism." He said that back in the mid-thirties he had been a member of an underground cell of government employees that had included Nathan Witt, John Abt, Lee Pressman, and Alger Hiss. Reporters immediately knew that they had their headline. Witt, Abt, Pressman, and others had been named by Bentley, but they were all relatively small fry. Hiss, the president of the Carnegie Endowment for International Peace, was another matter. Newspapers the following day carried some variant of a headline that read, "TIME EDITOR CHARGES CARNEGIE ENDOWMENT HEAD WAS SOVIET AGENT."[4]

Mundt and other committee members quizzed Chambers about his testimony, drawing more names out of him and exploring what he knew about Hiss's activities. Nixon, in his first question ever to Whittaker Chambers, went to the heart of the matter: "Mr. Chambers, you indicated that nine years ago you came to Washington and reported to the Government authorities concerning the Communists who were in the Government."

Chambers said that he had. Which authorities? Mr. A. A. Berle, the Assistant Secretary of State. Did he name Hiss? He did. "Mr. Chambers, were you informed of any action that was taken as a result of your report?" No, none.

Nixon: "It is significant, I think, that the report was made . . . at a time when we could not say by any stretch of the imagination that the Russians were our allies; and yet, apparently, no action was taken."[5]

It was even worse than that, it turned out. Chambers said he had repeated his story to the FBI in 1943, and again in 1945, but still nothing had happened.

Over the following two days, HUAC called the men named by Bentley and Chambers before it to question them about the accusations. With one exception, to a man they were long on indignation about the charges but short on details about their pasts. They took refuge in the Fifth Amendment, refusing on the grounds of self-incrimination to answer specific questions, especially about their own CP relationship. This mass use of the Fifth Amendment made the congressmen furious. These witnesses were not under indictment, membership in the CP was no crime, and the three-year statute of limitations on espionage had long since run out. Yet they would not answer. "It is pretty clear," Nixon commented to one, "that you are not using the defense of the Fifth Amendment because you are innocent."[6]

One of the accused, who also claimed his innocence, offered to appear—nay, insisted on appearing—before HUAC to answer Chambers' charges and to answer any and all questions the committee might wish to ask him. The afternoon of Chambers' testimony, Alger Hiss sent a telegram to Stripling requesting an opportunity to come before the committee and testify under oath. It was quickly arranged, and on August 5 Hiss made his first appearance before HUAC.

Tall, thin, handsome, smartly dressed, the Carnegie Endowment president carried himself with assurance, making the sharpest possible contrast with Chambers. He might well appear confident—he had some very powerful friends. The previous evening, Dean Acheson, former Under Secretary of State, had brought him a copy of Chambers' testimony, and just that morning Hiss had written to John Foster Dulles, Dewey's chief adviser on foreign policy and chairman of the board of the Carnegie Endowment. Hiss told Dulles that Acheson had helped him prepare his defense.[7] It was assumed that if Truman won in November, Acheson would be Secretary of State; if Dewey won, it would be Dulles. In addition, Hiss had highly placed friends from the Washington social community and from the State Department in the front rows of the spectator section.

Nixon remembered that Hiss read his opening statement "in a clear, well-modulated voice." Hiss denied membership in the CP, said he had never followed the Communist line, and that he had no friends in the CP. He reviewed his government career, dropping names of men he had worked for or who had recommended him that could not fail to impress. He had served for a year as clerk to Supreme Court Justice Oliver Wendell Holmes, and worked for Solicitor General Stanley F. Reed, who later also went on the Supreme Court. At the request of Assistant Secretary Francis B. Sayre, he had joined the State Department in 1936, where he remained until January 1947, when he went to the Carnegie Endowment. He had drafted the American position paper for the Yalta Conference, and then advised President Roosevelt at that meeting. "His manner," Nixon thought, "was coldly courteous and, at times, almost condescending." [8]

Hiss went on to deny ever having heard the name Whittaker Chambers: "The name means absolutely nothing to me." Stripling showed him a photograph of Chambers. "If this is a picture of Mr. Chambers," Hiss said, "he is not particularly unusual looking. He looks like a lot of people. I might even mistake him for the Chairman of this Committee."

Nixon noted that "Hiss's friends from . . . the Washington social community . . . broke into a titter of delighted laughter." After Mundt admonished both Hiss and the audience, Hiss said that he had not meant to be facetious, "but very seriously I would not want to take oath that I had never seen that man. . . . Is he here today?" And Hiss looked around the room. "Not to my knowledge," answered Mundt. "I hoped he would be," said Hiss with an air of disappointment.

"It was a virtuoso performance," Nixon wrote. It was indeed. Hiss was bluffing, and the first person to catch on was that master bluffer and amateur actor himself, Richard Nixon. [9]

Nixon sensed the bluff partly because of his prior knowledge. Although Chambers' naming of Hiss had caused a sensation in the press and came as a surprise to most reporters and congressmen, the truth was that Hiss's association with the CP was common gossip among those in Washington whose business it was to ferret out the Reds. As Father Cronin later said, "There was no great mystery about . . . these facts." [10] Ever since 1943, J. Edgar Hoover had pestered first FDR, then Truman, with warnings about Hiss. But no one had produced documentary evidence, and the Democrats had good reason to ignore the stories, which once broken would damage the Administration. What the State Department did do was ease Hiss out of his policy-making role, and then out of government altogether. He may have been a bright young man with an unlimited future during the New Deal and through the war years, but by early 1946 he had become a major potential embarrassment. Nixon's contribution to the Hiss case was not so much exposing the man as insisting that something be done about him.

The other reason Nixon suspected Hiss of bluffing was his conduct at the hearing. Nixon alone noted that for all his self-assurance, Hiss never once stated categorically that he did not know Whittaker Chambers. Every one of his answers was qualified by such phrases as "to the best of my recollection." Nixon, who had himself run a successful bluff against Voorhis and who had spent enough time in the courtroom to sense when a witness was lying, knew—in his own words—"that those who are lying or trying to cover up something generally make a common mistake—they tend to overact, to overstate their case." Hiss had overstated his.[11]

Nixon's feel for the situation was far short of proof. Neither he nor anyone else had produced one shred of documentary evidence of Hiss's guilt. Everything rested on the word of Chambers, an admitted ex-Communist, who, as will be seen, had told his fair share of lies to the committee. All Nixon really had was a hunch that Chambers had told more of the truth than Hiss had, and the courage to persist in the inquiry in the face of Hiss's powerful denials.

That it took courage for Nixon to hold to his hunch cannot be doubted. When Hiss finished, the audience burst into applause. Rankin rushed from his seat to shake hands with Hiss. He had to push his way through a crowd of people congratulating the beaming Hiss. The press, for its part, was convinced that at long last HUAC had committed its fatal blunder. One reporter asked Nixon, "How is the Committee going to dig itself out of this hole?" Mary Spargo of the Washington *Post* told him, "This case is going to kill the Committee unless you can prove Chambers' story." Ed Lahey of the Chicago *Daily News*, a reporter Nixon respected, was furious. He told Nixon that HUAC "stands convicted, guilty of calumny in putting Chambers on the stand without first checking the truth of his testimony."

At lunch that day, the news got worse. Nixon learned that Truman had held a morning press conference while the hearing was going on. There a reporter had asked the President, "Do you think that the Capitol Hill spy scare is a red herring to divert the public attention from inflation?" Truman agreed with the characterization; although he did not use the "red herring" phrase himself, he was widely quoted as having done so.[12]

WHEN HUAC RECONVENED after lunch, the scene was a madhouse. Angry members berated the staff for not having checked on Chambers before putting him on the stand. One Republican complained, "We've been had! We're ruined." Mundt said that HUAC was indeed ruined "unless the Committee was able to develop a collateral issue which would take it off the spot and take the minds of the public off the Hiss case." Eddie Hébert said that the only way to get "off the hook" was to turn the whole affair over to the Justice Department and hold no more hearings. "Let's wash our hands of the whole mess," Hébert said, and leave it to Attorney General Tom Clark to decide who was lying, Chambers or Hiss.[13]

That was exactly the last thing Nixon wanted to have happen. Justice had had the accusations against Hiss, from many quarters, including the FBI, for a long time, and had done absolutely nothing to develop them. Further, at least as far as Nixon was concerned (as he showed in his questions to both Bentley and Chambers), the Justice Department itself was being investigated here. It had much to answer for, and was in fact Nixon's real target—after all, Hiss had been eased out of government. Hiss by himself, even if proved guilty that afternoon, could not bring down the Truman Administration in the November elections, but convincing evidence that the Justice Department had ignored persuasive evidence might well contribute to a Dewey victory. That very afternoon, Truman issued an executive order instructing federal agencies (read FBI) to release no information on government employees to committees of Congress (read HUAC).

What Nixon had to prevent was a cover-up. That he did so is his great claim to fame in the Hiss case. He told his colleagues that turning the case over to Justice would not rescue the committee's reputation, but rather destroy it for good, as it would be a public confession of incompetence and recklessness. He reminded them of how Hiss had qualified all his important answers. Then he pointed out that Hiss had given HUAC a golden opportunity. It had been virtually impossible for HUAC to prove that this or that accused man had been or was a Communist—all he had to do was deny it or take the Fifth Amendment—and it would be just as impossible with Hiss. But the committee did not have to prove that Hiss was a Red, Nixon explained. All it had to do was prove that Hiss was lying when he said he did not know Chambers. Further, having given Chambers' charges such wide currency, the committee had an obligation to find out who was lying.

Nixon's arguments prevailed, helped by Stripling, who pointed out that a smear campaign against Chambers had begun. The whispers were that Chambers was an alcoholic, insane, and a homosexual. Such rumor campaigns, Stripling said, were typical

Communist tactics. Mundt finally agreed to appoint a subcommittee to question Chambers further, in executive session. Mundt put
the eager Nixon at the head of the subcommittee and instructed
Stripling to subpoena Chambers to a hearing in New York on August 7, two days away.[14]

NIXON HAD SET himself up as a dragon slayer, in the teeth of the
President, the Administration, a large majority in Congress, and
almost the entire press corps. In his later account of the case, Nixon
reported that he expected some criticism, "but I was not prepared
for an assault on the Committee and its members which, in fury
and vehemence, had never even been approached in the Committee's past history." Nearly everyone assumed that Chambers was
lying. Nixon's Republican colleagues in the House told him that
he should call off the investigation. Particularly disturbing to Nixon
was the attitude of Christian Herter, who said, "I don't want to
prejudge the case, but I'm afraid the Committee has been taken in
by Chambers."[15]

Nixon reread the testimony, over and over. He remained convinced that Hiss was lying and that the Justice Department was
guilty of a cover-up. He remained determined to go ahead.

Eleven years later, Nixon told reporter Earl Mazo that he realized this was his "first real testing." Nixon continued, "Very few
men get in the merciless spotlight of national publicity in a case
that may make or break a party. . . . The Hiss case was a very rugged experience . . . as difficult an experience as I've ever had.
From the standpoint of responsibility . . . the resourceful enemies
I was up against . . . the battle day in and day out . . . the terrible
attacks from the press, nasty cartoons, editorials, mail . . . and there
was always a great doubt whether you are going to win and
whether you are on the right side or not. I was convinced that I
was."[16]

ON SATURDAY MORNING, August 7, in Room 101 of the Federal
Courthouse in Foley Square, New York, Nixon's subcommittee,
consisting of himself, McDowell, and Hébert, took testimony in
executive session from Chambers. Nixon asked Chambers for supporting details on his relationship with Hiss, and Chambers gave
them in abundance. He said he was a close friend of Hiss and his
wife, had stayed in their home, borrowed money from them, given
them gifts, called them by their nicknames. Asked if Hiss had any
hobbies, Chambers said he and Priscilla Hiss were amateur orni-
thologists. "I recall once they saw, to their great excitement, a
prothonotary warbler."

Nixon asked if Hiss had a car. Chambers said yes, a Ford roadster. "It was black and it was very dilapidated . . . I remember very clearly that it had hand windshield wipers." He added that Hiss had given it to the CP "so it could be of use to some poor organizer in the West or somewhere."[17] Chambers' mass of detail about the Hisses was convincing. So was his confidence. "Would you be willing to submit to a lie detector test on this testimony?" Nixon asked near the end.

"Yes, if necessary," Chambers replied.

"You have that much confidence?"

"I am telling the truth."[18]

THE FOLLOWING WEEK, HUAC questioned people named by Chambers as Communists—without any breakthroughs—and once again had Bentley on the stand. These public confrontations were getting the committee nowhere. Nixon and Stripling, meanwhile, had the committee staff searching through Washington for documentary evidence that would link Hiss with Chambers—rent receipts, car transfer papers, anything.

Nixon went off on his own search for the truth. On at least three occasions that week, he drove to Westminster, Maryland, to visit Chambers on his farm. In a memo on the case that he wrote a half year later (and then used as the basis for his chapter on Hiss in his 1962 book, *Six Crises*), Nixon said that the visits were "mainly for the purpose of attempting to convince myself on the issue of whether or not Chambers, in speaking of Hiss, was speaking of a man he knew, or was telling a story which he had concocted."[19]

The two men sat on rocking chairs on Chambers' front porch, overlooking the rolling hills of Maryland, and talked about Communism. Chambers was America's leading ex-Communist (as distinguished from former Communists, who left the CP and did their best to put it out of their minds). He was as obsessed with Communism in 1948 as he had been in 1938, although now as an enemy rather than a member of the CP. He was an intellectual of high quality and great sensitivity—his translation of the German novel *Bambi* was an absolutely superb piece of work—who had long ago concluded that the modern world faced a life-and-death struggle between Communism and freedom.

Nixon told Chambers bluntly that many HUAC members questioned his credibility and insisted that he had to have some personal motive for doing what he was doing to Hiss. "Certainly I wouldn't have a motive which would involve destroying my own career," Chambers replied—he was making $25,000 per year as a senior editor at *Time*, which was $10,000 more than Nixon was making as a congressman. Chambers explained that he had come forward to warn his country of the scope, strength, and danger of the Communist conspiracy in the United States. He insisted that the case was much bigger than a clash of personalities, telling Nixon, "This is what you must get the country to realize."

Nixon was convinced by the conversations that Chambers was telling the truth. The clincher came when Nixon was leaving after his last visit. "I was still tying to press him for any personal recollection which might help us in breaking the case," Nixon wrote in his February 1949 memorandum. "The conversation came around to religion and he said that Mrs. Hiss was a Quaker and that he also was a Quaker. . . . I told him that I was a Quaker, and then suddenly Chambers snapped his fingers and said, 'Here's something I should have recalled before. Mrs. Hiss used to use the plain language in talking with Alger.' As a Quaker I knew that Chambers couldn't know such intimate matters unless he had known Hiss."[20]

Nixon's parents, Frank and Hannah, had retired and moved to a farm near York, Pennsylvania, less than an hour's drive from Westminster. Nixon called them regularly and realized that they were worried about all the newspaper uproar surrounding their son and the case. After leaving Chambers, he decided to drive over and spend the night with them, to reassure them and to do some thinking of his own.

When Hannah called him to dinner that night, he did not hear her. When he did sit down at the table, he could not eat. Hannah said that "he would go to one part of the room and stop and think. Then he would go to another part of the room and stop and think again. Then he would pace nervously and talk to himself. 'I just feel that I should get out of it,' he would say at one moment. But the next moment he would be saying, 'I can't drop it now.'"

Frank and Hannah were distressed by their son's behavior. She told Frank, "If Richard doesn't give up the case, he won't be here to carry on." Although she did not want to interfere, Hannah could no longer restrain herself. She told her son, "Richard, why don't you drop the case? No one else thinks Hiss is guilty. You are a young congressman. Older congressmen and senators have warned you to stop. Why don't you?"

"Mother," he replied, "I think Hiss is lying. Until I know the truth, I've got to stick it out."[21]

"MAKING THE DECISION to meet a crisis is far more difficult than the test itself," Richard Nixon wrote in *Six Crises*. In a famous passage, he went on to describe his method of meeting a crisis (which he generalized, but which in fact was highly personal—for example, Dwight Eisenhower never went through anything like what Nixon described when he met his crises).

Nixon wrote in an almost mystical fashion about the experience. When one is filled with doubt and soul-searching about whether to fight or flee, Nixon wrote, "almost unbearable tensions build up, tensions that can be relieved only by taking action, one way or the other. . . . It is this soul-searching and testing which ultimately gives a man the confidence, calmness, and toughness with which to act decisively."

From the experience, Nixon said, "a man . . . learns not to worry when his muscles tense up, his breathing comes faster, his nerves tingle, his stomach churns, his temper becomes short, his nights are sleepless." He might become "physically sore and mentally depressed." But these were all, he claimed, "natural and healthy signs that his system is keyed up for battle."

Nixon wrote about crises the way some men write about a religious experience, others about combat, still others about sexual conquests. He said it separated "the leaders from the followers," that "we are all tempted to stay on the sidelines, to live like vegetables, to concentrate all our efforts on living . . . longer, and leaving behind a bigger estate." Meeting crises involved creativity. "It engages all a man's talents." It was the ultimate test: "Did he risk all when the stakes were such that he might win or lose all?"

Nixon asserted that "a man who has never lost himself in a cause bigger than himself has missed one of life's mountaintop experiences. . . . Only then does he discover all the latent strengths he never knew he had. . . ."

"Crisis can indeed be agony," Nixon insisted. "But it is the exquisite agony. . . ."[22]

AFTER RETURNING to Washington, Nixon had a series of consultations. First he went to William Rogers, counsel for the Senate Investigating Committee, which had also heard Bentley but not Chambers. He wanted Rogers' advice as to whether to proceed or not. Nixon told Rogers what he knew and showed him the still-secret August 7 Chambers testimony before his subcommittee. Rogers read it and urged him to press on.[23]

Nixon next met with Bert Andrews, the chief Washington correspondent of the New York *Herald Tribune*, the leading Republican paper in the nation. Andrews was a Pulitzer Prize winner for a series of articles critical of State Department security procedures, later published in book form as *Washington Witch Hunt*. Along with James Reston of *The New York Times*, Andrews had recommended Hiss to John Foster Dulles for the post at the Carnegie Endowment. Andrews was widely respected, and his credentials for objectivity could not have been better.

Nixon gave Andrews the August 7 Chambers testimony to read. When Andrews finished, he said, "I wouldn't have believed it, after hearing Hiss the other day. But there's no doubt about it. Chambers knew Hiss."[24]

That evening, at dinner, Nixon showed the no-longer-very-secret Chambers testimony to Congressman Kersten, who was also convinced by it. But he warned Nixon that he had heard a rumor (which was quite correct) that Hiss was trying to get Dulles to make a statement in his behalf. Kersten suggested that Nixon should take the Chambers testimony to Dulles to read, and to do so as soon as possible.

The following morning, August 11, Nixon called Dulles, who agreed to a meeting that evening at the Roosevelt Hotel in New York. It would be a critical meeting for Nixon. As Dewey's chief foreign-policy adviser, Dulles was at the epicenter of power in the Republican Party. The Republicans had discussed making Communist infiltration into government a major issue, but now it appeared likely to backfire on them. Not only had Hiss been utterly convincing in his appearance before HUAC, but even worse, Dulles, as chairman of the board of the Carnegie Endowment, was Hiss's employer and benefactor. The potential for damage to the Dewey campaign from the Hiss case was very high, giving Dulles strong motivation to tell Nixon to back off.

When Nixon got to the Roosevelt, he found not only John Foster Dulles there, but also his brother, Allen, New York banker C. Douglas Dillon (later Under Secretary of State), and Christian Herter. This was, in effect, the senior brain trust of the Republican Party, and had this group decided to withhold its approval, Nixon would have had to drop the case.

Nixon approached the group with appropriate humility. Dulles later recalled, "Hiss had a reputation at the time that was very high indeed. Dick had gotten a lot of evidence, but it was clear he did not want to proceed with Hiss until people like myself had agreed that he really had got a case to justify going ahead."[25]

Nixon passed around copies of the August 7 Chambers testimony. When he finished reading, Dulles began pacing the floor, hands behind his back. "There's no question about it," he finally said. "It's almost impossible to believe, but Chambers knows Hiss." Allen Dulles and the others agreed.

Nixon asked if he should go ahead with the investigation. "In view of the facts Chambers has testified to," Dulles replied, "you'd be derelict in your duty as a Congressman if you did not see the case through to a conclusion."[26]

WITH THAT STAMP of approval, Nixon plunged ahead. He returned to Westminster to get more details from Chambers. He brought his parents down from York to the Chambers farm, so that they could see for themselves that Chambers was no crackpot. He developed a close and warm relationship with Chambers' family, best described by Chambers himself in his 1952 book, *Witness*: "Throughout the most trying phases of the Case, Nixon and his family, and sometimes his parents, were at our farm, encouraging me and comforting my family. My children have caught him lovingly in a nickname. To them, he is always 'Nixie,' the kind and the good, about whom they will tolerate no nonsense. His somewhat martial Quakerism sometimes amused and always heartened me. I have a vivid picture of him . . . standing by the barn and saying in his quietly savage way (he is the kindest of men): 'If the American people understood the real character of Alger Hiss, they would boil him in oil.' "[27]

Convinced Nixon may have been that Chambers was telling the truth and that Hiss ought to be boiled in oil, but he still wanted reassurance. He asked Bert Andrews to drive up to Westminster with him, to ask Chambers tough, reporter-type questions, not to test Chambers' veracity so much as to test his ability to convince others.

Andrews asked Chambers if he was a drunk. No. Had he been in an insane asylum? No, never. After further blunt questions, Andrews had an insight: "Chambers was a man who would answer all questions but volunteer nothing." And that leads to one of the great puzzlements of the Hiss case. As Andrews put it in his book, *A Tragedy of History*, "Looking back, I wonder why in the world Nixon and I never asked him if he had any documentary evidence. I truly believe he would have produced it."[28]

Why not indeed? This was Nixon's biggest single mistake, not only at this stage but again later in the case. But he was hardly alone. Beginning with Chambers' original confession and accusations to Berle in 1939, continuing through Chambers' testimony to the FBI in 1943 and again in 1945, on to the HUAC hearings in 1948, literally dozens of people had an opportunity to ask Chambers the simplest, yet most crucial of questions: "Do you have any documentary evidence to support these charges?" No one asked the question. Why not, to repeat, is a puzzlement.

The day after the visit with Andrews, Nixon drove up to the farm again, this time with Stripling. Again, Chambers overwhelmed the two men with details about Hiss, reinforcing their conviction that he had indeed known the man. But as they drove back to Washington, Stripling made the comment, "I don't think Chambers has yet told us the whole story. He is holding something back. He is trying to protect somebody." [29]

ON MONDAY, AUGUST 16, in Washington, Nixon's subcommittee again met in executive session, this time to hear Hiss. Nixon pretended to objectivity—"I will say that both you and Mr. Chambers are as convincing witnesses as I have ever seen"—but he bombarded Hiss with questions about his personal life. Before he got well started, however, Hiss interrupted to say that he wanted to see Chambers' August 7 testimony. He added, "I have seen newspaper accounts, Mr. Nixon, that you spent the weekend . . . at Mr. Chambers' farm in New Jersey."

> NIXON: That is quite incorrect.
> HISS: It is incorrect?
> NIXON: Yes, sir. I can say, as you did a moment ago, that I have never spent the night with Mr. Chambers.[30]

Although Hiss had misplaced the location of Chambers' farm, Nixon was equivocating in his answer (not to mention the innuendo in that "spent the night" phrase). But Nixon was a paragon of truthfulness compared to Hiss. As the details emerged, it became obvious that Hiss was in deep trouble, not at all the self-assured witness of a week and a half ago. In Nixon's words, "Now he was twisting, turning, evading, and changing his story to fit the evidence he knew we had." [31]

Hiss's evasions bothered Eddie Hébert. At one point he interrupted to give "a man-to-man impression. . . . Either you or Mr. Chambers is lying."

> HISS: That is certainly true.
> HÉBERT: And whichever one of you is lying is the greatest actor that America has ever produced.[32]

Nixon pressed Hiss on the names of his maids, the makes and years of the cars he had ever owned, where he had lived. Finally, dramatically, Hiss declared that he had perhaps known Chambers after all, but under a different name. It was possible, Hiss asserted, that "the name of the man I brought in—and he may have no relation to this whole nightmare—is a man named George Crosley. I met him when I was working for the Nye committee. He was a writer. He hoped to sell articles to magazines about the munitions industry." [33]

This fantastic story became even more fantastic as Nixon went after Hiss. Hiss claimed that he hardly knew "Mr. Crosley," but under questioning said that he had let Crosley stay in his home, and loaned him his old car, a Model A Ford, "slightly collegiate," Hiss said, with "a sassy little trunk on the back." He had given Crosley free use of his apartment. Yet he hardly knew the man.[34]

The questioning returned to Hiss's personal habits. Nixon asked him if he had a hobby. Hiss mentioned bird watching. Congressman McDowell asked, "Did you ever see a prothonotary warbler?"

> HISS: I have, right here on the Potomac. Do you know that place?
> MUNDT: What is that?
> NIXON: Have you ever seen one?
> HISS: Did you see it in the same place?
> McDOWELL: I saw one in Arlington.
> HISS: They come back and nest in those swamps. Beautiful yellow head, a gorgeous bird.[35]

That warbler would soon become the most famous bird in America. Meanwhile, the subcommittee agreed to arrange a face-to-face public meeting between Chambers and Hiss in Washington on August 25.

THAT EVENING, mulling over the situation, Nixon decided that "we would be playing into his [Hiss's] hands by delaying the public confrontation," because that would give Hiss time to make his story fit the facts. So at 2 A.M. on August 17, Nixon called Stripling and told him to summon both Chambers and Hiss before the subcommittee in New York City that very afternoon, in a suite in the Commodore Hotel.

Nixon and McDowell were there from the committee, along with Stripling and four staff members. After some preliminary skirmishing with Hiss, who sat across from the two congressmen, Nixon ordered Chambers brought into the room, then told the two men to face each other. "Mr. Hiss," he said, "the man standing here is Mr. Whittaker Chambers. I ask you now if you have ever known that man before."

Instead of replying, Hiss asked to have Chambers say something. Chambers did. Not satisfied with that, Hiss asked that Chambers read a passage from a magazine, so that he could further test his voice.

"Just one moment," Nixon interjected. "Since some repartee goes on between these two people, I think Mr. Chambers should be sworn."

HISS: That is a good idea.

[Chambers was then sworn in by McDowell.]

NIXON: Mr. Hiss, may I say something? I suggested that he be sworn, and when I say something like that I want no interruptions from you.

HISS: Mr. Nixon, in view of what happened yesterday, I think there is no occasion for you to use that tone of voice in speaking to me, and I hope the record will show what I have just said.

NIXON: The record shows everything that is being said here today.

Hiss then went through an elaborate examination of Chambers' teeth, asking if they had been fixed some time since 1935 and then demanding to know the name of the dentist. Nixon said, "Before we leave the teeth, Mr. Hiss, do you feel that you would have to have the dentist tell you just what he did to the teeth before you could tell anything about this man?"[36]

Hiss said that he did. This charade went on for some minutes, until Nixon suggested that Hiss ask Chambers some questions. Hiss asked if Chambers had ever sublet an apartment from him. No, Chambers replied. Had he ever spent time with his wife and children in Hiss's apartment?

CHAMBERS: I most certainly did.

HISS: You did or did not?

CHAMBERS: I did.

HISS: Would you tell me how you reconcile your negative answers with this affirmative answer?

CHAMBERS: Very easily, Alger. I was a Communist and you were a Communist.

Hiss decided at this point to drop the charade, or at least part of it. He said, "I will . . . positively identify him without further questioning as George Crosley." Stripling wanted to know if he could produce three people who would testify that they had known Chambers as Crosley. "I will if it is possible," Hiss replied. "Why is that a question to ask me?"[37] The obvious answer—because Hiss was the one who had invented Crosley—hung in the air. (In the event, Hiss could produce only one person who had ever heard of Crosley—his wife, Priscilla.)

Hiss, who had only a few moments past insisted that he would have to examine Chambers' dental records before identifying him as Crosley, now went to the other extreme. "The ass under the lion's skin is Crosley," he proclaimed. "I have no further question at all. If he had lost both eyes and taken his nose off, I would be sure."

That point established, Nixon turned to Chambers to ask if the man facing him was Alger Hiss, a member of the CP and a man at whose house he had stayed. "Positive identification," Chambers replied.

Hiss walked toward Chambers. "May I say for the record at this point, that I would like to invite Mr. Whittaker Chambers to make those same statements out of the presence of this committee without their being privileged for suit for libel. I challenge you to do it, and I hope you will do it damned quickly." [38]

When Hiss walked toward Chambers to dare him to make his charges in public, Nixon wrote in his 1949 memorandum (material he chose not to include in *Six Crises*), "he actually shook his fist and gave the appearance of one who was about to attack. But I was convinced it was purely a bluff. A staff member walked up behind him and actually touched only his clothes and asked him to sit down. Hiss wheeled on him as if he had stuck him with a hot needle in a sensitive spot, and shouted to take his hands off." [39]

For the next hour, Nixon hammered away at Hiss's story. Hiss said he had known Crosley for only a short time, yet had sublet his apartment to the man (and according to Hiss, Crosley never paid the rent) and thrown in free use of his car to boot. He had driven Crosley to New York, had him as a guest in his home for a week at a time, yet never read a word he had written, had never checked on him, and anyway had not seen him since 1935.

Through this fog of deception one fact showed clearly—that Hiss had deliberately deceived the press, the public, and HUAC in his initial appearance when he insisted that he had no idea who that man was when shown a photograph of Chambers. If Hiss had been half as good a bluffer as he thought he was, he would have recognized that the moment had come to call off the bluff, fold his hand, and leave the game. Instead, he tried to carry it off—as he still was trying forty years later.

Hiss insisted that the subcommittee question his wife; Nixon agreed to do so the next day. McDowell asked if Nixon had any further questions.

NIXON: I have nothing.
McDOWELL: That is all. [To Hiss] Thank you very much.
HISS: *I don't reciprocate.*
McDOWELL: Italicize that in the record.
HISS: I wish you would. [40]

When Hiss left the room, Stripling turned to Chambers. In his slow Texas drawl, he deadpanned, "How are you, Mr. Crosley?" The ensuing laughter broke the tension. Nixon was jubilant. He had proved the essential point, that whatever the relationship and under whatever name, Hiss knew Chambers. Nixon got on the phone to reporters. *The New York Times* carried a headline the next day that read, "ALGER HISS ADMITS KNOWING CHAMBERS," and a story that contained a summary of the confrontation, all provided by Nixon.[41]

STILL NIXON could not rest. He was hardly sleeping now, as Donald Appell, a member of the HUAC staff, discovered when Nixon asked him to spend the night because he did not wish to be alone in the Commodore Hotel suite. Late that evening Nixon called Bert Andrews on the telephone. Appell went to sleep. When he woke three hours later, at 2 A.M., he heard Nixon still talking to Andrews on the phone.[42]

The following morning, Hiss brought his wife to the suite in the Commodore to corroborate his story about Crosley. Nixon was almost somnolent. His questions to Priscilla were perfunctory at best. It lasted only ten minutes. She said she had a vague recollection of this man Crosley, and that was about all.[43]

Later, Nixon said he learned a fundamental lesson from this experience. He could have pressed Priscilla and broken her story, he felt, had he known the lesson in advance. It was that "the point of greatest danger is not in preparing to meet the crisis or fighting the battle; it occurs after the crisis of battle is over. . . . The individual is spent physically, emotionally, and mentally. He lets down . . . he is prone to drop his guard and to err in his judgment." What he really needed was some sleep.[44]

HUAC HAD ARRANGED for a public confrontation between Chambers and Hiss in Washington on August 25. In the week preceding, Nixon "put in longer hours and worked harder than I had at any time in my life." He was at it eighteen to twenty hours a day. He was directing a search for anyone who might have known Chambers as Crosley, and for any evidence supporting Chambers' story about his relationship with Hiss. The tension was such that he noticed that he was "mean" with his family and friends, quick-tempered with his staff. "I lost interest in eating and skipped meals without even being aware of it. Getting to sleep became more and more difficult."

Two days before the hearing, the HUAC staff hit the jackpot. It discovered a Motor Vehicle transfer certificate that proved that Hiss had given the old Ford with the sassy little trunk to a CP member. One day before the hearing, Bert Andrews dropped by Nixon's office. "You look like hell," Andrews said. "You need some sleep." At Andrews' insistence, Nixon went home, took a sleeping pill, and slept twelve hours.[45]

The session the next day, August 25, was long, bitter, and disastrous to Hiss. Nixon and Hiss jabbed and sparred, about when Hiss had known Crosley, under what circumstances, what happened to the car, and so on. Nixon showed him the title transfer for the car, with his signature on it, and asked him to identify his signature. Hiss hedged, said he wanted to see the original.

MUNDT: Could you be sure if you saw the original?
HISS: I could be surer.

The hearing room broke into laughter. Even Hiss's friends shook their heads in disbelief. Eventually, Hiss repeated his challenge to Chambers "to make statements about me with respect to Communism in public that he has made under privilege to this Committee." He was on the stand for five full hours. At one point, when they were discussing Hiss's apartment, Hiss protested, "The important charges are not questions of leases, but questions of whether I was a Communist." Nixon jumped right on that one: "The issue in this hearing today is whether or not Mr. Hiss or Mr. Chambers has committed perjury before this committee, as well as whether Mr. Hiss is a Communist."

When Hiss finished, Chambers took the stand. He repeated his charges and insisted that Hiss's story was a complete lie.

NIXON: Mr. Chambers, can you search your memory now to see what motive you can have for accusing Mr. Hiss of being a Communist at the present time?
CHAMBERS: What motive I can have?
NIXON: Yes. I mean, do you—is there any grudge that you have against Mr. Hiss over anything he has done to you?
CHAMBERS: The story has spread that in testifying against Mr. Hiss I am working out some old grudge, or motives of revenge or hatred. I do not hate Mr. Hiss. We were close friends, but we are caught in a tragedy of history. Mr. Hiss represents the concealed enemy against which we are all fighting, and I am fighting.[46]

TWO DAYS LATER, on August 27, HUAC released all the transcripts, from both secret executive sessions and from the public testimony, under the title *Hearings Regarding Communist Espionage in the United States Government* (actually no one had yet raised the question of espionage). Included were editorial comments from the staff, which termed Hiss's testimony as "vague and evasive" and Chambers' as "forthright and emphatic." It was convincing. A Gallup poll showed that four out of five Americans approved of HUAC's inquiry and thought it should continue. Major newspapers, normally critical of HUAC, such as the Washington *Post*, *The New York Times*, and the New York *Herald Tribune*, agreed editorially that the committee was onto something.[47]

IN THE FIRST WEEK of September, Nixon and Pat went over to Ocean City, Maryland, for a three-day weekend. Bert Andrews had made the arrangements and practically insisted on their going. Nixon told Andrews later that it was a "wonderful vacation. The weather was perfect, except for the fact that we tried to take two weeks of sun in three days with the usual results. We both had a chance to relax completely." Always the politician, Nixon assured Andrews that the beaches in Maryland were "as good as any we have in California, and better than most."

When he returned to Washington, Nixon wrote a four-page letter to John Foster Dulles, with a blind copy to Andrews. He summarized the hearings, told Dulles that Hiss's guilt was beyond doubt, and urged him to ease Hiss out of his position as president of the Carnegie Endowment.[48] Dulles would not fire Hiss, but the Endowment did grant him a leave of absence, and Dulles—partly at Andrews' urging, partly because of Nixon's presentation—refused to issue a statement of support for Hiss.

Nixon, Andrews, and others urged Dulles—and, through him, Dewey—to make the domestic Reds, and particularly Hiss, a major campaign issue, but neither Dulles nor Dewey would do it. For one reason, Dulles was too closely associated with Hiss. For another, Dulles did not want to upset the European allies, with whom he expected shortly to be working as Secretary of State, and who would think the Republicans were indulging in Red-baiting. But most of all, Dewey would not do it. He had been burned in 1944 when he tried to establish a link between FDR and CP leader Earl Browder, and anyway, as GOP National Chairman Hugh Scott put it, Dewey "thought it degrading to suspect Truman personally of being soft on Communism. He wasn't going around looking under beds." In other words, Nixon was on his own—his party would not stand behind him, but Dulles would not oppose him either.[49]

CHAMBERS MEANWHILE had appeared on the radio program *Meet the Press*. There he took up Hiss's challenge, saying, "Alger Hiss was a Communist and may be now." When asked if he was prepared to go to court to defend the charge, he replied, "I do not think Mr. Hiss will sue me for slander or libel."

For three weeks it appeared that Chambers was correct, for

Hiss did nothing, to the consternation of his supporters. Finally the Washington *Post* declared, "Mr. Hiss has created a situation in which he is obliged to put up or shut up. Mr. Hiss has left himself no alternative." At the end of September, Hiss filed a $50,000 libel suit, charging that Chambers had damaged his reputation by accusing him of having been a Communist.[50]

NIXON SPENT the fall months campaigning, not for himself but for fellow Republicans. He had already been re-elected, winning both primaries in the 12th District. He was much in demand, and his usual speech was a summary of the Hiss case, followed by a denunciation of the Democrats for protecting Hiss.

After their big win in 1946, the Republicans had been supremely confident in 1948, and their confidence was backed both by common sense and the polls. Common sense told them that the Democrats could never elect Harry Truman, a two-bit machine politician from Kansas City who was President by accident and who had lost control of his party when the left wing walked out to organize the Progressive Party (under Henry Wallace) and the Solid South had simultaneously walked out to organize a fourth party, the Dixiecrats (under Strom Thurmond). The polls confirmed the obvious—Dewey was sure to sweep to victory.

The results of the election, Nixon later said in a grand understatement, were "an unpleasant surprise for me and all Republicans." In fact, Truman's victory was an unprecedented blow to the solar plexus of the Republican Party, and its impact on American politics went far beyond giving Truman four more years in office.

Truman, almost single-handedly, had managed to win, and, in the process, brought a Democratic Congress in with him (so long as he was willing to forgive the Dixiecrats, as he was, in return for their votes in organizing the Congress). It turned out that the American people were not ready for the counterrevolution, not ready to abandon the New Deal, not ready to believe Republican charges that the Democratic Administration was shot through with Communists and fellow travelers, and certainly not ready to accept the Republican accusations that the Democrats were unwilling to stand up to the Russians or clean house at home.

It was not that the American people were hostile to the anti-Communist crusade. In fact, by making so much of an uproar about the Communists, the Republicans probably did Truman a favor, making him the chief beneficiary of the near-hysteria that was sweeping the country. That was only fair, since the Truman Doctrine speech had been an important contributing factor to that hysteria. It was just plain dumb of Nixon and other Republicans to try to convince people that Harry was soft on the Reds after Harry had stood up to them in Greece and Turkey, called for a worldwide policy of containment, accelerated the atomic-bomb-testing program, met Stalin's challenge in Berlin head on, instituted loyalty oaths for federal employees, and otherwise done so much to lead and even feed the anti-Communist crusade. Dewey and Dulles had been right in their instinctual judgment that they should avoid raising the Communist infiltration issue, but they were unable to keep other Republicans, including Nixon, from crying that the Truman Administration was soft on Communism. The charge backfired.

For Nixon and Chambers, the Democratic victory was a potential disaster of the first magnitude. With Truman re-elected and the Democrats once again in control of Congress, and thus of the committees, the odds were that HUAC would be dissolved and that the Justice Department would never indict Hiss. The slander suit had been filed in Baltimore—a jury there would be likely to believe native son Hiss. If Chambers lost the suit, he could then expect to be indicted himself by Justice for perjury.

Politics were closely woven into the entire fabric of the Hiss case. Nixon, Chambers, Stripling, and other HUAC members had all been jubilant up to the election, certain that they had proved their case. Chambers was completely confident about the suit. But the day after the election, they were all in a deep depression. Triumph had been turned that quickly into disaster, not by anything that had happened internally in the case, or by any new evidence, but by Truman's unexpected victory.

Nixon decided to shake the depression, and get some needed rest, on a cruise to Panama. Pat had been after him to take a vacation—they had not had a real one in two years. Frank and Hannah could take care of the girls at their farm. Along with some other congressmen, Nixon booked passage for a December 2 departure on a ten-day cruise. "This time," he told Pat when he brought the tickets home, "absolutely nothing is going to interfere with our vacation." She smiled and replied, "I hope you're right, but I still have to be shown."[51]

ON DECEMBER 1, as Pat was finishing the packing, Nixon read a United Press story in the Washington *Daily News* reporting that unnamed senior officials at Justice said that the department was "about ready to drop its investigation" of perjury of either Hiss or Chambers "unless additional evidence is forthcoming." That was the worst possible news, but it was directly contradicted by a story Nixon then read in the Washington *Post.* In his column, Jerry Kluttz announced that "some very startling information on who's a liar is reported to have been uncovered" in the Hiss-Chambers slander action.

Nixon, in great agitation, got on the phone to Stripling, then went to the office. There he had the first in a series of pieces of incredible good luck. Nicholas Vazzana, one of Chambers' lawyers, had decided on his own to tell HUAC that the *Post* was right, that new evidence did exist. He found Nixon and Stripling in the office, and after some stalling and evasiveness, he told the story.

It was simple enough. Someone had finally thought to ask Chambers if he had any documents to support his charges. Ironically, it was Hiss's chief lawyer, William Marbury, who did so. Chambers had then produced copies of documents, sixty-five in all, that he said had been stolen from the State Department by Alger Hiss, then given to him to be given to a Russian agent. Chambers gave photostatic copies of the documents to Marbury and to the Justice Department.

This development threw everything into turmoil. Suddenly Chambers was a confessed perjurer (he had told HUAC that he had never engaged in espionage, nor had the CP ring Hiss had belonged to in the government). But just as suddenly, the charges against Hiss escalated from perjury to treason.

When Vazzana left, Nixon and Stripling lunched together. Stripling thought Nixon appeared nervous and highly irritable, which surprised him, since he thought the escalation in the charges changed the nature of the case, to HUAC's great advantage. Still, Nixon was shaken.

Allen Weinstein, much the closest and most careful student of the Hiss case, speculates that Nixon felt angry at Chambers. Nixon certainly had good reason. Chambers had never said a word to him about any documents, much less any spying, and now he had given the evidence to Justice, not the FBI or HUAC. When Stripling suggested that they drive to Westminster to confront Chambers, Nixon snapped back, "I'm so goddamned sick and tired of this case. I don't want to hear any more about it and I'm going to Panama. And the hell with it, and you, and the whole damned business!"

Stripling pressed Nixon, pointing out that if he did not act, nothing would be done before January, when the Democrats would take over and the Hiss case would be quietly dropped. The furious Nixon would not budge. "Hell, I'm not going to Westminster. I'm going to Panama, and you can do what you damn want to, but I'm through with it."

Stripling decided to go see Chambers himself. Just before leaving, he called Nixon one final time, urging him to come. "Goddamn it," Nixon exploded. "If it'll shut your mouth, I'll go."

They drove up in a stone-cold silence, hardly looking at each other. When they arrived and confronted Chambers, he explained that Marbury had asked for evidence, that he had produced the documents, and that Marbury had then decided that they were so hot he had an obligation to turn them over immediately to Alex Campbell, chief of the Criminal Division in the Justice Department. All that had happened two weeks ago.

Nixon was aghast. Justice had been in possession of the stolen documents for two weeks and had done nothing about them, except to leak to the press the UP story that it was dropping the case. Here was cover-up with a vengeance, and for purely political reasons, an obstruction of justice by the Justice Department itself.

Nixon berated Chambers for his stupidity in giving the documents to Campbell. Chambers replied that "I wouldn't be that foolish. My attorney has photostatic copies, and also I didn't turn over everything I had. I have another bombshell in case they try to suppress this one."

"You keep that second bombshell," Nixon said. "Don't give it to anybody except the Committee." Why he did not issue a subpoena then and there on Chambers for the remaining documents is another of the many mysteries in the case. In any event, he did not —he and Stripling drove back to Washington empty-handed.

"Well, what do you think he's got?" Nixon asked Stripling. "I don't know what he has," Stripling replied, "but whatever he has, it'll blow the dome off the Capitol. Certainly you're not going to Panama now?"

"I don't think he's got a damned thing. I'm going right ahead with my plans." [52] In *Six Crises* Nixon explained that he could not cancel his vacation because he "didn't have the heart to tell Pat."

Back in Washington, Nixon phoned Bert Andrews, who rushed over to Nixon's office, where he heard the story of the trip to Westminster. Now it was Andrews' turn to explode. "You were too nice to Chambers," he told Nixon. "Did you slap a subpoena on him?" Nixon said that he had not thought of that. "Look," Andrews said, "before you leave town get hold of Bob Stripling. Tell him to serve a blanket subpoena on Chambers to produce *anything* and *everything* he still has in his possession." [53]

When Andrews left Nixon's office at 12:30 A.M. on December 2, Nixon got on the telephone to Assistant Director Louis B. Nichols of the FBI. According to a memorandum on the call that Nichols prepared, Nixon "specifically urged that we not tell the Attorney General that we were told of this information [about Chambers' bombshell] as the Attorney General undoubtedly would try to make it impossible for the Committee to get at the documents. He also asked that the Bureau not look for the documents themselves." J. Edgar Hoover, who was no friend of Attorney General Tom Clark's and who had been trying to get Hiss for years, kept his unbroken record of cooperation with HUAC intact. He made no search for the bombshell.[54]

That morning, December 2, Nixon decided to take Andrews' advice about the subpoena, but not Stripling's about canceling his cruise. On his way to Union Station to catch the train to New York for the departure, he stopped off at the HUAC office and signed a *subpoena duces tecum* on Chambers for any and all documents in his possession relating to the Hiss Case. From the train, Nixon used the radiotelephone to call Stripling at 9 A.M. ordering him to serve the subpoena that day. Stripling did so later in the morning.[55]

AND so the Nixons went off on their long-delayed and much-needed vacation. At dinner the first night out, Nixon remarked that he and Pat had taken the cruise so that they could be sure of ten days of rest, uninterrupted by telephone calls.

Stripling, meanwhile, had sent two HUAC staffers to Westminster, where Chambers led them to a pumpkin patch. There he reached into a hollowed-out pumpkin and produced rolls of microfilm that contained copies of State Department documents from the mid-thirties, some in Hiss's handwriting. This was indeed bombshell stuff, the biggest spy case in the history of the State Department.

Stripling wired Nixon on ship: "SECOND BOMBSHELL OBTAINED BY SUBPOENA," and again, "CASE CLINCHED. INFORMATION AMAZING. HEAT IS ON FROM PRESS AND OTHER PLACES. IMMEDIATE ACTION APPEARS NECESSARY. CAN YOU POSSIBLY GET BACK?" Andrews also wired several times.[56]

Nixon received the wires at the captain's table the evening of December 3. He read one from Stripling aloud. Pat threw up her hands. "Here we go again," she said. Nixon radioed Stripling to make arrangements to get him off the boat, which was then near Cuba. Stripling went to Secretary of Defense James Forrestal, who issued orders to the Coast Guard in Miami to fly a PBY out to the ship, pick up Nixon, and return him to Miami. When the PBY arrived, Nixon climbed into a lifeboat and the crew rowed him over to the plane. When they arrived in Miami, there was a crowd of reporters and photographers on hand to meet him—as a consequence, he got his picture on the front page of *The New York Times*, leaving the plane, rushing off to Washington to do his duty and save his country.

There are a number of unanswered questions about this event. Why did Forrestal, a member of the Truman Administration, cooperate with Nixon so handsomely? Who informed the press of the arrival time in Miami of the PBY? What did Nixon tell Pat? (She stayed on board and finished the cruise, alone.) Had the whole melodrama been staged? (According to William "Fishbait" Miller, doorkeeper of the House, Nixon told him the morning he left that he expected to be summoned back because of dramatic developments in the Hiss case.) Or was it all just a string of lucky coincidences? Whatever the case, the event certainly produced high drama and great publicity for Nixon.[57]

BEFORE THE pumpkin papers, Nixon had said that the question in the case was, Did Hiss and Chambers know each other? Hiss said the question was, Was he a Communist? Suddenly both questions seemed terribly inconsequential. The question now was, Was Alger Hiss, trusted adviser to FDR and friend of Supreme Court justices, of two future Secretaries of State, and of nearly everyone of importance in the State Department for the past fifteen years, a Soviet spy who had betrayed his country?

But the pumpkin papers also revealed that Chambers had been a spy himself, and unlike Hiss, he was clearly guilty, because he had the top-secret material in his possession. The only "proof" that Hiss was involved was Chambers' word that Hiss had given the documents to him—and Chambers was by now a self-confessed perjurer.

An intense struggle now began between the Justice Department, the FBI, and HUAC for control of the pumpkin papers and thus of the case. HUAC had the great advantage of physical possession; Justice had the great advantage that only it could decide who to prosecute, and for what. It was a classic struggle between the executive branch and the Congress over the immediate issue of first claim on evidence and the far more significant long-term issue over control of security procedures and national policy itself.

Justice moved fast. Alex Campbell indicated to the FBI that the department was contemplating indicting Chambers, but not Hiss. Nixon had to move fast, because a Chambers indictment by itself, not to mention the probable conviction, would undercut Chambers' credibility—and he was the sole witness against Hiss. Hiss would walk away, Chambers would go to prison, and Nixon's political career would be over. To prevent such catastrophies, Nixon undertook to mobilize public opinion.

NIXON GOT to Washington late on December 5. The following day he called a press conference in the HUAC offices, where he and Stripling gave the press its first glimpse of the microfilmed documents. (The press reciprocated with a photograph that became world famous, showing Nixon and Stripling examining the film with a magnifying glass—with which, incidentally, it is impossible to read microfilm.) While waiting for the conference to begin, a photographer casually asked Stripling, "What's the emulsion figure on these films?" He explained that the numbers would show the year of manufacture. Stripling called an Eastman Kodak official who after a check told him that the film had been manufactured in 1945. Chambers claimed he had made the copies in 1938, after his break with the CP; now it appeared that he had manufactured the evidence after the war.

"The news jolted us into almost complete shock," Nixon wrote in *Six Crises*. "This meant that Chambers was, after all, a liar." According to Nixon, he, Stripling, and the staff "sat looking at each other without saying a word." According to Stripling, Nixon lost his composure and began exclaiming, "Oh, my God, this is the end of my political career." He demanded that Stripling and the staff "do something," and cursed them in "abusive" language. He wanted to call off the press conference, but Stripling insisted that he would have to go through with it. "Tell them we were sold a bill of goods . . . that we were all wet."

Nixon called Chambers. "Am I correct in understanding that these papers were put on microfilm in 1938?" Chambers said they were. Nixon informed him that Eastman Kodak had not made the film until 1945. "What is your answer to that?"

After a long pause, Chambers said, "I can't understand it. God must be against me."

Nixon snarled into the phone, "You'd better have a better answer than that. The subcommittee's coming to New York tonight and we want to see you at the Commodore Hotel at 9:00 and you'd better be there!"

Hanging up, Nixon prepared to face the music with the press. Minutes before the scheduled beginning, however, Eastman Kodak called back. There had been a mistake—the film had been manufactured in 1937. Stripling let out a Rebel yell and leaped on Nixon's couch, then began waltzing Nixon around the room. When things quieted down, Nixon said sadly, "Poor Chambers. Nobody ever believes him at first." (No one present thought to call Chambers with the good news, who made an unsuccessful attempt to kill himself.[58])

The press conference was a roaring success, with appropriate headlines and front-page photographs. That afternoon, Nixon and Mundt took the train to New York, where they arrived at 7:30 P.M. Justice Department officials met them at the station and accompanied them to the Commodore, arguing the whole way. It was a power play by the Truman Administration, direct, unequivocating, unashamed. The officials demanded that Nixon give them the microfilm, call off his investigation of the case altogether, and leave it to the Justice Department.

As far as Nixon was concerned, that would be turning the case over to the very people who were ultimately guilty, who were also his political enemies, and who had every reason and opportunity to cover up. He engaged in what he called a "violent verbal battle" with the Justice representatives, flatly refusing to give them anything and insisting on proceeding with the hearing.[59]

At the hearing, which lasted from 9 P.M. to midnight, Chambers explained his bizarre behavior. Some of the documents had been copied by Priscilla Hiss on her typewriter, he said, while others had been microfilmed by a Communist photographer in Baltimore. In either case, Hiss would return the originals to his desk in the State Department the following morning, while Chambers would give the copies to a Soviet intelligence agent. After deciding to leave the CP, but before doing so, Chambers made copies of the copies as a life preserver—these became the pumpkin papers. If the CP threatened him, he could threaten blackmail in return.

On December 7 and 8, in Washington, HUAC held public sessions designed to keep the pressure on Justice. Former State Department officials testified that the documents were indeed valuable and that just their removal from the office was a serious breach of security. Some were still too hot to reveal.[60]

After the December 8 hearing, Nixon told FBI agents, as they reported it to Hoover, that he was "extremely mad at the Attorney General and at Alex Campbell for not having more vigorously prosecuted this whole matter, but . . . [he] had nothing but praise for the Director and the Bureau."

Hoover was unimpressed. "This fellow Nixon blows hot & cold," he scribbled on the memo.[61] Nixon had more success with Justice, where he had a number of lower-level informants who continually leaked to him inside information about the Attorney General's plans. Thus on the morning of December 8, Nixon learned that Justice still intended to indict Chambers before a New York grand jury, for lying when he had denied under oath any knowledge of espionage. Nixon counterattacked that evening at the hearing (which was well attended by reporters). He charged that in planning to indict Chambers instead of Hiss, "the Administration is trying to silence this Committee."[62]

THAT WAS clearly true, and the top man in the Administration, the President himself, participated in the effort. It was the first in a long series of head-on clashes Harry Truman would have with Richard Nixon. At his weekly press conference on December 9, Truman characterized the HUAC investigation as a "red herring," and plainly implied that his victory at the polls showed that the American people agreed with him. He promised that the Justice Department would find and prosecute the guilty, and assailed HUAC as "headline hunters not interested in prosecutions." [63]

Both Truman and Nixon were extremely partisan, and both were high risk takers. This confrontation was a gamble on public opinion, and Nixon won. Expressing overwhelming sentiment, the Washington *Post*, usually friendly to Truman, said: "The President's attitude suggests a desire to suppress the whole business and the indictment of Mr. Chambers at this time would certainly be a step in that direction. If this is the Administration's policy, it is incredibly shortsighted." [64]

Hoover, acting on his own, had meanwhile ordered an intensive search for Priscilla Hiss's typewriter, and on December 13 his agents found it. Nixon, meanwhile, had made the pumpkin papers available to the FBI, but only after Justice Department officials threatened him with a contempt citation. [65] Samples from Priscilla's old letters and from the pumpkin papers matched exactly, and now the FBI had the machine that had typed them, and it was hers.

That was the piece of evidence that the grand jury found conclusive. When Hiss was confronted with it during the proceedings, he reportedly said, "Until the day I die, I shall wonder how Whittaker Chambers got into my house to use my typewriter." A ripple of laughter ran through the jury room. [66] That afternoon, December 15, the last day of its existence, the grand jury voted 19 to 0 to indict Hiss on two counts of perjury: that he lied when he said he had not stolen State Department documents and given them to Chambers, and that he lied when he said he had not seen Chambers after 1935. He could not be indicted for espionage, because the three-year statute of limitations had long since run out.

So Nixon won the first round. In the process, he learned some unsavory lessons, not only about the extent of Communist infiltration into the government and about spy rings, but also about what lengths the Administration was willing to go to in order to prevent embarrassment. He was introduced to that intricate game that is Washington politics, in which the only thing that counts is success, and where anything goes. The case was filled with leaks, lies, deceptions, the deliberate use of the Justice Department for partisan political purposes, the manipulation of the press and public opinion, and brazen attempts at cover-up.

Nixon also learned about personal crisis management. He analyzed his own actions and reactions carefully, all within the context of his discovery that he thrived on crisis, actually enjoyed it, and did his best when he was under pressure. He also learned to be alert in the postcrisis stage, because he tended to let down at that time. What he did not learn—or at least never mentioned in his extensive writings on the Hiss case and the subject of crises—was that there came a point when the tension was unbearable, and at that point he would lash out in an uncontrollable fit of temper. He did it with Stripling at least twice, and he would do it again at some stage in every future crisis of his life.

But overall, the Hiss case had been quite an educational experience, and Nixon was a quick learner. It also made him into a world figure with an unlimited future.

CHAPTER ELEVEN

THE SECOND CAMPAIGN
1949–1950

BY THE BEGINNING of 1949 the bulk of the American public had been convinced that Alger Hiss was a Communist spy guilty of perjury, espionage, and treason. Richard Nixon was the man who exposed him, and if not for Nixon, it was unlikely that he ever would have been exposed. This fact meant that Nixon now had a national political base that was the envy of every other congressman in the country.

Still, he had problems, chief of which was that the Republicans were now in the minority, and even though Hiss's indictment guaranteed HUAC a new lease on life, Nixon was a minority member and would not head any subcommittees. The prospect before him was so bleak, in fact, that he wrote Herman Perry on January 3, 1949, that he hoped he would not remain on HUAC, even though Joe Martin had asked him to stay.[1]

In any event, he did remain on HUAC, where he was something of a moderating influence. For example, he turned back a Republican attempt to prove that FDR's closest adviser, Harry Hopkins, had been responsible for shipping uranium to the Soviet Union under the guise of Lend-Lease,[2] and he steered HUAC away from a proposed investigation of Communist influence on school textbooks.[3]

Throughout the 1949 session of the Eighty-first Congress, Nixon worked hard for his supporters in the 12th District, where agriculture remained the largest industry and fortunes were riding on federal water projects. Nixon managed to get $500,000 for dams for the district.[4] In the House, he led the fight against weakening

Taft-Hartley, in the process engaging in a spirited debate on the floor with John Kennedy and Vito Marcantonio over labor policy.[5]

THIS WAS ALL pretty small stuff for a man with a national reputation. Nixon needed a larger stage, and he wanted to garner the rewards for his role in the Hiss case before the public forgot about him. The most natural step would be up to the Senate. Luck was with him, because California's Democratic senator, Sheridan Downey, was up for re-election in 1950. Even luckier, Downey was in ill health and there were persistent rumors that he did not intend to run again. It was a perfect opportunity for Nixon to reap the maximum benefit out of his sudden fame.

On June 5, 1949, Nixon had a long conference with Bill Knowland, California's Republican senator. Knowland's support would be critical, partly because he was who he was, partly because Governor Earl Warren, the nominal head of the Republican Party in California, was up for re-election in 1950, and he was notorious for running his own campaigns on a nonpartisan basis, never endorsing any other Republican, much less campaigning for him. Nixon asked Knowland—whose father published the Oakland *Tribune*—for an immediate endorsement for the Senate, but Knowland would go no further than indicating that he was favorable to a Nixon candidacy. On June 8, Nixon wrote Pat Hillings, a lawyer and friend from Arcadia, that Knowland would support him if he could be convinced that Nixon had "the best chance to win."[6]

To convince Knowland, in the summer of 1949 Nixon undertook a tour of the state, not to make public speeches, but to line up heavyweight support. He began with his old backers from the Committee of 100. In mid-July, he talked privately to Bewley and Day in Bewley's Whittier office, Day recalled, prior to a gathering of the committee, Nixon saying "he'd decided that he wanted to run, and he wanted us to push for it when we went into that meeting." At the gathering Nixon told Frank Jorgensen, "It is admittedly a long shot, [but] it presents such an unusual opportunity that the risk is worth taking," and argued that staying in the House as part of a "vocal but ineffective minority" would do no one any good.[7] But Herman Perry said he was unalterably opposed. "You're going to crucify this young man if you send him out and run him," he warned.[8] Others urged Nixon to stay in the House, gain some seniority, get to be chairman of an important committee, represent the 12th District and see to its needs. "You've got a good, safe district," Jorgensen said.[9]

That prospect must have seemed unbearably dull to Nixon, who was thinking in much bigger terms. Day expressed his feelings well when he turned to Perry and said, "When your star is up, that's when you have to move." When Perry protested that Nixon could not win, Day retorted, "He could whip Abraham Lincoln, if necessary, in the senator fight." Perry and the others were unconvinced, but agreed to go along.[10]

Nixon then toured the state, seeking support. Herbert Hoover encouraged him, as did a group of bankers in San Francisco. Publisher Norman Chandler and political reporter Kyle Palmer promised the enthusiastic support of the Los Angeles *Times*. Chandler also helped convince the editors of the two largest northern California Republican dailies, the San Francisco *Chronicle* and the Oakland *Tribune*, to get behind Nixon. All this helped bring Knowland into line, and he too promised an endorsement.[11]

NONE OF THIS support would do Nixon much good if Alger Hiss got off the hook. Indeed, it does not stretch things much to say that Nixon's fate rested with the jury that would decide the Hiss trial. If it convicted Hiss, Nixon's already high reputation would soar; if it found Hiss not guilty, Nixon would be vulnerable to charges of witch-hunting.

The trial had begun on May 31, 1949, and would continue through June and into July. In mid-June, Nixon had a two-hour telephone conversation with Victor Lasky, a reporter for the New York *World-Telegram* and one of his growing number of friends among Republican newsmen. The day after the call, Lasky wrote Prosecutor Thomas Murphy. He began with an apology: "He [Nixon] hopes you don't resent his interest and I assured him you [Murphy] are not that kind of guy." Then he wrote, "As you probably realize Dick has a heck of a lot at stake in the outcome. Anyway, I got a couple of things which he thought you should like to know, based on his many dealings with our boy, Alger, in the House committee."

At his trial, Hiss had made a good first impression in his direct testimony, and his list of character references would have been the envy of a saint—it included two Supreme Court justices who told the jury of their own high opinion of Hiss. Lasky told Murphy that Nixon had reminded him that Hiss made a similar good impression in his first testimony before HUAC. "Dick's sure when you begin hammering away at him, at his inconsistencies, that impression will disappear. Dick, who is a lawyer, feels strongly Alger should be kept under cross at least three days, if possible." Nixon said it was "worth boring the jury rather than let Alger get off the stand with his exterior veneer unshaken." He offered sundry other techniques for discrediting Hiss.[12]

In the jurors' minds, the case came down to the typewriter and the question of who typed the stolen documents, but only because —at least in Nixon's view—Judge Samuel Kaufman refused to allow Murphy to present two witnesses to the jury. One was Hede Massing, former wife of Gerhard Eisler and a self-confessed Soviet agent. Massing was prepared to testify that she had known Hiss as a Communist in the late thirties, but Judge Kaufman would not allow her to testify as Hiss's political associations were not at issue. The second was William Rosen, the CP agent to whom Hiss had given his old Ford automobile. Kaufman anticipated that Rosen would take the Fifth Amendment (he had said that he would) and that this would be prejudicial to Hiss.

Eight jurors voted to convict Hiss; four voted to acquit. The hung jury made Nixon furious and made him vulnerable. Without a Hiss conviction, his chances for the Senate were poor to nonexistent. Thus cornered, he reacted instinctively, attacking in all directions, hurling accusations. The judge and the jury, he protested, were prejudiced. The foreman, Hubert E. James, had been a Henry Wallace Progressive Party supporter in the 1948 campaign, which in Nixon's view was tantamount to being a Communist. Mrs. James, according to Nixon, was a member of the "left-wing group" of the League of Women Voters.

In posttrial interviews, five of the jurors supported Nixon's charge that Foreman James was predisposed to judge Hiss innocent and used his influence to that effect. Juror Helen Sweatt argued publicly that if James had not been foreman, Hiss might well have been convicted. Nixon told an FBI agent "that if proof could be obtained, reflecting that James became a juror with the preconceived idea of Hiss's innocence, that would be a violation and James should be prosecuted." [13]

Nixon lashed out at the judge. He pilloried Kaufman for alleged bias. He said the judge's "prejudice for the defense and against the prosecution was so obvious and apparent that the jury's 8 to 4 vote for conviction frankly came as a surprise to me." He dramatically demanded a House inquiry into Kaufman's fitness to serve on the federal bench, knowing full well that the Democrats in charge of the congressional committees would do no such thing. But Nixon did provoke a response out of Truman, who took the unusual step of defending Kaufman publicly. On July 14 Truman said Kaufman was "a good judge. I appointed him. [He] acted all right." [14]

Getting Harry Truman in on it suited Nixon just fine. He charged that "the entire Truman administration was extremely anxious that nothing bad happen to Mr. Hiss. Members of the administration feared that an adverse verdict would prove that there was a great deal of foundation to all the reports of Communist infiltration into the government during the New Deal days." [15]

Nixon demanded not only a new judge for the second trial (announced for the fall) but a new prosecutor as well. Most observers had given Murphy high marks for his presentation of the case, and even Nixon began by claiming "I mean no disparagement" of Murphy in suggesting that "it might be wise—considering the importance of the case—to appoint a special prosecutor to work with him. I think Mr. Murphy might welcome such assistance." [16] But Murphy neither wanted nor needed a special prosecutor, and he immediately went to work on a second trial. It was generally thought that there would be a new judge.

From mid-July to the end of January 1950, Nixon waited in suspense. His fate was in the hands of those unknown and as yet unselected jurors. There would be a new judge but the accuser and the accused would be the same. A second hung jury (not to mention the unthinkable, a verdict of innocent), and Hiss would never be brought to justice. Nixon's chances of rebounding from such a blow would be about zero.

WHILE HE WAITED, Nixon stayed at work, and out of sight. "As far as the Senate race is concerned," he wrote Pat Hillings, "I think it is just as well to let it roll along at the present time [July 1949] without saying too much about me individually." In the meantime, "a lot of quiet ground work can be done which will mean a great deal to us in the event I decide to run." If nothing else, Nixon concluded, staying quiet would keep the "left-wing boys" from attacking him. [17]

The "ground work" began with the hiring of a campaign manager. Nixon turned first to Frank Jorgensen, his chief fund raiser and a man Nixon trusted. Jorgensen was in charge of a special fund Nixon's supporters maintained to help him with his political expenses, such as mailings, plane trips back to the district, and radio spots. Jorgensen already had $10,000 available. But Jorgensen declined the job of campaign manager although he did agree to serve as ramrod and financial chairman. [18]

Jorgensen suggested Murray Chotiner, citing his success in previous Knowland and Warren campaigns. [19] Nixon knew Chotiner well from his own 1946 campaign. He knew Chotiner was tough, amoral, and ruthless, and that he would run a slashing, anything-to-win campaign. That suited Nixon's needs and mood exactly. He was betting on the conviction of Alger Hiss. It was a big bet. One can never predict the outcome of a jury trial, and Nixon's whole career was at stake. But if he won the bet, if Hiss was convicted, he would collect his all-time biggest pot, a ticket to the Senate. Providing, of course, that he kept up the momentum, even increased the size and scope of his attack. With a Hiss conviction, Nixon could focus his campaign for the Senate seat on a national level, making foreign policy the major issue and centering his attack on Truman and Acheson.

This was an America in which paranoia ran so deep that it was politically profitable to charge that Truman and Acheson, those coldest of Cold Warriors, were soft on Communism. Nixon knew they were ideal targets for a Chotiner-style campaign. But, it should be noted, Nixon was by no means the only Republican to stress anti-Communism, nor was he the most extreme. Moreover, the Democrats in the State Department had been stressing the world-wide threat of Communism from the time Truman had "scared hell out of the American people" in March 1947.

"By God, that's right!" cried Nixon and his friends. "And why haven't you done something about it?" This left the Democrats bewildered and angry. With some justice, they wondered what more they could have done to stand up to the Russians, especially in view of the funds available, funds drastically limited by the very Republicans who now charged them with something close to treason.

American politics, like all sectors of American life, was attempting to adjust to the realities of the atomic age and the Cold War. The adjustment was painful, marked by excesses on all sides. America had to learn to live in a world in which she had a permanent enemy that was capable (or soon would be) of destroying the United States. Also there was the sudden emergence of a Big Two, the superpowers—Russia and America. Neither was prepared by training or experience to undertake world leadership, but take it they must and did. The five years since the end of World War II had been marked by some of the great upheavals of all time, including Indian independence and division, the Chinese Communist victory, independence for the Philippines and Indonesia, the emergence of modern Japan, the establishment of Israel, massive movements of displaced persons within Europe, and more. Peoples, governments, politicians were confused in this confusing situation.

It is no surprise that one of the leaders of the defense of the West, Dean Acheson, could feel that he was "present at the Creation." In these earliest years of the Cold War, precedents were indeed being set, habits formed. One of the first was for the party out of power to accuse the party in power of neglecting the nation's defenses, and of being soft on Communism in general. This played nicely on the twin threats to the Republic, destruction from without through Russian atomic missiles and destruction from within through Communist infiltration into the highest ranks of our government.

Fear. Nixon knew that fear was the way to get to the public. Fear of Alger Hiss and his kind; fear of Stalin and his bombs and rockets; fear of change; fear of someone getting ahead in the arms race; fear.

Fear of Communism had failed as a partisan issue in 1948, insofar as it was tried, but just a year later it was rapidly becoming the biggest issue. Many intervening events had strengthened the position of the anti-Communists—the Hiss indictment, the atomic spy-ring case, the Red victory in China, the Russian test of an atomic bomb. People found it easier to blame these developments on spies and traitors than to begin reappraising America's position in the world. The government's response to the Russian bomb included a campaign to get every homeowner to dig his own fallout shelter, and a companion piece showing how to survive atomic attack at the workplace. In short, it was not Nixon who brought a sense of crisis to the 1950 campaign, although he surely contributed to it. Nor was it Nixon who created the widespread sense of fear, although he surely managed to profit from it.

JORGENSEN WAS a genius at putting the squeeze on his fellow businessmen. He got Nixon free office space, free printing, free layouts for advertisements, and other contributions in kind, as well as cash. He also knew how to get people involved. Even before Nixon announced, Jorgensen had Nixon-for-Senate committees organized all across the state. "In politics," he explained in a 1975 interview, "you set up committees for everything. You have a committee for beauticians, a committee for aviation, a committee for garbage collectors, a committee for masseurs. . . . Hell, I had committees from knife sharpeners down. You lose track of them, they get that long." Jorgensen also had the Italians organized, and the Jews, the Negroes, and the Chinese in San Francisco.[20]

NIXON THUS HAD a solid financial and organizational base when, on November 3, 1949, in Pomona, he announced that he was a candidate for the Republican nomination for the Senate. With the major Republican dailies already behind him, and with Knowland's support, he anticipated an easy victory in the primary, assuming a Hiss conviction, so he directed his appeal to conservative Democrats rather than hard-core Republicans.

He began by praising the Democratic Party for its record of distinguished service to the nation. "But today," he continued, the party "has been captured and is completely controlled by a group of ruthless, cynical seekers after power—committed to policies and principles completely foreign to those of its founders." According to Nixon, if Thomas Jefferson and Andrew Jackson could see "the phony doctrines and ideologies now being foisted upon the American people they would turn over in their graves. . . . Call it planned economy, the Fair Deal, or social welfare—but it is still the same old Socialist baloney, any way you slice it."

The choice, he said, was "between freedom and state socialism." He insisted that he was "well aware of the Communist threat" (not that anyone had ever accused him of being indifferent to it), but charged that there was an "even greater threat to our free institutions." That threat came from "a group of hypocritical and cynical men who, under the guise of providing political panaceas for certain social and economic problems, are selling the American birthright for a mess of political pottage."

This would be an all-out, no-holds-barred campaign. Nixon made that explicit. "There is only one way we can win," he concluded. "We must put on a fighting, rocking, socking campaign and carry that campaign directly into every county, city, town, precinct, and home in the state of California." [21]

The second Hiss trial opened two weeks after Nixon's announcement, before a new judge, Henry W. Goddard, who is described by Allen Weinstein as "a crisp, tough jurist." Goddard allowed more witnesses, including Hede Massing and William Rosen. Massing said she had met Hiss at a Communist gathering in 1935. Rosen took the Fifth Amendment.

Hiss, who evidently blamed his lawyer for his failure to win acquittal in the first trial, had a new lawyer, Claude Cross, and a new defense, which was that Chambers was insane. Nixon, who had everything riding on the jury's responses to that charge, knew how crazy Chambers often appeared to be, and must have been in an agony as he read accounts of this or that day's proceedings. Cross had Dr. Carl Binger on the stand as an expert witness. Binger said he was a psychiatrist, that he had studied Chambers during both trials, that he had read Chambers' translations of German novels, and that he was prepared to present a diagnosis; to wit, "Mr. Chambers is suffering from a condition known as psychopathic personality, which is a disorder of character, of which the outstanding features are behavior of what we call an amoral or an asocial and delinquent nature." Symptoms included "persistent and repetitive lying . . . stealing . . . acts of deception and misrepresentation ... vagabondage; panhandling; inability to form stable attachments, and a tendency to make false accusations."

Dr. Binger then attempted to connect Chambers with these symptoms. That was successfully done when Cross was doing the questioning, but when Murphy got his chance at the doctor, he demolished the man. Binger's credentials were suspect; "psychopathic personality" was a vague term but clearly did not mean "insane"; Binger had no basis for his statements that Chambers was "unstable," and so forth.

That Chambers had held his job at *Time* for ten years "could or could not be consistent with psychopathic personality," Dr. Binger declared. Well then, Murphy asked, what about the fact that he was married for nineteen years to the same woman and raised two children, "would you say that there perhaps was some evidence of a stability of attachment?"

Binger replied, "It could be. It depends on the nature and character of the attachment." [22]

Why Hiss allowed such a man to be the bulwark of his defense is another of the infinite number of enduring mysteries of the case.

On January 21, 1950, after less than twenty-four hours of deliberation, the forewoman in the second Hiss trial declared, "We find the defendant guilty."

Nixon was exultant. At a press conference, he struck once again his basic theme: "This conspiracy would have come to light long since had there not been a definite ... effort on the part of certain high officials in two Administrations to keep the public from knowing the facts." He received hundreds of messages of congratulations; the one he cherished most came from former President Herbert Hoover. "The conviction of Alger Hiss was due to your patience and persistence alone," Hoover said, thus ignoring Stripling, Andrews, and Murphy and the FBI, not to mention Chambers himself. "At last the stream of treason that existed in our government has been exposed in a fashion that all may believe." [23]

DEAN ACHESON, in his 1949 Senate confirmation hearing for Secretary of State, had declared, "I should like the committee to understand my friendship was not easily given or easily withdrawn. Alger Hiss had been an officer in the State Department most of the time I served there. We became friends and remained friends." At a press conference following Hiss's conviction, Secretary of State Acheson told the press, "Whatever the outcome of any appeal which Mr. Hiss or his lawyers may take in this case I do not intend to turn my back on Alger Hiss." [24]

Acheson's gratuitous and inexplicable pledge of continued

friendship with a convicted perjurer was a gift to Nixon of incalculable value. It pitted the two-term member of the House in head-to-head combat with the Secretary of State on an issue that was a certain winner for Nixon. Best of all, the Secretary himself was widely hated, in some part because of his policies, but rather more because he was so easy to hate. His phony British accent, his striped pants, his condescending attitude toward American congressmen, his supercilious manner, that silly bowler hat, all put people off. So did his role as the messenger with the bad news (that America could not have her way in the world, that we are not all-powerful, but that we are doing our damned-well best to hold the line, that containment is working in Europe but would not have worked in China). For Nixon then, giving him Acheson for an opponent was like throwing Brother Rabbit into the brier patch.

Nixon's first comment on Acheson's 1949 statement was to call it "disgusting." He said the Secretary suffered from "color blindness—a form of pink eye toward the Communist threat in the United States."

Nixon also went after the President. On the day Hiss was convicted, Nixon told the press, ominously, "I believe President Truman will have further reason to regret his red herring remark."[25] Five days later, he made an hour-and-a-half speech to the House. It was a self-congratulatory summary of his role in the Hiss case, coupled with a call for action.

His basic point was the size and scope of the spy ring Hiss and Chambers worked within, and to warn that "this Nation cannot afford another Hiss case." Nixon asserted that the conspiracy "was so effective, so well-entrenched and so well-defended by apologists in high places that it was not discovered and apprehended until it was too late to prosecute those who were involved in it."

After listing the various Justice Department attempts at cover-up, Nixon provided an analysis of the Truman Administration's motivations. "There are some who claim," he said, that Administration officials "failed to act because they were Communist or pro-Communist." He rejected that interpretation. "The reason for their failure to act was not that they were disloyal, but this in my opinion makes that failure even more inexcusable."

The Democrats did not act, Nixon said, because Truman insisted on treating the case on a "politics as usual" basis (the phrase was Truman's; he had used it in a press conference to castigate Republicans for their partisan use of the case). Nixon explained that "it is customary practice for any Administration . . . to resist the disclosure of facts which might be embarrassing to that Administration. . . . This is a statement of fact though, of course, I do not mean to justify that practice, regardless of the nature of the skeleton in the political closet." But in treating the Hiss case as "an ordinary petty scandal," Truman "rendered the greatest possible disservice to the people of the Nation."

Then came the recommendations. The first was to support the FBI. Although he had been privately critical of J. Edgar Hoover and the Bureau, with good cause, neither Nixon nor any other member of the House was ready to take on the FBI, so when Nixon called the Bureau "the finest police organization which exists in a free Nation today," the House gave a sustained round of applause, the only time it interrupted him throughout the speech.

Second, Nixon wanted to extend the statute of limitations on espionage cases from three to ten years. Third, he asked the House to give its "wholehearted support" to HUAC. He realized that it was unpopular, he said, but he insisted that it was necessary and explained that he had made a personal sacrifice in accepting membership on HUAC, "probably the most unpleasant and thankless assignment in the Congress." That was a rather breathtaking assertion from a man whose power, publicity, and prospects had just increased immeasurably through his membership on HUAC, but Nixon insisted that it was true.

Nixon's fourth recommendation was to "completely overhaul our system of checking the loyalty of Federal employees." Finally, he wanted an extensive educational program about Communism.[26]

The speech added greatly to his luster, not least because he sent copies of it to every major newspaper editor in the country, and scores of them reprinted it.[27] As the first detailed account of the case to appear, it was widely read and made a strong and favorable impact. It was a highly effective campaign document.

To HEAR NIXON tell it, however, one would have thought that the Hiss case was a liability to him. In the years that followed, he blamed the large number and intense emotion of his political enemies on the reaction to the case. In part this was simple political expediency—it obviously helped Nixon to claim, as he usually implied, that behind his enemies and critics there stood the CP. But mainly it was a consequence of his "Poor Richard" self-pity. "There are many reasons for the political animosity against me," Nixon admitted to one of his first biographers, Bela Kornitzer, before asserting the opposite, that it was a consequence of the Hiss case. "No one can consistently take strong positions in public life on the issue of Communism, and particularly subversion at home, without expecting to pay the penalty for the rest of his life."[28]

The Communists had made him their number-one target, he

told newspaper publisher Ralph Turner in January 1949, and through their smears had made his "sincerity, patriotism, honesty and even veracity the subject of vicious attacks." He also claimed that only his sense of duty, not any personal profit, kept him at the task of exposing Communists. And he continued to make wide, sweeping generalizations about the extent of Red influence in Washington, based solely on the conviction of one spy.

"The easiest course I could follow," he declared, "would be to get off the committee," which would save him from "vitriolic abuse" and free him to work in other fields where he could enhance his reputation "at less cost to my time and health." He did not say what those other fields might be. He did charge that "there is a wealth of evidence pointing to the continued existence of Communist espionage activity in government today," but gave no particulars, except to say that the Truman Administration opposed the exposure of Hiss and "opposes with even greater vigor the exposure of similar espionage activity of more recent, if not current vintage." [29] Nixon did not call Truman a traitor, but Truman might well have wondered what else to call a President who not just knowingly, but actually vigorously protected Soviet spies. Nixon never said Truman was a Communist, but what other motive could possibly impel the President to shield Communist agents?

AFTER DELIVERING his speech to the House on the Hiss case, Nixon returned to California and began touring the state in a station wagon, with Pat in the backseat and an aide to drive, as he put his campaign for the Senate into high gear. An advance man proceeded him into the towns and cities, arranging a breakfast meeting with the local businessmen, a lunch with this or that women's organization, an interview with the newspaper editor and another for the radio station, and gathering a crowd for a street-corner speech over the station wagon's loudspeaker. Thanks to the Hiss case Nixon had no problems with name recognition, and could concentrate on blasting the Democrats for abandoning the traditions of their party.[30]

Nixon had cross-filed (as had the Democratic candidates), which technically made him a candidate for the Democratic as well as the Republican nomination, and therefore gave him an excuse to pitch his primary campaign to the Democrats. In addition, his Republican opposition was so inconsequential that he could afford to ignore it. Thus the most conspicuous feature of his primary campaign was a handbill sent to all registered Democrats and captioned "As One Democrat to Another." It concentrated on the Hiss case and in no way identified Nixon as a Republican, which led the Democrats to cry foul. The Los Angeles *Daily News* wondered what had happened to Nixon's well-known "antipathy to perjury. . . . It is surprising that a man who poses as the soul of truth and honor would permit such a deceitful device to be used."[31]

Democrats-for-Nixon committees sprang up all across the state. Many of these were phony, organized by Jorgensen and controlled by Chotiner, but some reflected a widespread impatience with Truman among conservative Democrats in California. A number of prominent Democrats defected, including George Creel, who in 1917 had served Woodrow Wilson as head of the Administration's wartime propaganda agency. Adela Rogers St. Johns was a Democrat for Nixon, as was Ruth Turner, former president of the San Francisco League of Women Voters.

Whenever a prominent Democrat announced his support for Nixon, he always cited as his reason the worldwide Communist conspiracy, and the need to bring the Democratic Party back to the principles of its founders.[32]

IN THE MAINSTREAM Democratic primary, to Nixon's delight and benefit, the candidates were cutting each other up. Senator Downey, the incumbent, was being challenged by Congresswoman Helen Gahagan Douglas, a former opera and Broadway star and the wife of movie actor Melvyn Douglas. An active New Dealer, she was first elected to the House in 1944, after attracting the attention of California liberals in speeches at labor rallies. Although generally regarded as a left-winger, she had spurned Henry Wallace's Progressive Party in the 1948 election, which was a litmus test for fellow travelers. On domestic issues she was a New Deal Democrat. But on foreign affairs her record was mixed. Although she had been critical of the Soviet Union and the Chinese Communists, she had voted against the Truman Doctrine program of aid for Greece and Turkey on the grounds that the effort should have been linked to the United Nations. She had also voted against HUAC appropriations, and had been one of its severe critics. One of her supporters was Ronald Reagan, a leader in the Screen Actors Guild and a registered Democrat.[33]

Douglas ran an aggressive campaign of her own. She accused Downey of having a do-nothing record in Congress and of being a tool of big business. She claimed the California oilmen had Downey in their pocket. After about a month of this, Downey quit. He said he was physically not up to "waging a personal and militant campaign against the vicious and unethical propaganda" Douglas was using against him. Douglas reminded voters that the "illness gimmick" was not new to politicians facing defeat.[34]

Manchester Boddy, publisher of the Los Angeles *Daily News*, replaced Downey as Douglas' chief rival. He pitched right into the name-calling, charging that Douglas and her supporters constituted a "statewide conspiracy on the part of a small subversive clique of red-hots to capture, through stealth and cunning, the nerve centers of our Democratic Party."[35] Downey added to the fire. He said that "Mrs. Douglas does not have the fundamental ability and qualifications for a United States Senator. . . . She gave comfort to the Soviet tyranny by voting against aid to both Greece and Turkey." He also had linked her to Marcantonio, saying that like him she had voted to eliminate HUAC.[36] Douglas' "consistent policy of voting along with the notorious radical, Vito Marcantonio," then became a major feature of the Boddy campaign.*[37]

Had he been in complete charge of the Democratic campaign, Nixon could not have written so helpful a script. Everything that he said about the Democrats, they said about each other, in more extreme form. And he learned from them that Marcantonio made a perfect foil. According to reporter Earl Mazo, in one of those stories that is probably too good to be true, when Marcantonio read about Boddy's use of his name in his campaign against Douglas, a woman he intensely disliked and usually referred to as "bitch," he went to a friend of Nixon's and said, chuckling, "Tell Nicky to get on this thing because it is a good idea."[38] Boys will be boys. Poor Marcantonio seldom got to participate in feelings of comradery, he was almost always way out there by himself, but when it came to women politicians, Vito was right in there with the rest of the boys, even Richard Nixon, protecting the turf.

Douglas was not only a woman in a man's game, but she was a movie star as well, who ran around with Hollywood's "parlor pinks" and was a dedicated and ambitious New Dealer. She was what most of the boys, including even the New Dealers, called a "bleeding-heart liberal," a "do-gooder." Very rich herself, she had made housing for lower-income families her cause, which naturally threw her up against the realtors and developers. Her opposition to the Greek aid bill made serious people question her judgment; her opposition to HUAC made others wonder if she was a Communist.

Her presence caused resentment in the world of male politicians; her policies caused rage among conservatives. One of the boys who did not like having Helen around was Jack Kennedy,

---

* Linking Marcantonio and Douglas on the basis of their anti-HUAC votes, and implying that something sinister was going on, ignored the fact that many politicians had publicly called for HUAC's demise, including the President himself.

who came into Nixon's office one afternoon. "Dick," he said, "I know you're in for a pretty rough campaign, and my father wanted to help out." He handed Nixon an envelope with a $1,000 campaign contribution. "I obviously can't endorse you," Kennedy explained, "but it isn't going to break my heart if you can turn the Senate's loss into Hollywood's gain."[39] Of course, Joe Kennedy also helped out with Joe McCarthy's finances.

During the primary, Nixon was sorely tempted to get in a lick or two himself about Douglas' voting record, but Chotiner convinced him to hold his ammunition. "Quite frankly," Chotiner later admitted, "we wanted her to be the Democratic nominee on the basis that it would be easier to defeat her than a conservative Democrat. So nothing was ever said pertaining to Helen Gahagan Douglas in the primaray."[40]

Instead, Nixon continued to concentrate on general attacks against the left wing of the Democratic Party. Chotiner explained the reasoning in a manual he sent to every campaign worker: "We must appeal to Democrats to help win the election. Therefore, do not make a blanket attack on Democrats. Refer to the opposition as a supporter of the socialistic program running on the Democratic ticket."[41]

Thus in a Lincoln Day speech, Nixon told his audience that "today the issue is still slavery. . . . The Soviet Union is an example of the slave state in its ultimate development; Great Britain is halfway down the same road; powerful interests are striving to impose the British socialist system upon the people of the United States."[42]

That was quite a charge—secret forces at work driving us toward slavery—but it was not that speech that made the headlines. It was another speech, on the same topic, by Joe McCarthy in Wheeling, West Virginia, that did. He garnered the headlines because McCarthy was explicit—there were Communists in the State Department, they had been responsible for the loss of China, and he had their names. Nixon had painted a fearful picture of insidious, unnamed forces at work, but he had made no direct accusations.

Nixon, as noted, kept some distance between himself and McCarthy, but like McCarthy, he defined the central issue of the campaign as the threat of internal Communism.

In the mythology of American politics, no one had even heard of anti-Communism before McCarthy's Wheeling speech. In fact, his initial success shows only how much of a factor luck is in politics. Nothing he said at Wheeling was new. He did not say it particularly well. His gimmick about a "list" was imaginative but of no substance. What McCarthy had was luck. His timing was as perfect as it was accidental. America was ready for McCarthyism, and if he hadn't given his talk at Wheeling, someone else would have stepped into the role, so great was the demand that someone play it. McCarthy no more invented anti-Communism than Nixon did.

Douglas claimed that she was a more effective anti-Communist than Nixon, and there were a number of significant purely domestic economic issues that divided the candidates. But Nixon managed to convince most voters to make their decision on the basis of the question, Is Communism a threat? Douglas said specifically and emphatically that it was not. Nixon said it was.

And that was by far the most important factor in his ultimate victory. In the minds of many voters, events had proved Nixon right on the central question. In the fall of 1949, Mao and the Red Chinese had conquered the whole of mainland China, a loss that McCarthy said had been caused by traitors at the China desk of the State Department. In September 1949, Truman announced that the Russians had exploded an atomic bomb, an accomplishment made possible, according to McCarthy and his supporters, by spies in the Manhattan Project. In January 1950, Alger Hiss had been convicted of perjury, and less than a month later Klaus Fuchs had confessed that he passed top-secret atomic information to the Russians from 1943 to 1947. In 1950 nine Americans had been arrested in connection with the atomic spy ring, including Harry Gold, David Greenglass, and Ethel and Julius Rosenberg. Put it all together, said McCarthy, and what you have is conspiracy aiming to destroy the American Republic from within.

Things were obviously not so simple as the Republicans painted them. That there was an atomic spy ring is unquestionable; that it explained the Russian success is uncertain. In a sense, the only real "secret" was that the theory was correct and an atomic bomb did work, which was a "secret" the United States gave away at Hiroshima. That there were China hands who preferred Mao to Chiang is also unquestionable; that they were traitors is altogether another matter. But these complexities were lost on many voters, who concluded that Nixon was correct in his assessment of the danger of internal Communism.

McCarthy's charges were so extreme, his inability to back them up so obvious, that he made Nixon look like a scholar and statesman in comparison. At the same time, McCarthy's domination of the headlines with his Communists-in-government charges kept the issue alive without Nixon having to raise a finger.

Nixon's initial public response to McCarthy was negative. In a press conference on April 15, 1950, he said that only the CP was profiting from McCarthy's charges.[43] He called for an independent investigation by a blue-ribbon citizens' panel, but he did not endorse the charges.[44] And in May, when J. Robert Oppenheimer, the chief scientist on the Manhattan Project, was accused of being a Communist before the California Senate's version of HUAC, Nixon flatly declared: "I have complete confidence in Dr. Oppenheimer's loyalty."[45]

IN THE PRIMARY campaign, while Douglas and Boddy hammered each other, Nixon was able to concentrate on building his base for the general election. First, simply by reaching voters. He made more than six hundred speeches in the primary.[46] Second, by identifying himself closely with the China Lobby in support of Chiang Kai-Shek and his Nationalist Party in its stronghold on Formosa, Nixon blamed the loss of China on the Truman Administration. He never specifically charged the State Department with treason, but he did say that it was incredibly inept.

The China Lobby was a loosely defined, never well-organized political movement inside the Republican Party that managed to take in most of the prewar isolationists and members of the Old Guard. Its special concern was Nationalist China, which it charged had been sold out by the Democrats, but which could yet return to the mainland if only America would follow new policies. In its basic analysis of America's national security interests, the China Lobby wanted to concentrate American resources on Asia. It accused the Truman Administration of following a Europe-first policy, which was true, while it ignored Asia, which was less true. "While engaging in a cold war against the spread of Communism in some parts of the world," Nixon told a San Francisco audience, "we have adopted a policy of virtual isolationism elsewhere. Communism requires a worldwide resistance."[47]

Put another way, why didn't Truman stand up to the Communists in China the way he did to the Communists in Greece?

Third, Nixon went after the labor vote. He called for a conference of labor and management to work out differences on Taft-Hartley, and declared that "management should give labor a stake in business and industry, through profit sharing plans and similar devices." He got the endorsement of Dave Beck of the Teamsters Union, and the votes of large numbers of rank-and-filers.[48]

Fourth, he secured his financial base. Much of this was due to Jorgensen, who was almost as energetic as Nixon himself, but some of it was due to the stand Nixon took on that most basic of all California issues, water. As noted, he had already delivered dams to his district. He got deeply involved in the rights of California versus Arizona for Colorado River water, and accused Truman of discrimination against California.[49]

Truman, supported by Douglas, was attempting to limit farmers in California to 160 acres of land that could be irrigated with federally controlled water. Nixon was dead opposed, as were all the larger ranchers and farmers. Given the contrasting stands of Douglas and Nixon on the issue, the big operators naturally put their money into the Nixon campaign. Ray Arbuthnot, a rancher in Riverside County with a thousand acres of orange groves, was one of the heaviest contributors. The same was true of the oil money— as Douglas had voted for federal control of the tidelands oil, and Nixon against, California oilmen naturally supported him (in the primary, they split their bet, putting half their money behind Boddy, half behind Nixon.)[50]

Fifth, Nixon solidified and extended his support from small-business men. He spoke in virtually every small town in the state, and always made it a point to demand tax incentives for small business and venture capital—and, of course, to defend the basic provisions of Taft-Hartley.[51]

In the June 7 primary, Nixon polled a total of 1,000,000 votes. Douglas got 890,000; and Boddy, 535,000. Lesser candidates received some 200,000 votes. Nixon got 22 percent of the Democratic primary votes; Douglas got 13 percent of the Republican votes.

Less than three weeks later, Nixon's campaign got a tremendous boost when the Communist North Koreans attacked South Korea. He and the other China Lobby people had been warning that such an event was coming because of the Truman-Acheson policy of Europe first. Appeasement in Asia, Nixon charged, led to war. Like most other Republicans, Nixon praised Truman for his quick and vigorous response to the Communist challenge in Korea, then in the same breath criticized him for not doing enough beforehand to deter the enemy. Nixon and the others were especially critical of Acheson, because earlier that year he had reportedly declared that Korea and Formosa were outside the American defensive perimeter in Asia and thus—according to the Republicans —had practically invited an attack. Nor was Nixon satisfied with Truman's partial mobilization for the Korean War—he demanded a total mobilization to meet the worldwide threat.

The Korean War made Nixon an almost certain winner. It made him look like a prophet, and made his appeal to fear irresistible. At the end of spring 1950, anti-Communism, which had been growing at a steady rate ever since the end of World War II, came into its own. It had not happened suddenly, not was it inevitable, but when it came, it did so with a vengeance, and it stayed onstage far longer than most political issues. The air was poisoned with anti-

Communist talk and hate literature. The picture most Americans had by the end of June 1950 was of a Soviet Union led by a madman worse than Hitler and just as bent on world conquest, who had fifth columns all around the world striving to topple free governments, and who was being helped even in the United States by unwitting dupes and outright traitors. Since the people felt these fears so strongly, obviously politicians used it to help themselves.

Even Helen Douglas herself succumbed to the temptation to do a bit of guilt-by-association campaigning. In her first broadside in the general campaign, in what her campaign manager, Harold Tipton, later confessed had been a deliberate attempt to goad Nixon into an overresponse, Douglas charged that Nixon had "voted with Representative Marcantonio against aid to Korea," and that he had also voted with Marcantonio to cut European aid in half.

"They fell for it," Tipton declared proudly during the campaign, referring to his scheme to goad the Nixon camp into rebuttal. But Tipton should have been chagrined, because his research was sloppy and the Nixon response highly effective. Nixon replied indignantly that he had voted against an aid to Korea bill on the grounds that it did not include aid to Formosa, that events had shown that he was right, and that he did vote for the amended bill that included Formosa. As to European aid, Nixon's record as a champion of the Marshall Plan was so well known that the charge sounded and read as false as it was. In fact, Nixon had not voted to cut the aid in half, but for a one-year rather than a two-year bill, with a renewal provision.

Still Douglas persisted, making such silly charges as: "On every key vote Nixon stood with party-liner Marcantonio against America in its fight to defeat Communism." [52] As a grateful Chotiner later put it, "She made the fatal mistake of attacking our strength instead of sticking to attacking our weaknesses." [53]

The campaign had degenerated into a name-calling contest in which, as The New York Times noted, "each side accuses the other of hitting a new low in distortion." [54] Much of the dirt was thrown in broadsides, leaflets, and advertisements, which both camps issued with abandon. Again, Douglas struck first. She issued a red-white-and-blue broadside that repeated her charges about Nixon opposing aid to Korea, then another on yellow paper that read: "THE BIG LIE. Hitler invented it. Stalin perfected it. Nixon uses it." In the yellow paper she charged that Nixon on five occasions had lined up with Marcantonio. Nixon replied with a broadside of his own using the same "BIG LIE" title to show that once again she had totally distorted his record. [55]

In his opening radio broadcast (August 30), Nixon had demanded the resignation of Dean Acheson, urged total mobilization and higher taxes, and charged that Douglas "during the six years she has been in Congress, has consistently supported the State Department's policy of appeasing communists in Asia, which finally resulted in the Korean war."[56] A week later Douglas described Nixon as a reactionary "beside whom Bob Taft is a flaming liberal."[57] She also tried to link Nixon with McCarthy, calling them both "pipsqueaks . . . who are trying to get us so frightened of communism that we'll be afraid to turn out the lights at night."[58] She told one audience, "The temporary success of the Republican Party in 1946, with its backwash of young men in dark shirts, was short lived."[59]

Catchy characterizations became one of the hallmarks of the campaign. Chotiner came up with a beauty—in an August 30 statement, the Nixon headquarters asked, "How can Helen Douglas, capable actress that she is, take up so strange a role as a foe of communism? And why does she when she has so deservedly earned the title of 'the pink lady'?" Douglas came up with a characterization of her own, one that was to plague Nixon throughout his career. She called him "Tricky Dick."[60]

There were no Nixon-Douglas debates, but the two candidates did appear on the same platform once, at the San Francisco Press Club. Douglas spoke first and, among other things, mentioned her lack of campaign funds. When Nixon's turn came, he said he sympathized deeply with her problem, which was one that he shared. However, he told the audience, grinning, he was making progress. With that, he drew a letter from his pocket and read from it: ". . . I am enclosing a small contribution to your campaign for the Senate. I only wish it could be ten times as much. Best wishes to you and Mrs. Nixon." It was signed, Nixon announced, "Eleanor Roosevelt."

Douglas—and everyone else—gasped. When the excitement simmered down a bit, Nixon continued in deadpan fashion: "I, too, was amazed with this contribution—amazed, that is, until I saw the postmark: Oyster Bay, New York." The contributor was not the former First Lady, but the widow of Theodore Roosevelt, Jr.[61]

By far the most famous broadside of the campaign was issued by Nixon headquarters in mid-September. It was the notorious "pink sheet," printed on pink paper. The first printing was fifty thousand copies, but it was so popular that within a week Chotiner had a half million printed.[62]

It was headlined "Douglas-Marcantonio Voting Record." It appeared to be a carefully researched leaflet, filled with dates, reference data, and lawyerlike analogies. It charged that on 354 occasions Douglas and Marcantonio had voted alike. It contained a pious statement: "While it should not be expected that a member of the House should always vote in opposition to Marcantonio, it is significant to note . . . the issues on which almost without exception they always saw eye-to-eye, to wit: Un-American Activities and Internal Security." Nixon, the pink sheet noted, had voted "exactly opposite to the Douglas-Marcantonio axis."[63]

The broadside used a technique Nixon was beginning to perfect. The first sentence began, "Many persons have requested a comparison of the voting records of Congresswoman Helen Douglas and the notorious Communist party-liner, Congressman Vito Marcantonio of New York." Who those "many persons" were, no one could tell. That even one person would have thought to ask the question is doubtful, had not Mrs. Douglas charged the existence of a Nixon-Marcantonio axis.

Not surprisingly, the pink sheet found that the recorded votes of Marcantonio and Douglas were remarkably alike. They had voted together against HUAC, against contempt citations of uncooperative witnesses before HUAC, against the Greek aid bill, "against refusing Foreign Relief to Soviet-dominated countries UNLESS supervised by Americans," against a bill requiring loyalty checks for federal employees, against Mundt-Nixon, against the McCarran internal security bill, against the bill confirming title to tidelands oil to California, against bills providing Congress with access to executive files in investigations, and a half-dozen other items, which left most of those 354 times Marcantonio and Douglas had voted together unaccounted for.

Now, of those 330 or so unexplained times Douglas and Marcantonio had voted together, Nixon had been with them more than 100 times. The majority of the remainder were straight party-line votes without significance. Of the seventy-six key votes, Douglas had voted sixty-six times with Marcantonio, against him ten times. There was no Douglas-Marcantonio axis, as Nixon well knew, just as he knew that his larger, implied charge was untrue.

That charge was carried by the pink sheet just below the columns that detailed the record. "After studying the voting comparison between Mrs. Douglas and Marcantonio, is it any wonder that the Communist line newspaper, the *Daily People's World*, in its lead editorial on January 31, 1950, labeled Congressman Nixon as 'The Man to Beat' in this Senate race and that the Communist newspaper, the New York *Daily Worker*, in the issue of July 1947 selected Mrs. Douglas along with Marcantonio as 'One of the Heroes of the 80th Congress.' "

Without ever having said so, Nixon had charged Helen Douglas with being a Communist. She fought back by asserting that Nixon was "throwing up a smokescreen of smears, innuendos, and half-truths to try to confuse and mislead the voters." But she was on the defensive, forced to explain herself.

The pink color was, not incidentally, a way to bring the female issue into the campaign without ever having to actually do so. Nixon occasionally joked about movie actors getting into politics, but he never overtly appealed for an antifeminist vote. Still he managed to make sure, one way or another, that all his audiences remembered that his opponent was female. One of Nixon's favorite lines was to say that Helen Douglas was "pink right down to her underwear."[64]

THERE WAS MORE to the campaign than the battle of broadsides. Nixon roared up and down the state in his station wagon, making five- or ten-minute speeches at street corners over the loudspeaker, nearly a thousand in all. He delivered his talks with a crusading intensity of manner and purpose. His basic speech followed the outline of the pink sheet; his favorite line was "My opponent is a member of a small clique which joins the notorious party-liner, Vito Marcantonio of New York, in voting time after time against measures that are for the security of this country."[65] Of her vote against HUAC, he said, "If she had had her way, the Communist conspiracy in the United States would never have been exposed, and instead of being a convicted perjurer, Alger Hiss would still be influencing the foreign policy of the United States."[66] The Los Angeles *Times* helped in all this by writing in an editorial that although Douglas was not herself a Communist, she voted the party line on numerous occasions and was "the darling of the Hollywood parlor pinks and Reds."[67]

Nixon had his own potential embarrassment. Gerald L. K. Smith and his Christian Nationalist Crusade urged California voters to "help Richard Nixon get rid of the Jew-Communists." In his own contribution to the flood of broadsides, Smith thundered: "Helen Douglas is the wife of a Jew. You Californians can do one thing very soon to further the ideals of Christian Nationalism, and that is not to send to the Senate the wife of a Jew."[68] But early in the campaign, on September 6, Nixon issued a vigorous repudiation of the support of "any individual or organization which promotes dissension among racial or religious elements." He specifically mentioned Smith and said, "I want to make it clear that I do not want his support and that I repudiate it," But he could not leave it at that statesmanlike point, and went on to indulge in his own hyperbole. "I am the one candidate who can state that I have never sought or accepted the support of either a Fascist or a Communist organization."[69]

Harry Truman badly wanted Nixon beaten. To that end, he sent into the state the biggest guns in the Democratic party. Averell Harriman, Vice-President Alben Barkley, Secretary of Labor Maurice Tobin, Attorney General Howard McGrath, Secretary of Agriculture Charles Brannan, and indeed almost the entire Truman Cabinet (except for Acheson), all toured California pleading for a Douglas victory. So did Eleanor Roosevelt. Nixon called them the "foreign legion" and denounced them as carpetbaggers. He claimed that he had no outside help at all.[70]

In fact one outsider came to California to speak on Nixon's behalf, although not at his request and not on a shared platform. He was Joe McCarthy, and he blasted away with abandon. Referring to Acheson, McCarthy said, "He must go. We cannot fight international atheistic communism with men who are either traitors or who are hip-deep in their own failures. . . . The chips are down . . . between the American people and the administration Commicrat Party of Betrayal."[71] Nixon did not repudiate McCarthy, but neither did he embrace him.

One endorsement that Nixon did want was from Earl Warren, but throughout the campaign the governor held aloof. Chotiner dreamed up a way to force Warren's hand. He sent a campaign worker to Douglas' press conference to ask, repeatedly, if she intended to vote for Warren's Democratic opponent, FDR's son James. Douglas was grateful to Warren for not entering the fray, and for some weeks she managed to avoid the question. Finally, on November 3, the Friday before the election, she replied: "I hope and pray he [James Roosevelt] will be the next governor, and he will be, if the Democrats vote the Democratic ticket."

The following day, Warren replied. "I have no intention of being coy about this situation," he said, before coyly insisting that "I have kept my campaign independent from other campaigns. Mrs. Douglas' statement does not change my position. In view of it, however, I might ask her how she expects I will vote when I mark my ballot for United States Senator next Tuesday." The Nixon camp claimed that this was an endorsement.[72]

In fact, Warren did nothing throughout the campaign for Nixon, nor should it be added did Nixon do anything for Warren. They consistently maintained a hands-off relationship. Nixon put it in the best way he could when he commented about his feelings toward Warren. "We are not unfriendly. We are two individuals going our own ways."[73]

IN HIS CONCLUDING speech in San Francisco, Nixon summed up the differences between himself and Douglas. He was for California ownership of the tidelands oil, while Douglas had voted for federal ownership. He favored Taft-Hartley, which she had opposed. He opposed farm subsidies and federal regulation of farmers, while she favored those policies. He was against "socialized medicine," which he accused her of favoring—a distortion of Truman's program, which called for national health insurance. Nixon favored voluntary health insurance provided by private companies, but insured by the federal government. Most of all, he said, Douglas wanted more government ownership and control, while he wanted to "encourage to the fullest extent possible individual opportunity."[74]

NIXON HAD HAD extraordinary good luck throughout the campaign, beginning with Douglas' decision to attempt to establish a Nixon-Marcantonio axis, but it was as nothing compared to what came in the closing days. On October 25, the Chinese Communists intervened in Korea. Throughout the campaign, Nixon had demanded that Douglas state her position on the question of the admission of Red China to the United Nations, but she had refused to answer. Even now, when the Chinese Communists "have been thrown into the Korean war with the result American troops are being forced to retreat and are suffering heavy casualties," she refused to answer. "This is the last straw," Nixon declared. "I know that my opponent was committed to the State Department policy of appeasement toward Communism in the Far East, but I never dreamed she would stick to it even after we were attacked."[75]

IN THE MYTHOLOGY of the campaign, Nixon destroyed the reputation of a woman who was as pure as the driven snow. As Earl Mazo put it, "Nothing in the litany of reprehensible conduct charged against Nixon, the campaigner, has been cited more often than the tactics by which he defeated . . . Douglas for senator."[76] Nixon's critics made Murray Chotiner the evil presence behind the throne, with Nixon the willing front man. In truth, Nixon ran the campaign, not Chotiner, and he never regretted what he did. In January 1957, he had an off-the-record interview with British publisher David Astor. According to a subsequent *New Republic* column, when Astor asked Nixon to justify the 1950 campaign, he replied, "I'm sorry about that episode. I was a very young man."[77] As he had done in a similar instance after the Voorhis campaign, Nixon furiously denied the story. He insisted that he had done nothing of which he was ashamed.[78]

So what if there had been some dirty tricks? In politics, like business, you had to look out for number one. Thus did the attitude of the Committee of 100 in the 1946 election carry over to the next level up, where the big men of California encouraged the already-eager Nixon to use everything he could get away with, no matter how scurrilous, in an anything-to-win campaign against Douglas. The knowingly false slurs, the outright lies, the outrageous innuendos used against Mrs. Douglas had their precedent in the Voorhis campaign. They had not caused any guilt feelings there either.

It must be understood that Nixon really did regard Mrs. Douglas as a threat to the Republic, even though he knew she was a sincere anti-Communist. As he himself said explicitly when he announced his candidacy for the Senate, there was a "greater threat to our free institutions" than the Communist Party. That threat came from politicians providing panaceas that sold the American birthright for "a mess of political pottage." Translated, that meant the New Deal wing of the Democratic Party. There was no chance that the Communists would ever come to power in America, but there was a real chance that the New Deal, as represented by such luminaries as Harry Truman and Helen Douglas, would stay in power. And New Deal policies, Nixon said, meant socialism at home and surrender abroad. Further, it was the New Deal, not the CP-USA, that by holding power prevented the Republicans from holding power. Therefore, it was the New Deal, not the CP, that was the real enemy.

Convinced by this logic, Nixon and his fellows were capable of going to any extreme in the campaign. These young veterans of World War II had been eager and active participants in the struggle against Hitler and Tojo. In their formative years, they had known the experience of putting their lives on the line in a cause no less than freedom itself. In a war in which the enemy was as evil as Hitler, there could be no moral qualms. Any means were justified to reach the end. Then too the politics of extreme characterized the American scene in the postwar years, so much so that each election was regarded as Armageddon Now. "I am convinced beyond question that the election of 1950 will be the most crucial in our nation's history," Nixon said when he announced that he would be a candidate.

But rather than launching a frontal assault against the New Deal, Nixon and his friends tried to outflank the enemy by charging that the New Dealers were pro-Communist. That this was absurd made no difference, because the charge itself forced the Democrats to deny and threw them on the defensive. Through this technique, Republican candidates could persuade voters to look at their opponents not as Democrats who had brought them such good things as Social Security and minimum-wage laws, but as left-wing extremists who secretly wanted to bring socialism to America. This was the Big Lie technique, and the Big Lie was that Helen Douglas and Dean Acheson and Harry Truman were pro-Communist.

It should be noted that the Democrats also overstated their case, and not just in Helen Douglas' rather ridiculous attempt to pin a soft-on-Communism label on Nixon. Truman was often outrageous in the things he said about the Republicans, and aggressive and cocksure in his denunciations of the Soviet Union. He thrived on crisis. More than any other man, Truman had been responsible for escalating the Greek civil war to the level of worldwide crisis, and he had done it primarily through rhetoric that was doomsday in its tone.

Truman carried that sense of crisis over into American politics, where his own partisanship was legendary, and where every election was the next crisis, to be met with immediate and drastic action.

The President, and the times, created an atmosphere that perfectly suited Nixon. He too thrived on crises, he too spoke in exaggerated terms, hurling threats and predicting disasters. In addition, Nixon was on the offensive, which gave him the advantage of maneuver over his opponents, and he was rapidly becoming a master of innuendo. "In almost every statement he made," one of Nixon's staff members recalled about the 1950 campaign, "it was Helen Gahagan Douglas and Alger Hiss. . . . He got the two together somehow, ingeniously." He never said they were linked, but his audiences walked away with the names Douglas and Hiss firmly together in their minds.

Nixon was also adroit in his use of the Korean War as an issue. He was an enthusiastic supporter of the war, and of MacArthur, while simultaneously blaming it on the Administration's inept, if not treasonous, foreign policy. He never said, directly, that there was a conspiracy within the State Department that had delivered China to the Reds, but nevertheless, as he knew, that was what many of his listeners thought he had said—especially those likely to believe it already.

He then applied the suspicion of conspiracy to Helen Douglas, by linking her to the Truman-Acheson foreign policy, which really was especially brazen of him, since he also castigated her for failing to support the Greek aid bill, the cornerstone of the Truman-Acheson foreign policy. Nixon charged that his opponent had "consistently supported the State Department's policy of appeasing Communism in Asia, which finally resulted in the Korean War."

He also said that she "follows the Communist Party line."[79] He did not say that she was a Communist, or that the State Department's line and the CP's line were the same—but he could count on it that many people would make the connection for him.

WHATEVER ELSE might be said about Nixon's campaign, it worked. Douglas never had a chance. He won by a margin of 680,000 votes, the largest plurality of any Senate winner of that year and only slightly behind Warren's total vote. Nixon got 2,183,454 to Douglas' 1,502,507.[80]

"We hopped from one victory celebration to another far into the night," Pat recalled. "Dick was so exuberant. Wherever he found a piano he played 'Happy Days Are Here Again'" (which was a nice frosting on the cake).[81] Two weeks later, Senator Downey announced that he would resign on November 30, and Governor Warren appointed Nixon as his replacement, thus giving Nixon a leg up on seniority over other incoming freshmen senators.[82]

The momentum that had begun when Nixon first announced that he was running against Voorhis, five years earlier, was still building.

CHAPTER TWELVE

U.S. SENATOR
1951

ON JANUARY 9, 1951, Nixon celebrated his thirty-eighth birthday. At this relatively young age he was no longer a comer, but rather a politician who had arrived. The Hiss case had made him a national figure; the 1950 election made him a member of the nation's most exclusive club, and not just a member, but the senator who had won his seat with the largest margin of any senator elected or re-elected that year. His reputation among the big men in his party could hardly have been higher. "Your victory was the greatest good that can come to our country," Herbert Hoover wrote him after the election, and Herbert Brownell, Jr., twice Dewey's campaign manager, praised Nixon for his "brilliant campaign" in California.[1]

Insofar as Nixon had a problem, it was that he remained a member of the minority party. The Republicans had picked up some seats in both the Senate and the House in 1950, but not enough to control the Congress. But Nixon managed to convert his minority status into an asset—being a member of the opposition during an intensely unpopular war was ideally suited to Nixon's talents and style. He could attack and denounce, without letup, here, there, everywhere, shamelessly, about every event of importance.

In 1951 and 1952, developments in the domestic and international scene proved to be ideal for Nixon's purposes. The American defeat in North Korea by the Chinese Communists, Truman's relief of General Douglas MacArthur, Hiss going to prison, corruption in the Internal Revenue Service, Joe McCarthy's continuous uproar, and many other events would give Nixon unmatchable opportunities to flay away at the Democrats.

Grocery store owner Frank Nixon, hard-working and God-fearing, and his Quaker wife, Hannah, had five sons (shown at right with Harold, Donald, and Richard). Richard was a serious youngster; in Mary Skidmore's first-grade class in Yorba Linda (below, Richard is on the right end of the first row), he was reading a book a week and beating third-graders in poetry-recitation contests. Ms. Skidmore recalled that he always showed up with a clean, ironed shirt and tie, even when barefoot.

ALL PHOTOS: WHITTIER COLLEGE

As a teenager, he was awkward, standoffish, a bit stiff (above, left, with Hannah and Donald). He was a promising musician, more so on the piano than the violin (shown below left at Fullerton High). He could not relax as his brothers could (above, with Frank, Donald, and Harold). At Whittier College, he was a top student, a debater, organizer of a men's society, a third-string football player (right), and politician who held nearly every position in student government, ending up with the top job (right, from the 1934 yearbook).

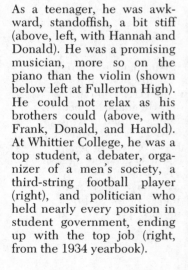

After one of the most successful years the college has ever witnessed, we stop to reminisce, and come to the realization that much of the success was due to the efforts of this very gentleman. Always progressive, and with a liberal attitude, he has led us through the year with flying colors.

RICHARD
NIXON
PRESIDENT
A. S. W. C.

Harold (above, with Dick and two unidentified girls) could get him to take some time off to enjoy himself; Harold's death while Dick was in college led him to resolve to try even harder, work harder. He graduated near the top of his class at Duke Law School, returned to Whittier to set up a practice, married Pat Ryan (above, right), and joined the Navy (shown here in 1945). In 1946 he ran for Congress and won; meanwhile Pat had borne their first daughter, Tricia. In 1947, *The Washington Post* called him the greenest congressman in town, but in truth he proved to be a sophisticated player of the political game. This photo (right) of the young congressman and his family was widely distributed.

CALIFORNIA STATE UNIVERSITY, FULLERTON

WHITTIER COLLEGE

AP/WIDE WORLD PHOTOS

Nixon made his name on the House Un-American Activities Committee (shown above in 1948 at a HUAC briefing, announcing a program providing for criminal prosecution of Communist Party leaders) and used his chairmanship of a subcommittee of HUAC to expose Alger Hiss. The conviction of Hiss made Nixon a national figure; in 1950 he went to the Senate, and in 1952, six years after entering politics, he was the vice-presidential nominee of the Republican Party (left, with Ike at the Chicago convention). His constant theme, that the Democrats were advocates of socialism at home and surrender abroad, infuriated his opponents, who lashed back with the charge that Nixon had a secret expense fund, paid for by California millionaires. He answered the critics on national television (top, right), insisting that he had done nothing illegal and would keep one gift, a dog named Checkers.

In 1954, Nixon was the spokesman for the Republicans in the off-year election; to his opponents he was Joe McCarthy in a white collar. But the Republicans loved him for the enemies he had made and renominated him for the Vice-Presidency in 1956.

Nixon tried as Vice-President to stay as close to Ike as he could, while remaining his own man. On political questions, Ike worked closely with Nixon (above, in 1952 in Chicago), and in campaigns the President sent Nixon out to blast the Democrats. In policy matters, Ike wanted Nixon to be the best-informed Vice-President ever, and he succeeded (left, Ike, Nixon, and Secretary of State John Foster Dulles leaving a National Security Council meeting, 1955). What Ike did not know was how often Nixon and Dulles disagreed with him on policy, as in Korea, Vietnam, and the arms race.

Nixon and Ike never became friends, but they were close associates. At the 1957 inaugural parade, Ike's grandchildren and Nixon's daughters got together (above, Anne and David Eisenhower, Julie and Tricia Nixon). Ike occasionally asked Nixon to play golf with him (right, Cherry Hills, Denver, 1953).

Nixon knew more foreign leaders than any previous Vice-President. Partly this was due to his closeness to Dulles (shown here with Nixon greeting Konrad Adenauer in 1953). He established some warm friendships (left, with Pat, the shah of Iran, and Empress Soraya, Washington airport, 1954). In 1955, Ike had a heart attack. Nixon met him at the airport in Washington following his recuperation in a Denver hospital (above, with John Eisenhower and Herbert Hoover, November 11, 1955). Nixon handled the crisis with skill and calmness, leading to stories about a "New Nixon," a man not quite so strident or reckless, a man of responsibility and moderation.

Always in a hurry, Nixon seldom had time for Pat and almost never danced with her, but an exception was made for the 1957 inaugural ball (above). Another crisis came in 1957, when Ike had a stroke; again, Nixon was a model of restraint and calm (shown here talking to newsmen outside the White House, November 26, 1957).

Nixon could dish it out, and he could take it. In 1958 he toured South
America, where he sought out confrontations with Communist agitators
(above, in Montevideo, Uruguay, interpreter Colonel Vernon Walters behind). In Caracas, Venezuela, the Reds struck back, when a mob attacked
Nixon's limo with baseball bats and lead pipes. Nixon never flinched
(below, the interior of the car after the riots).

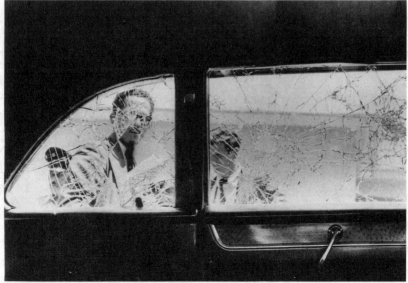

Pat had never wanted a politician's life for herself; she would have much preferred a quiet family life. But being famous brought its rewards, including associations with royalty, whether Hollywood style (above, with the Duke, John Wayne, at a Republican fund raiser in 1959) or the real thing (below, Dick and Pat host Queen Elizabeth and Prince Philip at a luncheon in Washington, 1957).

In 1959, Nixon went to Russia, where he exchanged insults with Nikita Khrushchev (above, in a rare moment of good feeling, with Milton Eisenhower). In 1960, Nixon and John F. Kennedy waged one of the bitterest and closest campaigns of the century. Kennedy challenged Nixon to a series of televised debates; against Ike's advice, Nixon accepted. Before the first debate, these hot-blooded Cold Warriors shook hands (below).

Politics was his life, and he could never resist a campaign. The only one open to him in 1962 was for governor of California, where he challenged the lackluster incumbent, Pat Brown (above). Nixon lost, badly, and decided to quit politics. He informed reporters that they would not have Nixon to kick around anymore, as this was his "last press conference."

Nixon in 1951 was the party's most sought-after speaker; he "blossomed into a Republican meld of Paul Revere and Billy Sunday."[2] He loved campaigning. The opportunity to blast the Democrats was only part of the appeal. He led a life of frenetic activity. He was constantly on the go, flying here, driving there, back and forth across America. He met state chairmen, county chairmen, the big and the small contributors, the party faithful, and he never, not ever, forgot a name. He was the most successful Republican fund raiser, partly because of his reputation, but more because of what he said and how he said it.

He took no money for his speeches to hundred-dollar-a-plate fund raisers (he did accept an honorarium for speeches to businessmen's conventions and other nonpolitical groups, a total of $6,611 in 1951), but nevertheless he reaped a reward. Whatever his bankbook said, his capital assets soared. There was scarcely a Republican in the country who did not owe Dick Nixon a favor, because it was Dick who had been willing to fly out to Montana, or up to Maine, or wherever, in the middle of the winter, to fill the party's depleted campaign chest. Through his constant campaigning, Nixon built a nationwide base for himself that through the decades would prove to be unshakable.

In 1951, he made a speech almost every other day, averaging three a week. By the end of the year he had appeared in twenty-five states. Just after being sworn in as senator, in the last week of January he spoke to the Maine Bar Association on the twenty-third, the Women's National Republican Club in New York on the twenty-fifth, a Republican gathering in Harrisburg on the twenty-seventh, and in Philadelphia on the twenty-ninth. On Lincoln's Birthday, he made appearances in Philadelphia, Louisville, Grand Rapids, and St. Paul.[3]

Wherever he went, he found—in his own words—a "desperate determination" on the part of Republicans to take the affairs of the nation out of the hands of Truman and the hated Democrats.[4] These discontented party faithful made an ideal audience for Nixon's standard speech, which above all else emphasized the need for change, complete and total and immediate change, in every aspect of national policy (save aid to Europe, the one issue on which Nixon supported Truman).

THE SPEECH THAT DID HIM THE MOST GOOD was one he delivered on June 28, 1951, in Boston, to the National Young Republican Convention. He called it "The Challenge of 1952," and for misleading allusions, half-truths, innuendos, and hyperbole it was unbeatable. It was also exactly what the audience wanted to hear.

The Truman Administration had failed on so many fronts,

Nixon proclaimed, that he despaired of listing them all. He said that no diplomatic gaffe in history had been worse "than the failure of our State Department to get the wholehearted support of our allies in Korea." He asserted that "the American people have had enough of the whining, whimpering, groveling attitude of our diplomatic representatives who talk of America's weaknesses and of America's fears rather than of America's strength and of America's courage." He charged that "Communists infiltrated the very highest councils of this administration," yet "our top administration officials have refused time and time again to recognize the existence of the fifth column in this country and to take effective action to clean subversives out of the administrative branch of our government."

The Administration that Nixon was accusing of being soft on Communism had, in the past five years, forced the Russians out of Iran in 1946, come to the aid of the Greek government in 1947, met the Red Army's challenge at Berlin and inaugurated the Marshall Plan in 1948, joined the North Atlantic Treaty Organization in 1949, and hurled back the Communist invaders of South Korea in 1950, all under the umbrella of the Truman Doctrine, which had proclaimed American resistance to any advance by any Communist anywhere. Nixon was talking about an Administration in which the FBI had uncovered the evidence and the Justice Department had prosecuted the case that put Alger Hiss in jail, in which the Attorney General had issued a list of Communist-front organizations and the President a sweeping executive order regarding subversives in government.

To liberals, Nixon's use of such words as "whining," "whimpering," "weaknesses," "fears," and "groveling" to describe the Truman Administration was not just an excess of partisan rhetoric but rather a distortion so gross as to defy comprehension. Many liberals saw Truman as a dangerously provocative statesman, a hard liner and a risk taker who was too eager to challenge the Soviets and too unwilling to attempt to cooperate with them. To such liberals (whose voice was loud because there were so many writers and intellectuals among them), Truman on the domestic front had abandoned the New Deal and inaugurated a witch-hunt.The gap between the liberal view of Truman and the one expressed by Nixon could not have been greater. It was a split that cut right through the nation.

The Young Republicans in Nixon's audience in Boston were, of course, enthusiastically on Nixon's side. If any of them had a criticism of what Nixon had said, it was that he went too easy on Truman. It was the kind of audience that brought out the worst in him.

As when he spoke on the Hiss case. He damned Acheson for speaking up for Hiss after the guilty verdict, and claimed that when the case was in the courts "two judges of the Supreme Court; the Governor of Illinois, Mr. Adlai Stevenson; Philip Jessup, the architect of our Far Eastern policy; and a host of other administration officials testified as character witnesses for Alger Hiss." Neither the justices nor the governor of Illinois were members of the Truman Administration; Jessup was a career diplomat; no other official of the federal government, much less a "host of others," testified in Hiss's behalf at his trials. And, of course, John Foster Dulles had hired Hiss for a prestigious job.

Nixon admitted that "the Republican party has some faults," but he quickly added, "one thing can be said to our credit which cannot be said for the party in power. That is, that we have never had the support of the Communists in the past [sic]. We have never asked for that support. We do not have it now, and we shall never ask for it or accept it in the future. And for that reason a Republican administration, we can be sure, will conduct a thoroughgoing housecleaning of Communists and fellow travelers in the administrative branch of the government because we have no fear of finding any Communist skeletons in our political closets" (again ignoring Dulles' relationship with Hiss).

Nixon insisted that a Republican housecleaning program would have to be "fair, sane, intelligent, and effective," because "indiscriminate name-calling and professional Red-baiting can hurt our cause more than it can help it" (not, evidently, because it was wrong to engage in smears).

He dazzled the Young Republicans with figures. Six years ago, he declared, "the United States was the most powerful nation on the face of the globe. . . . As far as people in the world were concerned, there were approximately 1,760,000,000 on our side and only 180,000,000 on the Communist side." In 1951, America had lost its lead in ground and tactical air strength, in submarines, and in atomic weapons. As to the Cold War lineup, "today there are only 540,000,000 people that can be counted on the side of the free nations—our side. There are 800,000,000 people on the Communist side, and there are 600,000,000 that will have to be classified as neutral. . . . In other words, six years ago the odds in people in the world were 9 to 1 in our favor, and today they are 5 to 3 against us."[5]

NIXON'S NEGATIVISM AND EXAGGERATION were typical of Republican congressmen elected in 1950. Even before the Chinese offensive in Korea, James Reston had reported, "On the political stump [the

Republicans] sound angry enough to make Joe McCarthy Secretary of State." [6] Events in December 1950 had turned anger to fury. The Chinese drove the Americans back from the Yalu River in what became a pell-mell retreat, almost a humiliating rout. At the same time, Truman announced that he was sending four divisions to Europe to meet the NATO commitment.

Why beef up Europe when American boys were on the run in Korea? Republicans demanded. Why send help to the British, who trade with our Chinese enemy through Hong Kong, who recognize the Communist government, and are a bunch of damned socialists to boot? Why not have it out with Red China here and now?

Having it out with China was a glittering prospect to the China Lobby. After Chinese intervention, conservative Republicans generally saw the Korean War as a full-fledged Sino-American war, and they wanted to do to Communist China what they had done to Nazi Germany and militarist Japan. They wanted nothing less than unconditional surrender. But Truman, after the defeat in North Korea, had reduced the war aims in Korea to securing the *status quo ante bellum* (from a goal of uniting a free Korea), and he absolutely refused to extend the war to China proper. He insisted that the Korean War had to be limited, for fear of starting World War III. What MacArthur and his many friends in the Republican Party saw as a great opportunity, to eliminate Red China, Truman saw as a potential disaster.

For their part, conservative Republicans advocated, simultaneously, either declaring war on China or bringing the American boys home.

A "Great Debate" began almost on the day Nixon was sworn in, a debate about fundamentals in American foreign policy. In its initial form, the Great Debate was over Truman's decision to send American troops to Europe. Did he have the right to do so? Not without congressional approval, cried the Republicans, who wanted to send them to Korea.

To a large extent, however, Truman had managed to undercut the Republicans by appointing the universally popular General Dwight Eisenhower as the NATO Supreme Commander. And on February 1, 1951, Nixon was in the audience as Eisenhower spoke to a joint session of Congress. The general urged Congress to put no limit on the number of troops that could be sent to Europe, affirmed the President's right to send such troops, and further recommended that the United States rearm Europe on a scale comparable to that of Lend-Lease days. This was a long, long way from the Old Guard's view of the world, but Republicans were deferential to the general in their comments, and remained so in investigative hearings. Only Senator Robert Taft of Ohio, the front-running candidate for the Republican nomination in 1952, went after Eisenhower in the questioning.[7]

Eisenhower's appearance prepared the way for a compromise resolution which stated that it was the sense of the Senate that no troops in addition to the four already earmarked divisions could be sent to Europe without specific Senate approval. This allowed the Senate to retain its sense of dignity, while conceding to the President the power he had already seized. Nixon voted for the resolution. But Dean Acheson dismissed it as without legal force.[8] In foreign affairs, Truman was building on and adding to the Roosevelt legacy of presidential command and control of policy and execution.

WHILE TRUMAN IGNORED THE SENATE, Nixon spent a good deal of his time there, although he wasn't working as hard as he had done during his freshman year in the House. His speaking schedule was such that he was more often on the stump than in the Senate chambers. Keenly aware of the importance of the pecking order in the Senate, he took care to establish a relationship with all the Republican senators, plus the conservative Democrats. He had an ability to listen to all sides sympathetically, and to explain the point of view of a right-wing West Coast Republican to an East Coast liberal Republican.

It was a session characterized by name-calling, snarls, threats, charges—a time of negativism and political cynicism. The United States was stuck with a President whose approval rating had fallen to 27 percent, with a war that was frustrating and confusing and that America was losing, with a Democratic Party that thought it ruled by divine right, and with a Republican Party that was so desperate for power that it would do anything to gain that power.

In this milieu, Nixon flourished. His attacks on Truman's foreign policy and conduct of the Korean War were incessant, the standard theme of his speeches, wherever delivered. He intermixed with them expressions of his outrage at the petty graft of the Truman Administration, its influence peddling, political cronyism, and tax settlements. But in always attacking, always accusing, always smearing his opponents, Nixon was by no means alone. It was during this session that Joe McCarthy called George Marshall a traitor. It was in this session that Senator Taft, who had previously distinguished himself by his broad, reform-minded conservatism and his political integrity, entered what his biographer William S. White called his "sad, worst, period."[9]

INEVITABLY, NIXON BECAME INVOLVED in the struggle for the 1952 Republican presidential nomination; just as inevitably, his name started popping up as a possible vice-presidential candidate. The leading contenders for the top place on the ticket were, in order of importance, General Eisenhower (if he would only declare himself a candidate and a Republican), Senator Taft, Governor Warren, and Harold Stassen. Taft was the leader of and hero to the Old Guard. The Old Guard hated Tom Dewey and his so-called "me-tooism" almost as much as it hated FDR, and as far as its members were concerned, Ike, Warren, and Stassen were all guilty of being Dewey men. After all, people pushing hardest for Eisenhower were all old Dewey men; Warren had run with him in 1948, and Stassen had many friends in the Dewey camp.

So strongly did the Old Guard feel about these men that Nixon often heard the comment at Republican gatherings: "I'd rather lose with Taft than win with any of those three." In these circumstances, the struggle for the nomination would necessarily be a bitter one. As Nixon put it in a letter to Kyle Palmer, "The boys realize they are playing for big stakes and they're putting the pressure on as I have never seen it put on before." [10]

Nixon was often thought of and called a member of the Old Guard, but things were not that simple. On foreign affairs, he was far more often on the side of the eastern, liberal Republicans, although on China he was as one with the China Lobby, which had strong Old Guard connections (the Old Guardsmen were a strange breed of isolationists—they wanted to get out of Western Europe, liberate Eastern Europe, and fight all out in Asia).

Nixon proved to be a skillful participant in the intricate pre-convention maneuvering for the presidential nomination. His position was a delicate one. He could hardly lead a movement for another candidate in opposition to Warren, the Republican governor of his own state. As an internationalist who continued his support for the Marshall Plan and other aid programs, all of which Taft and the Old Guard opposed, he could be expected to support General Eisenhower. But as the man who got Alger Hiss, and who thundered about Acheson's betrayal of America and responsibility for the loss of China, he seemed to have a natural affinity for Taft. Finally, Stassen had endorsed Nixon in 1946 and again in 1950, and Nixon had praised Stassen on a number of occasions. In short, Nixon had a boot in all four camps.

Through this maze Nixon steered a course that antagonized as few as possible. He was aware that, for all his fame, he was a junior senator whose ultimate fate rested in the hands of the party elders, or rather whoever could take control of the divided party.

In February, Palmer asked him to send along some political gossip. Nixon replied with a three-page single-spaced letter. In his talks around the country, Nixon said, he found many Republicans who thought that Warren could have won in 1948 and who were therefore supporting him for 1952. However, he added, "there is no question but that the hard core of the party, except Maine and New York, are for Taft." His personal opinion was that "Taft would be difficult to elect." Still, Taft "has the mid-west and south sewed up," and unless his foes could come up with "an electable candidate [read Eisenhower], Taft will win the nomination handily." What it all meant, Nixon said, was that "California, Pennsylvania and New York will probably have to get together on someone else if Taft is to be defeated." Nixon thought Taft's chances would be hurt if Truman withdrew from the race, as was widely rumored, because "it is now assumed that any candidate would be harder to beat than Truman." Senator Paul Douglas of Illinois, for example, would beat Taft easily. Nixon had a high opinion of the liberal Douglas—"He is certainly as able a man as the Democrats have in the Senate, both from the standpoint of brain power and political ability."

Eisenhower was the obvious man to stop Taft, and Nixon said that from what he heard, if the general declared himself to be a Republican candidate, "there would be no question whatever that he would get the nomination."

Nixon concluded, "My own opinion is that the Republicans must assume the worse, i.e., that Truman will be dumped and we will be faced by a tough candidate. This means, if we are to win, we had better get together on our strongest electable man and start building him up now. Otherwise, Taft will win the nomination virtually by default." He thought it "vitally important" that Senator James Duff, leader of the Pennsylvania Republicans and a prominent Ike supporter, Earl Warren, "and even the New York crowd [read Dewey] give some kind of an understanding in the near future as to what their program is going to be." [11]

THE CANDIDATE NIXON MOST WANTED was Eisenhower, and he wanted him for the most obvious reason—Ike's tremendous popularity. The Old Guard might feel it was better to lose with Taft and retain party purity, but not Nixon, who knew that nothing is better than winning.

Nixon had first met Eisenhower in the summer of 1950 at the redwood retreat of San Francisco's Bohemian Club, where fourteen hundred of the richest and most conservative men in America gathered each year to engage in high jinks and high politics. Herbert Hoover was the acknowledged chief at these annual gatherings, and the highest honor was to have lunch with him at his Cave

Man Camp. On the occasion Nixon was invited, Ike sat on Hoover's right, Nixon at the foot of the table. Later that day, Eisenhower gave a short address to the gathering at the lakeside amphitheater. The general gave a ringing defense of NATO. Nixon said later that "it struck me forcibly that Eisenhower's personality and personal mystique had deeply impressed the [pro-Taft] skeptical and critical Cave Man audience."[12]

Nine months later, in May 1951, Nixon met Eisenhower for a private conversation. By then, Eisenhower was headquartered in Paris, where he was Supreme Commander of the NATO forces. Nixon was in Europe as a Senate observer to the World Health Organization conference in Geneva, and he made a side trip to Paris to see Eisenhower.

Nixon was awed by Eisenhower. The general's reputation alone was enough to inspire such feelings, but in addition he was "erect and vital and impeccably tailored." Then, as happened with nearly everyone he met, Ike's informality, casual manner, intense curiosity, and sincerity of emotion put Nixon "so completely at ease that we were able to talk very freely."

Eisenhower's first impression of Nixon was favorable. He had heard many good things about the young man, from people he trusted and looked to for advice, and he had done some reading on the Hiss case. He told Nixon, "The thing that most impressed me was that you not only got Hiss, but you got him fairly." Nixon was justifiably proud of that comment, which he frequently quoted.

Eisenhower had also read some of Nixon's speeches, and told him he liked the emphasis Nixon put on the need for economic and ideological strength as well as military factors in fashioning American policy. "Being strong militarily just isn't enough in the kind of battle we are fighting now," Eisenhower declared. Then the general gave the senator his standard pep talk for NATO, and the meeting ended. Nixon came away from it convinced that of all the candidates Eisenhower had by far the best grasp on foreign policy and should be the next President. "I also decided that if he ran for the nomination I would do everything I could to help him get it."[13]

SOMETIME LATER, Taft came to Nixon to ask for his support. Nixon responded that much as he liked and admired Taft, and certain as he was that in domestic affairs Taft was the best man, he had decided that foreign affairs took precedence in 1952 and that he had therefore decided to support Eisenhower (who in January had announced that he was a candidate). He assured Taft that if he won the nomination "he would have my wholehearted support," and promised him that "under no circumstances would I lend myself to a 'stop Taft' movement at the convention."[14]

ALTHOUGH EISENHOWER WAS HIS MAN, Nixon was careful not to antagonize needlessly any of the other candidates, nor the senior players in the nomination game. He tried to work a friendly reference to Warren into all his speeches, and he was sensitive to Knowland's feelings. He rejected an offer to advertise his weekly radio program, for example, because Senator Knowland, acknowledged leader of the China Lobby and Warren's leading supporter, also had a radio program, and he did not advertise. Nixon feared that if he took out an advertisement, "people will use that to drive a wedge between the two of us." [15]

When asked to speak at the California Republican Convention in 1951, Nixon graciously sidestepped the invitation, explaining, "Bill is coming up for election next year, and I think it is best that he take the spotlight on such occasions." [16]

In May, Nixon was one of forty-five Republicans invited to a private New Jersey estate for a Stassen strategy conference. Stassen produced polls and surveys to show that he could emerge the winner from an Eisenhower-Taft deadlock (which was also Warren's only real hope). If there were a deadlock, and if Nixon could swing a major portion of the California delegation to him, Stassen promised Nixon second place on the ticket. Nixon was noncommittal.

Nor was Taft ready to give up. He sent a mutual friend, Tom Shroyer, to talk to Nixon. "I thought he was quite sympathetic in our first conferences during the latter part of 1951 and early 1952," Shroyer remembered. "Nixon liked Taft, but he did seem to have a few doubts about Taft's chances to win." [17]

Nixon seemed to keep his independence, but insiders in the Eisenhower camp knew where he stood. His seat in the Senate was directly behind that of Henry Cabot Lodge, Jr., of Massachusetts, and Lodge was the prime mover in the Eisenhower cause. "It was clear to us," he remarked later, "that Nixon was friendly to our group. His hands were tied [by the unit rule that committed the California delegation to Warren], but it came to a point where a relationship was established . . . where one of us would see him on occasion on the Senate floor and sound him out, get his advice on various things, never going too deep, still going deeper than we could with someone who was completely on the outside." [18]

Nixon meanwhile cultivated his old friends among the press corps, and made many new ones. He had a warm and lengthy correspondence with Palmer and saw him frequently. Ralph de Toledano, who wrote a book on the Hiss case, and who worked for *Newsweek*, became a confidant, as did Earl Mazo. Adela Rogers St. Johns, the magazine writer who had known Nixon as a boy in Whittier, and who was strong for Taft, was another. Hedda Hopper, Hollywood gossip columnist, wrote often, primarily to insist that

Nixon see to it that Charlie Chaplin, suspected of being a Red, was never, ever, let back into this country. Nixon's replies were warm and sympathetic. Bert Andrews remained close, and there were others, including Herb Klein, who had moved to the San Diego *Union-Tribune*, and Earl Behrens, political editor of the San Francisco *Chronicle*. Indeed, Nixon probably had more friends in the press corps than among the politicians.[19]

Nixon used his friendships to spread his views. He was often a guest at Ralph de Toledano's home, where he met with George Sokolsky and other pro-Taft reporters, and attempted to convince them that Taft could not win, that Eisenhower could, and that Eisenhower would make a fine President.[20]

NIXON'S CREDENTIALS with the right wing of his party, thanks to the Hiss case, were so good that he could afford to expose and criticize one of the pillars of the Old Guard. He had made himself into a leading critic of the Truman Administration's so-called "scandal a day," and had come down especially hard on the Democratic National Committee chairman for influence peddling with the Reconstruction Finance Corporation.

When Guy Gabrielson, the Republican National Committee chairman, insisted on retaining his position as president of the Carthage-Hydrocol Company, Nixon insisted on a conflict-of-interest investigation by a Senate committee. Although Gabrielson was cleared of the charges, Nixon nevertheless demanded his resignation, on the grounds that the RNC chairman had to be as pure as Caesar's wife. Nixon told Kyle Palmer that "our major objective if we want to win in '52 is to kick out Gabrielson. Of course, I realize this will be a tough assignment, but having him at the top of the National Committee is worse than useless in those states where the vote will be close and we need to appeal to the independents and the Democrats." Gabrielson did not resign.[21]

NIXON THE DEFENDER OF THE MORALITY of the Republican Party soon seized an opportunity to become Nixon the upholder of the Constitution. Back in 1948, Truman, by executive order, had closed the executive department's loyalty and security files to congressional committees. Truman's argument was that he could not allow HUAC and others to paw through the raw files, which were filled with rumors and unverified charges. His hope was that the gag order would cause HUAC to dry up and wither away due to a lack of documentation. But the effect was to strengthen the position of the professional anti-Communists. Joe McCarthy was the first to realize that Truman's order could be made into a positive asset.

McCarthy charged that a former State Department consultant and current Johns Hopkins University professor, Owen Lattimore, was the "top Russian espionage agent" in America, then said that he could prove it if only he had access to State Department loyalty files. Actually, McCarthy had the Administration coming and going, because he also warned that the files were being "rifled." In the event that Truman did rescind the order and no proof against Lattimore appeared in the files, McCarthy could say—as he would after Truman released them later in 1951—that the files had been "raped." [22]

Nixon leaped into the middle of the fray, charging cover-up and a blatant misuse of executive privilege. He was eloquent in his defense of Congress' right to information originating in the executive branch. "Every time a Congressional committee begins to ferret out facts which might embarrass the Administration," Nixon thundered in an October speech, "an agency head can ring down an iron curtain between the Executive Departments and the people and successfully thwart attempts to bring out the truth." He reminded the President that Grover Cleveland, a Democrat, when confronted with an embarrassing personal scandal, had issued orders to his aides to "tell the truth." Truman's motto, Nixon charged, was to "tell the truth only when you have to."

Nixon admitted that "some information should be classified on national security grounds," but then made a ringing declaration of the people's right to know. "The public interest is best served by allowing as much information as possible to reach the people. If we grant such tremendous power to the Administrative Branch of the Government we may find ourselves heading rapidly toward a military dictatorship." His conclusion was simple, direct, and unarguable: "Classification should be solely on the basis of the security of the nation rather than on the basis of the security of the Administration which desires to remain in power." [23]

NIXON HIMSELF, no longer a member of HUAC (which spent 1951 chasing Reds among the Hollywood stars), was pretty much out of the Communist-hunting business. He did keep after Alger Hiss. On March 12, 1951, the Supreme Court rejected Hiss's appeal for a review of his case. An exultant Nixon issued a press release that began by saying the opposite of what most people assumed he felt: "The decision should under no circumstances be an occasion for elation or gratification." Why not? "Because not since the days of Benedict Arnold have the American people been the victim of such a brazen and inexplicable act of treachery by a man who commanded the faith and confidence of our highest officials."

Then he offered Hiss an opportunity to recant and join Whittaker Chambers as a public hero by revealing the details of his sordid past. Hiss, Nixon said, should "come clean and tell what he knows about the Communist spy network here and abroad. With the information he could give we would be able to strike a mortal blow against the potential enemies of this country. By continuing to remain silent he only aggravates the crime for which he has been convicted." [24]

On April 4, Nixon wrote Austin Canfield of the American Bar Association, asking "if steps might not be taken to expel Alger Hiss from membership in the ABA for life." He said it would be "a most salutary action. Otherwise, after serving approximately a year and ten months he will be out on parole and probably will find plenty of clients who will be willing to subsidize him in the future." [25]

By summer, books about the case were beginning to appear. Nixon read a review of one of them in the *Minnesota Law Review* by Charles Alan Wright of the University of Minnesota. Wright was pro-Hiss, and Nixon wrote to a businessman friend in Minneapolis about his reaction. "Frankly, it shocked me so much that I cannot refrain from writing to you and urging that if you have any influence with the regents at the University of Minnesota it would be well to bring to their attention the type of fellow Wright is." Of course, Nixon added, he did not object to the author's right to his own opinion, but he did want the regents to know that Wright was "a completely biased and unobjective scholar." Nixon's conclusion was that "on the ground not of his obvious left wing bent but on the ground of his educational deficiencies I would think that Wright should not remain on the faculty." [26]

In January 1952, Nixon wrote in alarm to John Foster Dulles, reporting that he had heard a rumor that Dulles had said that Hiss would be vindicated within five years. Nixon asked if it could possibly be true. Dulles replied by return mail: "The statement attributed to me is totally without foundation. I would be very much surprised if he were vindicated as the evidence against him seemed to me quite conclusive." [27]

In May of 1952 Nixon wrote a review of Chambers' book, *Witness*, for the *Saturday Review of Literature*. He called it a great book, especially for showing Americans that men could become Communists "with the best of motives." He faced the always troubling question about Chambers: Why believe a self-confessed liar? Nixon said his own answer was "not one in justification but in extenuation. Is it not better to tell the whole truth in the end than to refuse as Hiss did to tell the truth at all? Is it not better to be one who has been a Communist than one who may still be one?" [28]

That same issue carried a second review, by none other than Charles Alan Wright, who entitled his piece "A Long Work of Fiction." Wright concluded, "I think Hiss is innocent. And I am sure that if the verdict was right and he is guilty, it is the purest chance that the jury guessed the correct answer." [29]

Professor Wright was to reappear in Nixon's life. In 1973, President Nixon hired him as one of his Watergate defenders, calling Wright a "distinguished constitutional scholar." It was Wright, by then a professor at the University of Texas, who handed over the first Watergate tapes to Judge John J. Sirica, announcing as he did so that "this President does not defy the law." [30] These tapes revealed, among so many things, that in moments of crisis, President Nixon would tell his aides to go back and study the Hiss case.

NIXON DEALT WITH A PROBLEM that bothered all Republican senators—how to react to Joe McCarthy's rantings and ravings—by turning it into a political plus. He was careful never to criticize McCarthy's motives, and often agreed with his Old Guard friends that "Joe might well have something." But he was equally careful to warn against hurling unsubstantiated charges, and he frequently told McCarthy privately that he had to do more homework (to Nixon's amazement, he discovered that McCarthy knew so little about Communism in America that he had not even heard of Earl Browder).[31] Thus both the Old Guard and the more moderate Republicans thought of Nixon as a friend and ally, as he indeed was. More, he was the bridge between the two factions.[32]

Typically, he claimed that his role was one he undertook reluctantly and at great personal sacrifice.[33] "I felt I should try to broker their feud," he later said of the Eisenhower-McCarthy relationship. "I soon learned that the go-between is seldom popular with either side." [34]

In December 1950, Nixon had acted as peacemaker in a direct fashion. He and Pat had attended a dinner dance at the swank Sulgrave Club in Washington. The hostess, evidently for her own amusement, had invited both the columnist Drew Pearson and Joe McCarthy. Pearson was attacking McCarthy in his "Washington Merry-Go-Round" column on an almost daily basis, dwelling on Joe's questionable income tax returns.

McCarthy started heckling Pearson. He told the fifty-three-year-old Quaker pacifist, "You know, I'm going to put you out of business with a speech in the Senate tomorrow. There isn't going to be anything left of you professionally or personally by the time I get finished with you."

Pearson deadpanned: "Joe, have you paid your income taxes yet?"

McCarthy, red-faced, challenged Pearson to step outside and fight. Pearson declined.

In the downstairs cloakroom, as the party was breaking up, McCarthy grabbed Pearson by the neck and issued another challenge. Then he kneed him twice in the groin. Pearson was struggling for air. Nixon walked in; as he did, McCarthy saw him, then drew his arm back and slapped Pearson hard enough to snap his head back. "That one was for you, Dick," Joe bragged.

Nixon stepped between the two men and pushed them apart. "Let a good Quaker stop this fight," he said. Pearson grabbed his coat and fled. "You shouldn't have stopped me, Dick," McCarthy complained.

Later that evening, McCarthy called a reporter to boast that he had just kicked Drew Pearson "in the nuts." The Old Guard was delighted. Senator Arthur Watkins said that he had heard two different reports about where Pearson was hit and he hoped that both were accurate. Another Old Guardsman told Joe that he could not understand how McCarthy could be so stupid as to kick Pearson in the groin "because . . . it is well known that Drew Pearson has nothing there." Joe loved telling the details of the struggle; when he did, his voice became high-pitched, and he giggled like a teenager.[35] In comparison to Joe McCarthy and his friends, Richard Nixon appeared measured and moderate.

EARLY IN THE MORNING of April 11, 1951, Truman announced that he had fired MacArthur. He gave as his reason insubordination. As Commander in Chief, Truman had ordered MacArthur, in unmistakable terms, to stay out of the Great Debate over American foreign policy, but MacArthur had nevertheless spoken out on several occasions, calling for all-out war against China and insisting that "in war there is no substitute for victory." Truman's dismissal of MacArthur combined the drama of two mighty egos locked in personal challenge with the much larger question of Asia first versus Europe first.

Nixon was an early and major contributor to the ensuing uproar. Within two hours of reading Truman's bombshell, Nixon had dictated a statement, edited it himself, had it run off on the mimeographing machine, and issued it to the press.

"The happiest group in the country over General MacArthur's removal," he declared, "will be the Communists and their stooges. They have been doing a hatchet job on him the past ten years and now the President has given them what they have always wanted —MacArthur's scalp."

Nixon searched for a motive, and found it in the Administration's's Europe-first policy, more specifically in its desire to appease the Labour government in Britain. The British had been urging Truman to keep the war in Korea limited to the peninsula and had expressed total opposition to extending the conflict to the Chinese mainland. The Republicans were already highly agitated by the internal policies of the Labour government; its insistence on appeasing the Red Chinese, even when the United Nations was at war with them, made the Republicans absolutely furious.

"The President has lined up with Dean Acheson and the British bloc of appeasers . . . against the overwhelming majority of the American people," Nixon declared. "The only possible explanation for the President's action is that he felt it was necessary to get rid of MacArthur so that Acheson would be free to make a deal with the Chinese Communists along the lines proposed by the British. We can now expect that the State Department will go ahead with its original plan of turning over Formosa to the Communists and of recognizing the Chinese Red government just as the British have been urging."

Nixon wanted victory, not appeasement, and to get it he wanted to take foreign policy out of the hands of Truman and Acheson. He called for "the great weight of American public opinion to be brought to bear in favor of the policies of MacArthur which will bring victory and peace in the Pacific." [36]

In a second press release, Nixon said that Truman "has tried to make it appear that the choice was between a little war in Korea or a much bigger war in Asia." He called this "a complete distortion of the facts," and insisted that "the choice is not between a little war or a big war; the choice is between continuing the Korean war with no real hope of ending it or of adopting a new policy which will allow our Commanders in the field to end the war with a military victory." He denounced Truman for playing "partisan politics . . . with the lives of American men and boys on the battlefield." [37]

On the Senate floor on April 11, Nixon showed his outrage. He blamed Acheson for the war, citing the Secretary's statement that Korea and Formosa lay outside the defense perimeter of the United States. When Republican Senator John Bricker of Ohio asked him "who was the chief advocate of the philosophy that the Chinese Communists were agrarian reformers," Nixon named Owen Lattimore and Philip Jessup, but quickly added that they were "only two members of the whole clique which has constantly held to that theory in the past, and some even hold to it today." Bricker then pointed out that Jessup had been one of Truman's advisers when the President met General MacArthur on Wake Island some months back. Nixon said that there was "no question" that the firing of MacArthur "means the pro-Lattimore-Jessup bloc in the State Department has prevailed."[38]

The Korean War in general, and MacArthur's firing in particular, set off the second phase of the Great Debate in America. It was between those who wanted to crush the Communists in Asia and those who wanted to contain them. Much of that debate centered around interpretations of the recent past; naturally, these interpretations were as far apart as were the two sides' views on what to do next. According to the Democrats, China had gone Communist because of the inept and corrupt nature of Chiang's regime, and nothing that the United States might have done would have made any difference. According to the Republicans, China was "lost" because the United States withdrew its financial and military support from Chiang's government. The debate thus posed one of the fundamental problems in American foreign policy for the second half of the twentieth century: Should the United States support right-wing dictators who were fighting Communists? It raised another perennial problem: What are the vital interests of the United States?

One of the things that made the Republicans so furious was that when the question of vital interests came up in Greece, Truman was quick to send the necessary aid, even though the Greek government was, as Nixon rightly pointed out, "weak, corrupt, and had an army that was not properly organized." But having accepted the principle of supporting *anyone* who was fighting Communists in Europe, Truman had abandoned the principle in Asia.[39] What made the Democrats furious was that the same Republicans who now demanded all-out war in Asia and who damned Truman for his refusal to continue to send aid to Chiang were the same men who in 1947 were in control of Congress and insisted on simultaneously lowering taxes and balancing the budget.

On the Senate floor, Nixon, although the youngest Republican in the body, led the assault against Truman. "The direct result" of Truman's decision to withhold aid from Chiang, he said, was that "China did go Communist." Had Truman supported Chiang, the generalissimo would still be fighting on the mainland, and the Red Chinese would have no troops to spare for Korea. (At this point, Nixon again cited his figures on the worldwide lineup of free peoples, Communists, and neutrals, repeating that during Truman's years in power, the numbers had shifted from 9 to 1 "in our favor, to 5 to 3 against us.")

One of the notable features of Nixon's assessment of the responsibility for the Korean War was his refusal to join McCarthy,

Bricker, Senator William Jenner of Indiana, and others in assigning some of the blame to General George C. Marshall. Shortly after the end of World War II, Truman had sent Marshall to China to attempt to mediate between Chiang and Mao. Nothing substantial came of the effort, which was indeed hopeless from the beginning, and in the end Marshall had expressed serious doubts about Chiang's ability to use American aid effectively. This led the far right wing of the Republican Party to charge that Marshall was a traitor—Joe McCarthy was already calling him that—who was among those responsible for the loss of China.

But Nixon knew that among the men who counted in the Republican Party, as with the top people in business, industry, the media, the professions, and the military, no one in America, not even General Eisenhower, had so high a reputation as George Marshall. Only a fool could suspect Marshall of treason; only a knave would accuse him of it. Nixon was no fool. On the Senate floor, Jenner attempted to pin blame on Marshall in a series of leading questions to Nixon, but Nixon managed to get through a rapid-fire exchange with Jenner without once mentioning Marshall.[40]

So much for history—what of the future? Nixon, as noted, wanted victory in Asia, and his program for achieving it was clear-cut, straightforward, and exactly what MacArthur recommended. He wanted to unleash Chiang from Formosa (when the Korean War had begun, Truman had announced that the U.S. Seventh Fleet would patrol the Formosa Strait, not only to keep Mao from attacking, but also to prevent Chiang from counterattacking), thereby creating at least a diversion that would drain Chinese troops from Korea. Nixon urged the use of strategic bombers to destroy targets inside China. He wanted the United Nations to put up or shut up —either the member states should send troops in significant numbers to Korea or it should pull out, the United States leaving with it. He wanted to force the British to stop selling goods to Red China, and in addition to impose a naval blockade on Red China.

The Democrats replied that the program would not work, that supporting Chiang was like building on quicksand, that bombing China would bring Russia into the war and could lead to an escalation into World War III, that neither air bombardment nor naval blockade could possibly bring Red China to its knees, that breaking with the European allies over the issue of trade with Red China would be a penny-wise and pound-foolish policy, that, in sum, in the words of Truman's Chief of Staff, General Omar Bradley, "it would be the wrong war in the wrong place at the wrong time against the wrong enemy."

To which Nixon rejoined, Where then would be the right war?

Further, What would be the end of it all? Would America have to live forever with a Communist threat? Why not do to the Communists what we did to the Nazis? Senator Brien McMahon explained the Democratic position, that Korea was a holding action while America built up free-world economic and military strength, and that ultimately the containment policy would lead to total victory through the internal revolution that was bound to come in the Communist countries, helped along by a vigorous American propaganda campaign, "a kind of intellectual invasion," as McMahon called it, "which will do more to weaken the Kremlin than any other thing we could possibly do in the military field."

Nixon responded, "Then the position of the Senator from Connecticut, as I understand it, is that he does not have any alternative proposals in the military or political field in dealing with the immediate military problem in Korea. He rejects the proposals of General MacArthur; but . . . he has no other proposals; and so far as his program is concerned, what he proposes is a continuation of the Korean War until we win on the ideological and economic fronts." [41]

Throughout the debate, Taft gave Nixon the strongest possible support, frequently injecting "That's right" or "I agree completely" when Nixon made a point. But most of all he helped him politically by allowing Nixon to lead the Republican attack. Late in the afternoon of April 11, Nixon introduced Senate Resolution 126, which stated the Republican position succinctly: it called upon the Senate to declare "that the President of the United States has not acted in the best interests of the American people in relieving . . . MacArthur and that the President should reconsider his action and should restore General MacArthur to the commands from which he was removed." Of course it had no chance in the Democratic Senate. [42]

Had there been a national referendum on Nixon's resolution, he would have won it overwhelmingly. Truman's Gallop poll rating plummeted to 27 percent. Nixon's mail—five thousand telegrams and ten thousand letters in the first three days after MacArthur's removal—ran 100 to 1 against Truman. [43]

To defend itself, the Truman Administration began publishing selected documents, designed to show that MacArthur had been insubordinate. Nixon lashed out against what he called "one of the most vicious smear campaigns in history." Some of the published material included parts of MacArthur's top-secret cables to Truman. Nixon charged that classification of documents had therefore lost any meaning; the old test was whether or not publication would weaken the nation's security, but "the new test seems to be

... whether it would affect the political security of the Administration. . . . The usual cheap political tactics of leak and counter-leak to prove a point are not good enough in this situation." [44]

By the end of April 1951, Truman was exploring the possibility of a cease-fire and peace talks with the Chinese. The idea of a settlement short of victory was unacceptable to Nixon and many others. "I believe the only way we can end this war," Nixon declared on May 1, "is not by a ninety-day-long 'peace talk' but by military victories and economic blockades to shut out all foreign trade . . . such as now continues to aid Red China. There can be no 'political ' settlement. . . . " [45]

IF THERE WAS NO possible political settlement, "What then is the end of it all? Are we going to have to remain an armed camp for twenty-five years?" Nixon put that question to himself on one of his radio broadcasts that spring. He did not really answer it, but he did insist that his California listeners ("some of whom," he acknowledged as he switched subjects, "say that we should not help Europe") recognize that "if Europe is allowed to go Communist, it will mean that within five or ten years we will be faced with a war which we are likely to lose." It was therefore imperative, he said, that America help Europe to become strong enough to defend itself. [46]

Nixon's strong, public, and frequent defense of Truman's European policy separated him from McCarthy, Jenner, Taft, and others who were furious over Truman's Europe-first policy. The China Lobby and its friends, led by MacArthur himself, wanted everything to go to Korea. But Nixon was not advocating sending more troops or tanks to Korea—he wanted to send more ships and planes, with the troops and tanks going to Europe. His insistence on the crucial importance of aid to Europe linked him to the Dewey wing of the party and especially to those who were pushing hardest for an Eisenhower nomination. Dewey and his friends noted and appreciated Nixon's stand.

So did Averell Harriman, who served Truman as his director of the Mutual Security Agency (MSA). Nixon wrote Harriman about a California friend who had been critical of Nixon's votes for the "giveaway programs" in Europe. The friend had recently driven through France and West Germany, and had since written Nixon, "I have changed my mind about the Marshall Plan, it is doing good." Nixon commented, "It is too bad that we can't afford to send all the voters over there!" and Harriman replied with a warm letter of thanks for all Nixon's help. [47]

Indeed, Nixon was ready to go further in support of Europe

than the Democrats. He fought on the Senate floor for higher appropriations for NATO, and was co-sponsor of an amendment that raised the Voice of America funds from $63 to $85 million.[48] He also came to Truman's aid when other Republicans criticized the Secret Service for assigning men to guard the President's daughter, Margaret Truman. To one constituent who complained, Nixon wrote that the expense was entirely justified and that criticism of Truman on this point was out of order. He sent a copy of the letter to one of Truman's aides, remarking, "I just wanted you to know that all of the Republicans aren't s.o.b.'s all of the time!"[49]

FOR PAT AND THE GIRLS, Nixon's total preoccupation with politics was something they just had to bear. He seemed never to be home, and he hardly had time for Washington social life, which Pat detested in any event. Nevertheless there were many functions they simply had to attend, forcing Pat to leave the girls with sitters, which as she later told Tricia, made her feel guilty. When they saw their parents packing for a trip, the girls would burst into tears, which did not help Pat's guilt feelings. She would hug and kiss them, then notice that they were still crying as she shut the door and left.

Once when they were leaving, Julie threw herself on the floor, crying uncontrollably. Hannah Nixon was there to care for the girls. Nixon begged her, "Mother, take her in your arms, or something." Hannah picked up Julie, and the Nixons left.[50]

After Nixon had made it to the Senate, the couple had moved into a new home, on the corner of Tilden Street in Spring Valley in northwest Washington. The house cost $41,000; the Nixons paid half down and took a mortgage on the remainder. His salary was up to $12,500 plus a tax-free $2,500 expense allowance, and he was supplementing his income through stock-market investments based on tips he (along with McCarthy, Everett Dirksen, Karl Mundt, and some other Republicans) was getting from several wealthy Texans, including Clint Murchison, H. R. Cullen, and H. L. Hunt.[51] But despite his improved financial position, Pat still made all the curtains, draperies, and slipcovers for the new house. She attended a sewing class, learned quilting, and made a quilted spread for their double bed. She did her own housework, cooked the meals, ironed her husband's shirts, and raised the children.

Her wardrobe was skimpy, so skimpy that during the 1950 campaign some of her old friends from Whittier got together and made her three knitted suits. When she did attend a social function, her old black cloth coat was lost in a sea of fur. Nixon did not notice, but then he did not notice what other women were wearing either.

Pat once said, "I can hardly recall his paying a woman a compliment, except to remark on her hat." As for herself, she said that "I never buy anything because I like it. I think, 'Will it pack?' 'Is it conservative?' " She devoted herself to her husband and her children, and her only complaint was that she did not have enough time with them. "A wife's first duty," she said, "is to help and encourage her husband in the career he has chosen."

Which meant, she might have added, doing things his way. Clothes were one example. He disapproved of women in pants, so much so that he encouraged Murray Chotiner, who was preparing a pamphlet for Republican volunteers, to incorporate a prohibition against women in slacks at Republican functions. Pat did not wear slacks in public. Chotiner's advice to the wives of politicians reflected Nixon's view: "Never embarrass your husband"—"Always look at your husband when he is talking."

At Washington functions in 1951, as on the campaign trail in 1950, Pat kept silent, partly because of her husband's wishes, partly because she was shy. Tom Dixon, who was with Nixon throughout the campaign, said, "I think he would have made it very miserable for her if she hadn't [kept silent]. She was . . . weak with him. His ego had to be toadied to. . . . She had a little of the martyr complex in her to take that with so little grumbling." [52]

But she hated political life, the cocktail parties, the reception lines, the gossip and small talk that she could never do well, the lack of a home life, the terrible things that were said about her husband. Nevertheless, Pat always managed to smile as she reached out to shake the next hand. [53]

In the summer of 1951, both Nixon's parents had operations. They spent some of their recuperation period living with their son's family in Washington. Nixon's brothers, Eddie and Don, came for visits. Nixon hardly saw any of them, but he did report to a friend that they were all doing well. As for the girls, he said that Tricia was in kindergarten "and seems to love it." He also reported that "Julie is more of a tomboy at this point than a lady. Needless to say they both are enjoying our new home where they have room to play." [54]

Pat told Earl Chapman, a California friend (they had taught school together), that Nixon frequently worked so late that he spent the night in his Senate office. "He'll work over there until the small hours of the morning. . . . He'll curl up on the couch and get a few hours' sleep. Then he'll get a little breakfast and shave, and go right down to the Senate chambers to work." [55]

He did not much care what he ate. He never had a problem with overweight, partly because he burned up so much energy (although it was almost all mental—he had no hobbies and played no games), mainly because he limited his intake. He ate lunch in his office, often a tuna-fish sandwich and a glass of buttermilk. The one game he did try was that favorite among politicians, golf. In 1951 he took some lessons and played a few times at a public course. He did not like it well enough to join a club. Nor was he a frequent drinker, although on occasion he could be a heavy one. Generally, Nixon put all of himself into his career. As Pat said, "He can keep right on thinking and working at politics from the time he wakes up until he goes to sleep."[56]

His office was like a magnet to him, as Pat revealed when she told the story of the time he promised to take the family on a picnic. The appointed Sunday was hot and humid. Nevertheless, Nixon kept his promise in his own way. "We packed a basket and got on our holiday clothes," Pat related, "and Dick drove us down to the Senate Office Building. We marched into his big air-conditioned office, spread a blanket on the floor in front of his desk and sat on it to eat our lunch."[57]

THE PEOPLE NIXON DID SPEND TIME WITH, aside from his fellow politicians, were on his staff. He had thirteen people on it, and called them all by their first names. He drove them hard, inundating them with memos, urging them to get the mail out faster, to work hard, to produce more. His secretaries arrived early in the morning and often worked until midnight, sometimes even later. When the Senate was in session they worked on Saturdays and occasionally even on Sundays. Nixon was a bear for detail, giving his staff precise instructions on how to prepare form letters, how to handle crackpots, how to deal with requests from constituents and from other congressmen, and so on. The male members of the staff —Bill Arnold, Jack Irwin, and Jim Gleason—were aides, not advisers. They came, mostly, from Southern California. He turned to them for administrative help, not for policy advice or new ideas.[58]

Nixon had no chief of staff. He delegated no power. But he did have a majordomo in the office, his personal secretary, Rose Mary Woods. They had first met in 1947, when Nixon returned from his European trip with the Herter Committee. Woods was then on the committee staff. When the congressmen returned from Europe, she had handled their expense accounts. Most of the congressmen had given her a few notes and bills and told her to "fix it up." Not Nixon. He had handed in a neatly typed form, with everything filled out and properly signed. Even more amazing to Woods, although Nixon had made more side trips than the others, his was by far the smallest expense account. She had been impressed.[59]

Woods was a thin, intense woman who looked a bit like Pat, including a reddish tint to her dark hair. She had come to Washington from a small town in Ohio during the war, and had worked in four different government offices by the time she met Nixon. She had all the qualities that make for a top-notch secretary. She was intelligent, fiercely loyal to her boss, an excellent stenographer and typist, tight-lipped, and dedicated to her work. In addition to all that, she was personable, a popular guest at Washington parties.[60]

When he became a senator, Nixon asked Woods to come work for him. She accepted, probably expecting another one- or two-year stint. Instead, she would stay with him for a quarter of a century. She became, for Nixon, one of the three most important women in his life—the others were Pat and Hannah. There was no sexual attraction involved. At one time or another, Nixon's critics charged him with almost every conceivable sin, but no one ever accused him of adultery or womanizing. Adela Rogers St. Johns recalled seeing Nixon at a Republican rally in Hollywood, surrounded by a galaxy of movie stars. "You never saw such beautiful flesh," she said, "and he acted like a man utterly unsexed. It was as if he didn't know they were there."[61] What attracted Nixon to Woods was her professional skills, plus his feeling that he could trust her—and he was absolutely right. So closely did Nixon work with Woods, and so completely did he trust her, that he had a special telephone hookup that rang in her apartment if he did not answer his phone at home.

He did not take her for granted, or at least not so much as he did Pat. When he saw Woods down in the dumps, he would take her out to lunch, or make some cheery comment to let her know that he cared. To a lesser extent he would do the same with the rest of the staff. Woods later said that "one of the best parties I ever went to" was one Nixon had for his staff, who were his first guests in his new home. After cocktails and dinner, Nixon sat down at the piano and played requests for more than two hours, while everyone sang along with him.

Fortunately for Nixon, Pat knew that she did not have to be jealous of other women, and Pat and Rose Mary got on famously. "Hi, Rosy!" Pat would call out when she came into the office. They shared jokes and confidences and problems, and sometimes even clothes. Rose Mary had affection and respect for Pat. "She's a real trouper," Woods said. She recalled seeing Pat on one trip sitting on a platform in Chicago, wearing only a thin wool suit in freezing weather. But Pat, Rose Mary said, "looked warm." That afternoon they flew to Texas, where it was blazing hot. Pat was still in the wool suit, but she "looked cool, pleased to be there." Rose Mary herself was just as adept at appearances—she too always looked perfectly groomed and tastefully, if inexpensively, dressed.[62]

Nixon kept her on the go. "I fly with a typewriter strapped on a table across my lap," she told one reporter, "so I can type without interruption during landings, take-offs, thunderstorms and rough air. I've typed on chairs, couches, card tables and boxes." She took dictation on the fly too—"As he heads for the Senate floor . . . I'll run along beside him taking dictation. In a few minutes he can give me a list of twenty phone calls to make, twice as many notes to write, have me change luncheon dates, assign people to dig up facts on a handful of subjects. He doesn't look as though he walks fast, but I have to trot to keep up—and take dictation at the same time."[63]

NIXON HAD PUT ON SOME WEIGHT since his navy days, especially in his face and most of all in his jowls. He scowled a lot, which befit most of the subjects he talked about, and when he did, it exaggerated the frown line that ran up the middle of his forehead. His hair had grown darker than ever, and he was wearing it longer, swept back over his head in curls kept in place with a liberal use of hairdressing. His dark eyebrows and cheeks (he needed a shave five minutes after shaving) added to the gloomy appearance, as did his rounded shoulders and awkward gestures. But when he smiled, it spread across his whole face and lit up the room. Many women said they found him sexually attractive, which may only have been an expression of wanting what they could never have.

Perhaps they were attracted by power. After one year in the Senate, Nixon had made himself into one of the most important Republicans in that body. He was virtually the party spokesman on the most important political event of the year, MacArthur's dismissal, and one of the Republican leaders in the more general attack against Truman's foreign policy. He was solidly established with East and West Coast Republicans, with the Dewey camp as well as the Taft wing, with the China Lobby and the friends of Joe McCarthy, with the party chairmen throughout the nation who could deliver the votes at national conventions, with conservative and moderate reporters, in fact with nearly everyone who counted in the Republican Party. His youth, his drive, his enthusiasm, his speaking abilities, his partisan approach to politics, his reputation, his position as a senator from the second-largest state, and his single-minded concentration on politics combined to make him a natural for more important assignments and tasks. Taking it all in all, the shy little Quaker boy from Yorba Linda who had entered politics only five years ago was doing sensationally well for himself.

CHAPTER THIRTEEN

THE DRIVE TO
THE VICE-PRESIDENTIAL
NOMINATION
January–August 1952

HERB BROWNELL, one of Eisenhower's inner group of managers, manipulators, and advisers, once explained Nixon's appeal to the Eisenhower camp. "Nixon seemed an almost ideal candidate for vice-president," Brownell said. "He was young, geographically right, had experience both in the House and the Senate with a good voting record, and was an excellent speaker." [1] His youth balanced Eisenhower's maturity; his California background balanced the Dewey–East Coast orientation of the Eisenhower people; his credentials with the Old Guard balanced Eisenhower's moderate image; his support for Chiang made him popular with the China Lobby, while his support for the Marshall Plan made him popular with Eisenhower and his friends. And his slashing attacks on Truman and the Democrats made him popular with Republicans everywhere.

Based on his experiences as Supreme Commander during the war, and on his personality, Eisenhower insisted on developing a team concept in any organization of which he was a part. Brownell said that in "the original conception of the *team*," Nixon fit perfectly. Brownell and his associates, primarily General Lucius Clay, an old friend of Eisenhower's and former head of the American occupation of Germany, and Senator Henry Cabot Lodge, Jr., wanted to have Eisenhower, "who was experienced on the world scene, running with a young, aggressive fellow, who knew the domestic issues and agreed with [Eisenhower's] policies." Then Eisenhhower "could be presented to the country as one who would stand up against the Communists in the international sphere, and

249

Nixon would lead the fight in the discussion of the domestic issues."[2]

Dewey added that Nixon "had a very fine voting record in both the House and the Senate, good, intelligent, middle of the road, and at this time it was important to get a Senator who knew the world was round." Since the Old Guard dominated the Republican side of the Senate, such men were difficult to find. "His age was a useful factor. He had a fine record in the war. Most of all, however, he was an extraordinarily intelligent man, fine balance and character."[3]

WITH THESE ATTRIBUTES, and with the support of Eisenhower's inner circle, how could Nixon miss? Very easily, in fact—Nixon knew the political history of the Republican Party well enough to know that there were a thousand pitfalls between him and the nomination. The first was appearing overeager. Nixon avoided that. All through the maneuvering that went on before the convention, from early 1951 until July 1952, his name appeared on every speculative list of potential vice-presidential nominees, but he always dismissed the possibility as so remote as to be impossible. Thus when Brownell talked to him at a Gridiron Club dinner in Washington about the second spot on an Eisenhower ticket, he said that he was flattered to be considered but could hardly expect to be nominated.[4]

A second potential pitfall for the vice-presidential candidate was to support the wrong man for the top spot. To be a serious contender, a candidate had to deliver something of value to the eventual winnner; to do that, he had to decide in advance who the eventual winner was going to be. As noted, Nixon had bet on Eisenhower; as will be seen, he would deliver the goods that would give Eisenhower the nomination. But in the process, he had to avoid the third pitfall of so alienating the Old Guard as to lose his position as the bridge between the two wings. Nixon had to manage the delicate act of supporting Eisenhower without appearing to do so, and without ever criticizing Taft. His standard line was that Taft was a wonderful man, a great man, but he just could not be elected, and the Republicans absolutely had to win the 1952 election.

In the first half of 1952, Nixon continued to make as many speeches as possible. He concentrated on blasting the Democrats and never criticized any of the Republican candidates. He had a neat way of combining the two themes. He would plead for the selection of "the man who can best sell our program to the most people," and then quickly add, "I challenge you to name any one of the prominently mentioned Republican candidates who wouldn't be a tremendous improvement over what we have in the White House now...."[5]

His basic speech continued the themes he had used in 1951. In February, in Philadelphia, at a meeting of the Pennsylvania Manufacturers Association, Nixon blamed Truman for the loss of 100 million people a year to Communism over the past seven years. "It is immaterial," he declared, "whether these losses have been sustained because of the questionable loyalty of some of those who made our policy or because of their stupidity or honest mistakes of judgment."

He continued to urge all-out war in Korea, where General Matthew Ridgway had stopped the Chinese advance but was not undertaking a general offensive. Nixon called for the extension of the war to the mainland, utilizing Chiang's forces on the ground, supported by American ships and planes to blockade and bombard the enemy. "There are only two alternatives," he insisted, "continuing the Korean war without any real hope of winning it, or ending it with a political settlement." He rejected stalemate, and had only scorn for an armistice. "[A] settlement," he said, "would amount to appeasement, because the price of settlement which the Communists insist upon is a seat in the United Nations and control of Formosa—laying the foundation for eventual Communist domination of all Asia and in the end an inevitable world war."

After a half hour or so of criticism, Nixon's peroration was positive. He said that he had "had the privilege of traveling through and speaking in twenty-five states, and no one can travel through America . . . without realizing . . . we have the resources and . . . we are on the side of freedom, of truth, of justice against godless totalitarianism, slavery and oppression. All we need is leadership—courageous, strong, decent, firm American leadership. . . ."[6]

ON MAY 8, 1952, at Dewey's invitation—it was a combination of command performance and a tryout—Nixon gave the principal speech at the New York State Republican Party's annual hundred-dollar-a-plate fund-raising dinner at the Waldorf Astoria. The party bought a half hour of radio time to broadcast it. Nixon had his timing down perfectly. He came in at exactly twenty-nine minutes (without notes, as he remembered it; with notes, according to Dewey) and got a standing ovation.

More important, Representative John Taber and Senator Irving Ives of New York turned simultaneously to Dewey to say that it was a great speech. Dewey himself turned to Nixon, after Nixon sat down, snuffed out his cigarette, and said, "That was a terrific speech. Make me a promise; don't get fat, don't lose your zeal, and you can be President someday."[7]

Dewey had already made up his mind. Before the speech, he later admitted, "I checked with a lot of people who worked with him in both the House and the Senate. Everybody whose opinion I respected said he was an absolute star, a man of enormous capacity. They liked and admired him. So I pretty much made up my mind that this was the fellow." Nixon's performance reinforced that decision. "He demonstrated he does not speak from what someone else writes and also has a very fine understanding of the world situation."[8]

After the dinner, Dewey took Nixon to his suite for some blunt talk about the vice-presidential nomination. "The two of us sat around for about an hour or an hour and a half," Dewey later said. "That was the occasion on which I discussed with him" the nomination. The story of the meeting leaked; when asked about it, Nixon replied modestly that he "couldn't believe Governor Dewey was serious."[9] As Dewey remembered it, Nixon's response was that he would be "greatly honored."[10]

Dewey's next step was to get Nixon approved by the men around Eisenhower. A few weeks after the Waldorf speech, Dewey arranged a meeting at the Mayflower Hotel in Washington for Nixon, Herb Brownell, Lucius Clay, and Harold Talbott, Dewey's chief fund raiser. They had a long discussion about both foreign and domestic affairs. "Nothing was said about the vice presidency," Nixon wrote in his memoirs, which seems improbable, "but it was clear that they were trying to . . . size me up," which seems certain.[11]

Nixon's original posture had been to dismiss the speculation about the vice-presidential nomination. He soon had to drop the pose. In its place he adopted a coy attitude, wondering aloud whether it would be wise for him to accept a nomination if offered. One evening he and Pat had dinner with Alice Roosevelt Longworth, Theodore Roosevelt's daughter and the grande dame of the Old Guard. He asked her whether she thought he should accept. "Father used to tell me that being Vice President was the most boring job in the world," she replied. But, she went on, "if Eisenhower gets the nomination, someone will have to go on that ticket who can reassure the party regulars and particularly the conservatives that he won't take everyone to hell in a handcart, and you are the best man to do it." Nixon recalled Longworth saying, "If you're thinking of your own good and your own career you are probably better off to stay in the Senate,"[12] which if true was an astonishing misjudgment by a woman who prided herself on her political shrewdness.

In 1952, of the eight twentieth-century Presidents, one was a senator when he became President (Harding), two were governors (Wilson and Franklin Delano Roosevelt), two were Cabinet members (William Howard Taft and Hoover), and three were Vice-Presidents (Theodore Roosevelt, Coolidge, and Truman). Under the circumstances, the idea of the freshman senator from California turning down the chance to run with an almost sure winner who was making his backers promise that he would have to serve only one term was absurd. The real question is why Nixon went to such lengths to pretend otherwise, to act eventually as if the nomination in Chicago came as a great surprise to him, and to insist ever afterward that such was really the truth. Any answer is speculative, but it is worth noting that whatever Nixon's motives, he was not unique; many other politicians played the same game. Nixon just played it better.

Perhaps, as Nixon insisted, he did not seek the nomination, did not gear his actions to getting it, was concerned solely with the good of the Republican Party, and was surprised when the party decided that he was what was good for it. But he could not have done better, nor would he have done anything differently, if he had actively sought the nomination and geared all his actions to getting it. In the process, he showed himself to be a political virtuoso at the national level.

IN JANUARY 1952, Senator Lodge announced that he was putting Eisenhower's name on the ballot in the New Hampshire primary, and Eisenhower issued a statement saying he would accept a Republican nomination but would not campaign for it. He soon had to come down off that high horse, for although he easily beat Taft, Warren, and Stassen in the spring primaries, he was still, at the end of May, behind Taft in total number of delegates. And Taft's delegates were unshakable—they didn't want the general, no matter how popular he was; they wanted Taft. These were the people who had told Nixon all along that it was better to lose with Taft than win with anyone else. And these were also the people who controlled the party machinery, from national chairman on down. And in most states in 1952, delegate selection was done through the party conventions rather than in open primaries.

California did have an open primary, the last (scheduled for June 3). It was a winner-take-all primary with seventy votes involved (second only to New York). In deference to Warren's popularity, neither Eisenhower nor Taft was on the ballot. Warren was still an active candidate, despite a thumping that spring in the Wisconsin primary. Warren's hope was for a Taft/Eisenhower stalemate. The convention might then turn to him. His great strength was control of the California delegation, which operated under the rule that required everyone to vote as a unit. All elected California delegates, including Nixon, were pledged to vote for Warren until he released them.

Neither Nixon nor Knowland, the other two powers in the California Republican Party, would dare to buck Warren, tempted though they may have been. Nixon needed an Eisenhower nomination to have much of a chance of his own (although some commentators were predicting that he could have the second spot on a Taft ticket), and Knowland was tied to Taft (there was even more speculation that a successful Taft would select Knowland for the second spot). But Knowland was bound to Warren by personal loyalty—Warren had first appointed him to the Senate—and he took the position that no California delegate should so much as even talk about an alternate to Warren for the Presidency.[13] Within the restriction of running in the primary as a delegate pledged to Warren, Nixon did insist on the right to name twenty-three members of the seventy-man delegation. He picked Ray Arbuthnot, Pat Hillings, Roy Crocker, Jack Drown, Frank Jorgensen, Roy Day, and other old supporters, many of them from the Committee of 100.[14]

Shortly before the June 3 primary, Nixon declared in a radio broadcast from San Francisco, "I have constantly stated that the Republican convention should select the very strongest possible nominee at Chicago." He said that Warren was "a much stronger candidate" then Taft or Eisenhower, but "if the convention does not turn to Governor Warren, our delegation will be in a position to throw our vote to the candidate who will be selected."[15]

Behind the scenes, Nixon worked for Eisenhower. Knowland was running for both the Democratic and Republican nominations to the Senate and Murray Chotiner was his campaign manager. But Knowland was such a sure thing (and in the event won both primaries, so he did not have to campaign in the fall) that Chotiner spent much of his time helping Nixon. In late May he wrote Nixon a long letter on the Republican chances in 1952, taking the line that Taft was a fine man but could not be elected. Nixon sent copies of the letter to all the Republicans in Congress, plus his friends in the press corps.[16]

THE REPUBLICAN PARTY had received hardly any electoral votes from the South (the old Confederacy) since 1876, yet southern Republicans provided one-third of the delegate votes at the 1952 national convention. The complete absence of a genuine Republican Party in the South proved to be a major complicating factor in the process of selecting a nominee. Insofar as there was a Republican

Party in such states as Georgia, Louisiana, and Texas, it was composed exclusively of officeholders, actual or potential. These "regulars" controlled the party machinery, and were loyal to Taft—after all, his father had first appointed some of them.

Meanwhile, southern supporters of Eisenhower had attended the party conventions at the state level, had sworn that they were committed to the Republican cause no matter who was nominated (these were lifelong Democrats), and then had used their numbers to elect pro-Eisenhower delegations. The "regulars," charging that "Republicans for a day" had stolen their party, held competing conventions and sent their own, pro-Taft delegations to Chicago.

In short, Eisenhower and Taft had competing delegations from a number of southern states, of which the most important were Georgia and Texas. Each side charged the other side with theft.

There were enough delegates involved to make their seating the decisive question at the convention. If the Taft delegations in the disputed states were seated, he would win; if the Eisenhower delegations, Eisenhower was the winner. Since Guy Gabrielson was a Taft man and, as RNC chairman, in charge of convention procedure, Taft was in the stronger position.

This is where California came in. If California supported the Taft forces from the South, Taft would win the nomination. If California supported the pro-Eisenhower southern delegations, the victory would be Eisenhower's. If California split, there might be a deadlock.

Lodge turned to Nixon. "I couldn't think of anybody else who could keep the California delegation in line," he later explained. And Bill Pfeiffer, who was Dewey's state party chairman, confessed that Nixon was "a fifth column" assigned by Lodge to undermine Warren's control of the California delegation.[17]

ONE WEEK AFTER WARREN WON THE PRIMARY, Nixon used his franking privilege to mail twenty-three thousand questionnaires to his 1950 precinct workers, asking their opinion on "the strongest candidate the Republicans could nominate for President." Since the people of California had just said that Warren was their choice, the governor was understandably upset. He got even angrier when he learned that Eisenhower was far in front in the straw poll. Warren rushed Bernard Brennan, a close political associate who had worked for Nixon in 1950, to Washington to persuade Nixon not to publish the results. Nixon agreed, but the news leaked anyway, and Warren felt that he had been stabbed in the back.[18]

NIXON'S USE OF THE FRANKING PRIVILEGE was illegal but commonplace. Equally commonplace, but perfectly legal, was his practice of accepting money from his political supporters to help defray the expenses of his office. His salary was $12,500 per year, plus some $6,000 in speaking honorariums. He had a staff of thirteen people, all paid for by the government, free office space, and one free trip a year to California. Altogether, the government provided him with about $70,000 per year to run his office.

It was not enough, at least not for a man who began campaigning for the next election the day after the last one was held. He made many more than one trip a year to California; he had a huge volume of mail to handle, much larger than senators from the smaller states; he had to pay to produce his weekly radio reports; he frequently had to hire extra typists (Pat came into the office from time to time to help with the typing, but she was not on his payroll); he had other expenses, all part of the small change of politics. Wealthy politicians, Bill Knowland or Jack Kennedy, for example, could pay such expenses out of their own pocket. Nixon could not.

Ever since Nixon had entered politics, his friends had maintained a small fund to help out. In November 1950, at Chotiner's suggestion, Nixon had made it more formal. At a meeting held shortly after the election, Nixon and his advisers had agreed that he should begin campaigning for 1956 at once, on a year-round basis. Dana Smith, a Los Angeles lawyer, had agreed to serve as treasurer and chief money raiser for what was in practice the 1956 Nixon re-election campaign fund.

Smith had started with telephone calls and private letters to heavy contributors. He had accepted a minimum of $100 and a maximum of $500. Contrary to what later came to be widely believed, the money had not poured in, indeed it hardly came in at all. In late June 1951, Smith and Chotiner had gone on a statewide barnstorming operation, but they had come up with more good wishes and verbal encouragement than they had cash money. In September 1951, Smith had tried to broaden the base. He had written a form letter to several thousand Republicans asking them "to help Dick to sell effectively to the people of California the economic and political systems which we all believe in." Smith had said the goal was $25,000, and had stressed the $500-per-contributor limit, "so that it can never be charged that anyone is contributing so much as to think he is entitled to special favors." There had been some seventy responses, mainly from Southern California small-business men, with a preponderance of independents in the oil industry, real-estate men and stockbrokers, and a scattering of ranchers, merchants, lawyers, and manufacturers.[19]

The effort had fallen short of the goal by some $7,000. Nixon then decided it was time to turn to the regular party organization. On June 9, 1952, he wrote Smith, "I think the time has now come for us to have a showdown with Republican Finance on obtaining assistance for our program." He suggested that $10,000 a year from Southern California and $5,000 from the northern half of the state would be reasonable sums to demand. He said that the most important justification was "that the purpose of all these off-year expenditures is, in the final analysis, to assure the [1956] election." Another justification was that "this type of expenditure is taken care of customarily by Republican Finance in other states like New York and Pennsylvania."

"I feel very strongly on this matter," Nixon told Smith. So strongly, in fact, that he was ready to threaten the party—"I intend to condition my future co-operation with Republican Finance on whether they support our program." He pointed out quite rightly that he never took a speaker's fee for an appearance at a Republican fund raiser, and it was just as true that he was one of the hottest fund raisers in the party. Of course, although he was not making any money from the speeches, he was piling up political capital. Of course, being Nixon, he had to deny the obvious—thus he told Smith, "As you are aware, appearing at such a dinner is not politically advantageous."

In his conclusion, Nixon said that he felt "tremendously indebted to our special group for what they had done to make our programs possible in the past, but I don't feel that they should continue to bear this burden indefinitely." Smith noted sadly in his reply that the party was free with its promises but never let go of any cash, that the $18,000 he had collected was almost all spent, and that he hoped to be able to "scare up enough more money here and there to see us through the summer."[20]

Most of the money went for mailings, nearly $5,000 of it for Christmas cards alone. The rest went into airfares, radio costs, extra office help, and the like. Nixon did not keep any of the money for himself, but the fund certainly helped him pay his political bills.

Later, much was made of the composition of the contributors in relation to Nixon's voting record. On public-housing issues, he always came down on the side of the private developers and realtors; on oil issues, he sided with California's oilmen. But he would have voted the way he did no matter who contributed to the fund, or even had there been no fund. In no way could Nixon be said to have been "bought." As Smith emphasized, "I do not know of any instance in which . . . Senator Nixon . . . ever did anything for any contributor . . . which he would not have done for any responsible constituent."[21]

Smith's statement could neither be proved nor disproved. It is true that the files of Senator Nixon's office were filled with requests to federal agencies for various problems of various constituents, many of them not noticeably heavy contributors. It is also true that Nixon's office requested information about or urged speed in the resolution of problems specific to contributors to the fund. In one case, the office interceded on behalf of Dana Smith himself in a Justice Department case in which a firm owned by Smith's family was asking for a $500,000 rebate.[22]

Such inquiries were commonly made by politicians in behalf of their constituents and contributors. Nixon was neither making nor breaking rules. What was unique about Nixon was that he was the only politician in the country who engaged in such practices while simultaneously demanding the resignation of both the DNC and the RNC chairmen for having made similar phone calls to federal agencies in behalf of their friends.

Nixon paid an immediate price for his hypocrisy. On June 7, twenty-one Republican congressmen sent a petition to Gabrielson asking him to select Nixon as the keynote speaker for the convention. They said he was "one of the most outstanding orators in the Republican party, and he can press the Republican cause very effectively." But Gabrielson had not forgotten Nixon's demands that he resign over the conflict-of-interest charge, even after he had been cleared. He chose General Douglas MacArthur instead.[23]

On July 1, Nixon went to Chicago for the preconvention maneuvering, working closely with Lodge. Lodge was in a desperate situation. Because the RNC had ruled for the pro-Taft delegations, he was in danger of losing the nomination for his man even before the convention formally opened. Desperation inspired genius: Lodge dreamed up an amendment to the convention rules that had the effect of taking the jurisdiction over disputed delegations away from the RNC and placing it in the hands of the delegates as a whole. In that vote, none of the contested delegations could participate.

One of the many beauties of the amendment was Lodge's name for it—he called it Fair Play. It would allow California, pledged to Warren, and Minnesota, pledged to Stassen, to vote with the Eisenhower people without abandoning their favorite-son status.

Nixon's problem was that without Fair Play, Eisenhower would fall short, but for him to support it openly would be a violation of his pledge to Taft that he would do nothing to block Taft's nomination. It would also mean a break with Earl Warren, who had nothing to gain from supporting Fair Play. Warren's aim was deadlock.

Nixon wanted no deadlock, and on July 3, he issued a statement condemning the RNC for granting temporary recognition to the pro-Taft Georgia delegation. Nixon warned that the RNC's action could "ruin" the Republican Party and he reinforced Lodge's call for Fair Play.[24]

On the afternoon of July 4, Nixon flew to Denver, where he boarded the special train bringing the California delegation to Chicago. Roy Day, on Nixon's instructions, had been going through the train saying, "Isn't it too bad that Taft is such a wonderful person, but he's just not electable. It's just a shame." Day would shake his head and look forlorn, then spread the gloom to "anybody I could find to talk to."[25]

Now Nixon joined him, going up and down the train, telling delegates that the Eisenhower momentum was unstoppable and that California had better get behind the general while it could still extract a price for its support. If by some miracle Taft did get the nomination, it would come only through the use of his power in the convention to seat the regular delegations from Texas and Georgia, which would deprive the Republicans of the corruption issue in the campaign and insure Taft's defeat in the general election. Warren, Nixon confided, did not have a chance, and if California stuck with its favorite son too long, the state would be left out in the cold. To his own handpicked twenty-three delegates, Nixon revealed that what California could get out of an Eisenhower nomination brought about with California support was a vice-presidential nomination for Nixon.[26]

Warren's supporters were furious at Nixon's breach of Knowland's injunction that the California delegates not even think about an alternative to Warren. Some of them tried to get Nixon thrown off the train. He did get off at a suburban station, but only to avoid reporters' questions when the train arrived in Chicago fifteen minutes later, carrying a bitterly divided delegation.

The reporters who were waiting at the station sensed a big story. There were conflicting leaks about what had happened during the trip. Buff Chandler, wife of the publisher of the Los Angeles *Times* and a supporter of an Ike-and-Dick ticket, told John S. Knight of the Knight newspaper chain some inside stuff about Nixon's activities. He interviewed other delegates, put two and two together, and ran a headline in the Chicago *Daily News:* "GOP TICKET: IKE AND NIXON, PREDICTS KNIGHT."[27]

Naturally, all the principals involved denied everything. Lodge was by no means home free, and he had to keep men like Congressman Walter Judd of Minnesota, Governor Dan Thornton of Colorado, and other vice-presidential hopefuls dangling. He declared indignantly that there had been no discussion of a running mate for Eisenhower. Nixon reinforced the denial by buying six copies of the paper and telling reporters, "That will probably be the last time we'll see that headline, and I want to be able to show it to my grandchildren." [28]

The Eisenhower people went to some lengths to keep alive the fiction that no decision had been made on a running mate. Brownell talked to Chotiner, asking him, as the man who had run campaigns for both Knowland and Nixon, which of the two would make the better campaigner (the chances of Eisenhower accepting Knowland, a bitter-end Asia-firster who opposed all "giveaway" foreign-aid programs except those going to Chiang, were zero). Chotiner, although he had worked more closely with Knowland, sensed the direction the wind was blowing and, as he later reported, "I gave [Brownell] my candid opinion, which was that Nixon had a shade as a campaigner and also appealed more to independents and young people." Brownell wanted to know how Warren would react to Nixon's selection. "I said I didn't know but that there had not been any warmth between the two." [29]

THE CONVENTION MOVED with ponderous slowness through the various amendments and challenges involved in Lodge's Fair Play. It was so complex that even as experienced a player of the game as Senator Taft got lost in the parliamentary maze. But the debate was sharp. In upholding the claims of the Georgia pro-Taft delegation, Senator Everett Dirksen of Illinois pointed a finger toward Dewey in the New York delegation and declared, "My friends on the eastern seaboard, re-examine your hearts on this issue because we followed you before and you took us down the path to defeat." Some delegates booed Dewey, others booed Dirksen.

Although the first ballot for the presidential nomination did not take place until July 11, the real climax to the convention took place on July 7, at the initial caucus of the California delegation. At issue was what to do about Fair Play. The majority report of the credentials committee had supported the Taft delegations; a minority had issued a separate report in favor of the Eisenhower delegations. Warren, clinging to his hope of a deadlock, wanted to split the California vote, which would have given Taft sufficient votes to prevail on the convention floor, thus blocking a first-ballot victory by Eisenhower and leaving open the possibility of a deadlock. Knowland supported Warren.

At this critical juncture, Nixon rushed to the microphone to plead the moral issue. If California split its vote, he said, the delegation would be guilty of cynically splitting the difference on a matter of ethics. "I feel that any candidate who is nominated . . . would have far greater difficulty in winning in November with those contested Taft delegates than otherwise." He denounced the "Texas grab" and warned that if the Taft delegations were approved, "we will be announcing to the country that we believe that ruthless machine politics is wrong only when the Democrats use it." His eloquence carried the delegates, who voted 62 to 8 for the minority (pro-Eisenhower) resolution. Minnesota, supporting Stassen as a favorite son, also voted for the minority resolution, which then carried on the convention floor, 658 to 548, thereby giving Eisenhower the disputed southern votes, and thus the victory. Nixon had managed to make himself the key to Eisenhower's nomination, and when the decisive moment came he had opened the door.* [30]

NIXON STILL HAD TWO HURDLES TO CROSS. The first was securing Eisenhower's nomination without any first-ballot California votes. "We don't want them from California," Jim Hagerty told a reporter who wondered why the Eisenhower people did not turn to that delegation for the few extra votes needed to nominate.[31] If California put Eisenhower over the top, and Eisenhower then offered Nixon second spot on the ticket, it would appear altogether too cynical a deal. In addition, it would alienate Warren and Knowland, and thus hurt Republican chances in the general election. So California remained committed to the unit rule and to Warren; Lodge meanwhile made a deal with Stassen to switch the Minnesota vote after the first ballot, which by his count was enough to put Eisenhower over.

Nixon's second hurdle was Pat. She hated campaigning, and after the 1950 election had sighed with relief at the thought of not having to go through another one for six years. On July 10, the night before the balloting began, he spent the evening and early-morning hours arguing with her. She did not want to make a national campaign, did not want to be separated from her daughters, did not want to do all the traveling involved, did not want to incur the social obligations involved in being the wife of the Vice-President. He could not get her to change her mind.

At 4 A.M., Nixon called Chotiner. "What are you doing?" he asked. "Sleeping," Chotiner replied. "Do you want to come

* How deeply Warren resented Nixon's actions Warren himself revealed when he swore in Nixon as President in 1969. The then Chief Justice told Herb Klein that he could not help thinking "that but for Nixon he might have won a compromise nomination for President himself in 1952."

down?" Nixon asked. Chotiner went down to Nixon's room, where he was sitting talking with Pat.

"What do you think?" Nixon asked him. "If this thing is offered to me, do you think I should take it?"

"I could tell that Pat had been talking against it," Chotiner recalled, and his reply to Nixon was directed at her. "Dick," he said, "you're a junior senator from California and . . . the junior senator from California doesn't amount to anything. There comes a time when you have to go up or out. Suppose you . . . lose? You're still the junior senator and haven't lost anything." All of which was so obvious it hardly needed saying. So was what came next: "If you win . . . and at the end of four years you become all washed up, you can open a law office in Whittier and have all the business in town. Any man who quit political life as vice-president as young as you are in years certainly hasn't lost a thing." [32]

It was all very persuasive, except to Pat, who continued to hold out. She was still arguing when Chotiner left at 5 A.M. According to Nixon, Pat finally said, "I guess I can make it through another campaign." But according to Pat's biographer, Lester David, Pat was "sure she had won and that he would refuse an offered bid." [33]

ON THE MORNING OF JULY 11, Nixon went to the convention floor. California cast its seventy votes for Warren and refused to switch even at the end of the balloting when Eisenhower needed only a few more votes to win the nomination. Nevertheless, Eisenhower was nominated at the end of the first ballot, when Warren Burger announced that Minnesota had switched its vote from Stassen to Eisenhower. Then the convention adjourned for lunch, and Nixon decided to go back to his room in the Stock Yard Inn to take a nap, and be near a telephone.

Meanwhile, Eisenhower and his people had gathered in the Conrad Hilton Hotel to pick a vice-presidential candidate. This was a fairly large group, containing a number of governors and senators who were not part of the Dewey brain trust. These men were not privy to the prior deals that had been cut with Nixon, and it was important to Lodge and the other insiders to get their approval before acting. The group therefore went through the motions of considering Taft, Senator Everett Dirksen, and one or two others. Dewey later recalled that "I waited until they had gotten down through the list. I didn't say much about it, until finally they had gotten from the East all the way across to the West. Then I named Nixon as the logical nominee." [34]

Paul Hoffman, one of the top administrators of the Marshall Plan and a leader of the Citizens for Eisenhower organization, thought that an excellent idea. "I looked on him as one of the Republicans who had an enlightened view on foreign affairs," Hoffman later explained, "and I thought that a man of his views should run with General Eisenhower."[35]

Eisenhower thought so too. He had made up a list of acceptable running mates, seven names in all, with Nixon's at the top. The general hardly knew Nixon personally, in fact thought he was forty-one or forty-two years old, not his actual thirty-nine. But he knew Nixon's reputation, knew what Nixon had done for him at the convention, knew that his most trusted advisers were all-out for Nixon, knew that none of the other candidates could bring so much to the ticket, knew most of all that Nixon was the ideal man to help bridge the gap between the Taft and Eisenhower forces, which a victorious Eisenhower had made his first objective. (Over the vigorous protest of his advisers, some of whom had been spat upon by Taft delegates, Eisenhower's first action when nominated had been to cross the street to Taft's hotel, go to Taft's room, and ask Taft for his support.[36])

"I HAD JUST STARTED TO DRIFT TO SLEEP," Nixon wrote in his memoirs, "when the bedside phone rang." It was Brownell. His message was "We picked you."

"The general asked if you could come see him right away in his suite," Brownell continued. "That is, assuming you want it!"

Nixon wanted it. He was hot, sleepy, grubby, did not have a clean suit. He badly needed a shower and a shave. But he skipped all that, threw on the clothes he had been wearing, and got into a limousine Chotiner had produced. Preceded by a police motorcycle escort, he set out for Eisenhower's room at the Blackstone Hotel.

Eisenhower was coldly formal. He told Nixon he wanted his campaign to be a crusade for all that he believed in and the things he felt America stood for. "Will you join me in such a campaign?" Nixon, somewhat bemused by the pretentious lines, answered, "I would be proud and happy to."

After dictating a telegram of resignation to the Secretary of the Army, Eisenhower turned again to Nixon. He was still stiff and formal, but what he said more than made up for how he said it. "Dick, I don't want a Vice President who will be a figurehead. I want a man who will be a member of the team. And I want him to be able to step into the presidency smoothly in case anything happens to me.

"Of course," Eisenhower added, "we have to win the election first," and he got down to business. He made it clear to Nixon that he intended to take an above-the-battle posture in the campaign, leaving the attacks on the Democrats to Nixon. Specifically, he wanted Nixon to hit the Democrats on the basis of the Republican formula for victory, C_2K_1, which stood for Communism, Corruption, and Korea. Eisenhower said that as a young, upstanding man, Nixon could "personify the remedy" for Democratic corruption, and that he should make "the Hiss case . . . a text from which I could preach everywhere in the country."[37]

AFTER THE MEETING, Nixon and Chotiner drove to the convention hall, where the delegates were about to begin the process of nominating a vice-presidential candidate. Nixon had to think about who he was going to ask to nominate him and what he was going to say in his acceptance speech that evening, so he probably did not have time to reflect on what had just happened. Still, it was absolutely stunning.

After six years in politics, at thirty-nine years of age, Nixon was on a ticket with one of the most popular Americans of the century. And Eisenhower had promised him an active role in the Administration, bringing up the inevitable preoccupation of every Vice-President, the fact that he was a heartbeat away from the White House.

Bill Rogers, who was in Eisenhower's suite when Nixon arrived, said that he appeared "surprised as hell," an example of how good an actor Nixon was, almost as good an actor as he was a politician.[38]

AN EXHAUSTED PAT NIXON went to lunch with Helene Drown, evidently thinking that her husband was going to turn down the nomination. An old movie was being shown on the restaurant television, but just as Pat took the first bite of her sandwich the station interrupted the movie to flash a news bulletin—General Eisenhower had just selected Richard Nixon to be his running mate. "That bite of sandwich popped right out of my mouth," Pat said later, "and we practically ran back to the [convention] hall."[39]

At the hall, reporters surrounded her. She said she was "amazed, flabbergasted, weak, and speechless. . . . We heard rumors, but we heard rumors about a lot of people. I wasn't prepared for this."[40] Then she was caught up in the swirling crowd and could not get to her husband's side.

NIXON, MEANWHILE, HAD FOUND KNOWLAND, and asked the senior senator to place his name in nomination. Knowland agreed. Then Nixon walked down the aisle to the Ohio delegation, where he asked Senator Bricker if he would second the nomination. Bricker refused. "After what they have said and done to Bob Taft over the last few months," he said, tears in his eyes, "I just cannot bring myself to do it. I would appreciate it if you would ask somebody else."

Nixon was taken aback. He said later that "for the first time I realized how difficult and how important my role as a bridge between the party factions was going to be." The experience also gave him a theme for his acceptance speech. Governor Alfred Driscoll of New Jersey agreed to give the seconding speech.[41]

There were no other nominees, and at 6:33 P.M. Nixon was nominated by acclamation. Joe Martin, the man who had given Nixon his first big break by putting him on HUAC, was at the gavel. He asked Nixon to come up to the rostrum.

As this was going on, Jack Drown found Pat, still caught up in the milling crowd on the convention floor. He pushed and shoved to make a path for her up to the rostrum, where she finally made her way to Nixon's side. She was wearing a white, polka-dot dress and a white beret. Someone managed to get her an orchid corsage. Nixon had on a rumpled light suit, a tie covered with charging elephants, and a heavy growth of beard. "A tremendous grin" spread across his face, *The New York Times* reported, as he flung his arms around those nearest him. When Pat arrived, she kissed him on the cheek. Although he did not turn to her, he did wrap his left arm around her shoulders as he continued to shake hands with his right hand. She kissed him again, at the request of photographers, this time more on the ear than the cheek, then took her place on the platform beside Mamie Eisenhower. He never looked at her.[42]

As Eisenhower threw his hands over his head, his version of Churchill's famous V for Victory, "endless waves of cyclonic cheers" swept through the hall. The band played the GOP theme song, "There's Gonna Be a Great Day."[43]

JULIE AND TRICIA WERE WATCHING ON TELEVISION (this was the first convention to be televised). When the camera zeroed in on Pat, they waved madly at her. To their great excitement and delight, she waved back. Friends later reported that Tricia, aged six, announced, "I want everybody to vote for my daddy." Julie, aged four, cried, "I want Mommy."[44]

"I felt exhilarated," Nixon wrote, "almost heady." Pat told him later that the excitement of that moment made her forget, briefly, the long campaign ordeal they had ahead of them.[45]

IN HIS ACCEPTANCE SPEECH, Eisenhower called on the Republican Party to join him in a "crusade." When the cheering died down,

Nixon stepped to the podium. It was his great moment, and he got the most out of it. He began with a line that fit the mood of the delegates: "Haven't we got a wonderful candidate for President of the United States?" That set the cheering off again. When it stopped, Nixon pledged himself to put on a "fighting campaign for the election of a fighting candidate," and to work for a Republican sweep in the House and the Senate. He praised Joe Martin and Senator Styles Bridges of New Hampshire, said it was important that Republicans sweep the Congress so that they would become Speaker of the House and majority leader.

The crowd quieted in anticipation of what was coming. "And then may I say this one word about a man that I consider to be a very great man," Nixon went on. "I am a relatively young man in politics. . . . But I do think I know something about the abilities of men in legislative life." He said the man he had in mind was "one of the really great senators, one of the greatest legislative leaders in the history of America," and it was "one of the greatest trage-dies" that he was leader of the minority rather than the majority party in the Senate. "And I say," he concluded, "let's be sure that Senator Bob Taft is chairman of the majority policy committee after next January."[46]

The crowd went wild, or at least the nearly half who were bitter-end Taft supporters. It was their first chance to cheer, since nothing had gone their way at the convention, and they put on a demonstration that was longer and noisier than Eisenhower's.

Thus did Nixon begin his work as healer. But he caused some consternation in Eisenhower's inner circle, many of whom were still furious at Taft and who resented the enthusiastic demonstra-tion. Nixon felt that it was at this moment that he earned the enmity of Eisenhower's palace guard.[47] Perhaps so, but certainly Lodge, Brownell, Hagerty, and others knew that Eisenhower himself had urged Nixon to praise Taft, and that Eisenhower's selection of Nixon had been based on his ability to pull the party together. Still, it cast a small shadow on the gala evening, a shadow that went on into the future.

BACK IN WASHINGTON, photographers rang the bell at the Nixon home, rushed past the frightened baby-sitter, and woke up the girls. They told them to pose for pictures. The flashbulbs and the excitement frightened the children, who broke into tears.[48]

The night the Nixons returned to Washington, they got in after the girls had gone to bed. Tricia came pattering down the hall and into their room. She put her hand on Pat's pillow and said, "I just wanted to be sure you were home. I came in here every night while you were away to see whether you had come back yet." When Pat told her about what had happened in Chicago, Tricia asked what it meant to be Vice-President. "Well," Pat said, "the vice president is a man who is elected to help the president."

"Oh," Tricia exclaimed with dismay, "you mean that you're going campaigning *again!*"[49]

It was Tricia's fate that throughout her childhood her father was *always* campaigning. The preparations for this one began the day after the convention. When Nixon arrived back in Washington, he set up his headquarters in the Washington Hotel. Chotiner had agreed to serve as his campaign manager. Bill Rogers also agreed to help in the campaign, as an assistant and adviser, after Nixon "assured me that nothing ever happens to a candidate for vice-president."[50]

On July 27, en route to California, Nixon stopped in Denver to see Eisenhower, who had established his headquarters at the Brown Palace Hotel in that city. But Eisenhower was up in the mountains, fishing. Nixon joined him. Eisenhower tried to teach Nixon the art of casting a dry fly, without success. No real business was done. Nixon flew off to speak at a civic reception in San Francisco, then at a Republican convention in Columbus, Ohio, at a meeting of the California state central committee in Sacramento, and at the Illinois State Fair in Springfield. His theme was C_2K_1.

The Democrats had meanwhile nominated a ticket of Governor Adlai E. Stevenson and Senator John Sparkman of Alabama. There was already ill feeling between Stevenson and Nixon, because of Nixon's denunciation of Stevenson for a deposition he gave in the Hiss case—Stevenson had attested that as far as he knew Hiss's reputation was a good one. Much worse was to come. Stevenson, witty, urbane, sophisticated, regarded Nixon as one of the Neanderthals of American politics. Nixon regarded Stevenson as a man who combined the worst excesses of Truman cronyism and Acheson superciliousness.

Both men were good with one-liners, with the edge going to Stevenson. They warmed up in the precampaign period. Stevenson compared Nixon with the septuagenarian Democratic Vice-President, Alben Barkley, saying that "the Republican party makes even its young men seem old; the Democratic party makes even its old men seem young."[51]

EARLY IN AUGUST, Nixon went back to Denver for a series of meetings with Eisenhower. The two men's staffs also got to know one another. It was on this occasion that a lifelong friendship began between those two extraordinary secretaries Rose Mary Woods and

Ann Whitman, the latter Eisenhower's private secretary. No record exists as to the substance of Nixon's talks with Eisenhower, but some of it can at least be inferred by what happened later.

Eisenhower's closest advisers were typified by such men as Lucius Clay and Paul Hoffman. It was an older group, moderate and conservative not only in its politics but in dress, social style, and speech. Furthermore, many members of the group had worked for Harry Truman—Clay as head of the occupation in Germany, Hoffman as a key figure in the Marshall Plan. Eisenhower himself had served Truman as Army Chief of Staff, chairman of the JCS, and Supreme Commander of the NATO forces. These men had worked closely with Dean Acheson, knew him well, and at one time at least had respected and supported him.

Dewey, Lodge, Brownell, and Hagerty, the men who had engineered Eisenhower's nomination, were all to play important roles in the ensuing campaign, but they were not the men Eisenhower turned to for advice on policy matters. In those areas he trusted Clay, Hoffman, and William Robinson, publisher of the New York *Herald Tribune,* and these men were disturbed by Nixon. His charges against Truman, Acheson, and the Democrats were too strident, too loose, too exaggerated. It made them uncomfortable. More specifically, if everything went according to plan, come January they would have to govern, so it was in their interest to hold down the sweeping charges and the blanket promises that were integral to Nixon's speeches.

On August 20, Hoffman sent Nixon a report on "National Security and Our Individual Freedom," suggesting that he make "civil liberties and the rights of minorities a major theme for your public addresses." In his last sentence, Hoffman said that "Arthur Sulzberger [of *The New York Times*] and Bill Robinson are both emphatic in their view that this is an opportunity you should embrace." [52]

Nixon knew that the vice-presidential nominee's position in a campaign is always ambiguous, that he could not go off on his own, but he also knew that if he started out by communicating directly with Eisenhower's advisers, he would never be able to carve out his own identity in an Eisenhower Administration. So rather than replying himself to Hoffman's letter, he had Chotiner do it. Chotiner told Hoffman that "Dick will study the material you furnished him." So much for making civil liberties the "major theme" of a Nixon campaign. [53]

Nevertheless, the meetings in Denver did bring Nixon around to new positions on important issues. He revealed them in a long interview with *U.S. News & World Report.* One major problem was what to do about McCarthy. Eisenhower's advisers wanted to disown him; Eisenhower himself was not so sure he could afford to do so; they did all agree that Nixon, at least in the public view, was much too close to McCarthy. They wanted some distance put between the two.

Nixon complied, without offending McCarthy. He said "McCarthyism" was Truman's creation. He said he recognized "that many sincere, honest anti-Communists do not share McCarthy's interpretation of some of his findings." Then he went into a "on the one hand, but on the other" routine about how those who cried that innocent people were being injured often discovered that the so-called innocents were guilty after all. Besides, "any committee . . . is bound to make mistakes. Unfortunately, it is probably inevitable that some innocent people may be falsely accused, but on the other hand that did not mean the investigation should not be made."

Korea was an even more difficult problem. Nixon had been one of General MacArthur's chief cheerleaders, urging his full program of all-out war with China. That was not Eisenhower's idea of how to conduct the war at all, and either Eisenhower himself or one of his advisers put Nixon straight on the matter. In his interview, Nixon said that although he had once wanted to go for total victory in Asia, the time had passed to do so. With truce talks already going on, it was just too late—although he still wanted to blockade China and warned that if the Red Chinese did not accept an armistice "then certainly consideration should be given to bombing across the Yalu." That sounded tough, but was a long way short of his previous call for a major strategic bombing campaign inside China.

For the rest, Nixon was well within the mainstream of the Republican Party as he expressed views on basic issues that he retained through his political career. On civil rights, he was for progress, but it should be at the state level and voluntary. Segregation in Washington, however, should be abolished at once ("I think we've got to have the District of Columbia as an example to the rest of the world of nondiscrimination."). He opposed the poll tax, was in favor of antilynching legislation. He opposed compulsive legislation by the federal government, arguing that it would set back race relations by fifty years. He supported Taft-Hartley, although he was willing to accept some amendments to the bill. He wanted freedom from price and acreage controls for farmers. In the event of a recession, he was prepared to rush forward public works programs to maintain employment. He favored federal aid to education, but only for those ten or twelve states that were too poor to provide good schools. He fully supported the Marshall Plan and NATO. He was opposed to high taxes but wanted a balanced budget.[54]

Properly briefed in Denver, but still maintaining his independence insofar as it was possible, Nixon geared himself up for the next campaign.

CHAPTER FOURTEEN

THE THIRD CAMPAIGN
August–November 1952

IN THE SAME WEEK as the level-headed *U.S. News* interview, Nixon showed another side of himself in an interview with the Kansas City *Star*. In the *Star* interview, he was unreasonable and immoderate, and overstated his case—the same tactics he used in going after Voorhis and Douglas. In so doing, he pandered to the worst instincts of his most conservative backers.

Nixon began the interview by citing his favorite figure, the 600 million people lost to Communism since Truman became President, and hinted that there was something more to Truman's failure to go after Hiss and other traitors than simple political expediency or stupidity. But he did not say directly what those other, apparently sinister, motives might have been.

He did say, "There's one difference between the Reds and Pinks. The Pinks want to socialize America. The Reds want to socialize the world and make Moscow the world capital. Their paths are similar; they have the same bible—the teachings of Karl Marx." He did not say that the Democrats were Pinks, only the New Deal wing of the party. Still, the logic of the statement was that Nixon had accused the liberal wing of the Democratic Party of wanting, nay plotting, to turn the United States over to Moscow's rule.

On a personal level, Nixon said that his only income was his salary (which was not true; at least one-third came from speaking honorariums and stock-market tips), and then introduced a theme that he would play increasingly in the weeks to come. The Nixons, he said, were just ordinary folks trying to make a go of it in this era

271

of Democratic incompetence, "as familiar as most Americans are with the household budget crimp resulting from 'the twin pincers of high taxes and high prices.' "[1]

His self-portrait, which he built up in his press conferences, statements, and interviews, stressed the "Poor Richard" theme. The very day he was nominated he had told *The New York Times* proudly, "My wife has never been on the Federal payroll."[*][2] That was not strictly true—she had worked for the OPA through the war —but it was true that she put in long hours in his Senate office without pay. He went into detail about their lack of material possessions. He drove a used car, had heavy mortgages on his home in Washington, and on a small house he had bought in Whittier, where his parents now lived (they had sold the place in Pennsylvania and gone back to California). He described his humble background, in the eyes of some of his relatives making Frank and Hannah sound much poorer than was the case.

But behind all these, and other, exaggerations there rested a basic truth. Nixon was not interested in money, not even in what it could buy. He had not entered politics to get rich. His self-portrait says he entered politics to slay dragons. Beginning with the CIO, continuing through Hiss and Douglas, on to Acheson and Truman, and now Stevenson, he was the knight on crusade. And as befit St. George, he was the embodiment of purity. He could have maintained his law practice, he said, and as a senator made handsome fees, but he had spurned that temptation. He insisted on the highest possible ethical standards. "Regardless of the merits of Mr. Gabrielson's position," Nixon had pontificated of the RNC chairman, "his effectiveness has been irreparably damaged because the charges against him will constantly be used to camouflage and confuse the issue and to protect those who are really guilty of corruption."[3] (Gabrielson did go, after the nominations; he was replaced by Arthur Summerfield.)

The image Nixon tried to present of himself as the most honest man in Washington, a twentieth-century Honest Abe, stuck in the craw of the Democrats. They saw him as the dirtiest man in town, worse even than McCarthy, a smear artist without parallel. Their image was nearly as wide of the mark as Nixon's own. In the pre-Labor Day lull in late August, Ernest Brashear wrote a piece for the *New Republic* that managed to get just about everything wrong, beginning with the charge that Nixon was the tool of "big business and the vested interests." In a rewrite of history that turned the

---

* A reference to Democratic vice-presidential nominee Senator John Sparkman of Alabama, whose wife worked in his office.

facts on their head, Brashear helped establish what became a standard Democratic myth about Nixon—his reprehensible conduct in the 1950 campaign against Helen Douglas. Brashear wrote: "Helen Douglas' heart was set on a constructive campaign, seeking solutions for the mounting urban and rural problems of California." Poor Helen was just "heartsick" when Nixon forced her to defend herself. Brashear said all this about a woman who had started the campaign by charging that there was a Nixon-Marcantonio axis.[4]

ON SEPTEMBER 2, Nixon began a four-day trial run for his campaign with a barnstorming tour of Maine. He declared that he would make "Communist subversion and corruption the theme of every speech from now until the election," and added, "If the record itself smears, let it smear. If the dry rot of corruption and communism, which has eaten deep into our body politic during the past seven years, can only be chopped out with a hatchet—then let's call for a hatchet."

He was out for blood. He explicitly rejected the idea of a "nicey-nice little powder-puff duel." He hit Stevenson for his Hiss statement, chided him for "referring to the Communist menace in America as phantoms," charged that for every Administration scandal that had been revealed "there are ten which haven't yet been uncovered," insisted that respect for public officials "can only be restored by a thorough housecleaning of the sticky-fingered crew now contaminating the national capital," claimed that Eisenhower would "liberate" the Soviet satellites in Eastern Europe while Stevenson offered only "a negative policy of containment," and warned that the American people would condemn themselves to "ultimate national suicide" if they continued to put Democrats in the White House.[5]

Nixon's condemnation of containment was new. From the time of the Truman Doctrine and the Marshall Plan through the formation of NATO and the return of American troops to Europe, Nixon had been a supporter of containment. But the Republican platform for 1952 had denounced containment as the abandonment of Eastern Europe to the Russians, and promised that Republican policy would be to liberate the area. The Republicans, in other words, were ready to go over from the defensive in the Cold War to the offensive. They were aware that such a platform would have great appeal in the ethnic working-class sections of industrial cities, areas that usually voted overwhelmingly Democratic. Having failed to make foreign policy an issue in 1948 and having lost, the Republicans were determined to make something of the subject in 1952. John Foster Dulles had drafted the fire-breathing plank. Eisenhower had been upset by it, and had persuaded Dulles to add some softening words, but he was still unhappy with the plank, because he had no idea how to go about liberating Poland. Nixon, however, was eager to criticize the Democrats for having offered and administered the policy he formerly had enthusiastically endorsed.

Nixon's supporters were not looking for consistency in his record, and his charges about the Democrats drew a good response. What Nixon did not know was that his attacks were causing Eisenhower's closest advisers to shake their heads again. Not the politicians among them—not Lodge or Hagerty or Dewey—but the policy people, Clay, Robinson, and Hoffman. They were as unhappy as Eisenhower with Nixon's loud call for liberation, and they cringed at the charge that the opposition would lead the country to national suicide. But the politicians in the inner circle, the men like Dewey and Brownell and Hagerty, who had lost the White House in 1948 by being too respectful of Truman and the opposition, rather liked what Nixon was saying and how he said it. "Anything to win" was not just Nixon's motto in 1952.

Thus did the Republican Party bring out two sides of Nixon. One side, encouraged by an older, old-fashioned kind of stodgy Republican conservatism, was the moderate and reasonable Nixon who supported the Marshall Plan in the face of heavy voter opposition, the Nixon who toned down the proceedings in HUAC, the Nixon who knew the importance of NATO and was ready to accept America's new role in the world. The other side, encouraged by some bitter losers (Dewey and his men) and by some of the new, tough, no-holds-barred Republicans coming out of the West and Midwest (Knowland, McCarthy, Jenner), was the wild slashing Nixon who drew no line in what he said about the Democrats, or at what he advocated for dealing with the Communists. Both sides of the man were authentic; both represented a part of the real Nixon.

ONE OF NIXON'S OPENING THEMES was political corruption in the Truman Administration,[6] where deepfreezes and mink coats had become symbols for gifts given to government officials for favors rendered. In going after graft, however, Nixon practically invited the Democrats to look behind his veneer. And Nixon was vulnerable, although surprisingly, for such an intelligent politician, he did not recognize the danger. The process had started at the Republican Convention, when disgruntled Warren supporters (who had previously been approached by Dana Smith as potential contributors to Nixon's fund) had spread a rumor that the senator had a supplemental salary paid for by California millionaires. But in the excitement of the convention, none of the reporters had checked out the story.

On September 14, Nixon appeared on *Meet the Press*. After the program one of the interviewers, Peter Edson, a Washington political columnist, took Nixon aside. "Senator," he said, "what is this 'fund' we hear about? There is a rumor to the effect that you have a supplementary salary of $20,000 a year, contributed by a hundred California businessmen. What about it?"

Nixon replied that there was no salary involved, that the fund was strictly for campaign purposes, that Dana Smith was the treasurer, and that Edson should talk to Smith about it. Edson was impressed by Nixon's straightforwardness; he said later that Nixon "didn't attempt to duck the question in any way."[7]

Edson called Smith, who was also open in explaining the fund and its purposes; he even suggested that other states adopt the plan to keep senators who were not wealthy from having to bow to outside "pressure." The following day, reporters Ernest Brashear and Leo Katcher called Smith about the fund. They got the same answers. Smith further explained, "We realized his salary was pitifully inadequate for a salesman of free enterprise . . . the best salesman against socialization available." Well, one of the reporters asked, was not Governor Warren a salesman of free enterprise too? "Frankly," Smith replied, "Warren has too much of the social point of view, and he never has gone out selling the free-enterprise system. But Dick did just what we wanted him to do."[8] If the Democrats had been smarter, they would have gone after that last line, not the fund itself.

On September 16, Nixon arrived in California, prepared to make his first major campaign swing up the West Coast in his train, the *Nixon Special*. Jack Drown was managing the train schedule and operation; Rose Mary Woods was in charge of preparing press releases, statements, advance copies of speeches, and general correspondence; Murray Chotiner was on board to handle strategy and tactics; Bill Rogers was there to give advice; Pat was along to supply moral support and generally to be the candidate's wife.

Pat had already brought him some excellent publicity; on September 6 *The Saturday Evening Post* had done an extremely flattering story on the Nixons, under her by-line (as told to Joe Alex Morris), entitled "I Say He's a Wonderful Guy." In the article, she said people were always asking her if she didn't get bored listening to the same speech over and over.

"I don't get bored" was her reply, "because every one of Dick's speeches is different. He talks about the same issues, of course, but not in the same words or the same way. There's always a new angle or a local story, and I'm always eagerly waiting to see how he'll do it this time. I haven't been disappointed—or bored—yet."[9]

ON SEPTEMBER 17, Nixon kicked off his West Coast campaign with a rally in Pomona, the place where he had started both the Voorhis and Douglas campaigns. His parents were there to lead a flag-waving delegation from Whittier; Governor Warren was there to introduce him. A week earlier, Stevenson had traveled through central California, up to Oregon and Washington, on the same route Nixon was following. Nixon promised to "nail down those lies" Stevenson had told. He lambasted the "Truman regime" for its "greedy, gouging, grumbling history."[10]

The next day the whistle-stopping began. The first stop was Bakersfield, where Nixon called out to the crowd, "Who can clean up the mess in Washington?" The audience responded, "Ike can." The next stop was Tulare, where the eleven-car train started to pull out of the station before Nixon could finish and get the crowd chanting "Ike can." He spread his arms as the train moved out and implored, "If you believe as I believe, come along on this great Crusade. . . ." Hundreds of people, magnetized by Nixon's out-stretched arms, followed along until the train picked up speed.

When Nixon went inside, he was furious. He cussed out Jack Drown, telling him to "never let that happen again." Bill Rogers remarked, "I thought you planned it that way," and assured Nixon that it was great stuff, getting the people to follow the train like that. Nixon relaxed and laughed.[11]

The same day, September 18, the New York *Post* carried a sensational banner headline, "SECRET NIXON FUND!" It was followed by a two-line banner that said, "SECRET RICH MEN'S TRUST FUND KEEPS NIXON IN STYLE FAR BEYOND HIS SALARY." The story itself, by Leo Katcher, was an account of the fund which in no way justified the headline.[12] In his column that day, Peter Edson reported Smith's explanation in a straight news story without any hint that Nixon kept the money for himself. Edson's story was buried in the editorial pages, while the allegations implicit in the *Post* headline began to draw the nation's attention.

Nixon had advance notice of the story, although not the headline, and late on the night of the seventeenth held a strategy session in the lounge of his private car. As Rogers was the only man on the team who did not know about the fund, Nixon and Chotiner explained it to him, then asked his opinion. "I don't see anything to worry about," Rogers said when they finished. "There is nothing illegal, unethical, or embarrassing about this fund. If your opponents try to make something out of it, they will never get anywhere. . . ." Chotiner dismissed the whole thing as "ridiculous, a tempest in a teapot."[13]

Had it been another candidate, Rogers and Chotiner almost certainly would have been correct. But Nixon had set himself up as the definition of propriety, and had made himself peculiarly vulnerable. Futhermore, Nixon had made the Democrats so mad that they had lost their perspective, and all too eagerly seized on the fund to attack him. But they made a basic mistake in charging that the money was used to "Keep Nixon in Style Far Beyond His Salary." Had they bothered to check, they would have known that whatever other sins Nixon was guilty of, they did not include high living.

On September 19, Nixon began to realize he was in trouble. Rose Woods reported a big upsurge in phone calls and telegrams coming into the train, raising additional questions, offering advice. Reporters from the East Coast, smelling a big story, began boarding the train. The Sacramento *Bee*, in an editorial, accused him of being "the pet and protege, the subsidized front man," for a "special interest group of rich Southern Californians." And Stephen A. Mitchell, the new chairman of the DNC, made a formal demand for Nixon's immediate resignation from the ticket.[14]

Some of Eisenhower's people thought that resignation was not a bad idea at all. Even though they knew that Nixon's speeches, filled with ranting and raving about Trumanism, were being delivered on Eisenhower's orders, he went too far. Eisenhower's advisers as a whole, even the political groups, were increasingly uncomfortable with Nixon, and became acutely so when it appeared his personal integrity was suspect. These men, led by Clay, Robinson, Hoffman, Brownell, and Sherman Adams (the governor of New Hampshire who served as Eisenhower's campaign manager), were all fiercely loyal to Ike. Their partisanship was singular —the only Republican they cared about was Eisenhower. They could not bear the thought of their hero's reputation being besmirched, and they felt a personal responsibility for having put him into such an awkward and embarrassing position. To Clay, Robinson, and Adams the thought of Eisenhower's being associated with, much less having picked, a man apparently guilty of two-bit graft was unacceptable. Never liking Nixon much anyway, they saw a chance to get rid of him.

When they approached Eisenhower with the thought, the general, who was a supposed political novice, immediately saw how much was at stake. His first comment to Adams was "Well, if Nixon has to resign, we can't possibly win." [15] That seemed obvious enough—if Eisenhower's first political decision turned out to be the selection of a cheap crook as his potential successor, how on earth could anyone vote for him? Yet almost no one else around him saw that basic truth, and Eisenhower's advisers continued to watch for the opportunity to dump Nixon.

NIXON RESPONDED TO MITCHELL'S DEMAND with a counterattack. "It's an attempt to pull a political smear," he told reporters. "Why doesn't he ask Sparkman to resign because his wife is on the government payroll?" [16]

That afternoon, at a whistle-stop in Marysville, he dealt with the fund. As the train getaway whistle blew, he called out, "Hold the train!" Jack Drown got it stopped.

"I heard that question," Nixon shouted at the crowd. Pointing to a young man, Nixon declared, "He said, 'Tell them about the $16,000.' "

Nixon told them, in his own way. "You folks know I did the work of investigating the Communists in the United States," he began. "Ever since I have done that work, the Communists and the left-wingers have been fighting me with every smear they have had.

"I want you folks to know something. I'm going to reveal it today for the first time.

"After I received the nomination for the vice-presidency, I was warned that if I continued to attack the Communists and crooks in this administration, they would smear me, and, believe me, you can expect that they will continue to do so.

"They started it yesterday. They said I had taken money— $16,000. What they didn't point out was this: what I was doing was saving you money." Then he explained that the money went to pay expenses in excess of the amounts allowable by law to a senator, so "rather than using taxpayers' money for these expenses, what did I do? . . . [I had them] paid by people back home who were interested in seeing that the information about what was going on in Washington was spread among the people.

"What else would you have me do?" he asked. "Put my wife on the payroll, like Sparkman does?" Pat worked in his office, he said, long and hard hours, and never took a penny of the government's money.

"Take fat legal fees on the side?" He could do that easily enough, he said, but it would be a violation of public trust.

"You can be sure that the smears will continue to come," he predicted, "and the purpose of these smears is to make me, if possible, relent in my attacks on the Communists and the crooks in the present administration. As far as I am concerned, they've got another guess coming. What I intend to do is go up and down this land, and the more they smear me the more I'm going to expose the Communists and the crooks and those who defend them until they throw them all out of Washington." [17]

It was an impromptu speech, delivered with great emotion. Nixon had had no chance to think through all his problems and possible responses. But already, in this initial reaction, he had in mind the outline of his formal response. He knew what he was going to say, he was just looking for the best platform from which to say it. Meanwhile, he was busy beating hecklers to the punch by opening his whistle-stop talks with his basic rejoinder quoted above. [18]

Nixon's defense got a strong, positive response from his audiences, so much so that Chotiner told him, "Dick, all we've got to do is to get you before enough people talking about this fund, and we will win this election in a landslide." Rogers agreed. He predicted that the attack would boomerang because it had come too early and had been grossly exaggerated. [19]

ON THE TWENTIETH, reactions across the nation began to appear in the press. Karl Mundt labeled the whole thing a "filthy left-wing smear." Arthur Summerfield studied the procedure for replacing a nominee and discovered that the formal, legal responsibility belonged to the RNC. That piece of information put him solidly in Nixon's camp, because he realized that the party would probably split irretrievably in a fight over Nixon's successor. Summerfield promptly committed the RNC to a policy of "down the line support for Dick." Taft said that Nixon had done nothing wrong and that he absolutely must stay on the ticket. In Los Angeles, Dana Smith made public the list of contributors to the fund, showing that the group was made up primarily of small-business men, not millionaires. He also listed the disbursements, which proved that Nixon was telling the truth when he said none of the money had come to him for his personal use. [20]

Nixon's defense did not convince his opponents, in either party. The DNC issued a "notice" to editors and reporters, citing criminal law on "bribery and graft . . . by members of Congress." The California franchise tax board announced that it was investigating the Nixon fund. [21] Truman directed the Attorney General to study the possibility of criminal prosecution of Nixon and the contributors. This was later denied, then reconfirmed. The DNC instructed workers to gather up all the "Ike and Dick" buttons and posters they could, with the thought that after Nixon resigned, the material could be used to embarrass the Republicans.[22] The Washington *Post* printed an editorial demanding Nixon's resignation.[23]

The *Post* had always been a bitter enemy and its editorial did not bother Nixon. But Bill Robinson's paper, the *Herald Tribune*, was another matter altogether. Robinson was known to be one of Eisenhower's closest friends. In his editorial on September 20, Robinson concluded: "The proper course of Senator Nixon in the circumstances is to make a formal offer of withdrawal from the ticket. How this offer is acted on will be determined by an appraisal of all the facts in the light of General Eisenhower's unsurpassed fairness of mind."[24]

Robinson's editorial nearly crushed Nixon. He had to assume that if it was not inspired by Eisenhower, it at least had been approved by the general. (In fact, Eisenhower had learned about it after it appeared; when it did, he wrote Robinson, "I have a feeling that in matters of this kind no one can afford to act on a hair-trigger. But if there is real wrong at stake, there will be prompt and conclusive action by me. That has always been my way of acting.")[25] Bert Andrews, Nixon's old friend, was head of the *Trib*'s Washington bureau and close to Robinson. Altogether it looked to Nixon as if the East Coast Republicans had become a hanging jury.

He was right about that. Robinson also sent a telegram to Eisenhower that ended, "My own personal view is that Nixon's continuation on the ticket seriously blunts the sharp edge of corruption issue and burdens you with heavy and unfair handicap."[26]

Stassen, who had thrown his support to Eisenhower at the convention and who was thought to be a part of the Eisenhower team, joined the chorus. He sent Nixon a rambling two-page telegram that practically begged Nixon to leave the ticket for the good of the Republican Party.[27]

Sherman Adams called Paul Hoffman in California. "He asked me to begin an immediate investigation of the Nixon Fund," Hoffman said, "to find out if it was clean." Hoffman retained Gibson, Dunn and Crutcher, a highly respected Los Angeles law firm, to give an opinion on the legality of the fund, and the well-known Price Waterhouse accounting firm to go over the books. Some fifty lawyers and accountants went to work at once.[28]

So far Nixon had heard nothing from Eisenhower himself. The general's silence hurt badly. Actually, Nixon was getting a break, because if Eisenhower had sent him the letter he had drafted on what to do about the uproar, Nixon would have been even angrier and more apprehensive. In the draft, Eisenhower suggested that Nixon invite Senator Paul Douglas, the Democratic chairman of the Senate Committee on Ethics in Government, "to examine your complete records and to make his findings public." [29] But Eisenhower had second thoughts about asking Nixon to put his fate in the hands of a Democratic senator, and instead issued a statement that declared, "I believe Dick Nixon to be an honest man. I am confident that he will place all the facts before the American people fairly and squarely." He concluded, "I intend to talk with him at the earliest time." He did not mean it, and went to great lengths over the next couple of days to stay out of touch. [30]

Eisenhower wanted to wait and see. But even without talking to Nixon, he was able to get a message through. The reporters on the Eisenhower train had voted 40 to 2 that the general should dump Nixon. On September 20, he called them up to his lounge for beer and off-the-cuff remarks. "I don't care if you fellows are forty to two," he said. "I am taking my time on this. Nothing's decided, contrary to your idea that this is a setup for a whitewash of Nixon." Then he added, "Of what avail is it for us to carry on this crusade against this business of what has been going on in Washington if we, ourselves, aren't clean as a hound's tooth?" The colorful phrase made headlines across the country. [31]

NIXON HAD REVIEWED HIS SITUATION in a September 19 meeting with Chotiner. Murray could not contain his anger. "If those damned amateurs around Eisenhower just had the sense they were born with," he said, "they would recognize that this is a purely political attack and they wouldn't pop off like this."

At 2 A.M. on the twentieth, Nixon, tired and discouraged, turned to Pat and said perhaps he should resign. She was accustomed to her husband's dark moods in the early hours and knew that they had always been followed in the morning by a determination to fight back. More important, she immediately saw what only Eisenhower had previously seen; as Nixon recalled it, "She said flatly that if Eisenhower forced me off the ticket he would lose the election." Pat also made the point that "unless I fought for my honor . . . I would mar not only my life but the lives of our family and particularly the girls." [32]

Pat's commonsense reply bucked up Nixon. She had to help him pay the price. The crowds in Oregon were hostile and threatening. Pat was pushed and jostled. People threw pennies into their car. Hand-held signs proclaimed "Bundles for Dick," "Shh! Anyone who mentions $16,000 is a Communist," and, in a reference to the Truman scandals, "No Mink Coats for Nixon, just cold cash." Pointing to the sign, an angry Nixon said, "That's absolutely right —there are no mink coats for the Nixons. I'm proud to say my wife, Pat, wears a good old Republican cloth coat." [33]

Early in the evening of September 21, in his hotel in Portland,

Nixon got a call from Tom Dewey. Dewey, always the broker, said the way to circumvent the "dump Nixon" movement on the Eisenhower train was to go on national TV to explain the fund. "At the conclusion of the program," Dewey advised him, "ask people to wire their verdict in to you." If the replies ran no better than sixty to forty in Nixon's favor, he should offer his resignation; if they were ninety to ten, he could stay on. "If you stay on," Dewey concluded, "it isn't blamed on Ike, and if you get off, it isn't blamed on Ike." [34]

Ninety to ten! George Washington couldn't get a ninety-to-ten vote out of the American people. Dewey's call plunged Nixon back into depression. Chotiner tried to cheer him up; Rogers later said that at that point, "Dick was ready to chuck the whole thing, and frankly it took the toughest arguments of some of us to hold him in check." Chotiner made the point Pat had introduced, that if Nixon were dumped the Republicans were sure to lose the election. Nixon at one stage muttered, almost to himself, "I will not crawl." [35]

AT 10 P.M., SEPTEMBER 21, Eisenhower finally called Nixon. He tried to buck up Nixon, then said that he had not decided what to do. Nixon let the line hang silent. Finally Eisenhower continued. "I don't want to be in the position of condemning an innocent man. I think you ought to go on a nationwide television program and tell them everything there is to tell, everything you can remember since the day you entered public life. Tell them about any money you have ever received."

"General," Nixon asked, "do you think after the television program that an announcement could then be made one way or the other?"

"Maybe," Eisenhower said.

Nixon, furious, said that Eisenhower had to stop dawdling. "There comes a time in matters like this when you've either got to shit or get off the pot," Nixon said. Catching himself, he added, "The great trouble here is the indecision."

There was another long silence. Finally, Eisenhower said, "We will have to wait three or four days after the television show to see what the effect of the program is." Then he signed off with the advice: "Keep your chin up." [36]

IN HIS ACCOUNT OF THE CONVERSATION, Nixon wrote that Eisenhower "was certainly not used to being talked to in that manner," which only showed how little Nixon knew about the general. Eisenhower was a professional soldier who had heard plenty of rough talk in his day. He himself used curse words as exclamation points, injecting them regularly into his conversation. He had been close friends for more than three decades with Generals George S. Patton and Walter B. Smith, men who were famous for their barracksroom language. No, contrary to Nixon's image, Eisenhower was not embarrassed when Nixon said over the phone that he would have to shit or get off the pot.

Eisenhower's face did turn red, but what the general found objectionable was not Nixon's word choice but his brashness. In Eisenhower's world, juniors did not tell their seniors what to do or when to do it. And Nixon was young enough to be Eisenhower's son, or his aide.

The myth is that Eisenhower was naïve about politics. The truth was that he was a master at the game, which he played with as cold a calculation as Harry Truman or Franklin Roosevelt. In the war, if one of his subordinates had told him to shit or vacate, he would have sent that general home on a slow boat. But he knew that in politics he did not have that kind of power. In the war, every American officer in Europe had been directly under his command and dependent upon him for his continuation in office. In the campaign in 1952, no Republican officeholder owed his position to Eisenhower, with the single exception of Nixon, who was the vicepresidential candidate because of Eisenhower. Even at that, Nixon would still be a U.S. senator if the Republicans lost or he left the ticket.

It all meant that the general had to put up with Nixon, which was irritating but possible. There was precedent—during the war Eisenhower had never learned to like Field Marshal Bernard Law Montgomery, but he had learned how to work effectively with him. In politics as in war, friendship was nice, but winning was better. Eisenhower wanted to win this contest with Stevenson, and if putting up with this young whelp Nixon was one of the costs, well then, that was a price the general was ready to pay.

At this stage in their relations, Eisenhower and Nixon knew little about each other on a personal give-and-take basis. They had not yet had an opportunity for a serious talk, alone, on any subject.

In addition, their staffs were much different and mutually antagonistic. The men around Eisenhower were the men who had helped run World War II in Europe or on the home front; the men around Nixon were the junior officers. Nixon's advisers were outraged at Eisenhower's advisers for their hostility to Nixon and their single-minded determination to protect the general at no matter what expense to Nixon. Eisenhower's advisers were furious with Chotiner and Rogers for their refusal to do as they were told. Throughout the fund crisis, the relationship between the two camps was characterized by tension, hostility, and mistrust.

As for the two principals, Nixon had no choice but to swallow his anger at Eisenhower for not backing him unhesitatingly during the crisis, while Eisenhower had no choice but to swallow Nixon's crude remark and get on with the contest.

CLICHÉS BEST DESCRIBE THE SITUATION. Everything came down to one speech, Nixon's career hung in the balance, it was all or nothing. It came down to clichés because the whole thing was so contrived. The fund was not a real issue, and the Democrats were criminally stupid in making it into one. They might have made Nixon's general integrity into an issue, gone after Nixon's record, especially in the Voorhis and Douglas campaigns. They could have cited him for first supporting containment and then condemning it. They might have pinned him to the wall on the implications of some of his grosser innuendos. Instead, they charged that he had taken a few thousand dollars from his supporters and used the money to buy new drapes for Pat. It was almost as if the whole thing was a drama in which Nixon had somehow contrived to be simultaneously the playwright, the leading actor, and the director.

The first requirement was financing. The RNC was reluctant to pay for a half hour of nationwide television (cost, $75,000) just to explain the fund, but Chotiner persuaded Summerfield to come up with the money. Nixon had his stage, living rooms from coast to coast. The buildup was carried out for Nixon on the front page of every newspaper in the country. The only advertising necessary was to make certain people knew when the show would go on. The potential size of the audience was staggering.

Nixon had so managed events that he ended up getting one half hour of prime-time television, before the largest audience in the history of mankind, to speak as a man accused of being a high liver and a cheap crook. The rebuttal was an almost sure thing, but he still had to write the dialogue. On the flight to Los Angeles, where the speech would originate, Nixon jotted down some of the lines he had been using on his campaign stops. Chotiner sat down beside him. He repeated an observation he had made earlier, that in all the uproar one voice had been strangely silent. Although the fund gave Stevenson an ideal opportunity for one of his quips, he had said not a word. "I smell a rat," Murray said. "I bet he has something to hide."

That evening the papers reported that Stevenson had a cash fund provided by private individuals and by firms that did business with the state of Illinois. Stevenson acknowledged that such a fund did exist, and said the money was "left over" from his last campaign. It was used, according to the explanation, to supplement the salaries of state officials.[37]

Stevenson was not candid about his fund, but the press did not push him on his evasive replies to questions about where the money came from and what it was used for. To Nixon, this "blatant double standard" was infuriating.

In Los Angeles, Nixon took a room in the Ambassador Hotel, where he insisted on being alone as he prepared his speech. Pat stayed with Helene Drown at her home.[38]

GOING INTO THE SPEECH, Nixon had some great strengths. Every orator, however accomplished, needs feedback from a live audience, so that he can judge how well this or that line works. One of the most famous political speeches in American history (and one that Nixon had heard on a recording in Paul Smith's history class at Whitter College) was William Jennings Bryan's Cross of Gold speech at the 1896 Democratic Convention. Bryan had delivered it without notes, and his apparent spontaneity, as much as what he said, had swept the delegates off their feet and given him the nomination. But Bryan had been delivering the same speech to Nebraska audiences for months, and he knew exactly which lines worked. In the days before his TV talk, Nixon had tested his basic lines. The business about Sparkman's wife being on the payroll had gotten a good response, and so had Pat's Republican cloth coat. He spliced them in.

Nixon also had a long memory and a nice sense of how to turn the tables. He recalled FDR's line in the 1944 campaign about how his dog, Fala, had been left behind at an overseas conference and a destroyer had been sent to the Aleutians to bring the dog back. FDR had responded to Republican cries of outrage by saying, "The Republicans are not content to attack me, or my wife, or my sons. No, not content with that, now they even attack my little dog, Fala." Nixon had an idea about how to turn that one back around again.

But Nixon's greatest strength going into the broadcast was the weakness of the charges. Dana Smith had done an excellent job with the books and could prove that the money had all been spent for legitimate campaign expenses. The Price Waterhouse report corroborated these facts. And the firm of Gibson, Dunn and Crutcher had given its opinion; there was nothing illegal about the fund.

Nixon was also on strong ground with regard to a broader charge, one raised by the New York *Post* in the original headline. He did not lead a life-style "Far Beyond His Salary." To prove it, all he had to do was list his assets and liabilities. The trouble with a full financial disclosure, however, was that it involved an invasion of privacy that Nixon said he found repugnant. When he had told Pat that he intended to do it anyway, she had protested: "Why do you have to tell people how little we have and how much we owe?"

"People in political life have to live in a fish bowl," he had replied, a line that he confessed in his memoirs "was a weak explanation for the humiliation I was asking her to endure." [39]

DNC Chairman Mitchell had also given Nixon an opportunity when he said that senators who could not afford to maintain their offices should not go into politics (one is forced to wonder sometimes whose side Mitchell was on). Nixon recalled a line of Lincoln's and he had Pat Hillings call Paul Smith to get it exact.

TUESDAY, SEPTEMBER 23. In the morning, Nixon went for a swim, then a long walk with Rogers. He went back to his notes, although he refused to rehearse. About an hour before it was time to leave for the studio, Sherman Adams phoned Chotiner to find out what Nixon was going to say. Chotiner said he didn't know.

Adams said, "Oh, come now, Murray, you must know . . . he has a script, doesn't he?

"No."

"What about the press?" Adams asked.

"We've set up television sets in the hotel for them, and we have shorthand reporters to take it down, page by page," Chotiner answered.

"Look, we have to know what is going to be said," Adams insisted.

"Sherm," Chotiner replied, "if you want to know what's going to be said, you do what I'm going to do. You sit in front of the television and listen." [40]

That was not good enough for the Eisenhower camp. The phone rang again. This time it was Dewey; he wanted to talk to Nixon. Both Hillings and Chotiner tried to put him off, but he insisted.

Dewey got right to the point: "There has just been a meeting of all of Eisenhower's top advisers, and they have asked me to tell you that it is their opinion that at the conclusion of the broadcast tonight you should submit your resignation to Eisenhower."

Nixon had to assume that the word had come from Eisenhower himself. It put Eisenhower and Nixon face-to-face in a power struggle. The meaning of Dewey's message was this: Eisenhower had not at all approved of Dewey's earlier suggestion that Nixon ask the audience to vote. The general was determined to reserve the final decision to himself. He ordered Dewey to make the phone call because it was Dewey who had created the problem in the first place with his "let the people decide" idea.

It was a test of wills, matching two strong personalities from two very different traditions. In the general's world, Dewey's words to Nixon were a direct order from a commander to a subordinate. In Nixon's world, the boss had to say it himself, without equivocation, and then hope that his running mate would respond. Furthermore, Nixon, again unlike Eisenhower's subordinates in the Army, had his own power base, the party regulars, who were threatening a full-scale revolt if Nixon was dumped. He had just received hundreds of telegrams of support, from Jerry Ford and Warren Burger, among others.

Instead of saying, "Yes, sir!" Nixon told Dewey, "It's kind of late for them to pass on this kind of recommendation to me now. I've already prepared my remarks, and it would be very difficult for me to change them now." Dewey assured him that he did not have to change his remarks, only to put in a sentence at the end offering his resignation to Eisenhower.

When Nixon did not respond, Dewey offered another suggestion. It was that Nixon also resign his Senate seat! Then, Dewey explained, he could run in and win a special election and vindicate himself.

There was another long pause. Desperate, Dewey asked, "Well, what shall I tell them you are going to do?"

Nixon exploded. "Just tell them that I haven't the slightest idea what I am going to do, and if they want to find out they'd better listen to the broadcast. And tell them I know something about politics too!"

He slammed down the receiver and ordered everyone out of his room. "I sat alone for at least thirty minutes," he later confessed. "The call was really a blockbuster.

"It was Chotiner who really saved the day as far as I was concerned," Nixon continued. "He was truly a tower of strength. He came into the room as I was shaving about ten minutes before departure time, and said, 'Dick, a campaign manager must never be seen or heard. But if you're kicked off this ticket, I'm going to call the biggest damn press conference that has even been held. . . . I'm going to tell everybody who called you, what was said, names and everything.' "

"Would you really do that?" a surprised Nixon asked.

"Sure," Murray replied. "Hell, we'd be through with politics anyway. It wouldn't make any difference."

They rode over to the El Capitan theater studio with Nixon in the front seat, Pat, Hillings, and Chotiner in the back. No one spoke. They arrived fifteen minutes before air time. "Even riding over to the broadcast I still hadn't decided for sure how I would conclude it," Nixon later said—that is, whether to submit his resignation or call for a poll.[41]

The set consisted of a desk with a bookcase behind it. Nixon told the camera crew he did not know whether he would sit through the speech or get up, but in any case they should keep the camera on him. He and Pat went into a small room just off the stage. Three minutes before air time the producer, Ted Rogers, came to get him.

Nixon got cold feet. "I just don't think I can go through with this one," he told Pat, his voice trembling.

"Of course you can," Pat replied, taking his hand and leading him onto the stage. He sat behind the desk, and Rogers indicated that he was on the air.

"MY FELLOW AMERICANS," he began earnestly, "I come before you tonight as a candidate for the Vice-Presidency ... and as a man whose honesty and integrity has been questioned." He began his defense with a rhetorical question: Was the fund morally wrong? It was, he said, if he had used any of the $18,000 for himself, or if he had given special favors to any of the contributors. On the first point: "Not one cent of the $18,000 ... ever went to me. ... Every penny of it was used to pay for political expenses that I did not think should be charged to the taxpayers." On the second point: "And I want to make this particularly clear, that no contributor ... has ever received any [special] consideration."

Then he listed his assets and liabilities in detail. "It isn't very much," he concluded, "but Pat and I have the satisfaction that every dime we've got is honestly ours. I should say this—that Pat doesn't have a mink coat. But she does have a respectable Republican cloth coat. And I always tell her that she'd look good in anything." Then he used the Lincoln quote: "The Lord must have loved the common people because he made so many of them."

He got in the point about Sparkman's wife, and called on Stevenson to explain his fund. He challenged Stevenson and Sparkman to make full revelations of their financial histories, as he had just done, because "a man who's to be President and a man who's to be Vice-President must have the confidence of all the people." (At this point Eisenhower, watching on TV in Cleveland, jabbed his pencil into his notepad and broke it. If three out of the four candidates made their finances public property, Eisenhower knew that he would have to do so too—which he eventually did, although he complained bitterly about it.)

Nixon said he expected the smears against him to continue. To forestall one, he admitted that he had accepted a gift from a Texas supporter. Now he was ready to use the story mimicking FDR. "You know what it was? It was a little cocker spaniel dog in a crate that he sent all the way from Texas. Black and white spotted. And our little girl—Tricia, the six-year-old—named it Checkers. And you know the kids love that dog and I just want to say this right now, that regardless of what they say about it, we're going to keep it."

Except for the Checkers bit, none of what Nixon said was new. What was new was the size of the audience. Some 58 million people watched, the largest TV audience in history (and it kept the record until 1960, when it was broken in the first Kennedy-Nixon debate). Virtually every American who was likely to vote in November was in the audience. Some viewers thought Nixon utterly sincere and completely convincing. They could identify with Nixon, with his used car and his mortgages and his wife's cloth coat. Others in the audience thought it was one of the most sickening, disgusting, maudlin performances ever experienced. (Lucius Clay thought the speech "the corniest thing I ever heard"; he later said he realized he was wrong "when I saw the elevator operator crying.")

Nixon got up, walked in front of the desk, and launched into his concluding remarks. "And now, finally, I know that you wonder whether or not I am going to stay on the Republican ticket or resign." In Cleveland, Eisenhower and his advisers leaned forward —they did indeed want to know. Nixon was speaking directly to the general now. "Let me say this: I don't believe that I ought to quit, because I am not a quitter. And, incidentally, Pat is not a quitter. After all, her name is Patricia Ryan, and she was born on St. Patrick's Day [well, almost]—and you know the Irish never quit."

Then came the direct challenge to Eisenhower. "The decision, my friends, is not mine. I would do nothing that would harm the possibilities of Dwight Eisenhower to become President; and for that reason I am submitting to the Republican National Committee tonight, through this television broadcast, the decision which it is theirs to make. . . . Wire and write the [RNC] whether you think I should stay or whether I should get off; and whatever their decision is, I will abide by it."

Next a warning to the Democrats: "Just let me say this last word: Regardless of what happens, I am going to continue this fight. I am going to campaign up and down America until we drive the crooks and Communists and those that defend them out of

Washington." He clenched his fist and thrust it forward, his face and whole body breathing defiance.

A parting sentence: "And remember, folks, Eisenhower is a great man, believe me. He is a great man. . . ." And the time was up. As the producer signaled to Nixon to cut, he was saying, ". . . Wire and write the National Committee . . . I will abide . . ."[42]

PAT, CHOTINER, HILLINGS, AND ROGERS came up to congratulate Nixon, who apologized for running over. "I loused it up," he said, shaking his head, "and I'm sorry." Chotiner patted his back reassuringly: "Dick, you did a terrific job." Nixon would have none of it. "No," he insisted, "it was a flop . . . I couldn't get off in time."

But what really upset Nixon was his failure to give the address of the RNC. He had just taken a terrible risk by directly disobeying Eisenhower's known wishes and attempting to remove the general from the decision-making process—and he forgot to tell people where to "wire and write." But his friends insisted that he had been terrific, and he began to brighten when the producer ran in and said, "The telephone switchboard is lit up like a Christmas tree."

When he returned to his hotel, there was a crowd to cheer him. Someone shouted, "The telephones are going crazy; everybody's in your corner!" He took a call from movie producer Darryl Zanuck, who told him it was "the most tremendous performance I've ever seen." He began to feel that the speech had in fact been a great success.[43]

It had indeed. Despite the lack of an address, tens of thousands of telegrams jammed the wires. The RNC in Washington alone reported the receipt of 300,000 letters and telegrams signed by more than a million people. Republican committees at the state levels received additional thousands of wires. They ran 350 to 1 in favor of Nixon.[44]

STILL ONLY EISENHOWER'S VOTE COUNTED. When Eisenhower went out to speak to the audience in Cleveland (which had listened over the radio and was chanting "We want Dick!"), he said, "I like courage. Tonight I saw an example of courage. . . . When I get in a fight, I would rather have a courageous and honest man by my side than a whole boxcar full of pussyfooters."[45]

But he also told the crowd he was asking Nixon to come see him tomorrow for "a face-to-face" talk, so that he could "complete the formulation of my personal decision. It is obvious that I have to have something more than one single presentation, necessarily limited to thirty minutes, the time allowed Senator Nixon."[46]

After the talk, Eisenhower sent his own telegram to Nixon. He praised him for his "magnificent" performance, but refrained from endorsing him and emphatically rejected the idea that Nixon's fate would be decided by the RNC: "My personal decision is going to be based on personal conclusions." In case Nixon still did not get the point as to who was in charge, Eisenhower added, "I would most appreciate it if you can fly to see me at once. Tomorrow I will be at Wheeling, W.Va." He concluded, "Whatever personal affection and admiration I had for you—and they are very great—are undiminished." Not enhanced, just undiminished.[47]

THEY WERE CELEBRATING in Nixon's suite, banging out "Happy Days Are Here Again" on the piano, when a reporter brought in a wire story about Eisenhower's Cleveland remarks. "What more can he possibly want from me?" Nixon demanded of Chotiner. He said he would not humiliate himself further by going to Wheeling. Instead, he would fly to his next scheduled stop, in Missoula, Montana. He called Rose Woods into his room and dictated a letter of resignation. She typed it up, but showed it to Chotiner before sending it, and he ripped it up, saying to Rose, "I don't blame him for being mad, and it would serve them right if he resigned now and Ike lost the election. But I think we ought to let things settle a little bit longer before we do anything this final."[48]

Now, instead of sending a wire resigning, Nixon decided to defy the general. He wired Eisenhower that he intended to resume his campaign tour and that he would be in Washington in five days "and will be delighted to confer with you at your convenience any time thereafter." An hour later, Summerfield called Chotiner, urging that Nixon come to Wheeling as requested. Chotiner said he would not come until the general had bestowed his blessing. "Dick is not going to be placed in the position of a little boy coming somewhere to beg for forgiveness."[49]

Nixon's defiance might have done him in, but he was saved by the common sense of Bert Andrews. Andrews called to praise the speech, but when Nixon told him of Eisenhower's response and his own determination not to go to Wheeling, Andrews gave him some serious advice. "Richard," he said, "you don't have to be concerned about what will happen when you meet Eisenhower. The broadcast decided that, and Eisenhower knows it as well as anyone else. But you must remember who he is. He is the general who led the Allied armies to victory in Europe. . . . and he is the boss of this outfit. He will make this decision, and he will make the right decision. But he has the right to make it in his own way, and you must come to Wheeling to meet him and give him an opportunity to do exactly that."[50]

Nixon decided to fly to Wheeling after all. First he did some campaigning in Missoula, where his party arrived at 3 A.M. At 8 A.M. he was at Hell Gate High, where he told the students, "I know a lot of you are going to say, 'I don't want to go into politics, it's a mean game, it's a rough game, it's a dirty game.' But just let me tell you this . . . politics is a tough game, but if you think it's dirty, it's your job to clean it up." And he said that only through politics could one "realize that in America all you have to do is to come out and tell the American people the truth; and if you do, they believe in you and they are for you."[51]

He was feeling as upbeat as he sounded. All the signs pointed his way. He had the satisfaction of getting a crow-eating telegram from Stassen, and another from Dewey, each praising the speech. Indeed, as Earl Mazo wrote, "The entire Republican hierarchy was singing hosannas, including the leaders who felt the program's emotional pitch to be revolting."[52] A wire service reported that Summerfield had been able to contact 107 of the 138-man RNC, and that they had voted 107 to 0 to keep Nixon on the ticket. The plane trip to Wheeling turned into a victory ride.

When the plane rolled to a stop at the Wheeling airport, Nixon started helping Pat put on her now famous coat. Eisenhower rushed up the steps to the plane, hand outstretched. Astonished, Nixon mumbled, "General, you didn't need to come out to the airport." "Why not?" Eisenhower grinned. "You're my boy!"[53]

Eisenhower was a good enough general to know when he had lost a battle. He was stuck with Nixon—but then that was the outcome he had always wanted. Even if Nixon had taken the decision from him through the weight of public opinion (or at least Republican Party opinion), Eisenhower had not lost the war. Nixon was in Wheeling, and in the limousine ride to the stadium for a rally, Eisenhower took the opportunity to let Nixon know, gently but firmly, who was boss. He said he had heard rumors about Pat having paid $10,000 in cash for interior decorating at the Nixon home. Was it true?

Actually, Eisenhower already knew that it was a lie; he had checked with people who had been in the Nixon home and they had assured him the furnishings were mostly handmade by Pat and could not possibly have cost $10,000. Just asking the question, however, made the point that he had the right to do so, and Nixon had to answer.

Nixon assured him that the rumor was false. He then warned that it was only the beginning: "Our opponents are losing. . . . They will be desperate and they will throw everything at us, including the kitchen sink."[54]

At the stadium, Eisenhower praised Nixon, with the emphasis

on the personal pronoun: "So far as I am concerned, he has not only vindicated himself, but I feel that he has acted as a man of courage and honor and so far as I am concerned stands higher than ever before." He then turned the mike to Nixon, who launched into a comparison of Truman and Eisenhower. When Truman's friends were charged with corruption, Nixon said, Truman's response was, "This is just a smear; I am not going to listen to any of them. . . . I am not even going to wait until the evidence is in before I make up my mind." Nixon said he was "glad General Eisenhower didn't do that. . . . I think his action was in happy contrast to what we have had in the past seven years. . . . What Eisenhower did was to say to me, 'Dick, take your case to the American people; bring out all the facts; tell the truth; and then we will make the decision as to what should be done." (Note the "we" instead of "I"; Nixon was not done with the power struggle yet.) "Well, folks," Nixon continued, "if he will do that with me, just think what he is going to do when he becomes President. It is going to be the cleanest, the most honest Government America has ever had." [55]

The drama was just about over. When Nixon finished, he saw Bill Knowland in the crowd gathering to congratulate him. "That was a great speech, Dick," Knowland said, shaking his hand. Nixon's eyes filled with tears; he put his head on Knowland's shoulder and sobbed. The curtain came down. [56]

As PLAYWRIGHT, LEADING ACTOR, and director of the drama, Nixon had achieved his first objective, holding his place on the ticket, thanks to the thousands of telegrams to the RNC. But as a gauge of public response around the country, the telegrams and letters to the RNC were wholly inadequate. They represented only that small portion of the audience which was so susceptible to Nixon's message it was moved to send in a telegram. Less than 2 percent of the audience "voted" for Nixon. Still, given the size of the audience, that 2 percent was enough to create the impression of a landslide miraculously engineered by the embattled Nixon in one brilliant thirty-minute television presentation.

That impression is incorrect on every count. Nixon was not embattled, no matter how he felt or what his advisers perceived. His place on the ticket was secure. The Republicans in 1952 would do anything to win. Eisenhower knew that if he dumped Nixon he might well end up like Dewey, snatching defeat out of the jaws of victory. Given those circumstances, and adding to them the hollowness of the Democratic charges, there never was a chance that Nixon would be dumped. Indeed, insofar as this was a genuine crisis, it was one manufactured in no small part by Nixon himself.

Eisenhower played his own role in the charade. He pretended that he would be an objective judge in determining Nixon's fitness to serve as Vice-President, which was obviously absurd. Eisenhower was not above milking the thing for all the drama it could hold either, as he managed to create an atmosphere of high stakes and great suspense around the television appearance: Would the idealistic young senator from the West prove his innocence? Could he convince the general, world famous for his Solomon-like wisdom, that it was his accusers, not he, who were cheats, liars, and crooks? But the truth was that Eisenhower no more needed convincing on these questions than he did on the cost of Nixon's home furnishings.

The impression that the speech was a personal triumph for Nixon is also incorrect. He held on to that part of the Republican Party faithful who were always his supporters no matter what, but he failed to use his unique opportunity to win new supporters. Instead, he made new enemies.

Despite the flood of telegrams, a majority in the audience found the speech objectionable, if not nauseating. In the years that followed, one never heard Republicans bring it up, while Democrats quoted it to one another gleefully, and enjoyed heckling Nixon by calling out, "Tell us about Checkers." What people remembered about the speech was Nixon's corny seriousness about a dog, his Uriah Heep manner in explaining his family finances, his awkward attempts at jokes, his use of that miserable little coat to make a political point, his threatening gestures at the end as he pledged war to the death with the Communists and the crooks.

In the 1970s, an anti-Nixon documentary entitled *Milhous: A White Comedy* featured segments of the Checkers speech. The speech was not used in Republican campaign films. It was the Nixon haters, not his supporters, who chuckled delightedly to themselves whenever they thought of Checkers.

At the time, as later, Nixon did *not* get even that 60 percent approval rating that Dewey had said would be insufficient. But Dewey knew about such things. The 90-to-10 vote he had called for was not preposterous at all; it was a nearly normal response from people moved to send in wires to such appeals. In fact, even at 350 to 1 on the wires, Nixon did not win a majority of the viewers.

What did Nixon learn from the crisis? He said it had made him tough: "After it, very few, if any, difficult situations could seem insurmountable. . . . Nothing could match it. Nothing could top it because not so much could again depend on one incident." He said he learned that "it isn't what the facts are but what they appear to be that counts when you are under fire in a political campaign."

Finally, two central lessons: "The best advice I can give to young men entering politics is to take to heart the Caesar's-wife admonition and to follow it to the letter" and "In politics, most people are your friends only as long as you can do something for them or something to them."

Nixon celebrated the anniversary of the speech each year thereafter. Pat Nixon never liked to think about it, and refused to talk about it.[57]

BOB STRIPLING, the former HUAC counsel who had helped Nixon uncover Hiss, had gone to Texas and struck oil. In 1952, he worked for the Eisenhower campaign. Toward the end of the campaign, he visited Nixon in his New York hotel suite. "Strip," Nixon told him, "those sons of bitches are out to get me. They got Mr. [J. Parnell] Thomas [former HUAC chairman who had gone to jail for taking kickbacks from his staff], they tried to get me, and they'll try to get anybody that had anything to do with the Hiss case."[58]

Nixon thought that the smear campaign against him resulted from the Hiss case, when in fact he had given, and would continue to give, his opponents many more immediate reasons than Hiss for wanting to get him. Moreover, since Eisenhower was adopting an above-the-partisan-battle posture, Nixon was the most visible Republican and thus the most obvious target for the Democrats.

But if Nixon was paranoid about his opponents' motives, he was realistic about their actions. From Truman down, the Democrats turned on their chief tormentor. Truman ordered Nixon's OPA record investigated. Nothing turned up there.[59] Justice Department officials tried to substantiate a rumor that Nixon, while engaged in navy contract terminations in 1945, had shaken down one of the companies involved for a personal loan. Nothing turned up there either.[60]

The Democrats should have checked certain other stories as thoroughly before making their charges in public, although their timing was such that further accusations could not be rebutted and put to rest until after the election. On October 20 the St. Louis *Post Dispatch* ran a front-page story charging that Nixon and Dana Smith had gone to Havana six months earlier, that Smith had lost large sums of money at the gambling tables, and that he had written a check on the fund account to cover his losses. The truth was that Nixon was on vacation in Hawaii at the time.[61]

On October 28, the DNC charged that Nixon and his family owned real estate "conservatively valued at more than a quarter of a million dollars." The figure included a "swanky new drive-in restaurant" owned by Don Nixon and appraised at $175,000, Frank and Hannah's small farm in Pennsylvania, and a retirement cottage they had purchased in Florida. Nixon replied that Don was renting the restaurant, and that it was "despicable" for the Democrats to attack his parents, who had sold the farm and whose modest properties in California "reflected the sum total of an entire life of hard work."[62]

Five days before the election, Drew Pearson wrote that he had gotten copies of Nixon's tax returns. Among other things, Pearson charged that the Nixons had falsely sworn to a joint property value of less than $10,000 in order to qualify for a $50 veteran's tax exemption on their California taxes. The outraged Nixon investigated and discovered that another California couple, coincidentally named Richard and Patricia Nixon, had filed for the exemption. Three weeks after the election Pearson printed a retraction.

Someone in the DNC tried to use two forged letters against Nixon. The letters purported to show that Nixon had taken more than $52,000 in 1950 from the oil industry. Just before the election, the DNC sent the story to the New York *Post*, but after its experience with the Nixon fund, the *Post* declined to print it. After the election, Pearson tried to revive it. Nixon demanded a full investigation by the Senate Subcommittee on Privileges and Elections; the investigation proved the letters were forgeries.[63]

Nixon was stung by the dirty tricks, enough so that he wrote Adela Rogers St. Johns asking her advice on how to deal with them.[64] "The taste for politics soured," he wrote in his memoirs. He realized that Pat had been put through pure hell: "I knew that from that time on, although she would do everything she could to help me and help my career, she would hate politics and dream of the day when I would leave it behind and we could have a happy and normal life for ourselves and our family."

He had no such dreams. Painful though the experiences were, he wrote, "my only recourse—and my instinct—was to fight back." And he quoted his favorite line from TR, the one about the man in the arena "whose face is marred by dust and sweat and blood."[65] If the Democrats wanted to fight with dirty tricks, Nixon was ready to oblige.

TERRIBLE THINGS WERE SAID in the 1952 campaign, especially by Nixon about his opponents, so terrible in fact that Nixon later apologized for his conduct—the only time in his career he did so. In his memoirs, written in 1978, he wrote, "Today I regret the intensity of those attacks." His apology came immediately after a sentence in which he pointed out that Dean Acheson's "clipped moustache, his British tweeds, and his haughty manner made him the perfect foil for my attacks on the snobbish kind of foreign service personality and mentality that had been taken in hook, line, and sinker by the Communists." [66]

Nor could he see any redeeming features in Adlai Stevenson, a man he described as "more veneer than substance. . . . Beneath his glibness and mocking wit he was shallow, flippant, and indecisive." [67]

But Stevenson had a way with words, and could sting Nixon as no other Democrat could. Nixon, Stevenson said, was "the kind of politician who would cut down a redwood tree, and then mount the stump and make a speech for conservation." [68] In his rebuttals, Nixon laid it on. He called Stevenson "a weakling, a waster, and a small-caliber Truman" who owed his career to a political organization infested with "mobsters, gangsters, and remnants of the old Capone gang." [69]

As the campaign neared its end, Nixon got as wild and reckless in his general statements as the Democrats had been in their specific charges against him. He kept his material so general that his opponents could only cry foul, not prove that he had lied. Nixon was pulling huge crowds, had been ever since the Checkers speech, crowds that sometimes were larger than Stevenson had drawn. The big audiences pepped him up and he became increasingly strident.

On October 27, in Texarkana, he lumped Stevenson, Acheson, and Truman together, calling them all "traitors to the high principles in which many of the nation's Democrats believe."*[70] On October 30, in Los Angeles, Nixon said that "Stevenson holds a Ph.D. degree from Acheson's College of Cowardly Communist Containment." [71]

On October 13, Nixon went on national television for the second time. He used most of his half hour to give a detailed account of the Hiss case. Then he drew what he said was the obvious conclusion: "We can assume because of the cover-up of this administration in the Hiss case that the Communists, the fellow-travelers, have not been cleaned out of the executive branch of the government." He said, "There is no question in my mind as to the loyalty

---

* The remark made Truman furious and he never got over it. He insisted that Nixon had called him a traitor. Nixon always denied it by pointing to the exact language he had used, but as Truman once snapped, "I can read, can't I?" In 1961, Truman told Merle Miller that Nixon was "a shifty-eyed, goddamn liar." "All the time I've been in politics, there's only two people I hate, and he's one. He not only doesn't give a damn about the people; he doesn't know . . . the difference between telling the truth and lying."

of Mr. Stevenson," but argued that Stevenson had disqualified himself for public trust by "going down the line for the arch-traitor of our generation," a reference to Stevenson's character deposition for Hiss. He was willing to grant that Stevenson "really believed Hiss was a man of loyalty, veracity, and integrity when he came to his defense in 1949," but that only made things worse. "If Stevenson were to be taken in by Stalin as he was by Hiss, the Yalta sell-out would look like a great American diplomatic triumph by comparison." [72]

TAKEN ALL IN ALL, 1952 is recalled as one of the bitterest campaigns of the twentieth century, and the one that featured the most mudslinging. Few of the participants could look back on it with pride. There was Joe McCarthy, constantly pretending to confuse the names "Alger" and "Adlai." There was Harry Truman, a late but enthusiastic participant, denouncing Ike personally (he was the only Democrat who would do so), saying that the general didn't know any more about politics than a pig did about Sunday, and charging that he was a "captive general" controlled by Republican big-business men. There was Eisenhower himself, usually so careful to hold to the high ground, being dragged in the mud, forced to stand next to Senator Jenner of Indiana, who had called George Marshall a traitor. Eisenhower's closest friends hung their heads in shame when he failed to defend General Marshall, and even, at Joe McCarthy's behest, removed a paragraph praising Marshall from a Milwaukee speech.

One participant who could take some pride in his performance was Adlai Stevenson. He was not only witty, but thoughtful, intelligent, concerned, and committed. He envisioned an America that would be caring and sharing. He offered a domestic program that would build on and extend the social gains of the New Deal. His speeches, his vision, his personality won him millions of loyal and enthusiastic followers. Many of them loved him not least because he was the most successful Democrat in getting under Nixon's skin.

What Stevenson could not do was cut into General Ike's tremendous popularity. The source of that popularity was, obviously, the man's achievements, record, personality, and good looks, but it should not be overlooked that some of that popularity resulted from the programs Eisenhower was advocating. He took a firm stance in the middle of the road, rejecting the entreaties of the Old Guard that the country move to the right. He promised a balanced budget, but not a tax cut; he supported Taft-Hartley, but favored some amendments; he wanted to encourage collective bargaining and the right to strike; he pledged himself to collective security abroad, with specific guarantees to NATO and the U.N.; he would continue foreign aid; he promised to extend Social Security. In short, to the discomfort of Old Guardsmen, he was not promising to dismantle the New Deal.

Eisenhower also broke with the Old Guard over Eastern Europe. The party platform, as noted, called for liberation, but Eisenhower refused to use that word. He did, however, say he would "aid by every peaceful means, but only by peaceful means, the right to live in freedom." He ridiculed those who wanted to invade or bomb China as people who did not know what they were talking about.[73] Eisenhower was evidently unaware that Nixon had called loudly for liberation, and for bombing China. The two men almost never came together during the campaign.

The big issue in 1952 was the increasingly unpopular Korean War. Eisenhower took a moderate position, rejecting either escalation or abandonment of the South Koreans. The high point of his campaign came in Detroit, on October 24, when he announced that, immediately after his election, "I shall go to Korea." He never said what he would do there, but the announcement itself electrified a nation that was already strongly pro-Eisenhower.

AFTER THE CHECKERS SPEECH, Nixon might have calculated that the middle of the high road was now the place for him to travel, right beside General Eisenhower. But that was neither his style nor his role. He wanted to lash out, and Eisenhower privately encouraged him to do it. He continued to say things that should not have been said, to make his enemies more bitter than he needed to.

ON ELECTION DAY, Nixon voted early, then went for a car ride with Bill Rogers. They drove down to Laguna Beach, parked, and took a long walk along the ocean shore. In the afternoon, they returned to Nixon's suite in the Ambassador Hotel. By 6 P.M. in California, Nixon knew that the Eisenhower/Nixon ticket had won an overwhelming victory.

Eisenhower had 34 million votes to Stevenson's 27 million, or 55 percent to 44 percent. The Republicans had taken control of the House, 221 to 213, and of the Senate, where Nixon's vote would break a 48-to-48 tie in favor of the Republicans. In House elections, the Republicans got 28,470,000 votes, the Democrats 28,715,000 votes.* Eisenhower ran almost 6 million votes, or 10 percent, ahead of his party.

What effect did Nixon's position on the ticket have on the

---

* There was no Republican Party in the South, which was the cause of the Democrats getting the most votes but fewer seats—the Republicans got *no* votes in the South in House elections.

election? No exact answer is possible, since no one had an opportunity to vote directly for or against him. Nixon may have attracted Eastern European voters in Chicago, Detroit, and elsewhere to the Republican Party, with his call for liberation and his anti-Communism. In general, however, he did not attract Democrats to the ticket, and he may have repelled some Republicans. Anti-Communism in its extreme form, as practiced by McCarthy, was *not* a vote getter in 1952, as shown by the results in Wisconsin, where McCarthy ran a full 100,000 votes (7 percent) behind Eisenhower. As the most partisan Republican, Nixon had to take some of the blame for the failure of the party to use Ike's coattails to sweep to commanding majorities in Congress.

Nixon nevertheless made a contribution to Eisenhower's victory. It was Nixon who made the ticket acceptable to the Old Guard. Men who were threatening to sit out the campaign got behind the Republicans with their money and enthusiasm because Dick Nixon was the vice-presidential nominee. Still, overall, if Nixon had any effect on the presidential election, it was to cost Eisenhower some votes.

In Eisenhower's view there were pluses and minuses about Nixon's performance in the campaign. The pluses were his service as a bridge to the Old Guard, his eagerness to blast the Democrats, and his image as St. George. The minuses were that Nixon was too right-wing and irresponsible in his views ("immature" was the word Eisenhower most often used), that Nixon was too strident in attacking the Democrats, and that he made himself too squeaky clean in his Checkers speech. In short, Eisenhower was ambivalent about Nixon, liking him for some of the same things he disliked about him.

Nixon was equally ambivalent about Eisenhower. He was awed by General Eisenhower, as everyone else was, but more than a bit suspicious about Eisenhower the politician. He also had major foreign-policy differences with the President-elect, such as what to do in Korea and China, where Eisenhower's program was much closer to that followed by Truman and Acheson than it was to the one advocated by MacArthur and Nixon. For six years Nixon had habitually criticized presidential announcements; now he would have to learn to bite his tongue and support policies he did not believe in.

As had been the case since the nominating convention in July, the relationship between Eisenhower and Nixon was dominated by a fact neither of the two men ever mentioned. Nixon needed Eisenhower but Eisenhower did not need Nixon. Whether said aloud or not, Nixon knew it to be the case, and prepared to calculate his actions on the basis of that fact.

CHAPTER FIFTEEN

VICE-PRESIDENT
1953

FOLLOWING THE ELECTION, Nixon flew to Miami for a vacation. He stayed at the home of Charles "Bebe" Rebozo in Key Biscayne. Rebozo took Nixon fishing and to a University of Miami football game. He introduced Nixon to Key Biscayne society. The two men went for long walks on the beach together. Rebozo was the perfect companion for an exhausted politician. He never introuced a subject, never volunteered an opinion, never argued. "Bebe Rebozo is the only person Nixon can relax with," one close observer said, "particularly when he's under pressure. He's the only person Nixon really trusts."[1]

Nixon had first met Rebozo after the 1950 senatorial campaign. At Senator-elect George Smathers' suggestion, Nixon had gone to Florida for a postelection vacation. Richard Danner, Smathers' campaign manager, had met him in Vero Beach. "He was tired, worn out, and wanted to relax," Danner recalled. "He was not dressed for Miami weather." Danner took him to a store to buy some suitable clothes, then to the Key Biscayne Hotel, where he had introduced Nixon to Rebozo. The next day, Rebozo had called to ask if Nixon would like to go out on his boat. Nixon agreed. He had spent the day belowdecks, working on a speech. Rebozo had spent the day puttering around his boat, leaving Nixon to himself. "I doubt if I exchanged a dozen words with the guy," he later said. He had worried all day about whether he had done the right thing, but was reassured when Nixon sent him a warm letter of thanks from Washington.[2]

Nixon had returned two more times while he was a senator. He and Bebe quickly became friends. Both were self-made men who admired each other for their accomplishments. In addition, Rebozo had that quality that is essential to any politician's friend, complete trustworthiness. Whatever Nixon said to Rebozo was kept in confidence.

Rebozo, born in November 1912, in Tampa, was two months older than Nixon. His parents were Cuban; he was the youngest of nine children; by 1952 he was well on his way to wealth thanks to a combination of shrewd real-estate dealings and a lot of hustle. He had been married and divorced twice (to the same woman). He was a quiet, unobtrusive man, discreet, willing to stay in the background. He enjoyed being around politicians, with no preference as to party affiliation, and enjoyed entertaining them. By the beginning of the fifties, he counted among his friends Florida's Democratic governor, Claude Kirk, and its senator, George Smathers. Lyndon and Lady Bird Johnson had been his houseguests, along with Senators Russell Long of Louisiana, Richard Russell of Georgia, and Stuart Symington of Missouri. From the politicians' point of view, Rebozo was the perfect host—he picked up the checks, did whatever it was they wanted to do, fishing, swimming, golf, drinking, or girls, and never asked a favor.

A mutual acquaintance remarked, "Bebe doesn't present Nixon with any intellectual problems, so Nixon does not feel threatened." Another cuttingly observed, "Nixon likes to be alone, and with Bebe along, he is."[3] Rebozo was always there, ready to mix the martinis or broil the steaks or talk sports as they watched football games, or spend the day fishing on his boat. Or, if Nixon wanted it that way, to sit silently for hours on end.

When in Florida, Nixon played an occasional round of golf (he even took some lessons), but his favorite activities were swimming in the surf and fishing on the ocean. On November 15, 1952, he cut his foot severely on a piece of metal jetty while swimming off Key Biscayne. At Pat's insistence, he went to the hospital, where five stitches were taken in the wound. He spent the following day on Rebozo's boat, fishing.[4] When he returned to Washington, Nixon wrote Rebozo, "You were wonderful to give us so much of your time, and, believe me, you were just what the doctor ordered. . . . We have put your name at the top of the list for the inaugural ceremonies."[5]

For his part, Rebozo was thrilled to have the Vice-President as a friend. In December, he wrote Rose Mary Woods, who had also been his guest: "I don't know when I have so thoroughly enjoyed someone else's vacation as I did your recent one. I sure hope that the Boss finds it necessary to return often and brings you with him." As to the invitation to the inaugural, it was "certainly wonderful, the thrill of a lifetime."[6]

BACK IN WASHINGTON, Nixon spent the first three weeks of January catching up on his correspondence, with the hope of having a clean desk by January 20. Simultaneously, however, he had to reorganize his staff, because although he would soon be the presiding officer in the Senate, his staff allowance was going to be cut from $70,000 to $47,970. Nor would he enjoy as much office space. He did not want a staff for advice. He had no chief of staff, and his executive secretary, Bob Ladd, was responsible only for "running the office." Dorothy Cox kept the calendar for his office appointments, and Rose Woods handled requests "for luncheons, dinners, and all other engagements." Everyone pitched in to help with the correspondence. To get caught up on his work, and to prepare for operating with a reduced staff, on January 6, Nixon sent out a basic staff memorandum. He had each of the nine people he was retaining sign it, and as his staff increased over the years he had new members sign it also.

In the memo Nixon laid down firm rules. "No one in the office is authorized to sign my name to any correspondence. . . . I shall personally do all autographing myself." Another rule: "Commencing immediately, this office will not handle any cases whatever dealing with Federal government agencies." Instead, all such inquiries should be referred to California's senators. "The rule includes a strict prohibition against introducing a constituent to an agency by telephone or otherwise." Noting that inevitably members of the staff would be asked questions about Nixon's views or personal life, he ordered, "No matter how routine the inquiry is, even though you think you know the answer . . . such inquiries are to be referred to Bob Ladd and are not to be answered by anybody else."

The reduction in his staff allowance forced Nixon to be cold-blooded. He told his staff that due to the loss of four secretaries, each remaining member would have to take on more of a load. He realized this would cause "a considerable amount of overtime work," which he wanted the staff members to divide equally among themselves. In the next paragraph, without apology, he informed the staffers that they were going to have to take a percentage salary reduction immediately, and that when he added one more secretary, as he intended to do soon, there would be another "proportionate reduction" of some $500 per year per staff member. In short, more work for less pay.[7]

Nevertheless, none of the staffers quit, a good indication of their personal loyalty to Nixon. They served him well, not only working long, hard hours, but by getting to know him intimately. They could anticipate how he would respond to this or that invitation or request. They knew whom to address by a first name when answering his mail, whom to brush off with a form reply, what little personal touch to put into letters to friends, what letters to give to Nixon for his personal reply.

Nixon kept a close watch on the letter-writing operation. On one reply that Bob Ladd had prepared, Nixon scribbled: "Do not write a letter to a politically sophisticated person that is copied from a State Department line—we have to at least fool them into thinking they are getting my own opinion—reword!"[8]

He went over drafts of letters prepared for VIPs with a sharp blue pencil, almost always making some changes in phrasing, sometimes eliminating whole paragraphs and adding new ones. Letters often went through three or four drafts before he was satisfied. Like Eisenhower, he could not keep from tinkering with final products; to the dismay of their secretaries, each man would send back a perfectly typed, totally acceptable letter, ready for the mail, with a "the" crossed out in blue pencil, replaced by an "a," or an "and" substituted for a "but," with orders to retype the whole thing.

ON JANUARY 12, at the Hotel Commodore in New York, Nixon joined Eisenhower and his newly appointed Cabinet for a preinaugural meeting. Eisenhower had called the meeting so that he could read his Inaugural Address and get comments, but he also wanted to introduce his Cabinet members to one another. Few of them were acquainted; few of them were politicians. Eisenhower had not consulted with Nixon on any of the appointments. His principal advisers were Lucius Clay, Herb Brownell, Sherman Adams, and Cabot Lodge. The key figures in the Cabinet were Charles E. Wilson, president of General Motors, the Secretary of Defense-designate; George M. Humphrey, president of the Mark Hanna Company, the Secretary of the Treasury-designate; and John Foster Dulles, the Secretary of State-designate. None of these men had ever won an election (Dulles had lost one in New York for the U.S. Senate). Neither had Brownell, the Attorney General-designate, but Brownell had been involved in national politics for years. So had Henry Cabot Lodge, Jr., who was the prospective ambassador to the United Nations. Lodge had just lost a bid for re-election to the Senate to John F. Kennedy. Lodge and Nixon were the only men in the Cabinet who had served in Congress, and the only full-time politicians.

At that first meeting, Nixon limited his remarks to endorsing whatever Eisenhower said. But he did not hold himself back for long. Even before the end of the month he was making a place for himself among this group of high-powered men, defining an area of expertise in which he was the acknowledged master. It was politics. He had won more votes than any man present. He knew more congressmen than any man present, more Republican county chairmen, more contributors, more of the party faithful. And by instinct and impulse, by experience and reputation, he was more partisan by far than any man present.

INAUGURAL DAY WAS APPROPRIATELY GLORIOUS. It was cold, but the sun shone. Nixon took the oath of office at 12:23 P.M. It was administered by Senator Knowland, who used two old Nixon family Bibles for the occasion. Nixon wore striped morning trousers and a club coat; Pat wore a black cloth coat over a gray suit, with a white semisailor hat. Hannah and Frank Nixon took care of their grandchildren, who were in the main stand for the ceremonies. That evening, the Nixons attended the twin inaugural balls, one at the National Guard Armory and the other at Georgetown University. In taking office just eleven days after his fortieth birthday, Nixon became the second-youngest Vice-President (John C. Breckinridge was just thirty-six years of age when he assumed the office in 1857).[9]

AT THE FIRST CABINET MEETING, Eisenhower read his draft of the State of the Union speech and asked for comments. Nixon spoke first. He said he wished the President had laid into the Democrats more. Eisenhower said he wanted to be forward-looking and positive, then gave Nixon a lecture in statecraft. Pointing to the slim Republican majorities in Congress (eight votes in the House, a tie in the Senate, broken in the Republicans' favor by Nixon's vote), he said he had to have Democratic support to put his program through. He wanted to reduce the bureaucracy, ferret out the Reds, balance the budget, reduce if not eliminate federal regulatory agencies, and make peace in Korea.[10]

Eisenhower's instinct was to reach out to a defeated enemy, to bring him onto the team, as he had helped do with Germany after the war, as he had done with Taft after the nomination. Nixon's instinct was to keep pounding, to never let up. These more or less involuntary responses were reinforced by the position each man held. Safely elected, Eisenhower's task was to govern. It was perfectly clear that to do so he had to have Democratic support, most specifically that of the southern Democrats. These southerners, in general, were the natural allies of the Republicans on economic and social issues, but they were, nearly to a man, staunch supporters of FDR and Truman, of Marshall and Acheson, on all foreign-policy matters. Eisenhower wanted them appeased, not irritated.

Nixon had no responsibility to govern, but his position required him, on all policy matters, to agree with whatever Eisenhower decided, even though he increasingly found himself in sharp disagreement with the President. Nixon wanted Eisenhower to issue a "repudiation" of the Yalta Accords (so did Taft and the Old Guard), not because such an unprecedented act would have any effect on events in Eastern Europe, but as a way to repudiate FDR's leadership. Yalta represented everything about FDR that members of the Old Guard hated (including Hiss's presence as an adviser), to the point that they made the most irresponsible charges about "betrayal" and even "treason." The Democrats, for their part, were almost as guilty of exaggeration in their defense of Yalta (except for the boundary shift in Poland's favor, not one provision of the Yalta Accords has ever been met). But Yalta had become one of the great symbols of the age, and vengeful Republicans, led by Nixon, wanted it "repudiated."

There were overwhelming diplomatic reasons for Eisenhower to resist repudiation, but what bothered him most was the probable effect on the Democrats, who would be furious at this brazen attempt to rewrite history and make FDR responsible for the plight of Eastern Europe. Still, that was exactly what Nixon wanted to do.

Nixon's position virtually required him to take such a stand. After all, Eisenhower had chosen him as a bridge to the Old Guard. He was the only man in the Cabinet who had close connections with the Republican senators, including the new committee chairmen. He was the only one whose first and almost only concern was the Republican Party. He was, in effect, the party's liaison with the Eisenhower Administration.

In addition to all that, Eisenhower played a double game with Nixon. Time and again in the years ahead, Eisenhower would call Nixon into his office to criticize him for having gone too far in a specific statement. But he would then add, either at the time or later, some general remarks about the good work Nixon was doing in blasting the Democrats. The President wanted it both ways, and in general he got it—at Nixon's expense. The advantage to Nixon was the solidification of his leadership role with the Republican Party; the cost was increasing enmity from the Democrats.

THE NIXONS continued to live in their Tilden Street home in Spring Valley, but almost everything else in their lives changed. Bus companies put the house on their regular tours, for people to gawk at it. Reporters hung around, hoping for a story. The public's appetite for details about their lives was insatiable, and the reporters' zeal knew few bounds. The newspapers told of the girls' doll collections, of Tricia's herd of miniature horses, her giant sea turtle skull, of Julie's parakeets and goldfish, her sets of tiny furniture. Photographers invaded Tricia's classroom at the Horace Mann Public School.

Nixon's salary was $30,000, more than double what he made as a senator, plus a $10,000 allowance for expenses. Still the Nixons were unable to save much. Pat complained that the doctors were charging them "twice as much as they did before," and that she needed many new clothes. "We were also buying gifts for visitors, and though we were told that no entertaining was necessary, we did it anyway." She kept even, she said, because "I shop very carefully, and I count the pennies."

Pat planned the menus (except for breakfast, Nixon ate at home only once or twice a week), drew up the shopping lists, and drove to the supermarket herself to select the items. She would do the cooking too, usually making twice or three times the amounts the family needed and freezing the remainder. But she gradually learned that she could afford to hire a maid to do much of the housework. She took on a full-time Swedish maid and had a man come in half a day a week to clean the floors and windows. But she never let them be photographed, and worked assiduously to maintain the image of herself as a typical housewife. She allowed photographers to take pictures of her pressing Dick's suits and running a vacuum cleaner. It was not all fanciful—she apparently found it difficult to let go of years of habit and give the housework over to someone else.

In her early forties, she continued to possess great energy. She was up at six-thirty each morning, prepared breakfast for her husband and children, and drove off for another day of receptions, coffees, luncheons, teas, and official ceremonies. Insofar as possible she tried to maintain a normal life for the girls, who for the most part were able to handle their sudden fame with aplomb. They were developing their personalities too—Tricia was reserved, quiet, intense, in Pat's words, "introverted like I am." At home, Tricia was known as "the Thinker," Julie as "the Speaker," for her outgoing traits. Pat herself, despite her hectic life, managed to keep looking youthful. There was no gray in her hair, no wrinkles on her face, no fat around her waist.

She still altered the girls' clothes herself, and sometimes her own, but she began to add to her wardrobe, partly at Dick's insistence. She went to auctions, looking for bargains. In public, especially when reporters were around, she was tightly controlled, always smiling but with nothing to say. But in private, with people she trusted, she relaxed, told jokes, teased her husband. Earl and

Rita Mazo became good friends; Mazo found her "a very *haimisheh* girl," a Yiddish word meaning informal, unpretentious, warm. He recalled the time Nixon was pontificating in his study when Pat walked in with a tray. "Try some of these," she said. "They're better than that baloney he's handing out."

What she wanted most—a normal family life—she could not have. Her husband's schedule simply would not permit it. He would make promises that he would be forced to break; on the night of a Brownie Scout father-daughter dinner, for example, one of the big events of the year for Julie, he called home at the last minute to say that he could not make it. Julie's tears added to Pat's disappointment, but she bit her tongue and said nothing. For better or for worse, she was a politician's wife, and knew what had to be done.[11]

NIXON'S OFFICE QUARTERS were in Suite 361 of the Old Senate Office Building. They were too small for his needs; his files, bulging with clippings and correspondence, overflowed into storage areas scattered through other parts of the building. His only duty, aside from just being around in the event of the President's disability or death, was to preside over the Senate. This was routine stuff. He left disputed points of order to the staff parliamentarian. It became his custom to call a session to order, sit through the opening prayer and the majority leader's announcements, and then turn the tedium over to freshman members. He had a small private office just off the Senate floor, where he was on hand to break tie votes.[12]

Because Nixon had no administrative experience whatsoever, Eisenhower tried over the years to give him jobs that would provide him some taste of running a show. He started in August 1953, when he appointed Nixon the chairman of the President's Committee on Government Contracts. The committee's task was to eliminate discrimination against minorities on work done under government contract. The committee had no enforcement powers; it worked entirely by persuasion and publicity. It had a membership of sixteen and held monthly meetings to review the work of twenty-five staff members in Washington, Chicago, and Los Angeles. The staff did surveys of about five hundred contracts a year, looking for evidence of discrimination, and it processed complaints charging contractors on government jobs with specific acts of discrimination. It was all rather ho-hum stuff, but Nixon plugged away at it, and the increasing number of complaints the committee received indicated that it was doing something useful. When Governor Jimmy Byrnes of South Carolina called the President to protest some of the committee's activities, Eisenhower knew that Nixon was on the right course.[13]

NIXON HAD A FAR GREATER IMPACT, and learned a great deal more, from his position as a member of the Cabinet, of the National Security Council, and his participation in Eisenhower's weekly meetings with the Republican leaders of Congress. He was there because Eisenhower wanted him there, and Eisenhower wanted him present partly because he thought FDR had made a serious blunder in not keeping Harry Truman informed, partly because he wanted Nixon to have the experience, but primarily because Nixon filled a real need—he could always be counted on to point out the political implications of any decision.

"I come from the legislative side," Nixon remarked in one early meeting. "I know the political problems."[14] By implication, and in fact, the Cabinet members did not. Neither did the President. Nixon undertook to educate them. "Go to the Hill only in dramatic circumstances," he advised the President in July. "Truman came so often there were occasions when he didn't have a full House."[15] On the other hand he advised reluctant Cabinet members, who were accustomed to making their big business decisions in private and unaccustomed to having to explain their actions, that they should accept, not reject, invitations from *Meet the Press* and other talk shows. He pointed out that they were in such demand that they could set the terms of the discussion, and the host would have no choice but to agree. He urged them to take advantage of the built-in audiences such shows gave them, and promised again, "they will change the format for you."[16]

Nixon was constantly educating the Cabinet on publicity, on how to get the story out. He explained such tricks of the trade as getting the master of ceremonies at a function to send copies of their speeches to local editors. They should also send copies to all congressmen, and to the RNC mailing lists. He told them that speeches thus circulated "get much used for editorializing in hinterland newspapers." "We get so darn busy doing things," Nixon added, "that we don't get credit for it. We forget the sales angle."[17]

One of Eisenhower's major objectives was to cut defense spending. Nixon had serious doubts about the wisdom of that policy, but he kept them to himself and acted as a loyal member of the team. He warned Eisenhower that there was "extremely effective opposition in the Senate" to defense cuts, especially Air Force cuts, opposition led by Senators Lyndon Johnson and Stuart Symington. "They are already taking the line that you are endangering national security," he told Eisenhower in May. He urged the President to speak out forcefully on the theme that enough is enough, thus drawing on his prestige as a military man. And he suggested that Eisenhower call in the Republicans in Congress who were veterans of World War II "and line them up solidly behind your program." They could say that they were once again "proud to follow Ike." [18]

When the Democrats raised conservation and monopoly questions about the Republican-sponsored Hell's Canyon dam, Nixon told the Cabinet to counter by emphasizing the Administration's commitment to building the St. Lawrence Seaway. "We should be giving it a really big publicity push," he advised, because "it has a liberal tone to it, so let's get the maximum benefit from it." [19] Nixon's advice on defense and the seaway was taken.

NIXON HAD SOME UNFINISHED BUSINESS from the past he wanted to get at. On January 25, he recommended to the President that the Administration appropriate to the Vice-President's office $150,000 in order to "conduct an investigation and analysis of the Hiss case." Nixon said he wanted to prove conclusively that Hiss was a spy as well as a perjurer, and that he thought with access to executive files and a high-level staff, he could do so. But Eisenhower could see no point to pursuing a man who was already convicted and in prison, and anyway did not want to start his Administration with anything so emotional and controversial as the Hiss case. He turned Nixon down. [20]

CONGRESSIONAL INVESTIGATIONS were a major problem for the Eisenhower Administration. The department heads, like the President, wanted to look to the future, to get on with their work of balancing the budget, streamlining the government, ending the Korean War, establishing a new defense policy, and eliminating regulations and red tape. But the Republicans in Congress, like Nixon, wanted to use their new access to executive files to embarrass the Democrats. They were convinced there were all kinds of unsuspected ghosts in numerous overlooked closets, and it made many of them more eager to investigate the past than to legislate for the future. Dulles complained that there were ten separate investigations of his department alone going on, which made it impossible for him to get any positive work done.

But Nixon, as anxious as McCarthy to prove that things had been as bad under the Democrats as he had said they were, urged the Cabinet to cooperate with Congress. He also gave the members advice on how to do it. "Sit down with the Committee Chairman," he said on February 12, 1953, "and settle on what ought to be investigated." He emphasized that they ought to talk to the chairmen alone, ignoring the other members of the committees.

The congressmen expected to give the most trouble, or already doing so, were subcommittee chairmen, led by Senators McCarthy and Jenner. Nixon felt that those two were much too dangerous for inexperienced Cabinet members to approach on their own, and suggested instead that he, Deputy Attorney General William Rogers, and General Jerry Persons, the White House liaison man with Congress, meet privately with McCarthy and Jenner, then report back. Eisenhower accepted the suggestion, but then warned that if investigations into the past were "pursued on the basis of politics, we'll all be in trouble in 1954." It was "bad enough," he said, "to have routine Democratic allegations" about Republican ineptness; "we can't risk the charge of pursuing partisan politics in investigations." But Nixon, who knew how tightly the Republicans had gotten the investigation bit into their teeth, said it could not be helped, and again urged the Cabinet to cooperate.

His position was with the Administration, but his sympathies were with the investigators. He explained, over and over, to irate department heads that they had to cooperate with the committees, no matter how much of their time it took. He also advised them to ignore, as best they could, the hostile attitude most Republicans took toward *any* Administration official. "It will take time," Nixon said, "much time, for the Republicans to develop a new 'majority' attitude." He again suggested that he be given liaison responsibility with the committee chairmen, on the grounds of his own special experience in investigations. Eisenhower agreed, telling his Cabinet, "Leave negotiations to Persons and Nixon." [21] Persons had responsibility for liaison with Congress for the President; Nixon had it for the Cabinet. He was making a secure, significant base for himself.

Secure enough that he could even risk a little joke from time to time, something not done frequently in these meetings of men in three-piece suits with serious matters on their minds, suitable scowls on their faces, and Republican conservatism in their hearts. Still, Nixon would try for a laugh. In May, at a meeting of the Republican leaders, when the topic was an intricate reorganizational problem, Nixon broke in, smiling, to suggest a "bipartisan approach. Name a commission of Hoover and Truman and three others!" "Now look!" Eisenhower rejoined, grimacing. "We will have to have the three others as referees." [22]

WHEN THEY REALLY NEEDED A REFEREE was in their dealings with Joe McCarthy. Every member of the Administration feared trouble with the senator, and looked to Nixon for help. Nixon was McCarthy's friend, his confidant, his fellow anti-Communist investigator. Most people thought that whatever differences there were between them, they were differences of degree, not of philosophy.

Nixon was smarter, more cautious, more persistent, but McCarthy's friends were his friends, and McCarthy's enemies were his enemies. Stevenson put it more succinctly when he said that Nixon "was McCarthy in a white collar."

But there was a fundamental difference between the two men. McCarthy was a loner who cared not one fig for the Republican Party. Nixon was a loner who cared very deeply about the Republican Party, because he had tied his fortunes to it. And the party, in the context of 1953, meant Dwight Eisenhower. Whatever Eisenhower wanted, Nixon wanted—only on the rarest of occasions in the fifties did Nixon make a public hint about his private disagreements with the President. On all basic issues, Nixon was the model of cooperation and support.

McCarthy could not cooperate with or support anyone. Initially, Nixon did not recognize this fact about his friend. At a staff meeting before the inaugural, C. D. Jackson, a *Time-Life* editor serving as a speech writer and Cold War expert, had told Eisenhower that any attempt to cooperate with Joe was doomed to failure, as it would only embolden him further. He urged an all-out attack. But Nixon and Persons, always the most conservative of Eisenhower's advisers, had said that an attack on McCarthy would only divide the party and publicize the senator even more. "The best way to reduce his influence to the proper proportion," Nixon declared, "is to take him on as part of the team." An open confrontation with McCarthy, Nixon feared, would split the Republican Party down the middle.[23]

On January 22, the Administration's second full day in office, McCarthy held up confirmation of Walter Bedell Smith, Eisenhower's old chief of staff and close friend, as Under Secretary of State. McCarthy's complaint was that Smith had once said something nice about a State Department official whom McCarthy had called a Communist. Eisenhower asked Senator Taft and Nixon to talk to McCarthy—they did, and McCarthy withdrew his objections. Smith was confirmed.[24] The Administration thought this indicated that McCarthy would get on the team. What it should have noticed was that McCarthy was so outside the team that he had dared attack Eisenhower's very first nomination, and the President's old friend at that.

A week or so later, McCarthy objected to the nomination of Dr. James B. Conant, president of Harvard University, as High Commissioner to Germany. Conant had said that there were no Communists on the Harvard faculty, a statement McCarthy found so preposterous that he could only conclude that the man who said it must be himself a Communist. Eisenhower again turned to Nixon, who talked McCarthy out of opposing the nomination. Eisenhower was delighted with the result: McCarthy wrote him to say that although he was "much opposed" to Conant, he would not make a floor fight against his nomination because "he doesn't want to make a row."[25]

Two days later, Eisenhower put forward the name of Charles E. "Chip" Bohlen for the post of ambassador to Russia. Bohlen was a career Foreign Service officer who had been at Yalta. In confirmation hearings, he refused to reject Yalta, defending the agreements as the best possible. McCarthy thereupon went after Bohlen with a vengeance. He turned to his FBI sources, obtained a copy of the raw file on Bohlen, and discovered that it contained vague allegations about homosexuality. With a great flourish, McCarthy demanded that the FBI files be made available to the Senate before it voted on confirmation.

Eisenhower tried to head him off once again with Nixon, but this time Nixon was only partly successful. He was unable to keep McCarthy from opposing Bohlen on the floor of the Senate, but he did get McCarthy to refrain from alluding to the homosexuality charge. As Persons later explained, "McCarthy had two speeches ready to use in fighting us. Both were pretty rough, but one was *real* dirty. So he [asked Nixon] which he ought to give. So Dick told him—and he didn't use the real *dirty* one."

That the Administration considered this a victory indicates how ready it was to fool itself about McCarthy, and how eager to placate him. McCarthy did not drop his demand for Senate access to the files; eventually Eisenhower gave in to the extent that he had Taft and Senator John Sparkman of Alabama, a Democrat, look at them. They assured their fellow senators that there was nothing detrimental in them. Bohlen was finally confirmed.[26]

Nixon's personal relations with McCarthy remained excellent. When the senator gleefully announced that he had added Roy Cohn, an Assistant U.S. Attorney with a reputation as the Justice Department's top Communist buster, to his staff, Nixon attended a private party celebrating the announcement. J. Edgar Hoover was also there.[27]

About this time, Nixon, Rogers, and Persons invited McCarthy to a private evening at Rogers' house. Earl Mazo, who got the story from Nixon, said it was "a fine friendly evening." McCarthy agreed that he had been a bit extreme, perhaps even irresponsible at times. But he insisted that he was sincere. Nixon believed him. He said he never accepted the view that "Communism to McCarthy was a racket." Rather, Nixon said he felt that the senator "believed what he was doing very deeply." In Rogers' living room, Nixon applauded McCarthy's implied promise to cooperate, and said he did not want him to take his eye off a single Communist.[28]

McCarthy may have been as sincere as Nixon thought he was, but he was not very bright. In March, he negotiated a "treaty" with Greek shipowners who agreed not to send goods to Communist China in their ships. Stassen, head of the Mutual Security Agency (MSA), in charge of foreign-aid programs and a Cabinet member, denounced McCarthy for "undermining' the Administration. Eisenhower was upset at McCarthy's outright violation of the law, not to mention his effrontery. But Nixon, who was disturbed by the poor relationship between Eisenhower and McCarthy, "felt I should try to broker their feud."[29] He told the President that the public approved of McCarthy's private boycott against Red China, and that he therefore felt strongly that this was not an issue on which to have a showdown. Instead, with Eisenhower's permission, he arranged a meeting between McCarthy and Dulles, after which the Secretary of State issued a statement praising the senator for acting in "the national interest." Eisenhower chipped in to help when he told a press conference that Stassen had meant to say that McCarthy was "infringing" on policy, not "undermining" it. For his part, McCarthy pledged to touch base with the State Department in the future before negotiating any treaties.[30]

McCarthy seemed to have won, but when European ships continued to carry goods to China, he got mad again. Mad enough that he fell into an obvious trap laid for him by two members of his Senate subcomittee, Democrats Stuart Symington and John McClellan. They told McCarthy it was shameful the way his initiative had come to naught, and urged him to send a letter to the President demanding to know, in the name of the subcommittee, what exactly was American policy with regard to this European trade with the enemy. Just asking the question put Eisenhower in an embarrassing position. If he took a strong stand against such trade, he would antagonize the NATO allies; if he gave an evasive reply, the Old Guard would be furious. Either way, the Republican Party would suffer. McCarthy sent his letter anyway. Eisenhower, knowing what was in it, let it lay unopened on the desk.

Nixon, at the President's request, called McCarthy. He asked him if he really wanted to go through with this, and pointed out to him how helpful it would be to the Democrats, how harmful to the Republicans. McCarthy saw the point and asked Nixon to intercept the letter. The incident was closed.[31]

In June, Nixon, Rogers, and Persons had McCarthy over for another private dinner and talk. They told him about all the rewards that were in it for him if he would only get on the team. It was a glittering prospect. McCarthy could have power, influence, perhaps—who knew?—even the top job itself. McCarthy smiled and agreed to accept their advice.

A month later, McCarthy went after the CIA. He threatened a full-scale investigation of the Agency. His immediate target was William Bundy, whom CIA Director Allen Dulles had appointed to the post of liaison officer between the NSC and the CIA. McCarthy challenged Bundy's fitness on the grounds that he was Dean Acheson's son-in-law and had contributed $400 to the Alger Hiss defense fund. McCarthy issued a subpoena to Bundy to appear before his subcommittee, but Allen Dulles flatly refused to allow any CIA employee to appear before any congressional committee. McCarthy than declared that the CIA was neither "sacrosanct" nor immune from investigation.

Both Eisenhower and Allen Dulles turned to Nixon for help, which they badly needed, because the prospect of McCarthy rummaging around in the CIA files was appalling. Nixon went to McCarthy. He said he had seen Bundy in action at NSC meetings and that "he seemed to me a loyal American who was rendering vital service to the country."

"But what about his contribution to Hiss?" McCarthy demanded.

"Joe," Nixon replied, "you have to understand how those people up in Cambridge think. Bundy graduated from the Harvard Law School, and Hiss was one of its most famous graduates. I think he probably just got on the bandwagon without giving any thought to where the bandwagon was heading."

The next day Nixon had lunch with McCarthy and the other Republicans on the subcommittee, Everett Dirksen, Karl Mundt, and Charles Potter. Along with Nixon, they got McCarthy to agree very reluctantly to drop his investigation of the CIA.[32] Nixon leaked a story to the press that McCarthy would soon be shifting his attention from Communism to charges of corruption under the Truman Administration.[33]

AS BEFIT A VICE-PRESIDENT, Nixon stayed in the background, not only in dealing with McCarthy but in other things too. It was obviously wise for him to do so, as the potential traps were so dangerous and ubiquitous. In a February 10, 1953, letter, Walter Trohan of the Chicago *Tribune* had warned him of some of them. "I assume you know that all people who are out to destroy you are not in the Democratic party," Trohan wrote . "You have aroused considerable envy within the Republican party, and stand in the way of the ambitions of powerful people." Nixon's job, Trohan thought, was to "just sit. This can do you more good than harm. Few people ever got in trouble in Washington by keeping their mouths shut." Trohan feared there was a "danger that you might get impatient and press." He urged Nixon not to do it. "You are far from enmity at the moment," he concluded, "and have plenty of time to play for your future." [34]

Adela Rogers St. Johns gave him similar advice, and in a March 7 reply Nixon assured her he was taking it. "I am deliberately avoiding making any statements for publication at this time," he told her, and added that "I have been developing some very good contacts among newspaper men on an informal and quiet basis." [35] Harold Hinton of *The New York Times* noted Nixon's success in a highly favorable article on the Vice-President in a March 31 by-line story. Nixon, Hinton said, "has been extraordinarily discreet in his public and private utterances during the ten weeks he has been Vice President." [36]

NIXON'S BEHIND-THE-SCENES DIPLOMACY with McCarthy was not so successful as he liked to think it was. The senator was always agreeing to behave, then forgetting the next day. In August, McCarthy was threatening to uncover the Reds in the Agriculture Department. Nixon advised the Secretary of Agriculture, Ezra Taft Benson, to "take a firm stand, like Allen Dulles, if McCarthy gets out of line," but he also reminded Benson that he had an obligation to supply a congressional committee with "the true facts." Nixon added that it was "important to take a cooperative approach with Joe, even if it means knocking down his errors." He also advised Benson, "Watch him all the time!" [37]

McCarthy was impatient with the Administration for its seeming slowness in cleaning the Commies out of Washington. So was Nixon. In addition, Nixon wanted maximum publicity for the housecleaning. He explained his motives at a Cabinet meeting. The Communists' first objective, he said, was infiltration into government. They were there, in large numbers, and "we've got to get them out." He said he did not want "to give a 'witch hunt' impression," but neither did he want to abandon the Communist-hunting field to McCarthy and his associates. To get out ahead of McCarthy, he urged the department heads to get maximum publicity out of each and every firing. [38]

Eisenhower wanted to get rid of the Reds too, and he was even keener than Nixon on streamlining the government payroll. But he was a bit leery about claiming that everyone let go was a Communist. When C. D. Jackson announced at an October 2 Cabinet meeting that Commerce alone had fired 2,500 employees, Eisenhower interrupted him to say, "If we have 2,500 security risks in one office, I'm going to quit!" Jackson then admitted that they were not "all" security risks.[39]

Nixon rather thought they were. The Vice-President, along with Attorney General Brownell, wanted to turn the criterion for government employment away from "loyalty" and make the test one of "security." Loyalty oaths, he said, were difficult to administer, and, anyway, no Communist ever hesitated to sign one. Nixon wished that the word "loyalty"' could be completely removed from the Administration's test of fitness to serve, and reminded the Cabinet that Hiss could have stayed in government under the loyalty test. Also, a man could be as loyal as Uncle Sam himself, and still be a security risk because of drunkenness, or homosexuality, or some other trait that made him subject to blackmail. Under the security criterion, almost every one of the thousands who were losing their jobs as the Republicans retrenched government agencies could be claimed to be a risk. Then, Nixon urged, the Republicans could announce the figures, which would fulfill their campaign promises to reduce the bureaucracy and fire the subversives. In addition, it would steal the headlines from McCarthy and prove that the Republicans had been right all along in charging that the Truman Administration was shot through with traitors. The only price, Nixon said, would be "a great hue and cry from the liberals."[40]

But Eisenhower hesitated. He did not want to get into a numbers game, and refused to believe that everyone being dismissed was a security risk. Besides, it was patently unfair to those who lost their jobs—many of them would have trouble finding new employment if all of them were branded as security risks.[41]

Nixon learned in a personal way how right the President was. Bill Brock, a Negro, the star halfback at Whittier College when Nixon was a student there, had become an electronics engineer by profession and a Socialist in his politics. After World War II his politics changed and he joined the Republican Party. He had a job with Hughes Aircraft in California, but in March 1953, he was fired on the grounds that his past politics made him a security risk. He wrote Nixon, saying he had long since abandoned the Socialist Party and its thinking, and pointing out that his firm had a number of ex-Nazis working for it, men "who not too long ago were actively engaged in deadly war against the United States." He asked Nixon to help him if he could, and signed off with a reminder that they were fellow Orthogonians.[42]

In the individual case, Nixon responded handsomely enough —although it took him nearly a year to do so. He had his staff check with the FBI. According to the staff report the FBI said "this fellow is alright; that he has cooperated with them and has disclosed the names of all his associates and they believe it would be a good thing to clear his record." He also checked with McCarthy, who said he had nothing on Brock. Thus reassured, Nixon told the staff to "go over and have a talk with the Security people at the Pentagon and go to bat for him."[43]

ON SEPTEMBER 29, 1953, AT St. Matthew's Cathedral in Washington, Joe McCarthy married his secretary, Jean Kerr. The wedding was a gala event, of course, but more interesting for what it revealed about McCarthy's position in the world of politics. Pope Pius sent his "paternal and apostolic" blessings to the couple. Numerous senators and representatives were there, including John Kennedy (whose younger brother Robert was on McCarthy's staff, and who had written the letter for McCarthy demanding to know what Eisenhower intended to do about trade with Red China). Allen Dulles was present, as was Alice Roosevelt Longworth and other Washington socialites. The President sent his congratulations, along with three of his aides, including Persons and Adams. But the most prominent dignitaries present were the Vice-President and his wife. McCarthy gave Nixon an extravagant handshake and the biggest smile as he walked down the aisle.[44]

RICHARD NIXON'S CHILDHOOD DREAMS had included extensive travel to faraway places, where he could see the classic buildings of antiquity, magnificent gardens, strange people and customs, the pomp and circumstance of state dinners in great halls. As Vice-President, those dreams came true beyond his wildest imagining. In his eight years in the office, he would make nine overseas trips, to every inhabited continent, covering 159,232 miles and including sixty-one countries.[45] He was always an official visitor, so he got a royal welcome almost everywhere he went.

It all started at an NSC meeting in March 1953 when Eisenhower casually asked him, "Dick, what are you going to do this summer?"

"Anything you say, Mr. President," Nixon answered.

"Well, I think you should take a trip to the Far East. Take Pat along."[46]

One factor in Eisenhower's thinking was that Nixon needed to be publicly associated with something other than Red-baiting. He also wanted his Vice-President to know the world and its leaders better. Furthermore, he felt that Truman had neglected the Asians, and hoped that Nixon might cultivate some friendships in that part of the world. Finally, he had a specific message he wanted Nixon to carry to Dr. Syngman Rhee, the South Korean leader.

Eisenhower urged Nixon to visit as many countries as possible. Nixon put nineteen, plus Hong Kong and Okinawa, on his itinerary. None had ever before had a visit from an American President or Vice-President. The trip, which Eisenhower's press secretary, Jim Hagerty, called a "goodwill trip," was the first of its kind.[47]

Nixon worked hard to do a good job. He spent hours reading State Department material on each country he was to visit, and more hours in briefings with experts. He was a quick study, as always, and retained what he learned. He was curious about the leaders he was going to meet, and eager to learn their views. He saw the trip as an opportunity to prepare himself to step onto the world stage. To a quite remarkable degree, he met that objective, as he visited countries and met leaders with whom he would be intimately associated over the next two decades. In those two decades, not incidentally, it can be argued plausibly that Nixon was the most important American politician in Asian affairs, the one with the most impact on developments there. Events in Asia, in turn, were often decisive in his career. His first visit to the continent, and his first serious thinking about its problems, came in 1953.

Nixon displayed his determination to learn, not just be entertained, when he told State Department officials to arrange his schedule so that he could meet students, laborers, businessmen, opposition political leaders, military men, and so forth. The officials replied that such a schedule would be unusual, unorthodox, and undiplomatic. They wanted him to concentrate on the government, the heads of state, ceremonial functions, official affairs. But Nixon insisted on having it his way. Pat too wanted to visit the schools, hospitals, clinics, and orphanages, as well as go shopping in the marketplaces. The State Department objected; like her husband, Pat insisted.[48]

THEY LEFT ON OCTOBER 5 for a seventy-day trip. Tricia and Julie came to National Airport to see them off. "It was a painful farewell," Nixon later wrote, "especially for Pat, who had never been away from the girls for more than two weeks." [49] After brief stops in New Zealand and Australia, they flew to Djakarta, Indonesia. President Sukarno, who had recently led his people to independence from the Dutch, made a poor impression on Nixon. He said Sukarno's "tastes were as rich as his people were poor," thereby implying that Indonesian poverty was Sukarno's fault, not that of the Dutch. He did not approve of Sukarno's magnificent palace (built by the Dutch), nor his lavish entertainment ("one night we ate off gold plate to the light of a thousand torches while musicians played on the shore of a lake covered with white lotus blossoms and candles floating on small rafts"), nor his womanizing. Nixon's final judgment was that Sukarno knew how to lead a revolution but not how to build a nation.[50]

Next stop was Kuala Lumpur, Malaya, where High Commissioner Sir Gerald Templer was leading the struggle against insurgent Communists while preparing the country for independence. Templer, a field marshal, told Nixon that the way to fight Communists in Asia was not through conventional warfare, but by enlisting the native leaders and convincing them that it was their war, fought for their independence and their country. And it would be their decision as to whether Malaya stayed in the British Commonwealth or not.

Nixon was impressed by Templer, who returned the compliment. After Nixon left, Templer wrote a friend: "I found him an extremely nice man in every way. He was very anxious to learn and to help. He has got charming manners and in fact he was the very reverse of everything that one had expected after reading press reports of the American election. He is easy in his conversations and got on extremely well with the many Asians that he met. ... I was really very impressed with Nixon indeed. He seemed to me potentially to be a much bigger man than Adlai Stevenson who, as you know, stayed with us a few months ago."

Nixon and Templer discussed the problem of containing Communism in Asia. Templer suggested that an attempt should be made to split China and Russia apart; Nixon agreed with the aim but thought the possibility doubtful. Nixon wondered if trade with China should be resumed; Templer thought it should. They discussed the possibility of some form of collective security in Asia, based on the NATO mode. Templer said that Chinese encroachment in Southeast Asia had to be stopped; Nixon agreed.[51]

IN FRENCH INDOCHINA, Nixon stayed first in Saigon, and visited Emperor Bao Dai at his mountain resort in Dalat. The emperor was widely regarded as a French puppet. He had no real power, and thus was seldom in Hanoi, the capital of his country. After having once been associated in a loose sort of way with Ho Chi Minh's Vietminh rebels, he had thrown in with the French. Meanwhile the war between the French and the Vietminh, by 1953 seven years old, had grown in intensity and scope. Since 1946 the United States had supported the French, and the Eisenhower Administration had increased that support. At American urging, the French had agreed to greatly expand the Vietnamese Army loyal to Bao Dai, for the good reason that the Americans promised to pay for it. Thus although the United States had no formal commitment of any kind to Emperor Bao Dai or Vietnam, Nixon was in practice visiting an ally when he went to Dalat.

Nixon feared that Bao Dai might be wavering. He had been told by the State Department that the French and Bao Dai were war-weary and ready to enter into negotiations with the Vietminh. He was therefore delighted to hear Bao Dai say that the State Department was mistaken, that he would have nothing to do with negotiations. He explained to Nixon, "There is no point in trying to negotiate with [Communists]. At the least we would end up with a conference which would divide my country between us and them. And if Vietnam is divided, we will eventually lose it all." That was convincing to Nixon.

Nixon flew on to Vientiane, the capital of Laos, one of the countries in the so-called "Associated States of French Indochina" (the others were Cambodia and Vietnam). There he met with Prince Souvanna Phouma, the Paris-educated Prime Minister. Nixon was happy to note that, like Bao Dai, Souvanna Phouma would not consider negotiations with the Communists.

Then on to Hanoi, Vietnam's capital, where the French Commissioner General put on a grand show for him ("the occasion might have been a mayoral banquet in Dijon or Toulouse, with starched linen napkins, sparkling crystal goblets, and silver candelabra"). Nixon was disturbed by the French attitudes toward the people of Vietnam. Their obvious contempt of the Vietnamese was in contrast to Templer's relations with the people of Malaya.

The French Army gave Nixon an opportunity to watch shells made in America being hurled at Vietnamese Communists. Officers took him to a depot where he was outfitted with battle fatigues and a helmet, then drove him in a convoy of American-built jeeps to the front lines, north of Hanoi, where he watched an artillery barrage.

That afternoon he visited the refugee center at Sontay, which he found "heartrending" (because of the miserable conditions) and "hopeful" (because these people were running away from Communism).

Nixon offered two toasts at banquets given by French officials in Hanoi. In the first, he declared: "We know that you are determined to resist aggression, even as we are determined to resist it. And we are resolved, as our past actions have proved, that you shall not fight unaided." In his second toast, Nixon noted that "there has been talk of negotiation with the aggressors." He admitted that "we all want peace," but insisted that negotiations "would in effect place people who want to be free and independent in perpetual bondage. Under the circumstances we leave with the confidence that this struggle . . . will finally come to a victorious end." That was consistent with Eisenhower's views.[52]

Next, in Cambodia, Nixon visited the ancient ruins of the temples at Angkor Wat and talked with King Sihanouk, who made a poor impression on him ("vain and flighty").

Nixon left Indochina convinced that the French had failed there because they had neither trained nor inspired the Vietnamese people. The Vietnamese needed confidence in themselves and a leader. Nevertheless, indeed for this very reason, he felt the French had to stay until the Communist threat was eliminated. This too was Eisenhower's position, and the President was doing all he could—short of sending in American troops—to keep the French fighting in Vietnam.

America's leaders simply ignored the logical fallacy inherent in their position: because of French condescension and refusal to grant independence, the Vietnamese would never be able to defend themselves without French help, so the French must stay; but so long as the French stayed, the Vietnamese would not be able to defend themselves. They could not win with the French, but they would lose without them. Eisenhower hoped that a declaration by the French of independence for Vietnam would reverse the situation, but then the French would never continue fighting for an independent Vietnam. The consequent American policy was a commitment to stalemate, at an expensive cost (although not in American lives), with no end in sight. But anything was better than negotiations and a consequent Communist take-over of some part of Vietnam. Aside from world balance-of-power considerations, and American national interests, the Republicans hardly wanted to hear the Democrats demanding, "Who lost Vietnam?"

In Taipei, Formosa, Nixon talked for seven hours with Generalissimo Chiang Kai-shek, with Madame Chiang serving as interpreter. Chiang talked grandly of his hopes to invade the Chinese mainland and reunite the country under his leadership; Nixon delivered a message from Eisenhower—"that American military power would not be committed to support any invasion he might launch."[53]

The other great symbol and leader of the anti-Communist cause in Asia was Syngman Rhee in Korea. In his talks with Rhee, Nixon had a delicate diplomatic task, given to him by Eisenhower. The President wanted Nixon to get Rhee to guarantee that he would not launch an invasion of North Korea. The task was difficult, not only because Rhee was constantly making public statements about his intentions to invade, but also because Nixon agreed with Rhee and disagreed with Eisenhower. Nixon, like Dulles and much of the Old Guard, had opposed the armistice in place that Eisenhower had accepted in July 1953. They wanted to fight on to victory, just as Rhee did, not abandon half of Korea to the Communists.

Nor was just the Old Guard unhappy with the settlement. Tom Dewey wrote Nixon on November 9, congratulating him on how well the trip was going, then bringing to his attention a story by Joe Alsop. Alsop had written, "I believe, as does every sensible man in the Far East, that the Korean truce was the worst error of American policy in many years." When Eisenhower agreed to the armistice, Alsop insisted, "we were on the verge of victory, the communists near collapse." Nixon replied from New Delhi on December 1. "I think the Alsop analysis is in many respects very close to the truth," he wrote. "I certainly agree with what he says on Korea." [54]

But Eisenhower had decided that the cost of victory was too high, and had settled, and now ordered Nixon to get Rhee's agreement to the settlement. In his first meeting, Nixon gave Rhee a letter from Eisenhower that insisted that the United States would not tolerate a reopening of the war by Rhee and asked for specific reassurances from him. Rhee tried to ignore the letter, but Nixon insisted. Rhee spoke of his duty to the three million enslaved Koreans in the North. He said a peace that left Korea divided "would inevitably lead to a war which would destroy both Korea and the United States. . . . " The most he would pledge was "that before I take any unilateral action at any time I shall inform President Eisenhower first."

That was hardly satisfactory. At the next meeting, Nixon pressed him again. Rhee explained that his policy was to keep the Communists guessing, that it was good for the United States and the free world that the Communists thought Rhee was a madman out of control, that his unpredictability was a positive asset that tied down enemy troops. "Any statements I have made about Korea acting independently were made to help America," Rhee said in conclusion. "In my heart I know that Korea cannot possibly act alone." [55] That was the assurance Nixon needed but did not really want.

IN JAPAN, Nixon carried a message from Dulles. He and the Secretary of State had become quite close, with Dulles relying on Nixon for inside political information, especially about the doings of Congress. They were frequently on the telephone with each other, exchanging intelligence, with Dulles doing most of the asking, Nixon supplying the answers. They also supported each other in Cabinet and NSC meetings, generally advocating a more aggressive policy than Eisenhower was willing to pursue.

On one thing Eisenhower, Dulles, and Nixon were in full agreement, the need to get America's allies to do more in their own defense, and as a part of that policy to get on with the rearmament of West Germany and Japan, potentially the two strongest partners in the anti-Communist coalition. But the Japanese Constitution, written in large part under Douglas MacArthur's direction, forbade Japanese rearmament. Hatred of the "Japs" was still high, eight years after the war, and even broaching the subject of Japanese rearmament was sure to cause a storm. Dulles wanted the possibility raised first in Tokyo, to blunt its political impact in the States, and thought the Vice-President the perfect man to raise it. Nixon agreed.

He did so at a luncheon with Japanese reporters, and what he said made headlines around the world. "Now, if [Japanese] disarmament was right in 1946, why is it wrong in 1953?" Nixon asked. "And if it was right in 1946 and wrong in 1953, why doesn't the United States admit for once that it made a mistake? . . . I'm going to admit right here that the United States did make a mistake in 1946." The reason, he said, was that the United States had misjudged the intentions of the Soviet leaders. "It is because we want peace and we believe in peace that we ourselves have rearmed since 1946, and that we believe that Japan and other free nations must assume their share of the responsibility of rearming."[56] Like his refusal to negotiate in Vietnam, Japanese rearmament would become a standard Nixon theme for the next twenty years.

IN THE PHILIPPINES, Nixon met and was much impressed by President-elect Ramón Magsaysay. In Burma, "the most exciting stop on the trip," he had his first direct confrontation with Communist mobs. In it, he established a pattern that he would follow in similar confrontations over the years. After a Thanksgiving Day lunch in Pegu, outside Rangoon, he was scheduled to walk to a Buddhist shrine. But a local official told him that the Communists had organized a demonstration along the route, with anti-American signs and a sound truck whipping up the crowd. There was a possibility of violence—as had happened a week earlier when a guerrilla band had ambushed and killed some government officials on the same road. The Secret Service agent with Nixon suggested that the Vice-President and his wife leave by car, using the back door.

Nixon brusquely rejected the advice. As he put it in his memoirs, "No crowd of Communist demonstrators should be allowed to alter the itinerary of the Vice President of the United States." He took Pat's arm and walked out the door, telling the Secret Service agent and Burmese security officials to stay behind them, and not show their guns. As the Nixons walked into the crowd gathered outside the door, it gave way for them.

Encouraged, Nixon grew even bolder. He walked up to a man carrying a sign that said in English, "Go Back Warmonger." "I am Nixon," he said gratuitously. "What's your name?" Naturally flustered, the man backed away. Nixon pressed. He said the signs were all wrong, that America wanted peace, not war. The real warmongers were the Communists in Korea and Vietnam. "That is different," the man replied in English. He explained that those were wars of national liberation. Nixon made a caustic reply, paused, smiled, and asked how many children the man had. Flustered again by this non sequitur, the man began to sputter. The spirit went out of the protesters, who began to disperse.

The experience, Nixon wrote later, taught him that "the only way to deal with Communists is to stand up to them. Otherwise, they will exploit your politeness as weakness."[57] What he really learned was how easy it was to fluster a protester caught totally off guard. All this made great copy back in the States.

NIXON DID NOT care for Nehru at all. He was bored with the Indian leader's problems—which seemed to center on the question of U.S. aid to Pakistan—and irritated by his "softly modulated British English." Indira Gandhi, Nehru's daughter, he found to be "in every way . . . her father's daughter." He did not mean the comment as a compliment.

After New Delhi, Nixon went on to Pakistan, where he met Ayub Khan, commander of the armed forces and soon to be the country's political leader as well. Nixon, like everyone in the Eisenhower Administration, was disturbed by Nehru's neutrality and his apparent unconcern about the Communist menace; Ayub Khan, Nixon was happy to note, "was seriously concerned about the communist threat." Ayub Khan somehow convinced Nixon that he was not terribly concerned about the Pakistan-India problems, only that the Soviets would make India into a pawn and thus threaten Pakistan. At the end of his visit, Nixon indicated to the press that he would support Pakistan's requests for military aid. Nehru then called him "an unprincipled cad."[58]

Nixon's last stop was Iran, where the CIA had just run a coup that toppled the supposedly pro-Communist regime of Prime Minister Mohammed Mossadegh and brought into power a government supporting the young Shah, Mohammed Riza Pahlevi. "I sensed an inner strength in him," Nixon wrote of the Shah, who, although nervous and quiet, asked penetrating questions. "I felt that in the years ahead he would become a strong leader." [59]

THROUGHOUT THE TRIP Nixon enjoyed good, if not sensational, Stateside press coverage. His most effective device for getting publicity was to break away from the official party and shake hands with the crowds lining the streets. *U.S. News & World Report* declared, "The Vice President is touring Asia with the energetic enthusiasm of an American Congressman stumping his home district." American businessmen and diplomats in the countries he visited were sometimes appalled, and complained about his "baby-kissing antics," which they said were unbecoming to the dignity of his high office. *U.S. News* said that he was warned that such conduct would cause Asians to laugh at him, "but it hasn't worked out that way." Indeed, "the folksy, handshaking part of the trip" was a great success. [60]

The New York Times agreed. After surveying its correspondents in each of the places he visited, the paper concluded, "The reports were that the common man of Asia liked this big, friendly, informal, democratic, serious young American. . . ." [61]

From Rangoon, Maung Maung reported that Nixon's "skill in handling difficult situations, his readiness to shake hands with all and sundry, his intuition for saying the right thing, his ruthless efficiency and determination to be successful, and last but not least his charming wife, are assets that should carry Mr. Nixon far in his political ambitions." [62]

Pat was a great hit everywhere, and indeed in her own quiet way contributed to the cause of Asian women. In Japan she gave the first press conference ever held exclusively for women reporters. In Malaya she was the first woman to have dinner in Kuala Lumpur's previously all-male club. She visited hospitals, orphanages, and schools, chatting gaily with people wherever she went. [63]

On their return to the States, December 14, seven senators, the ambassadors from all the countries visited, and a delegation from the State Department met the Nixons at the airport. They drove to the White House, where Eisenhower met them on the porch, saying, "It looks like we have a little interest in you, Dick." [64] They had a cup of coffee together before the Nixons went home to hugs and kisses from the girls.

LATER, EISENHOWER MET WITH NIXON to discuss Syngman Rhee. The President was satisfied with the results of the talks; on January

2, 1954, he wrote Rhee: "From his talks with you, the Vice President is satisfied that you will not renew hostilities unilaterally. In reliance on this, I feel warranted" in extending economic and military aid to South Korea.[65] Nixon's first venture into diplomacy had been a success.

On December 23, Nixon went on nationwide radio and TV to report to the people. For the most part, his speech stuck with old themes, made fresh by his allusions to his recent experiences. The Communists, he said, had "waged war in Korea, and they are waging war now in Indochina and Malaya. They have stirred up revolution in Burma and Indonesia and the Philippines. . . . If they take this area . . . the balance of power in the world . . . will be on their side, and the free world eventually will be forced to its knees." This was because if Indochina fell, Thailand would go next, then Malaya, then Indonesia, and finally Japan. He insisted that there was no easy way out of this problem, that it had to be faced. Negotiations were futile: "The time is past when we should try to reach agreement with the Communists at the conference table by surrendering to them." That was what had happened in China, and today "China is the basic cause of all of our troubles in Asia."[66]

Privately, he was even more worried than he sounded in public. All Eisenhower seemed to care about was getting Rhee to promise not to fight; the President was not interested in what Nixon had to say about the situation elsewhere in Asia. Nixon had told Dewey, in his letter from New Delhi, that while "it has been my policy to talk optimistically every place we have been, when I get back I would certainly appreciate the chance to sit down with you and a few other interested people and face up to some of the hard facts I think we may be ignoring." He suggested a private all-day conference to that end.[67]

WHILE NIXON WAS IN THE FAR EAST, McCarthy had gone out of control again. On national TV (the networks had given in to his demand for free time to reply to a Truman blast at the Republicans) McCarthy denounced Truman, but also declared that "the raw, harsh, unpleasant fact is that Communism [in government] is an issue and will be an issue in 1954." This directly contradicted Eisenhower, who in a press conference had just said that he "hoped the Communist-in-government question would not be an issue in the 1954 congressional campaign." Hagerty thought that McCarthy was trying to take control of the Republican Party from Eisenhower, that he wanted to make Communism an issue in 1954, then make himself the Republican nominee in 1956. C. D. Jackson told James Reston that McCarthy's speech was "a declaration of war against the President."[68]

What really worried Eisenhower was the possibility that McCarthy might start to probe into the Atomic Energy Commission, and specifically into charges that J. Robert Oppenheimer was a Russian spy. On December 3, 1953, Eisenhower ordered a full-scale, but quiet and he hoped secret, investigation by the FBI of Oppenheimer. Eisenhower was desperate to avoid the spectacle of McCarthy hammering away at Oppenheimer—who was highly vulnerable because of his many Communist friends—in a public hearing. Eisenhower's concern was less with Oppenheimer personally, more with the effect such a circus would have on the morale of atomic scientists in the AEC. He also did not want to let McCarthy give the country the impression that all scientists were disloyal. "We've got to handle this so that all our scientists are not made out to be Reds," Eisenhower told Hagerty. "That goddam McCarthy is just likely to try such a thing." [69]

Two weeks after Nixon arrived back in the States, Eisenhower turned to him for help. Nixon agreed to do what he could. He, Pat, and the girls went to Key Biscayne for Christmas; on December 30, Nixon and Rogers met with McCarthy, who had flown down at their invitation. Hagerty noted the results in his diary: "McCarthy knows about [Oppenheimer's] case and Nixon talked him out of using it because of security reasons." [70]

There was another issue Eisenhower wanted McCarthy kept away from, that of security at the Army's communications center at Fort Monmouth, New Jersey. McCarthy was after Army Secretary Robert Stevens for his "laxness" in protecting America's secrets. Eisenhower no more wanted McCarthy going after the Army than after the AEC, and had asked Nixon to see to that one too.

So at the December 30 meeting in Key Biscayne, Nixon told McCarthy, "Don't pull your punches at all on Communists in government. It doesn't make any difference if they are in this administration or in previous ones, if they are there, they should be out. On the other hand, remember that this is your administration. That the people in this administration, including Bob Stevens, are just as dedicated as you are to cleaning out people who are subversive. Give them a chance to do the job. Go to these people, discuss the matters with them and give them a chance to do the job." [71]

Then Nixon and Rogers suggested that McCarthy would be wise to concentrate his subcommittee investigations on something other than Communism. Otherwise, they warned, he would become known as a "one-shot" senator. What else? McCarthy wondered. Well, they said, since he was so hot to get the Democrats, why not do some probing into income tax cases settled out of court by the Truman Administation. McCarthy brightened at the thought, said he accepted the advice, and told the press that in 1954 his committee would be investigating the tax cases the Truman people had settled "at ridiculously low figures." Nixon told reporters that McCarthy planned a new role for his subcommittee.[72]

THAT SEEMING SUCCESS with McCarthy put a nice touch on the end of 1953, which had been an extremely good year for Nixon. He had his office set up and running smoothly, he had established a place for himself in the Cabinet and on the NSC, he had rendered valuable service to the President as a liaison to McCarthy and the Old Guard, he had kept a low profile in the press and avoided nasty name-calling fights with the Democrats, he had seen more of Asia than any other American politician, had learned a great deal in the process, and got some useful publicity for himself and some good feelings for America to boot. All in all, it could hardly have been a better year. He had good cause to celebrate on New Year's Eve, 1953.

CHAPTER SIXTEEN

THE FOURTH CAMPAIGN
1954

IN 1953 NIXON HAD DONE EVERYTHING RIGHT. In 1954 things started going sour on New Year's Day. When Joe McCarthy returned from Key Biscayne, reporters asked him about Nixon's statement that his subcommittee intended to concentrate on income tax investigations, not Communism. "That's a lie," McCarthy snapped back.[1] So much for any deals. Two weeks later, Nixon—and many others— were shocked when a Gallup poll reported that McCarthy's popularity had soared 16 percent since August, up to a full 50 percent who had a favorable opinion of the Wisconsin senator. Among Republicans, McCarthy had a whopping margin of 62 percent in favor, 19 percent opposed, and 19 percent with no opinion.[2] Simultaneously with this proof of his national political base, McCarthy discovered Dr. Irving Peress, an army dentist.

Upon being drafted into the Army, Peress had refused to sign a loyalty oath (he was a member of the American Labor Party). Nevertheless, he got a routine promotion (required by the doctors' draft law). McCarthy hauled Peress before his subcommittee, where the dentist took the Fifth Amendment. A few days later, the Army got rid of Peress by giving him an honorable discharge.

To McCarthy, that was proof enough of a Communist cover-up within the high ranks of the Army. "WHO PROMOTED PERESS?" he demanded to know, in headlines all across the nation. He summoned General Ralph Zwicker, in command at supersecret Camp Kilmer; Zwicker refused to name the men responsible for Peress' promotion and honorable discharge. McCarthy browbeat Zwicker in a most abusive fashion, telling the general (a much-decorated veteran of the campaign in Northwest Europe) that he did not have "the brains of a five-year-old child" and that he was "not fit to wear" his uniform.[3]

Secretary of the Army Robert Stevens then ordered Zwicker not to testify further, and McCarthy decided to go after Stevens himself. He summoned him to appear before the subcommittee on February 25. Nixon tried to broker. Working with Persons, he called a meeting in his office. Stevens, Persons, Rogers, Knowland, and Dirksen were also there. Stevens and his counsel, John Adams, expressed the hope that they could go before the subcommittee, confess that the Army had made a mistake in the Peress case, then move on to a denunciation of McCarthy for his abuse of General Zwicker. Nixon quickly disabused them of that notion. He pointed out that it was McCarthy's committee, and the senator would control the hearing. Nixon said frankly that Stevens would get the worst of it if he took on McCarthy. Furthermore, Nixon insisted that Stevens could not "order" Zwicker to ignore McCarthy's subpoenas, because the only official in the executive branch who was immune from a congressional subpoena was the President. Compromise was imperative, before Stevens got torn apart. Stevens thereupon accepted the suggestion that he meet the next day with McCarthy for lunch in Senator Dirksen's office.[4]

Dirksen's office was next door to Nixon's. Karl Mundt was also present for the lunch (the main course was fried chicken). The meeting was stormy, with McCarthy ranting away, but eventually agreeing to a compromise formula. McCarthy promised to stop abusing his witnesses in return for Stevens' promise to permit further testimony by Zwicker and to release "the names of everyone involved in the promotion and honorable discharge of Peress."[5] Mundt got both Stevens and McCarthy to sign a written agreement to that effect—*except* that the agreement contained no reference to McCarthy's promise to behave. This crucial omission has never been explained, but with so many political professionals involved, it is difficult to believe that it was an oversight.

In any event, when Stevens, McCarthy, and the others emerged from Dirksen's office, they found themselves surrounded by photographers and reporters (the meeting was supposed to be secret—who tipped off the press is unknown). Nixon discreetly stayed in his office. McCarthy held an impromptu press conference. He displayed the agreement and crowed that Zwicker would be coming back to testify. He neglected to add that he in turn had promised to act responsibly, and not Stevens, Mundt, or Dirksen thought to point this out to the press.[6]

In his diary the next day, Jim Hagerty expressed the White

House point of view on these developments: "Adams, self, Persons, Martin . . . have meeting with Nixon and Bill Rogers. . . . Piecing together yesterday's mess seems that the Senators really jobbed up on Stevens. . . . Pres. very mad and getting fed up—it's his Army and he doesn't like McCarthy's tactics at all."[7]

The President soon got madder. The press announced that the Army, and its commander in chief, had surrendered. *The New York Times* headline—"STEVENS BOWS TO MCCARTHY AT ADMINISTRATION BEHEST"—was one of the milder ones.[8]

At Eisenhower's request, Nixon joined with White House Chief of Staff Sherman Adams, Persons, and Stevens in drafting a statement for Stevens to issue. In it, Stevens belatedly mentioned Joe's promise to behave, and insisted that he would "never accede to the abuse of Army personnel. . . . " But McCarthy denied making any promises, and the press would not believe it, so the President decided to issue a statement of his own.

He announced his intention at a Republican leadership meeting on March 1. Senator Leverett Saltonstall (R., Mass.) protested. He said the Army had made a mistake and had not admitted it. And Nixon recorded in his diary that "Knowland very emphatically defended the Senators for the action they took at the luncheon with Stevens. He said that the Army's conduct in this case was inexcusable," and that if the President made a statement (he had proposed saying that in fighting Communism one should not destroy Americanism) he would only make matters worse. Knowland "tore sheets of paper off his note pad for emphasis. I don't know when I have seen him quite so stirred up on a matter as he was on this one."

Eisenhower turned to Nixon and said he was going to have a talk with the Vice-President about the whole matter "and attempt to get the thing in perspective."[9]

The President badly needed perspective. The case had grown much bigger than Stevens versus McCarthy. What was involved was nothing less than the future of the Republican Party. McCarthy, in Hagerty's view (and that of many others), was making a bid for party leadership. He was emboldened by his 50 percent approval rating, and even more so by the deep unhappiness of many of the Old Guard with the Eisenhower Administration. For all Eisenhower's popularity, he had not satisfied the Old Guard on a number of crucial issues—he had refused to go for victory in Korea, he was holding back from a commitment to Vietnam, he had neither balanced the budget nor cut taxes, he had not dismantled the New Deal, he had continued Truman's Europe-first policy and Truman's program of foreign aid, and worst of all he had not gone after the Communists in government with sufficient vigor. Added to all this was the ingrained Republican habit of opposing the executive branch on general principles.

Nixon told Eisenhower that if he issued his tough statement, it would cause him and the party "more trouble than he or his White House staff and liberal friends who were urging it could imagine." Eisenhower was convinced. When he held his press conference, on March 3, he considerably softened his language.[10]

Simultaneously, Nixon worked on McCarthy, trying to get him to give a bit too. But McCarthy would have none of it. Later, Nixon remarked, "Frankly, we tried to mediate with McCarthy until we were blue in the face. At the famous so-called Chicken Luncheon which was held in my room [the Zwicker problem] was supposed to be worked out that way.* . . . Our efforts failed with the result which anybody could have anticipated—a suicidal bloodletting for both the administration and McCarthy."[11]

Nixon did not want to have to choose between Eisenhower and McCarthy, but if he did, there could be no doubt as to which side he would support. The night of the Chicken Lunch, Nixon discussed the McCarthy problem with James Bassett of the RNC. After three drinks, Bassett recorded in his diary that Nixon said of McCarthy, "It's probably time we dumped him."[12]

IT WAS ALREADY TOO LATE. On March 6, Stevenson made a national broadcast that hit the Republicans in their most vulnerable spot. "A political party divided against itself," he said, one that was "half McCarthy and half Eisenhower, cannot produce national unity." He hit the Republicans on Eisenhower's "New Look" in defense, and on their figures on the number of federal employees released from service on security grounds—"It looks as though the Great Crusade has practiced a Great Deception."[13]

McCarthy demanded equal time to reply. Eisenhower decided to outmaneuver him by putting Nixon forward to make the reply. On March 8, at a Republican leaders' meeting, the President announced, "I think we probably ought to use Dick more than we have been. He can sometimes take positions which are more political than it would be expected that I take. The difficulty with the McCarthy problem is that anybody who takes it on runs the risk of being called a pink. Dick . . . would not be subject to [that] criticism." After the meeting, in a private conference in the Oval Office, the President told Nixon to be positive in his reply to Stevenson.[14]

* A major problem for any Nixon biographer is that, for all his fabulous memory for names, in his memoirs and later interviews, he often got his places mixed up. The Chicken Lunch was not held in his office, but rather in Dirksen's.

Nixon worked five days on preparing the speech; he told Jim Bassett, who was helping him, that it was the most difficult speech he had ever had to write. He considered it, as did most others, the opening salvo for the fall elections. At one point in the writing, Nixon confessed a startling fantasy to Bassett. Nixon said "he'd love to slip a secret recording gadget in the President's office." He explained that he would use the recording "to capture some of those warm, offhand, greathearted things the Man says, play 'em back, then get them press-released."* [15]

Nixon did not need Eisenhower's help in thinking up one-liners; it was the overall speech that was bothering him. He had simultaneously to assault the Democrats (a task he relished) while he rebuked McCarthy (without actually mentioning him by name, much less reading him out of the party) and defend Eisenhower's New Look (with which he disagreed) and foreign policy (about which he was ambivalent). No wonder he found it difficult to write.

The day before he was to give the speech, Nixon got a vivid example of how close the Republicans were to a severe split. Senator Knowland called him, furious because of an unflattering leak from the White House, and announced that he intended to resign as majority leader in the Senate (Taft had died the preceding year). Nixon persuaded him to wait until after the speech. Then he went to a Cabinet meeting. There the discussion was about Knowland, and about Roy Cohn, whom moderate Republicans wanted to fire from the subcommittee staff on the grounds that Cohn was a bad influence on McCarthy. Nixon explained that Knowland felt he had been undercut by the Administration, that "Bill was talking about having the Republicans take the initiative to fire this guy," but was now backing off. Still, Nixon thought that "Cohn is vulnerable" and that the moment had come to strike.

"What do we do about Knowland?" Eisenhower asked.

"He's excited," Nixon said.

"Yes," Eisenhower replied, "he's very emotional." The President complained that Knowland would shoot off his mouth before consultation and "this is only March—we have to live with him until [Senate adjournment in] July."

---

* Actually, Eisenhower already had a tape recorder in the Oval Office. He had also recommended to his Cabinet that the members tape-record all their phone calls, explaining, "You know, boys, it's a good thing when you're talking to someone you don't trust to get a record made of it. There are some guys I just don't trust in Washington, and I want to have myself protected so that they can't later report that I said something else." [16] Nixon was present when Eisenhower made these remarks. Eisenhower's machine was activated by a switch under his desk; he often forgot to turn it on. The quality of the tapes was poor.

Nixon defended Knowland, saying that "we must recognize the difficult position of the party leadership." Then he admonished Eisenhower not to allow the White House to put out anything "unless you let the leadership know first." Eisenhower decided he did not want any part of the Knowland-McCarthy-Cohn fight. "Don't bring it to me," he told Nixon. "They're talking about Cohn, not about a Senator. That's not for me." [17]

After the meeting, Eisenhower called Nixon to the Oval Office to talk about the next day's speech. The President suggested that Nixon did not need advice on a political speech, then proceeded to give him some detailed advice anyway. He said he wanted Nixon to be positive, not negative, to concentrate on the virtues of the Republican program, not the evils of the Democratic past. He urged Nixon to smile once in a while. Nixon recorded in his diary, "I told him that I planned to stick a few barbs into [Stevenson], and then he suggested he was perfectly content that I do so but that he thought it was best to laugh at him rather than to hit him meanly." [18]

NIXON DELIVERED HIS SPEECH on Saturday night, March 13, from a television studio in Washington. He drew an audience of some 10 million people. Sitting alone, at a desk—a repetition of the setting for the Checkers speech—he gave his talk from memory, without notes. He devoted the first portion to defending the New Look. In so doing, he showed once again what an excellent debater he was, as he took the side he opposed and made it sound convincing.

The New Look emphasized balancing the budget by cutting defense spending—some 20 percent overall—while relying on America's lead in nuclear weapons for security. An essential part of the New Look was saving money by getting out of the Korean War and staying out of the Vietnam hostilities. Nixon had wanted to drive to the Yalu for victory in Korea, and to support the French in Vietnam (where the French garrison at Dien Bien Phu was already in deep trouble). Like most conservatives, Nixon wanted a strong defense, across the board, as well as a balanced budget and lower taxes. Neither he nor any other conservative ever figured out how to achieve such an elusive formula, but he persisted, privately, anyway. In public, however, Nixon was foursquare in defense of Ike's policies.

The Eisenhower Administration, Nixon declared, had discovered that the Kremlin's plan "was to destroy us by drawing us into little wars all over the world with their satellites. . . . " Their plan was to force the United States to stay armed to the teeth, to be prepared to fight anywhere—anywhere in the world—that they, the men in the Kremlin, chose. Why? Because they knew that this would "force us into bankruptcy; that we would destroy our free-dom in attempting to defend it." But Eisenhower saw the trap, and "rather than let the Communists nibble us to death all over the world in little wars," the President decided that in the future the United States "would rely primarily on our massive mobile retal-iatory power which we could use in our discretion against the major source of aggression at times and places that we chose."

(This was a restatement of a speech Secretary of State Dulles had made two months earlier. Dulles had said that Eisenhower and the NSC had made a "basic decision" that in the future the United States would confront any possible aggression by "a great capacity to retaliate instantly by means and places of our own choosing." But Dulles, like Nixon, was only making the best case he could for a policy he had fought against; Dulles too had wanted to fight on in Korea and get into Vietnam.)[19]

Nixon said that the ending of the Korean War, plus the New Look, would lead to a balanced budget, an end to inflation, and eventually to lower taxes. Stevenson had said that Eisenhower was sacrificing American security by cutting defense funds; Nixon as-sured his audience that Eisenhower, "the greatest military leader in the world today," knew what he was doing. "He is an expert. He is the one who made the final decision on this policy. And I believe that we can and that we should have confidence in him."

Nixon quoted Dulles favorably, then added gratuitously, "And incidentally, in mentioning Secretary Dulles, isn't it wonderful that finally we have a Secretary of State who isn't taken in by the Communists, who stands up to them? We can be sure now that the victories that our men win on the battlefields will not be lost in the future by our diplomats at the council table." Furious Democrats made these most-quoted sentences from the speech. Moderate Re-publicans were embarrassed by them.

Then Nixon made a statement that would come back to haunt him. Presumably because Dulles was not "taken in" by the Krem-lin, as supposedly Acheson had been, Nixon said that in the year the Republicans had been in charge, "in not one area of the world have the Communists made a significant gain." He did not mention that Vietnam was falling fast.

Next Nixon fired a series of "questions" at Stevenson. Did he want to continue the Korean War? Did he want to send more troops to Korea? Did he favor "having more Korean type wars all over the world?" In every instance, Nixon's own answer at Cabinet and NSC meetings had been yes; on television, he asked the questions scornfully, as if no honest man could give yes for an answer.

Finally he turned to Joe McCarthy. One of Stevenson's criticisms had been Eisenhower's refusal to speak out on McCarthy. Nixon, the master at turning the tables, adroitly used the criticism both to defend Eisenhower and to attack Harry Truman: "It is true that President Eisenhower does not engage in personal vituperation and vulgar name-calling and promiscuous letter writing in asserting his leadership, and I say, 'Thank God he doesn't.' "

Nixon never mentioned McCarthy by name, though he did make an oblique attack: "Men who have in the past done effective work exposing Communists in this country have, by reckless talk and questionable methods, made themselves the issue rather than the cause they believe in so deeply." Then he turned that one around too in a memorable passage that was also widely quoted: "I have heard people say, 'Well, why all of this hullabaloo about being fair when you're dealing with a gang of traitors? . . . After all, they're a bunch of rats. What we ought to do is go out and shoot 'em.' Well, I'll agree they're a bunch of rats, but just remember this. When you go out to shoot rats, you have to shoot straight, because when you shoot wildly it not only means that the rat may get away more easily, you make it easier on the rat."

Finally, Nixon got into a numbers game with Stevenson. He asserted that he had in his hand a breakdown of the files of the 2,400 people who had been dismissed from government employment since the Republicans took office. Then he rattled off figures —422 dismissed because of subversive activities or associations, 198 for sexual perversion, 611 for having criminal records, 1,424 for "untrustworthiness, drunkenness, mental instability, or possible exposure to blackmail." All of them, Nixon claimed, had been hired by Harry Truman, fired by Dwight Eisenhower.[20]

In Cabinet meetings, and in Republican leaders' meetings, Nixon had consistently and vigorously urged that Republican spokesmen give maximum publicity to the numbers of security risks the Administration had fired. But Attorney General Brownell hesitated to do so for fear of smearing the reputation of every employee let go, and even more for fear that the Republicans could not make the charges stick. Besides, it smacked too much of McCarthyism. The President himself could not believe that there were more than two thousand legitimate security risks in the government. So the department heads did nothing, the Republican senators did little, and it was Nixon himself who had to make the dismissals into a major issue.[21]

Overall, Eisenhower was pleased with the speech (he should have been, given the unstinting praise Nixon heaped upon him, and the way Nixon supported the New Look). He telephoned Nixon with congratulations, calling the speech "magnificent . . .

the very best that could have been done under the circumstances."
He was especially pleased because Nixon had managed to smile a
couple of times. But most of all, he was pleased because he convinced himself that Nixon had managed to take care of McCarthy
without splitting the party.

This was a profound misjudgment. The Administration's approach to McCarthy had been hesitant at best, caused in part by
Nixon's constant warnings about the political risks of taking him
on, in part by Eisenhower's personal perception of how a President
ought to behave. Nixon had taken the lead in trying to get
McCarthy to tone his recklessness down a bit, and especially to
leave a Republican Administration alone, but his efforts had failed.
His "compromises" were all one-sided, the Chicken Lunch being
the supreme example, with McCarthy getting his way. Nothing that
the Administration had done to date had had any effect on cutting
McCarthy down. Nixon's "rebuke" to McCarthy in the March 13
speech was less than a summer squall on Joe's sunny horizon. The
senator, on the verge of his showdown hearings with Stevens and
the Army, was at the peak of his influence. Asked to comment on
Nixon's speech, McCarthy said he was "sick and tired" of the "constant yack-yacking" from "that prick Nixon." [22]

Much was later made of the behind-the-scenes attack on
McCarthy supposedly carried out by the Eisenhower Administration, with Eisenhower giving the campaign its direction.[23] That
there was such an effort is unquestioned; whether it was large or
small depends on one's perception (in the author's, it was minuscule); its results are clear: they amounted to nothing at all.

What was to bring McCarthy down was not what Eisenhower
or Nixon did, but his own stupidity. In taking on the Army, he was
taking on the President, making the struggle into McCarthy versus
Eisenhower, a match he could never win. Had he seen this ele-
mental truth, he could have backed off, dispatched with the hearings in a day or so, and gone on to find Reds hiding out in the
universities, a far more promising hunting ground than the Army.
Backing down had never hurt his popularity—just a couple of
months earlier, he had hastily abandoned proposed investigations
into the Protestant churches of America when an overwhelmingly
hostile public reaction became known. Had McCarthy backed
away again, Nixon's speech would have blown itself out and he
would have had clear sailing.

The Administration did make two contributions to the senator's downfall, but they both hinged on McCarthy's going ahead
with the hearings. The first came from Nixon, who leaked to various senators a long report from the Army detailing McCarthy's and

Cohn's threats and attempted intimidations over the past several weeks. The second came from Eisenhower himself, but it was a response to an initiative from McCarthy.

The purpose of the hearings was to determine the truth of Army Secretary Stevens' charge that McCarthy had attempted to secure preferential treatment for a former aide, Private G. David Schine, and of McCarthy's countercharge that the Army had tried to pressure him into calling off his search for Communists in the Army. The proceedings began on April 22 and were a national sensation, carried live on television, the first such political spectacle. Eisenhower thought the Senate ought to be ashamed of itself for letting such proceedings go on, and many of his countrymen felt embarrassment more than anything else in regard to the hearings.

As the hearings went on, McCarthy grew wilder. "Point of order," he would shout as he berated witnesses and fellow senators alike. Soon McCarthy was talking of "twenty-one years of treason," apologizing for supporting Eisenhower in 1952, and snarling at his witnesses. Meanwhile the Republicans were tearing themselves apart on the question of whether to support McCarthy or not. Nixon watched some of the hearings, then told reporters he was giving up, because "I prefer professionals to amateur actors." He had opposed televising the hearings, because "there is inevitably too much of a tendency . . . to play to the cameras rather than the facts," but McCarthy ignored him.[24]

Although the President would not speak out against McCarthy, in the privacy of his meetings with Republican leaders he said he was "considerably disturbed and embarrassed. The worst thing about this McCarthy business is that the newspapers are all saying that the leadership in the Republican Party has switched to McCarthy and that we are all dancing to his tune." He complained that everything had come to a standstill while everyone spent the day watching the hearings. Knowland interrupted to say that "not one single bill has been delayed because of McCarthy," although he did admit that McCarthy had "distracted attention on the Hill." Eisenhower, ignoring Knowland, went on: "We are being painted as fearful, helpless individuals and it's about time we did something about it."[25]

As McCarthy began to realize how badly he was hurting himself, he decided that rather than cut his losses he would go for broke. He decided to subpoena Sherman Adams. To Eisenhower, even the thought of the senator getting the dour, unimaginative, stubborn, and hot-tempered Adams in front of the committee, with McCarthy asking the questions, was unbearable. Eisenhower told

Hagerty, "Congress has absolutely no right to ask [White House personnel] to testify in any way, shape, or form about the advice that they were giving to me at any time on any subject."[26]

Three days later, on May 17, the President told the Republican leaders that "any man who testifies as to the advice he gave me won't be working for me that night. I will not allow people around me to be subpoenaed and you might just as well know it now." Both Nixon and Knowland protested that it would be a terrible thing if Eisenhower challenged Congress' right to subpoena (Nixon in the Hiss case had insisted that Congress' claims were paramount, its power to subpoena unchallengeable). Eisenhower told them, "My people are not going to be subpoenaed."[27]

He gave the orders the next day. The key sentence read, "It is not in the public interest that *any* of their [employees of the executive branch] conversations or communications, or *any* documents or reproductions, concerning such advice be disclosed." This was the most sweeping assertion of executive privilege ever uttered, but at the time few noticed and fewer commented on Eisenhower's boldness in establishing the principle (primarily because most of the press had turned against McCarthy by this time), which quickly came to be regarded as precedent.

Deprived of Adams and other potentially headline-making witnesses, McCarthy was reduced to ranting and raving. Special army counsel Joseph N. Welch became something of a folk hero with such comments as "Little did I dream you could be so reckless" and "Have you left no sense of decency?"

The hearings ended, mercifully, on June 17. McCarthy won a technical victory, in that a majority of the seven-man subcommittee largely exonerated him from charges of "improper influence." But seven weeks later, the Senate established a select committee to consider censure charges against McCarthy. On December 2, with the elections over, the Senate finally voted, 67 to 22, to "condemn" McCarthy for contemptuous conduct toward the Senate. Those Republican senators present and voting split exactly, twenty-two senators for censure, twenty-two against. McCarthy was a broken man, although he hung around for two and a half more years, shunned by most of his fellow senators. When he died, on May 2, 1957, he was a hopeless drunk. Vice-President and Mrs. Nixon, Roy Cohn, and Bill Knowland were the most prominent people in attendance at his funeral.*[28]

---

* That McCarthy's death was suicide is best shown in this passage from Thomas Reeves' masterful biography of him: "Back in Washington, Joe ambled into the office . . . where two colleagues were having a drink. He

In his memoirs, Nixon wrote that "my own feelings about Joe McCarthy were mixed. I never shared the disdain with which fashionable Washington treated him because of his lack of polished manners. In fact, I found him personally likable, if irresponsibly impulsive." His worst sin, according to Nixon, was a tendency to exaggerate his facts, but overall "McCarthy was sincere." [29]

THROUGHOUT THAT SPRING, Nixon was in almost daily telephone contact with Secretary Dulles, who was worried at the prospect of the State Department being dragged into the hearings. Nixon, at Dulles' request, worked behind the scenes with Republican senators to make certain that did not happen. [30]

Dulles' concern in the spring of 1954 was with the upcoming Foreign Ministers' conference in Geneva. It had been called to deal with Korea; the agenda was broadened by the French, who were seeking a way out of Vietnam, and would include Red China, Britain, and the Soviet Union among the participants, but not the Vietminh nor Bao Dai. The Eisenhower Administration was flatly opposed to a negotiated peace at Geneva that would give Ho Chi Minh any part of Vietnam, but it had accepted the invitation to Geneva because it was necessary to prolong the life of the Joseph Laniel government in Paris; behind Laniel loomed the shadow of Pierre Mendès-France, the advocate of French withdrawal from Vietnam. The conference was scheduled to begin in late April 1954. Dulles consulted closely with Nixon often by telephone about which senators to take along. The obvious choices were Alexander Wiley (R., Wis.), chairman of the Senate Foreign Relations Committee, and Theodore Green (D., R.I.), but Nixon told Dulles that Wiley and Green would be "a burden and a risk," and suggested instead H. Alexander Smith (R., N.J.) and J. William Fulbright (D., Ark.). [31]

These telephone conversations sometimes got terribly convoluted, full of politicians' jargon and shorthand, concerned primarily with the egos of the individual senators, most especially Knowland. Typical examples: "N. asked if the Sec. would mind if he talked with Knowland. The Sec. said he wouldn't want F. [Ralph Flanders (R., Vt.)] to think he had been working against him behind his back, but if N. could talk with K. without his saying anything. N. said this might be a problem." [32] "Re K., N. said to be sure he knows before

---

filled a drinking glass to the brim with liquor and downed the contents in several uninterrupted gulps. He told his astonished observers that he had been to Bethesda Naval Hospital several times to 'dry out' and that on the last occasion his doctor had said he would die if he had one more drop. He then proceeded to refill the glass and drink it dry."

but not too much in advance. Say to him—this is the best we can do and we would like your support. . . . N. said at least this move will keep the thing out of a bad situation for a few weeks. The Sec. referred to his message to the Pres. re his getting N.'s judgment. The Sec. will tell the Pres. N. concurs."[33]

Nixon also gave Dulles advice and information on the situation in the Far East, based on his contacts from his trip. One of Dulles' great fears, and Nixon's, was that Nehru would assume the leadership of the neutral nations and then tilt them toward Russia. Nixon had thrown his own support to Pakistan on the basis of that danger, and told Dulles he had worked in other ways to lessen Nehru's influence. "I was talking to the Finance Minister of Ceylon," Nixon said, and asked him about reports that Ceylon would join Nehru in opposing American aid to Pakistan. The Finance Minister of Ceylon "told me [Nixon] to disregard such reports. He urged that we take a firm position with Nehru. He said, 'I have known the Indians all my life and a policy of weakness and flattery brings from them only contempt.' "[34] Nixon felt that Ceylon, Pakistan, and Burma would act as a pro-American block whenever there were meetings of the neutrals.[35]

NIXON'S INTEREST IN FOREIGN POLICY continued and expanded after his Far East trip, to the point that he spent almost as much time on foreign policy as on domestic politics. His main concern was stopping the spread of Communism in Asia. After his return to the States at the end of 1953, he had met privately with Tom Dewey, C. D. Jackson, and others to express his fear that the Administration was not doing enough to help the French in Vietnam, nor was it building the kind of collective security system in Asia that NATO was in Europe.

In a long letter of January 4, 1954, Jackson built on the themes Nixon had stressed. "I believe that in view of the high priority you place on the problems of Asia," Jackson began, Nixon would be interested in pushing a proposal for a CIA-State-Defense-USIA coordinating board that would set in motion "psychological warfare and para-military operations" in Southeast Asia, "using Thailand as a secure and sympathetic base." Jackson said that, like Nixon, he was convinced "that the free world must develop a secure defense perimeter in Asia for the conduct of its long-range policies, and that such development must rest on indigenous strength and capabilities."

In his private talk with Dewey and Jackson, Nixon had argued for an "area" concept for Southeast Asia. Jackson was all for it. So, he said, was William Donovan, the wartime director of OSS and currently ambassador to Thailand. "In fact," Jackson wrote, "Wild

Bill is so much in favor that he has to be restrained." Jackson said that "your recent trip, plus the recent military developments which put Ho Chi Minh right on the border of Thailand, make this a good time" to push an "area" plan.[36]

Thus Nixon committed himself early to what became the Southeast Asia Treaty Organization (SEATO). He worked on Dulles with the idea, and lobbied with sympathetic senators. The latter were hard to find, outside the Democratic Party. To Nixon's Republican friends, all these foreign-aid programs had gone too far, were too expensive, showed no profit. These Republicans would not even support NATO. They were, as Hagerty put it in his diary, "more worried about winning an election than saving the world and winning the peace."[37]

Nixon got a better response from the President and the Secretary of State, when Dulles on March 29 made a speech calling for "United Action" in Vietnam. The hope Dulles expressed was that the United States, the United Kingdom, France, New Zealand, Australia, Thailand, the Philippines, Cambodia, and Laos would all intervene in Vietnam together. Out of this suggestion, SEATO eventually was born.[38] For the moment, however, it was Eisenhower's way of putting off the French demands that the United States intervene immediately and unilaterally in Vietnam. Eisenhower insisted that he would not go in without allies.

The President also insisted on congressional support (knowing that he would never get it). On April 2, Dulles, Nixon, and Chairman Admiral Arthur Radford of the Joint Chiefs met with the leaders of both parties to ask for a congressional resolution that would give the President the authority to use American air and sea power in Vietnam. The politicians were aghast. They cried out, "No more Koreas." The only way Eisenhower could get such a resolution, they said (thus protecting themselves as carefully as Eisenhower was protecting himself), was if the British and other allies joined in, and if the French promised independence to Vietnam.

Meanwhile, French Army Chief of Staff Paul Ely had come to Washington to ask for help. Together with Radford, and with Dulles' and Nixon's knowledge and approval, Ely approved plans previously prepared by planners in Paris and Washington for Operation Vulture, an air strike against the Vietminh around Dien Bien Phu.

Dien Bien Phu, where a French force was fighting for its life, had by April of 1954 become a worldwide symbol for the French effort in Vietnam, because the French had attached so much prestige to the garrison there. It was clear that the fall of the garrison would mean the end of French rule in Vietnam.

That was where Operation Vulture came in. Its advocates, including Nixon, hoped that when the fall of Dien Bien Phu was imminent, Eisenhower could not resist the pressure to intervene, and by then only an air strike would suffice. There was, however, great confusion about Vulture. Radford, Ely, and Nixon all believed it involved two or three atomic bombs, while Dulles thought it would be a "massive B-29 bombing" by U.S. planes using conventional bombs.[39] In fact, the planes were flexible on the choice of weapons.

On April 5, the French said that they wanted Vulture implemented. Eisenhower told Dulles that "such a move is impossible," that without congressional support any air strike would be "completely unconstitutional and indefensible," and concluded, "We cannot engage in active war."[40]

Nixon was not ready to give up. The next day, at an NSC meeting, he told the President that he should not "underestimate his ability to get the Congress and the country to follow his leadership." As a first step, he suggested sending more American technicians and equipment to Vietnam. Nixon also criticized Dulles' United Action plan, saying it was "all right as far as it goes but that, if it were limited to resisting overt aggression alone, it would not meet the real future danger in Asia," which was subversion. For that problem, Donovan's "area" idea, which would include psychological and paramilitary warfare, was necessary.

Clear-cut as these arguments seemed to Nixon, he noted sadly in his diary that "the President had backed down considerably. . . . He seemed resigned to doing nothing at all. . . . "[41]

On April 16, Nixon made another attempt to force the President to intervene. He appeared before the American Society of Newspaper Editors for an "off-the-record" luncheon talk. As Roscoe Drummond summed it up in the *Herald Tribune*, Nixon spoke "on the problem of Southeast Asia, on the magnitude of America's stake in keeping it from falling to Communist domination and on the urgency of avoiding a deceptive settlement, which would in effect be a sell-out to the Communists, at Geneva."[42]

Nixon was asked, from the floor, whether he thought American troops ought to be sent to Vietnam if the French pulled out. Nixon began his reply by saying that he did not believe that "the presumption or the assumption which has been made by the questioner will occur, and I recognize that he has put it as a hypothetical question." (In fact, all Cabinet and NSC discussions that week had taken it for granted that the French were going to cut and run.) Given his major reservations, Nixon continued, if sending American boys was the only way to stop Communist expansion in Indochina, then, "I believe that the executive branch of the government has to take the politically unpopular position of facing up to it and doing it, and I personally would support such a decision."[43]

When the story leaked, it was headline news across the country. Nixon protested that he had been double-crossed, without explaining what he had expected would happen to such sensational news given to a room filled with newspaper editors. The editors, incidentally, interpreted Nixon's remark as a trial balloon by the Administration, when in fact it was an attempt by Nixon to jolt Eisenhower into action.

In this, Nixon was unsuccessful. Eisenhower and Hagerty called Nixon that afternoon to ask what he had said. Hagerty wrote in his diary that Nixon "played dumb," and commented, "Think it was foolish for Dick to answer as he did but will make the best of it."[44] The next morning, Hagerty talked to Eisenhower, who "asked me to . . . have State Department put out statement on hypothetical question without cutting ground from under Nixon." Eisenhower was willing to protect Nixon though not to listen to his advice.[45]

The following week, at the leaders' meeting, House Majority Leader Charles Halleck said that Nixon's statement "had really hurt," and that he hoped there would be no more talk of that type. Nixon entered into his diary Eisenhower's response: "The President . . . immediately stepped in and said he felt it was important that we not show a weakness at this critical time and that we not let the Russians think that we might not resist. . . . He . . . pointed out that it was not well to tell the Russians everything as to what we would or would not do."[46]

Encouraged by the President's permissive attitude, Nixon pressed again for intervention. At an April 29 NSC meeting, Nixon got the idea that Eisenhower was "greatly concerned about what was the right course to take." Nixon was ready to tell him, but Stassen jumped in first, telling Eisenhower that he thought American ground troops should be sent in, unilaterally and immediately. Eisenhower cut Stassen off, saying that he "could not visualize a ground troop operation in Indochina that would be supported by the people of the United States and which would not in the long run put our defense too far out of balance."

Nixon interjected that it would not be necessary to send in ground troops. He said in his opinion bombing missions by the U.S. Air Force would be sufficient to hold back the Communists.[47] The next morning Nixon met with the President and Robert Cutler, of the NSC staff, to discuss further the idea of an air strike to save Dien Bien Phu. Cutler wanted to tell America's allies that if the United States went into Vietnam, it would use atomic bombs.

Nixon thought it was not necessary to tell them "before we got them to agree on United Action." Nor was he convinced that atomic bombs were required; he said "it might not be necessary to have more than a few conventional air strikes . . . to let the Communists see that we are determined to resist."[48]

But Nixon could not convince Eisenhower, who refused to intervene. On May 7, Dien Bien Phu fell. At Geneva, meanwhile, the rumors were that the French were ready to surrender northern Vietnam to Ho Chi Minh and the Vietminh, sign an armistice, and get out of Indochina. Whatever the French did, Nixon wanted to avoid any compromise that would lead to Communist gains. He urged Dulles not to be a part of any Geneva settlement "that would result in the surrender of any part of Indochina to the Communists." When the Geneva Accords were finally completed, on July 21, the United States refused to sign, a decision Nixon agreed with and supported. Failure to sign, however, did not mean the United States would oppose the settlement, which much to Nixon's dismay gave North Vietnam to the Communists.[49]

A number of things stand out about Nixon's first major foray into foreign policy. First, he failed to convince the President and could not get the intervention he wanted. Second, he was forthright and vigorous in advocating what he believed in, even though he knew that what he was saying was not what the President wanted to hear. Third, he knowingly took great political risks, as the only elected politician to speak out for intervention. All the others, including Knowland, had backed away. The supporters of intervention, except for Nixon, came from State, Defense, the JCS, and the NSC, not from Congress. Fourth, this early in his career, after only slightly more than a year as Vice-President, at the age of forty-one, he had made what was almost a lifelong commitment to saving the people of Indochina from Communism. To that end he had a detailed program, a program that would hardly change at all over the next two decades.

The program was many-sided. It included never negotiating with the Communists, forming an area-wide collective defense system, and avoiding the use of American ground troops by putting heavy emphasis on supplying and training Indochinese to defend themselves, supported by massive U.S. air strikes and a naval blockade. It involved keeping the Communists guessing about American intentions, most specifically about whether or not the United States would use atomic weapons. Nixon wanted to search for, then support without stint, a strong Vietnamese anti-Communist leader. It meant never surrendering, even if avoiding defeat required a quick injection of American troops. Long term, he

wanted to strengthen the economy of Vietnam, treating the Vietnamese as partners, not clients. He wanted to use the powers of
the Presidency to persuade the American people of the necessity
for action.

It was a bold, comprehensive, well-thought-out program that
might have worked. But Eisenhower would not implement it.
Nixon, nevertheless, stayed with it, until he himself had a chance
to implement at least parts of it, from 1969 to 1973.

ALTOGETHER, APRIL WAS A BAD MONTH for Nixon. He was frustrated
in Vietnam, had to endure the Army-McCarthy hearings, and got
some unfavorable publicity over his "send the American boys to
Vietnam" statement. In addition, he underwent a personal humiliation. He had accepted an invitation to deliver the commencement
address at Duke University, but on April 5 the Duke faculty voted
61 to 42 against awarding the university's most famous graduate an
honorary degree. Nixon thereupon canceled his commencement
talk. All this made the front pages everywhere, though buried deep
in the story was the information that only 103 faculty members out
of a total of 606 had attended the meeting and voted.[50]

The next month, Nixon went to Whittier College to deliver the
commencement address. Even there he was insulted. The president of the college had to form two reception lines after the ceremony, one being for those who did not want to shake Dick Nixon's
hand.[51] Nixon's friends had proposed naming a Whittier street after
him, but that aroused so much opposition it was called Mar Vista
Lane instead.

WHO COULD HE BLAME BUT HIMSELF? He was the one, after all, who
delighted in deliberately goading the Democrats, as he did again
throughout the 1954 campaign.

As Nixon saw it, in 1954, he battled valiantly and almost single-
handedly against the Democrats. "They have a 'murderers row' to
come out at the drop of a hat and issue statements and fight for
their party," he remarked. "We have practically nobody to stand
up and fight back."[52] It left him badly discouraged. He told one
friend, "I'm tired, bone tired. My heart's not in it." To others he
confided that his only consolation was that this would be his last
campaign.

He did not allow his pessimism to affect his involvement. He
threw himself into the campaign with his usual enthusiasm and
recklessness. A major reason was his sense of what was at stake.
He agreed completely with C. D. Jackson, who wrote him on
March 9 that the November elections "are just about the last

chance the Republican Party has." [53] Nixon told an April 17 Cabinet meeting, over which he presided, that "the success of the Eisenhower Administration will depend on the 1954 elections. If the Republicans lose, the Eisenhower program will be torpedoed," and the party would go with it. [54]

Nixon held such a cataclysmic view because he suspected the Democrats were engaged in a plot. As he explained to the Cabinet, the Democrats were going to run on Eisenhower's coattails, by claiming that they were better supporters of the President's policies than were the Republicans—which in such areas as support for NATO and foreign aid, for maintaining tax levels until the budget was balanced, subsidies for farmers, extension of Social Security, and a number of other issues was perfectly true. But Nixon warned that Democratic "helpfulness now is a tactic for success in 1954," and that with majorities in both houses of Congress, the Democrats would sabotage the Eisenhower program, then sweep to victory in 1956.

Nixon next launched into a sales pitch for the kind of campaign he wanted. He warned the Cabinet against assuming that because the off-year elections usually went to the party out of power, they would do so in 1954. He cited the Democratic victory in the 1934 elections as an example, and said that it all depended on how well public relations were handled. "Our program is good," he said, but he doubted that the public relations were good enough "to convince the people." Therefore he urged the Cabinet to get active, and to concentrate on close districts where there already existed a strong Republican organization. "I think we have to cold-bloodedly pick out the key districts for 1954," he said, and "fight our battles there." Just the appearance of a Cabinet member in such districts could be decisive. He insisted that "local issues are overrated in local elections," and wanted the department heads to go to the people and explain the Republican program. [55]

Specifically, he wanted them to defend Republican economics. "In the past," he said, "the Democrats were expansive, the Republicans were not. But now we have the shoe on the other foot." The Republican program, he declared, created jobs and goods, providing a base for maximum expansion and a growing standard of living. He told the Cabinet members to stop being so defensive about Republican economics, to point out that it was not the Republicans who went around trying to artificially prime the economy, that Republican faith in the free market could bring—was already bringing—the best times America had ever enjoyed. [56]

Unfortunately, he did not take his own advice. Instead of a high-tone, positive campaign pointing to Republican virtues, early on Nixon started hurling accusations at the Democrats. A climax of sorts came in Milwaukee, where on June 26 he attempted to blame Republican failure to meet campaign promises (such as liberating Eastern Europe, unleashing Chiang, unifying Korea under Rhee, and defending Indochina) on the Democrats. "To sum it up bluntly," he declared, "the Acheson policy was directly responsible for the loss of China. And if China had not been lost, there would have been no war in Korea and there would be no war in Indochina today." [57]

Eisenhower was distraught, Dulles hardly less so, by what Nixon said. They had to have Democratic support for their foreign policy, and were not likely to get it if Nixon kept kicking Acheson in the teeth. Eisenhower drafted a letter to Nixon ("I quite understand the impulse—particularly before a partisan audience—to lash out at our political opponents. . . . But I am constantly working to produce a truly bipartisan approach, and I rather think that keeping up attacks against Acheson will, at this late date, hamper our efforts") then decided not to send it. Instead, he asked Nixon to stop by the office.

A woodshed would have been more appropriate. The President scolded Nixon. He said that a number of senior Democrats, led by the southerners on whom he counted so heavily, had complained to him about Nixon's Milwaukee remarks. Nixon argued that he had been careful not to attack the Democrats, but only Acheson. Eisenhower said that in the context of a campaign talk the two were inseparable and the Democrats were "smarting" about it. Nixon then argued that the bipartisanship of foreign policy in previous years had applied only to Europe, not to Asia.

Eisenhower said that Nixon had his history wrong. 'The reason we lost China," Ike explained, "was because the U.S. insisted upon Chiang Kai-shek taking Communists into his government, against Chiang's judgment at the time." And it was George Marshall, not Acheson, who had made that recommendation. Again he told Nixon to hold it down, then concluded by pointing out that McCarthy had frequently referred to "twenty years of treason." This, said Eisenhower, "is an indefensible statement," and he insisted that by no implication could Nixon be considered to be saying the same thing. Nixon replied that he would be making no more speeches for the balance of the summer, and said he was "perfectly willing to delete such references from future ones." [58]

EISENHOWER'S BAWLING OUT only added to Nixon's woes. Nothing he did seemed to work, Congress droned on, Washington was hot and dull. Washington social life, he admitted that summer, was "unattractive and extremely boring. The difficult part is that you can't allow your boredom to show." In Washington everyone he met was either a political associate or an enemy—his friends were in California or Key Biscayne. He had no talent for making new ones. Leonard Hall, chairman of the RNC, thought that Nixon "ached for people to like him," but did not know how to go about achieving that. He was, according to Hall, "not cold but offish. No one would look forward to spending a week with Nixon fishing."[59]

Mrs. Stewart Alsop, whose husband usually supported Nixon in his column, gave one of her famous parties that summer. She invited the Nixons, but found both of them "wooden and stiff . . . terribly difficult to talk to." When the dancing began, "Nixon danced only one dance, with me. He's a terrible dancer. Pat didn't dance at all. They stayed only half an hour. It was as if the high school monitor had suddenly appeared. I couldn't wait for him to go."[60]

That summer Pat told a reporter, "We don't have as many good times as we used to." She hated politics, and the effect they had on Dick, and the things his enemies said about him—and the things they drew. It was also that summer she canceled their home subscription to the Washington *Post* because she did not want the girls to see the front-page Herblock cartoons portraying their father as a sewer-dwelling demagogue.

A reporter who interviewed her for the *New Republic* that summer entitled his piece "No Trouble in Our House" and wrote: "Mrs. Nixon has learned rapidly. She knows when to be the silent, demure partner of the great man who is only a heartbeat away from the White House. . . . She always has the right reply, the right greeting, the gracious smile."[61] To another reporter, Pat insisted of her relationship with her husband, "We've never quarreled."[62]

Jessamyn West heard differently. She told Fawn Brodie, "My mother told me that Aunt Hannah had a call from Dick to come back to Washington. Pat was not speaking to him. 'What will you do?' my mother asked her, troubled at the idea of her sister being asked to referee a quarrel between the Vice-President and his wife. Aunt Hannah replied, 'I will go back to Washington and say nothing. I will just help out Pat in every way I can.' And she did."[63]

About the only joy in Pat's life, aside from the girls, came from the family pets. On Nixon's forty-first birthday, Checkers had presented the famly with a litter of five purebred cocker spaniels. In addition, Julie and Tricia had pet cats.[64]

Pat did have hopes for a brighter future. She had made Dick sit down and talk about their plans, about the need the girls had for a home life, about what Chotiner had said when they initially discussed the Vice-Presidency, back in Chicago in the summer of 1952 (that if Nixon retired in 1957, he would be forty-four years old and have excellent prospects, say, for example, in a law firm in Whittier). A successful law practice in Whittier, surrounded by their friends and relatives, watching the girls grow up and go through high school and college—what an appealing prospect, at least to Pat. She was persuasive—that night she got Dick to sign a statement pledging that he would retire from politics after 1956. After signing, he put the paper into his wallet, not into her purse.[65]

At this time, Nixon was a patient of Dr. Arnold Hutschnecker, a New York internist specializing in psychosomatic problems. Dr. Hutschnecker has been guarded in what he has said about his treatment, and Nixon evasive about their relationship. Nixon's psychobiographers have made much of this matter, citing rumors that Nixon sought psychological help to deal with sexual inadequacy, or a death wish, and then found the analysis too painful to bear and cut it off. But no one (other than the doctor and the patient) knows. Len Hall did point to one obvious psychological problem that Nixon had, and for which he may well have sought help, his chronic insomnia. On numerous occasions, but especially after a speech, Nixon was on the telephone until 3 or 4 A.M. Overall, he averaged about five hours' sleep per night.

Hutschnecker's own direct statement about his relationship with Nixon was: "At the time I was engaged in the practice of internal medicine, and Mr. Nixon came simply for occasional checkups and to discuss how to deal with the stresses of his office, including the many official dinners he had to attend—in short how to stay fit. There was no evidence of any illness."[66]

IN MID-SEPTEMBER, the active campaign began. Nixon had mapped out a strenuous schedule, calling for forty-eight days of speechmaking in thirty-one states. He explained to RNC officials at a Cincinnati meeting that the party had to "run scared." If the Republicans lost this one, he contended, "we are done . . . we might as well fold up our tents and go away." He insisted on all-out party support for every Republican candidate, and was impatient with protests that this one was "too liberal," that one "too conservative." "We've got to get forty-eight votes in the Senate," he declared, "and let's get that into our heads." He was as good as his word, giving vigorous support to liberal Clifford Case of New Jersey, who was running for the Senate and who eventually won by only 3,200 votes, with Nixon at least sharing the credit for his victory.[67]

Nixon's first stop was the Ohio Republican State Convention, in Columbus: "The election of a Democratic Eighty-fourth Congress . . . will mean the beginning of the end of the Republican Party. It is that simple." St. Louis, the next day: "[The Democrats] either did not understand the magnitude of the [Communist] threat, or ignored it." Omaha, September 20: "[We are] kicking Communists, fellow travelers, and bad security risks out of the federal government by the thousands. The Communist conspiracy is being smashed to bits by this administration. . . . Previous Democratic administrations . . . covered up rather than cleaned up." Lansing, September 21: "The issue is the inexcusable actions of a few leaders of the previous administration who by underestimating the danger of Communist infiltration, by ignoring the warnings of J. Edgar Hoover . . . rendered a terrible disservice to their country and discredit to their party."[68]

The Democrats fought back, delighted at the opportunity to make Nixon and McCarthy, rather than Eisenhower, their target. Stevenson said Nixon was off on an "ill-will tour," that the Republican Party had "as many wings as a boardinghouse chicken," and that "caught between contradiction, apathy, and McCarthy, they act as confused as a blind dog in a meathouse."[69] Nixon, he said again, represented "McCarthyism in a white collar."

The polls were predicting a Democratic sweep, and Nixon was afraid they were right. Meanwhile, Eisenhower was vacationing in Denver. Nixon resented Eisenhower's above-the-battle posture. The President's absence necessarily made Nixon the chief Republican spokesman, which meant he had to take the burden of answering Stevenson's quips, which in turn made him bear the brunt of the Democratic charges. It was a can't-win situation—the more he attacked, the more vulnerable to counterattack he made himself. Meanwhile, Eisenhower sat in Denver, doing nothing—after all, he was not up for re-election, and, as he said privately, he wouldn't mind at all if five or six of the most reactionary Republican senators got beat.[70]

(Nixon, for all his pep talk to the RNC about getting behind every Republican, was as appreciative as Eisenhower of the support of southern Democrats. On July 17, he sent a personal check for $100 to the Allan Shivers campaign fund for the governorship of Texas. "I am handling it in this way [he sent the check to Dan Thornton of Colorado, to be passed on to Shivers] because I realize it would be embarrassing to him in a Democratic primary if any publicity were given to the fact that he was receiving contributions from Republicans.)"[71]

Eisenhower's indifference bothered Nixon sufficiently for him to place a conference call to Brownell and Persons. "Don't give the President the idea that things are in good shape," he exclaimed.

"They're not. If we don't get moving and get the issues working for us instead of killing us, we're going to lose fifty seats."[72] What bothered him even more was the way in which the big guns in the Administration—Brownell, Wilson, Humphrey, and other Cabinet members—took their attitude from Eisenhower and laid back too.

Chotiner managed Nixon's activities. He remarked that with a few exceptions, "Dick was about the only man [in the top echelon] willing to stick his neck out and campaign for Republicans though he knew that if the party won, they would say it was because of the administration, and if it lost, they would say it was his fault. He felt the people didn't stand by him who should have."[73]

Nixon was also disturbed by complacency among the Republicans, the lack of organization, the second-rate candidates, and the absence of a guiding philosophy or theme. In early October, on a plane ride between campaign stops, he dictated a memorandum on the problems and what to do about them. He had Rose Woods take it down, type it up, and send it off to Postmaster General Arthur Summerfield, RNC Chairman Len Hall, and other party leaders.

In Nixon's analysis, the party that was most united, best organized, and capable of getting out its votes would win in off-year elections. In presidential election years, the Republicans had to pick up a fair share of normally Democratic votes to win, but in the off years, with a light vote, that was not the case—the Republicans could win simply by getting out their own vote. The tactic, therefore, should be: "Don't stir up interest in the election in preponderately Democratic areas." Instead, concentrate all activities in heavily Republican areas. He explained that if Republicans campaigned in an area that was 2 to 1 Democratic, they might be able to reduce the margin to 5 to 3, but in the process get many more people going to the polls "and your loss will be greater than your gain." Remember, he said, "whenever you go into an area to stir up your own people you also bring out the other people."

He thought that "all Republican speakers from the President down should begin to emphasize," first, confidence, second, the good news on the economic and world front, and third, "those issues in which we are strong and the other side is weak." The "strong" issues for the Republicans were "peace, Communism, corruption, taxes." The "weak" issues were unemployment and farm prices. Republicans should stay away from them, "because these two issues are *defensive* from our standpoint and the others are *offensive*." He reminded Republicans that the Democrats "can always *outpromise* us on economic issues. Only our *performance* on economic issues can win for us, and performance may not take place in time to win for us on those issues by election day." (The unemployment rate, at about 5 percent, was said by the Democrats to be a scandal.)

He recommended concentrating on Communism in the large cities, because "this is the only issue on which we can make an effective appeal to [urban] Democrats." But McCarthy and McCarthyism he wanted to stay away from entirely. "Our handling of this issue has gained us no new support," he admitted, and cost the Republicans a great deal: "The greatest damage has been done in splitting the Republicans and causing apathy in our ranks." He thought "we can remedy to an extent" the situation "by emphasizing vigorously the Administration's anti-Communist record and by attacking the other side for its past and present softness on the issue."

His conclusion was direct, honest, and hard-hitting. "I believe this is an election we have no business at all to lose. We have an immensely popular President and a good program. . . . If we lose, it will be only because of division and apathy in our own organization and by failing to adopt the correct strategy." Above all, organize, organize, organize.[74]

And attack, attack, attack. In Los Angeles, Nixon charged that "the housing scandals that the Truman Administration failed to check constitute the biggest scandal in American history." In Artesia, he said, "in 1952 the issue was 'kick the rascals out.' In 1954, it is 'keep the rascals out.' "[75] In Washington, on October 18, he charged that the Democratic Party had been taken over by its left wing, the Americans for Democratic Action (ADA). "The people know from bitter experience that this clique is notoriously soft on the Communist threat at home and is blatantly advocating socialization of American institutions." He heaped scorn on the idea that the Democrats would give Eisenhower better support than the Republicans.[76] In Van Nuys, California, he revealed that "when the Eisenhower administration came to Washington, we found in the files a blueprint for socializing America. This dangerous, well-oiled scheme contained plans for adding $40 billion to the national debt by 1956. It called for socialized medicine, socialized housing, socialized agriculture, socialized water and power, and perhaps most disturbing of all, socialization of America's greatest source of power, atomic energy." When reporters asked for copies of this "blueprint," Chotiner explained to them that Nixon was not referring to any specific document, but was using figurative language to describe the Democratic program.[77]

In Butte, Montana, on October 22, Nixon announced the discovery of another "secret memorandum," this one sent by the CP to Communists in California. According to Nixon, it urged the Communists to "fight out the issues within the ranks of the Democratic

Party," which he said "proved" that the Communist Party was "determined to conduct its program within the Democratic Party."[78]

He continued to play the numbers game. During the course of the campaign, the number of federal employees appointed by Truman and dismissed by Eisenhower as security risks grew magically, from 1,456 to 2,200 to 2,486, and eventually to 6,926. In Rock Island, Illinois, on October 21, he said, "The President's security risk program resulted in 6,926 individuals removed from the federal service. . . . The great majority of these individuals were inherited largely from the Truman regime. . . . Included in this number were individuals who were members of the Communist Party and Communist-controlled organizations." In Denver, eleven days later, he claimed that "96 percent of the 6,926 Communists, fellow travelers, sex perverts, people with criminal records, drunks, and other security risks removed under the Eisenhower security program were hired by the Truman administration."

The Democrats vigorously disputed these figures, with good cause. Philip Young, head of the Civil Service Commission (and appointed by Eisenhower), admitted toward the end of the campaign that he knew of no single government employee who had been fired for being a Communist. He also revealed that of a total of 3,746 employees who had been dismissed or who had resigned for security reasons since May 1953, nearly half had been hired by the Eisenhower Administration.[79]

When Stevenson charged that Republican economics, the emphasis on a balanced budget and a free marketplace for the private sector, were leading to stagnation, and warned that the Russian rate of growth was surpassing that of the United States, Nixon struck back immediately. In Beverly Hills, on October 28, he said, "Mr. Stevenson has been guilty, probably without being aware that he was doing so, of spreading pro-Communist propaganda as he has attacked with violent fury the economic system of the United States and praised the Soviet economy. . . . [Stevenson's] dislike for our own economic system is his own business, but when he links such criticism with praise of the rapid growth of the Soviet economy, he is performing a grave disservice to us and the rest of the free world."[80]

Cabell Phillips of *The New York Times*, after describing the Vice-President as the chief strategist and "one-man task force of the GOP," offered an analysis of Nixon's methods: "Like most politicians, Mr. Nixon talks in hyperboles, makes sweeping generalizations of sometimes dubious validity, and is adept at planting the dark and ominous inference. But he does it with extraordinary finesse."[81]

Nixon's style continued to arouse passions and practically invited hecklers. On October 29, in San Mateo, during a nationally televised speech, when he was just getting into his climax, a voice boomed out from the audience, "Tell us a dog story, Dick." Nixon ignored the heckler, but when he finished his speech and the crowd started filing out, he called to the doorman to restrain the man as he tried to leave. "I would be ashamed if any member of my party wouldn't allow a speaker to address his audience," Nixon declared. He said that he had so far been in twenty-two states and made more than two hundred speeches, "and this is the first time I have been heckled." Angry, his face flushed, he concluded his impromptu address by telling the doorman, "O.K., boys, throw him out." (A month later the heckler, a Mr. James Heavey of San Francisco, sued Nixon for $150,000, charging that Nixon's "goon squad" had "assaulted him, battered and falsely detained him." Nothing came of the suit.) [82]

Nixon pushed himself so hard, and had such a sense of fighting the incoming tide alone, that, as he later remarked, "I was feeling low because I didn't think we were getting enough help in the campaign and were carrying it pretty much alone." [83] Eisenhower bucked him up with cheery little notes. On September 29, from his vacation headquarters in Denver, the President wrote, "Good reports have been reaching me from all parts of the country as the result of your intensive—and I am sure exhaustive—speaking tour. . . . Please don't think that I am not unaware that I have done little to lighten your load." Then he pointed out the benefit to Nixon: "One thing that has come of this is that you are constantly becoming better and more favorably known to the American public. This is all to the good." Eisenhower's note encouraged Nixon to keep at it. [84]

Others in the Republican Party exhorted him to keep it up. Charlie Halleck told Nixon, "You've got to give 'em hell, Dick! Sam Rayburn's just been to town [Indianapolis]. He was murdering us!" Dewey advised Nixon to "hit harder . . . people like a fighter." Stassen sent a letter: "I wish to commend you on the splendid and hard-hitting contribution you are making to this campaign." [85]

Eisenhower, meanwhile, finally roused himself, got out of Denver, and hit the campaign trail. In the second half of October, he traveled more than ten thousand miles and made nearly forty speeches. He concentrated on the eastern half of the country and stayed in states where moderate Republicans needed help, leaving the Old Guard strongholds in the Midwest and West to Nixon. The reason the President came out of his torpor was a warning he had received to the effect that if the Republicans lost control of Congress, "the extreme right wing will try to recapture the leadership of the party." Eisenhower thought the threat a serious one, and deplored it, because "if the right wing really recaptures the Republican Party, there simply isn't going to be any Republican influence in this country within a matter of a few brief years. A new party will be inevitable." [86]

The night before the election, Nixon joined Eisenhower for a national broadcast. Stevenson had just chided Eisenhower for saying that prosperity under the Democrats had come about at the cost of war and bloodshed, and that only the Republicans knew how to keep a peacetime economy growing. Nixon called Stevenson's speech "one of the most vicious, scurrilous attacks ever made by a major political figure on a President of the United States."

Going further, Nixon said that Stevenson was practicing Hitler's technique of the "Big Lie." He said that Stevenson had given a textbook example of how not to run a political campaign: "The Stevenson-Truman campaign to elect an anti-Eisenhower A.D.A. Left-Wing Congress is a prize example." The Democratic campaign, he charged, "has consisted of the following ingredients in approximately the proportions mentioned: Quips—50 per cent. Innuendo and name-calling—45 percent. Honest discussion of the issues—5 per cent." Then he claimed that the Democrats' secret aim was to "socialize basic American institutions . . . and return to the Acheson foreign policy." [87]

ON ELECTION DAY, Nixon flew back to Washington with Chotiner. He pulled from his briefcase seven pages of handwritten notes on yellow legal-pad paper, handed them to Chotiner, and said, "Here's my last campaign speech, Murray. You might like to keep it as a souvenir. It's the last one, because after this I am through with politics." [88]

The results should have reinforced his depression. The Republicans lost seventeen seats in the House and two in the Senate, and thereby lost control of both houses of Congress. As Chotiner had predicted, everyone in the Republican Party seemed to blame Nixon; especially infuriating was the commonly expressed view that Eisenhower's last-minute campaigning saved the party from an even bigger loss. But instead of letting all this lead to his retirement from politics, Nixon roused himself and fought back.

He started the day after the election, when Eisenhower called him into the Oval Office for an initial postmortem. The President said that he had noticed The New York Times was taking Nixon apart for his "smears." Nixon responded, "I never said an untrue word in the campaign," and vowed that he was "not going to take this New York Times attack without fighting back." [89]

He did so with enthusiasm. He gathered together excerpts from his speeches in the last two weeks of the campaign and sent them out to Republican columnists, reporters, and editors. His covering letter to Roscoe Drummond was typical: "In view of the fact that some people are saying that I am supposed to have smeared the Democratic Party . . . I thought you might like to see the basic evidence. . . . My entire campaign was based on the record." He dared anyone to "name any statement I have made in this campaign which is untrue."[90] To reporter Victor Lasky, he explained, "My attack was on the ADA left-wingers in the Democratic Party, and as usual, they are trying to throw the cloak of injured innocence around a larger number than themselves."[91]

In the first Cabinet meeting after the election, Eisenhower turned to Nixon, asking him to organize meetings with party leaders "to decide immediately the significance of the election, and what we are going to do to avoid any trouble." The President also wanted advice on how to live with a Democratic Congress, remarking, "I expect much help from Dick Nixon on this." Finally, Eisenhower asked Nixon, as the resident political expert, to analyze the election results for the Cabinet.

Nixon said that considering 1954 was an off-year election, "the swing is so small that it was really a dead heat." The Democrats had not won the mandate; indeed, given how far below the usual off-year swing the election had been, it was a Republican victory. Credit for that, Nixon said pointedly, "has got to go to the program and to the campaign at the top." The reasons for the losses were poor candidates and weak organization. "There were just too many turkeys running on the Republican ticket." He took a little windup toy drummer from his pocket, released the catch, and set it in motion on the table. As the little drummer beat his way around the table, Nixon declared, "Gentlemen, we should take a lesson from this: this is not the time to be depressed, and we have got to keep beating the drum about our achievements." Eisenhower loved it.[92]

Looking to the future, Nixon found one especially bright spot in the election returns. He pointed it out to Victor Lasky: "Did you realize that west of the Mississippi we gained one Senate seat and broke even on House seats? Incidentally, a shift of one vote a precinct in Oregon, Wyoming and Montana would have given us a margin of five seats in the Senate." The Republicans were on their way to building on a Solid West to match the Democrats' Solid South, and the West was much the fastest-growing area of the country.[93]

In a December 28 letter to a California friend, Nixon described one of the problems he felt he had throughout the campaign—the

media. "Radio and television commentators as well as a great proportion of the working press are on the other side," he claimed.
"They stick the needle into us every night and every day, and
frankly I simply don't know how we're going to be able to counteract it until we've developed a corps of people ourselves who will
at least give us an even break in reporting the news."[94]

To that end, Nixon turned to Whittaker Chambers, who had
many friends in the conservative press, and asked Chambers to
arrange a meeting, early in the New Year, at which they could
discuss the problems the Republicans, expecially Nixon, had with
the press. He was girding himself for 1955, and yet another round
in the never-ending battle of the Democrats.[95]

AND WHAT OF HIS PROMISE to Pat to retire? Years later, Nixon said
that "circumstances" forced him to change his mind. "Pat felt very,
very strongly about it," Nixon said. "Ever since the fund thing she
hasn't been keen on this business." Then he added, "Once you get
into this great stream of history you can't get out. You can drown.
Or you can be pulled ashore by the tide. But it is awfully hard to
get out when you are in the middle of the stream—if it is intended
that you stay there."[96]

"THE PRESIDENT HAS HAD
A CORONARY"
1955

"THE BIG TEST OF A MAN is not how well he does the things he likes," Nixon told reporter Helen Erskine in a 1954 interview, "but how well he does things he doesn't like. The thing that destroys a person is to be constantly looking for something else—thinking how much happier you'd be in another job." [1]

After his experiences in the 1954 campaign, Nixon could hardly help but think of how much happier he might be in another job. He had promised Pat he would quit politics, but no matter how serious he was at the time he signed his pledge, he never really meant it. Life without politics was unimaginable. Still, there were lots of jobs in politics—nowhere was it written in stone that he had to serve as Vice-President after 1956.

On January 5, 1955, Nixon had a long talk with Senator Earle Clements of Kentucky. Their subject was Vice-Presidents who had returned to the Senate, or gone into the Cabinet, when their terms were up. [2] The idea tempted Nixon, who—like every one of his predecessors—felt frustrated in his job. He could not speak his own mind, had to be the hatchet man in campaigns, which made him few friends and many enemies, and aside from whatever crumbs Eisenhower decided to give him, he had nothing real to do. In *Six Crises* Nixon quoted Charles G. Dawes (Coolidge's Vice-President), who described the Vice-President's job as "the easiest in the world." Dawes has explained that he had only two responsibilities—to sit and listen to senators give speeches, and to check the morning's newspaper as to the President's health. [3]

Nixon nevertheless found things to do. There was, first and

foremost, politics pure and simple. Nixon advised Knowland, now the minority leader in the Senate, and other Republican congressmen on ways to divide the Democrats, and on how to keep the southern Democrats voting with the Republicans. He urged his associates to do as he claimed he did, never attack the Democratic Party, just its left wing, and especially the ADA. He said he had learned long ago in the Senate cloakroom that the southerners were "very sensitive about the A.D.A., very bitter."[4]

Despite his disappointment at the refusal of Cabinet members to respond to his exhortations to hit the campaign trail, he kept after them. In January 1955, he told them to make maximum use of a recent economic report, one that was decidedly upbeat (1 percent inflation, steady growth in GNP, low unemployment, a balanced budget), because as he saw it, "everyone in the country trusted the President on the peace issue," but many remained fearful of a depression under the Republicans. Nixon urged them to use the report in their speeches, including their Lincoln Day addresses.

Despite the loss of the 1954 elections, Nixon remained convinced that he had been hitting the right issues—the problem was not his issues, but his isolation. He not only wanted the Cabinet to join him in pointing to Republican prosperity, but also to continue to hit the theme of the numbers of Communists in government found and dismissed by the Eisenhower Administration. Nixon was solemn and earnest as he gave this opinion to the Cabinet. Eisenhower lightened the atmosphere by telling a couple of old army stories, the point of which was that if Bob Stevens had admitted a mistake in the Peress case, there never would have been any Army-McCarthy hearings, and the Republicans would still be in control of Congress.

Eisenhower laughed, then added, "And then, I'll tell you gentlemen another story I learned a long time ago. Don't try to be cute or cover up. If you do, you will get so entangled you won't know what you're doing."[5]

NIXON'S POLITICAL WORK included regular meetings with younger Republicans in Congress, sub-Cabinet people, the RNC, Persons, and others to figure out ways to do a better job of selling the President's program, and to begin building the Republican Party for the 1956 elections. Nixon's advice was as routine as the job—establish better liaison between the White House staff and Congress, set up regular meetings between the Cabinet members and the Republicans on the pertinent committee, don't depend on "mere errand boys" for important testimony before Congress, make "research and speech stuff" available to Republican congressmen, and so on. All this, he claimed, "will effectively put a 'new face' on our party."

When Nixon made that claim before the Cabinet, a number of members looked a bit skeptical. The President jumped in to support Nixon, by way of doing some reminiscing: "Some 30 or 35 years ago," he said, grinning, "I was assigned to writing speeches for Congressmen. I even had to think up the subject!" Shaking his head, Eisenhower added, "They worked me to death."[6]

Some weeks later, the Cabinet was discussing four resolutions from the Daughters of the American Revolution, all strongly right-wing and all in direct contradiction to Eisenhower's policy. "Where does the D.A.R. get such cockeyed resolutions?" the President asked.

"Women at conventions!" Nixon snorted. "They don't worry about resolutions." He assured the President that "the women love you," and repeated, "They don't know what is in those resolutions."[7]

He continued his active speechmaking schedule, usually giving two or more speeches a week. In direct contrast to his slashing attacks on the Democrats throughout 1954, in 1955 he concentrated on proclaiming Republican policy and praising Republican accomplishments. His basic theme was: "For twenty years our opponents have been beating us over the head with the claim that Republican economic policies meant depression and that Democratic policies meant good times. The Eisenhower record has destroyed this myth once and for all, and it seems to me that it is time we did a better job of letting the people know what has happened." He sent copies of his speeches to all prominent Republicans, urging them to use his material in their speeches and help spread the good news. One of his form letters (it went out as a cover note for a copy of a speech he had just made to the Young Republican Convention) concluded, "It seems to me that instead of continually stating the obvious, 'We have to have Ike,'—we should recognize the responsibility we all have to do our part as well."[8]

MORE THAN ANY OTHER MAN IN THE COUNTRY, Nixon worried about the Republican Party after Eisenhower. But he was not alone in his concern, only more intense about it. A common response from Republicans, when asked what the party was going to do after Eisenhower retired, was "When we come to that bridge, we'll jump in the river." For himself, however, Nixon saw more promising possibilities. The post-Eisenhower Republican Party would need a leader, and he was in the best position of all the contenders for the role. Before he could become party leader, however, two things had to happen: Eisenhower had to retire, and Eisenhower had to give Nixon his blessing.

In the spring of 1955, retirement was very much on Eisenhower's mind, and the subject of many of his conversations. The President was keeping all his options open, but again and again in private talks he insisted that, barring some unforeseen emergency, he would step down after 1956. The struggle to replace him, therefore, had begun almost immediately after the 1954 elections.

On June 4, 1955, Nixon received a memo from Robert Finch of his staff. "Walter Trohan called," Finch began (Trohan was a reporter for the Chicago *Tribune*). "He was very much concerned about the Rockefeller buildup which he says is on the way." Nelson Rockefeller had recently replaced C. D. Jackson as Special Assistant to the President. He not only had a potentially key position in the White House (from which he was already milking maximum publicity), but good looks, unlimited ambitions as well as unlimited personal financial resources, and the support of those East Coast Republicans who never could stomach Nixon.

Finch's memo continued: "Trohan wants to have a group of your friends to an off-the-record session which he will host simply for the purpose of going over your plans and how they might be helpful." Finch concluded, "Is this worth pursuing?"

Nixon felt that indeed it was. He scribbled at the bottom of the memo: "Bob—keep in close touch with Trohan. Get intelligence from him. Feed him our stories. This meeting is an excellent idea if he is sure of the loyalty of those concerned."[9]

Nixon's position required secrecy. He could not make an open bid for leadership, not so long as Eisenhower was healthy and on the job and closemouthed about his intentions. But just as obviously, Nixon could not merely sit around and wait for Eisenhower to make up his mind. He had to solidify as much support as possible, and as soon as possible. In the process, he needed to soften his image. He already had the right wing of the party behind him, primarily because of his record but also because that wing could never accept Nelson Rockefeller. What Nixon needed was more strength in the center. He turned to Chotiner for help.

On July 9, in a memo, Chotiner gave Nixon a long list of suggestions. He thought Nixon ought to write an article on civil rights, and another on his work as the head of the Government Contracts Committee. Chotiner advised Nixon to "get a liberal" to write an article on "This Man Nixon" for a "suitable publication"—but did not tell him how to arrange that feat. Another suggested article, on the "Pains and Penalties of Politics," should emphasize "the difficulty in getting good people to hold public office because of the sniping that takes place." It would be a development of the "Poor Richard" theme with which Nixon had already had so much practice—one might have thought that only because he had a gun at his head did he stay in politics.

Chotiner's advice, generally, was run-of-the-mill—Nixon should have his office put out more "human interest" stories and more material on "The Work Nixon Does." Further, Nixon should "attend as many events as possible of minority groups." Chotiner, in short, was as obsessed as Nixon himself with "getting the story out," that is, with public relations. But even the greatest of PR men need *something* to work with: Chotiner advised Nixon to persuade Eisenhower to "give you a new assignment or project." [10]

What Nixon really needed was access to television. By the mid-fifties, the evening news programs on the major networks were attracting millions of viewers, but they were only ten or eleven minutes long, fifteen counting commercials, so there was intense competition to get on. Nixon almost never made it. Compounding that problem, his major television appearances, from Checkers through the 1954 campaign, had all been characterized by slashing attacks on the opposition. This reinforced his bad-guy image. The best way to counter that impression—get Nixon on the evening news, announcing some new and positive program—was difficult to arrange, primarily because most of Nixon's work was for the party, behind the scenes.

In January, Nixon got a vivid lesson in the value of television to a politician. Eisenhower decided to allow television reporters to film his press conferences. Hagerty then censored the film, usually removing about 10 percent, primarily because of jumbled syntax rather than security reasons. He released the rest to the networks.

The results, Nixon reported to the President after a trip to California, were sensational. Everyone loved it. What impressed Nixon most was the way in which the President "can go directly to the people, instead of through the press." Putting it into perspective, Nixon said the televised news conferences were even better than Roosevelt's fireside chats. He congratulated the President on how well he had done in facing the cameras and lights. Eisenhower shrugged and replied, "I've faced cameras too long to mind them now." [11]

EISENHOWER DID TRY TO GIVE NIXON ASSIGNMENTS that would result in extensive and positive coverage. In July 1954, he had sent Nixon to a Governor's Conference, there to announce the Administration's program for an Interstate Highway System. Nixon staggered the audience with the scope of the proposal. The plan advocated a comprehensive program, including roads for farm-to-market travel and rapid intercity and interregional travel. Nixon called for spending $5 billion per year for the next ten years, in addition to the $700 million already being spent annually. His speech had an "electrifying effect" on the governors and on the public.[12]

But not on the Democrats, who objected to the financial arrangements (they wanted to pay for the system through increased taxes on the trucking industry, instead of the Republican method of a federal gasoline and tire tax), and killed the bill in 1955. Overall, in fact, the Democrats were proving to be much more difficult to work with than Nixon had predicted.

For example, they were impossible on the question of schools. The great economic boom of the fifties, which created the pressing need for new highways (Detroit sold almost 8 million automobiles in 1955, a record until a full decade later), was matched by the great baby boom of the postwar period, which created a pressing need for new schools. The Republican answer was a billion-dollar program of federal loans and grants to the states for the construction of schools. But however great the need, political considerations killed the bill. The Old Guard Republicans refused to support it, because they were alarmed at the possible intrusion of the federal government into education; the Democrats wanted to add to it federal assistance for teachers' salaries, and make it more generous. Further complicating the situation was the problem of desegregation; liberal Democrats wanted to deny funds to any state that continued to segregate its schools, something Southern Democrats would not accept.

Eisenhower turned to Nixon for help in Congress on both the Interstate System and the school construction bill. Nixon was an enthusiastic supporter. He had long ago learned that schools and roads were the smart politician's bread and butter. In his diary, Hagerty reported that Nixon told a January Cabinet meeting, "It would be a good thing for the Republican Party to get behind such programs and said that in California Earl Warren got the reputation of being a great liberal because he built schools and roads. We are now ready to build roads and it is very popular. We will find that the school construction program is even more popular. So if we combine roads and schools we can really go someplace."[13] But in fact, despite Nixon's and Eisenhower's and Persons' strenuous efforts, they could not get anywhere with the Democratically controlled Congress, and no such bills were passed in 1955.

THE EASIEST WAY FOR NIXON to get publicity for himself was to go abroad. In February 1955, he made his second goodwill trip, this one to Mexico, Central America, and the Caribbean. He was gone for a month, in which time he visited ten countries, plus two American possessions, the Virgin Islands and Puerto Rico. Pat went along, which led to a front-page photograph in *The New York Times* showing a tearful goodbye to Julie and Tricia. Throughout the trip, Nixon used the same techniques he had developed in the Far East —extensive handshaking with the crowds, discussions with leaders of various groups, intensive briefings before his meetings, and so forth. As in the Far East, he learned a great deal, and met foreign leaders with whom he would have extensive contact in the future.

He also did some serious diplomatic work. In Cuba he reassured the government by promising that the sugar quota would not be cut. In Guatemala, where the CIA had the previous year engineered a coup that replaced leftist Jacobo Arbenz with a pro-U.S. government headed by Colonel Castillo Armas, Nixon pledged additional aid. But he also met with leaders of the Guatemalan labor union, and recommended stronger free trade unions in Guatemala as a deterrent to Communism. In Honduras he promised to promote private investment in the country, as well as more aid. Farther south, President Anastasio Somoza of Nicaragua and President José Figueres of Costa Rica (both were military men) were engaged in a blood feud. Somoza told Nixon that Figueres was trying to have him assassinated; Figueres said that Somoza was trying to take away Costa Rican territory in an endemic border war. Nixon got each dictator to promise to ease tensions. In the Dominican Republic he was effusive in expressing his thanks to Generalissimo Rafael Trujillo for his support of the United States in the United Nations.[14]

When he returned, Nixon gave a full report to the Cabinet and the NSC. "We must keep our eyes on this part of the world," he declared. "They are close to us, they are our best customers, they buy more from us than all Europe, and more than all the rest of the world, Europe and Canada excluded." A major problem, he said, was "so much one-man rule," but he could not see what the United States could do about that, so he proceeded to give a personality sketch of the various dictators.

Fulgencio Batista of Cuba, Nixon said, was "a very remarkable man . . . once an army sergeant. Reads voraciously. . . . He wants to do a job for Cuba, not for himself. . . . Is concerned with social development . . . Will give stability to Cuba. . . . He will deal effectively with the Commies (who are more numerous than in the U.S.). . . . Sugar is all important. . . . We must realize that Cuban purchases from us will drop to the extent that we cut their sugar."

He found Mexican President Cortines to be "honest, capable,

with a real feeling for his people," but also noted that his mansion was "more costly than the White House." Meanwhile, within one hundred yards of the mansion, "people live in caves." In Guatemala, a country with "much potential for advancement," he found Castillo Armas to be "a good middle-roader" with "overwhelming popular support." Nixon predicted that Castillo Armas "will accomplish in two years what the Commies failed to do in ten." In Honduras the United Fruit Company was leading the nation toward prosperity and progress. Somoza had "dealt effectively with the Nicaraguan Commies," but he hated Figueres so much it blinded him to everything else. As for Figueres himself, Nixon found him to be "complex, cocky, popular with his people." In the Dominican Republic, Nixon was disturbed by Trujillo's "moral flexibility," but praised him for keeping the place "clean" and providing "drinkable water." The Dominicans, he found, had an "obsession with progress" and were "proud of being on time." Haiti, by way of contrast, was "a picture in poverty and pregnancy. We can only hope and pray that they find some resources to help them along."

Summing up, Nixon said the essential problem in the area was government. "The Spaniards had many talents," he asserted, "but government was not among them. So the question facing us is, how far is dictatorship necessary?" He did not answer the question, but he did declare that "we must deal with these governments as they are and work over a period of time towards more democracy." Meanwhile, the United States had to be aware of the possibilities of a coup, because "in these countries, a very few organized people can take over—so we should concentrate on winning them." [15]

Those were all rather commonplace Republican views, reflecting Republican aims in the region—stability and a favorable climate for investment. What was unusual about Nixon was the way he followed up on the promises he made while in Central America. He pressed the State Department to improve the quantity and quality of technical magazines, journals, and books going to USIA libraries. He pushed hard, both in public speeches and in Cabinet meetings, for increased expenditures for the Inter-American Highway. He called for the creation of a Caribbean bloc. He urged the Export-Import Bank to take a "fresh new look" at its lending policies in Latin America, as part of a program designed to increase trade between the U.S. and its neighbors.[16]

Nixon's trip led to some firsthand knowledge on his part of conditions in the Caribbean and Central America, some limited improvements in U.S. relations in the area, a few marginal gains in the local economies, and some serious misjudgments about the social and political forces coming to the fore. The trouble was that the region was a backwater in the Cold War, hardly of any interest at all to the Eisenhower Administration. At Nixon's urging, Eisenhower did free up some funds for the Inter-American Highway, but otherwise the President seemed hardly to have noticed Nixon's departure or return. The newspapers had buried what little news they printed about the last weeks of Nixon's trip on the back pages, and *The New York Times'* photograph of his homecoming, which showed Julie rushing up the steps of the plane to greet her father, was on page 33.[17]

Meanwhile, Nixon's chief rival for the position of chosen successor to Eisenhower, Nelson Rockefeller, was working on the biggest project of all—an arms control proposal to the Soviets to be made at the upcoming Geneva Summit Conference—and making sure he got a huge amount of publicity for his efforts.

THE SUMMIT AT GENEVA, the first since Potsdam, ten years earlier, raised fears that Eisenhower would be taken in by the Soviets. Nixon advised the President on how to deal with them. He sent Eisenhower a photograph of Nikita Khrushchev, the Party Secretary and the emerging leader in the Kremlin. Khrushchev was laughing heartily in the photograph, holding up a champagne glass, while his belly shook—the very picture of a lovable bear of a man. But Nixon saw through the Red plot. He informed Eisenhower that the scene was "part of a concerted effort to make the world think that the Russians are truly changed, a human, approachable, hail-fellow-well-met bunch of characters with whom any reasonable man can argue or bargain on a reasonable basis and that ANY FAILURE TO REACH AGREEMENT IS NOT THEIR FAULT." The effort was based on the Kremlin's conviction that the conference would fail; the aim was to convince the world that the onus for the failure lay with the West.

In acknowledging Nixon's memo, the President merely noted that it "has come in." Nothing more. But Eisenhower did give Nixon a task to carry out while he, the President, was in Geneva—he wanted the Vice-President to conduct a Cabinet meeting, and a meeting of the legislative leaders.[18] Nixon did as Eisenhower wished, and carried out the job with aplomb (the subjects discussed were arrangements for meeting the President at the airport on his return, and Nixon's favorite topic, how to get the Cabinet members to make more partisan speeches).[19]

EISENHOWER'S ATTITUDE at this time was as ambiguous as the bare record indicates. He did not yet know whether he would run in

1956 for re-election. As part of his determination to keep his options open, the President wanted to build up a potential successor to whom he could hand over the job with a feeling of confidence, both in his ability to get elected and in his ability to serve. It was a subject he discussed often with his friends and advisers.

Ann Whitman's transcription of a tape-recorded Oval Office conversation between Eisenhower and his close adviser Lucius Clay reads: "President gave the names of four people...he thought could be built up: Bob Anderson [Secretary of the Navy], Dick Nixon, Herb Brownell and Herbert Hoover, Jr. [Under Secretary of State]. He said Brownell might not quite have 'saleable' character. Said Hoover was completely charming, lucid and clear in presentations."[20]

With the former head of the Marshall Plan, Paul Hoffman: "They were talking about possible successors to the Presidency. President said my number one man would be Bob Anderson; my second, or along with him, would be young Hoover. It would be a little harder because of his name. But he is sound and learns rapidly. Then I would take Dick Nixon. A man that would be almost my ideal would be Charlie Hallack."[21]

With his economics adviser, Gabe Hauge: "President thinks Bob Anderson would be the finest candidate we could have.... Hoover just hasn't quite got the fire—a little too much of his dad. Charlie Halleck just loves politics, a great virtue. Dick Nixon, he has made some enemies, is not considered very matured—but he's got pretty good experience. Then you have Cabot Lodge, who in many ways would be the best President—but a blueblood from Boston, you could not elect him."[22]

In these and many other conversations, the President would ramble on and on about potential candidates to replace him. What stands out about them is how seldom he put Nixon first or even second, and how negative his comments about the Vice-President were. What also stands out, however, is that he *never* mentioned Rockefeller.

Nixon's great advantages over all his rivals was that he was where he was. Nobody was going to get the Republican nomination in 1956 without Eisenhower's blessing, and the President had spent a lifetime identifying his enemies. He knew who supported his policies, and who didn't (thus his high esteem for Halleck). In this situation, Nixon's being Vice-President helped him considerably—he had no choice but to heartily endorse anything the President proposed. If he had stayed in the Senate, Nixon almost certainly would have done as Knowland was doing, that is, criticized the President for accepting an armistice in Korea, for his failure to support the French at Dien Bien Phu, and so on. That was another feature of Eisenhower's rambling about possible successors—except for Halleck, he never mentioned a Republican congressman, for the good reason that every one of them had been critical of him on some issue.

The Vice-Presidency also benefited Nixon because it allowed him to stay pretty much clear of Republican infighting in California. Because of its size and wealth, California had earned a near-permanent place on the national ticket. (In the ten elections from 1944 through 1984, only in 1964 and 1976 did the Republicans run without a Californian. The Democrats have never run a Californian, and have paid a high price for that neglect.) The three giants from California were Warren, Knowland, and Nixon. Warren was hardly likely to give up his place as Chief Justice to become a candidate; Eisenhower would never accept Knowland, for whom he often expressed deep contempt ("In his case there seems to be no answer to the question, How dumb can you get?"); that left Nixon. Inside the California Republican Party, meanwhile, Knowland and Goodwin Knight, the governor, were locked in a struggle for control. Nixon was able to stay neutral.

The best thing about being Vice-President was that it meant that Nixon's name was automatically on any list of possible successors, whether drawn up by Eisenhower or by a columnist doing some speculating—something that happened almost every day. Being the front-runner, however, carried with it the cost of practically guaranteeing the development of a "dump Nixon" movement on the part of all the other candidates.

One of Nixon's assets was his standing in the Republican Party. Here too the Vice-Presidency helped him, because it made him even more attractive as a speaker at conventions and fund raisers. In addition, the demands of his job were so slight that he could afford to make extensive speaking trips. He did so with enthusiasm, lambasting the Democrats with gusto. As a result, he was, without question, the most popular Republican among the party professionals.

In sum, Nixon's greatest strength was also his biggest weakness—his partisanship, which was reinforced by his role as Vice-President. It endeared him to the Old Guard, made the Democrats furious, and left Eisenhower and his advisers wondering if Dick would ever mature (they would shake their heads about Dick's going too far even as they sent him out to make yet another reply to Stevenson).

In the event that Eisenhower decided not to run again, there was obviously going to be an intense struggle within the party over the replacement candidate. Already, Eisenhower's closest friends were telling him that Nixon would be a disaster, while Republican professionals were telling him that he had to choose Nixon to succeed him. In the event Eisenhower did decide to run, there was just as obviously going to be a major drive to dump Nixon, as well as one to keep him. Complexity piled on complexity as the speculation went on.

The unknown factor was the President's health. If for any reason Eisenhower had to resign, or if he died before the 1956 convention, Nixon would be President and then be a cinch for the nomination. But Eisenhower was looking good, indeed seemed to be thriving on the Presidency. When he returned from Geneva, he went to Denver for a vacation. Nixon visited him there. On September 6, he reported to a friend that Eisenhower "seemed to be in exceedingly good spirits and I am sure that the change from the sometimes 'hot air' of Washington to the cool and invigorating atmosphere in Denver is proving beneficial to him." [23]

EISENHOWER'S POPULARITY IN THE SUMMER OF 1955 was at a peak. He had scored a great triumph at the Geneva Summit Conference with his proposal that arms control agreements be monitored through an "Open Skies" arrangement that would allow each side to fly unlimited reconnaissance missions over the other's territory. Further, just the fact that the President had met with the leaders in the Kremlin helped create a "spirit of Geneva," a thawing in the Cold War, that lifted spirits worldwide. For the five years before Geneva, war scares came on almost a monthly basis, and major wars were fought in Korea and Indochina. The year following Geneva was the calmest of the first two decades of the Cold War.

Eisenhower had few illusions about the spirit of Geneva. He knew that Khruschev had already rejected Open Skies and that Geneva would not even slow down the arms race. Still, a start had been made. The world scene was calm. America was on a major economic boom. As he relaxed in that lovely Denver air, he had good reason to feel satisfaction with what had been started, and optimistic about continued progress.

THE AFTERNOON OF SEPTEMBER 24, the Nixons attended a wedding. They got home shortly after 5 P.M. Nixon had just settled down to read the batting averages, after scanning the headlines, when the phone rang. It was Jim Hagerty, who identified himself, then said, "The President has had a coronary."

Nixon was speechless for so long that Hagerty feared the line had gone dead. Finally Nixon asked, "Are they sure? . . . Doctors can make mistakes. I don't think we should announce it as a heart attack until we are absolutely sure."

"We are absolutely sure," Hagerty declared, and added that he was going to tell the press in half an hour. Before hanging up, he added, "Let me know where you can be reached at all times."

"I went back into the living room and sat down again," Nixon later wrote. "For fully ten minutes I sat alone in the room, and to this day I cannot remember the thoughts that flowed through my mind. . . . I probably was in a momentary state of shock. . . . It was like a great physical weight holding me down in the chair." [24]

The delicacy of his position could not be overstated, and is so obvious that it need not be described. He felt the need for advice and counsel, and thought immediately of Bill Rogers. He recalled how helpful Rogers had been during the fund crisis, how loyal he was, and what a good sense he had for public relations. He called Rogers, who agreed to come right over.

Then Nixon thought of Pat, went upstairs, and told her the news. Next he called Rose Mary Woods, who was still at the wedding reception, and asked her to return to her apartment so that she could handle the incoming calls on her extension of his home telephone number. As he hung up, Tricia came running down the stairs, crying. "The President isn't going to die, is he, Daddy?" she asked. Nixon reassured her.

Rogers arrived, and the two men talked. They knew almost nothing about Eisenhower's condition, so they concentrated on Nixon's position. Nixon said he realized that Eisenhower's family, his staff, the Cabinet, the political parties, the press, indeed the whole nation would be extremely sensitive about his actions. Above all, he could not appear to be seizing power, but simultaneously he had to be prepared to provide for continuity of government, and to assume the leadership role if necessary. Rogers advised him to hold no press conferences for as long as possible, nor allow any photographs. That was good advice, but the problem was the avalanche of reporters who had descended on the Vice-President's house. Nixon decided to spend the night with Rogers; to get the Vice-President out of his house without being seen, Rogers called his wife, who drove over and parked on a side street. Then, as Tricia went out the front door to look at the TV cameras (and attract the attention of the press), Nixon and Rogers went out the back door. [25]

Once safely in Rogers' living room, Nixon called Jerry Persons, who came right over. They discussed getting a civilian specialist to Denver to assist the army doctors at Fitzsimons Army Hospital. They turned to the Constitution, noting that it did not provide for a situation in which the President was incapacitated for a temporary period. It did say that the Vice-President should become President "in case of the removal of the President from office, or of his death, resignation or inability to discharge the powers and duties of said office...." But the Constitution was silent on the overwhelming question, Who decides when the President is unable to exercise his powers? Compounding the constitutional ambiguity were the unanswerable questions about the President's condition. Could he function? Make decisions? Sign papers? Would he be an invalid? Would he recover at all?

Nixon spent much of the evening on the telephone, talking to various Cabinet members. Together, they reached the common-sense, indeed inevitable, conclusion that their best course was to carry on in an atmosphere of "business as usual," with the emphasis on the "team" Eisenhower had built and its ability to function in an emergency.[26]

At 2:30 A.M., Nixon went to bed in Rogers' guest room. He did not sleep. Instead, he thought his way through his situation. He concluded that if Eisenhower recovered within a few weeks, "it would be foolish for me to do anything that the press could in any way interpret as being self-serving." In the more likely situation, that recovery would take some months, and that in the meantime the Vice-President had to take over some—if not all—of his duties, "it was equally important that nothing I did made it appear that I was seeking his power." In the worst case, if Eisenhower died, Nixon would be President; "if that happened it would be even more important that my conduct beforehand be above question."[27]

When Nixon got up in the morning, he knew that his only viable option was to do nothing, or at least as little as he could get away with.

That ran against the grain for Nixon. In a crisis, he sought his solution in action, not inaction. In this crisis, he later wrote, the problem "was how to walk on eggs and not break them.... I had to ... provide leadership without appearing to lead."[28]

HIS LONG-TERM PROBLEM was protecting and strengthening his position as Eisenhower's logical successor. The news of the President's heart attack had set off a torrent of speculation. The morning after Eisenhower went into the hospital, James Reston's story on the front page of *The New York Times* began, "Vice President Richard M. Nixon today fell heir to one of the greatest responsibilities and political opportunities ever presented to so young a man in the history of the Republic. The general feeling here [Washington] was that the 42-year-old Californian was in a better position than anyone else to get the Republican nomination, if, as seems almost certain, the stricken President retires at the end of his first term."[29]

That morning, a Sunday, Nixon drove home, picked up Pat and the girls, and went to services at the Westmoreland Congregational Church. When he returned home, Nixon invited ten or so reporters into his living room for coffee and a talk. They bombarded him with questions about the political implications. He refused to speculate, telling them that his only concern was with the complete recovery of the President.[30]

The immediate struggle was over leadership while the President recuperated. As the man who would become President if Eisenhower died or was incapable of carrying on, and as the only man besides Eisenhower elected by the whole nation, Nixon was in a strong position. But Sherman Adams, the head of the White House staff, did not much like Nixon, and even if he had, he was not about to turn power over to the Vice-President and his people so long as Eisenhower had a breath left in him. In addition, Adams was furiously jealous of his right to control access to Eisenhower, and in this emergency he felt that he should be the one to serve as a liaison between the President and the world. On Monday, September 26, Reston reported that Adams and the so-called "Eisenhower Republicans" were anxious to keep control in Adams' hands and away from Nixon, because they were not going to hand over power to Nixon, and with it the 1956 nomination.[31] Richard Rovere observed in *The New Yorker* that Adams "regards himself as the President's appointed caretaker and is doing everything he can to cut Mr. Nixon down to size."[32]

For their part, Republican professionals did not want to see their party stolen from them by Sherman Adams. Senator Styles Bridges sent a telegram to Nixon, which advised, "You are the constitutional second-in-command and you ought to assume the leadership. Don't let the White House clique take command."[33] And C. D. Jackson wrote Nixon, full of praise for the Vice-President's "straightforward dignity and visible unselfishness," and urging him to lead.[34]

Eisenhower, meanwhile, gave Nixon needed support. On the second day, the President talked with Hagerty. Eisenhower realized that in 1920 Mrs. Woodrow Wilson had become so upset with Secretary of State Robert Lansing for calling Cabinet meetings without President Wilson's knowledge (Wilson was so ill he saw no one but his doctor and his wife) that she insisted that her husband fire Lansing. To make certain that there was no repetition, Eisenhower had Hagerty send a message to the effect that all regular meetings of the NSC and the Cabinet would be held, under the chairmanship of the Vice-President.[35]

On September 29, Nixon met with the NSC; the next day, with the Cabinet. He issued a press release which emphasized that "the subjects on the agenda for these meetings were of a normal routine nature." He also called in photographers to observe the harmony among Eisenhower's "family" and to record how the teamwork was so effective that the government was functioning "as usual." [36]

Nixon opened the Cabinet meeting with a prayer, then turned it over to Dulles, who gave an overlong review of foreign affairs (where there were no pressing crises going on). After other department heads gave their reports (they too had nothing of a pressing nature), Dulles turned to the subject of Adams and Eisenhower. Stating the obvious, he said that the "big question will be, Who has access to the President?" He warned about "hustlers" who would try to get in to see Eisenhower, and said "it is very important that we reinforce Sherm's position." He insisted that Adams go to Denver to be at Eisenhower's side, where he could handle all liaison activities. Nixon stressed that while the President was "temporarily absent," the Cabinet members should "see to it that government moves along without delay, that we don't pile up problems on the President's desk." But he reminded them that when new policy decisions had to be made, "only the President can make them." He also emphasized the "vital importance" of keeping before the public the image of an "Eisenhower Administration" that was fully in support of the President.

At the conclusion of the meeting, Dulles, in his own pompous but sincere way, praised Nixon. "I realize that you have been under a very heavy burden during these past few days," the Secretary of State said, "and I know I express the opinion of everybody here that you have conducted yourself superbly and I want you to know we are proud to be on this team and proud to be serving in this Cabinet under your leadership." [37]

Actually Nixon, like the President, the country, even the world, was extremely lucky in the timing of the heart attack (as well as in Eisenhower's steady recovery). The world scene was quiet in the fall of 1955. Had the attack come later, when the 1956 campaign was already under way, Eisenhower and the Republicans would have been in a far more difficult situation. Further, as Brownell noted at the Cabinet meeting, "happily there is nothing immediately pressing in domestic affairs." Congress was not in session, so there were no bills for the President to sign or veto. If there ever was a time when the United States in the Cold War could get by without a functioning President for a few weeks, it was the fall of 1955.

But Nixon was far more than lucky. He earned the high praise he received for his conduct during the crisis. He was level-headed, sensible, controlled. He made no attempt to seize power and, despite prodding by the Old Guard, did not undercut Adams; indeed, he agreed heartily with Dulles that until the President was in better health, no one except Adams should be allowed to see him.[38] Nixon refused to indulge in the smallest speculation about the future, and entered into no intrigues. Instead, he spoke on every possible occasion about what a great man Eisenhower was, and how marvelous the "team" Eisenhower had put together was, and how successfully everyone was carrying on the routine work of the government. At an October 2 press conference, he said that he and everyone in the Cabinet had pitched in for "the common objective of carrying on the President's program in his absence." Referring to the Wilson Cabinet of 1920, he noted that "in past history there have been internal disputes and jealousies." There were none in the Eisenhower Cabinet.[39]

That was stretching things a bit, but only a bit. The first two weeks after Eisenhower's attack, there was a pulling together of the top government officials to a quite remarkable degree, and an absence of infighting. In large part, this was due to Eisenhower's steady recovery—after the second day, it seemed likely that within a few weeks he would be whole again, in command, and then woe betide the man who struck out on his own on the assumption that Eisenhower would not return. But Nixon's contribution should not be slighted. Even if he had little or no choice about his general response (to do as little as possible), he carried out the details in an exemplary fashion.

It was not an easy time for him. As he noted later, "For me . . . this period continued to be one which drained my emotional as well as physical energies, for it was, above all, a period of indecision."[40] One of Eisenhower's speech writers, and a man who was no friend of Nixon's, Emmet John Hughes, gave Nixon his due. During the first two weeks after the attack, Hughes wrote, Nixon was "poised and restrained . . . a man close to great power *not* being presumptuously or prematurely assertive. This discreetly empty time was surely his finest official hour."[41]

Nixon played a major role in seeing to it that nothing happened in those two weeks. The Russians also helped. What made this presidential illness so much greater an emergency than any that had gone before, including Wilson's, was the possibility of a surprise nuclear attack. A remote possibility, to be sure, but still Nixon had to assume that the thought had at least crossed the minds of the men in the Kremlin. In that event, "Would the President be well enough to make a decision?" And if not, Nixon continued, "who had the authority to push the button?"[42] Fortunately, these dread questions did not have to be answered. During the crisis, the Russians stayed discreetly silent.

Eisenhower had frequently criticized FDR for not bringing Harry Truman into his inner circle, even when Roosevelt's health was obviously failing. Not until he actually became President did Truman learn about the atomic bomb. Eisenhower had said he was going to make certain that Nixon was prepared to take over if anything happened, but he had not been as good as his word. He had many secrets from Nixon, one of which had to be revealed following the heart attack. Foster Dulles told his younger brother that, in view of the President's condition, Nixon had to be fully briefed on current CIA methods and operations. Allen Dulles took Nixon on a tour of CIA headquarters, and told him about the U-2 spy plane program and about CIA plans to use the plane for deep photographic reconaissance flights into the Soviet Union.[43]

Nixon did not complain about previously being left in the dark about the U-2. In this, as in many other ways, he was a model of propriety.

ON OCTOBER 8, two weeks after the attack, Eisenhower called Nixon to Denver. He told the Vice-President how much he appreciated all that he and the Cabinet had done, and asked Nixon to arrange, through Adams, for the Cabinet members to fly to Denver, one at a time, in order of rank (Dulles first), for consultation. He also handed Nixon a letter. The Foreign Ministers were about to meet in Geneva to follow up on the summit meeting. Eisenhower wanted to make sure that everyone understood that Dulles spoke for him. Therefore, in his letter to Nixon, he told the Vice-President that Dulles had "my complete confidence." He also warned Nixon against making any anti-Communist attacks while the meetings were going on. Returning to Dulles, Eisenhower told Nixon, "He must be the one who both at the conference table and before the world speaks for me with authority for our country."[44]

Clearly Eisenhower feared a possible power grab by Nixon, or more precisely some blunder, even at this late date. The fear was unfounded—Nixon did exactly as he was told. Nor was Eisenhower unaware of what Nixon had done. Two days later, he told Hagerty that his illness "has turned public attention pretty sharply toward Nixon. He is a darn good young man." Good enough to be President? On that point, Eisenhower had his doubts. He said that "the country still considers him a bit immature," even though "his judgments are given accurately and thoughtfully." Adams said that Nixon "lacks the experience. He has not quite reached a maturity of intellect."

Eisenhower had not yet decided on retirement—he wanted to wait to see how complete a recovery he had. His character was such that his primary consideration was his country's future. He wanted the best for the United States. In his own mind, as in the minds of millions of his fellow citizens, he himself was undoubtedly the best. But what if he was incapable of serving?

The conversation turned to Nelson Rockefeller. Dulles was complaining that Rockefeller was trying to replace him as the President's principal foreign-policy adviser (which led Eisenhower to comment, "I am astonished at the sensitivity of big people to what they consider encroachment in their fields"), and indeed Dulles was in the process of squeezing Rocky out of government. Eisenhower admitted that Rocky was "a gadfly," and observed that the problem with Rockefeller was that "he was too used to hiring brains instead of using his own."[45]

In other words, except for Eisenhower himself, there was no ideal nominee for the Republicans in 1956. When Dulles came to Denver, on October 11, Eisenhower said that his "concern was that the country might fall into the hands of persons who had no real principles and who just believed in 'give-away' for the purpose of trying to buy votes and favor. . . . He expressed the hope that, if possible, a successor to him should be found within the inner circle of his Administration. . . . He said he thought that the successor should be reasonably young, preferably in his forties. But he was not sure that he could see around him a person who had the desired youth and vigor, and who at the same time had maturity of judgment."

In his memo of the conversation, Dulles continued, "I said I thought that maturity of judgment was almost too much to expect of any one in the forties."[46]

Throughout this period, Nixon and Dulles were in daily telephone contact. Their conversations, monitored and later summarized by Dulles' secretary, consisted for the most part of Dulles telling Nixon what he could not do. On October 17, for example, Nixon said that he planned to make a speech on Eisenhower's Open Skies proposal. His theme would be that "during the past week a dramatic development [the U-2 program] has occurred which should spur acceptance of the President's proposal." Dulles interrupted him to say that no such thing had happened. Nothing was as clear as Nixon thought it was, Dulles said, and told Nixon to drop the delicate subject of spy flights. Nixon wondered if it would be all right for him to say that it was "unfortunate" that the Soviets were "attempting to stimulate by proxy an arms race in the Middle East." Dulles said yes, he could say that.[47]

Nixon not only had to accept the fact that Dulles could tell him what to say and not say, but also Eisenhower's stinginess with his emotions. However much pain it caused him, Nixon nevertheless recorded the facts in his 1962 memoir, *Six Crises*. He counted up the number of times during his eight years serving under Eisenhower for which Eisenhower expressed personal thanks. It was an embarrassingly, even devastatingly, short list. Only three times in eight years had Eisenhower said thanks.[48]

"This was characteristic of Eisenhower," Nixon wrote. Actually, it was not—the President was usually quick to thank people who had helped him. A possible interpretation of his coldness toward Nixon is that he indeed felt coldly toward his Vice-President. But another possible interpretation is just the opposite—that he felt warmly toward Nixon, indeed regarded him almost as a son. How else explain his most common complaint about Nixon, that the Vice-President "just hasn't matured"? He continued to make that complaint past Nixon's fiftieth birthday. Eisenhower came out of one of those nineteenth-century American families in which the son could never, not ever, live up to his father's expectations. Eisenhower treated his own son that way.

But Nixon was not Eisenhower's son, which only compounded the President's ambiguity. Try as he might, he just could not get close to Nixon personally. In no way were they ever friends. Nevertheless, Eisenhower could not fail to be impressed by Nixon's abilities—his intelligence, his capacity for hard work, his loyalty, his political insights, his willingness to speak up inside the NCS and the Cabinet, but be quiet outside, and most of all his contribution to getting through the heart attack without a crisis. The President's feelings were further complicated by his sense of guilt. Eisenhower knew that although he was the one who complained most often about Nixon's partisanship, he was also the one who sent Nixon out after the Democrats.

Whatever his motives, the President failed to thank Nixon for his efforts. Nixon spent twenty pages of *Six Crises* describing in detail all that he had done for Eisenhower, then wrote: "There was no personal thank you." Then came Nixon's denial that Eisenhower's indifference hurt: "Nor was one needed or expected."[49] On October 18, Eisenhower did write a sort-of-thank-you note to Nixon, but as always, the President chose his words carefully: "I am most keenly aware of your devotion and dedication to the best interests of the people of the United States."[50]

A SIMPLE "THANK YOU" would have been nice, but much, much better would have been an endorsement. Nixon hoped for it, but

Eisenhower was not about to give it. On December 13, by which time he was recuperating at his Gettysburg farm, the President had a three-hour conversation with Hagerty about the 1956 nominee. Eisenhower threw out almost every name imaginable—Tom Dewey (that left Hagerty speechless), Earl Warren, Milton Eisenhower, and scores of others. There was something wrong with every one of them.

"What about Nixon?" the President asked Hagerty. "I told him that I thought Nixon was a very excellent vice-presidential candidate on the ticket of Eisenhower and Nixon, but that I did not believe that Dick on his own could get the nomination."[51] The following day, Eisenhower resumed the discussion, throwing out possible combinations (George Humphrey–Milton Eisenhower; Dewey and Warren). Hagerty pronounced them all acceptable, "but I still have my own opinion—Eisenhower-Nixon."[52] And from that moment on, Hagerty never wavered. Of all the people close to Eisenhower, he was by far Nixon's strongest supporter. The two men were not friends, but Hagerty greatly admired Nixon, and had a realistic sense of Nixon's importance within the Republican Party, and as a campaigner.

Nixon's enemy was Adams, who was urging the President to run again, but to dump Nixon as his running mate. Adams provided Eisenhower with the results of current polls, which indicated that Nixon could cost Eisenhower three or four points in a race with Stevenson, and others that showed if Eisenhower did not run, Warren was the strongest candidate. A third poll showed Stevenson winning in a Nixon-Stevenson race. Adams did not call to the President's attention later polls, taken after the heart attack, which showed a substantial Nixon improvement.[53]

ON DECEMBER 26, Eisenhower called Nixon into his office for a private chat. The President said he was going to Florida, where he would be holding political discussions with Milton Eisenhower and some of his close friends. Nixon's future would be a part of those discussions, obviously, but the main point Eisenhower wanted to settle was whether he should run for re-election. That he wanted to do so, Nixon took for granted (and quite rightly; as Nixon put it, "few real leaders can turn their backs on such a challenge . . . . Eisenhower was not a quitter—he liked to finish a job which he had started.").[54] But should he? He told Nixon that "he could not see how he could run in good conscience with that 'sword of Damocles [his weakened heart]' hanging over his head."

For that very reason, if Eisenhower ran, the vice-presidential nomination would be worth far more in 1956 than it had been in 1952. Everyone understood this basic fact; the Republicans, correctly, feared that the Democrats would make it a major campaign issue. Nixon's fate was tied to Eisenhower's actions. Clearly, it was in Nixon's best interests for Eisenhower to run again, of course with Nixon in the second slot, if only because in the event Eisenhower retired, Nixon could anticipate that getting the nomination for himself would be as difficult as Hagerty had predicted, if not impossible. So in the private talk the day after Christmas, Nixon did his best to persuade Eisenhower to run again, promising him that the Eisenhower team was now so competent that "the job need not be nearly so burdensome as it had been."

The President acknowledged the advice, then hit Nixon with a hammerblow. He said he did not think he could face another campaign, and that when he had agreed to run in 1952 he had declared he would serve only one term. He had hoped that in four years the Republicans "would be strong enough to elect another candidate." But, he continued, pacing the floor, that had not happened. It was "most disappointing," he said, that Nixon's popularity had not risen "as high as he had hoped it would." He stopped, looked at Nixon, and delivered the blow. He said "it might be better" for Nixon to take a Cabinet office.

As Nixon caught his breath, the President rushed on, trying to convince himself as much as Nixon that such a course really would be best for Nixon. The Vice-President could have any post he wanted in a second Eisenhower Administration, Eisenhower said, except Attorney General or Secretary of State (the two most important and prestigious positions). But if Nixon became Secretary of Defense, he would gain some badly needed administrative experience. He could keep his name before the public. He could mature.

Nixon could not believe the President was serious. The parallel with Henry Wallace was all too obvious (in 1944, FDR had dropped Wallace from the ticket, putting him in the Cabinet as Secretary of Commerce; as a consequence, in 1945 it was Harry Truman, not Wallace, who became President). Nixon knew, and felt that Eisenhower had to know, that if he moved to the Cabinet, the press and politicians would interpret such an action as a demotion, so serious a demotion as to probably ruin Nixon's chances to ever be President. On the other hand, Nixon simply had to do whatever the President told him to do; he certainly could not force his way onto the 1956 ticket against Eisenhower's wishes.

The problem was that Eisenhower would not say what his

wishes were. In the weeks that followed, Eisenhower brought up the Cabinet possibility on five or six different occasions. Nixon always gave the only answer he could: "If you believe your own candidacy and your Administration would be better served with me off the ticket, you tell me what you want me to do and I'll do it. I want to do what is best for you." And Eisenhower always answered obliquely. "No, I think we've got to do what's best for you," he would say, then repeat once again that he thought the Cabinet was best.

Whatever Nixon thought, Eisenhower was serious, so serious he sweetened the offer. He had Dulles bring up the subject with Nixon. Dulles said that he felt Nixon "ought to be President one day," and that the office was within his reach. But he thought Nixon "might better prepare" himself by serving in the Cabinet. Then came the sweetener: Dulles, who was in poor health, said that after his resignation, Nixon could become Secretary of State. That glittering possibility caused Nixon to do "some private agonizing," but his conclusion was the same: "I could not switch jobs without the disastrous appearance that 'Nixon had been dumped.' " [55]

OVER THE NEXT SIX MONTHS, Eisenhower continued to urge Nixon to take a Cabinet post, without ever saying directly that he wanted him off the ticket. For Nixon this was a period of "agonizing indecision," one that took "a heavy toll mentally, physically, and emotionally." [56] Bryce Harlow, of the White House staff, said later that Nixon "went through a period of absolutely indescribable anguish." [57] Seeking an explanation for Eisenhower's seemingly inexplicable cruelness, a friend speculated, "I think the President was naïve. . . ." [58]

Nixon knew better. As he put it in Six Crises, Eisenhower "was a far more complex and devious man than most people realized" [59] . . . Despite Nixon's great success in handling his biggest challenge to date—getting through the President's heart attack and recovery without a crisis—at the end of 1955 the Vice-President was even more insecure than he had been after the 1954 campaign. He was sure he was being "set up" by the White House staff, and that he had no friends at all in Eisenhower's inner circle (he was right about the first point, wrong on the second, because Hagerty remained steadfast for another Ike-Dick ticket). Given Nixon's vivid imagination, his ability to see in advance every possible outcome, just thinking about the future must have been near torture. He might end up like John Nance Garner, FDR's first Vice-President, long since forgotten, or at the other extreme, like Harry Truman. There were innumerable possibilities in between the extremes.

And not only did Nixon have to live with these uncertainties in his future, he had in addition to live with the fact that there was almost nothing he could do about it. Everything depended on Eisenhower.

CHAPTER EIGHTEEN

HOLDING ON TO
THE VICE-PRESIDENCY
January–August 1956

THROUGH THE FIRST MONTHS OF 1956, Nixon lived in an agony of suspension because the world's most famous decision maker refused to make a decision. At any moment following his announcement that he would seek a second term, Eisenhower could have decided to dump Nixon or to keep him, and that would have been that. There was precedent aplenty, either way. But Eisenhower left the decision to others, most specifically to Nixon himself—something Nixon, like the reporters and columnists and politicians, could not believe.

Adding to Nixon's discontent was the obvious fact that the prize was so great. Back in 1952, some of Nixon's friends could honestly advise him to reject the Vice-Presidency in favor of staying in the Senate, but in 1956 no real friend of Nixon's could doubt that the best possible place for him was right where he was, one (damaged) heartbeat away from the Presidency. Yet throughout the period of indecision, Eisenhower continually told him that he would be better off elsewhere, then urged him to make his own choice. It was impossible for Nixon to understand exactly what Eisenhower did want. There was good reason for Nixon's confusion—on the subject of Nixon's future, Eisenhower contradicted himself on an almost daily basis.

Milton Eisenhower once said that in 1956 "a more sensitive man" than Nixon would have taken Eisenhower's hint and left the ticket.[1] Perhaps. And perhaps Eisenhower felt that, as had been the case in the Army, a hint from the CO was sufficient. In addition, Eisenhower hated to fire someone who had served him loyally and to the best of his ability—that trait had been one of his weaknesses as a soldier, as he himself often confessed—and he believed that Nixon had done as good a job as possible as Vice-President. Another Eisenhower characteristic, as soldier and as President, was to keep his options open for as long as possible. He really did not know the answers to the chief questions: What would be best for Nixon? for the Republican party? for the country? The last was the most important because of the real possibility that the Republican vice-presidential nominee of 1956 could become President before 1960.

In the narrative that follows, Eisenhower will often be seen expressing doubts about Nixon. What should be noted throughout, however, is what Eisenhower kept in the forefront of his mind— the possibility that the vice-presidential nominee might well become President. Eisenhower was an old man whose love for his country, like his service to it, was unmatched. He wanted what was best for the United States. That was why he decided to run again —he was sure he was the best. That was also why he finally picked Nixon as his running mate—he thought Nixon had his shortcomings, but he would rather turn the country over to Nixon than any other possible candidate. In itself, that was the highest possible tribute he could pay Nixon.

Nevertheless, the lack of a clear-cut and enthusiastic endorsement from the President cut Nixon deeply. It forced him to circumscribe his behavior (he could not "run" for the Vice-Presidency, because only one vote counted, that of the President himself); it put him into a purgatory of "agonizing indecision";[2] it forced him to operate behind the scenes in his attempts to influence the President's decision. Nixon campaigned hard for the vice-presidential nomination in 1956, but unlike his previous campaigns, this one had to be carried out privately.

BACK IN MARCH 1955, Nixon had told a meeting of GOP workers, "The Republican party is not strong enough to elect a President. We have to have a presidential candidate strong enough to get the Republican party elected."[3] Recognizing this fundamental truth, throughout the period when Eisenhower was making up his mind about re-election, Nixon urged him, almost begged him, to agree to run again.

On February 7, 1956, a week or so before doctors planned to run some tests and then tell Eisenhower whether he was physically capable of running again or not, Eisenhower called Nixon into the Oval Office for some political talk. The President opened by saying he had seen Len Hall the night before, and Hall had assured him that he need make only three or four speeches in the campaign. "I think Hall is wearing rose-colored glasses," Eisenhower commented. The President was sure the RNC would be after him to do more, much more, just as it had in 1952 after giving similar promises about an easy campaign. What did Nixon think?

Nixon told the President to think back to 1944, when "Roosevelt did not make a campaign. He made certain nonpolitical swings here and there, but he pretty much won those campaigns on fireside chats, no television, and inspection tours." Eisenhower could follow the FDR precedent, but vastly improve upon it because of the magic of television. Nixon grew expansive as he described the possibilities on TV, "this new medium that has never been used up to its potentialities." Nixon thought that with a half-dozen television programs, well advertised in advance, "fireside chats if you will," Eisenhower "could campaign this time and win."

Nixon advised the President to "lay down the law right at the beginning" about not coming into any state to support any candidate. Otherwise, he would be deluged with last-minute pleas to come here or go there to save this or that seat. Five or six TV programs would be just about right. "I don't say that because I am trying to give an argument to make your mind up; I honestly believe that that is the best kind of a campaign for you to put on at this time."

Eisenhower said that sounded fine, but he had been through this before, and he was still dubious about the RNC's promises— he feared they would be forgotten the minute he accepted the nomination. And besides, why should he work for Republican candidates who, when they got to Congress, would not support him? Not on his school construction bill or his health insurance bill, or on foreign aid, or on the tariff, or on immigration quotas, or on a variety of other proposals. He had even told Hall he was thinking of running as a Democrat. If he ran as a Republican, he might bring the Congress with him, and he confessed he dreaded the prospect of Republican control. "Why should I help such people as [Knowland] to get chairmanships?" he asked Hall. "It becomes a terrible thing to do to our country almost." He preferred southern Democrats to western Republicans as committee chairmen. The Republican Party, he told Nixon, "is hopelessly split." He could not understand why there was no teamwork among Republicans: "I am at my wit's end to try to understand it."

Nixon rushed to defend the party, to assure the President that it was not "so badly split" after all. He insisted that the party had grown up in the last four years, citing the number of converts to foreign aid as an example. Indeed, Nixon declared, the President had "accomplished almost a miracle in getting the Party together." He had brought the Old Guard "a long ways," and the Party "is more united today than it has been for twenty-five years." Nixon said he felt "in eight years the Republican Party can be made over to a reasonably conservative progressive Party—and an internationalist Party." Eisenhower had his doubts.[4]

Eisenhower told different people different things about Nixon. When Hagerty pointed out to the President that "Nixon is stymied" and urged Eisenhower to go out of his way to praise the Vice-President, Eisenhower replied that he feared Nixon would become "atrophied" if he spent eight years in the office. He should get into the Cabinet—"he has a very fine understanding in the foreign field, in the security field, he is thoroughly grounded in the workings of this government." But—there was always a "but" when Eisenhower talked about Nixon—"people think of him as an immature boy." Still another "but"—"but it would be difficult to find a better Vice President."[5]

On February 9, Eisenhower discussed the matter with Dulles. The President said Nixon should become Secretary of Commerce. Dulles doubted that Nixon would take the post, and suggested instead that Nixon succeed him as Secretary of State. Eisenhower laughed and said Dulles was not going to get out of his job that easily, then added that "he doubted in any event that Nixon had the qualifications to be Secretary of State."[6]

That same day, the President talked to Nixon again. "As one of the coming men of the party," he said, "if we can count on me living five years, your place is not serving eight years as Vice President, but to take one of the big departments, HEW, Defense, Interior, any one of which is entirely possible. However, if you calculate that I won't last five years, of course that is different." Nixon was speechless—what could he possibly say? Finally, he muttered that whatever the President wanted him to do, he would do. The President replied, again, that it was Nixon's decision to make, a proposition that no one, least of all Nixon, could accept.[7]

Four days later, Eisenhower talked to Hall about the Vice-Presidency. He tried out all sorts of possibilities—Earl Warren, Governor Frank Lausche of Ohio (a Democrat and a Catholic, both of which appealed to Eisenhower), Tom Dewey, former governor Dan Thornton of Colorado, Bob Anderson ("my first choice"), "any number" of southerners (but the segregation issue made that impossible, he admitted), Brownell, Milton Eisenhower, and others. But then what to do about Nixon? The obvious answer, if Eisenhower really wanted to dump Nixon, was to accept Dulles' advice and promise Nixon the post of Secretary of State, the one Cabinet position Nixon could not have turned down. But Eisenhower wanted to keep Dulles on the job, and as noted, he did not think Nixon up to it (how then, one has to ask, could he have possibly felt Nixon was up to the Presidency itself?).

Hall said what was self-evident, that if the President wanted it done, "it was the easiest thing to get Nixon out of the picture willingly." All the President had to do was tell him so. Instead, Eisenhower told Hall to talk to Nixon. Hall should say, "What do you want to do? What is the best thing for you to do, for yourself, and that means the good of the party." But, Eisenhower warned, Hall should be "very, very gentle."[8]

Instead, Hall presented the President's case in a blunt manner, implying if not saying directly that Eisenhower wanted him off the ticket. Nixon's face darkened. "He's never liked me," Nixon said of Eisenhower. "He's always been against me."[9] Nevertheless, Nixon dug in. He was not about to give up his position on the basis of guarded hints from Hall or anyone else—if Eisenhower wanted him off the ticket, Eisenhower had to give the order, personally and directly.

MEANWHILE, NIXON WORKED TO SOLIDIFY his hold on the party regulars, and thus on his job. He gathered in intelligence, primarily from the conservative reporters he had cultivated over the years, and also from his friends among the Republican congressmen. As a result, he was much better informed than most of the columnists, who were doing all sorts of speculating on the manifold possibilities. Thus Nixon knew that Dewey was not interested, that Bob Anderson thought his own chances were nil, that Warren would never leave the Supreme Court, and so on. Not all his informants were conservatives; at the end of February, Kyle Palmer called with some "constructive criticism" from the chief Washington reporter of *The New York Times*, James Reston. Palmer said that Reston was "dispassionate, objective, friendly," and that Reston had told him, on a confidential basis, "that there was a definite move on for Eisenhower not to go overboard" in support of Nixon. In passing this word along to Nixon, Palmer told Rose Woods, "Reston thinks that—as I do—the decision may depend upon the way in which our man handles himself."[10]

Nixon knew that much already, and was in fact handling himself with great care. He held no press conferences, made no inflammatory remarks, despite provocation. On February 17, for example, Stevenson, who was the front-runner for the Democratic nomination, charged that Nixon was "uniquely qualified by his experience for a campaign on the lowest level." Two weeks earlier Truman had again upbraided Nixon for calling him a traitor in 1954; Truman said it made him "want to punch somebody." In both cases, Nixon refused to comment.[11] He continued to speak at party fund raisers, but his speeches were all positive, a defense of the Republican record rather than an attack on the opposition.[12] At his forty-third birthday party, sponsored by his old friends in the Chowder and Marching Club, and at other gatherings, he quietly got commitments from delegates to the convention. By April, he had some eight hundred pledges, a comfortable majority.[13]

Nixon also cooperated fully with Ralph de Toledano on the production of a campaign biography. De Toledano, whose admiration for Nixon was very great, gave Nixon the manuscript, for corrections and improvements. Nixon added material on the already-long section about the smears against him, and gave even more emphasis to refuting Truman's complaint that Nixon had called him a traitor. When the book came out, in the summer of 1956, Nixon was delighted with it, as well he might have been, since it was a piece of puffery. With his encouragement, friends did some fund raising and bought thousands of copies for free distribution.[14]

But neither a flattering biography nor eight hundred delegates in hand meant a thing without Eisenhower's blessing. All Nixon could get from the President, however, was the obviously impossible advice to make his own choice. Of course, Eisenhower had his own future to think about, and until he decided what he was going to do, Nixon knew he could not expect the President to make a decision about the number-two spot. So, like everyone else in the country, including Eisenhower himself, he waited for the doctors' report. Once that was issued, and Eisenhower had reacted to it, Nixon could expect a decision that would at least relieve the misery of not knowing, and hopefully one that would allow Nixon to hit the campaign trail as the designated running mate.

ON FEBRUARY 29, at a press conference, Eisenhower made his announcement. The doctors had told him he was capable of doing the job; he had therefore decided that he would be a candidate for re-election.

The first question was "Who will be your running mate?" Eisenhower refused to answer, "in spite of my tremendous admiration for Mr. Nixon." The President said "it is traditional . . . to wait and see who the Republican Convention nominates" before announcing the vice-presidential candidate. That was too coy by half for the veteran reporters. One asked, "Would you like to have

Nixon?" Eisenhower replied, "I will say nothing more about it. I have said that my admiration and my respect for Vice-President Nixon is unbounded. He has been for me a loyal and dedicated associate, and a successful one. I am very fond of him, but I am going to say no more about it."[15]

So, after all that suspense, Nixon once again had Eisenhower's admiration and respect, but not his endorsement. It threw him into a depression. A friend of Nixon's remarked that Eisenhower's refusal to come out flatly for Nixon was "one of the greatest hurts of his [Nixon's] whole career." The friend added, "I think the President . . . sincerely felt that Nixon had a better political future from a Cabinet post. But Nixon had a much shrewder judgment and reached the conclusion very early in the whole episode that either he had to go all the way and win . . . or get out and be finished."[16]

After Eisenhower's press conference, Nixon decided to get out. That night he told Ralph de Toledano that he had decided to quit. De Toledano told him in a March 2 letter that "it would be a calamity if you quit now. . . . Many, many people have pinned their hopes on you. If you back down, you will be letting them down." Nixon agreed to defer a decision.[17]

The next week, things got worse. At the President's March 7 press conference, Nixon was again the number-one topic. Marvin Arrowsmith of the AP asked the President about reports that his advisers wanted him to dump Nixon from the ticket and that "you yourself have suggested to Mr. Nixon that he consider . . . taking a Cabinet post. Can you tell us whether there is anything in those reports?"

Eisenhower replied that as to the "dump Nixon" reports, "I will promise you this much: if anyone ever has the effrontery to come in and urge me to dump somebody that I respect as I do Vice-President Nixon, there will be more commotion around my office than you have noticed yet." As to the second, "I have not presumed to tell the Vice-President what he should do with his own future. . . . The only thing I have asked him to do is to chart out his own course, and tell me what he would like to do." Did that mean "that if he elects to remain on the ticket you are content to have him as your running mate?" Evidently not: "I am not going to be pushed into corners here and say what I would do in a hypothetical question that involves about five ifs." The most Eisenhower would say was "I have no criticism of Vice-President Nixon to make, either as a man, an associate, or as my running mate on the ticket."[18]

Nixon's unhappiness was complete. Arrowsmith's question about the Cabinet post was based on a *Newsweek* story that Nixon believed had to have come as a result of a leak from the White House. It looked to Nixon as if Eisenhower really did want to get rid of him. If so, Nixon was ready to go—he had been offered the presidency of a large California firm, and a partnership in a New York law firm, either of which would pay far more than the Vice-Presidency. He felt he could not take seriously the Cabinet offer ("I would have been like Henry Wallace.") and he could not "chart out his own course," whatever Eisenhower said.

Nixon took out his legal pad and drafted an announcement that he would not be a candidate in 1956, and told two or three friends that he would call a press conference the next day, March 9, to announce his retirement. He mentioned it to Vic Johnston, of the Republican Senate Campaign Committee, who rushed to tell Hall and Persons. Those two dashed to the Capitol, cornered Nixon, and asked him not to do it. They said his friends would call him a "quitter." They insisted that his departure would split the Republican Party. He agreed to tear up the retirement announcement and defer his decision for a few weeks.[19]

EISENHOWER'S "CHART OUT HIS OWN COURSE" phrase became the subject of innumerable newspaper columns that week. Most commentators agreed with Nixon's private judgment, that "I can only assume that if he puts it this way, this must be his way of saying he'd prefer someone else." Disturbed by the speculation, Eisenhower made Nixon's future the subject at one of his famous stag dinners. Some of his rich friends present thought he should make a change, on the grounds that Nixon would cost him votes. But Charles Jones, president of Richfield Oil, strongly disagreed. An old friend of the President's, Jones looked at him and said, "Ike, what in the hell does a man have to do to get your support? Dick Nixon has done everything you asked him to do. He has taken on the hard jobs that many of your other associates have run away from. For you not to support him now would be the most ungrateful thing that I can possibly think of." [20]

Still another old friend of the President's, George Whitney, told him, "I think it is fairer to Nixon, and better for the future of the country, that he spend the next four years in some position where publicly he can demonstrate how good he is in his own right . . . where he can get administrative ability and other qualities of leadership that are so essential in the top job . . . rather than stay in a position which . . . has the outward appearance of a secondary job." [21]

Eisenhower said he heartily agreed. But it was difficult to get Nixon to see that point, he added, because of "the constantly bubbling political pot." The President explained to Whitney that "rarely does a man who is primarily a politician look ahead to the preparation of individuals for leadership in positions of great responsibility." Alas, the politician's attitude was "do the thing that seems most popular at the moment."[22] Eisenhower once again bemoaned Nixon's complete lack of administrative experience.

On March 13, the day of the first 1956 primary election, in New Hampshire, Eisenhower met with Fred Seaton, Sherman Adams' deputy. In one paragraph, the President presented all his ambiguities about Nixon. "I am happy to have him as an associate, and I am happy to have him in government," the President said. Then the "but"—"That still doesn't make him Vice President. He has serious problems. He has his own way to make. He has got to decide whether he puts his eggs into the basket of the improbable future four years from now. I don't know exactly what he wants to do. I am not going to say he is the only individual I would have for Vice President. There is nothing to be gained politically by ditching him. He is going to be a 'comer' four years from now. I want a bevy of young fellows to be available four years from now. Nixon can't always be the understudy to the star."[23]

THAT SAME MORNING, MARCH 13, Nixon followed Seaton into the Oval Office. Eisenhower opened the conversation by complaining about columnist Bill Lawrence's "vicious story that I am giving you the works." The trouble with the press, Eisenhower said, was that reporters "can't believe the unvarnished truth—they can't believe I actually said to you, 'Anything you want to do, I would go along with it.'"

Nixon could not believe it himself, but before he could say anything, Eisenhower went on. "I don't want to influence you," he said. "I want you to preserve your independent decision until the last minute. If you want to continue . . . "

Nixon interrupted. "As I told you before, it is a difficult decision." He assured the President that the press was not getting this "Ike dumps Nixon" line from him or his office, that "the stories they have written are off the top of their heads."

The President agreed that the press was impossible. Did Nixon see "our good friend Chris Herter [governor of Massachusetts]" on *Meet the Press* yesterday? Nixon had not. Eisenhower said the reporters had "tied Chris in knots—it was a pretty stupid performance. . . . When they asked his views on the world situation, he just didn't know." The President said the State Department should put out a short list of accomplishments since January 1953, so that

Republican speakers could cite it when asked. He complained that Reston was always critical. Nixon agreed: "I feel Scotty Reston is very conceited, but not a great thinker."*

Then Nixon brought the discussion back to the central point. "It's true," he said, "that in the last couple of weeks, there has developed some misconception in the minds of some people that there is some conflict between you and me." Eisenhower assured him that it was not so. Nixon explained his difficulty. "What position *can* I take?" When the press asked about his intentions, "I can't appear to be coy or clever." He doubted that a move to the Cabinet "could be sold," because the press would say "Nixon is afraid to run again, or the President is afraid to have him."

Eisenhower said his concern was "Where are you going to be four years from now?" If Nixon stayed in the Vice-Presidency, "you will always be thought of as the understudy to the star of the team, rather than a halfback in your own right." Nixon said he hoped he did not have to make a decision until convention time. Meanwhile, he urged Eisenhower to "look over all the available candidates, see who is the strongest. Whatever you decide, I will accept it gracefully." He did not want the President to keep him on merely out of a sense of obligation—"we must not have that type of thing." He continued, "These are important times; these are big decisions. I think you ought to decide it at the time—on the basis of what we think is the best thing to do." Then he reminded the President of the probable cost of making a switch; "friendly columnists will say, 'Nixon has done a good job; it's a terrible thing for the President to fire him.' "

Eisenhower knew that would be the case, but he mused anyway: "What I would really like to do is get a good Catholic, or an outstanding Jew—but I just don't know any good man to fit the description.' "

The two men engaged in further political gossip, until Nixon —for the only time in the many months devoted to this decision— brought up Pat's feelings. "I have one serious problem," he said, "—my family. Pat is not at all happy about the prospect of staying in Washington." Eisenhower replied, "I like Pat so much, I do not want her to be upset." Nixon confessed that "if she feels in August

* Reston had just reported in the *Times* that Adams and Brownell were "masterminding" a White House "holding operation" to head off the Vice-President, and added, "Mr. Nixon does not like this and he is not without power to influence the outcome. . . . President Eisenhower could, of course, come out flatly against Mr. Nixon, and that would end it. But he is not yet sure he wants to do that and besides he does not like direct action." [24]

as she does now, I will have difficulty in doing *anything*," i.e., even taking a Cabinet post.

Well, Eisenhower said, "I am going to tell the press, Look, I would be very happy to have Nixon on any ticket on which I happen to be. That is my final word. I will see you after the Convention." Nixon said "that ought to settle it," but added, "I am doubtful that a Cabinet post will work." Eisenhower remained unconvinced: "I want to make your position very strong four years from now," and for that purpose the Cabinet was best. He added that it was "silly for the press to try to promote a fight between us —it is like trying to promote a fight between me and my brother."

As Nixon got up to leave, he again assured Eisenhower that "I will do whatever job is best, even though I have this serious personal problem." [25]

In sum, after sixty-three minutes of intense discussion, Nixon's status was no clearer than it had been at the beginning.

WHAT DID EISENHOWER REALLY THINK OF NIXON? Did he want him on the team or not? The questions are far more complex than they seem. Eisenhower must have answered them hundreds of times, to reporters in press conferences and to intimate friends in private, but the problem is he answered them differently on different occasions, thereby making any judgment tentative and speculative.

Eisenhower may well have wished he could rid himself of Nixon, but he had spent his career facing reality. He was stuck with Nixon, in large part because of his own decision to put Nixon on the 1952 ticket. Nixon had used the Vice-Presidency, plus the reputation he had built in the Hiss case, to establish a wide, deep, and loyal base for himself in the Republican Party. As a consequence, the Eisenhower-Nixon relationship can be compared to the Eisenhower-Montgomery or the Eisenhower-de Gaulle relationship during the war. General Eisenhower never much liked Field Marshal B. L. Montgomery or General Charles de Gaulle, but he had to work with them, and on a basis that recognized that although Eisenhower was the Supreme Commander, Monty and de Gaulle each brought his own independent strength to the relationship. President Eisenhower's personal feelings for Nixon were ambiguous, but in the working relationship he had to deal with the fact that Nixon was the most popular politician among the party regulars, and for all that Eisenhower disliked the party regulars, he recognized that he could not get along without them, which meant he was stuck with Nixon.

IN NEW HAMPSHIRE, Senator Styles Bridges, always strong for Nixon, had made eighty-seven telephone calls the evening before the presidential primary ballot, urging his friends to write in Nixon's name. His friends in turn made calls, and the results were impressive. Eisenhower got 56,464 votes, but almost 23,000 voters had written in Nixon's name. As Bridges intended, it was an impressive demonstration of Nixon's vote-getting power, at least among Republicans.[26]

Despite Nixon's triumph, Eisenhower withheld his endorsement. At his next press conference, when asked to comment on the write-in vote, the President said "apparently there are lots of people in New Hampshire that agree with what I have told you about Dick Nixon. . . . I am very happy that Dick Nixon is my friend. I am very happy to have him as an associate in government. I would be happy to be on any political ticket in which I was a candidate with him. Now, if those words aren't plain, then it is merely because people can't understand the plain unvarnished truth"[27]

NIXON'S WOES WERE NOT YET OVER, despite New Hampshire. To this point, the Democrats had sat back, enjoying the spectacle of Republican infighting over their favorite man to hate, Richard Nixon. But in April they began easing themselves into the battle. They came along from the flank—with charges against Murray Chotiner, not Nixon himself.

Like Nixon, Chotiner had lots of enemies. His hard-hitting, aggressive campaigns were always on the border of unethical practices. He had left many victims in the wake. Democrats on a Senate subcommittee, investigating corruption and influence peddling in military procurement, began looking into some of Chotiner's lawyer-client relations. The initial results of the probe were promising; it appeared they could charge him with influence peddling, through Nixon.

There was another attempt to attack Nixon through Chotiner that year, by the anti-Semitic press, which damned Nixon for having "that Jew Chotiner" as his campaign manager. Murray deftly turned that charge into an immediate asset—he managed to get editorials in the Jewish press all over the country, decrying racism and pointing with pride to Nixon's record of fighting discrimination on the Government Contracts Committee.[28]

The segregationists didn't much like Nixon either. On March 19, Hagerty reported to the President on the results of a scouting trip he had taken in the South. Things did not look good, Hagerty said, partly because "not one person was for Nixon for Vice President for a second term." When Hagerty, who was for Nixon, pressed southerners on the cause of their attitude, they mumbled something like "too immature." But Hagerty's impression was that "Nixon is in some way connected in Southerners' minds with the

Negro difficulty." * He admitted that he was "startled by the intensity of the feeling in the South over the Negro question, currently at white heat." [29]

Nixon himself was heading south. Exhausted by the enforced inaction, he decided to spend two weeks at Bebe Rebozo's place in Key Biscayne and just relax.

HE RETURNED, FOURTEEN DAYS LATER, to find that he was still hung up. At an April 9 meeting with Eisenhower, the President continued to urge him to take HEW or Commerce. But, Eisenhower added, "I still insist you must make your decision as to what you want to do. If the answer is yes, I will be happy to have you on the ticket." Then the "but"—the President said that he kept getting reports "that in some areas there were still great oppositions to you." Followed by another "but"—"if we start now we can do a job on this opposition."

After Nixon left, still wondering what his boss really wanted, Hall entered the Oval Office. "I personally like and admire Dick, and he could not have done better," the President said. "I think he is making a mistake by wanting the job. I would think he would do better by taking a Cabinet post." [30]

IN HIS MEMOIRS, Eisenhower wrote that not until seven years later when he read Nixon's own account of this period, in *Six Crises*, did he realize that Nixon "regarded that period as one of agonizing uncertainty." What everyone else saw clearly and immediately, Eisenhower missed altogether, or so at least he claimed.[31]

Eisenhower really did believe Nixon would be better off with a Cabinet post. This did not mean he was opposed to Nixon as his successor, quite the contrary. As a man whose career had been marked by wide and deep experience in administration on an increasingly larger scale, until culmination in Overlord and the Presidency, Eisenhower naturally believed experience was essential to performance. In addition, as a man who had been a major for sixteen years, Eisenhower knew that patience was indeed a virtue.

Eisenhower felt strongly that Nixon needed administrative experience. The last time Nixon had administered anything larger than his office or campaign staff was in 1944 in the Pacific, as a

* No matter how ineffective, Nixon's work on the Government Contracts Committee, designed to insure minority representation in the labor force on government construction projects through persuasion and publicity, had given him a reputation as an integrationist.

junior officer commanding a small work detail. He also wished that Nixon would mature, and not be in such a hurry to do so. Eisenhower was clearly correct on both counts. To indulge in a look ahead, one of the characteristics of the Nixon Presidency, 1969–1974, was poor administration, marked by duplication of effort, vague lines of authority, and an inner staff more concerned with politics than government. And in the 1960 campaign, he did and said things that he later wished he had not, things the older and wiser Nixon of 1968 avoided.

The trouble with Eisenhower's analysis of what was best for Nixon and the country was the President's damaged heart. It was a subject the President tried not to think about. Nixon, however, could not get it out of his mind. If Nixon volunteered for the Cabinet, his replacement as Vice-President might well be in the White House before the 1960 Republican Convention. In that event, from the perspective of the always-in-a-hurry Nixon, his administrative experience would be worthless.

So Nixon dug in.

ON APRIL 25, two things happened. The Senate subcommittee issued a subpoena on Chotiner. Democrats explained to the press that they believed Chotiner had used his connections with Nixon on behalf of his clients. The next day, Chotiner failed to appear as ordered, risking a contempt citation.[32]

Also on the twenty-fifth, the President held a press conference. He used it to communicate with Nixon, more effectively than they could ever do face-to-face. Asked if Nixon had yet chartered his own course and reported back, Eisenhower replied, "Well, he hasn't reported back in the terms in which I used the expression . . . no."

When Nixon heard the remark, he wrote in his memoirs, "I knew the time had come to act." He had convinced himself that if he got off the ticket he would hurt Eisenhower more than help him. He reasoned that the party regulars would be so incensed at his dumping that they would stay out of the campaign. He knew Eisenhower felt that Republican dissatisfaction would not hurt him, because the right wing had no place else to go, but Nixon convinced himself that the President "needed more than just their votes." He needed their money, their enthusiasm, their organization. On that basis, Nixon decided he had to stay (when or how he told Pat he never revealed), and he asked for an appointment with the President the next morning, April 26.[33]

The meeting went well, despite the continued use of circumlocution in the Eisenhower-Nixon conversations. Nixon opened by saying that "freedom of action" should be maintained as late as possible. There should be an "open field" of candidates, "though this would perhaps create a bit of a hassle." He explained that "Party people" were expressing concern about "having too much argument between now and Convention time." They wanted "as much unity as possible."

Eisenhower said nothing. Nixon plunged on. "Obviously any man would welcome the opportunity to be a Vice-Presidential candidate on this ticket," Nixon said. Eisenhower nodded. Well, Nixon went on, "I have weighed all the considerations," and concluded it would be best all around if he stayed on the ticket.

There it was. He had charted his own course, and reported to the President. Eisenhower, who had created the situation, now had to live with it. He suggested that Nixon go outside and announce his decision to the White House press corps. Nixon demurred—would not a statement from the President himself be better? Eisenhower thought not. He called Hagerty into the office and told him to take Nixon out to the reporters to make the announcement. "And you can tell them that I'm delighted by the news."

But before Nixon left, he told the President that "there's another matter" that he felt he ought to know about. "It's the Murray Chotiner case." Nixon explained that Murray had been accused of representing two hundred gamblers and bookmakers in Los Angeles alone, and that he had collected high fees for representing clothing manufacturers who sold uniforms to the Army, and that he had got those fees because of his connection with Nixon. "The point is," Nixon summed up for Eisenhower, "the Democrats are going after him because he is involved with people who are bad people."

Nixon assured the President that neither he nor any member of his staff was involved, that Chotiner was merely an employee of his, that he "is a good man, and has been completely honest through the years," but that if "anything does turn up, the Administration has no relationship with him at all."[34]

Thus reassured, Eisenhower told Nixon to go make his announcement to the press. The conference went well. Nixon said he had told the President, "I would be honored to accept the nomination," and Hagerty added that Eisenhower had instructed him to say "that he was delighted to hear of the Vice President's decision." Nixon then explained that the basis of his decision had been the President's best interests. He was asked who sought today's meeting. "I would say that it was a mutual thing," stretching the truth, but getting closer to the facts when he added that Eisenhower had given him a general invitation to "talk about this matter

...when I had something to report to him. Consequently, the meeting was arranged in accordance with his wishes." [35]

Time magazine called it "the most predictable announcement of the year." Columnists sneered at Nixon's implication that he was putting the interests of Eisenhower ahead of his own interests, and derided the notion that he had seriously considered stepping aside. [36]

Those judgments were probably true enough, but they failed to see a deeper truth, which was that the outcome was always very much in doubt (and indeed continued to be). In meeting this crisis, Nixon had been forced to call on talents he did not ordinarily use —patience, quiet persuasion, logical arguments—as well as some that he did habitually use—perseverance, cold calculation of the forces at work, behind-the-scenes manipulation, all based on his assurance of his solid base with the party regulars. To use a poker metaphor, he had played a game of five-stud with the President, for the highest of all possible stakes, and had won.

NIXON'S ANNOUNCEMENT, supported by Eisenhower's apparent endorsement, appeared to settle the question of the 1956 Republican ticket. In May, Nixon had a string of successes. Almost thirty-three thousand voters wrote in his name on their ballots in the Oregon primary. The Chotiner case more or less collapsed when Chotiner refused to testify (on the grounds that his relations with his clients were privileged). Critics pointed out that Chotiner was using what amounted to a Fifth Amendment defense, and that Nixon used a different standard in judging Chotiner (innocent, because he had only taken a fee as a lawyer and was not a partner in the enterprise) than he did in judging Gabrielson (even the appearance of wrongdoing was enough to disqualify him as chairman of the RNC). In any case, the Democrats brought no indictment against Chotiner. [37] As Ralph de Toledano told Rose Woods, "They sprang it too soon," and therefore, "I don't think it will hurt the Boss at all." [38]

Nixon also began to attract bright young men, eager to serve in his campaign. On May 22, H. R. Haldeman, of the J. Walter Thompson advertising firm, wrote Nixon "to offer my assistance in the forthcoming campaign." He assured Nixon he had "a firm belief in you and your work," and volunteered his full-time services from the convention through the elections. There would be no charge "since my company would give me a leave of absence with salary." [39]

Loie Gaunt, Nixon's office manager at the time, had known Haldeman at UCLA and had kept up some contact since. She told Nixon she felt his offer "a genuine and sincere one," and that "he would be a good worker." Nixon asked her to have Ray Arbuthnot get together with Haldeman and make an evaluation. He did, was impressed, and recommended Haldeman.[40] Haldeman joined the campaign staff, working full time through to the election as an advance man.

The only bad news for Nixon that May came from Sidney Weinberg, senior partner of the New York investment firm of Goldman Sachs. Weinberg was a strong Dewey man, and Dewey was strong for Nixon. So Weinberg had attempted to get Citizens for Eisenhower (which had bankrolled and managed Eisenhower's 1952 campaign) to change its name to Citizens for Eisenhower and Nixon. But Lucius Clay, Paul Hoffman, and some others had refused.[41] Not that they opposed Nixon—most of them did not—but, as Clay once put it to Eisenhower, because "I don't care one damn about the Republican Party. I care about you." Nixon's supporters, nevertheless, saw the refusal as an indication that the ticket was not yet as settled as it appeared to be.

IF NOT ALREADY UNSETTLED, it became so on June 8, because Eisenhower had a two-hour early-morning operation for ileitis. It was simple, straightforward, and recovery was rapid, but nevertheless it frightened the wits out of people. The immediate concern was subjecting a recent heart-attack victim to such a long operation; the long-range question was how much of a pounding Eisenhower's sixty-five-year-old body could take. The operation led to speculation that Eisenhower would withdraw from the contest, or even die; in the first instance, Nixon would be the front-runner for the nomination, while in the second he would be the incumbent. No one could do anything about the second possibility, but the first could be challenged. Or, as Nixon put it in his memoirs, Eisenhower's illness "resurrected the desire to 'dump Nixon.' "[42]

Rumors flew. According to the "What's Happening in Washington" column of the *Lawyer's Weekly Report*, a long list of prominent Republicans was suddenly working against Nixon, including Dewey, Brownell, Humphrey, Adams, Hagerty, and Clay. Next Drew Pearson reported that John J. McCloy of the Chase Manhattan Bank, Treasury Secretary Humphrey, and others were working to dump Nixon.

Every man named in these stories hastened to write Nixon, assuring him that the reports were not true. These reassurances were satisfying to Nixon, even if he knew—as they all knew that he knew—that he might become President at any moment, thus casting some suspicion on their motives, if not on the facts of their denials.[43]

The twenty-one Republican governors were willing to take a risk. At the Governors' Conference in June, they all signed a pledge of support for Eisenhower, but Nixon's name was omitted because he was "controversial," and because one of the governors had insisted, "For God's sake, keep Nixon's name off it."[44]

ON JUNE 30, Nixon got away from the uproar by making a thirteen-day trip to the Far East. It had long since been planned—the occasion was the tenth anniversary of Philippine independence and the upcoming second anniversary of the inauguration of South Vietnam's President Diem.

Back in 1954, the Geneva Conference had divided Vietnam into a Communist North under Ho Chi Minh and a southern half headed by the Emperor Bao Dai. The United States had not been a signatory to the Geneva Accords, but had promised not to oppose the settlement by force. The Accords called for nationwide elections within two years, but instead Ngo Dinh Diem, the Prime Minister in the southern half, organized a plebiscite in the South only that deposed Bao Dai and created the Republic of Vietnam, or South Vietnam. Diem then became president, and refused to hold the nationwide elections, instead proclaiming South Vietnamese sovereignty, and linking South Vietnam to the West. The Eisenhower Administration had given strong moral and some financial support to Diem. Also back in 1954, the United States had taken the lead in forming the Southeast Asia Treaty Organization (SEATO) and pledging SEATO to the defense of South Vietnam. Thus Nixon's trip to Saigon, Diem's capital, was in the nature of a continued American stamp of approval of Diem.

Nixon had been a strong supporter of Diem, as he was of all Asians fighting the Communists. His interest in Asia remained high. It was a subject he had returned to time and again in Cabinet meetings. For example, in April, when Sukarno of Indonesia was planning to come to the States for a visit, Nixon had urged the Cabinet members to make every effort to attend every possible social function, because "Asians attach much importance to having persons of importance in attendance." He persuaded Eisenhower to have the Washington schoolchildren let out for a Sukarno parade.[45] In preparation for his July trip, Nixon went through another intense briefing from the State Department. He was making himself into an expert on Asia.

The trip had the benefit of generating favorable publicity. Dick and Pat got their pictures on the front page of *The New York Times*, meeting President and Mrs. Ramón Magsaysay, and stories about the trip stayed on the front pages for the duration. He got some headlines too. In Manila he cautioned neutral nations against thinking they could outmaneuver the Communists. Those that did "are taking a fearful risk." He said that the United States respected neutrality, but had "no sympathy" with those nations that drew no moral distinction between the Communist and free worlds.[46] (The resulting protests from India and other neutrals forced Dulles, a week later, to say there were "very few, if any," nations of the "immoral kind.")[47] In Karachi, Pakistan, Nixon warned the nations of Asia against accepting any form of economic or military assistance from the Soviet Union, because the price of such aid was "a rope around the neck."[48] In Saigon, Nixon assured the South Vietnamese that they had the support of the American people in their fight "to make their young republic strong and safe from communist encroachment."[49]

HAROLD STASSEN HAS BECOME THE GREAT COMIC FIGURE of American politics, the perennial presidential candidate, the ultimate leader of lost causes. The Washington *Evening Star* made the classic comment about him: "There's one thing about Harold E. Stassen—he likes to go down with his ship, and he doesn't care how many times it's sunk."[50]

But in the summer of 1956, Harold wasn't so funny, at least not to Nixon. He was a presidential adviser, called by the press the "Secretary of Peace" and credited (wrongly) with the Open Skies proposal Eisenhower made to the Russians in 1955. He was thought to be a superior political manipulator, again credited (again wrongly) with blocking Taft in 1952 and seeing to it that Eisenhower got the nomination.

In early May 1956, Stassen returned to the States from a long and fruitless disarmament conference in London. Although by then Eisenhower had given his blessing to Nixon's announcement that he would be happy to serve once again as Vice-President, Stassen immediately began a "stop Nixon" campaign. Almost no one in the party was willing to join him in a challenge to the man who might succeed to the Presidency any day, but he pushed ahead nevertheless, spurred on by Eisenhower's ileitis operation. He took a poll, financed, according to columnist David Lawrence, by a "coterie in New York City . . . with the avowed object of developing statistical data to force Mr. Nixon out of the race."[51]

Delighted with the results of the poll, on July 20 Stassen marched into the Oval Office, where he told the President that Nixon's name on the ticket would cost the Republicans 4 to 6 percent of the electorate. Such losses, Stassen asserted, would in turn cost the Republicans control of Congress.

Eisenhower had earlier fretted over polls that roughly paralleled Stassen's, but according to his memoirs he found Stassen's attitude to be "astonishing." That could hardly have been true, since the fear that Nixon would cost votes had been a regular topic of his political conversations all spring. Eisenhower wrote that he told Stassen, "You are an American citizen, Harold, and free to follow your own judgment in such matters." [52]

The President's next visitor that morning was Art Larson, director of the United States Information Agency (USIA). Eisenhower brought up the subject of Stassen's poll, and commented that if Nixon was going to cost him 6 percent, "that's serious." [53] Then he prepared to leave for a meeting of the Presidents of the Americas in Panama, a trip he was undertaking in order to show that his recovery from the operation was complete.

The person who was genuinely astonished by Stassen's last-minute stop-Nixon move was Nixon. Even more astonishing to the Vice-President was the President's failure to order Stassen to back off. What made Nixon especially fearful was the obvious unsuitability of Stassen's proposed replacement for Nixon, Massachusetts Governor Christian Herter. Herter's name had not appeared on any of the President's lists of acceptable successors, nor in newspaper speculation. Herter was sixty-one years old, suffered badly from arthritis, came from Harvard, and was not a lively campaigner. All in all, he was about the worst possible choice Stassen could have made, but to Nixon that only made it more remarkable that Eisenhower had not put an immediate stop to Stassen's ploy.

On July 23, while Eisenhower was still in Panama, Stassen sent a letter to Nixon marked "Personal and Confidential," delivered by messenger to Rose Woods. Her boss was having lunch with Hall and Persons. She brought in Stassen's letter. Nixon scanned it, laughed nervously, and said, "Let me read this to you." [54]

Stassen had written that he was going to support Herter for Vice-President, and asked Nixon to join him—for the good of the Republican Party. That was hitting Nixon where it counted. Stassen asserted that Nixon on the ticket would cost 6 percent of the vote, which would make a "decisive difference in a number of Senatorial and House seats" and cost the Republicans control of Congress. He gave Nixon some of the details from his poll, then twisted the knife with the information that "the negative side is relatively highest among those best informed and among the younger voters," which—Stassen explained—meant that the 6 percent figure was likely to grow as the campaign progressed and the voters became better informed. [55]

That was uncomfortably close to the truth, as those three

professional politicians—Nixon, Hall, and Persons—immediately recognized. They agreed that "this could be serious."[56] It was true that Nixon's position with the party assured him the nomination (unless Eisenhower himself said no at the last minute), but his identification with the party cost the party votes. To Republicans, he looked like a moderate, but to independents and Democrats, he seemed an extreme partisan. And the Democrats hated him more than the Republicans ever loved him. Further, the Republican Party was a distinct minority, which meant that without independent and Democratic votes there would not be another Republican Administration. Eisenhower had those votes, and was going to win no matter who was on the ticket. Of course he wanted as big a personal victory as possible, and even more, he wanted to bring a Republican Congress in with him.

Or so he said. On a number of occasions he told Persons and others that he did not much care who won the congressional elections. He indicated frequently that he preferred southern Democrats as committee chairmen to mossback Republicans. If the President did not care what happened to the Republicans in Congress, why should Nixon? Besides, Nixon had long since convinced himself that what he brought to the ticket—Republican enthusiasm, money, organization—more than paid for what he cost with independents and Democrats. Hall and Persons agreed.

After lunch, Hall returned to the RNC, where he met with his principal assistants, Robert Humphrey and Richard Guylay. Nixon partisans all, they agreed that "the thing had to be closed off fast." Hall later remarked, "I didn't think Stassen would get anywhere, but he could create doubt in people's minds, and you'd have a lot of candidates." Dan Thornton of Colorado, for example, or Governor Theodore McKeldin of Maryland, or Governor Goodwin Knight of California (the one prominent Republican to support Stassen), plus others who, in Nixon's words, were "eagerly waiting in the wings."[57]

That afternoon, Stassen called a press conference, where he announced his support for Herter. He claimed that Eisenhower had agreed to an open convention (which was stretching Eisenhower's response to his dump-Nixon campaign considerably). Stassen also said he was "confident President Eisenhower will be pleased to have Chris Herter on the ticket."[58] Nixon said he would "be happy to abide by any decision the President and the delegates make with regard to the Vice Presidential nominee." He praised Herter and promised "my full support" if Herter got the nomination.[59]

Stassen's announcement, and Nixon's reply, got a big play in the press. Reporters speculated that because Stassen was on the White House staff, Eisenhower himself must be behind this last-minute stop-Nixon drive. Eisenhower's own comment, when he was asked in Panama about the Stassen press conference, disputed that interpretation, but still it was hardly the ringing defense of Nixon that Nixon wanted so badly to hear. Instead of repudiating Stassen on the spot, Eisenhower—who was peeved that Stassen had stolen the headlines from his Panama trip—told Hagerty to issue a statement stressing Stassen's right as an American to campaign for whomever he wished, but that he could not conduct independent political activity and remain a member of the "official family." Therefore, Eisenhower was going to put him on a leave-without-pay status until after the convention.[60]

Nixon, not knowing what to think, went off to Maryland's Eastern Shore for two days of brooding and walking along the beach. Friends reported that he was "eating his heart out" with apprehension.[61] When well-wishers called to heap scorn on Stassen, Nixon replied, "Don't underestimate Harold. He's smart and resourceful."[62]

Eisenhower returned to Washington on July 26, where he learned that the Republican Party had rallied behind Nixon. Among numerous denunciations of Stassen that Eisenhower received from prominent Republicans, the one that stood out was an endorsement of Nixon by 180 of the 203 House Republicans. That was a statement of party preference so direct and clear that Eisenhower could not ignore it. Eisenhower decided to put an end to the Stassen business then and there, although characteristically he acted behind the scenes, meanwhile keeping Nixon in some suspense.

Eisenhower had Sherman Adams call Herter and tell him that there was a job waiting for him in the State Department (although Adams never said so directly, it was Under Secretary of State, with an implied promise of the top job after Dulles' retirement, expected within a year or two). If Herter wanted to be a candidate for the vice-presidential nomination, Adams told him, that was his choice. However, if he did enter the race, the State Department position "would not be possible." Herter, naturally enough, disavowed any interest in the Vice-Presidency and said he would be happy to place Nixon's name in nomination at the San Francisco convention, less than a month away.[63]

AND THAT SHOULD HAVE BEEN THAT, and would have been had it not been for Eisenhower's ambiguity about Nixon. The next day, July 27, Eisenhower had a telephone conversation with his close friend

Cliff Roberts. Nixon's name came up. Eisenhower said, "I get peeved about too much talk in calling the other party 'soft on Communism.'" Roberts asked what Eisenhower thought of Stassen's move. "There's one little thing, it did stir up some interest. Our program has been so cut and dried, a little interest won't hurt." [64]

Eisenhower still held back from a public endorsement of Nixon. At an August 1 press conference, James Reston asked if it was fair to conclude that Nixon was Eisenhower's preference. Eisenhower said that Reston could conclude whatever he pleased, "but I have said that I would not express a preference. I have said he is perfectly acceptable to me, as he was in 1952 [when] I also put down a few others that were equally acceptable to me." He added that the Republicans were going to have an open convention and nominate the best men for the ticket. Merriman Smith reminded him that he had said some weeks earlier that if anyone came into his office to propose a "dump Nixon" move, he would create quite a commotion in his office. "Have you created such a commotion in the wake of Mr. Stassen's recommendation?" "No," the President replied, because "no one ever proposed to me that I dump Mr. Nixon. No one, I think, would have that effrontery." [65]

That was such an outright denial of the plain truth that it left everyone puzzled. Since Eisenhower had already eliminated the Herter threat, and since there was no other possible candidate at this late date, he knew that the ticket was going to be Ike and Dick. Why, then, did he not issue a ringing endorsement rather than that awful "he is as acceptable as anyone else" business he told Reston? Did he enjoy watching Nixon dangle? Or, more likely, was he only trying to keep some suspense about the convention in order to attract more interest and more viewers?

Nixon knew where at least one Eisenhower stood. When Drew Pearson wrote in his column that Milton Eisenhower was the man who instigated the Stassen move, Milton hastened to write Nixon, telling him it was not only not so, but that "I happen to think Harold Stassen's action was unforgivable, harmful and childish." [66] In thanking him, Nixon noted that he had received a heavy volume of mail support, "but none could mean more than the one I received from you." [67]

One reason Stassen went down with so many ships was that he could never tell when they were sinking under him, indeed couldn't even tell when the ship had hit the bottom. So in this case, he persisted in his efforts. On August 16, only days before the convention, he wrote Nixon again, asking him to step aside in the interests of the President and of the party. "It is my deep conviction that if you decide to take this step it would be best not only for our country but, in the long run, for your future career." [68]

Nixon was in North Carolina at the time, as a houseguest of evangelist Billy Graham, with whom he was developing a friendship. They played some golf together, and talked about religious and moral matters. The chief topic was desegregation. Nixon made a speech on the subject in Nashville, at Graham's request, at a major religious conference. Nixon took Graham's line, that integration was morally right but progress toward the goal would have to be slow. Mostly Nixon just relaxed—and ignored Stassen's letter.[69]

On August 19, the Nixon family flew to California. First stop was Whittier, where Julie and Tricia stayed with their grandparents while Dick and Pat went on to San Francisco. Frank and Hannah were going to bring the girls up in a couple of days.

The Democrats, meeting a week earlier, had nominated Stevenson again; Stevenson had thrown open the vice-presidential nomination to the Convention, an unprecedented action. After a struggle, Senator Estes Kefauver of Tennessee won the prize from Senator John Kennedy. Stevenson's action gave Stassen one last gasp, and he fired off his final salvo, a letter to every Republican delegate urging a vote for Herter. Eisenhower finally acted directly and personally—he called Stassen into his hotel suite, told Stassen that he had to stop, and capped his humiliation by ordering Stassen to give one of the seconding speeches for Nixon. Then the President told the press that Stassen had become convinced that "the majority of the delegates want Mr. Nixon," so he was ending his efforts.[70]

With that, Nixon was, at last, the nominee. He and Pat spent a delightful day in San Francisco; they rode a cable car, ate in a Chinese restaurant, and stayed at the Mark Hopkins Hotel on Nob Hill. Pat held a news conference, which she opened by saying, "I don't discuss politics," but she would answer questions about the girls and the Nixon home life. These centered on how much help she had around the house (almost none) to who bought the girls' clothes (she did). In the afternoon, she shook a thousand hands at a reception, and the next morning attended breakfasts with two state delegations. Finally cornered and asked directly how she felt about Stassen and the nomination, she replied that she would not be disappointed whichever way the balloting went.[71]

August 22 was the day for the balloting. Early that morning, Nixon got a call from Whittier. His father had suffered a ruptured abdominal artery and was not expected to live. Nixon canceled all his appointments, went with Pat to the airport, and flew down to Los Angeles. When they arrived at the Whittier hospital, Frank Nixon was in an oxygen tent, in great pain, but still able to talk. He told his son to return to San Francisco. "You get back there, Dick, and don't let that Stassen pull any more last-minute funny business on you."[72] Instead, Nixon stayed in Whittier. He watched on television as Herter put his name into nomination, and Stassen made his seconding speech. Then Nixon was renominated by a vote of 1,323 to 1.

The news of his son's triumph led to a rally by Frank, who was taken off the critical list. Nixon flew back to San Francisco to give his acceptance speech (which was primarily a eulogy of Eisenhower, "the man of the Century"). Then he returned to Whittier to be with his family. Frank had asked to be moved to his home, so that he could die there. He was unable to communicate, but stable, so the Nixons flew east. They spent a couple of days on the Jersey coast, where Dick played golf with Billy Graham. The Whittier doctors called—the end was near. On August 31, Nixon flew back to California. On September 4, Frank Nixon died. The funeral service was held on September 7, at the East Whittier Friends Meeting House. Nixon, Pat, Hannah, Don, and Ed attended together. They sat behind a curtain. Nixon allowed no photographs.[73]

HIS FATHER'S ILLNESS AND DEATH took much of the immediate pleasure and pride out of the nomination. It was not a time for celebration. Still, Nixon had much to be proud of and pleased by. He had secured his place as first in the line of succession. In addition, he had further strengthened his ties with the party regulars. He had shown that he had a power base of his own, not so great nor widespread as Eisenhower's, to be sure, but still greater than anyone else's.

He had survived. Now he could leave behind him the infighting with his fellow Republicans, and do what he liked to do most, take off after the Democrats.

CHAPTER NINETEEN

THE FIFTH CAMPAIGN
September–December 1956

WITHIN DAYS OF THE START OF THE 1952 CAMPAIGN, the fund controversy had made Nixon himself into a central issue. In 1956, because
of Eisenhower's health and because the Democrats were reluctant
to criticize the President directly, Nixon's personality, his partisanship, his fitness for the highest office in the land, once again became central issues.

As in 1952, Eisenhower in 1956 used Nixon to answer Stevenson's attacks on him. The kickoff for the campaign was a picnic for
six hundred Republican workers at the Eisenhower farm at Gettysburg. The morning of the picnic, September 13, Eisenhower called
Nixon with instructions. Noting that Nixon had been "talking the
new high level," he nevertheless said, "I think today you ought to
take notice of some of these attacks. . . . I think that when Stevenson calls this administration racketeers and rascals . . . I want them
to be called on it. I would like for you to do so." Nixon said he
agreed that Stevenson had been irresponsible. "Of course," Eisenhower interjected, "it isn't necessary to attack him personally." [1]

Nixon hit exactly the tone Eisenhower wanted. It was a warm,
sunny afternoon, with lots of food and drink and backslapping politicians. In his remarks, Nixon denied that the Democrats were the
party of the poor and the Republicans that of the rich. He held up
to scorn Stevenson's charges that the Eisenhower Administration
was shot through with corruption; he damned as "political fakery"
Stevenson's statement that the draft might soon be ended; he twit-
ted Stevenson for his failure to endorse the Supreme Court's decision in *Brown* v. *Topeka*, which ruled segregation by race in
schools unconstitutional.

Eisenhower was delighted—Nixon had made the points he wanted made, without casting doubts on Stevenson's patriotism or his attitudes toward Communism. The President thereupon tore up his prepared notes and spoke extemporaneously, and boldly, on the subject of his own health and the question it raised about Nixon's qualifications to succeed him. "I feel fine," Eisenhower asserted, and he certainly looked it. Then he stated flatly: "There is no man in the history of America who has had such a careful preparation as has Vice-President Nixon for carrying out the duties of the presidency, if that duty should ever fall on him."[2]

That was the ringing endorsement Nixon had wanted so desperately and needed so badly for almost a year, but however late, it was still welcome, and cherished. Late in the afternoon, as the party broke up into small groups, Nixon got a rare show of affection from Eisenhower, although not unmixed with a little pain. Eisenhower, who had been talking to Nixon, turned to others in the group around him and said, "Did you hear that? Dick says he's never seen the inside of the house here!" The President consulted with Mamie, called for a jeep, and drove Dick and Pat to the house for a tour.[3]

This little incident quickly passed around the press corps, and was cited for decades after as proof of Eisenhower's coldness toward Nixon, but at least in this instance the story does not prove the conclusion. Ike and Mamie had only started spending their weekends in Gettysburg within the past year, and except for Eisenhower's closest personal friends, none of whom were politicians, no one had been guests or had even seen the place. Eisenhower was a very private person, and the Nixons were indeed honored to be among the first to see his home.

Eisenhower gave Nixon another boost when he called Arthur Sulzberger, publisher of *The New York Times*. Sulzberger was an old friend and Eisenhower talked straight to him—the President asked for an endorsement from the *Times*, which had been undecided. Sulzberger said, "It is your running mate that bothers me." Eisenhower replied, "I sometimes wish I could put him clear before the public." Then he asked Sulzberger down to lunch, where he praised Nixon. The *Times* endorsed the Eisenhower-Nixon ticket.[4]

ON SEPTEMBER 18, the President came out to National Airport to see the Nixons off on their first campaign swing. In a last-minute pep talk, he reiterated points that had been worked out in the White House about how to conduct the campaign. The President reminded Nixon that there was no need to indulge in "the exaggerations of partisan political talk," nor to "claim perfection." Referring to Harry Truman's 1948 campaign cry, "Give 'em hell," Eisenhower said Nixon should "Give 'em heaven."[5]

In 1952, Nixon had campaigned from the back of a train. In 1956, he traveled the country in a DC-6B, which he found to be a vast improvement. The chartered airplane had a divided compartment at the rear where he and Pat could have privacy to read, nap, or write without interruption. The rest of the plane was filled with his staff and the press; since every seat was filled, Nixon was spared idle chitchat with local politicians riding along to the next stop. He had the largest press corps ever to accompany a vice-presidential campaign. When a reporter asked if he preferred planes or trains, he replied, "Planes, of course; more privacy, and you can get more work done."

Nixon's staff included Jim Bassett, the forty-four-year-old city editor of the Los Angeles *Mirror-News*, who served as press secretary. Herb Klein, thirty-eight years old, also on leave of absence from his paper, the San Diego *Union*, was assistant press secretary. Ted Rogers, a thirty-five-year-old NBC television producer, was the media adviser. Ray Arbuthnot worked as advance man. Jack Drown managed the plane as he had the train in 1952. Rose Woods did a bit of everything. Nixon had publicly dissociated himself from Chotiner, who played no role in the 1956 campaign. Father John Cronin of Baltimore, although not on the plane, was the principal speech writer.

Nixon himself, however, did most of the speech writing, going over drafts again and again until the moment of delivery. "He just . . . thought and thought and wrote and wrote," Klein told Richard Rovere. "He doesn't want ghost-writers. Oh, we help with research, and we give him ideas now and then, and sometimes we throw in a phrase or a sentence. . . . But it all goes through that meat-grinder of a mind he's got. . . . He has his own vocabulary and his own rhythms, and none of us can really catch them. And he'll never use anything that doesn't sound like him."[6]

At each airport, Nixon walked down the ramp with one arm around Pat, waving with the other as the band played and the local GOP cheered. Then there was a motorcade into the city center— on Nixon's express orders, no Cadillacs—and the rally. Generally he drew good crowds and got a polite reception, with fewer hecklers than he had attracted in the past.

His basic themes were what a great man Eisenhower was and how the GOP had delivered "peace, prosperity, and progress." Reporters who had to listen to him numerous times each day made up titles for his clichés. The "Old Shoe" was his statement that the United States "has prosperity and peace to boot." "Bush-Leaguer" was the title given to his assertion that "Adlai Stevenson just isn't in the same league with President Eisenhower." And his line that "every man can hold up Dwight Eisenhower to his children as a man who has faith in God, faith in America" was christened the "Weight-Lifting Act."[7]

Nixon was almost constantly on the move, with a schedule that accounted for nearly every minute of every day. Except in his private compartment on the plane, he seldom relaxed. He had no close friends among the press corps covering his campaign, and except for Drown and Arbuthnot, none among the staff. William Costello told the story of the time the weather forced a layover. Weary reporters and staff members took advantage of the break to go for a swim in the hotel pool. Suddenly Nixon appeared, wearing his swimsuit. He dove in, swam up and down the pool several times, climbed out, grabbed his towel, and returned to his room without saying one word to anyone, not even a nod.[8]

Pat, as she had done in the previous four campaigns, listened intently to every word of every speech. She suppressed whatever negative feelings she had about being on the campaign trail once again, with the girls back in Washington, and gave her man her unstinting support. Once, in Cheyenne, Nixon was hit with a virus attack. His speech that night was an ordeal for him—he could barely speak, his face was ashen, and he just did get through it. As the party boarded the plane, at midnight, a reporter standing next to Pat expressed his sympathy at having to carry on at such cost. "Oh," Pat replied defensively, "but it was a *good* speech!"[9]

Overall, Nixon ran the campaign with remarkable effectiveness and smoothness. He made himself easily accessible to the press, holding a press conference every day, sometimes two. *The New York Times* reported that he was "adroitly . . . running a campaign that has to be seen to be believed."[10] And on October 19, television newscaster David Brinkley wrote Len Hall, "I've just spent nine days scurrying around the country on the Dick Nixon special. And in my 15 years of covering presidential politics and candidates on trains, planes, cars, buses and helicopters, this is the best operation I've ever seen." Nixon himself, Brinkley said, "is a splendid campaigner." He concluded, "You will gather I was quite impressed, as I was. And when it comes to politics I am hard to impress."[11]

IN 1952, the party platforms had been far apart, but in 1956 the differences were not sharp. The Democrats asserted the right of all citizens to "equal opportunities for education," while the Republicans said segregation must be "progressively eliminated." The Democrats favored public as opposed to private development of water power, which was the focus of their one example of corruption in the Eisenhower Administration—the opening of the TVA system to private power interests (the Dixon-Yates group). The Democrats discovered that the Bureau of the Budget consultant who advised the government on the Dixon-Yates negotiations was also vice-president of the First Boston Corporation, Dixon-Yates's financial agent. The Democrats favored 90 to 100 percent parity payments to farmers; the Republicans, the flexible parity payments.

In 1956, race relations were not the burning issue they would become in the 1960s, partly because few southern Negroes had the right to vote and most northern Negroes habitually voted for the party of FDR and the New Deal. The Democrats were vulnerable on the race issue, however, because they were running for the Vice-Presidency a southern senator who had supported segregation, because a Democratic victory meant southerners would be committee chairmen in Congress, and because Stevenson refused to give a full endorsement to *Brown* v. *Topeka*. But the Republicans were slow to act on the opportunity, because they wanted to make further inroads in the Deep South and because their candidate, President Eisenhower, had also refused to endorse *Brown* v. *Topeka*.

Nixon, however, had consistently been forthright in his denunciations of segregation and his insistence on equality of opportunity. He did not duck; he told Father Cronin he wanted more material, not less, on the "race problem" in his speeches. One of his favorite paragraphs was about Nate George, "a great colored athlete at Whittier College." George, Nixon said, was working with young people in Los Angeles, where his wife was teaching in third grade. "They are as fine Americans as anyone could want to meet. I am proud to count them as my friends and as my fellow citizens." By the 1980s, such words would sound condescending, but in the mid-fifties, Nixon was almost the only prominent politician in the country saying them, and certainly the only candidate for high office doing so. He asserted that "America is fortunate that men and women like Nate George and his wife are citizens of this country. We need to give our 17 million Negro citizens an opportunity to develop their skills so that they can make the contribution of which they are capable to the American economy and to our culture and to our national life." [12]

When Nixon campaigned in Texas, the Democrats spread the

word that the Vice-President was a member of the NAACP, which was so thoroughly hated (and feared) throughout the South that in several states the legislatures were considering bills banning the organization outright. Nixon condemned such efforts. He freely admitted that he was an "honorary" member of the NAACP and said he supported the organization's goal of "equal opportunity for all of us." But he warned that "we are not going to solve this problem without a basic change of attitude in the hearts of men," and said that the issue "must not be made a political football." [13]

But of course politics were never far from Nixon's mind. In a telephone conversation with Father Cronin on October 6, he said "there is insufficient emphasis on the Negroes. From a vote-getting standpoint, the South appears lost, whereas the large Negro voting groups in states with heavy electoral votes can be most important." He continued to speak out for equality of opportunity, and to support the aims of the NAACP. [14]

One of his major campaign appearances was on October 19, when he was the featured speaker at the annual Al Smith dinner at the Waldorf Astoria in New York. His theme was brotherhood. He said that a majority of those present would live to see racial integration accomplished in the nation's schools, and made it clear that he would welcome the day. He warned, however, that "the most nearly perfect law is only as good as the will of the people to obey it." Then he extended the principle to universal proportions, stating that "the American Revolution will be incomplete until its goals of independence and freedom are realities all over the world." [15]

New York reporters had been reading about a "new" Nixon, but even so they could hardly believe their ears. They were even more dumbfounded when they asked Nixon to comment on Stevenson's latest crack, that Nixon was "a man of many masks," and the Vice-President refused. [16] Some columnists welcomed the emergence of this new Nixon, others deplored Nixon's abandonment of his former style, while still others refused to believe he was in any way sincere.

THE DEMOCRATS WERE EVEN MORE CONFOUNDED by the New Nixon than the reporters were puzzled or suspicious. They wanted to make Nixon their target, not Ike. To accomplish that purpose, they tried to goad him into lashing back, in the hopes that he would commit an indiscretion here, a blunder there, and thus get voters to ask themselves whether they really wanted this man who might succeed Eisenhower.

But Nixon, generally, avoided all such traps. Stevenson

mocked the new Nixon every chance he got. Nixon, he said, "has put away his switchblade and now assumes the aspect of an Eagle Scout." No answer from Nixon. On October 27, Stevenson said of Nixon, "This man has no standard of truth but convenience and no standard of morality except what will serve his interest in an election." He described "Nixonland" as "a land of slander and scare, the land of sly innuendo, the poison pen, the anonymous phone call, and hustling, pushing, shoving; the land of smash and grab and anything to win." Nixon did not reply. On November 5, Stevenson said that "people prefer men who 'don't have to be changed.' . . . A lot of people just don't believe that Richard Nixon is really at home in this role as the Little Lord Fauntleroy of the Republican party. They wonder if he doesn't yearn for his old tar bucket and brush. . . . " No response from Nixon.[17]

Not even Harry Truman could get Nixon to respond, at least not the way Harry wanted him to. At the start of the campaign, Truman brought up his favorite complaint against Nixon, that the Vice-President had called him a "traitor." Nixon limited his reply to off-the-record remarks and private letters (and in the process softened considerably what he had in fact said in 1954). "I have said," Nixon explained to one correspondent, "that certain members of the former Democratic Administration showed bad judgment in that they failed to appreciate the seriousness of the Communist menace and to take effective steps to combat it. That charge has never been refuted; the record speaks for itself."[18] At other times, he said he had been referring to the "principles" of Thomas Jefferson and Andrew Jackson when he used the word "traitor" in the same sentence with Truman's name.

On November 3, Truman tried again. "Why," he asked, "is the Republican Party offering us this over-ambitious, unscrupulous, reactionary boy orator as a possibility for the President? Why are they imposing this terrible choice on the people?" Nixon had no comment.[19]

THERE WERE REPUBLICANS TOO WHO WERE CONFOUNDED by this new Nixon. They wanted him to get off his high horse and do a bit of grappling down in the dust. Willard Edwards of the Chicago *Tribune* reported that the RNC was sending messages begging Nixon to slug it out with Stevenson. Nixon responded to their advice to "engage in verbal street-fighting, slashing, ripping, and swinging from his heels" with a message that he had no intention of becoming a "political Jack the Ripper."[20]

Nixon later confessed that he found it "frustrating . . . to suppress the normal partisan instincts and campaign with one arm tied behind my back while Stevenson bombarded us with malicious ridicule and wild charges." [21] But he did it. When Congressman Dewey Short introduced him at a rally, Short assured Nixon, "You're among friends—take off your gloves and sock them." Nixon pretended not to hear. In Ohio he told a news conference, "The problem this year is different from that in 1952. . . . In 1952 we were giving the people reasons to throw out a group, and now we are giving them reasons to keep an administration in. What I am doing now is to appeal to swing voters, whom we must have to win. It is essential to have a type of campaign persuasive to independents and Democrats." [22]

That was obviously good politics, because there was much in the Eisenhower record the Republicans could point to with pride. There was peace and prosperity, without inflation. In the past four years, the cost of living had gone up 2.8 percent while the real wages of factory workers had increased by 8.6 percent. The stock market was booming. Detroit could not make cars fast enough to stock the dealers' showrooms. Eisenhower had extended Social Security to cover an additional 10 million people, and in 1956 launched the gigantic Interstate Highway program, the largest public works project in the history of the world. The St. Lawrence Seaway was finally under way. Government controls had been eased, and taxes reduced. Eisenhower had brought peace in Korea, and at Geneva in 1955 a relaxation in the Cold War. Nixon would have been some kind of fool had he spent his time attacking Stevenson instead of talking about Republican accomplishments.

If Nixon held firm to the high ground in his speeches, he was at the cutting edge of technological possibilities in his presentation of the Republican case. Campaigning by airplane was innovative enough, but where he really moved the art of campaigning forward was in his use of television. He developed a technique that he liked so much he used it in every subsequent campaign—the national live televised news conference. On October 4, from NBC's Washington studio, he answered questions from eight reporters in eight different cities. In his remarks, he was as upbeat as the technology.

He opened with a statement: "For the great majority of Americans the Eisenhower years have been the best four years of our lives." He answered questions on farm policy and electric power development. From Philadelphia, Paul Warner asked him to comment on Stevenson's charge that the Republican Party had no concern for "the small-business man, the wage earner, the needy, the aged." That was bread and butter for Nixon—"We say that no one of the 167 million Americans is a little man. We say that every one of our American citizens has God-given dignity and unalienable rights and that he is bigger than any Government. . . . May I say in that connection also that I think that any political candidate who tries to divide Americans on a class basis is rendering a terrible disservice to our country."

Workers, he said, "have more jobs at higher wages, with greater take-home pay than at any time in history, and they have peace to boot." The old folks too were better off. More of them were covered by Social Security than ever before, and no longer did Democratic inflation eat away at their savings. They were the chief beneficiaries of "a sound Eisenhower dollar rather than a rubber Truman dollar."

A. C. Dunkleberger, editor of the Nashville *Banner*, asked about desegregation. Nixon urged "a moderate approach, a steady approach." Just passing laws was not going to accomplish the objective. So, he advised, "let's avoid extremes, which hurt the cause far more than they help it." If that sounded mealymouthed, he was forthright in his next paragraph: "America, the people of the United States, cannot afford the cost of prejudice and hatred and discrimination. We can't afford it morally, we can't afford it economically, and we can't afford it internationally." He added up the cost and put the total at $15 billion in national income, "and this at a time when we have to keep ahead of the Communist world, is a cost that we cannot afford." He reminded the audience that he was a world traveler, and said everywhere he went he found that American racism was the most powerful weapon in the arsenal of Communist propaganda.

His conclusion to the program soared over the mountaintop: "This is a nation of destiny and I believe that the man best qualified from both parties to lead America to its destiny is a man of destiny, the President of the United States." [23]

PHYSICALLY, NIXON NEVER LOOKED BETTER. He may have found travel on the high road to be "frustrating" to his "partisan instincts," but it was good for his health and reputation. His picture was in the papers almost every day. Usually he was smiling, comfortably, not that awful grimace he had used in '52 and '54 as he called the Democrats traitors to their own party. This time he looked at ease with himself, and with his material, and with his audiences. He feared he was putting them to sleep, but in fact he was impressing them. His self-confidence was high (as well it might have been, given all those good economic figures, "and peace to boot"), and it showed in his face, even in his gestures. He stood erect, with his head back. He carried no excess weight, not even in his jowls, which were somehow not so noticeable in '56 as they had been or would be. Herblock was in danger of losing a target for his cartoons.

Pat too was blooming. Although she appeared to be dangerously thin, her face pinched, she always had a smile on her face, her hand outstretched to greet yet another reception line. She was, as always, a major asset as a vote getter, and a major contributor to her husband's sense of self-esteem.

Nixon lost his temper only once during the campaign, and he learned a lesson from the experience. After a difficult session with a group of young college editors at Cornell University, Nixon climbed into his plane and berated Ted Rogers. "You son of a bitch," Nixon growled, "you put me on with those shitty-ass liberal sons of bitches, you tried to destroy me. . . . " Reporter Philip Potter of the Baltimore *Sun* separated the two men. Later, Jim Bassett upbraided Nixon. "You didn't go into this campaign with a gun at your head," Bassett said. "You fought for it. What scares the hell out of me is that you would blow sky high over a thing as inconsequential as this. What in God's name would you do if you were president and got into a really bad situation?"

Chagrined, Nixon replied, "I'll think about it." For the remainder of the campaign, Bassett said, "he was the kindest boss we ever had."[24]

ASIDE FROM NIXON'S QUALIFICATIONS to be President, in the event of Eisenhower's incapacity or death, the chief issues Stevenson tried to develop were an end to the draft and an end to nuclear testing. On these issues, Nixon was more than willing and ready to take Stevenson on directly.

He gave his standard reply on the draft to Alvin McCoy of the Kansas City *Star* in his televised press conference. The Republicans would like to find "an easy way" to provide for national security, he said, but "there isn't any easy way, unless we surrender and that we will never do." Therefore, "we aren't going to hold out any false hopes to the American people that they can end the draft." He pointed out that "we are trying to get our allies in Europe to strengthen their defenses and it's completely irresponsible to suggest at such a time that we in the United States are weakening our own position."[25]

Stevenson had made his call for an end to nuclear testing the centerpiece of his campaign, devoting the whole of a national TV talk on October 15 to it. He offered four reasons to stop testing. First, the United States already had bombs big enough to destroy any major city—why improve them? Second, a moratorium on testing could be monitored without on-site inspection because "you can't hide the explosion." Third, a prohibition on testing would halt the spread of nuclear weapons. Fourth, a test ban would eliminate fallout, especially of strontium-90, which Stevenson called "the most dreadful poison in the world." [26]

Those arguments were uncomfortably close to the truth—indeed, in his second term Eisenhower accepted them and became himself the leading advocate of an end to testing. But it was a complex subject, and Eisenhower wanted to avoid it during a political campaign. Thus his initial response was to insist that "this specific matter is manifestly not a subject for detailed public discussion—for obvious security reasons." [27] Nixon followed the same line. He gave Stevenson credit for being "a well-intentioned man," but insisted that "he does not have the experience and the judgment that President Eisenhower has." In short, in all matters of defense, trust Ike. [28]

Stevenson's advisers, in fact, had urged him to avoid any debate over defense issues with General Eisenhower, but by mid-October they were about ready to admit that they were wrong and Stevenson right. Despite Eisenhower's and Nixon's scorn of his military qualifications, Stevenson's appeal was making converts. The White House mail was running heavily in favor of a suspension of testing. But then Stevenson had the worst possible luck. Soviet Premier Bulganin sent Eisenhower a public letter urging a test ban. Bulganin noted with approval that "certain prominent public figures in the United States" were advocating a ban. Eisenhower sent a blistering reply to Bulganin, protesting his blatant interference in an American election, while Nixon went after Stevenson, already made thoroughly miserable by Bulganin's "endorsement." Nixon described Stevenson as a "clay pigeon" for Soviet sharpshooters, compared him to Neville Chamberlain, said that his test-ban proposal was "the height of irresponsibility and absurdity," and warned that "the Stevenson leadership would increase the chances of war." [29] Picking up on a line he had gotten from Dulles, Nixon said that the United States "could not afford a trial-and-error President at this time." [30]

WHAT HAD BEEN BAD LUCK for Stevenson turned into a full-scale disaster. Two major foreign-policy crises broke simultaneously in the last week of the campaign—the Israeli/French/British invasion of Egypt, and the Red Army invasion of Hungary. With World War III in the offing, more voters turned to General Ike than to Governor Stevenson.

The one potential danger in the election for the Republicans was the Jewish vote, which Eisenhower personally thought was decisive in New York, New Jersey, Pennsylvania, and Connecticut.[31] Nixon too was fully aware of the political power of America's Jews, not only as voters but as campaign contributors, fund raisers, and party workers. Nevertheless, the morning Israel invaded Egypt, he called Dulles from California. He told Dulles, according to Dulles' memo of the conversation, "that he wanted me to know that he felt no domestic political factors ought to stand in the way of our taking a firm position against the Israelis' aggression."[32]

Two days later, it was obvious that the French and the British were supporting Israel, in the hopes of getting the Suez Canal back. Nixon called Dulles again. "N. asked what is wrong condemning the Br. and Fr." Dulles said he was for condemnation, as was the President. "N. urged strongly against calling Congress back." Dulles assured him there was no such thought. "N. asked can it be said our policies are designed to protect the independence of small countries but it is also designed to keep American boys from being involved." Yes, Dulles replied, he could say that. "N. asked how the Sec. analyzed it politically, and the Sec. said N. is the expert. N. said we will lose some Israeli votes but they agreed there weren't many. N. said our policy is still one that has kept American boys out and at such a time you don't want a pipsqueak for Pres."[33]

In his memoirs, Nixon wrote that "in retrospect I believe that our actions were a serious mistake. Nasser became even more rash and aggressive. . . . Britain and France were so humiliated. . . . they lost the will to play a major role. . . . I have often felt that if the Suez crisis had not arisen during the heat of a presidential election campaign a different decision would have been made."[34] About this last point he was certainly wrong—Eisenhower never wavered on or regretted his decision to force the invading parties out of Egypt, no matter what. At the time, Nixon heartily endorsed that policy.

What made Eisenhower and his associates particularly furious with the NATO allies was that they had struck at just the moment when the Soviet Union was at its weakest in the court of world opinion. The Red Army invasion of Hungary, coming after Khrushchev had practically invited the East European nations to liberalize their regimes, outraged people around the world. But the simultaneous invasion of Egypt diverted the world's attention and allowed Khruschev to get away with a brutal crushing of the freedom fighters in Hungary. Nixon coined a phrase when he called Khrushchev the "Butcher of Budapest," but rhetorical flourishes did nothing for the Hungarians. Nixon supported Eisenhower's decision to stay out, despite calls for help from the Hungarian freedom fighters.

Stevenson could not fault Eisenhower's responses—he too opposed aggression against Egypt, and did not want to challenge the Red Army in Hungary. The only way he could figure to use the world crisis to his advantage was to point to the possibility that Nixon might have to handle the next one. He had already described the Vice-Presidency as "this nation's life insurance policy," and said that victory for Ike and Dick would mean that the nation would "go for four years uninsured." [35] On election eve, in a nationwide television broadcast, he let out all the stops. "Distasteful as this matter is," he declared, "I must say bluntly that every piece of scientific evidence we have, every lesson of history and experience, indicates that a Republican victory tomorrow would mean that Richard M. Nixon probably would be President of this country within the next four years. . . . Distasteful as it is, this is the truth, the central truth, about the most fateful decision that American people have to make tomorrow." [36] What most people found distasteful, however, was what Stevenson said, and the way he said it.

IKE AND DICK WON BY A LANDSLIDE, 35 million to 25 million. But the victory, especially for Nixon, was bittersweet. Eisenhower got all the credit for the sweep, while Nixon got blamed for the failure of the Republicans to carry either house of Congress. Nixon was caught in a can't-win position. In 1954 he had been blamed for the Republican loss because he was too partisan in his campaign; in 1956 he was blamed because his character was still a central issue.

The first point was true enough—Eisenhower's victory was a personal one, and he would have won even with Harold Stassen as a running mate (a Gallup poll just before the election showed that Eisenhower had a 76 percent favorable rating to Nixon's 45 percent, while only 8 percent had an unfavorable view of Eisenhower, to 28 percent for Nixon).[37] The second point was patently unfair—Nixon was not the one who drove independents and Democrats who voted for Eisenhower away from the Republican candidates, but the candidates themselves.

Eisenhower himself saw that immediately. On election night, Dick and Pat joined Ike and Mamie at the Sheraton-Park Hotel. The early returns had them elated, but when the congressional count began to come in, Eisenhower grew increasingly depressed. He had won one of the biggest presidential landslides in history, but he was the first man elected President in 108 years who did not carry at least one house of Congress with him.

"You know why this is happening, Dick?" he finally said. "It's all those damned mossbacks and hard-shell conservatives we've got in the party. I think that what we need is a new party." His thoughts turned to the crowd waiting in the ballroom. "You know," Eisenhower said, "I think I will talk to them about Modern Republicanism." Nixon was aghast. He had tied his fortunes to the Republican Party, as it was and without any preceding adjectives. He strongly urged the President to avoid any such language, but Eisenhower did it anyway. When he announced that his victory was a victory for Modern Republicanism, party regulars took it as a boast that he had won by himself, and as a threat to the Old Guard. As Nixon laconically noted in his memoirs, this caused "a slightly sour note in some Republican circles." [38]

It would have been even sourer if Republicans had known that their President soon began scribbling on legal pads during especially dull meetings a list of those who he felt might join him in a new party, which he wanted to call the Americans for Modern Republicanism Party (AMR). Nixon's name headed all his lists. Fortunately for Nixon, the thought of a third party always remained a fantasy with Eisenhower, unlike Teddy Roosevelt, who did break with the Old Guard Republicans of his day. As Eisenhower must have known, Nixon outside the Republican Party was as unimaginable as Truman outside the Democratic Party.

IMMEDIATELY AFTER THE ELECTION, Nixon flew to Miami for ten days of "just plain relaxing." He stayed with Bebe Rebozo on Key Biscayne. His family flew down a week later, in time for Thanksgiving. [39] While he was there, congratulations on the victory poured in from all over the country, which helped make up for some cold weather. To Ray Arbuthnot, Nixon wrote, "I am feeling much better after this campaign than in 1952 and 1954. I guess it's because we didn't work as hard!" He said he was so pleased with the newspaper reporters who had covered his campaign that he was inviting them all to the inaugural party. [40]

The reporters, for the most part, returned those warm feelings. They were impressed by the new Nixon. Carl Greenberg, political editor of the Los Angeles *Examiner*, spoke for many of his colleagues when he wrote Nixon on November 12, referring to the Truman-Stevenson attacks, "I don't think I'd have been able to display the graciousness that you did, in view of the obvious antagonism some of these birds displayed, although I think your course took the steam out of them." [41]

IN HUNGARY, meanwhile, the Red Army had crushed the rebellion and reimposed a brutal dictatorship. Thousands of former freedom fighters fled, crossing the border at night into Austria, as many as 3,000 or 4,000 a night, to a total of more than 100,000. Thus did a world that had just recently gotten the last of the displaced persons of World War II settled face a new phenomenon, the Cold War refugee. In this case the situation was almost as embarrassing to the Americans as to the Communists, because the Hungarians came out steaming mad at the United States. They claimed that they had been encouraged to revolt by the Voice of America, then left to their own devices when they responded. There was an additional immediate problem, the housing and care of the refugees. Tiny Austria had just received its independence a year earlier, in the Austrian State Treaty of 1955, after pledging itself to permanent neutrality. Now it had a victorious, cocky Red Army less than fifty miles from Vienna, and had to be careful not to antagonize the Russian bear. Nevertheless, the Austrians did the best they could for the refugees, but of course their means were limited, and they called on the United States for help.

Eisenhower was disturbed by the charge that the Americans had encouraged the revolt, and on simple humanitarian grounds he wanted to help. He was prevented from acting decisively, however, by the McCarran-Walter Act, which limited immigration to the United States on a quota system—and Hungary's quota was pitifully small. He did offer asylum to 21,500 Hungarian refugees, but only on a temporary basis, as required in the existing law. He appealed for private donations to help the refugees, but almost no money was raised, not even by the Red Cross. The President also asked for new legislation on immigration to permit him to admit Hungarian refugees on a permanent basis, but the idea aroused considerable opposition in Congress, where "don't let the barriers down" was the cry.

Eisenhower, and Dulles, deplored this attitude. Admitting Hungarians was not only the moral thing to do, especially in view of the American involvement in encouraging the revolt, but it would make good propaganda. Perhaps most important, they knew that the majority of the refugees were young, well-educated students, usually unmarried, who would make outstanding additions to the nation's body politic. Since the problem was with Congress, and beyond that with public opinion, they turned to Nixon for help.

On December 7, Dulles called Nixon. "The Sec. said he has been giving thought to N's going to Austria," the notes read. "N. said it would be interesting to him if the Sec. thinks it is useful. The Sec. said he mentioned it to the Pres yesterday and he said he would be glad to have the two (the Sec and N) work it out. . . . N. does not want to go if it will be interpreted as a grandstand play."[42]

Nixon and Pat went off to New York for some Christmas shopping. On December 13, Eisenhower called him back to Washington, to tell Nixon he wanted the Vice-President to go to Austria in order to focus public attention on the plight of the refugees. When he returned, he should prepare a report that would become the basis for new legislation. Code name for the mission would be Operation Mercy.[43]

Nixon flew to Vienna on December 18, accompanied by Bill Rogers, ambassador to Austria Llewellyn Thompson, and Congressman Robert Wilson of San Diego. The Austrian government gave a dinner in his honor, but Nixon wanted to see the border, not the glitter of Vienna, and that evening he had Thompson get him a car for a drive to a refugee center near the border. There he met refugees who had just crossed that night.

The refugees were students, and some of them spoke English. To their surprise, Nixon asked them, "Do you feel that the Voice of America and Radio Free Europe played a part in encouraging the revolution?" They had not expected so blunt a question, but they replied, "Yes." The exchange broke the ice. One of the Hungarians, in response to another question, said the best place to cross the border was in a deep woods some miles to the north. Nixon wanted to go there. "You will have to travel the way we do," he was warned. Nixon climbed into the back of a large hay wagon, pulled by a tractor.

Just being at the border between Eastern and Western Europe is a powerful experience for most Americans. Nixon was there, for his first visit, at a moment of high drama—searchlights, guard towers, dogs patrolling along the barbed wire, the possibility of seeing an occasional figure dashing away from the wire and toward freedom, perhaps to be gunned down at the last minute. Nixon was looking at the only frontier posts in the history of the world designed to keep people in rather than out.

Nixon did not actually see any escapes, but his party did pick up a young man who said he had hidden in the woods on the other side for three days before dashing over the wire some five hours earlier. They got back to the refugee camp at 6 A.M., then to Vienna in time for a quick shower and a 9 A.M. meeting[44] (no jet lag for Nixon, who attended meetings all day). He called his visit to the frontier "the most thrilling of my life." Chancellor Julius Raab asked him when he found time to sleep. Nixon replied that he lived according to schedule. "Time for sleeping comes every Tuesday," he cracked.[45]

Nixon returned on Christmas Eve, and the day after Christmas met Eisenhower in the Oval Office to give an oral report. Ann Whitman took notes. Nixon's first comment was "about the high calibre of the refugees. They are young, in most cases the people that 'had' to leave the country—i.e., the leadership type—to avoid deportation. The President recalled that once Marshal Zhukov had once said if you got rid of the leaders of a country, you could do anything you wanted to." Congressmen opposed to opening America's doors had warned that Communist spies would join the refugee groups. Nixon told Eisenhower that was virtually impossible, because the refugees knew one another well, and what each had done during the revolt. Eisenhower said "such danger is almost zero—the Communists did not have to go to such elaborate means to get spies into our country."

Nixon pointed out that "other countries regard these particular refugees as tremendous assets, rather than liabilities." Holland, for example, with the highest population density in the world, had taken in a few hundred and wanted more. West Germany was pledged to take 10 percent of all who came over. But there were still twenty thousand with no place to go. "The Vice President pointed out the danger in leaving people too long in refugee camps because of morale problem." Eisenhower wanted to get the Latin American nations in on the operation because "they are in general underpopulated and can use the skills the Hungarians have." But as for the United States, Eisenhower could not see what more it could do under existing law. Nevertheless, "the President pointed out that he did not want to stop processing [individuals, for entry into the United States], particularly since if we do, the pick of the refugees will go to other countries." Nixon "emphasized that it is important that we not drag our feet—that we stay in the forefront and continue to take applications at current rate."

They talked about the McCarran-Walter Act. "The Vice President urged that here was an opportunity to get some needed flexibility into our Immigration laws. He pointed out also the injustice to the 10,000 Eastern European refugees who are anxious to come to this country—who crawled under barbed wire to come out—and who have been long in camps, mainly in Germany."[46] He never said so publicly, but by now he must have regretted his vote in 1952 to override Truman's veto of McCarran-Walter.

On New Year's Day, Nixon released his report to the press. He called for immediate legislation that would regularize the status of refugees brought into the country under the emergency provisions of McCarran-Walter (which provided for asylum in special circumstances for limited numbers; they were allowed to stay for an indefinite period, but they had no fixed legal status). Nixon also called for flexible authority for the President to issue nonquota visas without an annual ceiling to admit "additional numbers of Hungarian and other refugees from Communist persecution." He remarked, "We should not place a ceiling on what we will do in fulfilling our traditional national mission of providing a haven of refuge for victims of oppression."[47]

There were no American votes to be won by relaxing the immigration quotas, not even for the victims of Communist oppression, and Nixon knew it. Even before arriving in Vienna, he saw in the Hungarian refugees both an obligation and an opportunity for the United States. What he saw, at firsthand, reinforced his convictions. He worked hard to get America to meet its obligation and profit from its opportunity.

Unfortunately, the Lord himself would not have been able to move Congress on the immigration issue. At a meeting with congressional leaders on Hungary on New Year's Day, Sam Rayburn pontificated, "I represent a district less excitable than any other in the United States." But, he said, "my people are terribly concerned, afraid the wrong type will get in. I don't know that you ought to allow more in. Already there is unemployment in Dallas." Nixon tried to make Mr. Sam understand. He told the story of a refugee who had bought materials and made his own radio so that he could listen to the Voice of America. The boy used his shoe money. Nixon quoted him as saying, "I can get along without shoes, but it is hard to live without hope." Mr. Sam was not impressed. Neither was Congress as a whole. McCarran-Walter was not amended.[48]

At least, Nixon thought, he could goad his country into doing something for the relief of Hungarians still in Hungary. In mid-January he went to New York to talk to Herbert Hoover, who explained to him how he organized the 1922 relief expedition to the Soviet Union, at a time when that country faced massive starvation. Hoover suggested that the same pattern of relief could be used in Hungary, and that Ezra Taft Benson could do the job Hoover had done in 1922. Nixon pushed the idea with Sherman Adams, Bobby Cutler of the NSC, and others, to no avail. Cutler told him coldly, "The time is not opportune to act."[49]

So, rather like the election, Nixon's year ended with a bittersweet experience. He had learned while in Austria, and seen much, and generated some front-page publicity for himself and for the refugees, and added to his stature as an emerging world leader —but he failed to get anything done for the Hungarians. It seemed to be his fate that no triumph was ever complete, or even clear-cut.

CHAPTER TWENTY

SEARCHING FOR A ROLE
1957

SAFELY RE-ELECTED and assured of a job in Washington for at least the next four years, in January 1957, Nixon bought a new home. It was a secluded house, quite large, with eight bedrooms and five baths. Located at 4308 Forest Lane in Wesley Heights, it was a fieldstone English Tudor house formerly owned by Homer S. Cummings, FDR's first Attorney General. It was on a dead-end street and had a large backyard surrounded by dense woods. Nixon sold his three-bedroom house on Tilden Street for $45,000, and paid $70,000 for the new home.[1]

It was magnificently furnished. After the Nixons moved in, in late March, *The New York Times* reported, "NIXON'S NEW HOME ADORNED WITH GIFTS FROM FORTY NATIONS." Bess Furman wrote the story. Pat took her on a tour. The home, the reporter wrote, "is filled with conversation pieces. The visitor sees souvenirs and gifts from the more than forty countries visited by the Nixons, but nothing looks cluttered. Mrs. Nixon, the tidy housekeeper who achieved this paradox, . . . disclosed that the family now had for the first time more than one bath, a live-in maid, bookshelves, a barbecue pit and a large slice of a park for background and view. 'The girls just adore it all,' she said. 'They've already had their Girl Scout and Brownie troops here for a cook-out.' "[2]

The redwood outdoor furniture was also a gift. Nixon wrote a gracious thank-you letter to Helene and Jack Drown for it. He said he and Pat had always wanted to have a real California-style outdoor living room, and "the patio in the new house was one of the features which appealed to us most when we first looked at it.

However, we didn't realize what a really favorite spot it would be until we walked in and saw it all set up with the wonderful furniture and equipment which you and the Arbuthnots so generously gave us."[3]

The "conversation pieces" included matching pictorial scrolls from Japan, a candelabrum from Korea given by Syngman Rhee, Oriental rugs from Mme. Chiang Kai-shek, a Persian rug from the Shah of Iran, and a Buddha head from the king of Afghanistan.

Gifts are a problem for any politician. Graciously rejecting a gift is always a difficult proposition, whether it comes from the head of a government, or from a political supporter, or from a complete stranger. Nixon got far more gifts than any previous Vice-President because he traveled more. In accepting them, he was well within the precedent established by various Presidents over the years, and doing exactly as Eisenhower was doing (Ike and Mamie accepted some very expensive gifts from their close friends, and kept much of what was given them by foreign leaders).

The new home allowed the Nixons to do a great deal more entertaining than they had in the past, when they had been forced to rent a hotel ballroom for their big parties. Pat was proud to show her home, and Nixon began to enjoy playing gracious host.[4] They became more active in the Washington social scene, and in New York too. They were often guests of celebrities, whether from the world of politics, entertainment, or business. Arthur Godfrey had them on his farm for a weekend; there Nixon met for the first time Air Force General Curtis LeMay, and was much impressed by him.[5]

Lewis Strauss, chairman of the Atomic Energy Commission, was one of the great party givers in Washington and had been for decades. In late July he held a big one. The next morning, he wrote Nixon: "You are the first guest in twenty-five years who ever took the trouble to go backstairs and thank the hired help. They were bubbling over the experience, and I suspect that . . . they will vote Republican hereafter. They think you are terrific!" Nixon, in reply, said it was he who should be thanking Strauss, because Strauss had been so considerate of Julie and Tricia. "You made them feel that they were just as important and just as grown up as their elders."[6]

Aside from a weekend at the Eisenhower farm in Gettysburg, the most prestigious invitations in Washington in the late fifties were to play golf with Eisenhower or to attend one of his stag dinners. As Nixon improved his game (from 130 down to the high 80s), and as Eisenhower in his second term started reaching out to Nixon in his own awkward way, the President and the Vice-President played together occasionally. On October 2, 1957, for example, Eisenhower sent a note to Nixon. He said he might be able to break away for a round that afternoon. "In the event I do go, I wonder whether you would play with me. . . . Please don't think of changing your plans." Nixon, naturally enough, dropped everything and went out to the links.[7] There was no doubt who was the Commander in Chief.

Golf and swimming were Nixon's principal physical exercises, and they were sufficient to keep him looking fit and strong. Still, he was getting older. In December, when he was just short of his forty-fifth birthday, he began wearing reading glasses. "My arms just got too short for me to see those telephone numbers," he explained to a friend.[8] *The New York Times* reported it a bit differently; the paper said that Nixon had to read a citation to the king of Morocco at a dinner, in candlelight, and that the words had blurred. Nixon had stumbled over the citation; the next day he got glasses. The *Times* gave as its opinion that the glasses made him look "more mature."[9]

NIXON'S STAFF EXPANDED, but only by one man. When the position (designated Legislative Assistant) opened, Nixon asked Bob Haldeman for suggestions. Haldeman recommended John Ehrlichman, a young Seattle lawyer who had helped in the campaign, but Ehrlichman could not take the job. Then Haldeman himself became a candidate, but Nixon instead chose Charles McWhorter, a rising young star in the Republican Party with credentials far superior to Haldeman's. McWhorter, thirty-five years old, had been a war hero in Europe in World War II, had twice been chairman of the Young Republicans, and was a member of the well-known New York law firm of Donovan, Leisure, Newton & Irvine.[10] Herb Klein, meanwhile, went back to the San Diego *Union,* but he continued to send Nixon long letters that gave the details of the political situation in Southern California.[11]

The staff was loyal and efficient. It knew the boss well, and could anticipate his reactions to almost any situation. He had a heavy volume of mail, far too big for one man to even contemplate handling himself, so the vast majority of his letters were drafted by the staff members. They almost always got it right. Generally, Nixon would draft a form letter on a subject (lowering taxes, or defense spending, or whatever) for use with people who just wrote in, but even in those cases the staff would add some personal touch in response to a particular point. There were of course hundreds and hundreds of invitations that had to be turned down—to give speeches, to attend meetings or parties—and it had to be done, as it was, politely but firmly. There were also requests for favors, sometimes subtly disguised, sometimes not, that had to be dealt with delicately, especially when they came from the rich and powerful.

In April, Jack Hughes of the staff sent Nixon a memorandum on a meeting he had had with Leland Kaiser, of Kaiser Aluminum. "Mr. Kaiser wants an introduction to the Chairman of the Securities Exchange Commission so that he can discuss the suit [against Kaiser], informally and directly, with him," Hughes wrote. "Mr. Kaiser feels that the Chairman would benefit from hearing his side of the case in this matter." Hughes bucked the decision up to Nixon, asking for guidance.[12]

Before Nixon saw the memo, Rose Mary Woods intercepted it. She wrote a memo of her own: "This would be intervening with an agency—we could not set up an appointment for anyone who wanted to see about a case. We never make appointments on these matters. Sorry. This is policy—we would not do it for the Boss' family."

Nixon saw the Woods memo and scribbled on it: "Talked with Mr. Kaiser and told him no could do. He understood our position and appreciated our interest. RN."[13]

Once Nixon did break his otherwise inflexible rule never to intervene for anyone. In December, Billy Graham asked for some help for his father-in-law, Dr. Nelson Bell, who published a magazine called *Christianity Today,* which went out to 160,000 fundamentalist ministers. Bell wanted a favorable tax ruling on his publication, and at Graham's request, Nixon had spoken to the Treasury Department to get it to expedite the ruling. Then Bell got anxious that the ruling might go against him, so he called McWhorter to suggest that Nixon's office once again "intervene in order to 'put in a good word.'" McWhorter told Bell, "It is not the practice of our office to intervene in such matters, but I will bring it to [Nixon's] attention." Nixon told McWhorter that in this case he did want to intervene, because "this isn't a usual case—no profit involved."[14]

Members of the staff were often asked questions about Nixon by the press. To help them give accurate answers, Rose Woods compiled a list of facts about the Vice-President. It included his hat size (7¼), height (5' 11"), suit (42 long), shoe (11D), and so forth. His favorite Bible verse was the 23rd Psalm, his favorite play was *South Pacific,* with *The King and I* a close second. His favorite books were *War and Peace,* Robert La Follette's autobiography, and Whittaker Chambers' *Witness.* He used a Remington Rollelectric razor; his TV makeup was a blend of shades 22 and 23.[15]

Nixon appreciated his staff's effort, and tried in his own way to show it, with an occasional staff party, a kind word here or there, or a birthday gift. But he was not close enough to members of the staff to be really comfortable with any one of them, and he could be quite blunt in laying down the law. One memo to the staff read: "Whenever I do radio or TV no one is to be in the room but the technicians. I don't like any of my staff in the room. The staff people can go out and listen on the monitor or whatever they want."[16]

His closest friends were Bill Rogers, the Drowns, Arbuthnot, Billy Graham, Bebe Rebozo, and a group of reporters and their wives, including the de Toledanos, the Mazos, and *Herald Tribune* Washington correspondents Bert Andrews, Roscoe Drummond, and Don Whitehead.[17] It was notable that although he knew every senator on a first-name basis, and got along with most of them well enough, none were really close friends. The same was true of the Cabinet members, except for Dulles, with whom he continued to exchange almost daily phone calls, and often visited at home for a late-night drink or a weekend meal.

ON SATURDAY, FEBRUARY 2, 1957, Nixon had lunch at Dulles' residence. Dulles, who tried to put everything down on paper, later wrote a memcon (memorandum of conversation) about their discussion. Dulles wanted Nixon's help in getting Stassen out of the Cabinet (as Eisenhower's adviser on disarmament, Stassen had direct access to the President and sat in on Cabinet and NSC meetings). Nixon was eager to help cut Harold down a bit, which was accomplished by putting him under Dulles in the State Department hierarchy—at which point Stassen resigned to run, unsuccessfully, for governor of Pennsylvania.

Another topic taken up at lunch was a proposed Nixon trip to the Gold Coast, which was about to become the independent nation of Ghana. Eisenhower wanted Nixon to represent the United States at the independence ceremonies. Dulles' memcon reads: "He spoke about the mission to the Gold Coast. He wanted to be sure we really felt this amounted to something and the President really wanted him to go. He said there had been gossip that he himself promoted these missions and they did not serve a vital government purpose. I assured Nixon that both the President and I thought this was important." Nixon accepted that judgment, then got Dulles to agree that he could expand the trip to include Liberia and Ethiopia. Later, he added Morocco, Uganda, Sudan, Libya, Italy, and Tunisia to the itinerary.[18]

He left on February 28, accompanied by Pat and a four-member official delegation, including E. Frederic Morrow, who was on Sherman Adams' staff and was the first Negro to have a position on the President's executive staff and an office in the White House. Thirty newsmen went along, more than half of them from the American Negro press.

The tour followed the by-now familiar pattern. Nixon landed in Morocco and immediately set off on a motorcade through Casablanca, perched on the roll-down top of a blue convertible. He acted like a candidate for office, shaking hands, passing out ballpoint pens left over from the 1956 campaign, and answering cheers with a shout of "Long live his majesty, the Sultan." In Ethiopia, wearing a top hat and striped pants, he reviewed an honor guard in the rain. In Accra, capital of Ghana, he made a handshaking tour of an outlying village and passed out autographed cards to villagers dressed in togas and sandals. In private talks with the leaders of the new nation, he diplomatically explained why the United States could not extend more economic and military aid.[19]

The truth was that Eisenhower had given him almost nothing to offer the Africans, except good wishes. In Accra, the most he could offer Prime Minister Kwame Nkrumah was an Eisenhower Fellowship on behalf of the Eisenhower Foundation. It financed one year of study in the States for one student from Ghana. Nkrumah retaliated for this stinginess at a huge state dinner by putting the leader of the Red Chinese delegation at the head table and relegating Nixon (and the chief Russian delegate) to a place at the back of the hall. Some of the American delegates were indignant at this slight, but Nixon laughed and told reporters, "So what." [20]

There was another American guest at the Ghana ceremonies, an unofficial one invited by Nkrumah himself, Rev. Martin Luther King, Jr. The young civil rights leader stole the spotlight from all the official representatives, including Nixon. At an impromptu press conference at Ghana University, the world press hung on King's every word. King took the opportunity to express the wish that Nixon would make a tour of the American South, "to study the desperate situation and report to the President on the extent of the violence." Shortly afterward, Nixon managed to "bump into" King. Nixon "smiled broadly, and began a friendly chat which ended with the Vice President inviting Mr. King to confer with him in Washington later this month." [21]

Upon his return to the States on March 21, Nixon released a long report he had prepared for the President. It was full of platitudes about the importance of Africa, a continent of "tremendous potentialities, the most rapidly changing area in the world today." He encouraged "progress towards independence and self-government," and predicted that Africa "could well prove to be the decisive factor in the conflict between the forces of freedom and international communism." The great problem was to encourage independence "and at the same time develop governmental institutions which are based on principles of freedom and democracy."[22]

The place where that problem was most immediately pressing was Algeria, where the Arabs were in revolt against France. Senator John Kennedy had made headlines in July with a long speech on Algeria, in which he proposed a resolution in support of independence. At a legislative leaders' meeting, Nixon gave his own views on Algerian independence, a subject he said he had dared not raise in his public report. He noted that the United States had encouraged independence for Ghana and other emerging African nations, but admitted "we did it because we knew it was inevitable." Algeria was a different matter. If it became independent today, he said, "there would be a terrible revolution, one million French against 8 million Algerians." Still, the United States could not simply run away from the situation. The "right way," according to Nixon, was to work "quietly, behind the scenes, to get the French to take a reasonable position and to work to prepare the Algerians for independence." The "wrong way" was Kennedy's way, to call for independence now. That would "only harden French determination."

Eisenhower said he understood and accepted all that, but strong as Nixon's arguments were, they had to give way to even stronger ones. "The United States could not possibly maintain that freedom—independence—liberty—were necessary to us but not to others." The Republicans simply could not argue against the Algerian cause. "Perhaps," the President concluded, "Republicans might best just chide Mr. Kennedy a bit for pretending to have all the answers."[23]

SHORTLY AFTER HIS RETURN FROM AFRICA, Nixon kept his promise and met with Martin Luther King and his colleague Rev. Ralph Abernathy in his office. They discussed the Administration-sponsored 1957 civil rights bill. It was the first civil rights bill since Reconstruction, and had been greeted with great enthusiam. But in the Senate, the southern Democrats had chipped away at it, for example, insisting on a jury trial for state officials who refused to register Negroes to vote. Roughly half the Negro community had taken the attitude that the bill was so emasculated that it should be killed, but the other half thought that something was better than nothing. King and Abernathy were with the latter group. "The present bill is far better than no bill at all," King told Nixon. The bill would help get Negroes registered, King believed, and he promised to have two million Negroes on the voting roles in the South in time for the 1960 elections if it passed.

After the meeting, in a follow-up letter, King wrote: "Let me say how deeply grateful we are to you for your assiduous labor and dauntless courage in seeking to make the Civil Rights Bill a reality. This has impressed people all across the country, both negro and white. This is certainly an expression of your devotion to the highest mandates of the moral law. It is also an expression of your political wisdom. More and more the negro vote is becoming a decisive factor in national politics." King concluded with a sharp reminder: "The negro vote is the balance of power in so many important big states that one almost has to have the negro vote to win a presidential election."[24]

WHATEVER NIXON'S MOTIVATION, he was foursquare for civil rights. He played an active role as chairman of the Committee on Government Contracts. Because the committee dealt with case-by-case discrimination, because it had to wait for cases to be brought to it, and because it had no enforcement powers, progress in eliminating discrimination in employment was agonizingly slow—but there was some movement, and at least the committee was trying, which was more than could be said for any other agency of the government (although one feature of the pending bill created a Civil Rights Division in the Justice Department).

In the fifties, "civil rights" meant Negro rights. Senator Jacob Javits wanted to broaden the definition, and asked Nixon to extend the work of the Committee on Government Contracts to include action against discrimination because of age. Nixon replied that "with regard to age, as with sex or with the physically handicapped, there is a difference relating to job performance by the applicant or employee which is not present in the matter of race, religion, color or national origin." He said he knew that "the problem of the aged worker is real," but told Javits he would have to look somewhere else for help.[25]

Through the summer, Nixon was the leading champion of the civil rights bill, not so much in public as in legislative leaders' and Cabinet meetings. The House had passed the bill pretty much as the Administration drafted it, but the Senate, as noted, had badly weakened it with amendments. The immediate question was how much the Administration should insist upon in the conference committee of the two bodies, and beyond that whether or not to accept the bill if the Senate prevailed. The key issue remained the right to a jury trial for anyone cited in a civil rights case, as the Senate bill provided. The amendment was a brilliant stroke by the southerners, because the right of an accused to a trial by a jury of his peers was so deeply ingrained in the American tradition, and so sacred, that it attracted support from northern liberal Democrats.

Nixon had warned the Republican legislative leaders that such would be the case. On August 6, he gave his analysis: "The so-called liberal forces will before long start supporting jury trial." He mentioned Senator Paul Douglas and labor leaders Walter Reuther and George Meany as examples. Nixon pointed out that NAACP lobbyists "are all talking in terms of accepting something like this," because, he said, they wanted "something," and because "basically, they are pro-Democrat first, pro-civil rights second." He warned that "[Senator] Mike Mansfield [D., Mont.], Jack Kennedy, the liberal newspapers will all sing, 'this is not a bad bill.' " For his part, Nixon wanted to hold out for the original Administration proposal.[26]

A week later, at the next leader's meeting, Nixon declared, "If this bill goes to conference and dies, we have made a serious error." Therefore, he was willing to compromise. If the Justice Department could come up with an amendment on jury trial that "we all could accept, then we can take the heat and be proved right in the end." Still, he feared that if the Administration dug in and refused to accept the Senate bill (and if that bill survived the conference despite Administration objections), "then the way has all been paved in the press for the Democrats to be the heroes of civil rights and we will be painted as the villains. They will say they are willing to do a bill, but we stubbornly oppose."

But the Republican congressmen were not all that happy with the bill themselves. They had gone along, because Eisenhower demanded it, but they had a hard time seeing any profit for the Republican Party in civil rights. Nixon disagreed. He told them of Martin Luther King's promise to register two million Negroes by "touching off a massive Negro registration drive." Nixon added that King had told him that although his civil rights movement was nonpartisan, he wanted Nixon to know that both he and Abernathy had voted Republican in 1956. So there was hope that the Republicans could regain the Negro vote, lost to FDR during the Depression. Nixon warned his fellow Republicans, "As a result of all this clamor, something *is* going to happen that will get more Negroes voting."

Joe Martin of Massachusetts, the House minority leader, was clearly skeptical about Republican chances to pick up some of the Negro vote. "Yeh," he growled when Nixon finished. "I might even get 2 or 3 in my district!" [27]

On August 29, the emasculated Senate bill cleared the conference and was passed by both houses. Eisenhower had conflicting advice on whether to sign or not. Martin Luther King, the NAACP, and a reluctant Nixon all advised him to sign; Ralph Bunche, Jackie Robinson, and A. Philip Randolph were among the many Negro leaders urging a veto. Eventually, on September 9, Eisenhower did sign. Nixon received a congratulatory telegram from Clarence Mitchell, director of the Washington Bureau of the NAACP. Nixon replied, "I share your disappointment that the bill in its final form was not as strong as we would have liked. The very fact, however, that the Congress has at last taken some constructive action in this field is a significant victory for the cause in which we are all interested."[28]

In 1957, the schools were the cutting edge of the civil rights revolution. Back in 1954 the Supreme Court, in *Brown* v. *Topeka,* had ruled segregation by race in the schools unconstitutional. Enforcement of that ruling was the responsibility of the federal government, but that enforcement had been, at best, slow and hesitant, partly because the President himself did not agree with the ruling, partly because of near-fanatic white southern resistance. In 1956 Texas had challenged the Court's right to make such a ruling, and Washington's right to enforce it. Eisenhower had shrunk from the challenge. In early 1957, federal district courts had ordered the integration of specific schools, mainly in the border states but also at Central High in Little Rock, Arkansas, beginning with the opening of the new term in September. Outraged southerners, including Governor Orval Faubus of Arkansas, declared their intention to resist.

Complicating the situation, the postwar baby boom was placing unprecedented strains on the nation's schools. Local funds had run out just when they were most needed. Short of a major increase in state and local taxes, hardly likely, only the federal government could provide the necessary funds for new schools, more books and teachers, and the other inescapable expenses of educating the nation's youth. This was a problem Eisenhower had faced; his Administration was promoting an aid to education bill.

The Republicans wanted to give scholarships only, and avoid any direct grants to the states. The Democrats proposed large direct grants. Complicating everything, Adam Clayton Powell, Jr., the Negro Democratic congressman from Harlem, added an amendment denying any funds to states that practiced segregation.

"It's a tough problem," Nixon told the Republican leaders on July 23. "The people see a crisis," he continued. "It will be very bad for our candidates in close districts if they oppose any action."

He thought the Republicans ought to support some grants. "Our Washington mail doesn't reflect the very real concern of the housewives of this country," he stated.

Senator Everett Dirksen, Senate minority leader, was unimpressed. "If you ever go down this road of returning taxes to the states," he warned, "you'll never get back. The Treasury will never be safe." Charlie Halleck broke in. "Dick," he said, "you may be right, but the pressure for these grants is from teachers who are trying to get on the Federal gravy train." Halleck reminded Nixon that they had just "gotten killed by the Postal lobby" (which had won a pay increase), and began to make a prediction. "If ever the teachers get a lobby . . ." he said, and broke off, unable to find the words to express the fears that thought raised.[29]

"Well," replied Nixon, "I recognize all these factors. But I don't think any of our fellows should be under the impression that it's a popular thing to oppose Federal grants."

Eisenhower settled the matter. "I agree with Dick," he announced. He would accept a compromise that included direct federal grants, "because of the urgency of this situation." He explained that "the great problem is this, it would be a national calamity if our youngsters grew up without an education."

Charlie Halleck was not ready to give up. The schools already cost too much, he said. In Indiana, personal-property taxes were terribly high, all because of schools. Why, said Charlie, "it costs me $250 per year in taxes to own a Cadillac sedan."[30]

Eventually, in 1958, the Nixon-recommended compromise did become law, the National Defense Education Act. It provided low-cost loans for college students, fellowships for graduate students, and direct grants to the states for upgrading science and mathematics courses.

IN THE FALL OF 1957, the big story in education was also the big story in national politics, the integration crisis at Little Rock Central High. Governor Orval Faubus of Arkansas defied a court order to integrate the school; Eisenhower responded by sending in federal troops to enforce the order. Nixon was not involved in making the decision, but he was a strong supporter of it. He also responded favorably to a two-man delegation of Negro leaders (Jackie Robinson and Roy Wilkins), who asked him to urge the President to meet with a group including NAACP officials, Dr. King, Jackie Robinson, and A. Philip Randolph. They pointed out that the President had met with Senator Richard Russell and Governor Faubus, and asked for a chance to give the Negro point of view on Little Rock. The delegation came to Nixon, Rowland Evans reported in the

Herald Tribune (in a story he cleared with Nixon's office), because "Nixon is correctly regarded as the spearhead of Republican efforts to capture a larger share of the Negro vote in 1958 and 1960." Nixon was enthusiastic about a meeting, and promised to do all he could to persuade the President to invite the leaders to his office. Alas, the President, never comfortable with Negroes, could not find the time.[31]

Still Nixon kept at it. He wrote long letters to southern newspaper editors who were up in arms over the Little Rock "invasion," pleading for common sense. Each letter was personal, relating to the particular situation, but each contained some form paragraphs. The key one read, "Fundamentally, over and beyond the legal aspects, I believe the issue is a moral one, and is of such transcendent importance that all Americans must face it. Moreover, we must work out ways so that this tremendous change, which affects all aspects of life, can be made without completely disrupting or threatening the very fabric of our system of government and, more important, the relations between the races."[32]

Republicans throughout the South wrote Nixon to protest in the strongest terms against the President on Little Rock. Most of them said that the chances of breaking up the Solid South and breathing life into the Republican Party there had been set back by twenty years or more. In his form reply, Nixon admitted "that we have suffered a temporary set-back in our efforts to establish a true two-party system in the South," but insisted that a great opportunity now presented itself to the despairing southern Republicans. "You and other Republican leaders in the South can do much to help provide a rallying point for those men and women of moderate and conservative inclinations who are opposed to extremism in any form," he wrote. "They will soon come to realize that their most effective political vehicle is the Republican party, both nationally and locally."[33]

On a personal level, Nixon's daughters attended an integrated school, and he had refused to sign a restrictive covenant when he bought his new home.

IN AUGUST, the President wrote a six-page single-spaced letter to Meade Alcorn, the new chairman of the RNC, on the subject of how to revive the fortunes of the Republican Party. After many detailed suggestions, Eisenhower concluded, "I suggest a consultation with Dick Nixon whenever you get a chance. He has a remarkably clear conception of what is necessary."[34] Alcorn took the advice. Nixon's conception was organize, organize, organize.

In Eisenhower's second term, as in the first, Nixon was the

liaison man between the Administration and the party. He took on, as a regular chore, the defense of Administration policies from the grumbling of unhappy Republicans. He had a basic mailing list of 663 prominent Republicans across the nation, who got copies of his speeches and statements, all of which extolled Eisenhower's middle-of-the-road approach to taxes, defense spending, civil rights, and the other issues. When the Administration proposed its budget in the spring for the coming fiscal year, Nixon got a deluge of letters from conservatives complaining about the deficit, and the absence of a tax cut. Nixon developed a long form letter defending the budget, explaining the need for the expenditures and the irresponsibility of cutting taxes when the budget was unbalanced.[35]

KEEPING DISGRUNTLED REPUBLICANS IN LINE, making speeches at Republican meetings, giving advice on politics to the legislative leaders and the Cabinet, exposing discrimination through the Government Contracts Committee, and representing the United States in faraway places were all important tasks, but by no means were they sufficiently significant in size or scope to satisfy Nixon. He had energy to spare, he wanted to be involved, he had much to offer, and he evidently was beginning to feel the need for a little administrative experience.

On February 2, Dulles recorded in his memcon of their discussion that day, Nixon "indicated he would like to undertake some substantive task, preferably involving little publicity. He had in mind such tasks as disarmament, international economic development, or possibly such a task as the development of the OAS [Organization of American States]. I said that I was confident that things of this sort would come along and promised the Vice President that I would be on the lookout for opportunities of public service of this character which he might perform."[36]

As a scout, Dulles wasn't much good. The most he could produce in the next six months for Nixon was a vice-chairmanship for the Federal Service Campaign for National Health Agencies (a fund-raising effort) and a spot on the President's Council on Youth Fitness.[37]

In September, Nixon pressed Dulles on finding something for him to do. Dulles talked to the President "about giving Nixon a greater role in preparing our Congressional plans." Later, over the telephone, he told Nixon, "I suggested we could do a better job in mapping out the substance and general strategy and tactics of presentation. I thought if the VP could take a leading role in this respect, it would be a great advantage to the program. I said that, for example, on MSA [Mutual Security Administration—i.e., foreign aid] it might be desirable to break the program up and present it in parts instead of a total. Military assistance and defense support might actually be included in the Defense budget."

Dulles told Nixon that after some reflection, "the President indicated he was prepared to talk with the VP along these lines." But he was unsure of where Nixon would fit in, and afraid of a hostile reaction from his congressional liaison group (meaning Adams and Persons) if Nixon started coordinating directly between the Administration and Congress. Dulles continued, "I said I did not of course think in terms of the VP doing liaison work and dealing with members of Congress, but merely functioning at the upper strategy level. He should coordinate the entire program." [38]

When Eisenhower agreed, and said he would draft a letter to Nixon outlining his duties, Dulles called Nixon, who was in White Sulpher Springs, and told him the news. He wanted Nixon to return to Washington immediately, because the President was leaving in the morning for his summer vacation. Nixon said he would try, then mentioned that he was surprised the President accepted the idea so quickly. What about the White House group? Dulles assured him that he had told the President there would be no problem. [39]

Nixon made it to the meeting. Eisenhower explained his thinking: Nixon should assist in the preparation of the legislative program insofar as it related to national security matters. This would include State, USIA, Defense, and others. Dulles—surprised at hearing his department mentioned—jumped in to say "that the Vice President would not be expected to play any role in terms of actually discussing with individual Congressmen the question of how they would vote and persuading them." Nor, he hastened to add, would Nixon's new role "interfere at all with the direct dealing of the President with Congressional leaders." Eisenhower nodded.

Nixon said he "would be glad to undertake this function. He felt that his Congressional experience and constitutional role plus his attendance at NSC meetings and his trips abroad, etc., enabled him perhaps to make a contribution."

All this business about a role for Nixon was as vague as it sounded, indeed it was empty of content. Neither Dulles nor any of the other department heads involved were ever going to surrender to the Vice-President any of their power, much less allow him to be the coordinating agent between them. Nor was the White House staff ever going to cooperate in such an experiment. So many people with turf to defend left Nixon with no new ground to occupy.

Dulles made this brutally clear after the meeting. He gave Nixon a ride in his limousine. "We briefly discussed matters of procedure. I indicated that I thought that the meetings on this subject should normally be held at the State Department."[40] Not, that is, in the Vice-President's office. Like every Washingtonian, Nixon knew that he who hosts a meeting, runs it.

Eisenhower's letter to Nixon on the subject of his new role was as poorly worded as the whole idea was bad. The trouble was obvious—one simply could not suddenly inject the Vice-President into basic governmental organization relationships. Thus Eisenhower's letter contained such vapid observations as "there is an interrelationship between expenditures and taxation, and the domestic economy." After three pages of such stuff, Eisenhower got to the point. "Consequently, while the main mission I would see for you would be the consultation with the State Department in helping them plan their legislative presentations, you would at the same time find it needful to coordinate with Governor Adams and the liaison group here in the White House so that the entire legislative program could be presented in the most advantageous manner." Then, realizing that he was trying to make a point that just wasn't there, Eisenhower concluded, "I hope you see what I am getting at, and I assure you that both Foster Dulles and Governor Adams would welcome your thinking and your help on such matters as these."[41]

The facts were, however, that there was no role for Nixon, nor could there be. The nature of the Constitution and the Vice-Presidency precluded it. What Nixon had been groping for, a position somewhat akin to that of an executive assistant, in which he would stand between the President on one side, and the Cabinet and Congress on the other, cannot exist in the American system.

As Nixon quickly found out. On September 30 he went to the Bureau of the Budget to begin preparation of next year's legislative program affecting foreign affairs. He was told that this was the responsibility of the Department of State and of the Bureau of the Budget. He protested that he had "a special dispensation from the President this year in relation to this matter." The Bureau told him that was very nice, but that the responsibility belonged to it. Nixon bowed out as gracefully as he could.[42]

NIXON'S POSITION gave him no real role in the Administration, but he had to support it, even when he sharply disagreed with policy and played no part in the making of it. Nuclear policy, for example, was made exclusively by Eisenhower, Strauss, and the JCS. Even Dulles was excluded from the key discussions, which took place in the privacy of the Oval Office. Recalling FDR's neglect of Truman, and Truman's consequent unpreparedness for office, Eisenhower wanted to keep Nixon informed—but he did not want him participating in policy discussions.

Strauss, on the other hand, aware that Nixon might become President at some unforeseen moment, did want Nixon involved in the nuclear program. Earlier, Strauss had invited Eisenhower to come to Nevada to watch a test of a nuclear warhead. Eisenhower had been interested, but Hagerty convinced the President it would have bad public-relations repercussions.[43] In May 1957, Strauss invited the Vice-President. Nixon was keen to go and sent a letter of acceptance, but someone—perhaps Eisenhower himself, or Hagerty—vetoed the idea.*[44]

ON OCTOBER 4, 1957, the Soviet Union fired into orbit the world's first man-made satellite, named Sputnik. This impressive achievement came as a distinct surprise to Eisenhower and his Administration. It created a crisis of confidence in American science and technology and education, and generated an overwhelming public demand that the country do something, anything, to catch up.

Sputnik created an almost panic situation within the United States. Everything seemed to be in crisis—including Richard Nixon's future. Even before Sputnik, the Democrats had been attacking the Republicans for Eisenhower's defense policy, charging that the President had allowed his desire for a balanced budget to override his responsibility for the nation's defense. Sputnik, by demonstrating the Russian lead in rockets, seemed to prove the point, and provided the Democrats with the first solid issue to use against Eisenhower since 1952. Within days, indeed within hours, of Sputnik's first orbit, it was obvious that Eisenhower's reluctance to spend money on defense was going to be a major issue in the 1960 election.

Eisenhower's response was to downplay Sputnik and insist that America's defenses were perfectly adequate. From Nixon's point of view, while such an attitude might work for General Ike, it could never work for him. People who trusted Eisenhower because he was who he was could not be expected to extend that same trust to Nixon. For Nixon it was imperative that the United States do something spectacular in weapons technology before the 1960 election. In addition to the politics of the thing, Nixon was genuinely worried about the apparent Russian lead. But it was all

---

* So far as this author is aware, no President has ever watched a nuclear explosion.

very frustrating, because Eisenhower could not be convinced that he should be excited, or that he should start some crash programs to catch up, and Nixon obviously could not go off on his own.

The day after Sputnik went up, Nixon told his staff that he was attending an NSC meeting in two days to discuss Sputnik. "Until then we will not have a party line," he told Rose Woods, who put it out in a staff memo. "I want to get it directly from the President so that we don't go off at all ends and will give you the word then." Meanwhile, the staff should admit to inquiring reporters that the United States was "too weak in basic scientific research," but that the reason the country was behind in missiles was "because the preceding Administration put all their eggs in one basket (the long-range bomber) and only when the Eisenhower Administration came in did we try to catch up on the missile program." Finally, Nixon told the staff to "take a crack" at persuading reporters that the problem was interservice rivalry—each service was conducting its own missile development program, and there was no coordination of effort.[45]

Backbiting and blame fixing dominated the news. The Army blamed the Navy, the Air Force blamed the Army, and so on. The Democrats now had their own version of the classic Republican question, "Who lost China?" Democrats demanded, "Who lost to Sputnik?" On October 9, Nixon talked to Dulles about how to answer. Dulles made a memcon. "N asked for confirmation of the fact that the missile field had been almost wholly neglected by the Democrats. I said this was the case and contrasted greatly with the Soviet activity in this field. I recalled the knowledge I had obtained in Moscow in 1947 of the VIP treatment being given to the German missile scientists. I said I thought we should get some real documentation on the lack of support prior to 1953, and N said he thought he could get this information."[46]

A week later, they again talked over the telephone. Dulles' secretary took notes. "N said between 1946–1952 the spending was for airplanes rather than rockets. The satellite program was treated as a 5th cousin because the military were not too keen about it nor was there keenness among some in the Executive. N said we can tear the Democrats to pieces. The data is classified and Defense was reluctant to give it but N has it. While the Soviets were making a big push we were doing nothing."[47]

The problem with that line of defense was that neither had the Eisenhower Administration done very much, as Nixon well knew. By letting each service work on its own missile, Eisenhower had practically guaranteed a low-level and diluted effort. He had rejected occasional suggestions that he concentrate the research and development in one organization, under a czar, on the model of the Manhattan Project and its director, General Leslie Groves, partly because he thought such an approach would cost more rather than less, partly because he believed competition would spur progress. Even after Sputnik, the President resisted the idea of a czar.

Nixon was in the forefront of those pushing for a centralized, and much expanded, organization. Just saying that it was all the Democrats' fault was not going to help Nixon much in the 1960 election; for himself, and for the nation, he wanted the United States well out in front before 1960. He discussed the approach to take with Dulles. "N said what is required is for us to take the initiative before there is a Congressional investigation. They agreed it will be rough. N said the best argument is if Congress says we are behind we say then we must pool the best brains. The Sec said we have to. You do this automatically in case of war." [48]

Later, again over the telephone, they talked about the czar idea. "N thinks it would get support—it is imaginative. They both think that balancing the budget should not have priority." [49] That was the heresy of heresies, so far as Eisenhower was concerned. Except when the nation was actually at war, the President could see no justification whatsoever for an unbalanced budget, and indeed felt that federal deficits were as dangerous to the health of the Republic as were Russian missiles. He was virtually alone in holding such views, but he held to them steadfastly until the day he left office—much to the dismay of Richard Nixon, who knew he would have to run in 1960 on the Eisenhower record.

Although Nixon felt the President was not spending nearly enough money on rockets, and began saying so—guardedly—in public, he was solidly with the President on a related issue, cutting taxes. Eisenhower had given the country a big tax cut in 1954, but the Republicans—especially the small-business men (the ones in Southern California bombarded Nixon with letters on the subject) —wanted more. On October 11, a week after Sputnik, Nixon told the Cabinet "we need to remember, when we hear this clamor of cutting taxes, that our people will be urging it for political reasons." But Nixon felt that, to the contrary, it would be bad politics. "I think we would make a great mistake if we encouraged, even privately, any expectation of a tax cut." More money would have to be spent on missiles and defense generally. "We must be in a position to take a strong line against a tax cut so as to maintain a balanced budget and to provide security." [50]

In California the defense industry, then in its infancy, was eager to get to work. On October 14, Frank Jameson, one of Nixon's original supporters, called Nixon's office and left a message. "He feels that you should champion the cause of vigorous thinking and action in this field. He is willing to fly to Washington to see you and to bring several people who are actively engaged in missile research and development and who would provide more detailed information." Nixon replied, "Put him off right now. Tell him I am having great numbers of people talking to me about missiles at this time."[51]

Through leaks to selected reporters, Nixon let it be known that he was "taking a stronger line on the satellite situation than some people in the Administration."[52] "Some people" meant the President, who continued to downplay Sputnik. In response to almost irresistible demands that he spend more, for fallout shelters, for bombers, for bombs, for more research and development of missiles and satellites, Eisenhower said there was nothing to worry about. Only Eisenhower could have gotten away with saying no; his unique prestige as a military leader among his countrymen made him unassailable on the question of national defense.[53]

Nevertheless, Nixon disagreed. On November 6, he had a talk with Arthur Larson, who was writing a speech for the President on defense. Nixon told Larson that the main thing was to make sure this speech could not be characterized as "too little and too late." Therefore, he wanted the speech to emphasize the importance of "rushing through the Defense Department whatever is necessary." To save money, the policy had been to allow no overtime work on any of the rocket projects. Nixon wanted that policy changed. He also wanted the speech to call for "a missile manager, a completely new set-up in which someone is going to manage the money for all missile programs."

That afternoon, Nixon flew down to Key Biscayne for a vacation at Rebozo's place. When he arrived, he called Rose Woods with a message for Larson. He had been thinking on the plane, Nixon said, and he wanted Larson to have the President say: "Regardless of the cost in money, or effort, I intend to see that the United States maintains superior strength so that we can always be in a position to defend our freedom without compromising with slavery."[54]

Instead, the President said the opposite. "Hasty and extraordinary effort under the impetus of sudden fear . . . cannot provide for an adequate answer to the threat." Additional expenditures, at levels the Democrats (and Nixon) were calling for, were "unjustifiable."[55]

Adding to Nixon's frustration, he continued to hear from his Southern California friends, wanting to know why they could not have a tax cut. In many cases they were the same men who were eagerly anticipating a great boom in R&D for missile spending in the state.[56]

CALIFORNIA WAS NIXON'S BASE, but California politics represented more of a snare for him than an opportunity. The state's size insured it a spot on the national ticket in 1960, but it also insured a split within the Republican Party, generally along north-south lines. Further, both the senior senator, Knowland, and the governor, Goodwin Knight, both Republicans, had presidential ambitions. In pursuit of that goal, Knowland had announced that he would not seek re-election to the Senate, but rather was going to run for governor in 1958 (and presumably as the favorite son and head of the California delegation to the 1960 convention). At this point, Knight dug in, saying he had no intention of giving up his job and would be a candidate for re-election.

In April, after a tour of the state, Bob Finch reported on all this in a telephone call to Rose Woods. She wrote a memo on the call: "On the governorship thing—Goodie is fighting back pretty effectively and is beginning to convince some prominent Republicans that a primary fight would be disastrous—Goodie is of course trying to create the impression that RN goes along with him. Also, story is going around that RN let Tom Dewey know that he was for Goodie. It looks like Goodie will get the support of the Hearst papers. More and more people are looking to RN to straighten this thing out. Several people have come to Bob [Finch] asking him to suggest to RN to try to persuade Knowland not to resign and to stay in the Senate. Problem is to try to keep RN's name out of this thing altogether—obviously he has to be protected."[57]

Nixon did stay out of it, as long as he could, but neither Knowland nor Knight would give way. In August, Nixon wrote his old friend and supporter Frank Jorgensen of San Francisco, a power in Northern California Republican circles. "I am inclined to think," Nixon wrote, "that it would be well for some of our friends to get in on the ground floor in the Knowland campaign." Nixon said he would be in California after Congress adjourned, "and at that time I shall have just as many meetings as I can on an off-the-record basis with our friends in various parts of the State." He was sure Knowland would not change his mind, and saw therein an opportunity for Southern California to demand the Republican nominations for U.S. Senate, and the state's lieutenant governor and attorney general.[58]

Northern California was not going to give up all those positions without a struggle. The current attorney general was Edmund G. ("Pat") Brown, but he had announced his candidacy for the governorship on the Democratic ticket. Two Republicans, Caspar Weinberger from San Francisco and Pat Hillings from Whittier, aspired to the post of attorney general. Weinberger had an outstanding record as an assemblyman and was one of the most popular Republicans in Northern California. Hillings, who held Nixon's old congressional seat, was a close friend of Nixon's. Both men wanted Nixon's support, but Nixon stayed neutral.

He also stayed neutral in the governor's race. In August, when Knowland began to press him for an endorsement, Nixon told Jorgensen, "Under no circumstances should our friends make any commitments to Knowland at this time. Under no circumstances should they even talk to him. Let Knowland come to you." [59] Privately, Nixon thought that Knowland had made a serious error in calling for a right-to-work bill in California. He felt that "the labor leaders are much more subtle than they were in 1950," when it was still possible "to tag our opponents as stooges for labor bosses." By 1958, that would be difficult, and besides, right-to-work was so controversial that it ought to be straddled, rather than embraced. [60]

As letters came in urging Nixon to exert his leadership and settle the Knowland-Knight contest, he remained determinedly neutral. "As you know," his form-letter reply read, "I have publicly stated that I will not personally endorse a candidate for Governor at this time [a year ahead of the election]." But, he said, "it would be out of character for me to refuse to indicate at some time before the primary the man for whom, as a California voter, I, personally, will cast my ballot." Meanwhile, "I do not believe it would be proper for me to dictate to my friends as to which candidate they should support." He realized that "there are those who believe one candidate rather than the other might prove to be more helpful to me in 1960," but insisted that "all of my friends make their individual decisions as to which man will make the best governor, and do so without regard to the effect on my own situation." [61]

Whoever won, Nixon wanted to reduce the governor's power, specifically with regard to the California Republican Party, which was dominated by Republican assemblymen and state senators, who in turn were beholden to the governor. Nixon urged his supporters to make their financial contributions to the Los Angeles County Republicans (where Bob Finch had recently taken over), not to the state organization. Thus in October, he wrote Jack Warner, of Warner Brothers, to thank him for his generous assistance "in the financial campaign for the Republican Party in Southern California." [62]

MORE IMMEDIATELY IMPORTANT TO NIXON than 1960 was the state of the President's health. Inevitably, Nixon had to think about it, as did the President himself. Eisenhower was particularly worried about the line of succession in the event he died or had to resign. Nixon would become President, of course, but that would put Sam Rayburn, as Speaker of the House, next in line.

On February 8, Attorney General Brownell led a long, detailed Cabinet discussion on the Constitution and the Presidency, covering such subjects as succession, presidential disability, and who should decide when the President was incapable of carrying out his responsibilities, or indeed when he was fit to resume them. It was all theoretical talk and got nowhere. As Nixon observed, any attempt to amend the Constitution to put the Secretary of State next in line in place of the Speaker of the House (as Eisenhower wanted to do) "would be taken by the Democrats as a slap at Sam Rayburn." So nothing was done.[63] Anyway, Eisenhower was feeling fine so there was no sense of urgency.

Nine months later, the afternoon of November 25, 1957, Nixon received a telephone call from Sherman Adams. He asked Nixon to come to the White House "right away." When Nixon arrived, Adams was blunt: "The President has suffered a stroke."

"How serious is his condition?" Nixon asked.

"We'll know more in the morning," Adams replied. "Right now he's more confused and disoriented than anything else. . . . This is a terribly, terribly difficult thing to handle." Then he looked directly at Nixon. "You may be President in twenty-four hours."[64]

Adams did not tell Nixon that the President, two hours after his stroke and to the horror of his doctor, his wife, his son, and Adams himself, had appeared in the doorway of his bedroom to say that he felt fine and intended to preside at a state dinner that evening. Mamie insisted that he could not possibly do that. He tried to argue with her, but he lost his temper and his words came out as gibberish. He couldn't find the ones he wanted to say, and those he did use were scrambled. Finally Mamie persuaded him to go back to bed. As he left the room, he mumbled, "If I cannot attend to my duties, I am simply going to give up this job. Now that is all there is to it."[65]

At Adams' suggestion, Nixon substituted for Eisenhower at the state dinner. The next day, the two men called on the President, still resting in his bed. Nixon assured him that the dinner had gone well and offered to substitute for the President at a NATO conference scheduled for mid-December. Eisenhower felt all right— there was no pain and his pulse was normal—although he still had difficulty with words. But there was no more talk of a resignation.

The following day, the President undertook a light work load, meeting with Adams and signing some papers, in an attempt to calm a jittery press corps and reassure a nervous nation. Nixon, meanwhile, at Hagerty's suggestion, held a press conference in the White House—his first. He was calm, collected, very much in control. James Reston, who covered the conference for *The New York Times*, opened his account, "Vice President Richard M. Nixon emerged today as the Administration spokesman." Reston thought that "he seemed slightly nervous at first in the face of a battery of camera men, but handled a wide range of questions with skill and confidence."

In his summation, Reston went further: "This was clearly a more assured young man than the Nixon of twenty-six months ago who stayed in the background at Denver, while Governor Adams presided over the Administration during the early weeks of the President's heart attack. Nixon even looks different. He seems to have lost a little weight. His hair is cut closer on the sides and on top. His speech is more vivid and articulate and his manner more patient and courteous."

Nixon's main theme was business as usual and nothing to worry about. He opened with a statement: "I would like to scotch once and for all any reports that the President is in a condition that would make it necessary for him to consider resigning." The reporters treated him gently, even apologizing for some of their questions. "No questions are embarrassing," Nixon assured them.

What they wanted to know was, Who's in charge? Nixon insisted that it was a team effort. He had called a Cabinet meeting that morning, he said, but neither he nor anyone else had "presided," and all discussions had been routine. No decision had been made as to the NATO head-of-state meeting, but, "I would say that the President is champing at the bit. He is very anxious to get back to his office." Regular Cabinet and NSC meetings would go on, beginning Monday, December 2, after the Thanksgiving holiday and weekend. The *Times* headline read, "NIXON NOW SPEAKS FOR WHITE HOUSE." [66]

The following day, Thanksgiving, Eisenhower insisted on taking Mamie to church, to show himself in public. On Friday, the Eisenhowers drove up to Gettysburg for the weekend. He was recuperating nicely, his speech almost recovered. But he lost his temper when he read the Sunday papers. Walter Lippmann recommended that he delegate his powers to Nixon; there were a number of editorials and columns urging him to resign. On the radio, Drew Pearson made such an appeal and, to Nixon's vast amusement, went on to say what a wonderful man Dick Nixon was. The effect of all this on Eisenhower was to strengthen his determination to take up his full duties on Monday morning.

Eisenhower's determination frightened his aides and his doctors, who wanted him to stay in Gettysburg and rest for at least a few more days. Persons called Dulles at 1:42 P.M. to tell the Secretary about Eisenhower's decision to return to work. Dulles said, "That in itself is a very bad sign, the fact that he does not realize that he needs rest." He told Persons, "Someone must get control of the situation." [67]

Hanging up, Dulles called Nixon. As his note taker recorded the conversation, "Sec said we are liable to run into a situation where the President is incapable of acting and does not realize it. Sec said he was very much disturbed about the situation." Nixon said, "It looks like his judgment is not good and the people around him are not able to exercise judgment or control." Dulles replied "that for the first time he got the impression that the President was sensitive about the VP," but assured Nixon that he "had handled this thing to perfection."

Inevitably, on both men's minds was the question, Should we declare him incompetent? Dulles complained again about the "lack of judgment" of Persons and the other aides, but pointed out that if he and Nixon tried to overrule the decision and prevent Eisenhower from returning to work on Monday, "then that is a reproduction of the [Woodrow] Wilson problem, jealousy and usurpation of power." Dulles finally broke the tension by mentioning Drew Pearson's praise of Nixon, the very idea of which gave both men a good laugh. [68]

The following day, Eisenhower presided at the Cabinet and NSC meetings in Washington. Afterward, he had a long private meeting with Dulles, going over various matters. He said he wanted to go to the NATO meeting, and Dulles did not protest— in fact the Secretary encouraged him. It was Eisenhower, not Dulles, who brought up a possible resignation. The President said that if, three weeks after his attack, he was not able to go to Europe, "it would in his opinion raise a serious question as to whether he should not then 'abdicate.' " [69]

After Dulles left, Eisenhower met with Bill Rogers, who recently had replaced Brownell as Attorney General. Rogers later gave Nixon a memo on the conversation. Rogers assured the President that his staff and the Cabinet could shoulder much more of the work load, thereby easing the pressure on him. Eisenhower agreed. The President also indicated that he felt there was no need for so many formal meetings of the Cabinet and the NSC. Furthermore, he indicated, although indirectly, he thought there was no need to hold meetings when he was not able to be present, and even more that meetings should be called only by the President.

He told Rogers that it "was not necessary" for the staff, or Nixon, to call for meetings, and explained "this is in your [Nixon's and the Cabinet's] best interests too because of the possible impression of stepping in and exerting authority."

Eisenhower, in short, was more than a bit put out at Dulles and Nixon. He knew that Dulles had complained to Persons about the President's "bad judgment," and may have known about the Dulles-Nixon conversation in which they had (very guardedly) skirted around the subject of declaring the President incompetent. As Rogers recorded it for Nixon, Eisenhower "resented that we had called the Cabinet meeting and Security Council meeting and undertaken other activities in his absence." [70]

Eisenhower's irritation with Nixon was unfair, because Eisenhower himself had urged Adams and Nixon, the day after the stroke, to carry on with all regular business, and said specifically that if they had a Cabinet or NSC meeting he "would try to drop by." But when the power of the Presidency is at stake, everyone— most of all the President—gets sensitive and intense. Everyone fears and anticipates, as Dulles so neatly put it, "jealousy and usurpation." The wonder is not that Eisenhower got a bit irritated with Nixon, but rather that their relationship suffered no permanent damage.

IN THE EVENT, Eisenhower attended the NATO meeting, and there was no more talk about resignation, but still Eisenhower's stroke raised some grave questions surrounding the problem of possible incapacity, either physical or, worse, mental. What would happen if the President were in such bad condition that he was unable to recognize his own incapacity and therefore unable to delegate power to Nixon? What would happen if the President went clear out of his mind? What would happen if he were in an automobile accident and in an extended coma? What would happen if . . . The list was endless. The Constitution was silent.

Even before his stroke, Eisenhower had had Brownell working on the problem; after the stroke, he put the new Attorney General, William Rogers, on it. But neither man could think of anything suitable in the way of legislation (because, Nixon believed, "the Democratic congressional leaders would not approve any plan which might put Richard Nixon in the White House before the 1960 election").[71]

In January 1958, Eisenhower talked to Nixon about the problem. He then decided he would write a draft letter of resignation "to be effective when five people of his own choosing should decide it should be so." For the five, he suggested the Attorney General, the Senate and House majority leaders, the Surgeon General, and the Secretary of State. The letter would state that in the event of a presidential disability, "the committee could decide that the Vice-President takes over, and equally, could decide at a later time when the President was able to resume his duties."[72]

The President told his secretary, Ann Whitman, that "I am willing personally to test the legality of this," but it was clearly a terrible idea. Two Democrats, two Republicans, one doctor—the chances of their coming to a unanimous decision in what would inevitably be a highly charged political situation were almost nil, and a split verdict would surely lead to a constitutional crisis of the first magnitude.

Eisenhower soon recognized the dangers in his committee idea, and a month later called Rogers and Nixon into the Oval Office. He said he thought he had "licked the problem." He then handed them each a copy of a letter from the President to the Vice-President.

The letter said that in the event the President was disabled, and aware of it, he would inform Nixon and Nixon would take over. But if the President were so disabled he was incapable of recognizing it, Nixon would "decide upon the devolution of the powers and duties of the Office and would serve as Acting President until the inability had ended." Eisenhower expressed the "hope" that Nixon would consult with Dulles, Adams, and the doctors before acting, but emphasized that Nixon would be "the individual explicitly and exclusively responsible. . . . You will decide. The decision will be yours only." By the same token, "I will be the one to determine if and when it is proper for me to resume the full exercise of the powers and duties of the Office."

Eisenhower had encouraged Congress to act, either through legislation or a constitutional amendment, but nothing had happened. Therefore, he wrote Nixon, "in view of our mutual confidence and friendship," he had decided to make this agreement in advance, so that "you could without personal or official embarrassment, make any decisions that seemed to you proper in cases where my ability to discharge my powers and duties may be in serious question."

Eisenhower wanted and expected a commonsense approach from Nixon. He wrote that Nixon would take over presidential powers "only when you feel it necessary. I have no fear that you, for any fleeting or inconsequential purpose, would do so and thereby create confusion in the government. Circumstances would have to guide you . . . and if emergency demanded, you would have to act promptly."[73]

"THERE IS ALWAYS THE POSSIBILITY THAT, as in the cases of Garfield and Wilson, I might, without warning, become personally incapable of making a decision at the moment when it should be made." Eisenhower was referring to James A. Garfield, who was shot in 1881, a few months after taking office, and lingered for seventy-nine days before succumbing. In those seventy-nine days, he signed only one paper, and suffered from hallucinations. The doctors felt, however, that he would recover, which prevented Vice-President Chester Arthur from stepping in as Acting President. The Cabinet split. Some thought Arthur should take the oath (others argued that his vice-presidential oath was sufficient) and become Chief Executive until Garfield's recovery. Others argued that once Arthur was President, he was President—the Attorney General's opinion was that Garfield could not regain the office even if he regained his health. (Sam Rayburn had the same view in 1957.) Somehow the government muddled through the Garfield crisis, but that was in the 1880s. In the nuclear age, it would be impossible.

Wilson, in the fall of 1919, was felled by a stroke, which left the left side of his body paralyzed. For six weeks, he was critically ill and unable to function. For eight months, he could not attend a Cabinet meeting. Only his wife and his doctor had access to him. Mrs. Wilson decided what problems the President should deal with. Secretary of State Lansing took it upon himself to call twenty-one Cabinet meetings for "informal discussions." When Wilson had recovered slightly, he sent a stinging rebuke to Lansing—"No one but the President has the right to summon the heads of the executive departments into conference . . ."—and asked for Lansing's resignation.[74]

In Wilson's case, the results were serious. His illness coincided with one of the great debates in American history: the question was ratification of the Treaty of Versailles and with it American entry into the League of Nations. During the critical months of the debate, the pro-Treaty/pro-League side had no leadership, except for Wilson's stubborn refusal (passed on by Mrs. Wilson) to even consider compromise. Had Vice-President Thomas R. Marshall taken over as President, it is possible to conjecture that he would have agreed to a compromise that would have led to ratification. In that event, the United States would have been a founding member of the League of Nations. With what results, no one could ever know, but surely it would have made some difference.

EISENHOWER INTENDED TO KEEP HIS AGREEMENT with Nixon a secret. He kept one copy of the letter, gave one to Nixon, a third to Dulles, and a fourth to Rogers. No one else knew of its existence.[75]

But the Presidency cannot be handed over in secret. Reporters pressed him on the problem of succession in the event of incapacity. At a February 26 press conference, he assured the press that the problem was taken care of, that there would be no "period of uncertainty," and that it was all spelled out in writing. That led to a clamor for the letter itself that could not be denied. On March 3, Hagerty released the three key action paragraphs of the letter.

Disclosure led to mass confusion. The letter raised all sorts of questions. Would a bill signed by Nixon as Acting President become law? Or could it be challenged in the courts? Could a Nixon appointment to a federal position be challenged? Could the appointee's actions be subject to lawsuits? If Nixon vetoed a bill, he would be in direct conflict with Congress, which might then challenge him. Would a Nixon executive order to a department head be binding? What if a Cabinet member chose to disregard it?

Could there even be such a position as Acting President? Sam Rayburn, leader of those who were saying no, could cite Daniel Webster on the question. Webster said (at the time William Henry Harrison died and John Tyler took over; Webster was Secretary of State) that the powers and the office of the Presidency were indivisible, and that in succeeding to one the Vice-President succeeded to both. Rayburn could also cite a federal judge at the time of the Garfield case: "I start with this conclusion: that whenever the Vice President gets lawfully into the Presidency, the President gets lawfully out of it. There cannot be two lawful Presidents at the same time. . . . And when the President gets lawfully out there is no way in which he can get in again." [76]

The Twenty-fifth Amendment (adopted in 1967) is supposed to answer these questions, but God help the Republic if it ever has to be tested. On the problem of a President who is incapacitated and does not realize it, the amendment brings the Vice-President, the Cabinet, "or such other body as Congress may by law provide," the President pro tempore of the Senate, and the Speaker of the House into the decision to declare him incompetent and replace him with the Vice-President. At that point "Congress shall decide the issue" by a two-thirds vote (which would, not incidentally, be sufficient to impeach the President and remove him from office). The possible contretemps are endless.

Eisenhower wanted to make things simple. The reporters wanted to explore the various possibilities. Eisenhower would not let them. At a March 5 press conference, his letter to Nixon was the lead topic. Robert Spivack got started on a question "in connection with this pact between yourself and the Vice President. . . ." Eisenhower cut him off: "No, it isn't a pact." Spivack tried again: "Well, agreement or . . ." Eisenhower again interrupted, to explain once and for all: "We are not trying to rewrite the Constitution. We are trying just to say that we are trying to carry out what normal humans of good faith having some confidence in each other would do in accordance with the language of the Constitution. . . . I believe this: as long as the Vice President, as acting President, is carrying or discharging the powers and the duties of the office, he has to do anything that the President would be required to do at that time."[77]

That last phrase was the key one. Eisenhower was a soldier before he became a politician, and he wanted a clear chain of command, so that there would never be a period, however short, in which there was some question about who was the Commander in Chief. Thus he concluded his four-page letter to Nixon, "The existence of this agreement . . . will remove any necessity . . . on the part of friends and staffs to impede the right and authority of the Vice President" to act in an emergency.[78]

THE PRESIDENT'S LETTER was a most remarkable grant of power. Eisenhower had come to it reluctantly—he would have preferred a legislative or a constitutional amendment solution, and failing that would have liked to have brought in the Cabinet on the decision. But, as had been the case with the selection of his running mate in 1956, when he finally had to decide, he chose Nixon. It was a tremendous vote of confidence, both in Nixon's good judgment and in his ability to lead the nation.

CHAPTER TWENTY-ONE

A CONTINENT
FOR A THEATER
South America 1958

NIXON SPENT THE FIRST COUPLE OF WEEKS OF 1958 in Key Biscayne, at Bebe Rebozo's home, leaving Pat and the girls in Washington. He did some swimming, and a bit of fishing, but mainly he spent long periods walking alone along the beach, brooding, in what was becoming a habitual practice for him. Rebozo was always there when wanted, always out of sight when Nixon wished to be alone. After returning to Washington, Nixon wrote a note to Rebozo, thanking him for setting things up on such short notice. "One of the reasons why I enjoy myself so much and relax so completely in Florida is because everything goes so smoothly and back of it all is your guiding hand." [1] That spring, Rebozo bought a new house on a stretch of beach that Nixon particularly liked, one where Rebozo often anchored his boat so that Nixon could swim or walk. Rebozo passed the word via an aide that "the Boss and Pat should know that the place was theirs anytime they wanted to use it." Two weeks later, Nixon flew down alone for four days of solitude. [2]

In Washington, Nixon was notorious for his frenetic schedule and inability to relax. Aside from the Florida trips, his recreation came on the golf course, and even there politics was usually the subject of conversation. He continued to read the sports pages avidly, and with that marvelous memory of his he absorbed all the numbers. Batting averages, yards gained per carry, earned run averages, pass completion percentage, the whole never-ending stream of numbers was to Nixon what the Western novels were to Eisenhower, the perfect relaxation. Through the sports pages, Nixon could escape to a world in which there were no moral qualms and no one's motives were ever questioned. In addition, Nixon, like millions of his fellow countrymen, was a hero-worshiper, standing in awe of those who could do so well what he could never do at all, playing games for a living, testing themselves daily in the arena.

When Nixon took his daughters to a Washington Senators baseball game, a sports reporter for the Washington *Post* wrote a column on the Vice-President's detailed knowledge of the game. Nixon wrote a thank-you letter in which he confessed that "my favorite vacation, if I had an opportunity to take a week off at the right time, would be to travel with a baseball club. The dugout chatter and, particularly, the conversation on the train or plane between cities would be a welcome relief from some of the heavy discussions in which I participate in my office!" In other words, he continued, "I think you have one of the best jobs possible. If I could only write I would trade places with you today even up!"[3]

Nixon often complained that political campaigns every other fall, and speaking obligations in the odd-numbered years, caused him to miss much of the football season. But his position gave him access to the top people in sports, an access he cherished. In January, he attended the Baseball Writers dinner, where he sat next to Casey Stengel, manager of the New York Yankees. "We talked baseball all night," Nixon recalled. Stengel was impressed by Nixon's knowledge of the game, and by Nixon himself. He later told the bartender at the Waldorf that Nixon had converted him from Democrat to Republican. Nixon for his part was captivated by Casey's "unique personality." The next week, Nixon presented the Coach of the Year Award at a Football Coaches luncheon in Philadelphia (he had done so the preceding year also). He was much impressed by Woody Hayes of Ohio State, telling a friend that Hayes was "one of the best operators in the business."[4]

THANKS TO HIS ROLE IN THE 1952 AND 1956 CAMPAIGNS, plus his foreign trips, plus Eisenhower's illnesses, Nixon had become the most visible Vice-President since Teddy Roosevelt. As the probable Republican nominee in 1960, he attracted even more attention. One full-length biography had already appeared, de Toledano's *Nixon*, and there were a number of others coming along, including a hostile but well-researched effort by reporter William Costello, *The Facts About Nixon*, which was done without Nixon's cooperation, and Stewart Alsop's *Nixon and Rockefeller: A Double Portrait*, which was based on extensive interviews with both men.

His most favorable biographers, after de Toledano, were Bela Kornitzer and Earl Mazo. Kornitzer was a Hungarian refugee and writer who had done a successful group portrait of the Eisenhower brothers and their parents, called *The Great American Heritage.* His specialty was human-interest stories based on interviews with members of the family. He found Hannah Nixon to be cooperative, her son rather less so. "I suppose he will have to talk with Pat," Nixon wrote in a memo to his staff, "but he is to be told that under no circumstances could he interview the girls—we do not submit them to any questioning—this is just not done." Nixon said to tell Kornitzer that he could have one hour for his interview with the Vice-President, but "that is to be the only one. . . . He should see everyone else before he sees me and when he comes in to see me he should not ask if I can tell him some anecdotes or anything else stupid like that. No tape recorder."[5]

Mazo was a top reporter for the *Herald Tribune,* widely respected, and a close friend of Nixon's. His book, *Richard Nixon,* like Alsop's, was based on interviews with Nixon, but Nixon opened up to him more than he did to Alsop, and Mazo got into much more detail than any of the others. Mazo submitted his taped interviews with his subjects—Milton Eisenhower, Adlai Stevenson, Lyndon Johnson and so on—to them for comment and correction. In his comment, Nixon took the opportunity to ask Mazo to deal head on with the charge "Scottie Reston and others make, that 'no one knows where Nixon stands.'" Nixon commented, "I am the first to admit that my views on issues have changed through the years. In fact I would be very distressed if I did not feel that my mind was always open for new ideas." But, he insisted, "year in and year out my record has been perhaps as consistent as any man in public life today except, of course, for the extremists on the right and on the left."[6]

Costello, the unfriendly biographer, never did get to see Nixon, nor members of his family. Nixon and his friends were unhappy with the finished product; Nora de Toledano got her hands on the galley proofs of the book, read them, and called Nixon to say that it was "the worst hatchet job yet—appalling and incredible."[7] But that was the judgment of the wife of a competitor; actually Costello's work, while critical, was honest, forthright, and as objective as such works can be.

All these books were campaign biographies (and all were published well before the 1960 campaign). Each book contains material that cannot be found anywhere else, contributing to the body of knowledge about Nixon in significant ways. They are especially strong on his youth in California and early years in politics.

By 1958, Nixon had been in politics for a dozen years. During that period, he had said and done things that were coming back to haunt him, especially in campaigns. The "new" Nixon of 1956 hardly seemed compatible with the "old" Nixon of the early California days. In January, Marquis Childs reported that Nixon was apologizing for his past. According to Childs, Nixon had an interview with a British reporter. Impressed by Nixon's commitment to foreign aid and American responsibility for freedom around the globe, the reporter asked "how anyone who has spoken with your sense of responsibility and your awareness can have done what you did to Helen Gahagan Douglas in your senatorial campaign in 1950." Nixon, the story went, replied, "All I can say is that I was very young and very ambitious and I am sorry."[8]

When Nixon read the story, he was furious. New Nixon or old, he was not about to back down from that 1950 campaign. He wrote reporter Adela Rogers St. Johns that "there is no foundation in fact whatever for the comments in the Marquis Childs column. . . . Nothing I have ever said . . . could under any circumstances be interpreted in this way." Then he launched a vigorous defense of the 1950 campaign: "I personally checked the record on every fact used in 1950 and in no instance do I know of a single statement we used which is not supported by the facts." Just in case he had missed something, however, he had put de Toledano to work on the matter.[9] Mrs. Douglas, meanwhile, continued to bring out negative response in him; he wrote Westbrook Pegler about how amused he was when he heard that she had a mirror in the ceiling of her bedroom.[10]

When asked about the Hiss case, Nixon told his staff to reply, "Don't say I have an apology—say I am proud of the part I played in sending this traitor to jail."[11] He was equally aggressive in defending his 1946 campaign against Jerry Voorhis, both with his biographers and with reporters doing current stories.

NIXON'S IMMEDIATE CONCERN WAS FOREIGN POLICY. In this area, and especially in foreign aid, he was a great help to the President.

Every year of his Presidency, Eisenhower proposed big increases in foreign aid. Every year, the Republicans in the Senate cut his requests, by anywhere from one-third to one-half. On January 21, after Eisenhower's 1958 State of the Union speech repeated the call for more foreign aid, Dulles telephoned Nixon. "The Sec said there is a lack of agreement of the role of the Pres re mutual security. The Pres should talk personally and vigorously to Congress. The Sec does not think it will go through unless he does." Nixon said that he had heard that Rayburn and Senate Majority Leader Lyndon Johnson wanted to be called to the Oval Office and be begged by Eisenhower for their support and leadership, but Eisenhower would not do it because "the Pres is mad at Johnson for playing politics with Defense. N and the Sec agreed this is not a good argument. N said he should call them in and put them on the spot. N said Knowland is sensitive re the Pres' seeing Democrats. N said Knowland has taken a dim view on foreign aid. There is a feeling at the WH of not asking the Pres to see people where it will be unpleasant. N said to leave it to him." [12]

Foreign aid was an integral part of the worldwide defense against Communism, as Nixon tried to explain to Republicans in the legislative leaders' meetings. "Take the Shah of Iran," he told them. Since the CIA-sponsored coup of 1953, the Shah had been "very impressive in his feeling and actions toward us. But look at their long border with the Russians. They need strength to resist— it may be touch and go—we have to give aid where it is needed. If we cut back from what he now expects, we will undo all the good that has been done." [13]

Fighting Communists in the Third World cost money. "Everywhere out there," Nixon told another Cabinet meeting, "the press, the radio, the magazines, etc., have been heavily infiltrated by the Commies." He thought "we might have to buy more support out there to compete," by providing financial aid to America's friends in the Third World media. [14]

His advocacy of clandestine support for publishers and reporters who were on the free-world side was only one reflection of the importance he assigned to mood and perception in the Cold War. By early 1958 the Korean War had been over for almost five years, and some Republicans were urging Eisenhower to reach out to Red China with an offer of recognition and a seat in the United Nations. When Maryland lawyer John Dewicki, a friend of Nixon's from Duke Law School days, wrote to suggest that Nixon get behind a move to recognize China, Nixon said he realized that Dewicki had some strong arguments for such a course. But "my own view is that recognition of Communist China or its admission to the UN would have a catastrophic effect on the anti-Communist and non-Communist nations in Asia." [15]

He felt strongly about the issue. In April, as he prepared to leave the country for two and a half weeks, he sent a formal memorandum to Robert Cutler of the NSC. Nixon said that if the question of relationships with Red China came up in the NSC during his absence, "I wish to have my view put on the record as follows: I am unequivocally opposed at this time to recognition of Red China, admission of Red China to the United Nations and to any concept of 'two Chinas.' " [16]

He hammered at the theme that recognition would have an adverse effect on the other nations in Asia, which would naturally

wonder if the United States was abandoning them and might conclude that the time had come to cut the best deal they could
for themselves with China. If that happened, Nixon feared that
the United States would lose not only Asia but the Cold War
itself.

On February 8, Nixon and Dulles talked about the problem
over a Saturday lunch at Dulles' home. Latin America was the part
of the Third World closest to the United States, and Dulles wanted
Nixon to make a trip there, beginning with Argentina, where
Dulles asked Nixon to represent the United States at the inauguration of Arturo Frondizi as president. He explained that because
Frondizi was the first elected president in twenty years, and because of the widespread feeling that the United States had supported the dictator Juan Perón, it was important to show
enthusiastic backing for Frondizi. Nixon said he was not sure about
the inauguration, as he did not want to seem to be setting up a
counter attraction, but he would make a week or ten-day trip to
South America in the spring.

Then, Dulles recorded in a memcon, "we discussed at some
length the project for a study of economic warfare." Their concern
was that the Soviet Union "might develop a capability and purpose
to wage economic warfare against our free enterprise system by
getting control of raw materials. There might be a real question as
to whether our classical free trade methods based upon profits by
private enterprise could survive that kind of a struggle." [17]

It was a subject Dulles frequently discussed with the President. At its core was one of the great historic movements of the
second half of the twentieth century—the emergence of independent nations in Asia, Africa, and the Near East on the termination
of European and American colonialism. Would the new nations—
the Philippines, Ghana, Vietnam, Malaysia, Algeria, and the others
—join with the free world or go with the Communists? Eisenhower, Dulles, and Nixon all thought that the ultimate outcome of
the Cold War depended on the answer. As Dulles described the
danger, the industrial democracies could not survive if the Russians got control of the oil of the Middle East, the uranium of Africa,
and many of the other raw materials that were crucial to Western
industry and available only in the Third World.

That was what made foreign aid so crucial. The newly emerging governments desperately needed aid, which to some extent put
the United States into a bidding war with the Soviet Union. They
also desperately needed some dramatic economic progress, which
made centralized control and state planning under some form or
other of socialism look appealing to them. These radical trends had

to be fought, Dulles thought, all around the world, else America would lose the Cold War.

Throughout his career, Richard Nixon devoted much of his time, energy, and intelligence to the struggles for the Third World. It was never an issue that was particulary popular (witness the perennial difficulty in getting foreign aid through Congress), nor were there many votes in it. From his first days in Congress, when he gave strong support to aid to Greece and Turkey, to his last days in the White House, when he was still asking Congress for aid for South Vietnam, he fought for foreign aid. His critics charged that his single-mindedness led to American support for right-wing dictators whose excesses made revolution inevitable; his defenders claimed that events in those countries in Asia and Africa that went Communist proved how right he was; a biographer needs to note that whether right or wrong in his approach to the Third World, he never changed his mind or his position.

THE STATE DEPARTMENT, under Dulles, was as eager as Nixon to play a major role in the Third World, and used that excuse to broaden the proposed short trip to Argentina for Frondizi's inauguration to a two-and-a-half-week tour of South America, with stops at every country except Brazil and Chile. Nixon objected to the length of the trip, but not strenuously, because he recognized the need, and because he saw it as an opportunity to learn. He threw himself into an intensive program of briefings and readings on the political and economic problems of each country he would be visiting. Curious as always about new faces and new places, he nevertheless anticipated that the trip would be rather ho-hum. He told a number of reporters that it would produce little news and that it therefore would not be worth their publishers' expense to send them along.[18]

Shortly before he left, he received an invitation from Lewis Strauss that he hated to pass up—to watch a nuclear test in an upcoming series. Nixon replied that "I am most disappointed that it will not be possible for me to accept your offer," because he would be in South America during the testing.[19]

As things turned out, the explosion he encountered in South America was bigger, in its own way, than anything Strauss could have shown him.

IT WAS A STRANGE BUSINESS, all around. There was no real point to Nixon's trip, other than the purely ceremonial function of attending Frondizi's inaugural. He was not empowered to negotiate about anything; he was given no surprise announcements to make; he

had nothing to offer. The things the Latins wanted from the United States—a reduction of tariff barriers on their products, higher prices for tin, copper, and coffee—he was in no position to offer. The most Nixon could do would be to reassure the Latins that they were respected and that the United States did not take them for granted—propositions so patently untrue as to undo any good that Nixon's physical presence might accomplish.

Nevertheless, Nixon participated in the process of saying yes to every invitation from every country on the continent, save only Brazil (which he had visited in 1956 for another inauguration) and Chile (whose leader was scheduled to meet the President in Washington while Nixon was in South America). What Nixon, or the State Department, thought could be accomplished by a two-day visit to Peru or Venezuela or the others was as vague as the results. Although this trip became one of the most famous incidents of his Vice-Presidency, and forced even some of his bitterest enemies to give him some grudging respect, it is difficult to avoid the conclusion that it was all theater. Certainly no policy changes resulted from the trip, nor any change in U.S.–South American relations. For a time the trip boosted Nixon's personal popularity, but even that quickly faded in the heat of the 1958 campaign. But however insignificant politically, the trip provides some fascinating glimpses of Nixon the man.

THE PARTY CONSISTED OF PAT, who had a sore back but decided to go anyway; Samuel Waugh, president of the Export-Import Bank; Roy Rubottom, Jr., Assistant Secretary of State; and Director Maurice Bernbaum of the State Department's office of South American affairs. Nixon's personal staff included Bill Key, his administrative assistant; Marine Major Robert E. Cushman, Jr., who had been added to the staff as his national security adviser; his military aide, Air Force Major James Don Hughes; his interpreter, Colonel Vernon Walters; and Rose Woods.

Some twenty-five newspaper, radio, and television correspondents followed the official party in their own chartered plane. Reporters included Bob Hartmann of the Los Angeles *Times,* Tad Szulc of *The New York Times,* Earl Mazo of the *Herald Tribune,* Herb Kaplow of NBC, and Jinx Falkenburg, who had a TV and radio show. The following narrative of what happened in South America is based primarily on their day-by-day reports, filed the evening of the day the events happened.

They took off on April 27, in a cold rain. At the airport, Nixon read a short statement to a small gathering of newsmen and well-wishers. As she hugged her mother goodbye, Julie told Pat, "I'll see you in three little weeks." They landed in Montevideo, Uruguay, where Nixon's first words were "Even in California we've never had more beautiful weather!" On the ride into town, and later on his official rounds, Nixon frequently stopped the motorcade to get out of his car and mingle with the crowds, meanwhile shooing off alarmed police. People were at first astonished, then curious, and finally (at least in some cases) converted by the strange experience of having this world figure descend upon them, hand outstretched, asking through his interpreter what their problems were. Nor did they know what to make of Pat, who shook two thousand hands the first day, in addition to visiting a crippled children's hospital and an orphanage.[20]

The following day, Nixon suddenly switched his schedule. He told his driver to take the party to the National University, where a handful of students had held up signs reading *"Fuera Nixon"* (Go Home Nixon) when his motorcade had passed en route from the airport. Seeking confrontation and debate, Nixon and Pat walked unannounced and unescorted onto the Law School campus. He signed some autographs for excited students, then marched into a jammed classroom. Taking over the class, Nixon announced, through Colonel Walters, that he was there to answer any questions they had with regard to U.S. policy in Latin America.

The questions were predictable enough, and easy enough for someone who had been briefed as thoroughly as Nixon had been (and who knew Communist propaganda as well as he did), and he fielded them deftly—U.S. imperialism, unfair trade practices, economic exploitation, support for dictators, and the rest. The twenty-six-year-old leader of the Communist-dominated Student Union was there, and Nixon was able to demolish him in a brief debate. As the American party left, the students started chanting "Neekson-Neekson," and reporters heard them say to one another, *"Muy simpático."*[21] The American ambassador, Robert Woodward, told Nixon that he had been sensational. Latins, he explained, admired courage and were contemptuous of fear or timidity. Nixon was to hear this character analysis from all sides throughout his trip (especially from Walters); small wonder that he became convinced that personal machismo was the key to the Latin's heart and to a successful trip. And the widespread publicity his "debate" got in the Latin press convinced him that the universities, not government palaces, were the place to look for headlines.[22]

Bob Hartmann, summarizing the day, wrote that the visit was "a huge success," but warned that "it holds the seeds of disillusionment unless it is followed promptly by Washington action on behalf of Uruguay, which nobody knowing the real situation can quite visualize." Hartmann pointed out that "Nixon shook more wool workers' greasy hands and talked to more Uruguayan labor leaders and commen men than to brass hats," and concluded, "the best benefit of the two-day visit has been the demonstration of the youthful vigor and democratic demeanor of both Nixon and his wife."[23]

In Buenos Aires, on April 30, Nixon again worked the crowds, pressing the flesh and asking people about their complaints. Most residents, Hartmann reported, "watched curiously and waved amiably without enthusiasm." The American newsmen were surprised that no attention was paid to Pat, also busy shaking hands; local reporters explained that the Argentines had had enough of politicians' wives with Eva Perón.[24]

The following day, Nixon missed the whole reason for the trip —Frondizi's oath taking. In his top hat and tails, he arrived ten minutes after the ceremony. The fault lay with the American ambassador, who had misjudged the traffic, but Nixon took the blame on himself.

Halfway through the inaugural parade, Nixon left his balcony seat, went to his hotel, changed to street clothes, and—passing up the reception—drove to a celebration picnic of the Municipal Workers Union, where he ate barbecued beef and watched folk dances. One of the union leaders praised him for "finding time in a busy day to share a table with working men," and told the Vice-President that Argentine workers needed bread but prized freedom even more.

Ah, the voice of the people. Nixon made an impromptu speech in response: "I say it's possible to have both. Men can have more material progress when free than when slaves. . . . Free labor and dictatorship are completely incompatible. I can tell you from experience that free organized labor contributes not only free institutions but also to economic progress." He sounded, Hartmann thought, rather like Walter Reuther.[25]

At the University of Buenos Aires, Nixon repeated the scene he had played at the National University in Uruguay with similar results. Pat visited the Children's Polio Hospital, where she passed out candy to the small patients.[26]

The party made a one-day stop in Paraguay. Why it did so is something of a mystery, since the whole purpose of the trip was to show that the United States did not support dictators like Perón and wanted to demonstrate its approval of the new elected government in Argentina, and Paraguay was generally regarded as the toughest one-man dictatorship in South America. President Alfredo Stroessner was the dictator, and he greeted Nixon at the airport. In

Six Crises, Nixon explained that by staying only one day in Paraguay, he had indicated American disapproval of dictators. "This point," he wrote, "I am sure, was not missed. . . ." But, he added in an understatement, "it was not widely understood publicly." [27] Hartmann wrote that to "make up for the brevity of the visit, the Vice-President used every minute jumping from his car to greet rural school children or city folk." [28]

In La Paz, Bolivia, at thirteen thousand feet the world's highest capital (and airport), the Nixons kept up the hectic pace. At a press conference, when asked what was the point of spending so much time shaking hands and talking to common people, Nixon rejoined that he learned from the experiences. "I've found woeful lack of understanding in many important areas such as university circles, labor unions, press and radio. The United States must realize it is not enough to convince government officials. We also must reach peoples." Then, in another understatement, he added, "This can't be done in a two-and-a-half-week goodwill visit." Hartmann commented: "The weary entourage of the inexhaustible Vice-President packing to fly to Peru tomorrow has little hope Nixon will take his own advice." [29]

Of course he would not, nor anyone else's advice for that matter. When the party arrived in Lima, Peru, on May 7, it was greeted with reports that "Latin-American Communists have orders to play it tough from here on with Vice-President Nixon after their decisive defeats, soft soap and polite protests in previous countries on Nixon's route." Nixon was scheduled to visit San Marcos University, the oldest in the hemisphere, the following day, and the word was that the Communists were organized and determined to prevent his visit. To punctuate the threat, about one hundred students were gathered opposite his hotel in the Plaza San Martín when he arrived, shouting *"Fuera Nixon."* [30] His staff reported that thousands of leaflets were circulating in the city, summoning "students, workers, employees" to gather at San Marcos University to prevent Nixon from speaking. The leaflets referred to Nixon as "the most insolent representative of monopolistic trusts," and encouraged people to "JOIN US—GATHER TO SHOUT WITH ALL YOUR FORCES—OUT NIXON—DEATH TO YANKEE IMPERIALISM."

That evening, Nixon met with the ambassador, Theodore Achilles, the two State Department officials, Rubottom and Bernbaum, and three members of his staff, Cushman, Hughes, and Key, to discuss the problem of whether or not to go to San Marcos. Rubottom was opposed, as were most of the others. There was a real possibility of violence, Rubottom said, and if anything happened to Nixon it would create a news sensation. He added that both the rector of San Marcos and the Lima chief of police had expressed the wish that he cancel the visit.

Nixon agreed to cancel if the rector would publicly withdraw his invitation. But the rector replied that to do so would be an admission that he could not control his own institution, and refused. Nixon turned to the chief of police. But the chief said no too —he did not want to give the impression that he could not protect his high-ranking guest. Still, like Nixon's advisers and the rector, he hoped the Vice-President would cancel on his own.

Bill Key suggested an alternative visit, to the smaller and more conservative Catholic University, near San Marcos, where Nixon could expect a warm welcome. Nixon told Key and Jack Sherwood, in charge of the Secret Service detail, to work out the details of a visit to Catholic University in the event he decided to go there rather than San Marcos, but he insisted that the visit be unscheduled and unannounced.

As the meeting ended, Nixon asked Ambassador Achilles to stay and give his private opinion. Achilles replied with a long analysis of Latin character—the people admired courage and were contemptuous of fear, which was why they loved the bullfight. Above all else, Achilles declared, in dealing with Latins one should never lose face. If Nixon canceled the San Marcos visit, the Communists would crow about it for weeks and months afterward, and there would be "some very detrimental publicity reactions throughout the hemisphere." [31]

Nixon slept fitfully that night, as he geared himself up to face the situation. His intuition was to go to San Marcos, because, as he rather grandly put it in *Six Crises*, to back down "would not be simply a case of Nixon being bluffed out by a group of students, but of the United States itself putting its tail between its legs and running away form a bunch of Communist thugs." [32]

In the morning, Nixon laid a wreath at the tomb of General José de San Martín. There he made his decision. "San Marcos," he told Sherwood after the wreath-laying ceremony, and off the motorcade sped. Along the way, Nixon decided on the tactics he would employ: "take the offensive; show no fear; do the unexpected; but do nothing rash." [33]

When the motorcade arrived, there were more than two thousand students milling about, shouting out catcalls, carrying *"Fuera Nixon"* signs, and an occasional cry of *"Muera Nixon"* (Death to Nixon).

Nixon stopped the motorcade and got out of his car. Accompanied only by Walters and Sherwood, he walked toward the students, smiling, asking the police not to push them back. With Walters shouting the translation, Nixon called out, "I would like to talk to you. What's the matter, you afraid of the truth?" One of the demonstrators shouted back, "Go home." "I'll be glad to go home," Nixon replied, "but don't you want the truth first?"

The crowd slowly gave way as Nixon moved toward the university gates. Students near enough to hear what he was saying were impressed—Walters heard one of them say, *"El gringo tiene cojones"* (The Yankee has balls)—but it was all show without substance, as there was not the slightest possibility the three men could force their way through the gates and into the university, especially not with Nixon ordering the police to stay out of it.

As Nixon continued to try to engage the students around him in conversation, those in the rear began throwing oranges, bottles, and an occasional small rock. Tad Szulc, who was back with the motorcade, watching, reported: "Pale with anger, but keeping a tight smile on his lips, Mr. Nixon stood his ground for four minutes. When one policeman tried to arrest a demonstrator, Nixon said, 'Let him go, I want to talk to him.' "[34]

Then one of the rocks grazed Nixon's shoulder and landed on Sherwood's face, breaking a tooth. "Let's get out of here," Nixon said to Sherwood and Walters, "but move back slowly, keep facing them." When they reached their vehicle, a convertible, Nixon stood up in the backseat, Sherwood bracing him. Nixon threw his hands above his head and shouted, "Cowards, you are cowards! You are afraid of the truth! You are the worst kind of cowards!"[35]

As the car began to pick up speed, and Nixon sat down, Tad Szulc ran alongside shouting, "Good going, Mr. Vice-President, good going." Or so Nixon and Walters later reported; Szulc told Fawn Brodie that the story was not true.[36] A Peruvian reporter told Hartmann, "No doubt about it, Nixon made a good impression— he came out—he won."[37] Walters told Nixon, "Sir, you tried and at least they saw that you were not scared of them." Nixon, who said later that he had felt "the excitement of battle" as he spoke, was pleased with the performance. "Did you see how they pressed up to shake my hand?" he asked Walters.[38]

Rebuffed at San Marcos, Nixon ordered the motorcade to Catholic University, a few blocks away. There he entered an assembly unannounced as students conducted an election for student-body president. They crowded around him, applauding and asking for autographs. When order was restored, Nixon declared, "Nothing must interfere with free elections. I'll observe and you finish and then we'll try to answer some of your questions." When the balloting was completed, the entire group went over to the chapel where

Nixon, standing under a wooden figure of the crucified Christ, said: "Due to the fact that a small minority seemed to object to my visiting a neighboring university, I decided I would come here. The mark of a great university is the free expression of views." And for an hour and a half he answered questions, most of them hostile (the American tariff on lead and zinc was the principal complaint). But overall the Catholic University students were delighted to show up their rivals at San Marcos, and when Nixon left, there were shouts of *"Viva Nixon!"*

At noon, two hours after it left, the Nixon motorcade returned to the Plaza San Martín, there to discover that a mob blocked the entrance of the Grand Hotel Bolívar. Nixon told his driver to stop. "I didn't think that we should try to drive up because . . . that is probably what they expected. It is always best to do the unexpected if you can get away with it. I knew we had them on the run [an odd judgment, considering that the reporters present thought the members of the mob had come from San Marcos, where they had just succeeded in turning back the Nixon visit], and it was essential that we bust right through, walking. So we walked through them, waving and smiling and even shaking a few hands." [39]

Nixon paid a price for seeking confrontation. As Hartmann wrote, "This crowd was really worked up. Spit, fruit and pebbles again rained on Nixon and his party, including the two dozen U.S. newsmen." [40] Nixon fared worst of all. A tobacco-chewing agitator stood face-to-face with him at the door of the hotel and let fly a wad of tobacco spittle that caught Nixon full in the face. Nixon went through "a terrible test of temper control"; as he explained later, "One must experience the sensation to realize why spitting in a person's face is the most infuriating insult ever conceived by man." Nixon's instinct was to strike out at the agitator, but before he could recover from the shock of the spit, Sherwood threw the man aside. Nixon got in one blow, "planting a healthy kick on his shins. Nothing I did all day made me feel better." [41]

Pat watched all of this from a fourth-story window. "I've never been more proud of him," she said later. Hartmann shared her sentiments. "Throughout the ordeal," he wrote, "Nixon himself was completely self-possessed and bore himself with dignity and strength, a credit to his country." [42]

That afternoon, following some meetings with local officials and businessmen, Nixon held a press conference. In complete control, he was a model of good sense and statesmanship. Peruvian reporters tried to apologize, but he cut them off: "No apology is needed." Nixon explained that "this was not a personal affront to me. When one of the demonstrators spat in my face he was spitting on the good name of Peru, he was spitting on the memory of San Martín and all the men who through the years have fought and died for freedom of expression. . . . This day will live in infamy in the history of San Marcos University . . . because a small vocal minority denied freedom of expression without which no institution of learning can deserve the word great." Nixon said the mob exemplified cowardice "because the greatest cowardice of all is intellectual cowardice—being unable to hear facts and truth." He admitted that the Reds were claiming victory, because they kept him out of the university, but insisted that time would show that "they exposed themselves to the people of Peru for what they are—those who speak of freedom but deny it to others."[43]

After the conference, Nixon returned to his room to dress for a formal dinner. He was suffering emotional, mental, and physical fatigue, but he roused himself sufficiently to ask Bob Cushman to give him a rundown on reactions to the day's events. Cushman said most reports were favorable, but Rubottom and Bernbaum of the State Department had expressed concern that the incidents had embarrassed the Peruvian government and thus compromised the goodwill effect of the visit.

"I blew my stack," Nixon later confessed. He told Cushman to have Rubottom and Bernbaum come to his room immediately. Cushman reported back that they were dressing. Nixon said to tell them to come as they were. They arrived, half dressed, and Nixon "ripped into them." He told them they had an obligation to support his decisions, once made, just as he supported Eisenhower. Then he launched into a denunciation of Foreign Service people, who, he charged, "prefer to compromise, to avoid conflict, to play it safe." Such conduct, Nixon predicted, "will . . . only lead to inevitable defeat for the forces of freedom. The Communists are out to win the world. . . . We are doomed to defeat in the world struggle unless we are willing to risk as much to defend freedom as the Communists are willing to risk to destroy it."

One might have thought that the entry to San Marcos University had become the crucial battleground of the Cold War. Actually, it was a minor incident—as the reporters all confessed later, after seeing a real mob in action in Caracas, literally threatening the Vice-President's life. And Rubottom and Bernbaum were right, it was embarrassing to the government and the university, and it was true that Peruvian officials had asked Nixon to cancel the visit and go to Catholic University instead. As a political event, it was as meaningless as two little boys drawing lines in the dust with their toes and daring each other to cross. Nixon's last words to Rubottom and Bernbaum were "What we must do is to act like Americans and not put our tails between our legs and run every time some Communist bully tries to bluff us." [44]

As a personal event, in other words, the incident at San Marcos was of the first importance, a test of his courage. If Nixon did not show good sense in challenging the mob (he thought his personal presence would force the students to make way; he forgot that approaching them on foot with only two men as escort put him on their level, which meant that those not a part of the inner circle around him never saw Nixon; to them he remained a symbol of the United States, not a living human being projecting his personality), he most certainly showed his guts. Whether Szulc's "Good going, Mr. Vice-President, good going" was apocryphal or not, it summed up the sentiments of all the reporters present.

Indeed, praise rolled in from all over. Nelson Rockefeller sent a telegram. Eisenhower praised Nixon's "courage, patience, and calmness in the demonstration directed against you by radical agitators." Clare Boothe Luce nicely caught the Teddy Roosevelt image with a one-word telegram: "Bully." [45] Still, despite Nixon's claim that he had exposed the Communists for what they were, and thereby alerted the Peruvian government to the danger they posed, the stark truth was that Peruvian–U.S. relations were not improved by Nixon's goodwill visit.

NEXT STOP WAS QUITO, ECUADOR. Nixon's first decision there was to cancel a scheduled visit to Central University. Instead, he strolled around town, more or less aimlessly, shaking hands and asking people about their problems. The reporters trailed behind. He popped into a two-chair barbershop and asked for a trim. The reporters gathered around for what became an impromptu press conference. It was, Hartmann wrote, "the longest time he has sat still in 12 days."

He was asked about his feelings at San Marcos. "I did not have any fear," Nixon replied. "I am pretty much of a fatalist as far as accidents are concerned. Usually my reaction is one of tension, like that before the kickoff of a football game." He insisted that he never lost his temper, not even when he was standing in the convertible shouting "Cowards!" at the students. He explained, "I intentionally don't lose my temper when other people are angry." [46]

In Quito, Hartmann heard a warning: "The Communists reportedly are planning a final all-out effort to discredit Nixon in Caracas, Venezuela, the last stop on the 12,387-mile journey." [47] Nixon got similar warnings, including one from the CIA saying there were rumors of a plot to assassinate the Vice-President in

Caracas.[48] Still, everything went well in Quito—Nixon even reconsidered and met with some Central University students, to their delight. Ecuador issued a stamp with his picture on it.[49]

BOGOTÁ, COLOMBIA, ALSO WENT WELL. The police went to work on extremists before Nixon's arrival, arresting suspected conspirators by the scores, and surrounding him with officers wherever he went. Indeed, the police concentrated so exclusively on getting through the visit without an incident that Bogotá's pickpockets managed to lift the wallets of three American reporters, some members of Nixon's staff, and—amazingly—those of two Secret Service agents. Nixon made one concession to security, riding in a closed limousine rather than an open car.[50]

While in Bogotá, the press heard about more CIA warnings of an assassination plot at the next stop, Caracas. Asked about the threat, Nixon replied, "It's just one of those routine things." Asked what he was going to do about it, he replied, "I'm just going to ignore it." Unless the Venezuelan government asked him to stay away, there was little else he could do.[51]

Everyone on the trip knew that Venezuela was going to be tough. Not only were there the warnings about frenetic Communist preparations to create anti-American and anti-Nixon rallies, and the assassination threats, there were also special circumstances in Venezuela that made some kind of violence almost inevitable. Beyond the regular Latin American complaints about the United States, Venezuelan Communists had particular grievances they could exploit, along with some special weaknesses in the government and police. In January, Venezuela had overthrown dictator Perez Jimenez with a military junta. During the revolution, the people had turned on the police, in some working-class districts actually burning them alive. The new police force was inexperienced, afraid, and demoralized.

Worse, the United States had long supported Jimenez—Dulles had praised him, and Eisenhower had presented him with the Legion of Merit, calling his government a "model" for the rest of Latin America. The dictator's hated chief of police, Pedro Estrada, had escaped the revolution in a small plane and found refuge in Washington, D.C., while Jimenez himself was living in a mansion in Miami.[52] As if that were not provocation enough, there were widespread rumors that the United States intended to reduce its already low quota on imported Venezuelan oil.

The Communists worked on all this effectively, showering Caracas under leaflets, holding rallies, building tension. One newspaper showed a Negro being lynched, over a caption, "The American Way of Life." Another had an altered photograph of

Nixon, labeled "Tricky Dick." It showed him as a snarling beast with sharp fangs for teeth. Reports of these and other activities led Nixon to ask for assurances of protection from the Venezuelan government. They were given. Sherwood, meanwhile, decided to raise the Secret Service unit from four to twelve men.

Later, Nixon explained his reasoning for going ahead. "I felt that it was going to be bad," he admitted. "I thought the reception would be the coldest we ever had. But I believed it would be proper. That was my feeling about Caracas—proper, but no violence."[53]

If Nixon was guilty of seeking confrontation in Lima, nothing that took place in Caracas was his fault. What did happen was quite bizarre, without precedent, unique in the annals of international relations. No one could possibly have anticipated it.

There was a large crowd when Nixon arrived, gathered outside the gate and on the balcony of the airport terminal. People, mostly teen-agers, were shouting slogans and waving *"Feura Nixon"* signs. A group of dignitaries gathered at the foot of the ramp. At the airplane door, as Nixon waved at the crowd, Walters whispered into his ear, "They aren't friendly, Mr. Vice President." Nixon made a quick inspection of the military honor guard, then broke away to a nearby hangar, where some mechanics were standing around gaping. He shook hands, returned to the host committee, and said he had decided to skip the usual airport welcome speeches, because "no one could possibly hear what we said over the noise of this mob." He took Pat's arm and led the way toward the terminal building, over a red carpet specially laid out for the occasion. It was lined by soldiers and looked safe enough. But the soldiers simply stood, as did the police, as the mob began throwing little whistles, fruit, and other objects, along with vicious obscenities, at the Nixons.

Hartmann and the rest of the press corps had arrived an hour earlier, and they watched the scene from the terminal. Hartmann noticed the one friendly gesture: "Mrs. Nixon was given a bouquet by a small girl and stopped to hug her."[54]

As the Nixons approached the terminal door, directly under the observation balcony, which was packed with howling demonstrators, the army band struck up the Venezuelan national anthem. The Nixons came to attention. Then the unbelievable happened. A shower of spit began to rain down upon them. A torrent of the stuff, much of it brown, from the tobacco chewers. Pat's new red suit was covered with it. It was running down her face. Still Nixon stood, although he admitted that no one could hear the anthem anyway, due to the noise.

No one ever asked him directly how he could have stood there and let this happen to his wife. He did explain his own reasoning: "We preferred the indignity of spit to that of letting the mob see the Vice President of the United States duck and run away. And we also wanted to show them that we respected their national anthem even if they did not. . . . Pat shared this trial at my side. In one sense, I was horrified that she should be subjected to it. In another sense, I was proud that she was with me." [55]

As the anthem came to an end, Mazo heard adult mob leaders shout to the screaming kids, "Go, go, go." They dashed away from the balcony and reassembled on the street outside the terminal, blocking the path to the motorcade vehicles. All the while the police and Venezuelan officials watched solemnly. Mazo noticed that "the soldiers stood erect and at perfect attention, fixed bayonets gleaming in the sunlight." Sherwood and his agents pushed a way through the crowd inside the terminal, and finally the Nixons emerged on the street side. [56]

The mob closed in again as the Secret Service pushed back. Spit flew. A teen-ager grabbed Pat's hand and screeched a question about Nixon's torturing "little black boys" in Little Rock. "He was one of the very mean young boys," Pat later told Mazo. "I pretended that I didn't understand him. I just said, 'How are you? So nice to be here.' . . . They must have been told that we were horrible people." [57]

A bit farther along, Hartmann noted, "Pat reached between bayonets to shake the hand of an amazed girl demonstrator as the hate came off her twisted face."

Eventually they reached the limousines. Nixon got into one, Pat into another. The Foreign Minister, Sherwood, and Walters were with Nixon. As they swung onto the Autopista, a superhighway built by Jimenez that ran twelve miles into the city, the Foreign Minister was wringing his hands, apologizing for what happened. He took a handkerchief from his pocket and tried to wipe the spit from Nixon's shirt and suit.

"Don't bother," Nixon told him. "I am going to burn these clothes as soon as I can get out of them."

The Foreign Minister attempted an explanation: "The Venezuelan people have been without freedom so long that they tend now to express themselves more vigorously perhaps than they should. In our new government we do not want to do anything which would be interpreted as a suppression of freedom."

Nixon shut him up. "If your new government doesn't have the guts and good sense to control a mob like the one at the airport, there soon will be no freedom for anyone in Venezuela. Don't you realize that that mob was Communist-led?"

The Foreign Minister begged Nixon not to say that publicly, because the government did not want to "embarrass or anger the Venezuelan Communists. They helped us overthrow Perez Jimenez and we are trying to find a way to work with them."

Nixon gave it up as hopeless. Just then the motorcade turned into the Avenida Sucre, a six-lane highway leading to the Panteón Nacional in the center of the city, where the Vice-President was scheduled to lay a wreath at the tomb of Simón Bolívar. The avenue seemed clear, but suddenly there was a roadblock ahead. They were in the toughest working-class section of Caracas, where police had been torn apart in January. Nixon heard some dull thuds, and realized that rocks—big rocks—were being thrown against the limousine.

A mob began to descend on them from the side streets, waving placards with Nazi swastikas alongside the doctored photo of Nixon that made him look like a fanged monster. But the ambush failed, because there was a way through the roadblock which the driver successfully negotiated.

An open truck led the motorcade. In the back, there were six American reporters and some cameramen. Hartmann was there, along with Mazo. They were the first to see the next roadblock, just around a turn. This one included buses, driven by members of a Communist-controlled union. There was no way through.

As the motorcade stopped, yet another mob—about two hundred strong—emerged from the side streets. "Here they come," someone shouted. To Mazo it was "like a scene from the French Revolution." They were screaming, shouting, waving banners, placards, pipes, clubs, and bare fists. They swarmed around Nixon's car.[58]

"Seven Venezuelan motorcycle police," Hartmann wrote, "formed in a V around the Nixon car, rested one foot to the pavement and just sat there as the mob spilled past. The military police who had flanked the motorcade at the airport had disappeared." But at least the motorcycle police kept the crowd from the front of Nixon's car. To the rear, in the car carrying Pat, the driver pulled up bumper to bumper, so that the rear was protected. But the side windows and doors were unprotected.

Four of the Secret Service men dashed forward from cars in the rear. They took positions guarding the door handles, pushing people away with their bare hands, "coolly," as Hartmann saw it, but heroically. Then, Hartmann reported, "the mob smashed against the glass [of Nixon's car] with rocks, pipes, jagged beer cans and their naked fists. They kicked and hammered at the doors and fenders. Some who had carried signs jammed at the shattered safety glass with the wooden sticks."[59] Mazo thought that the mob was "bent on dragging the Vice-President from his limousine to tear him apart—the most degrading death possible, by Venezuelan standards."[60]

Hartmann noticed that two of the motorcycle cops had pulled their revolvers. "Frantically, fearing that one shot would set the mob off and every American would be murdered, the Secret Service men shouted to the Venezuelans to holster their guns. They did. The Americans never even reached for theirs." No guns were seen in the throng.[61]

The Nixon party sat there for twelve minutes. Inside his limousine, Nixon stayed calm. He glanced back once, to see how Pat was doing. The mob was ignoring her car, which came through virtually undamaged. She was talking calmly to the Foreign Minister's wife—about her daughters, and the weather in Washington. Looking ahead, Nixon wrote later, "I could see the truck filled with reporters and cameramen in action."[62]

As rocks and pipes hit the shatterproof windows, some glass sprayed into the face of the Foreign Minister. "It's my eye, my eye," he cried out, close to hysteria. "This is terrible. This is terrible."

The chant of the crowd had changed from "Feura Nixon" to "Muera Nixon." Another rock sent more glass flying through the interior, some of it hitting Walters in the mouth. Nixon asked him if he was all right, then saw the blood. "Spit that glass out," Nixon commanded. "You are going to have a lot more talking to do in Spanish for me today." To Walters, Nixon seemed "extraordinarily calm."[63]

The riot attracted more people, older people who appeared to be directing the assault on Nixon's car, until the mob numbered four or five hundred. Inside the car, the four men in the back—Nixon and the Foreign Minister, plus Walters and Sherwood on the jump seats—were helpless, except for Sherwood's pistol, which was their last line of defense. Their worst fear was a bomb tossed under the car, which would set off the fuel tank.

Then the second worst thing began to happen—the mob started rocking the car, in an attempt to turn it over. The Secret Service men on the outside were pushing and shoving people away, thereby interfering with the rocking, but they were unable to stop it altogether.

Sherwood pulled his revolver. "Let's get some of these sons-of-bitches," he swore. Later, another agent told Nixon, "I figured we were goners and I was determined to get six of those bastards before they got us."[64]

Nixon put his hand on Sherwood's arm. "Put that away," he ordered. "You take it out when they open the door and grab for me, and not before. You don't shoot unless I tell you to do so." Sherwood put the pistol back into his holster.[65]

Although Pat's car was not under direct attack, it did get hit by an occasional stray rock. Pat sat and watched, wondering if the windows in her husband's car would hold, whether the doors would be broken open, or the car tipped over. "I had visions of all those things," she said later. "I kept watching what went on ahead. I couldn't believe that nobody, none of the police, would do anything. I tried to calm the Foreign Minister's wife. . . . She felt horrible that this was happening in her country."[66]

Finally, somebody threw a tear-gas grenade. It hit near the back of the motorcade (Rose Woods, in limousine number nine, was almost overcome by it; she also had some broken-glass injuries). Finally a squad of Venezuelan soldiers showed up and cleared a path through the roadblock. Nixon's driver sped through it, his windshield wipers going full blast to clear the spit. The remainder of the motorcade followed.

They headed toward the Bolívar Tomb, where another, larger, and if possible even uglier mob awaited. Bill Key had been there an hour earlier, to check on arrangements, and tried frantically to send a radio message to the motorcade to stay away, because he feared for the Vice-President's life. But the message had not gotten through. Nixon, however, had the presence of mind to figure out if things had been this bad on the Avenida Sucre, they would be worse at the Bolívar Tomb. He told the driver to take an alley, turning away from the tomb.

At this, the Foreign Minister grew hysterical. "We can't leave our protection," he cried. "We've got to follow the police escort."

"If that's the kind of protection we are going to get, we are better off going it alone," Nixon snapped back.[67]

The motorcade emerged from the alley onto an empty boulevard. Nixon ordered the car stopped, then sent Walters back to check on Pat. Walters found Pat "sitting in a very composed fashion with her hands folded on her lap." "Mrs. Nixon," he said, "the Vice-President wants to know how you are. He says he is all right and we are going to the American Embassy residence." She replied quietly, "Tell him I'm all right too, but it was quite a sight to watch from back here."[68]

Fortuitously, they were across the street from a hospital. The Foreign Minister went in for treatment for his eyes. The press truck caught up with the party; Herb Kaplow leaped off and ran up to ask if anyone had been hurt. Nixon, getting out of the car, assured him that he was all right. The other reporters gathered around. "Let's go," Nixon said. "You can get your pictures later at the Embassy."[69] No one thought to write a description of what he looked like—whether ashen-faced with fear and worry, or red-faced from anger, but he must have been a sight, his suit covered with spit and broken glass, standing beside a limousine whose side windows were all broken, covered with spit and dents.

At the embassy, as he hurried inside, the reporters caught up with him. In a short, impromptu response to a dozen questions hurled all at once, he was calm and unruffled. "These incidents are against Venezuela," he declared. "No patriotic Venezuelan would have torn down his country's flag as the mob did to the Venezuelan flag and also to ours. I don't feel it at all as a personal offense. If anything, the future relations of the United States and Venezuela will be better than ever." When some Venezuelans attempted to apologize, he said, "As far as I'm concerned, the incident is closed."

Nixon told Bill Key to cancel all his appearances, and to tell members of the ruling junta that they should come to the embassy to see him. Then he went to an upstairs room, threw away his stained clothes, and went to bed. "It was," Mazo wrote, "Nixon's first afternoon nap in twelve years of public life. He slept for forty minutes."[70]

THAT AFTERNOON, cleaned up and refreshed by his nap, Nixon held a series of meetings with members of the junta (who were full of pious apologies) and with American businessmen. Then he held a press conference, where he insisted that the mob "does not represent the people of Venezuela." Asked about his personal feelings, he said, "It's not easy to endure the kind of action we have had to go through today. It's certainly not pleasant to go through a shower of spit and have a man spit directly in the face of my wife." He said he was going to stay in the American Embassy until he left the city, explaining, "I've got the right to risk my own personal safety but no right to risk the safety of others." Turning to the lesson to be learned, he said the day's events showed that the Communists, if ever they came to power, would impose a dictatorship far worse than that of Perez Jimenez.

The mention of Jimenez brought local newsmen out of their seats. What about Jimenez? they demanded. Why did you support him? Why is he living like a king in Miami? Nixon replied that he could not think less of Jimenez and his secret-police chief, Estrada, than they did, but pointed out that until this moment, no one in Venezuela had asked for their return under an extradition treaty.

As Venezuelan reporters gasped at this news, Nixon promised that "any time the government brings charges against Jimenez and Estrada with proof, they can get them back and we would be very glad to turn them over." (Estrada slipped away to Europe; three years later, under the Kennedy Administration, Jimenez was extradited to Venezuela and imprisoned.)

At the conclusion of the forty-five-minute press conference, the reporters all rose to give Nixon an ovation.[71]

BACK IN WASHINGTON, communications with Caracas were out; whether they were deliberately sabotaged or not was never discovered. Eisenhower was getting conflicting, but increasingly alarming, reports. From the President's perspective, it appeared that something akin to anarchy had taken hold in Caracas, that the Army was ineffective and the police nonexistent, and that the Vice-President of the United States was under attack by a mob of potential assassins. He ordered two companies of the 101st Airborne to Puerto Rico, and two companies of Marines from the Second Division to Guantánamo, where they were within two or three hours' flying time from Caracas. He also ordered an aircraft carrier and accompanying fleet to stations off the Venezuelan coast. He explained that it was "purely a precautionary measure" in the event the Venezuelan government requested assistance. Since the government was a major part of the problem, he could not have expected such a request; in fact, he started the troop movements in the event that he had to order a rescue operation in a hostile situation.[72]

It was called Operation Poor Richard, and when Nixon heard about it, he was appalled. Calm had returned to the city; the Army was in control. Moreover, he correctly anticipated that Eisenhower's mobilization, however tiny in fact, would cause every newspaper in Latin America to outdo its rivals in denunciations of gunboat diplomacy by the Colossus of the North.

By nine that evening, the Venezuelan radio was reporting an enormous invasion was imminent. Nixon issued a statement, saying there was "a very limited troop movement" under way, from one American base to another, and that he was sure the Venezuelan government had the situation well in hand and did not need any outside assistance. The furor died down.

Later, when Mazo asked him in an interview how he remained so calm, Nixon replied, "The most difficult period in one of these incidents is not in handling the situation at the time. The difficult task is with your reactions after it is all over. I get a real letdown after one of these issues. . . . You . . . get the sense that you licked them . . . though they really poured it on. Then you try to catch yourself . . . in statements and actions . . . to be a generous winner. . . ."

Nixon's pattern in a crisis was by now well established. When it was over, he would have a fit of nearly uncontrollable temper over an apparently minor matter, but it would be in private and directed against his own people, not the enemy. Thus his outburst against Rubottom after Lima.

In this instance, Mazo reported that after Nixon issued his statement and retired to "the intimacy of those closest to him, [he] released the bitter anger that he had submerged during that hard day. . . . He opened the safety valve and blew his top. Once relieved, he went to bed."[73] Mazo did not say who was the object of Nixon's rage. Eisenhower himself was the obvious candidate.

THE FOLLOWING DAY, after a three-hour lunch at the fabulous Venezuelan army officers' club (Hartmann commented that had it been built in the United States, there would have been an immediate congressional investigation), Nixon drove to the airport. The Army lined the streets, troops shoulder to shoulder, while everything but tanks escorted the motorcade. When the plane left the ground, everyone on board cheered. The party went to Puerto Rico for the night, to give the White House time to organize a reception.

Such an airport reception Washington had never before seen. More than fifteen thousand people gathered, including the President, all of the Cabinet, and about half of Congress. Tricia and Julie, naturally scared to death by the reports they had heard, rushed into their mother's arms as she descended the ramp.

The Nixons were heroes. Federal workers got the afternoon off, and the streets were jammed with cheering crowds as Eisenhower and the Nixons drove to the White House. After lunch, the Nixons drove home.

Marie Smith of the Washington *Post* was waiting for them. She got Pat to answer a couple of questions. Was she glad to be home? "We are always glad to be home," Pat replied, "and the people in all of these countries were kind and charming. A wonderful trip and just a small minority of communistic inspired groups participated in the disturbances." She said she was spending the evening at home with her daughters.[74]

Nixon himself was on a high, incapable of relaxing. He called a press conference, where he said that the United States must put Latin America in a "top priority position. We need a reappraisal of policies so we can counteract what has been a very serious Soviet propaganda and subversive offensive." That evening, he appeared at a Woman's National Press Club reception, where he was cheered heartily, and then returned to the White House for one of Eisenhower's stag dinners, where he was the center of attention as he had never been before with the President's millionaire buddies.[75]

In the following days, the favorite "have you heard" joke in Washington was that "Jack Kennedy is demanding equal time in Venezuela." The Nixons were greeted with spontaneous applause wherever they went. Thousands of telegrams of congratulation poured in from all over the country. Politicians could not outdo one another in praising the Vice-President. When a reporter who had previously heard Lyndon Johnson call Nixon "chicken shit" asked him about his embrace of Nixon at the airport, Johnson replied, "Son, in politics you've got to learn that overnight chicken shit can turn to chicken salad." A Gallup poll showed Nixon ahead of Stevenson and even with Kennedy.[76]

Chotiner was elated, and saw great opportunities. "Dear Dick," he wrote by hand: "The threat of Communism is still an issue; it was demonstrated on your trip. Keep it definitely in mind when preparing your report to the people. With best wishes, Murray."[77]

Nixon replied, "Dear Murray: I was having lunch with J. Edgar Hoover just a few days ago and he said that one very positive result of the South American trip was that it made anti-Communism respectable again in the United States!"[78]

In a press conference on May 21, however, he was more statesmanlike than political. His theme was that revolutionary new forces were stirring in South America and that the days of the ruling elite were numbered. To keep the Communists from seizing the opportunity, he said, the United States had to help the Latins, proving to them that private U.S. investment and government assistance to South America are not "for the purpose simply of keeping in power a group of the elite, making the rich richer and the poor poorer."

A reporter asked if it was not beneath the dignity of the Vice-President to "go around debating with labor unionists and radical students." Nixon replied, "In these question and answer sessions we covered every difficult and tough question you can imagine. I believe it's essential that we talk to those groups." Asked what his thoughts were in the limousine, he said, "You don't think in terms of world politics and hemispheric problems when someone is banging on your window." And he confessed, "I wouldn't have missed it for anything."[79]

THERE WERE CRITICISMS. Walter Lippmann called the tour "a diplomatic Pearl Harbor." The Boston *Globe* said it was "one of the most ineptly handled episodes in this country's foreign relations."

The New York *Post* said that Nixon "had established his valor in Peru. His insistence on a repeat performance in Venezuela indicates that he was utterly seduced by his press notices, and was incapable of recognizing his own limitations."[80] James Reston wrote that Nixon had been "sent south as a substitute for policy," and added: "As an exercise in national self-bamboozlement, the reaction here to the Vice President's trip is a classic. A national defeat has been parlayed into a personal political triumph, and even when the Nixons are decorated for good conduct under fire, the larger significance of this event cannot be overlooked."[81]

What that long-range significance might be, Reston did not say. If there was any, it is still difficult to locate three decades later. Certainly the trip failed to generate anything more than excitement —no goodwill, no change in policy. Nor can it be said that it did Nixon much permanent good, indeed did him precious little good in the 1958 elections. What Nixon discovered (as did Jimmy Carter in 1980 when mobs in Teheran were shouting "Death to Carter") was that the American people would instinctively rally around the Vice-President when he was under foreign attack, but only as a symbol. The affection for and pride in Nixon that seized the American people, it turned out, were for the Vice-President of the United States, not for Nixon the man.

CHAPTER TWENTY-TWO

THE SIXTH CAMPAIGN
1958

FROM THE BEGINNING, '58 looked as if it was going to be a bad year for the Republicans. In Nixon's long, solitary walks along the Florida beaches, Republican prospects in the off-year elections were the main subject he brooded over.

He was alone by choice and by need. Earlier in his career he had been a man who could—sometimes—listen to and take advice from people he respected, like Roy Day of the Committee of 100 back in 1946, or Bert Andrews and Bob Stripling in 1948, or Murray Chotiner in 1950 and 1952. But increasingly he liked thinking his own way through problems. When he sought other people's views, he did so to gauge public opinion, or to flatter them, not to find new solutions.

He made up his own mind; however, he almost never stuck to it. On the important issues of his era, except foreign aid and civil rights, at one time or another he came down squarely on both sides. This led one set of observers to conclude that he was the ultimate pragmatist, while another set saw him as the ultimate cynic. The first group claimed that he made up his mind on the basis of what was good for the country, and that changing circumstances caused his changes of mind. The second group charged that he made up his mind on the basis of what was good for Richard Nixon, and that he changed his mind as a part of his constant pursuit of the Presidency.

Because Nixon himself was so given to epigrams, he brought out the best—and the worst—in retaliation. "When Nixon's public and private personalities meet," said one such epigram, "they shake hands." If he ever wrestled with his conscience, said another, "the match was fixed." Even when his critics agreed with his conclusions, as in foreign aid or on civil rights, they charged that his motives were wrong, based as they were—so it was said—on his obsessive drive for the Presidency.

Nixon himself maintained that he was not obsessed with the Presidency. He had a highly realistic view of politics and his own position in the political world. In a series of interviews with Earl Mazo in 1958, he was both candid and insightful in speculating on his prospects for the 1960 nomination.

"No one can tell in advance what the issues will be six months later," he said, dismissing the idea that he took this or that position because of its possible effect on 1960.[1] "The only thing certain about a public figure's popularity . . . is that it is never stable, never static. It varies very greatly, up and down, sometimes very violently." He was a fatalist, he said, and he recognized that "the one thing sure about politics is that what goes up comes down and what goes down often comes up," which was as prophetic a line as ever he uttered.[2]

"I don't think that a leader can control to any great extent his destiny," Nixon said. "Very seldom can he step in and change the situation if the forces of history are running in another direction. That is why men like Taft, Clay, Webster . . . never made it, much as they wanted to be president, though all of them had leadership qualities that would have made them good presidents. They never made it because circumstances, in each case, called for somebody else." The same might well happen to him in 1960.[3]

Nixon recognized that he did not control events, that luck, chance, or fate could throw him up to the top or cast him down to the bottom. But he also recognized that if circumstances were such that he did become the nominee, the nomination would be worthless unless the Republican Party was revived.

As he walked the beaches, he reflected on the sad shape of the party. First of all, it was leaderless. Taft was dead, Dewey had retired from national politics, and Eisenhower was infinitely more concerned with the arms race and a balanced budget than he was with the fortunes of the Republican Party. Khrushchev, not Kennedy, occupied Eisenhower's mind.

"Frankly," Eisenhower told Arthur Larson early in the 1958 campaign, "I don't care too much about the congressional elections." Come to that, he added, "I'd just as soon see [Republican Senator Karl] Mundt get beat."[4] He certainly was not going to lift a finger to help Bill Knowland in his campaign for governor of California. Until the party made its 1960 nomination, no one could step forward to fill the vacuum in party leadership.

Adding to Nixon's frustration was his deep disagreement with the President over some basic policy issues, especially taxes, public works spending during the mild 1958 recession, the budget in general and spending on missiles and DOD in particular. He was coming to regard Eisenhower as an old fogy stuck in standpattism. So did many of his friends. In April 1958, Joe Alsop wrote his friend Isaiah Berlin, "One prays—how odd it seems!—for the course of nature to transfer the burden to Nixon (who exactly resembles an heir to a very rich family . . . now utterly distraught because Papa has grown a little senile and spends his time throwing the family fortune out the window—really he is like that. I lunched with him the other day, and he all but asked me how it was possible to argue with a ramolli papa without getting disinherited yourself!)"[5]

Others shared Alsop's view. In March, Charlie McWhorter had lunch with Carroll Kilpatrick of the Washington *Post*. In a memo McWhorter reported to Nixon that "Senator Fulbright told Kilpatrick confidentially that he never knew anyone who could so quickly see the point at issue in a problem, and that he, Fulbright, wishes you were President right now."[6]

The issues were all running against the Republicans, adding to Nixon's woes. Sometimes it was their own fault. John Bricker in Ohio, Bill Knowland in California, and others were campaigning on a right-to-work platform, which was rousing organized labor against them as nothing else could. Recession and its consequences, a falling GNP with a rising unemployment rate, also were hurting the Republicans badly. So was their farm policy—Benson's attempts to get the government out of farming, to reduce the stockpile, and to lower the parity rate were widely resented in the farm belt, and widely blamed for falling commodity prices.

In the face of the recession, Eisenhower refused either to cut taxes, as many Republicans urged, or to appreciably speed up the Interstate Highway program, defense spending, and the missile program. Eisenhower's standpat approach to the economy satisfied no one except Treasury Secretary Anderson, who was as fanatically devoted to a balanced budget as Eisenhower was.

Nixon thought Eisenhower was badly mistaken, but he never attempted to change the President's mind in any direct confrontation. Nor did he, nor could he, attempt to build a political movement to undercut Eisenhower. But he did give a public hint here and there of his disagreement, to indicate both that he was his own man and that things would be different if he were to become President. In private, outside the White House, he pushed as hard as he dared for new policies.

"I AM CONCERNED ABOUT THE TENDENCY in this Administration to be sort of a care-taker," Nixon wrote Father Cronin in August, to "keep the best of the past—things are good—let's don't rock the boat." Nixon believed "we must not approach the problems with resistance to change—etc.—we must go out and look for new ideas. We talk all about finding the way to the moon and the exploration of outer space—let's do a little exploration in the economic field."

Nixon was providing Cronin with notes for a speech Cronin was writing. Nixon told him, "This is a speech which I will pitch to the business community—one which I will circulate as being my economic philosophy but in addition to that it will have a progress touch to it other than the stand-pat conservative economics that Anderson and his crowd are constantly parrotting." And again, "I want to give Republicans something so that they can say this is the philosophy that we have. This is something we have to offer— it is not just a stand-pat philosophy." [7]

The philosophy was free enterprise unleashed. Major tax cuts, he had come to believe, especially in the higher brackets, would unloose a flood of investment capital, which would provide new jobs and pull the country out of the recession. The basic idea eventually became commonplace (and indeed became policy under Jack Kennedy and again with Ronald Reagan). But in 1958 the idea of cutting taxes at a time that government revenues were down because of a recession was unthinkable to Eisenhower and Anderson.

"While popular politically," Nixon said, "the idea that we can get more tax revenue simply by soaking the rich is phony and unworkable because the tax rates now are at such a level that we have dried up that source. You couldn't squeeze any more taxes out of the people in the higher brackets at this point than you could get juice out of a cueball." Lowering taxes "would have the effect of stimulating economic growth by unleashing capital and encouraging new capital. This, in turn, would lead not only to more revenue for the government, but even more important, it would inevitably produce more and better jobs for our people." [8]

In September, he unveiled his plan in a speech at Harvard University. He was careful in proposing it; he did not call for an immediate tax cut, which would have infuriated Anderson and Eisenhower, but only suggested revisions in the tax code, to be studied when the new Congress went to work in January 1959. He also had Charlie McWhorter call Anderson. "Tell him I am making this speech at Harvard and that I am projecting for the future and suggesting certain tax reforms—not as Administration policies but as matters that should be considered in the next session. I have deliberately not cleared it with Anderson because I did not want him to be on the spot. Anderson can say anything he wants—that Treasury has under continuing study this whole issue of tax reform." [9]

He was just as careful in preparing the speech. His instructions to Cronin were detailed and extensive. He said he wanted a "frontal attack on reducing the take from the higher brackets—immediately this is political—most people say privately it is right—point out that if our economy is going to grow, if we are going to have the incentives—if we are going to have the capital we have to move. Point out the barrenness of the New Deal, Fair Deal, ADA approach to economics." The Democrats said they wanted to raise the floor. Fine, responded Nixon, "but you cannot raise the floor without raising the ceiling as well or you get in a squeeze."

He wanted to go after labor, using West Germany as an example. "They have encouraged private enterprise and they have not had runaway labor. I want to hit this spiral of wage increases without increased productivity. I have to hit it frontally and make a positive suggestion or two. The approach I don't like and one that intends [sic] to backfire is I am appealing to the labor workers over the head of the union bosses."

He wanted to create a Republican philosophy, one that people could rally around, one that emphasized growth and progress in the economy and in national defense. "This idea that you can't do things—that we can't afford things—constantly in national defense we are always coming up to this we can't afford this." Nixon thought the nation could afford it, but he could not say so publicly: "At this point I can't have a break with the President on national defense but on the other hand I would go further than he does in saying that we do considerably more." [10]

In the speech, delivered on September 6, Nixon asserted that "there are strong reasons to believe that the stimulating effects of even a small cut in the corporate tax rate would lead to more rather than less revenue. . . . In the area of personal income the almost confiscatory rates in the highest brackets stifle and prevent risk-taking and encourage tax avoidance devices. The small loss of revenue caused by some reduction in these rates would inevitably be offset by the new investment and business expansion which would result." In a direct criticism of the Eisenhower/Anderson position on the budget, he declared, "We must not allow the fear of a temporary budget deficit to put us in a strait jacket which will keep us from doing what we ought to do to insure economic growth." [11]

NIXON WANTED WIDE DISTRIBUTION OF HIS HARVARD SPEECH. He told Cronin to "submit a prospective list for mailing this speech to people on the economic side—the egghead group—the business mailing list—the Young Republican Presidents—NAM—etc." [12] He sent it out, with a covering letter, to editors around the country. [13] On September 23, two weeks after delivering the speech, he wrote Henry Luce, reminding him that in recent discussions "we talked about the need for more Republicans getting out in public with an affirmative approach to our national problems." He said he had made his Harvard speech in that spirit, called it "one of the most important speeches I have ever made," and then complained that "not a solitary line about that speech has appeared in either *Time* or *Life*." Businessmen all over the country had heard about it, Nixon claimed, and were ordering multiple copies—one industrialist was going to distribute 150,000 copies in booklet form. "Even The Washington *Post* produced a highly favorable editorial in probably the first kind words they have had for me in the past six years." [14] But not a word from the Luce empire. Nor was there to be any—for the good reason that what Nixon was suggesting Eisenhower was ignoring. Nixon's ideas on taxation policy, strong as they were—as time showed—were not brutally rejected by the Administration. Rather, they were coldly ignored.

ONE OF THE CRITICAL ISSUES IN '58 was right-to-work. Taft-Hartley had given states the opportunity to outlaw the closed shop, and a number were seeking to do so, most importantly Ohio and California. Republicans in those states thought the issue was a winner. Nixon's instincts told him that right-to-work, at least that year, was a loser. But Chotiner was the only Republican in California who agreed with him. [15] The others wanted him to support right-to-work. Nixon had an aide call Kyle Palmer of the Los Angeles *Times*. "Tell him that I do not plan to say anything one way or the other. Will stay with position that I voted for Taft-Hartley bill which leaves this decision up to the states, would be improper for a federal official to take a position other than that." [16]

That was not good enough for the fat cats who paid for the campaigns. Chotiner wrote Nixon to warn him that NAM (National Association of Manufacturers) people in California wanted to know the answer to two questions: Would Dick support right-to-work? Would he stump the state for Bill Knowland? "If the answer is no to either one," Murray warned, "the group is supposed to be of a mind to write you off." [17]

Nixon remained neutral. Three days after Chotiner wrote, Nixon told Father Cronin, "Obviously I am not going to take a position on right-to-work—I am going to avoid that. I can't say I am for it or against it because if I say I am against it they will say I am against Knowland." [18] He never did say whether he was for it or against it, but he did insist that it was a loser for '58. And he deplored the split it was causing in the Republican Party.

THE REPUBLICANS WERE ALSO TEARING THEMSELVES APART over Sherman Adams, who became an even bigger issue than right-to-work that summer. In a neat reversal of what the Republicans had done to them in 1947 and 1948, the Democrats used their control of the congressional committees to uncover a little corruption in the Eisenhower Administration. Their target was Adams, and they hit him in June, with an investigation into his relations with Bernard Goldfine, a New England industrialist who had given Adams small presents (a vicuña coat became the most famous) and paid his hotel bills when he was in Boston. Adams, in turn (in return, the Democrats charged), made some phone calls to federal agencies in Goldfine's behalf.

The whole Adams furor had a surreal quality to it. What Adams did for Goldfine was the small change of politics. The total worth of the bills paid over five years amounted to little more than $3,000. It also turned out that Goldfine had given equal or greater amounts to a number of congressmen. But naturally enough, a balanced and relative view of the matter was not the Democrats' view.

A number of things made Adams particularly vulnerable and thus a profitable target. First and foremost, nobody liked the man. He was incapable of small talk and had never learned how to use the words that everyone else uses to make conversation possible, words like "hello" and "thank you" and "goodbye." Eisenhower once painted a portrait of Adams, done from a photograph as a surprise. When Eisenhower presented it to Adams, the chief of staff had not so much as a word of praise for the effort. "Mr. President," he muttered, ". . . you flattered me." He then turned on his heel and walked out of the Oval Office.[19]

Adams' role added to his unpopularity. He was the manager of the door, the one who decided who got in to see the President. Or rather, announced, because in fact the President made the decision, which Adams merely implemented. But congressmen and politicians ascribed absolute powers to Adams, calling him the most powerful man in Washington. This was so far from the truth that it is hard to figure out how such a view became so popular. Clearly one reason was Adams himself, who not only shared the view but promoted it. Another was Eisenhower's leadership style, what Fred Greenstein has so nicely characterized as "hidden-hand leadership."

Republican vulnerability on any corruption issue was obvious. Nixon and his friends had hit the Democrats so hard on corruption in 1952 that they had invited a counterattack. When it came, Nixon's first impulse was to open an offensive. As he remarked that summer, "I don't think anybody ever is as good on the defense as on the offense, but whenever anybody attacks, I believe the way to answer is not simply to defend, but to take the offensive." [20] In this case, he put his staff to work on reseaching gifts given to FDR and Harry Truman. The lists they worked up were quite impressive, but it turned out they could not be used. Despite coats (including a mink for Eleanor), jewels, and other valuable items, Eisenhower let Nixon know he didn't want a word of criticism. The reason was that Eisenhower himself had accepted lots of valuable gifts from his rich friends. [21]

Other Republicans sensed that there could be no effective counterattack and were prepared to retreat. A number of senators called for Adams' resignation, including Knowland and Barry Goldwater, Republican of Arizona. In the case of Guy Gabrielson back in 1951, Nixon had been alone in demanding the RNC chairman's resignation, and had at that time insisted on absolute purity as a prerequisite for a Republican officeholder. But in 1958 he knew how much Adams meant to Eisenhower, so he joined the save-Adams wing of the party. He accused Goldwater, Knowland, and the other critics of "acting like a bunch of cannibals." He charged that they were only helping the Democrats, and that "it doesn't take much guts to kick a guy when he is down." [22]

But defending Adams proved impossible. As the Democrats continued to hit the headlines with new accusations, Republican morale sank, and contributions all but disappeared. The polls predicted disaster for the Republicans. They would have anyway, but Adams made the perfect scapegoat. That he had to resign, for the good of the party, was obvious to every Republican in the country —except Adams. And Eisenhower was not the man to fire anyone who had been loyal to him and served him well, an Eisenhower characteristic that had worked to Nixon's advantage back in '56. The trick became how to get Adams to resign. The amount of time and effort that went into this simple proposition was quite incredible. One would have thought, from the way it was handled, that Adams was being asked to renounce the throne of England.

ON JULY 15, Nixon had breakfast with Eisenhower. The President never mentioned Adams by name, but he did bemoan the state of the party. Nixon then had a long talk with Adams. Emphasizing that he was not speaking for Eisenhower, he tried to talk Adams into resigning. Adams made it clear that if Eisenhower asked for his resignation, he would have it, but only if Eisenhower asked. [23]

Eisenhower could not bring himself to ask, and the issue stayed alive. In late August, just before Congress adjourned, Eisenhower and Nixon talked. It was the beginning of a complex minuet. Nixon explained to the President that the party could not stand up for Adams because he was going to hurt the candidates badly in the election. Eisenhower thought that "Sherm could use that as a good reason for his resigning" (which ignored the fact that Sherm had already rejected it as a reason for resigning), and hoped that Nixon could "have a talk with Sherm after Congress adjourns."

When Congress adjourned, on August 24, Nixon, Pat, and the girls took the train to The Greenbrier in West Virginia. Every vacation they had taken since 1947 had been cut short by politics, but Nixon promised this time would be different.[24]

The next morning, he got a call from the White House. Ann Whitman took notes: "The President reminded the Vice President of a long talk they had had about a certain individual; he said he did not think their plan should be forgotten. The President said 'Of course I could do it but I thought we had agreed that you should.' " Nixon said that he had heard the Democrats planned to reopen the Adams hearings in late September, "a move that was of course flagrantly political." Eisenhower sighed. "I was really hoping," he said, "that we could get the matter resolved before then."[25]

This last expression, Ann Whitman wrote in her diary, "the Vice President took (as did I) to be an order." Nixon was back in Washington that afternoon, leaving Pat and the girls in West Virginia. He saw Adams, then reported the results to Whitman: "He said he was as blunt as it was possible to be; that he had appealed to Governor Adams on the basis that the Republicans were going to lose seats in the Congress and they were going to blame loss on Governor Adams, that he would therefore find it more difficult to operate." But Adams rejected the arguments, saw Eisenhower himself, and convinced the President that he should stay.[26]

The following day, Eisenhower asked Nixon to play golf with him. On the course, Eisenhower explained, "I can't fire a man who is sincere just for political reasons. He must resign in a way I can't refuse." Then the President mused, "I think Sherm must have misunderstood what you said." Nixon thought he had understood well enough, it was just that he would respond only to word from the man himself. Nixon also quoted Adams' remark: " 'Who will take my place? I've never heard anyone suggested.' " Eisenhower flushed, then said curtly and coldly, "That's my problem, not his."[27]

Over the next few days, Eisenhower's determination hardened. One of his closest friends, Cliff Roberts, told him the affair was the cause of Republican "hopelessness," and Winthrop Aldrich told him that Goldfine really was a crook, that he was tarnishing the White House itself, and that "this man [Adams] has got to go or we [the Republican Party] are done." [28]

Nixon having failed to persuade Adams to resign, Eisenhower turned to Meade Alcorn, the new chairman of the RNC. Alcorn met with Nixon to plan a strategy. He wanted Nixon to join him and Persons in the confrontation with Adams, but Nixon excused himself. He did offer a suggestion—that Alcorn find some way to convince Adams that he was speaking for the President.

Evidently Alcorn did, because on September 17 Adams called the President. He said he was thinking of resigning but needed some time to think over his method and statement—he thought he would be ready in a month. Eisenhower replied with a lovely example of his jumbled syntax and contradictory meanings within one sentence that nevertheless got the point across: "If anything is done and we make any critical decision, as I have always said, you will have to take the initiative yourself." He did not want to put any pressure on Adams, or do "anything that looks cold and indifferent." Finally, he dropped the ax—he read Adams the statement he intended to issue when he accepted the resignation, a statement full of praise for Adams' integrity, ability, and devotion to his country. Less than a week later, Eisenhower accepted Adams' resignation. The boil had been lanced, but too late to do the Republicans any good in the '58 elections. [29]

As CONGRESS WOUND DOWN, politics heated up. The campaign was under way. It was obvious that Eisenhower was not going to participate; except for Agriculture Secretary Ezra Taft Benson, no one on the Cabinet was going to participate; if the Republicans were to have a national leader, it had to be Nixon.

His friends nevertheless urged him to stay out. General Douglas MacArthur wrote, "If I had one word of advice, it would be to abstain. . . . You have established an invincible position that time and your own immediate silence will immeasurably strengthen." [30] Tom Dewey told him, "I know that all those old party wheelhorses will tell you stories that will pluck your heartstrings, but you're toying with your chance to be President. Don't do it, Dick. You've already done enough, and 1960 is what counts now." [31]

Such advice—and it came from many others—was predicated on the assumption that the Republicans were going to take a bad licking, and that if Nixon entered the campaign with his usual stumping across the country, he would be blamed for the loss and branded a loser. That was true enough, but it ignored other facts.

After six years of the Eisenhower Presidency, the Republican Party was in disarray. It had no genuine leadership. Its percentage of the vote had fallen off in every election since 1946, with the single exception of 1952, and was now at its lowest ebb. It could no longer draw on Ike's popularity, which in any case had fallen for the first time below a 50 percent approval rating. Unless the party was revived, its 1960 nomination would be worthless.

In his memoirs, Nixon explained his decision to once again hit the campaign trail—"I was deluged by appeals from across the country to appear on behalf of Republican candidates. In the end, I took on the task because it had to be done, and because there wasn't anyone else to do it."[32] The further truth was that he never thought seriously of not doing it.

On August 22, Nixon and Dulles had one of their long telephone conversations. "N said this is the political season and Kennedy and the boys are starting on the [missile] gap. N suspects they may try to make an issue of defense policy in the campaign." That was going to hurt, Nixon knew, especially because Eisenhower was talking about suspending nuclear testing, not spending more on defense. "The Sec thinks the suspension of testing will be well regarded in the country. N agreed hesitatingly and said you can't tell—might get a mixed reaction on that." When Congress adjourned, Nixon added, "there will be an interval of a couple of weeks and then we will be in the middle of rough politics. The Sec has to stay out of it but would not rule out the possibility that he make a couple of good ringing defenses of our policies. N said that would be good. The Sec asked re foreign aid and N said they would pass it—how much? N said a lot has been done and he thinks we will get ¾s of the difference. N will be going away with his family and then to a beach alone later. And then on to the campaign. N said we don't want people to keep us on the defensive. Agreed. N will let them have it between the eyes if they get too tough."[33]

Nixon's problem was that he had to defend the Eisenhower Administration. It was difficult to attack the Democrats after six years of Republican rule. Nixon could not charge them with various and sundry errors and shortcomings; the only way he could take the offensive was to warn about what would happen in the event of a Democratic victory.

His basic speech, drafted by Cronin and extensively revised by Nixon, began with the question, "What would happen if the Democrats swept Congress?" Nixon's reply was a question of his own: "Which Democratic Party do you mean?" The southern conservatives, he said, "have a good record on foreign policy and government spending," but "their record is bad on civil rights." Then there was "the radical-ADA wing of the Democratic Party, which dominates the national organization." This wing "consists largely of a group whose thinking was solidified in the first four years of the New Deal. Since 1936, they have stopped thinking. But they have been planning and plotting to take over again and give us another dish of deficit hash on boondoggle bread."

Nixon claimed there were two divisions to the radical wing. "There is the ADA group with both feet planted firmly on Cloud Nine. On the next cloud are the labor politicians." What would happen if the radical Democrats took over? "It would be the end to government economy for the next two years. . . . Any hope of bringing the budget into balance will be gone. Taxes would have to go up sharply. Prices would again get out of hand. In the area of foreign policy, the appetite for appeasement would dominate." A Democratic victory, in short, would be a disaster.[34]

Nixon's emphasis on the two wings of the Democratic Party allowed him to make private appeals to the southern senators. After Little Rock, the Republican Party had little hope of breaking up the Solid South anytime soon, but Eisenhower and Nixon wanted to retain and solidify the alliance with southern conservatives. So Nixon told one of his aides to "call Bebe [Rebozo] and ask him to tell Senators Smathers and Johnson that although it isn't always carried in the papers, RN has been careful in every instance to make a distinction between the radical Democrats and the real Democrats." Bebe should remind them that Nixon often said nice things about southern senators, and warn them that "if the radical Democrat candidates are elected the real Democrats will no longer be able to control the party." In addition, "if Bebe thinks it advisable," he should tell them that "RN of course understands that they have to take him on. Also, Smathers might want to pass along to Symington, Mansfield, and Kennedy that under no circumstances is RN coming into their states, even tho he has been asked to many times." Nixon summed up: "It's just like Smathers privately says— he doesn't want too many [Democrats] to win because of the radicals. Naturally, Smathers can't say that publicly."[35]

Not all southern senators were on Nixon's "good guy" list. Senator William Fulbright of Arkansas, for example, was suspect. Nixon wanted to put his feet to the fire, because Fulbright voted a liberal line when in Washington, while talking a conservative line back home. "Last year in the Little Rock crisis," Nixon noted in a memo to an aide, "both Senators Fulbright and [John] McClellan [also of Arkansas] were absent and silent during most of the time, particularly the otherwise vocal Fulbright. We should put these Senators on the spot. To deal only with Governor Faubus gives him too much of a build-up, and even if Fulbright lines up with Faubus, it will help to tarnish him for future attacks on the Administration." [36]

ON CIVIL RIGHTS, Nixon and the Repubicans were caught in a hopeless situation. Neither Eisenhower's dramatic and decisive action at Little Rock nor the passage of the Administration's 1957 Civil Rights Act had drawn any appreciable number of Negro voters out of the party of FDR and back to the party of Lincoln, but they had seriously set back progress toward the creation of a Republican Party in the South. There was a widespread suspicion in Washington "that Nixon would welcome racial antagonisms to split the Democratic party and win in Eastern and Western states the Negro votes which could decide the presidential election." [37] The suspicion was unfounded. Nixon knew there was no profit for him or his party in racial antagonism. As to the split in the Democratic party, he did not have to lift a finger to bring it about or to maintain it, not when northern Democrats were calling for "freedom now" and southerners were responding "resistance forever."

As befit the moderate that he was on the race issue, Nixon did his best to keep it out of the campaign. Privately, he explained, "I feel strongly that civil rights is primarily a moral rather than a legal question. Laws play a necessary part, of course. But the approach of those who say 'Education alone is the answer' and 'Leave us alone and this thing will eventually work out' is not adequate. It is just as unrealistic to assume that passing a law or handing down a court decision will solve this problem. Where human relations are concerned, a law isn't worth the paper it is written on unless it has the moral support of the majority of the people. . . . Just passing laws and trying to enforce them isn't going to work any better than prohibition did." He thought the place to start mobilizing the moral conscience of the nation was among the young, because "they have a minimum of prejudice." Thus he believed that a moderate implementation of school desegregation was the "constructive" way. [38]

WHAT NIXON DID TALK ABOUT IN THE CAMPAIGN, aside from the catastrophes that would befall the country in the event of a Democratic victory, was the need for Republicans to get to work. In so doing, he was taking on a virtually impossible task, because Republican demoralization was so bad, Republican coffers so low, that there was a feeling of total hopelessness. Nixon shared it. [39] Nevertheless he assumed the responsibility of acting as party prod and cheerleader. It was a bit like being on the third string at Whittier College football games, when Whittier was playing Southern Cal.

Although there was no hope for Whittier, Nixon was up and down the sidelines, encouraging the players, slapping them on the back, telling them to get out there and fight.

He was alone in making optimistic forecasts. In Wyoming: "I find increasing evidence that the political pollsters and prophets who have been predicting a decisive Democratic victory are in for the surprise of their lives on November 4." In Wisconsin: "Thousands of moderate Democrats will turn the tide in close races in the Northern and Western states by voting for Republican candidates." [40]

On October 19, he sent all GOP candidates a telegram. "The tide that was running so strongly against us has taken a sharp turn in our favor," he said, without a shred of evidence. But he needed to exhort, not predict. "If we make the fight of our lives and mount a massive offensive . . . we can turn what appeared to be a certain defeat into victory. . . . All Republican candidates and spokesmen should radiate optimism and should be on the offensive." [41]

He undercut himself, however, by insisting on telling his audiences about the great sacrifice he was making for them. In Indianapolis on September 29: "Some of my Republican friends have even urged me to do as little as possible in this campaign so as to avoid being associated with a losing cause." In Garden City, Long Island, October 23: "Many friends have warned me of the political risks involved in being associated with a losing campaign." Then the reassurance that it did not matter: "What happens to me in this campaign is relatively unimportant. What happens to the Republican party is more important." Finally the explanation: "Win or lose, it is unforgivable to lack the courage to fight for the principles we believe in." [42]

Insofar as it reminded the Republicans of how much they owed to Dick Nixon, and how much he was sacrificing for their sake, the theme was helpful to Nixon. But insofar as it made Republicans wonder why they should exert themselves when the top people in the party were whispering to Nixon that he should stay away from a certain losing cause, it was bad for Republicn morale. Making things worse, with one exception the members of the Cabinet were sitting this one out, to Nixon's disgust, which only added to the impression that anyone with any brains was saving his money, time, and reputation in '58 and staying out. Adding to the malaise was the fact that the exception was Ezra Taft Benson, the most unpopular man in the Cabinet. Each time he spoke in the farm belt he lost more votes.

WHATEVER THE DIFFICULTIES AND COMPLEXITIES, Nixon plunged ahead, campaigning across twenty-five states and making innumerable speeches. Except when forecasting what the "radical-ADA wing" would do once in power, he was positive and upbeat, stressing Republican gains. Once again repporters began writing about a new Nixon. Cabell Phillips of *The New York Times* thought he had "matured." To Phillips, "He no longer has the unctuous countenance of a superannuated 'All-American Boy,' and has acquired instead a certain sedateness that better becomes his age and his station." Still, Phillips was not ready to forget the old Nixon, "a crafty, shrewd politician whose disarming youthfulness masks a ruthless ambition, for whom expedience takes the place of principles, and whose most effective weapon is the imputation of dubious loyalty to his opponents."

Phillips gives a word picture of Nixon on the campaign trail: "The brisk, buoyant march to the head table, the exaggerated handshaking with the other guests, follow a ritual pattern not unlike that used to show off a fighter in the prize ring. Mrs. Nixon, fragile and shy, is an important prop in this pageantry; there is always an extra measure of applause when the crowd recognizes her. His platform manner is that of a sales promotion manager pepping up his sales force. . . . His posture is mobile and expressive, and he scowls or smiles or betrays indignation or whips the air with a clenched fist, at precisely the right moment and with good elocutionary effect. His mood is earnest and evangelical and tinged now and then with righteous anger." [43]

As a member of Congress in 1948, when he was investigating Alger Hiss, Nixon lived on leaks from federal bureaucrats. As a member of the Eisenhower Administration, he detested leaks. He hated them so much, in fact, that he let his emotions show, and thereby damaged the image of the new Nixon, recalling to Phillips' mind the old Nixon.

The incident concerned American policy in the Far East. The Chinese Communists were shelling the tiny offshore islands of Quemoy and Matsu, which were held by the Chinese Nationalists. War threatened. Eisenhower's policy, as in an earlier crisis in the same place, was to defend Quemoy and Matsu. Many Democrats, John Kennedy among them, were questioning his wisdom of risking a world war over such a minuscule matter. Nixon had supported the President.

On September 27, someone in the State Department leaked a story to *The New York Times*. It was not much of a story—the gist was that the department had received five thousand letters on the Quemoy-Matsu situation and that 80 percent of them were critical of Administration policy. Although it was a common practice for the Administration to release mail counts when they were favorable, the leak of this adverse count made Nixon furious. On his own, he undertook to counter and denounce it.

The day of the leak, Nixon issued a statement. "I am shocked," he began. "What concerns me primarily is not the patent and deliberate effort of a State Department subordinate to undercut the Secretary of State and sabotage his policy. What is of far greater concern is the apparent assumption that the weight of the mail rather than the weight of the evidence should be the controlling factor in determining American foreign policy. . . . If we indulge in the kind of thinking which assumes that foreign policy decisions should be made on the basis of opinion polls, we might as well decide now to surrender our position of world leadership to the Communists and to become a second-rate nation." [44]

Nixon's overreaction, and his implicit threat to government employees who "sabotaged" policy decisions through leaks, caused not only Phillips but a number of other reporters to recall the old Nixon. Costello wrote, "It was a deliberate attempt to intimidate federal workers [which] exposed [him] again to a charge of 'fascist tendencies,' for no one could escape the inference that, if it were his administration, anyone running afoul of policy, even inadvertently, could expect only the swiftest and most merciless reprisals." [45]

Dulles was alarmed too. He told reporters he did not think there had been deliberate sabotage. Then he called Nixon, who got him to agree that "the man who put it out should have cleared it." Nixon urged Dulles to have a full-fledged press conference. Dulles thought he might, because otherwise "the Communists may conclude we may have reached the point where we are not able to take forcible action against them." That was a gross exaggeration too, but Nixon liked it. "N said to say that and also N understands it is the case a lot of it [the five thousand letters] was stimulated. N said could the Sec say that. . . . The Sec said he did not make the sabotage the burden of his argument. N said the Sec might at least indicate he thinks it was unauthorized and unwise. . . . The Sec said he can't say he has proof. . . . N said no, but that was the intent —say the Sec has no proof but that the effect was to undercut. . . . They agreed he could say that." [46]

But Dulles' attempts at explanation did little good. Over the following week, newspapers asserted that "Nixon goofed," that the incident unmasked his "fascist tendencies," and so on. He received nearly a thousand letters, 60 percent of them hostile, some violently so. A New York businessman wrote that he had felt the only hope for the nation was "the election of Dick Nixon in 1960, [but] now I am not so sure. You have committed an egregious blunder. . . . My advice to you, sir, is to eat crow promptly and in a big way." [47]

In response to the criticisms, Nixon prepared a long, defensive form letter. "Let me make two points very clear," he wrote. "I uphold without reservation the right and duty of Americans to express their views to government officials. I equally defend the right of our free press to seek out and publish such information as legitimate news." Then he made two more points clear. First, the mail should never decide policy—"For example, the fact that my mail at times has run as high as ten to one against integration has not caused me to change my view that fighting for racial justice is for me a moral as well as a legal obligation." Second: "For us to yield in the face of Communist pressures in Formosa would be disastrous," not because of any strategic importance "but because we must always fight for the principle that use of force to accomplish international objectives can never be condoned or rewarded." [48]

But the statement was not directed at the Communists, nor at public opinion. Shortly after the 1958 elections, Nixon confessed his real—many would have thought obvious—motive. He said that his statement was directed at "a group in the State Department that keeps trying to undercut Dulles' Far Eastern policies." He said he weighed the risk of "saying what I did" and decided he had to do it. "I believe the statement had the effect I intended it to have." Nixon argued that the warning implicit in his statement "will discourage State Department personnel who disagree with administration policy from assuming the right to buck it publicly." [49]

THE TEMPEST OVER NIXON'S STATEMENT on disloyal State Department employees had barely subsided when he was in trouble again. On October 13, he switched from defending the Administration's policy of defending Quemoy and Matsu to attacking his favorite enemies, Harry Truman and Dean Acheson. He denounced the Democratic Party's "sorry record of retreat and appeasement" and compared Eisenhower's foreign-policy record "with the record of failure of the seven years that preceded it." He damned the "defensive, defeatist fuzzy-headed thinking which contributed to the loss of China and led to the Korean war.

"In a nutshell," he concluded, "the Acheson foreign policy resulted in war and the Eisenhower-Dulles policy resulted in peace." [50]

Dulles was unhappy with Nixon's speech. He did not want the tense and complex Quemoy-Matsu situation made into a campaign issue. At a press conference the next morning, a reporter asked Dulles whether current aspects of foreign policy should be debated on the stump. Dulles answered that the practice was "highly undesirable" and added, "I would hope that both sides would calm down on this aspect of the debate." This was widely regarded as a rebuke to Nixon.

Nixon called Dulles. The Secretary agreed to issue a clarifying statement to the effect that of course when the Democrats attacked Eisenhower's foreign policy, someone had to reply. But that same morning, October 15, Eisenhower had his own press conference. The President said, "I do subscribe to this theory: foreign policy ought to be kept out of partisan debate. . . . I realize that when someone makes a charge another individual is going to reply. I deplore that. . . . America's best interests in the world will be served if we do not indulge in this kind of thing." The President's rebuke made headlines.[51]

It was a storm that could have broken only over Nixon's head. It was not his words but his theme that caused such an uproar. Many politicians and political observers were highly suspicious of the new Nixon, and always on the lookout for traces of the old Nixon, which was the reason for the reaction to his earlier statement. In his attack on Truman/Acheson he accused them of "retreat and appeasement," not "surrender and treason," as he had in 1952. Similarly, he charged that Democratic policies "contributed" to the loss of China—back in '52 the word was "led."

But however much Nixon moderated his words, the theme was still the same, the reaction as strong. Eisenhower and Dulles were resigned to a Democratic victory in November, and knew they would have to work with a Democratic Congress the next two years. Getting the Democrats all riled up over Nixon's irresponsible innuendos about their loyalty was exactly what they did *not* want.

But what was good for the country was not good for the Republican Party—at least as Nixon saw it. At a press conference in San Francisco, reporters asked him to comment on Eisenhower's statement earlier that day about the need to keep foreign policy out of the campaign. "This, I think, is a proper position for the President," he said, but added that "for us who have the responsibility of carrying the weight of this campaign to stand by and to allow our policies to be attacked with impunity by our opponents without reply would lead to inevitable defeat." Nixon went on: "One of the reasons the Republican party is in trouble today is because we have allowed people to criticize our policies and we have not stood up and answered effectively. . . . I intend to continue to answer the attacks. . . . That's my view of a political campaign."

Good enough, but it did not speak to the real point, which was that Nixon had not defended the Quemoy-Matsu policy, he had attacked Truman and Acheson. So when Eisenhower learned of Nixon's press conference, he sent the Vice-President a telegram to clarify things. "I want to point out the following," he began. "Both political parties have taken a common stand on the essential foundation of a foreign policy. Both of us are dedicated to peace, to the renunciation of force except for defense, to the principles of the United Nations Charter, to opposing Communist expansion, to promoting the defensive and economic strength of the free world through cooperative action." Such matters, the President declared, "do not lend themselves to political argument."

But, Eisenhower continued, when the Democrats attacked the "administrative operation of foreign policy," why then "these need to be answered whenever they occur." The President was specific; with regard to American policy in Lebanon and Formosa, "these actions, when criticized, should be supported by our side. No one can do this more effectively than you."[52]

In a separate telegram, the President told Nixon, "If there exists in your mind any possible misunderstanding, please call me on the telephone at your convenience."[53]

Nixon understood well enough. Four days later, in Baltimore, he declared, "I do not question the sincerity or patriotism of those who criticize our policies. Our differences are not in ends but in means.

"There is no war party in the United States. All Americans want peace.

"There is no party of surrender in the United States. . . .

"There is only one party of treason in the United States—the Communist party. . . ."[54]

He even reached out to Harry Truman. As always, they talked to each other through the newspapers. On the campaign trail, Nixon praised Truman's decisive response to the North Korean invasion, and for his sponsorship of the Marshall Plan. He called Truman "a gallant warrior." In Sioux Falls, on October 25, newsmen reported that Nixon's "cordiality towards Truman reached such a peak this week that Mr. Nixon was asked when and where the final peace would be made. The Vice President—who plays the piano too—replied, 'The hatchet will be buried when the National Press Club gets us up there to play a duet.' " The club immediately called Truman. Harry would have nothing to do with the proposal. "He has called me a traitor," Truman said, "and I don't like that. Why would I do a thing like this? I've refused to enter the Senate when he was there."[55]

THERE WAS ONE MORE FLAP TO ENDURE in the '58 campaign, this last one centering around Nelson Rockefeller. He was running for governor on the Republican ticket in New York, and beyond that, almost everyone assumed, for the Republican nomination for President in 1960. The common assumption was that a big win by Rockefeller in New York, coupled with a Democratic sweep in California, would make him the leading contender for the '60 nomination. Rockefeller's strategy in New York was to stick strictly to local issues. He not only would not defend Eisenhower's policies, he went out of his way to dissociate himself from them (on precisely the same issues—taxes and defense spending—that Nixon privately also disagreed with the President), to the point that he turned down an opportunity to appear on television with Eisenhower.

On October 23, Nixon came to New York for a major fundraising speech. Rockefeller decided to keep his distance, saying he would not campaign with Nixon and did not want Nixon campaigning for him. He had heard that the New York *Post*, a Democratic paper influential with New York's liberals, was going to endorse him, but that the endorsement hinged on his attitude toward Nixon. At the dinner, a Theodore Roosevelt anniversary at Garden City, Long Island, Nixon denounced the "defeatist" mood in the Republican Party and gave his usual pep talk. He knew he was in liberal country, where the only hope Republicans had was to attract independent and Democratic voters, so as Harrison Salisbury noted in *The New York Times*, "he dulled the sharpness of some of the barbs that he has directed against the 'radicals' and the 'radical wing' of the Democratic party." Dewey thought it was a *"tour de force* of the first magnitude," and told Nixon so, but the *Times* headline was "ROCKEFELLER FAILS TO SEE NIXON," and Salisbury's story emphasized that Nixon had mentioned Rocky only twice, while he praised Republican senatorial candidate Kenneth Keating on seven occasions.[56]

Dewey and other Republicans in New York began putting pressure on Rockefeller to patch up the apparent rift in the party. Rockefeller, whose political career was characterized by indecision, changed his mind about seeing Nixon. He arranged for a breakfast meeting. This too became headlines. It also enraged Dorothy Schiff, publisher of the *Post*. She wrote in her column that her newspaper "might well have endorsed Nelson Rockefeller" had he not broken bread with Richard Nixon. "To us," she explained, "Nixonism has replaced McCarthyism as the greatest threat to the prestige of our nation today."[57]

DESPITE ALL HIS CHEERLEADING, right down to the wire, Nixon tried to prepare himself for the worst on election night. But no one could have anticipated just how bad it was going to be. The Republicans suffered a massive defeat, unprecedented, and decisive. The '58 election gave the Democrats control of the government so completely that they held it for the next decade. They increased their majority in the Senate by thirteen seats, bringing the proportion to 62 to 34. They won forty-seven additional seats in the House, where they now had a 292 to 153 majority. They won thirteen of the twenty-one gubernatorial races, and thus controlled thirty-four of the forty-eight statehouses. Senators Bricker in Ohio and Knowland in California had lost badly, as had right-to-work. Among the few bright spots for the Republicans were Goldwater's victory in Arizona, Rockefeller's big win in New York (where Keating also won), and Hugh Scott's Senate win in Pennsylvania. But overall, the Republicans share of the vote had dropped precipitously. In 1956, Republican congressional candidates had run almost even with the Democrats—28.7 million Republican votes to 29.8 million Democratic—but in 1958, the Democrats had a margin of more than 5 million.

The morning after this doleful news, Dulles called Nixon. "The Sec said he is proud to be a New Yorker. N said he would add to that Oregon, R.I. and Arizona. The Sec does not feel discouraged about 1960 and N said you don't? The Sec said it seems to him it demonstrates there are not any national issues that predominated. N said it was all local. Right-to-work lost us 4 states, something else lost us 4 more and the recession lost us 2. N said the farm thing cost us. N said we kept the House losses to less than 50. The Sec said we need to be thinking pretty hard pretty soon about 1960 and what we are going to do in the meantime because there is a lot of work to be done." Naturally enough, Nixon agreed.

Dulles tried to buck up Nixon. "The Sec said N did a wonderful job. N felt he helped Keating. Keating and Scott will be helpful to the Sec." Then Nixon got back to the issue at hand. "N said this party has to be remade. There is one asset—a lot who were reelected are all right on foreign aid—those [Democrats] elected are spenders and Rayburn and Johnson will not be able to control them and the Pres can make an issue by vetoing some of these bills." [58]

That was thin gruel indeed, and failed to cheer Nixon for any length of time. Even when he wrote his memoirs, twenty years later, the thought of that election night made him "wince." So did the postmortems by the commentators, who were saying that the big winner among Republicans in 1958 was Rockefeller, and Nixon was the big loser. "It seemed that the worst fears of my friends and advisers had been realized," Nixon wrote. "My campaigning had had little visible effect, had gained me little thanks or credit, and had tarred me with the brush of partisan defeat at a time when . . .

Rockefeller [was] basking in the glory of victory. Perhaps Dewey had been right; I should have sat it out."[59]

Of course he knew that the party regulars would not forget that Dick was the only national figure to hit the campaign trail for the Republicans, but he also knew that the number of Republicans was relatively small and by all indications growing smaller. He could not see how Dulles could say that the results did not worry him with regard to 1960.

NO MATTER HOW BAD THE NEWS, it was not in Nixon's character to remain enshrouded in gloom. The day after the election, he went back to work. He began by sending a form letter to every successful Republican candidate, telling them that "I only wish that I, personally, could have done more." He claimed that the party "came out of this campaign stronger than we went in because of the very fact that we went down fighting."[60] To the losers he wrote that "I felt the losses we suffered this year as much as if I had been on the ballot." To both winners and losers, he said, "I look forward to working with you in rebuilding our Republican Party strength at every level over the next two years."[61]

Nixon wrote one letter to a Democratic loser, Congressman Brooks Hays of Arkansas, a moderate who had tried to broker between the President and Governor Faubus in the Little Rock crisis and had become a target of the segregationists as a consequence. Nixon paid Hays some handsome compliments: "I can say without qualification that there was no more tragic result of this last election, from the standpoint of the nation, than your defeat. When statesmanship of the type you represent in such an exemplary way becomes the victim of demagoguery and prejudice, it is time for men of good will to exert more positive leadership."[62]

Shortly thereafter, the New York *Herald Tribune* ran an article on the letter. The next day, Charlie McWhorter had a memo for Nixon. "Scotty Reston called; his remarks were as follows: 'Charlie —this is in the nature of an unfriendly call. We who work on *The New York Times* are well aware of the Republican propensities of the *Herald Tribune* and their reasons for giving excellent coverage to the activities of the Vice President. We of the *Times* are also ready and willing to cover activities of the Vice President. But we don't seem to be getting any cooperation.'" Then Reston mentioned the "Brooks Hays letter which was given to the *Trib*." Reston said there were times when he would be willing to help Nixon, "but this can not be played both ways. I am deadly serious about this, Charlie, and if he (the VP) wants to play it that way, then we want to know it."[63]

Nixon sent a memo back. Tell Scotty, he said, that it was just good reporting, not favoritism. A reporter from the *Herald Tribune* had asked Nixon if he had talked to Hays after the election. Nixon said he had not, but indicated that he had written. The reporter then asked Hays for a copy of the letter. "Above all," Nixon concluded his memo, "don't complain about the lack of coverage in the *Times*—just give Scotty the straight story." [64]

HAROLD STASSEN, who had lost a primary election for governor of Pennsylvania, blamed Nixon for the party debacle. On November 12, Stassen had a short meeting with Eisenhower in the Oval Office. When he emerged, he told reporters it was time to dump Nixon and embrace Rockefeller. Because he was in the White House when he said it, and had just met with the President, Stassen's remarks made headlines. Nixon was in Key Biscayne at the time; Eisenhower called him on the telephone to apologize.[65] Nixon had just had a wisdom tooth pulled. While under sedation he had mumbled a campaign speech, part of which was high praise for Pat for her behavior in Caracas, so he was too groggy to do more than mumble a reply.[66] Bob Donovan of the *Herald Tribune*, meanwhile, called Charlie McWhorter to say "that if the President had had the same 'guts' as FDR, he would have blasted Stassen out of the White House." [67]

But Nixon had to undertake his own defense. He wrote Charles Wilson, former Secretary of Defense, "As you have no doubt noted, some of the politicians like Harold Stassen, and political pundits like Scotty Reston, now claim that I was the 'architect of the Republican defeat.' I, personally, however, do not see how I could have followed any other course. It seemed vitally important to me, even though I knew we were going to lose, that we go down fighting. Had we done otherwise, our losses probably would have been even greater, and what spirit there was in the Party Faithful would have been completely killed." [68]

Barry Goldwater stood by Nixon. On December 16, he wrote, "I believe you are the person who must select the spot on which the party is going to stand; put the flag there; and then rally the forces around it." Not surprisingly, Goldwater thought "that spot must be to the *right of center*." Goldwater assured Nixon that if he did that, "then I can assure you that your team will begin to build, its strength will grow, and in 1960, not only you, but the party will be successful." [69]

Nixon's reply was noncommittal about where he was going to put the flag, but realistic about the prospects: "At this time the nomination in 1960 is not going to be worth anything to any Republican and I think you will agree there is considerable chance that nothing we can do will save the situation." He did promise to "make an all out fight," because "we owe it to the Party." [70]

The gossip, meanwhile, had it that the men who had backed Eisenhower in 1952 were now organizing behind Rockefeller for 1960. But Rockefeller himself denied any presidential ambitions. In December, he told Meade Alcorn (who he knew was Nixon's friend and would pass it along) that his only concern was in doing a good job for New York, and in helping the Republican Party. He also said some nice things about Nixon. Neither Nixon nor his friends believed a word of this. [71]

IT HAD BEEN A LONG TIME since Eisenhower had done anything helpful for Nixon, but he made up for it in late November, when he sent the Vice-President to England to represent the United States at the dedicaton of the American Chapel in St. Paul's Cathedral in London. The chapel, built with pennies contributed by British schoolchildren (no large donations were accepted), was dedicated to American servicemen killed in action while stationed in Britain during the war. A glorious piece of religious architecture, it is virtually impossible for any American to visit it without shedding at least a few tears. This was a choice assignment, and Nixon made the most of it.

His major speech was before the English-Speaking Union at London's Guildhall, where Woodrow Wilson and Eisenhower had previously spoken. Nixon was appropriately eloquent. He called for "a great offensive against the evils of poverty, disease and misery" in the underdeveloped areas of the world, on a scale far greater "than any the American people or Congress have ever yet dared to contemplate."

"What must be made clear and unmistakable for all the world to see," said the Vice-President, "is that free peoples can compete with and surpass totalitarian nations in producing economic progress. No people in the world today should be forced to choose between bread and freedom." [72]

The British were impressed, and for their part they went out of their way to impress Nixon, who for all they knew might well be the next American President. At cocktail parties, dinners, and private meetings, the British put forward their best people, from Churchill through Prime Minister Harold Macmillan to junior members of the Labour Party (to his great surprise, Nixon was much impressed by the Labour politicians he met). The only sour note came at Thanksgiving dinner at the American Embassy. Nixon sat next to Queen Elizabeth II, but he sat uncomfortably, because his tuxedo did not fit. It seemed that he only discovered someone had forgotten to pack his tux forty-five minutes before the queen arrived, and had to borrow one. Pat was chagrined. "I'll never let anybody else pack Richard's clothes again," she told reporters. "This is the first trip he ever went on that I didn't pack for him. It will never happen again."[73]

Drew Middleton did a wrap-up on the trip for *The New York Times.* Nixon, he wrote, "who arrived billed as an uncouth adventurer in the political jungles, departed trailing clouds of statesmanship and esteem. . . . In the higher echelons of government, the British found Mr. Nixon well informed—which they do not always expect in American politicians—ready to listen and a good but not over-eager expositor of United States policies." Middleton's summary was as grand as the occasion for the trip: "No man of imagination can go through a ceremony like a dedication of the American Memorial Chapel in St. Paul's without being deeply impressed by the stability of Britain. There he was, Richard Milhous Nixon from Yorba Linda, Calif., standing next to a Queen whose throne has existed for more than a thousand years on a site where Christians have worshipped for thirteen and a half centuries."[74]

When he returned, Nixon wrote Pat Hillings (who had left his seat from Nixon's old congressional district to run, unsuccessfully, for Attorney General of California). Nixon said the trip had been "pretty rugged," especially a half-hour question period with the students at Oxford, a press conference with the international press corps, and a *Meet the Press*–type program on BBC. "All in all, it was quite an intellectual exercise. I was, frankly, lucky to come out alive when you consider the number of mistakes I might have made!" Still, he complained about the press coverage, both in Britain and at home. He told Hillings, "I am more and more coming to your conclusion that greater use of television is the only answer to combat this type of activity and to keep the press honest. . . . The image that commentators and the cartoonists (Herblock, et al) have in the main painted of me is generally such an unfavorable one that I can't see how letting people look at the subject himself could be harmful!"[75]

To Herb Klein, Nixon complained that "our so-called 'liberal' friends will never say die. Now the thing they seem to find wrong about me is that I didn't do anything wrong! For example, the *Manchester Guardian* said 'the Vice President never put a foot wrong. The question is whether he did not put it right a little too often. Many people prefer to the smooth competence of a Nixon the impulsive mistakes of a Truman—that it is a matter of political psychology of the elusive quality that makes people trust a man.' I guess you just can't win!"

IN THE SECOND PAGE OF HIS LETTER to Klein about his British trip, Nixon returned to reality and got down to business. "I would be interested in having your appraisal of the Gallup polls which showed considerable strength for Rockefeller as against me and also a sharp increase in Kennedy's strength in his trial heat with me. I anticipated some falloff as a result of the campaign but I was somewhat surprised that it was as heavy as this. Your expert analysis would be welcome!"[76]

It was time to start gearing up for the 1960 Republican Convention. One thing about politics—so long as a man has the stamina, no defeat is final. There is always the next campaign.

CHAPTER TWENTY-THREE

THE MAN WHO STOOD UP
TO KHRUSHCHEV
1959

SENATOR ROBERT KERR, Democrat of Oklahoma, posed Nixon's problem in the year before the Republican Convention succinctly: "He's got to stay close enough to Eisenhower to win the nomination, and far enough away to win the election."[1]

Eisenhower's and Nixon's respective positions made it inevitable that their relationship would be full of complexity, difficulty, and antagonism, all of which had to be suppressed. Eisenhower had his last election behind him, which was the reason he cared so little about the 1958 campaign. The next election was Nixon's. This put Nixon in the awkward position of having to be simultaneously a loyal member of the Administration, a supplicant, and his own man. It put Eisenhower in the worrisome position of realizing that in two years he would have to hand over the Presidency to Nixon, or, worse, the Democrats. Were the opposition to take charge, Eisenhower anticipated an orgy of spending on defense and on social programs combined with a tax cut, a prospect he regarded with horror.

Nor could he regard a Nixon succession with optimism. Nixon's Harvard speech, and what Eisenhower knew he was telling major Republican contributors privately, indicated that Nixon too intended to raise defense spending and cut taxes. Eisenhower also worried about Nixon's ambition. On June 11, 1959, Ann Whitman recorded in her diary that the Boss had breakfast with Nixon. Nixon asked Eisenhower if he would take some of Nixon's friends—all rich men, potential contributors—for a weekend on a Navy yacht and play some golf with them at Quantico. Eisenhower, who

509

prided himself on not mixing politics and his social life (although of course he did), flatly refused. He commented on Nixon to Whitman, "It is terrible when people get politically ambitious—they have so many problems." [2]

Indeed. One of Nixon's problems was that he wanted to do more, be more visible, shoulder more responsibilities, but Eisenhower would not let him. Another problem was the age difference, which gave the two men different outlooks. Eisenhower, born in the nineteenth century, the son of a laborer in rural Kansas, put his emphasis on how much had been gained by Americans in the twentieth century. Nixon, born in the second decade of the twentieth century, the son of a grocery-store owner, put his emphasis on what had been lost. At a Republican leaders' meeting, when the discussion was about a tax exemption for tuition payments to private schools, Nixon declared that "what's involved is the whole erosion of the middle class." He said that in America "the very wealthy do very well, but the middle class is sinking." Nixon was speaking for what he regarded as a dispossessed middle class, for the professional and small-business men who had always been the core of his constituency, who resented the advances of the labor unions and the growth of federal regulations and the taxes they had to pay.

Eisenhower cut Nixon off, contradicting him in the process. The President said the middle class had not disappeared, but the proletariat had. The laboring man had become middle class, and was sending his sons to college. Where Nixon wanted to retrieve what had been lost, Eisenhower wanted to protect what had been gained. [3]

Not only their views but their concerns were different. Nixon's position forced him to concentrate most of his attention and energy on the 1960 nomination and election; Eisenhower's position led him to concentrate most of his attention and energy on what he could accomplish in the next two years. Eisenhower's goals were peace, disarmament, a balanced budget. Nixon's goal was votes.

AFTER SIX YEARS AS HEAD OF GOVERNMENT, Eisenhower had some strong ideas on structural changes needed to make the American system work more efficiently. One was a line-item veto, a proposal every President favors and every Congress refuses. Another was a limitation on congressional service—in Eisenhower's view, if the President was going to be limited to two terms, then so should individual congressmen.

These ideas came from Milton Eisenhower. Laudable though they may have been, there was not the slightest chance that they could be achieved in Eisenhower's Presidency. There was no need for Nixon to get involved in, or get behind, the proposals, and he did not. But one of Milton's suggestions could be implemented by the President, because it involved the executive branch only and did not require a constitutional amendment. It did concern Nixon directly, and he very much opposed it, while Eisenhower very much favored it.

Milton's idea was to take some of the burden off the President by creating two new positions, which he called "Assistant Presidents." One would be responsible for foreign affairs; the other, for domestic affairs. They would stand between the President and his Cabinet, as superadvisers. Although he did not use the term, Milton was groping toward the creation of what later came to be called the National Security Adviser on the foreign side, and a comparable position on the domestic side. Arthur Flemming, the leading Republican intellectual, and Nelson Rockefeller, a friend of Milton's, had worked with Milton on the proposal, which Eisenhower had embraced. No one else was involved.

The President sprang the idea on his Cabinet on January 24, 1959. Reaction was muted and cautious, but after the Cabinet meeting the two men most directly involved, the Secretary of State and the Vice-President, got together over the telephone to discuss the proposal. Both Dulles and Nixon were appalled, Dulles because he was always jealous of any encroachment on the State Department's exclusive control of foreign affairs and would fight to the death any idea that injected someone in the White House who would stand between the President and the Secretary of State as chief adviser on foreign policy, Nixon because the creation of two Assistant Presidents would make him even more superfluous than he already was and would inevitably be interpreted as a sign that the President had no confidence in his Vice-President.

"The Sec said this looked like it was pretty much designed to interpose between the President and the Cabinet. Sec. said this whole thing had taken him considerably by surprise. No one here had caught on what it was all about." Dulles complained that Eisenhower was trying to make it look like "a routine affair. . . . The VP said what concerned him was that it was a much more revolutionary plan than the President realizes. In effect it puts in two people between the Cabinet and the Pres." At the Cabinet meeting, Dulles and Nixon had muted their criticisms, although they had managed to persuade Eisenhower to hold up on implementation until a study could be made, and Nixon had made the point that "another President might have different ideas." In their phone conversation, they chipped away more vigorously. "The VP thought a considerable body of opinion would think this was just another move by this Pres. to get away from some of his responsibilities and to delegate a lot more authority to a 'Palace Guard' group."

The President had hoped that he could implement the change by simply announcing a restructuring of the executive branch. Nixon insisted that the Senate would have to be involved, if only to confirm the appointees. "N asked if any feelers had been put out to the Democratic Leadership. You don't want to get into a hassle unless you are sure it is going through. Sec said he was perplexed as to what was skillful and wise way to handle this whole thing. It gave him some concern. The Pres. is strongly convinced that this needs to be done and he has been absolutely sold by this small group—Milton, Arthur and Nelson. He feels the Government has become obsolete in its processes and needs overhauling. Sec said it was politically hazardous in the sense of making the Pres. into more of a Head of State and less the Head of Government."

Even in their private conversation, these two master politicians managed to make it sound as if their only objective was to protect the President, and that the protection of their own positions was the last thing on their minds. Only once did Nixon slip in the potential effect of such a change on his personal prospects. "N said Pres. may say he thinks this is necessary to run the Govt since the tasks of the Pres. are becoming excessive. Pres. may say he was not going to be candidate and was doing it for the good of the country whether or not it was politically profitable. Trouble was it could ruin the Party and increase the popular demand for a change and make N's prospects pretty dim."

What to do? "The question, N said, was one of strategy." Dulles thought there was "nothing to do but to go along with the study" and stall for time. "N said it would be the most revolutionary change in 150 years. These two people would have power equivalent to the Pres's in certain respects. They would have the advantage of speaking from the WH." Eisenhower had wanted to limit discussion to the Cabinet; Nixon correctly saw that the way to sabotage the proposal was to bring as many people into the discussion as possible, including Democrats. The more men involved, the less likely that anything would get done.[4]

Nixon knew that Eisenhower was terribly sensitive to the Democratic charge that he was not running the government, even though the truth, as Nixon well knew, was that Eisenhower kept power in his own hands. The way to get the President to back down was to convince him that the appointment of two Assistant Presidents would greatly strengthen the criticism that he was a do-nothing President. In March, by which time Dulles was in the hospital and Christian Herter was running the State Department, Herter called Nixon on the phone to ask his advice on how to proceed at a lunch at the White House that day, where the discussion was going to be about the Assistant President idea. "V.P. said his reservations have to do with the political and public relations implications and said CH could report him as saying this. It would look as if this President could not work as hard as others." That argument convinced Eisenhower, who dropped the idea. With Dulles' help, and some assistance from bureaucratic inertia, but primarily by finding the right argument and using it effectively, Nixon had managed to avoid a crisis.[5]

Although it turned out to be a tempest in a teapot in 1959, the basic idea would not die. Indeed, in 1959 it was not the idea itself that Nixon objected to, but rather the effect of its implementation on his own election chances. In 1969, with the appointments of Henry Kissinger, John Ehrlichman, and H. R. Haldeman, Nixon himself implemented his own version of Milton Eisenhower's idea.

Back in 1959, it was not just the Assistant Presidents idea that gave Nixon difficulty, but even more the attitude behind it. Obviously, Eisenhower in his last two years was going to put the long-term good of the country ahead of all other considerations, and would not gear his actions or his ideas to the immediate problem of electing Dick Nixon in 1960. This became a major reason for Nixon's defeat. Time and again, Eisenhower could have done things that Nixon urged on him that could have swayed votes, but he always refused.

NINETEEN FIFTY-NINE was a great year for the newspaper columnists. Eisenhower was making policy, but it was speculation about the future that intrigued the heavy thinkers. Some things were clear, some foggy. America was certainly going to have younger leadership in the sixties—when Eisenhower left office in January 1961, he would be seventy years old, the oldest President to date. The younger generation, the junior officers of World War II, were impatient to take over from the old men. The emphasis on youth also fit the national mood. For one thing, there were just so many youngsters around, the highest percentage of young people ever, as these were the peak years of the baby boom. For another, America felt optimistic, a mood with deep roots in the national tradition, but one that had been badly battered of late, what with the Depression and then World War II and Korea. By 1959, unbounded optimism had returned. Six years of peace and prosperity had brought confidence. One of Eisenhower's major goals in 1953 had been to ease the crisis atmosphere that had prevailed since 1929, and he was successful, so much so that people were almost yearning for crises again, fully confident that the nation could handle anything. The complacency of the Eisenhower years, coupled with the prodigious material progress that was achieved in the fifties, made Americans eager to seek out challenges that could be overcome. Poverty wiped out, racism eliminated, freedom protected everywhere, prosperity for all.

(In Nixon's Vice-Presidential Papers, there is a file of correspondence with a man in Wichita, Kansas, one Willard Garvey. Mr. Garvey was a home builder who thought big. He wanted to make everyone, everywhere, a homeowner, which he felt would be the most effective anti-Communist measure imaginable. He proposed to start by building houses in India. With $45 million in foreign-aid funds, Garvey said he would build homes to house 30 million Indians every year. As he put it to Nixon, "Kansas grew a home at a time, why not India?"[6])

Why not India? That spirit of no limits to the good America could do prevailed, and was the real reason the Democrats had enjoyed such a landslide in 1958. And it was that spirit that would decide the 1960 presidential election. Nixon knew this, but it was much more difficult for him to align himself with the future than it was for his Democratic competitors for national leadership, Kennedy, Johnson, and Hubert Humphrey. They were all free to criticize Eisenhower for his standpattism, for his insistence on preserving what had been won rather than promoting what could be done.

But if Nixon's position as Vice-President forced him on the defensive on the question of doing more, spending more, accomplishing more, it also gave him a major advantage in publicity possibilities. He not only drew more reporters than any of the senators, but he could choose where and when to go to achieve maximum publicity.

Not that the others did not know how to get their names in the papers. One of the reasons there was so much speculation about the nominations and the election was that this was a most newsworthy set of candidates. They were, in fact, quite fascinating, these men who were going to lead America through the sixties. Each had a powerful and unique personality, each was a professional politician of the first rank, each was fiercely ambitious. They towered over their contemporaries. Kennedy, Humphrey, Johnson, Nixon—the public could not read enough about them. And rightly so, because they truly were big men who had the added advantage —from the reader's point of view—of having serious flaws, and thus each made great copy.

In addition, the maneuvering of the candidates was a complex process that required close coverage. Much of the maneuvering was done to get headlines. For example, Humphrey flew to the Soviet Union, where he had a private meeting with Premier Nikita Khrushchev. Afterward, he claimed he had achieved some break-throughs, and that he had important new information to give privately to President Eisenhower. What he actually got was his picture on the cover of *Life* magazine.

This business of opposition politicians going to see foreign leaders and afterward claiming that they had secret messages to take back to their President or Prime Minister goes on in all the democracies. It always works in the sense of getting publicity; it never works in the sense of achievement of breakthroughs. Heads of government negotiate only with other heads of government, not subordinates, not even the Foreign Ministers, and most certainly not opposition leaders. Still, Nixon himself would use the technique extensively from 1963 through 1967.

At a Cabinet meeting, Eisenhower gave his view on such visits: "Humphrey—all he learned was what K told him. He came in here with all that 'important new information' stuff—Hah! Talk about baloney—and sliced very thin, too."[7] Nixon laughed with the rest of the Cabinet, but he had reason to feel some resentment. After his first overseas trip as Vice-President, Eisenhower had asked him to report to the Cabinet. Nixon had done a country-by-country tour that took nearly an hour. From that meeting on, Eisenhower never again asked Nixon to fill him in on the substance of his talks with foreign leaders. A further reason for resentment of Eisenhower's crack about Humphrey was that Nixon was just then preparing a trip of his own to Moscow. Eisenhower had shown no enthusiasm for such a trip, he was simply indifferent.

NIXON HAD HELD his own private conversation with a head of government, Fidel Castro of Cuba, and had produced a long memorandum for Eisenhower on his impressions of the young revolutionary leader. It had not brought about any changes in the President's attitude or policy, but the experience itself was a learning one for Nixon, who in the process added to his already long list of foreign leaders to whom he had talked privately.

Castro had come to power on January 1, 1959, but by April the United States still had not recognized his government. State wanted to do so, but the CIA warned that Castro might well be a Communist, or a dupe of the Communists, and urged caution. Eisenhower was in a quandary. At this time, Castro accepted an invitation to speak in Washington to the American Society of

Newspaper Editors. Eisenhower refused to see Castro, but Nixon was eager to meet the man, and Secretary of State Herter urged that he do so. Eisenhower did not object. On April 19, 1959, Castro and Nixon met in the Vice-President's formal office for a three-hour conversation.

Rather than seek out possible areas of accommodation, Nixon confronted Castro with his shortcomings in a vain effort to talk him into changing his behavior. Why don't you hold free elections? Nixon demanded. Castro explained, "The people did not want elections because the elections in the past had produced bad government." Why don't you stop the executions of Batista's people? Because, Castro explained, he was carrying out "the will of the people."[8] And so it went for three hours, as they talked past each other about a free press, fair trials for accused war criminals, and individual rights.

Nixon was ambivalent in his impressions. On the one hand, Nixon told Eisenhower that Castro had an "obvious lack of understanding of even the most elementary economic principles," but on the other, "he has the great gift of leadership." As to his politics, Nixon could not be sure. "He seems to be sincere," Nixon told the President. "He is either incredibly naïve about Communism or under Communist discipline—my guess is the former, and as I have already implied his ideas as to how to run a government or an economy are less developed than those of almost any world figure I have met in fifty countries."

To Bill Baggs, editor of the Miami News, Nixon wrote that Castro "has in abundance those unique qualities which make him a leader of men. . . . I hope that you will be able to keep in close touch with him. He impresses me as one who is extremely sensitive to public opinion and while he has some very definite views, I think it is possible that he may change his attitude."[9]

Nixon concluded his memo to Eisenhower with a policy recommendation. "Because he has the power to lead," he wrote, "we have no choice but at least to try to orient him in the right direction."[10] Instead, Eisenhower decided to try to eliminate him.

IN JANUARY 1959, Anastas I. Mikoyan, one of Khrushchev's deputies, came to the States for a visit. His subject was Berlin. Khrushchev had threatened to sign a separate peace treaty with East Germany and then to turn over the access routes to Berlin to the East German government. As the Western occupying powers in West Berlin had no agreements with the East Germans, if Khrushchev carried through on his threat there would presumably be some form of another Berlin blockade.[11] What Khrushchev was seeking was some way to stem the flow of refugees escaping East Germany through East Berlin. As had been the case in Hungary in 1956, the refugees tended to be young, well educated, unmarried, ambitious. So great was the flow becoming that Khrushchev faced the prospect of East Germany's becoming a country without any productive people. The Eisenhower Administration was standing firm, refusing to even discuss the situation in Berlin so long as Khrushchev continued to stand by his ultimatum. Nixon was in full support of the President.[12]

Nixon was not a part of the negotiating team, but he did sit by Mikoyan at the main banquet. Nixon had agreed to go on the basis that "the Sec said he felt he [Nixon] could contribute to the evening. N. said he would see the Sec before the dinner to see if there is anything the Sec wants him to needle Mikoyan about."[13] Propaganda, not meaningful negotiation, was Nixon's objective, but that was just as well, because Mikoyan had no authority to negotiate and nothing to offer.[14]

When Mikoyan was quoted in The New York Times suggesting that "relaxation of tension is possible," Dulles called Nixon. "Where lies responsibility for the Cold War?" he asked. "N would like to throw it back at Mikoyan to get the record straight. The fault is theirs and not ours. The Sec thought well of this. N said they talk about what we can do and yet everything they suggest would not end it but would have them wage it. This the Sec had said to N yesterday and N liked it."[15]

IT WAS THE LAST of the telephone conversations between the Secretary and the Vice-President. By February, Dulles was in Walter Reed Hospital with terminal cancer. Nixon was solicitous about his condition. He urged Henry Luce to call or visit. "I had a long talk with him before he made his decision to take a leave of absence," Nixon told Luce, "and the courage and stamina he has displayed under the most difficult and painful stress cannot really adequately be described. I do not always agree with him, as I am sure you do not, but I am confident history will record that he was truly one of the most heroic figures of this generation."[16]

Nixon himself was a frequent visitor to Dulles' bedside. At the doctors' suggestion, he discussed matters of state, not Dulles' health. He was especially eager to have Dulles' advice on how to talk to Khrushchev when he, Nixon, went to the Soviet Union. Dulles, not surprisingly, told Nixon to be firm. On May 20, for example, he said that when Khrushchev brought up competition between the Communists and the capitalists, "he really means competition . . . only in our world, not in his. He must be made to understand that he cannot have it both ways. Point the record out to him, that we have concrete proof of the Kremlin's activities around the world." Dulles was sitting in a wheelchair, sucking on ice cubes to dull the pain of the cancer in his throat, but despite his condition, he remained a militant defender of the free world against Communist lies.[17]

Four days after this meeting, Dulles died. His passing was a real loss to Nixon. The two men had formed a solid team. For six years, each had helped the other as occasion demanded. Indeed, their relationship went back to 1948 and the Hiss case, when Dulles was the first prominent figure in the Republican Party to urge Nixon to keep after Hiss. They enjoyed each other's company, whether over the telephone or at breakfast meetings at Eleanor Dulles' house, or cocktails at Dulles' home. On the personal level, Nixon said that "Foster Dulles was one of the kindest and most thoughtful men I have ever known."[18] Dulles was one of the few men in the world who had traveled more than Nixon had, and met more world leaders. He was one of the few men Nixon deeply respected. Listening to Dulles, Nixon wrote in his memoirs, "was an incomparable opportunity for me to learn. . . ."[19]

Henry Luce asked Nixon to write a tribute to Dulles for *Life* magazine. He also sent along a draft of what he wanted Nixon to say. Except for one paragraph, Nixon threw out the draft and wrote his own piece. He spoke of Dulles' loyalty, in the process of describing his own view of life in Washington: "In a city where a political leader learns that the number of his friends goes up and down with his standing in the public opinion polls, I found Mr. Dulles' loyalty to his friends was no more affected by the latest poll than was his adherence to his own policies." Nixon asserted that "he recognized the fundamental truth that a public man must never forget—that he loses his usefulness when he as an individual, rather than his policy, becomes the issue." Many political observers thought that rather the opposite was the case with Dulles. So too with Nixon's next assertion, that "history will also record that the 'inflexibility' and 'brinkmanship' for which he was criticized in truth represented basic principles of the highest order." As to Dulles' advocacy of liberation of Communist-dominated peoples, Nixon said he knew that "some of his critics" scoffed at the notion. "Yet," Nixon asked, "what other tenable position can self-respecting free peoples take? The Communists have no hesitancy in proclaiming their faith in the eventual domination of the world by dictators. Can we be less determined in our dedication to the cause of freedom from tyranny for all people?"[20]

It was an eloquent tribute, much better than the one Luce's

writers had drafted, and it enjoyed wide circulation both in *Life* and in a special, individual printing. In it, Nixon had expressed some of his deepest convictions. Together, he and Dulles had been the leading anti-Communists in America. Khrushchev hated them both—in his memoirs he described Dulles as "that vicious cur" and Nixon as a "son-of-a-bitch."[21]

NOW NIXON WAS PREPARING TO MEET KHRUSHCHEV. For the Russian Premier, it was a minor publicity stunt that he agreed to in late April because he wanted an invitation from Eisenhower to visit the United States, and thought that a bit of hospitality for the Vice-President might help get him that invitation. For Nixon, however, it was a major opportunity that he eagerly seized.

To get ready, as Nixon wrote in his memoirs, "I undertook the most intense preparation I had ever made for a trip or meeting." He talked to Macmillan about Khrushchev, to Walter Lippmann, to Humphrey, to anyone he knew who had ever met Khrushchev. He corresponded with Professor William Elliott of Harvard, a Russian expert. He read briefing papers from State, the CIA, the JCS, and the White House staff.

The official reason for his going was to open the first United States Exhibition ever held in the Soviet Union, on July 24, in Sokolniki Park in Moscow. It was part of a program of cultural exchange that had come out of the spirit of Geneva, following the 1955 summit meeting. It reflected American optimism, the notion that anyone who knows us must love us, and the idea that peoples who know one another would not go to war against one another, an idea that ignores the obvious fact that almost nobody knows each other better than the Germans and the French. Still, it was a widely held view, and the promised Nixon appearance on Soviet television caused the greatest excitement in the State Department and in the American Embassy in Moscow.

Dulles had encouraged Nixon. He had told him that he felt he could "hold his own" in conversation with Khrushchev, but more important that Nixon could use the forum of his television appearance "to expose at least some segment of the Russian people to the reasonableness and justice of the American position on world issues."[22] This sort of faith was widespread—the exhibition itself was built around the theme of the triumphs of capitalism, and its message was that capitalism, not socialism, could help everybody get richer faster.

The superiority of capitalism over Communism in the competition to produce consumer goods is the easy side in a debate, and Nixon eagerly seized it. But the hope that he and the exhibit could somehow talk the Russians into acknowledging that superiority was dangerously misplaced.

Eisenhower was less optimistic about the trip than Dulles. He gave Nixon a final briefing in the afternoon of July 22, a few hours before the flight took off for Moscow. Khrushchev was pushing hard for a summit, to be preceded by an exchange of visits, Khrushchev to the United States and Eisenhower to Russia. Eisenhower was hesitant—political summits, he often said, were like real ones, barren. Still, the President was tempted, as he dedicated his last years in office to the achievement of world peace. But before he would invite Khrushchev to America, he insisted on some progress in Geneva, where Foreign Minister talks about the future of Berlin were going on. He had just received a letter from the Kremlin, which ignored his precondition of progress at Geneva but instead assumed that the exchange of visits and the follow-up summit were all but set up. The President advised Nixon about the situation so that he would be informed, not because he wanted Nixon to enter into serious negotiations with Khrushchev. Indeed, the President explicitly reminded the Vice-President that "you are not a normal part of the negotiating machinery." If Khrushchev were to bring up the subject of the visits, Eisenhower added, Nixon should refer to "progress" in Geneva over Berlin as a precondition, but engage in no detailed negotiations.

As to how to approach Khrushchev, Eisenhower recommended to Nixon that he maintain "a cordial, almost light, atmosphere." John Eisenhower, the President's son and aide, kept notes on the briefing. He noted that "to this, Mr. Nixon expressed his intention of debating with Khrushchev and countering his points. He feels he has an excellent chance to probe and cause some blurting out of Khrushchev's real feelings." He added that he "particularly hopes to lay to rest some of Khrushchev's misconceptions about America."[23]

Nixon also wanted to establish himself as tough on Communism, contrasting himself to the Democrats. In a July 17 memo, he told his military aide, Major Robert E. Cushman, that the speech writers "are never again to use 'We endorse the principle of peaceful coexistence.' . . . This is the Acheson line in the State Department and I will not put it out!!!!!! Cushman, tell all of them—it is never to be used again . . . or whoever does it will be shipped [out] on the next plane." In place of "peaceful coexistence," Nixon proposed to offer "peaceful competition."[24]

The trip was exciting, and everyone who could manage an excuse wanted to go along. H. R. Haldeman, then doing promotion work for Nixon and the Republicans in Southern California, wrote Robert Finch, who was now chairman of the Los Angeles County

Republican Central Committee, "If RN is looking for a thoroughly-experienced non-professional staff man for the Moscow journey, give me shout."[25]

No one shouted for Haldeman, but nevertheless the Nixon party was a large one. Pat was along. Milton Eisenhower joined in, as did Admiral Hyman Rickover, the Navy's nuclear expert, Professor Elliott of Harvard, and a host of staff people from State and from Nixon's office. Some seventy newsmen followed in a chartered 707. Reston, who was among them, wrote that Nixon "had more reporters and photographers following him than at any time in his political career—and the Presidential race is getting close." Reston also noted that the potential for major mistakes or goofs was "never higher."[26]

"I was keyed up and ready for battle," Nixon wrote later, "as the flight neared Moscow."[27] He needed to be, because so were the Soviets. Ever since the Republicans took over in 1953, Congress had annually passed a Captive Nations resolution, one that required the President to proclaim Captive Nations Week, during which time Americans were urged to pray for the people living under Communist tyranny. Eisenhower had issued the proclamation just a few days before Nixon's departure, so presumably, as Nixon's plane touched down in Moscow, millions of Americans were praying for a change of government, if not a full-fledged revolution, in Russia and throughout the Communist world. The best thing that can be said about these annual proclamations, as far as Russian-American relations were concerned, is that the Americans were unaware of how deeply the Russians resented them. But calling the Russian people "captives" struck in Khrushchev's craw, indeed gagged the entire Russian leadership.

There were additional current problems that added to the difficulty of Nixon's position. On the day after he left the States, July 23, the front-page New York Times stories included: "SOVIET RENEWS THREAT ON BERLIN. Warsaw, July 22. The Soviet Union held out the threat today that it would back East Germany in attempts to force the West out of West Berlin."

"EISENHOWER HAS LITTLE HOPE FOR SUMMIT. Washington, July 22. President Eisenhower confirmed today that he entertained little hope now for a summit meeting. But he said that the road to such a meeting would remain open as long as there was any hope of agreement at the Big Four foreign ministers' conference."

"GROMYKO YIELDS SLIGHTLY: NOT ENOUGH, HERTER SAYS. Geneva, July 22. Andrei A. Gromyko made some concessions to the Western powers in the foreign ministers' conference today. But the Allies found them inadequate."

At this delicate moment, as Reston wrote in his column, "Vice

President Nixon arrived in Moscow, accompanied by a battalion of reporters, technicians and television experts in two gleaming new trans-Atlantic jet liners on a mission that had all the look of a propaganda invasion." [28]

The reception, predictably, was cool. Deputy Premier Frol Kozlov gave a welcoming speech to a small gathering. There were no bands, no anthems, no crowds. The Nixons went to Spaso House, the American ambassador's residence, where Llewellyn Thompson told him that the Soviet leaders were furious about the Captive Nations resolution.

Nixon could not sleep that night. At 5:30 A.M. he woke his Secret Service agent, Jack Sherwood, and took off to the Danilovsky market; he wanted to compare it to the Los Angeles produce markets he had worked in as a boy. As he had done around the world, he mingled with the crowd of farmers and workers. When he explained that he was in Moscow (there had been no advance publicity) to open the American Exhibition, several people asked him if he had any extra tickets. No, he replied, but said he would be glad to buy some tickets for them. Whereupon he told Sherwood to give the spokesman for the group a hundred-ruble note, enough for one hundred tickets. The man refused the bill. Money was not the problem, he said—it was just that there were no tickets available.

The following day, *Pravda* and other Soviet newspapers made this little scene into a headline event. They charged that Nixon had tried to "bribe" and "degrade" Soviet citizens by offering them money. They had photos of Sherwood extending the bill, and claimed that Nixon had deliberately picked out a poorly dressed man so that he could maximize publicity back home.

Later that morning, Nixon went to the Kremlin for his first meeting with Khrushchev. While the photographers took pictures, Khrushchev praised Nixon for his Guildhall speech and said he welcomed the kind of peaceful competition Nixon had called for. But when they were alone, Khrushchev launched into a tirade about the Captive Nations resolution. Red-faced and shouting, trembling with rage, he called it stupid. "It appears that, although Senator McCarthy is dead, his spirit still lives. For this reason the Soviet Union has to keep its powder dry." Nixon tried to change the subject, to no avail.

"People should not go to the toilet where they eat," Khrushchev retorted. "This resolution stinks. It stinks like fresh horse shit, and nothing smells worse than that!"

Nixon remembered from his briefings that Khrushchev had started life as a pig breeder. "I am afraid that the Chairman is mistaken," he replied, staring at Khrushchev. "There is something

that smells worse than horse shit—and that is pig shit." Khrushchev looked as if he would burst, but took a breath, smiled, and
agreed to change the subject.[29]

They left the Kremlin together and drove to the American Exhibition, which was opening that evening. Workmen were making
last-minute preparations. An American engineer asked the two
leaders if they would like to say a few words for the new color
television cameras. Khrushchev opened with some gibes about
American trade practices. Nixon replied, "There must be a free
exchange of ideas." Khrushchev seized his opportunity. "What
about this tape," he asked, pointing to the camera. Would Nixon
guarantee him that what he said would be shown in America, in
English translation? Nixon would. Well then, Khrushchev asked,
how long has America been in existence? "One hundred and fifty
years," Nixon replied.*

"One hundred and fifty years?" Khrushchev repeated. "Well,
then, we will say America has been in existence for one hundred
and fifty years and this is the level she has reached. We have existed not quite forty-two years and in another seven years we will
be on the same level as America. When we catch you up, in passing
you by, we will wave to you [waves to an imaginary America]. Then
if you wish, we can stop and say: Please follow up."

He went on to denounce the Captive Nations resolution, but
suddenly switched his mood, wrapped his arms around a huge bear
of a Soviet workman on the set, and rocked back and forth with
him. "Does this man look like a slave laborer?" he demanded.
Waving at other Soviet workers, he added, "With men with such
spirit how can we lose?"

Nixon returned to the free-exchange-of-ideas theme. "After
all," he told Khrushchev, "you don't know everything . . . "
Khrushchev cut him off. "If I don't know everything, you don't
know anything about communism except fear of it."

Nixon tried the competition theme again. He admitted that the
Soviets were ahead of America in rockets, but pointed out that
America was ahead in other things—"color television, for instance." "No," Khrushchev replied, "we are up with you on this,
too. We have bested you in one technique and also in the other."

NIXON: You see, you never concede anything.
KHRUSHCHEV: I do not give up.[30]

This went on for half an hour more, then continued when the
two men left the studio (the tape was shown on American television

* In his memoirs, Nixon corrected his slip and put the figure at 180 years.

later) and walked to a model kitchen filled with all the latest gadgets. "Anything that makes women work less is good," Nixon declared. Khrushchev pounced: "We don't think of women in terms of capitalism. We think better of them."

Nixon extolled the virtues of the model house, which he said cost $14,000 and was easily within reach of American workers. Khrushchev said the same was true in the Soviet Union. Besides, he pointed out, American houses "will not last longer than 20 years. We put that question to your capitalists and they said, 'In 20 years we will sell them another house.' We [Russians] build firmly. We build for our children and grandchildren. We use bricks."

Khrushchev accused Nixon of having his "own image of the Soviet man. . . . You think the Russians will be dumbfounded by this exhibit." But, he said, in Russia everyone had a house. In America, only if a person had dollars did he have a house—otherwise he slept on the pavement. "And you say we are slaves!"

Nixon accused Khrushchev of filibustering."You do all the talking and you do not let anyone talk. I want to make one point. We don't think this fair will astound the Russian people, but it will interest them. . . . To us, diversity, the right to choose, the fact that we have a thousand different builders, that's the spice of life. We don't want to have a decision made at the top by one government official saying that we will have one type of house. That's the difference."

Khrushchev said it was inefficient to produce so many types of washing machines or houses, and delivered another sermon on the superiority of Soviet products. Nixon heard him out.

NIXON: Isn't it better to be talking about the relative merits of our washing machines than of the relative strength of our rockets? Isn't this the kind of competition you want?
KHRUSHCHEV: Yes, but your generals say, "We want to compete in rockets. We can beat you."

Nixon said both sides were strong, and for that reason "neither one should put the other in a position where he in effect faces an ultimatum."

KHRUSHCHEV: Who is giving an ultimatum?
NIXON: We will discuss that at another time.
KHRUSHCHEV: Since you raised the question, why not now when people are listening. We know something about politics too. Let your correspondents compare watches and see who is filibustering. What do you mean [about an ultimatum]?

NIXON: I'll be very direct. I'm talking about it in the international scene . . .
KHRUSHCHEV (breaking in): That sounds like a threat to us. We too are giant. You want to threaten us. We will answer threat with threat.

By this time the two men were jabbing fingers at each other. Nixon asked, "Who wants to threaten? I'm not threatening. We will never engage in threats." [31]

Reston was among the reporters and officials (including Leonid Brezhnev) intently observing this exchange of bluff, bluster, and near-buffoonery. It resembled the 1946 Nixon-Voorhis debates for brazenness, except that this time Nixon got back as good as he gave, and the stage was an international one rather than a high-school gym in Pomona.

"While all this was going on," Reston wrote, "Ambassador Thompson and Milton Eisenhower were standing outside wondering whatever became of diplomacy and why didn't somebody pull a plug on the whole thing." Still, he noted that although the debate was a "disaster in terms of conventional diplomacy, Mr. Khrushchev was still smiling at the end. He had a good time. He had an argument with another politician today and an audience to go with it, and naturally this was a politician's idea of fun." [32]

When they finally emerged from the kitchen, Khrushchev spied an old Russian woman, wearing a babushka, cheering for him. He gave her a hug, again rocking back and forth for several minutes. Then William Randolph Hearst called out, "Hey, Dick!" Nixon wheeled and spotted him; so did Khrushchev, who had earlier had an interview with Hearst. Khrushchev grabbed both of Hearst's hands and shook them emphatically, shouting for all to hear, "My capitalist, monopolist, journalist friend. Do you ever publish anything in your papers that you disagree with?"

Hearst: "Oh, boy, do I." Khrushchev clearly did not believe him. Nixon chimed in, "You should see what some papers print about me." Khrushchev looked dubious. Nixon lectured him: "If there is one idea you must get out of your head it is that the American press is a kept press." [33]

That evening, Nixon opened the exhibit with a speech he had prepared before leaving Washington. Khrushchev had promised it would be printed in full in *Pravda* and *Izvestia,* so Nixon pitched it at the Russian masses. It was designed to make everyone wish he or she had been born in the U.S.A. "There are 44 million families in the United States," Nixon began, and "25 million of these families live in houses or apartments that have as much or more floor space than the one you see in this Exhibit." He claimed that 31 million families owned their own homes, that Americans had 56 million cars, 50 million television sets and 143 million radio sets. The average American family bought nine dresses and suits and 14 pairs of shoes per year. Then he asserted that what the statistics showed was this: "That the United States . . . has from the standpoint of distribution of wealth come closest to the idea of prosperity for all in a classless society." He drove home the point with an apt image: "The caricature of capitalism as a predatory, monopolist-dominated society is as hopelessly out of date, as far as the United States is concerned, as a wooden plow."

Impressive as the material achievements of the United States were, however, they paled beside other, more important triumphs. "To us, progress without freedom is like potatoes without fat." In America everyone was free to criticize the President, and he assured the Russians that this was done every day. He talked of freedom of religion and freedom of information. In what was probably a more telling example to the Russians, he spoke of freedom of movement. "Within our country we live and travel where we please without travel permits, internal passports or police registration. We also travel freely abroad."

Nixon concluded by stressing his basic theme of peaceful competition. "Let us extend this competition to include the spiritual as well as the material aspects of our civilization. Let us compete not in how to take lives but in how to save them. Let us work for victory not in war but for the victory of plenty over poverty, of health over disease, of understanding over ignorance wherever they exist in the world." [34]

It was a clever if shallow summary of the American way of life, but what effect it had on the Russian people cannot be known. Certainly it did not cause the Russian press to suddenly confess that it had been wrong all along in its portrayal of America, or to thereafter stop describing the United States as a land of racism, warmongers, and monopolists. It did bring great joy to the American community in Moscow; at a reception at the embassy that evening, it was deemed a smashing success. Nixon was the first politician to have gotten across to the Russians such a positive view of American life. "No matter what happens now," one guest told Nixon that night, "your trip to the Soviet Union will go down as a major diplomatic triumph." [35] That was stretching things considerably.

Still Nixon could not sleep. That night, his second in Russia, he stayed up until almost dawn going over his briefing notes.

THE FOLLOWING DAY was devoted to official calls and ceremonial functions, ending in a lavish dinner at Spaso House for Khrushchev and the Soviet hierarchy. Afterward, Khrushchev insisted that the Nixons make a midnight drive to the forest outside Moscow, where they stayed overnight at the Premier's fabulous dacha. The following day, again at Khrushchev's insistence, they went for a boat ride on the Moskva River. A flotilla of boats carrying Soviet leaders and American reporters followed. When the lead boat ran aground, "Khrushchev looked as if he were going to shoot the pilot . . . on the spot." Nixon tried to calm him down and save the pilot by remarking that his friend Bebe Rebozo, "a very experienced boatman," often ran aground too. But, Nixon noted, "as we climbed out of our boat into another one . . . I looked back . . . and saw the most forlorn, hopeless-looking individual I was to see in my visit in the Soviet Union."

At various points along the river, swimmers surrounded the boats, cheering Khrushchev and reaching up to shake hands. "Do you feel like captive people?" Khrushchev called out. "*Nyet! Nyet!*" they cried. "You never miss a chance to make propaganda, do you?" Nixon commented. "I don't make propaganda," Khrushchev replied. "I tell the truth."[36] Milton Eisenhower, who was along, later learned that the swimmers were all high-ranking party officials—that stretch of the river was off limits to ordinary citizens.[37]

THAT AFTERNOON, there was a five-hour lunch. The debate that had begun in the television studio continued. Although the audience was smaller, the two men continued to play to it, making debaters' points. Khrushchev wanted to know why the United States refused to support free elections in Vietnam, as called for in the Geneva Accords of 1954. Nixon countered with his own question: If Khrushchev was for free elections in Vietnam, why wasn't he for free elections in Germany? Khrushchev's reply, Nixon felt, exposed his true position—that "he was for elections only when he was sure that the Communists would win." That was, of course, exactly the point Khrushchev was trying to make—in reverse—about America's position on Vietnamese elections.

That evening, Nixon and Khrushchev went for a walk in the woods. Finally alone with the man, Nixon tried his hand at a bit of diplomacy. He brought up the possibility of an invitation from Eisenhower to come to the States. Nixon told him that "the eyes of the world" were on the Geneva meetings and urged him "to break the impasse on the Berlin question." That, Nixon said, would be a dramatic event." Khrushchev was noncommittal.[38]

Three years later, Nixon summed up his impressions of Khrushchev in *Six Crises*. "Intelligence, a quick-hitting sense of humor, always on the offensive, colorful in action and words, a tendency to be a show-off . . . a steel-like determination coupled with an almost compulsive tendency to press an advantage . . . to run over anyone who shows any sign of timidity or weakness—this was Khrushchev." Nixon described him as "particularly effective in debate because of his resourcefulness, his ability to twist and turn, to change the subject when he is forced into a corner or an untenable position." [39]

FOLLOWING HIS PRIVATE TALK WITH KHRUSHCHEV, Nixon sent a cable to Eisenhower. "Point I repeatedly emphasized," he said, "was that element of crisis, for which he was responsible, must be removed from picture by Geneva if there were to be future meetings." Khrushchev, he claimed, "seemed to back away from some previously stated positions. In view of this, Ambassador Thompson and entire party agree with me in strong recommendation we probe Gromyko at Geneva for a further period before you send reply to Khrushchev on possible visit." [40]

Eisenhower ignored the advice. While Nixon was still in Russia, he announced that Khrushchev would be visiting the United States for a ten-day tour. He did so because he discovered that the State Department had blundered and not made it clear to Khrushchev that an invitation was dependent on progress at Geneva (the meetings there broke up, stalemated, the day Eisenhower announced the visit).

Eisenhower's announcement brought forth howls of protest. Columnist William Buckley, for example, wanted to fill the Hudson River with red dye so that when Khrushchev entered New York harbor, it would be on a figurative "river of blood." Conservatives everywhere were outraged. Many mistakenly blamed Nixon. Barry Goldwater came to his defense. A few days after Nixon returned, Goldwater told a Constitution Day convention of We, the People, that "Nixon is a conservative," and he said that Nixon had told him that he was "shocked and surprised the invitation was made." It all showed how tricky this business of sitting down with the Communists could be.[41]

Eisenhower did not help matters any. At an August 12 press conference, reporters asked Eisenhower what it was he wanted Khrushchev to see in the United States. Eisenhower explained that his chief purpose was to fly Khrushchev from the White House to Camp David in a helicopter, during rush hour, so that Khrushchev could see all those cars, and all those houses along the beltway, the idea being to convince the Russian leader of the superiority of capitalism. In addition, Eisenhower said, he wanted to take

Khrushchev to Abilene, where the people could "tell him the story of how hard I worked until I was twenty-one. . . ." Referring to Nixon's kitchen debate with Khrushchev, Eisenhower reminded the press that the Russian dictator had said to Nixon, "What do you know about work? You never worked." Well, said the President, "*I* can show him the evidence that *I* did, and I would like him to see it."[42]

It was an unfair cut. As a boy Nixon had worked as hard as anyone could have, certainly at least as hard as Eisenhower and Khrushchev. But it was Nixon's own fault, because he had let Khrushchev get away with the comment in Moscow without reply. (Nixon did manage to tell Khrushchev that his father had been a shopkeeper, but it only brought from Khrushchev the caustic rejoinder, "All shopkeepers are thieves.")

FOLLOWING HIS DEBATES WITH KHRUSHCHEV, Nixon made a five-day trip through the Russian provinces, with stops in Leningrad, Novosibirsk in Siberia, and Sverdlovsk in the Urals. As usual, he broke away from official parties to meet and shake hands with workers and people on the streets. But the Russians were aware of his habits, and they had hecklers planted in the crowds, primed with questions about American racism, foreign military bases encircling Russia, and nuclear tests. In a cable to Eisenhower, Nixon said that "it is clear that the Soviets have been trying with their needling and planted hecklers to provoke me into some angry and ill-considered reactions." But he assured the President that "I have resisted the temptation to hit back violently, popular as that might be at home."[43]

At home the trip got extensive and highly favorable coverage from the army of reporters that had followed Nixon around. Reston thought that Nixon had chosen "the perfect way to launch a campaign for the U.S. Presidency." *Time* described Nixon as "the personification of a kind of disciplined vigor that belied tales of the decadent and limp-wristed West." *Life* put his picture on its cover, with the Kremlin towers in the background. Ralph de Toledano, writing for *Newsweek*, got carried away, claiming that Nixon's trip "could change the course of history."[44]

At most stops, Pat went off on her own. *The New York Times* called it her "mingle-with-the-Russians" campaign. Her favorite places to visit were children's hospitals. She walked through endless corridors, the newspaper reported, "without appearing tired in her pencil-slim high heels." She talked to the children in the wards, pulled pigtails, patted heads, and handed out candy. In Siberia she visited a Young Pioneers camp. Reporters asked what she liked best about Siberia. "Meeting campers," she replied, "but they make me homesick for my little girls."[45]

Pat more than held her own throughout the trip. At the first banquet, she asked Khrushchev repeatedly about his wife and the wives of other Soviet officials. Khrushchev explained that his wife had a sprained ankle, but at every subsequent formal gathering Mrs. Khrushchev was present. At the five-hour lunch, Nixon asked Khrushchev how the Soviets were progressing with solid fuels for their missiles. "Well," Khrushchev replied, "that is a technical subject which I am not capable of discussing." Pat, smiling, leaned across the table and remarked, "I'm surprised that there is a subject that you're not prepared to discuss, Mr. Chairman. I thought that with your one-man government you had to know everything and have everything firmly in your own hands." Mikoyan came to his boss's rescue: "Even Chairman Khrushchev does not have enough hands for all he has to do, so that is why we are here to help him."[46]

Clearly Pat's popularity with the Russian people she met was not shared by the Soviet leaders. Indeed they tried to keep her away from their people. She found it difficult to locate hospitals or camps, and on a number of occasions it was obvious that the people had been told not to show any enthusiasm. Herb Klein, acting as Nixon's press secretary, said that nevertheless "Pat went ahead regardless of obstacles and did the things that have endeared her to people throughout the world. She definitely made a major impression on the people and probably influenced the Kremlin leaders to show their wives more."[47]

ON THE LAST DAY OF JULY, Nixon returned to Moscow, where he worked without letup on his thirty-minute television speech to the Soviet people. For two nights, he did not go to bed at all. Ambassador Thompson kept telling him what he already knew, that this was an unprecedented opportunity for an American leader to talk directly to the Russian people. With the Republican Convention only a year away, Nixon was tempted to direct his remarks at the American people instead of the Russians, with an all-out blast at the police state he had just seen at first hand. But he was also aware that Eisenhower would be coming to Russia after him, and he did not want to give Khrushchev an excuse for denying Eisenhower the chance to make his own television speech in Moscow. "I was the first high American official to have this opportunity," he noted in *Six Crises*. "I did not want to be the last." Thompson and Professor Elliott helped him prepare the speech, but the final product was his alone.[48]

What he said was not tough enough to please conservatives at home, but it delighted the Americans in Moscow, because he told the Russians things they had never heard before. He opened with his impressions of Russia—a beautiful country, filled with wonderful people. He spoke of a common desire for peace, and expressed his sympathies for the millions of Russians killed in World War II. He dealt with the questions hecklers had raised on his trip, saying that the foreign military bases erected by the Americans around the Soviet Union were not "for purposes of attacking you but for purposes of defending ourselves and our allies." He cited Soviet spending on arms, asserting that "one-fourth of the entire production of the U.S.S.R. goes into armaments." To prove America's peaceful intentions, he provided a short history of the Cold War proposals made by the United States—the 1946 Baruch plan for international control of atomic energy, American support for a U.N. peace-keeping force in 1947, Eisenhower's Open Skies proposal at Geneva in 1955—and pointed out that the Soviet Union had rejected them all.

Nixon called for free exchange of information, telling the Russians that everything their Premier said was reported in the American press, while almost none of Eisenhower's words ever appeared in the Soviet press. He proposed an agreement—the Soviets would print all of Eisenhower's speeches and the Americans would print all of Khrushchev's. Further, each side should send radio and television broadcasts to the other, and in addition agree to a free flow of newspapers and magazines.

To give an example of what he meant, Nixon referred to the incident on the first morning of his visit, when he offered the one-hundred-ruble note to the workman who wanted tickets to the American Exhibition. The *Pravda* account, he carefully explained, was a lie, and warned that "all irresponsible reporters should never forget in the end the truth always catches up with a lie."

His conclusion was also a warning. "In every factory and on hundreds of billboards I saw this slogan: 'Let us work for the victory of Communism.' If Mr. Khrushchev means by this working for a better life for the people within the Soviet Union that is one thing. If on the other hand he means the victory of Communism over the United States, this is a horse of a different color. For we have our own ideas as to what system is best for us." [49]

"Western ambassadors here are astonished," Reston wrote in his account of the speech. They had never seen anything like it. The very idea that someone could go on Russian television and "accuse *Pravda*, the Communist journalistic bible, of distorting the truth" quite bowled the diplomats over. But Reston also noted that the speech played better in the United States than in Russia, and said that Western diplomats "are not terribly impressed by the diplomatic results."[50] As to the long-term effects on the Russian people, it probably had none at all—two days after Nixon left, for example, *Pravda* had a headline story about an interview with the recipient of the one-hundred-ruble offer. The man denied Nixon's story completely and insisted that Nixon had indeed tried to bribe him.[51] The most Nixon himself hoped for was that he had convinced "some of the Russian people of our desire for peace." But he was realistic: "I knew that I had had no success whatever in getting through to Khrushchev and the Soviet leaders." He left Moscow "depressed."[52]

DEPRESSION QUICKLY SHIFTED TO ELATION. Nixon came home via Warsaw. Khrushchev had been in Poland two weeks earlier, where he had been received with sullen looks and unfriendly stares, naturally enough, as he had been in charge of partitioning Poland between Germany and Russia in 1939 and of suppressing a Polish uprising in 1956. The Polish government, fearing to offend the Kremlin, had not announced Nixon's coming, but Radio Free Europe did, and people turned out by the hundreds of thousands to cheer the American Vice-President. Even the Polish honor guard broke all regulations and traditions—at the airport, the men cheered and applauded. On the streets, people shouted "Long live America!" "Long live Eisenhower!" "Long live Nixon!" "May you live a thousand years!" Dozens, hundreds, ultimately thousands of bouquets of flowers showered into the open cars Nixon and Pat rode in; when a rose scratched Pat's face, Nixon commented, "Better to be hit by roses than rocks," a reference to Caracas. When Khrushchev was in town, the government distributed flowers to throw at him, but the people kept them. To Nixon the Poles proudly exclaimed, "This time we bought our own flowers!"[53]

That night, Nixon sent a cable to Eisenhower. "In all my travels," he declared, "this was the most moving experience I have ever had. I felt it necessary to exercise great restraint to prevent any untoward incidents."[54]

OBVIOUSLY IT WAS NIXON'S POSITION in the American government rather than his personality that led the Poles to give him such a tumultuous welcome. He could hardly expect anything like it in Washington. Still, the turnout at the airport was a big one, and most commentators praised the Vice-President as "the man who stood up to Khrushchev."[55] He received hundreds of letters of congratulation, one from Eisenhower, another from J. Edgar Hoover, scores from Republican politicians and contributors. From Hollywood, movie actor Ronald Reagan wrote: "As the cold war continues I'm sure many people lose sight of the basic conflict and begin to accept that two nations are foolishly bickering with sane justice and right as well as wrong on each side. This 'tolerant' view ignores of course the fact that only Communism is dedicated to imposing its 'way and belief' on all the world. This is in direct contradiction to our belief (so forcefully expressed by you) that people should be allowed to choose for themselves." He was especially grateful that Nixon told the Russians "truths seldom if ever uttered in diplomatic exchanges."

Reagan thought Americans ought to answer Soviet charges about "imperialism" by constantly shooting back a question of their own: "Has Russia abandoned the Marxian precept that Communism must be imposed on the whole world?" He felt that "only when their answer to that question is affirmative can we truly believe in 'co-existence.' Until such time 'co-existence' means 'don't do anything while I steal your horse.' " He praised Nixon for "the great step you took in starting us back to the uncompromising position of leadership which is our heritage and responsibility," and signed off, "Ronald." [56]

There were critics, of course, commentators who regretted Nixon's confrontational style and wished that more had been done to ease world tensions, less to put the spotlight on Richard Nixon. And as Nixon dourly noted, "Some press observers suggested that if I became President I might not be able to get along with Khrushchev." [57]

Nixon's trip had no diplomatic substance, nor did it accomplish anything. Khrushchev did not even mention it in his memoirs. And it was quickly overshadowed by Khrushchev's own trip to the United States, where he showed that he was at least as good as Nixon at grabbing the headlines.

But the trip had a major impact on Nixon personally. He shed any illusions he held about the effect that confronting the Russians with the truth would have on them. He told Reston that "on the basis of what he saw of Mr. Khrushchev—and he saw a great deal in a short while—he thinks that Mr. Khrushchev's convictions about the supremacy of Communism and the weakness of capitalism are too deeply ingrained to be removed or even influenced much by a single trip to the United States." [58]

The day after his return, Nixon had a conference with the President and his White House staff. John Eisenhower kept the notes. "The Vice President described Khrushchev as a man with a closed mind, who will not be impressed with what he sees in America. The only approach which will be useful will be to give him a subtle feeling of the power and the will of America."

Nixon gave Eisenhower advice on how to deal with Khrushchev. He warned that Khrushchev "will try to wear anyone down who talks to him. As to social matters, the Vice President recommended stag events in business suits since Khrushchev, by principle, eschews tuxedoes. The women are accustomed to being entertained separately." The Russians, he said, would bring a "great entourage," and he suggested that "his trip should be managed by someone experienced in running political campaigns." He excused himself from acting as host, as it would be "improper since he had not done so with any other head of state." (Eisenhower gave the task to Henry Cabot Lodge, Jr.) Twice Nixon recommended that Eisenhower "give Khrushchev the greatest exposure possible," both because Khrushchev would have to return the favor when Eisenhower came to Moscow, and because "in the long run, exposure would hurt Khrushchev."[59]

Most of all, Nixon warned, don't expect to change Khrushchev's mind by arguing with him about the merits of the two competing systems. It was a lesson he learned so well that he never again, in all his many dealings with Communist leaders, made the mistake of trying to do so.

CHAPTER TWENTY-FOUR

POLITICS
1959–1960

At a November 27, 1959, Cabinet meeting, the President turned to his Vice-President. "Dick," he said, "I hope if someday I surrender this chair to you, I'll be able to give you a balanced budget."

The President was in a lecturing mood. He noted that he had only fourteen months left. He said that if he could not produce a balanced budget and halt the upward trend of expenditures, "then I'm defeated—and I don't like to be defeated." The economy was in an upswing, which had led many politicians—including Nixon —to advocate more spending on defense. The President would have none of that. "Even with this fabulous increase in tax receipts," he said, "the thing to do is to pay off the national debt, not add to it." [1]

Economy in government was one of Eisenhower's two major themes in his last years in office. To support his position, he had various horror stories. In June, he told the Cabinet he had discovered a branch in DOD that consisted of a chairman, making $15,000 a year, and two secretaries whose job was "working on a World War I project long since dead . . . to find spruce lumber for airplanes!!!" Nixon remarked that the story showed the difference between the Republicans and the Democrats—"they want government to spend more, we want people to spend more." [2]

Eisenhower's other major theme was peace. He spoke forcefully about the prospects. "I'm talking about waging peace, and not just with pretty words. We have got to give people a chance to make a living. If we can't have peace, we had better fall back to a Citadel." [3] Again, Nixon supported the President. The Democrats,

535

he said, "want to bust the budget, basing their whole case on the Berlin crisis. But more money, for missiles or for manpower, won't give us any greater strength for Berlin. We already have all the strength we need for Berlin." Eisenhower agreed wholeheartedly. He said that anyone who knew anything about the Communists realized that since Lenin's day "they're trying to make us spend ourselves into bankruptcy." For his part, he believed that "once you spend one dollar beyond adequacy, you're weakening yourself."[4]

Nixon's problem was that the national mood was running in the exact opposite direction from Eisenhower's thinking. Not only the Democrats, but also his only real rival for the Republican nomination, Nelson Rockefeller, were calling for increased defense expenditures, and arguing that Eisenhower was jeopardizing security on the altar of a balanced budget. Nixon agreed with that criticism —although never in Eisenhower's presence. In the middle of a June 9, 1960, meeting with the Republican congressional leaders, Eisenhower had to leave the room for an appointment with the Prime Minister of Peru. As soon as he left, Nixon took the floor. "What Rocky is saying about defense can have a big impact," he warned his fellow politicians. "We cannot allow this charge of weakness to stand. Not that the President's judgment is bad, but we just can't ignore Rocky's 'sitting duck' charge."[5]

THESE EXCHANGES ARE ONLY ANOTHER EXAMPLE of Nixon's fundamental problem going into the 1960 campaign. He had to support the President in public (and in Eisenhower's presence), no matter how strongly he disagreed and no matter if almost every other politician in America also disagreed. In March 1960, Charlie McWhorter had reported that Texas Republicans were furious with Eisenhower for proposing another civil rights bill (which Nixon did support, in private as well as in public). The Texans accused Nixon of "turning left" and "wooing the liberals." They thought the Vice-President was "not concerned with the support of conservatives since they have no place else to go."

Nixon scribbled at the bottom of McWhorter's memo: "Charlie, write . . . [and] point out that I am only supporting *Adm* positions in each case."[6]

Nixon needed Eisenhower's blessing to win the nomination, but he also needed to retain his bedrock support, the conservatives in the Republican Party. In addition, he had to hold the conservatives without alienating the Rockefeller liberal wing of the party. And he had to have Democratic and independent votes to win the election. It was all exceedingly complex, made the more so because, as the leading candidate, everyone wanted to force him to take positions on the controversial issues before the convention.

The American Society of Newspaper Editors wanted to know Nixon's stand on freedom of information (without saying so, the editors were alluding to his threats against State Department employees for releasing the adverse Quemoy-Matsu mail count in 1958). Nixon wrote Eugene Pulliam, chairman of the society and editor of the Indianapolis *News*, "The only justification for classifying information . . . is for the security of the nation, not for the security of the Administration which may be in power at the moment. . . . I recognize that it is a problem to keep government bureaus from hiding information under the guise of security. Vigorous steps . . . should be taken to avoid this. . . . I would lean toward more disclosure rather than less."[7]

One of the sharpest splits between the Administration and the Old Guard of the Republican Party was still over foreign aid. Nixon was under constant pressure to repudiate Eisenhower's program. He refused absolutely to do so; in fact, he took the lead in supporting the appropriations. In May 1960, he wrote a two-page letter to every Republican in Congress. "We must stand by our President on this," he said. "We must demonstrate the responsibility of our Republican Party, and we must support the cause of freedom and decency against Communist tyranny by appropriating the funds the President requested for Mutual Security."[8]

California Republicans were as troublesome to Nixon as those in Texas. They had been badly burned on right-to-work in the 1958 election, but they were not ready to give it up. The latest proposal was to have a statewide referendum on right-to-work. Most California Republicans were supporting it, and they wanted Nixon's help. He withheld it. Such issues, he said, "tend to divide our citizens along lines of class interest in ways which prejudice our two-party system."[9]

To Professor Elliott at Harvard, Nixon wrote: "The trouble with the right-to-work proposals is that those who favor them are immediately attacked as being opposed to union members as well as to dictatorial union bosses. We are confronted here with the perennial problem of not only being right, but being smart at the same time. Or, putting it another way, a man must be a politician before he can be a statesman!"[10]

Civil rights was an even more emotional and dangerous issue than right-to-work. Little Rock, the 1957 Civil Rights Act, Rogers' attempts to enforce that bill, and Administration sponsorship of a tougher bill in 1960 were hurting Republican attempts to break up the Solid South. Meanwhile, few northern Negroes were switching to the Republican Party. Nixon, nevertheless, remained a leading supporter of civil rights. He got the private support of Martin Luther King, and the public support of baseball star and civil rights activist Jackie Robinson, who was writing a column for the New York *Post*. Nixon had lunch with Robinson, who later wrote a favorable column on the Vice-President. Thanking Robinson, Nixon explained that "I have consistently taken a strong position on civil rights, not only for the clear-cut moral considerations involved, but for other reasons which reach beyond our nation's borders." Unless the federal government took "consistent, direct action," he said, "we will suffer in the eyes of the emerging nations and the uncommitted peoples. Beyond this, our present struggle with the forces of atheistic Communism is an economic as well as an ideological battle. To deny ourselves the full talent and energies of 17 million Negro Americans in this struggle would be stupidity of the greatest magnitude." [11]

Such views, widely reported by Robinson and others, were anathema in the South. In March 1959, Bryce Harlow of the White House staff told McWhorter that he had just been in Baton Rouge, where the word was that "Nixon will lose every Southern state" in the Republican Convention to Rockefeller. Harlow, disturbed, demanded to know why. Because, he was told, Nixon had "never given sufficient indication that he had any real interest in the South, its problem or its people, that while he vacationed in Florida, he didn't even associate with Florida Republicans." [12]

HARLOW'S INFORMATION was part of a steady stream of intelligence and gossip that flowed into Nixon's office. The Vice-President knew just about everybody in the Republican Party, and most of the national press corps. Many of these people were his supporters, and many of those who were not were nevertheless opposed to Rockefeller. [13]

In February 1959, Meade Alcorn had reported that "Rockefeller is absolutely murdering the Republican Organization in New York State. We have been unable to obtain even lower level jobs for our workers. Our Party in New York City is completely demoralized and disintegrating rapidly. No Republican regulars want to see Rockefeller or even hear his name." [14]

A week after that, Bob Finch—who had joined Nixon's staff as administrative assistant on a full-time basis—reported that "the oil people are extremely unhappy with Rockefeller." [15] Charlie McWhorter relayed the information that Claude Vardaman, Republican state chairman from Alabama, was upset by a Bill Rogers' statement that business would not want to go South until the race problem was settled. "Vardaman remarked that he thought you should speak to Rogers and try to get him to conduct himself in a way which makes it easier for your friends in the South to support you."[16]

In June, McWhorter told Nixon that Jerry Ford was with him all the way.[17] In August, McWhorter attended the Playboy Jazz Festival in Chicago. Mort Sahl was the master of ceremonies. Sahl "had a lot of anti-Nixon comment. The guy, in my opinion, is sick, sick, sick, but he does have a following."[18] About the same time McWhorter had lunch with James Reston, who told him that New Hampshire Republicans were urging Rockefeller to make an all-out fight in the New Hampshire primary in March, and that the Rockefeller people were thinking of challenging Nixon in the California primary, which Reston described as "going for the jugular." When McWhorter asked Reston for his estimate of the situation, "he replied that he thought Rockefeller was going to go right down to the wire with his campaign, and then pull out in your favor; that you would be nominated and defeated." Reston was not happy with this situation, McWhorter reported: "Reston commented that you and Lyndon Johnson are the two ablest American politicians of this century."[19]

In addition to McWhorter and Finch, Nixon got gossip from de Toledano, Mazo, Robert Donovan, Kyle Palmer, Hartmann, and other reporters who were in positions to pick up information.[20] Still Nixon wanted more. His staff hired agents to gather news.[21] He hired an agent to follow Rockefeller around and report on his activities. He was the young Seattle lawyer John Ehrlichman, and he took his assignment seriously, especially as the convention drew nearer. In early June 1960, Ehrlichman sent in a six-page report on a two-day Rockefeller visit to North Dakota. He reported in great detail on who met Rockefeller at the Fargo airport, what questions were asked by the press ("Reporters mainly easy on NR—didn't bore in as they do with RN"), Rockefeller's local television interviews, the reactions of the people on the street to Rockefeller's handshaking, and on and on.[22]

FROM HIS OLYMPIAN POSITION the President watched the intricate maneuvering of Nixon and Rockefeller with some dismay. He told Nixon that "my concern is that two people . . . who have supported me, should find themselves publicly at odds. . . . My own opinion is that people can be politically ambitious if they so desire without necessarily becoming personal antagonists." He concluded with a mild rebuke: "I think perhaps some enthusiasts, possibly both in Nelson's group and your own, are seeing things that don't exist."[23]

Back in 1956, the President had taken the obviously absurd position that the Republican delegates to the convention, not he, should choose the vice-presidential candidate. In 1960, he was more realistic in taking a neutral stance on the question of the nominee, because in 1960 he was not in a position to dictate. Still, his endorsement, if won, could be valuable, perhaps decisive. Indeed, by June of 1960 it was Rockefeller's only real hope, as he had declined to enter the early primaries against Nixon and, in a Stassen-like maneuver, was trying to get the nomination on the basis not of votes but of public opinion polls (he paid for them himself, which made them suspect) that indicated that he would run stronger against the Democrats than Nixon. Rockefeller spent large sums of money to gather in delegates, but refused to announce his candidacy publicly.

On June 11, 1960, Rockefeller tried to get an Eisenhower endorsement, although typically he went about it in a convoluted way. He called the President to ask "whether or not he should be an avowed candidate." Ann Whitman took notes. Eisenhower seized the opportunity to give the New York governor a little lecture. Insofar as Rockefeller had campaigned, he had done so on a platform of calling for more defense spending, more even than the Democrats were demanding. Eisenhower told him "he did not believe it was right to alarm people unnecessarily." As to Rockefeller becoming an open candidate, Whitman's notes read, "The President said he was afraid Nelson would be called 'off again, on again, gone again, Finnegan.' He suggested Nelson take his [New York] delegation to Chicago, if someone wants to propose his name on the floor fine—Nelson would have opportunity to put facts before the convention. He was sure everybody would welcome that. The President said he thought Nelson's chances were very remote." He reminded Rockefeller that if Nixon lost, then Rockefeller would be in a strong position for the 1964 nomination, and urged Rockefeller, in 1960, to "support whomever was nominated."[24]

Which did not necessarily mean that Nixon was Eisenhower's choice. Inevitable as Nixon's nomination appeared to be, the President was willing to at least consider some other possibilities. In May 1960, he wrote Oveta Culp Hobby, his former Secretary of HEW and a leading Texas supporter, to suggest that she do what she could to promote Bob Anderson as a Texas "favorite son." That thought led to another: "How about a lady 'favorite son'?" If Hobby would become a candidate, "at least it will remind people that there are ladies who believe in moderate government, fiscal responsibility, and official and personal integrity." Hobby was not interested.[25]

Rockefeller's reluctance to challenge Nixon left Nixon free to organize his presidential campaign, which he did through the first half of 1960. His people organized Dick Nixon Clubs in every state, complete with the regular political hoopla—radio broadcasts, a biweekly newsletter (with such items as "Hagerty Cites Nixon's Training," "North Dakota Republicans Support Nixon," and "Letter from Nixon Thrills Seventh Grader"), and, of course, fundraising dinners. Richard Kleindiest, formerly party chairman in Arizona, signed on as head of the club in that state.[26] Bob Finch ordered twenty thousand copies of de Toledano's almost embarrassingly favorable biography of Nixon for national distribution.[27]

Nixon himself bombarded his staff with memos on organization. To Finch, for example, he wrote that "we simply have to tap the bright new young people who are coming up in the Los Angeles area and who are presently being courted very effectively by the Democrats." He wanted some "Mexican projects" put in motion in Southern California, "and above all, organization of suburbia, with particular emphasis on those who have come into the State in the last five years or so." In all his memos he stressed that "emphasis should be on organization rather than on public relations gimmicks."[28]

Nixon personally went after movie star Ronald Reagan. On June 18, 1959, Nixon wrote Reagan that he had just read a copy of Reagan's speech, "Business, Ballots and Bureaus," a Reagan set piece that he delivered to business groups around the country under the sponsorship of the General Electric company, for whom he also hosted a television show. Nixon said that Reagan had done "an excellent job of analyzing our present tax situation and the attitudes that have contributed to it." He added that he was "greatly encouraged by the apparent trend on the part of the American people to question the 'Tax and tax, spend and spend . . . elect and elect' philosophy. Speeches such as yours should do much to cause some solid thinking about the inherent dangers in this philosophy with the final result being a nationwide demand for reform." He hoped Reagan "will have many opportunities to repeat your wise words," and added a postscript: "As I read your speech, I recalled our first meeting in 1947 when we discussed some of the labor relations problems in the motion picture industry."[29]

In a handwritten reply, Reagan thanked Nixon for his kind words. He assured Nixon that "the subject and material are my own. General Electric has never suggested in any way what I should or should not say." In giving the speech across the country, Reagan said, "I have been amazed at the reaction. . . . Audiences are actually militant in their expression that 'something must be done.' " The only negative opinion he had encountered was an editorial in a Teamsters Union newspaper, "which I accept as further evidence that sound thinking is on our side." He was "convinced there is a ground swell of economic conservatism building up which could reverse the entire tide of present day 'statism.' As a matter of fact we seem to be in one of those rare moments when the American people . . . are ready to say 'enough.' . . . Prohibition was ended in the same way when people (even those who opposed drinking) decided that the wrong method had been tried."[30]

Nixon replied, "I hope that you will continue your very effective speeches. You have the ability of putting complicated technical ideas into words everyone can understand. Those of us who have spent a number of years in Washington too often lack the ability to express ourselves in this way."[31]

NIXON MAY HAVE ENVIED Reagan's ability to put complex problems into simple language, but he was smart enough never to try to copy it. He was much too intense to attempt Reagan's casual style. Neither did he have Reagan's ability to relax. Politics was his life, and he concentrated single-mindedly on the struggle. Even his bedtime reading reflected his passion—he read either political history or biographies of American politicians.[32] When he went to Florida to stay at Bebe Rebozo's, he usually went alone (or with members of his staff), and his purpose was less to take a vacation, more to find time to think through his problems.

A family vacation was a rare event. When Pat and the girls wanted to get away, they ordinarily did so without Dick.[33] Pat was doing everything possible to give them a normal upbringing. Julie was then eleven, Tricia thirteen. They had stolen their father's heart, even if his activities kept him from spending much time with them. Pat told Ruth Montgomery of *Cosmopolitan* magazine of her determination to keep the girls "natural, unspoiled, and out of the limelight." Neighboring mothers agreed that she had accomplished that goal. "Tricia and Julie are exactly the kind of normal, fun-loving children that I like my daughters to play with," one mother remarked. "I don't know how Pat Nixon does it, with all the official obligations she has, but those girls are as comfortable as old shoes to have around." Another mother thought that "the Nixon girls are almost too perfect to be true. It's a bit discouraging, really. They have such nice manners that I sometimes wonder where I've failed with my kids."[34]

Although Tricia was now a teen-ager, her mother told Montgomery that "she has yet to have a date, or want one. She never plays jive records, or monopolizes the telephone. Actually, she has more fun playing with our menagerie of pets than going to parties or the movies." Pride of place among the pets went to Checkers. When Puff Ball, one of their four cats, had a birthday, the girls had a party for the cat, complete with a cake. They put poor Puff Ball in a doll's dress, hat, and veil. The girls set the table regularly; when their father was home for dinner they made an artistic production out of it, using candles and fresh flowers. They went grocery shopping with their mother, and she taught them how to use a steam iron.

Julie was more gregarious and outgoing than Tricia. After a month in California visiting the Drowns, she flew home alone. When Pat picked her up at the airport, Julie reported: "It was great! First I sat by an old man who went to sleep. That was pretty boring, so I moved back five seats and talked to that nice Mr. Hoffa." It was Jimmy Hoffa, head of the Teamsters. Julie's ambition was to be an actress; one of her favorite pastimes was to organize her friends for plays and shows for the adults.

Tricia's passion was baseball, and like her father, she was a fan of the Washington Senators, which took a lot of faith, as they were by far the worst team in the major leagues. When he was out of town, Nixon would call his daughter at night to find out how badly the Senators had lost that day. She knew every player's batting average. "The biggest thrill for Tricia is a trip to the ball park with her father," Pat related. "She hates flying, but nothing could have kept her off the plane when Dick asked her to meet him in Pittsburgh for the All-Star game."

"The girls adore their father," Pat told Montgomery. "He's very affectionate and so are they. They await him every evening, and the minute he walks into the house they throw themselves into his arms. After the hugging and kissing, Dick lets Checkers in, and it's complete pandemonium for a while, with everyone romping and laughing at once." [35]

Aside from his family, Nixon's relaxation centered as always around sports. In 1959, the year he took Tricia to the All-Star baseball game, he also attended the Patterson-Johansson heavyweight championship fight (in a party that included Tom Dewey, J. Edgar Hoover, Stuart Symington, Bill Rogers, and some forty heads of *Fortune* Five Hundred corporations), and the All-Star football game in Chicago. At the All-Star game, he gave a speech to the Football Writers Association in which he compared football with international politics. One member of the audience thought it "the best extemporaneous talk I have ever heard. Those hard-bitten writers sat on the edge of their seats!" [36]

In February 1959, he slipped on the ice outside his house and cracked two ribs. It was a painful, but not serious, injury. He told one friend that "when I cracked a rib playing football 29 years ago, the doctor told me then, just as my doctor told me this time, that while there is nothing more painful than a cracked rib there has never been a case in medical history where the patient didn't recover completely." [37] In fact, there was a bonus—he told reporters that he had never before had such thoughtful treatment from his daughters. They carefully helped him with his coat and performed many other tasks for him when he came home at night. [38]

Khrushchev came to the States in the fall of 1959. Pat hosted a lunch for Mrs. Khrushchev at the F Street Club in Washington—the guest list included the wives of the Cabinet members, Alice Roosevelt Longworth, Mrs. James Reston, the wives of the Joint Chiefs, and some thirty other prominent women. [39] Although her husband made $35,000 in salary, plus $10,000 in expense allowances, she continued to press his clothes and do the family mending. She was teaching the girls to be frugal too—their allowances were fifty cents a week, half of what their friends received. She did have a maid to help her with the other housework. Nixon could have supplemented his income with speaking and writing fees, indeed could have made himself a rich man, but he refused to do so. In December 1959, *National Geographic* sent him a check for $2,000 for an article he wrote on the Soviet Union. As was his custom, he contributed it to a nonprofit institution—in this case, to the National Cultural Center. [40]

AS ALWAYS, NIXON WANTED POWER, NOT MONEY. With no real opposition within the Republican Party for the nomination, the man who stood between him and the White House was whoever the Democrats nominated. Kennedy and Humphrey were the front runners, battling it out in the primaries. Eisenhower and other Republicans worried about the extensive press coverage the Democrats' contest was getting—in contrast, the unopposed Nixon was attracting little attention in the Republican primaries. Former Senator John Bricker of Ohio was among those pressuring him to begin active campaigning in April 1960 so as to get his name in the headlines, but Nixon was much too good a politician for that. As he explained to Bricker on April 18, he intended to gradually step up his appearances at fund raisers in the spring and summer, but "it would be unwise to start intensive campaigning at this point. I feel very strongly that the time to be fresh and strong, both mentally and physically, is the month before election. Then speeches will have lasting impact which could affect votes—now they may affect standings in the polls but by the time the election comes around they will be pretty well forgotten." [41]

Meanwhile, he contented himself with playing insider politics in Washington. The Democrats in Congress were proposing all sorts of programs, social, economic, and military. At Republican leaders' meetings, Nixon urged his friends in Congress to force a vote "on every cockeyed item, so that all these candidates are on record." He was especially eager to force Kennedy to vote, because "he is pretending to be more conservative than Hubert. It is not true—it's a case of the pot calling the kettle black."[42]

From January 1960 onward, Nixon predicted a Kennedy nomination. When his friends insisted that the Democrats would never nominate Kennedy, because of the religious issue, he laughed at them. He thought Kennedy's religion would be a plus for him, and urged Republicans to stay far away from the issue. He told one California Republican, Jack Irwin, that "aggressive anti-Catholics will do more to drive Republican Catholics and independent Catholics into the Kennedy ranks than all his campaigning could possibly do." He said he realized "there is very little, if anything, which can be done to stop their foolish statements," but he wished "the situation were otherwise."[43]

After the West Virginia primary, where Kennedy beat Humphrey in a state that was overwhelmingly Protestant, some Republicans were delighted. They felt that Kennedy would be much easier for Nixon to beat than Humphrey. Nixon knew better. He told Milton Eisenhower that the truth was the other way around. Kennedy's religion, Nixon said, "has helped him more than it has hurt him," and it would continue to do so. In addition, Kennedy "has unlimited money, a superb organization and a very effective ability to project himself well on television." Nixon thought that his own major problem was "the frightening weakness of the Republican Party throughout the country." He would have to run seven or eight points ahead of the party to win. In 1952 and 1956, President Eisenhower had been able to do that, "but it will take an extraordinary effort for me to pull it off."[44]

On July 13, on the night of the balloting in the Democratic Convention in Los Angeles, Nixon wrote columnist George Sokolsky. He said he was holding to his prediction that Kennedy would be the nominee. "This means that the election will be a close, hard-fought one. There have been press reports to the effect that I thought Kennedy was the easiest to beat. Nothing could be further from the truth. . . . In any event, it will not be a dull campaign!"[45] —another prediction that was right on the mark. To Dillon Anderson, Nixon wrote that "the only question in my mind about the Democrats is whether Johnson can be persuaded to be the Vice Presidential nominee."[46]

When Kennedy did win the nomination, Ronald Reagan sent

one of his handwritten letters to Nixon. He said he had watched the convention with great interest and not a little disgust. He thought the Democrats "could pick up some campaign money" by publishing their speeches and selling the book as "talks suitable for any patriotic occasion with platitudes and generalities guaranteed." He did not, however, include Kennedy's acceptance speech in that category, "because beneath the generalities I heard a frightening call to arms. Unfortunately he is a powerful speaker with an appeal to the emotions. He leaves little doubt that his idea of the 'challenging new world' is one in which the Federal Govt. will grow bigger and do more and of course spend more."

Reagan advised Nixon not to try to "out liberal" Kennedy, because "I am convinced that America is economically conservative and for that reason I think someone should force the Democrats to publish the 'retail price' for this great new wave of 'public service' they promise. . . . No Republican no matter how liberal is going to woo a Democratic vote, but a Republican bucking the give away trend might re-create some voters who have been staying home."

As "one last thought," Reagan wanted Nixon to tag Kennedy's *"bold new imaginative* program with its proper age. Under the tousled boyish hair cut it is still old Karl Marx—first launched a century ago. There is nothing new in the idea of a government being Big Brother to us all." Switching his comparison from the far left to the far right, Reagan said that "Hitler called his 'State Socialism' and way before him it was 'benevolent monarchy.' " He was certain "the American people do not want the government paid services at 'any price' and if we collectively can't afford 'free this and that' they'd like to know it before they buy and not after it is entrenched behind another immovable government bureau." [47]

KENNEDY HAD SURPRISED almost all political observers—although not Eisenhower or Nixon—by picking Lyndon Johnson as his running mate. Liberals were outraged—Johnson was the man who had emasculated the 1957 Civil Rights Act and stopped a new, tougher bill in 1960—but then the liberals were never going to vote for Nixon anyway, and Johnson's nomination immeasurably strengthened Kennedy's prospects in the South. Some Republicans wanted Nixon to counter by choosing a Catholic as his running mate. Eisenhower was one of them—he suggested his old friend and former chief of staff General Alfred Gruenther [48]—but that was an idea that Billy Graham, among others, thought madness. Graham wrote Nixon to advise him that Kennedy "will capture the Catholic vote —almost 100 percent of it—no matter what concessions you make to the Catholic church or how you play up to them." Even with a

Catholic on the ticket, Graham warned, "you would not crack . . . the Catholic vote." Graham thought that Nixon would only "divide the Protestant vote and make no inroads whatsoever in the Catholic vote," and reminded him that Protestants outnumbered Catholic voters by three to one. Graham wanted Nixon to choose Congressman Walter Judd, a former Protestant missionary. In his opinion, Judd was "almost a *must*," a man widely respected by fundamentalist Protestants, Graham said, who "would put much of the South and border states in the Republican column and bring about a dedicated Protestant vote to counteract the Catholic vote." He concluded, "You would do me a favor by destroying this letter after reading it."[49]

Nixon kept his own counsel, and made no promises. He did keep in close touch with the President, talking to him on the telephone at least twice a day during the Democratic Convention (Eisenhower was vacationing in Newport, Rhode Island). The man Nixon wanted for his running mate was Governor Rockefeller, but Rockefeller, in response to press speculation, was insisting that under no circumstances would he accept a vice-presidential nomination. When Nixon asked Eisenhower's help in persuading Rockefeller, the President responded, "I don't see very well how I can get down on my knees to him. He is apparently possessed of a popular appeal that people feel—but he is no philosophical genius. He has a personal ambition that is overwhelming." Eisenhower said that if he did ask Rockefeller, "Nelson would go out and tell it to the world." The only suggestion Eisenhower could make was that Nixon promise Rockefeller that if he ran for Vice-President, Nixon would step down after four years—an idea that had no appeal for Nixon. Noting that Rockefeller and Nixon were much closer on the issues than Kennedy and Johnson, Eisenhower mused that "the Democrats, in spite of their differences, manage to get together when the chips are down, like brothers." He wished the Republicans could do the same, but sighed again, "Nelson has a terrible amount of personal ambition."[50]

AFTER EIGHT YEARS AT THE HELM, Eisenhower hated to give it up, especially when he could not regard any of his potential successors as qualified to take over. Of Lyndon Johnson he said, "He is not a big man. He is a small man. He hasn't got the depth of mind nor the breadth of vision to carry great responsibility." Of Jack Kennedy he said, "incompetent," and pledged, "I will do almost anything to avoid turning my chair and the country over to Kennedy." He was nearly as negative in his expressions about Nelson Rockefeller.

Nor did he think much of the political parties. The Democrats were taxers and spenders who would bankrupt the country. The Republicans had no principles. About this time, Eisenhower told Ann Whitman that he personally was "disgusted with the Republican leadership; I don't know why anyone should be a member of the Republican Party."[51]

Eisenhower's negative attitudes toward the leading politicians and their parties were a consequence of his deep fear that no matter who succeeded him, his policies were going to be rejected. In some part because of Eisenhower's leadership, the fifties had been a time of peace and prosperity. The sixties, he feared, were going to be much different, precisely because whoever succeeded him was almost certainly going to cut taxes, unbalance the budget, and greatly increase defense spending. So strongly did he fear the effect of such policies on the nation that had the Twenty-second Amendment not prevented him from running again, he surely would have done so. As things stood, he felt rejected, as in a sense he had been. His approval rating in the polls was below 50 percent. The party platforms, as they were shaping up, were going to be repudiations of his policies. Eisenhower knew better but could not escape the thought that the election would be a referendum on his conduct of the Presidency.

His personal feelings about Nixon added another difficult aspect to the complex situation. Ike liked Dick well enough, but then Ike liked almost everybody. Eisenhower the President regarded Nixon the potential successor as unready. While Eisenhower disapproved of Nixon's aggressiveness and partisanship, his deeper concern was Nixon's immaturity. He wished Nixon had taken his suggestion back in 1956 and served the past four years as Secretary of Defense, thereby obtaining some badly needed administrative experience. He wished that he had an older substitute for Nixon, specifically Robert Anderson or Al Gruenther or Milton Eisenhower, but he realized that none of them had the necessary political appeal. He knew, in short, that he was stuck with Nixon, who, unprepared though he was, seemed to Eisenhower to be infinitely superior to Johnson, Kennedy, and Rockefeller.

IN A JULY 13 LETTER TO SOKOLSKY, Nixon had predicted that "what will affect the campaign most of all will be international developments." He thought that if foreign policy became the centerpiece of the campaign, it would help him; if domestic policy, then "the Democratic candidates, who inevitably can and will promise more than we will, would probably benefit."[52]

Actually, the number-one foreign-policy issue—relations with the Russians—was running against the Republicans. Eisenhower had hoped to negotiate a nuclear test ban treaty with Krushchev, and in the spring seemed on the verge of doing so. A summit meeting had been arranged for May, in Paris, but it broke up in acrimony after the Russians shot down a U-2 spy plane over their territory and Eisenhower got caught lying about the plane's mission. In the ensuing hubbub, Eisenhower was embarrassed, the Republicans disconcerted, and the treaty scuttled. Nixon had no involvement in any of this, but he was the one who was going to have to pay the highest price for it, as the Democrats leaped on the U-2 incident to show how inept the Republican Administration was in dealing with the Russians. The best Nixon could do was to stress how valuable the U-2 flights had been—the photographs from the spy missions had shown that Democratic charges about a "missile gap" were false—but he was denied even that claim, because Eisenhower and the CIA remained secretive about the flights and would not release the information. "In retrospect," Nixon told the Republican leaders, "years from now, people may still criticize the President for his initial statements, but they will recognize it was a great achievement to get as much information as we have from the U-2." [53] That was little comfort—what Nixon needed was not historians' approval of the U-2 program sometime in the distant future, but votes in 1960.

Nixon was also disconcerted by Kennedy's charges that the Eisenhower Administration had neglected the nation's defenses and allowed a missile gap to develop. Kennedy, increasingly, was centering his campaign about the theme of "more," whether in social and domestic policies or defense or a strong foreign policy. Kennedy, Humphrey, northern Democrats generally, and even Lyndon Johnson were charging that the fifties were the time of the great postponement. Republican complacency meant that problems were avoided that had to be faced, problems of race and poverty and schools and economic growth on the home front, and of the arms race and the Soviet challenge abroad. In a way, the Democratic charge was that Eisenhower had not understood how to use the power his policies had generated. America could afford to do much more, on every front, than it was doing. Nixon was disconcerted about these Democratic charges because on most of the specific points he agreed with them.

POTENTIALLY, THE BEST FOREIGN-POLICY ISSUE for Nixon was only ninety miles off the American coast. If the United States government could overthrow Castro sometime before the election and replace him with a moderate Cuban leader, and if Nixon could get some of the credit for it, his prospects would be infinitely better.

He therefore became, in his own words, "the strongest and most persistent advocate for setting up and supporting . . . a program [of] training Cuban exiles so that they could free Cuba from communist control."[54]

In March 1960, Eisenhower had approved a CIA program to create "a paramilitary force outside of Cuba for future guerrilla action."[55] Nixon was one of the few people outside the innermost circle in the White House and the Agency who knew about the program. The idea was to train Cuban exiles in Guatemala, then provide them with covert American support for an invasion that would be coordinated with guerrilla units set up inside Cuba. The original target date was September 1960, which would have been perfect for Nixon's purposes, assuming the invasion worked. But Eisenhower insisted that before he would implement the plan, the Cuban exiles had to agree on a head of government to replace Castro. His condition was not or could not be achieved. In the summer the target date was put back to October.

Throughout this period, Nixon pushed as hard for action as he dared. In April, he sent a memorandum to Major Cushman (who was serving as his liaison man with the CIA people in charge of the program). Nixon said the agents "ought to get off their tails and do something." Meanwhile, he was furious with the State Department, which was urging caution, primarily on the grounds that it was not at all sure Castro was a Communist. "I strongly disagree with their present policy of forbearance," Nixon told Cushman, "although I, of course, publicly will defend it. I think it is time that they begin to show some backbone in dealing with this situation, despite their obvious fear of Herbert Matthews of *The New York Times* and the other left-wingers who have been dictating American policy toward Latin America for too long a period."[56]

Years later, Cushman told reporter Peter Wyden, who was writing a book on the Bay of Pigs invasion, that Nixon would ask him, "How are the boys doing at the [CIA]? Are they falling dead over there? What in the world are they doing that takes months?" Cushman felt that Nixon thought of the operation as "mostly rifle training" and did not understand the complexities or the details. Himself a highly competent Marine, Cushman had his own doubts about the CIA plan.[57] Meanwhile, the CIA had launched some harebrained attempts to assassinate Castro, but it is uncertain whether Eisenhower knew about them[58]—it is clear that Nixon did not.

WHILE THE DEMOCRATS MET IN LOS ANGELES, Nixon was at Camp David, working on his acceptance speech and thinking about the problem of uniting the Republican Party for the campaign. Party regulars and the representatives of the Old Guard were solidly behind him. The liberals, especially Rockefeller and his adherents in the Northeast, were the problem. Rockefeller had resisted every attempt to convince him that he had a duty to sign on as Nixon's running mate, but Nixon had not yet made a personal appeal. "I knew," Nixon wrote in *Six Crises*, "that . . . he would not come to me—I had to go to him." Nixon called Herb Brownell in New York, and Brownell arranged for a meeting. On the afternoon of July 22, Nixon flew to New York and that evening joined Rockefeller for dinner at his apartment. When the meal was over, Nixon made his offer.

He did not make it directly, because he anticipated rejection, but he did tell Rockefeller he planned to expand the duties of the Vice-President in foreign affairs, and pointed out that "if we . . . should lose, he . . . would be in line for the presidential nomination four years hence." Rockefeller said what Nixon expected him to say, that he was not interested.[59]

They turned to the real business at hand, hammering out a platform that would unite the party, or, more exactly, a platform that Rockefeller could support. Rockefeller had anticipated this development, and gave Nixon a statement of principles that he had prepared. From 10 P.M. until 4:30 A.M., the two men went over the statement.

On a number of points, Rockefeller gave way. Nixon would not agree to his proposal for financing compulsory health insurance for the aged from Social Security payments, nor on his insistence that the federal government be given compulsory arbitration power in labor disputes. But the key issue, defense expenditures, was another matter. Rockefeller had called for a $3.5 billion increase, about 9 percent a year. While not necessarily accepting the specific figure, Nixon was in general agreement—indeed, had been pushing behind the scenes for more defense spending. But Nixon knew that Eisenhower was furious with what he regarded as Rockefeller's repudiation of the President's defense policy, and badly as Nixon needed Rockefeller's support, he needed Eisenhower's more. Rockefeller was aware of his dilemma but was not prepared to compromise.

The statement of defense that they finally agreed to read: "The United States can afford and must provide the increased expenditures to implement fully this necessary program for strengthening our defense posture. There must be no price ceiling on America's security." The second sentence was Nixon's, one that he had been using in his private correspondence for some time past.

Nixon may have felt that the statement was general enough to meet the President's approval, or at least to insure his silence. But when the "Treaty of Fifth Avenue" was reported to the President, Eisenhower said he found it "somewhat astonishing," especially as it came from two men "who had long been in administration councils and who had never voiced any doubt—at least in my presence—of the adequacy of America's defenses."[60]

Bill Robinson, vice-president of the *Herald Tribune*, was with Eisenhower in Newport. He, and others close to Eisenhower, felt that the statement "really involved a repudiation of the President's position on defense." Worse, Rockefeller was insisting on putting the statement into the platform. Eisenhower called Nixon on the telephone. Robinson overheard the conversation and recorded it in his diary. The President told Nixon "that it would be difficult for Nixon to run on the Administration record if the platform contained a repudiation of it. He also pointed out that he (Eisenhower) would still be President during the next six months and he intended to stick to his policies. Any position by Nixon or the platform in repudiation of these policies would bring discord and disunity in the Republican Party efforts. Nixon assured the President the platform would contain not one word which could be interpreted as being directly or indirectly critical of the Administration position on Defense or any other matter. . . . Nixon said that if the platform committee chose to take a position like that, he (Nixon) would have to repudiate the platform."[61]

The next day, the newspapers had the statement. Reporters wrote that Nixon had "surrendered" to Rockefeller. Eisenhower, visibly upset, called Nixon again. Nixon said he was innocent, that Rockefeller was the one who had released the statement, and he did so unilaterally. "What I'm trying to do," Nixon explained, "is to find some ground on which this fellow [Rockefeller] can be with us and not against us." Eisenhower said he would find it "difficult . . . to be enthusiastic about a platform which did not reflect a respect for the record of the Republican Administration. . . ."[62] Nixon then instructed his lieutenants to eliminate the offensive passage in the platform, substituting for it this statement: "The United States can and must provide whatever is necessary to insure its own security . . . to provide any necessary increased expenditures to meet new situations. . . . To provide more would be wasteful. To provide less would be catastrophic." That was general enough, and vague enough, to satisfy both Eisenhower and Rockefeller. Nixon had survived the crisis.[63]

He immediately had to face another. When he arrived in Chicago later that day, July 25, he found "the delegates in an angry and rebellious mood." They thought Nixon should have given Rockefeller "the back of my hand." Nixon held a press conference, where he stressed the number of points on which Rockefeller had surrendered to him. Then he undertook a twenty-four-hour blitz of the delegates. In an amazing display of energy, he managed to shake hands with, and be photographed with, every single one of the twenty-six hundred delegates and alternates. His performance quieted the criticism, and the convention went smoothly.

WHILE THE SPEECHES DRONED ON, Nixon picked his running mate. In *Six Crises* he wrote that his criteria were, first, a man capable of assuming the duties of the Presidency, and second, that he share Nixon's views on the major issues. Unstated but obvious was that he add strength to the ticket. His original list included U.N. Ambassador Henry Cabot Lodge, Jr., RNC chairman Thruston Morton of Kentucky, Congressmen Gerald Ford of Michigan and Walter Judd of Minnesota, Labor Secretary James Mitchell, and Interior Secretary Fred Seaton.

He was getting advice from all sides, and each of the potential candidates had something to recommend him, and someone doing it. Nora de Toledano called Rose Woods on July 22, for example, to say that she had been talking with Whittaker Chambers. Chambers felt that any attempt to match the Kennedy-Johnson ticket by choosing either a Catholic or a southerner "would be an impossibility. Whit was very very much for someone like Jerry Ford—caliber, ability—fresh approach."[64] Ford, for his part, was supporting Morton.

By the time Nixon arrived in Chicago, he had narrowed the list to Lodge, Morton, and Judd. Judd gave the keynote speech; Nixon liked it and afterward talked to him about the Vice-Presidency, but Judd said he would rather remain in Congress. Nixon liked Morton —they had come to the House together as freshman congressmen in 1947, and agreed on the issues—but as a midwesterner, Morton would add strength where Nixon was already strong. Lodge's assets were his prominent role as U.N. spokesman and, more important, his strength in the East, where Nixon needed help.

At midnight on the evening the balloting made him the Republican nominee, Nixon called a meeting of twenty top party leaders to discuss the selection of his running mate. Although Nixon did not indicate his preference among the three finalists, Jerry Ford had the distinct impression that he had already decided on Lodge. Nevertheless, Ford endorsed Morton. But when Governor Stratton of Illinois said that where Dick needed help was with the midwestern farm vote, Nixon interrupted: "If you ever let them [the

Democrats] campaign only on domestic issues, they'll beat us—our only hope is to keep it on foreign policy." That meant Lodge. Ford was "disappointed," not so much at the selection as at Nixon's sham meeting. He later wrote, "Making up his mind and then pretending that his options were still open—that was a Nixon trait that I'd have occasion to witness again." [65]

So Nixon chose Lodge. It was an odd selection, insofar as Lodge, in his last campaign, in 1952, had lost his Senate seat to Kennedy despite the Eisenhower landslide of that year. (Nixon assured Clare Boothe Luce, "People's memories are short and all that they recall about Cabot is that for eight years he has been on television speaking for America against the likes of Gromyko, etc." [66]) He could not do for Nixon what Nixon had done for Eisenhower in '52 and '56—Lodge was far from being a "rock 'em, sock 'em" campaigner. But then Nixon was not the man to adopt an Eisenhower-style "above the battle" posture in the campaign, and did not need his running mate to tear into the Democrats. Lodge was nationally known for tearing into the Communists in the U.N., which presumably would be helpful with the big-city ethnic vote. Further, Lodge was acceptable to both conservatives and liberals in the party; Eisenhower liked him, as did John Bricker of Ohio. But Barry Goldwater called the choice "a disastrous blunder," [67] a sentiment shared by many right-wing Republicans.

At 2:30 A.M., Nixon called Lodge in Boston, and Lodge accepted.

ROCKEFELLER INTRODUCED THE EXHAUSTED NIXON to the convention (the nominee had had virtually no sleep for three days). Nixon shook off his fatigue as he walked to the podium, where he delivered his acceptance speech to a wildly enthusiastic audience. He used part of his time to respond to the Democrats' and Kennedy's call for a "New Frontier." As Nixon put it, "They promised everything to everybody with one exception: they didn't promise to pay the bill." He pledged that "we are not going to try to out-promise our opponents in this campaign." The Democrats had charged that the United States was responsible for the failure of the Paris summit, and for recent Communist-led riots in Caracas and Tokyo. They said that American education and American science were inferior, that American prestige was at an all-time low. Nixon replied, "I say that when the Communists are running us down abroad, it is time to speak up for America at home."

There were other themes. He promised to campaign in all fifty states. He pointed to the difference between Republicans and Democrats: "We put our primary reliance not upon government but upon people. . . . We produce on the promises they make." In a nice phrase, he managed to both support the Eisenhower Administration and promise bold new action: "A record is not something to stand on, but something to build on." On the difficult defense-spending issue, he declared, "Militarily, the security of the United States must be put before all other considerations." He reminded the delegates that he was the man who had stood up to Khrushchev, and to the Communists in Venezuela. He indicated that he would be tougher with the Communists than Kennedy, and swore that "America will not tolerate being pushed around by anybody." Indeed, he promised to take the offensive. "It is not enough . . . to hold the line against Communism. The only answer to a strategy of victory for the Communist world is a strategy of victory for the free world. . . . When Mr. Khrushchev says our grandchildren will live under Communism, let us say his grandchildren will live in freedom."

On civil rights, he was forthright: "Each of us . . . should be doing his part to end the prejudice which one hundred years after Lincoln, to our shame, still embarrasses us abroad and saps our strength at home."

Nixon identified himself with idealism and challenge every bit as much as Kennedy. The competition with Communism, he declared, "means sacrifice." It meant "working together in a cause greater than ourselves, greater than our nation, as great as the whole world itself." In his peroration he recalled the man the Republicans had nominated in Chicago exactly a century earlier: "Abraham Lincoln was asked during the dark days of the tragic War Between the States whether he thought God was on his side. His answer was, 'My concern is not whether God is on our side, but whether we are on God's side.' " In that spirit, Nixon said, he accepted the nomination.[68]

If it was not his best speech, if it did not quite match Kennedy's charismatic effort, it was good enough to send the delegates into paroxysms of joy, delight Republican voters across the nation, and deeply impress many independents and even some Democrats. The *New Republic* was especially enthusiastic. The speech, it declared, had "sent millions into raptures" and was "one of the most impressively effective fifty minutes we ever witnessed. He rang every bell."[69] Now Nixon's task was to build on the enthusiasm as he faced yet another campaign, this one the most important and most difficult of his life.

CHAPTER TWENTY-FIVE

THE SEVENTH CAMPAIGN
PART ONE
1960

IMMEDIATELY AFTER NIXON'S ACCEPTANCE SPEECH, Colonel Earl Blaik, the legendary former football coach at West Point, sent him a letter of advice. "It is just as important to plan your campaign with the understanding of possible physical attrition as it is to plan the presentation of issues," Blaik wrote. Television was going to be the big factor, he predicted, and "you must always project as the relaxed, confident, fresh and unwearied candidate. Issues are important, but far more important is the impression created by the candidate." Therefore, Blaik said, "you must have sufficient rest, diversion and change of pace to eliminate fatigue which comes to us all, but in far greater degree to those whose daily routine is a repetition of speaking engagements, a matter of meeting individuals by the score, endless hours of flying, and the daily planning which is required for victory." Blaik also warned that an impossible schedule would exhaust Nixon's staff, and pointed out that "fatigue, strain, and just plain being worn out are all common denominators to the team that should have won but did not."[1]

In the margin of Blaik's letter, Nixon scribbled, "Right." But in the campaign that followed, he ignored the warning and failed to take the advice.

INDEED, HE HARDLY TOOK ADVICE FROM ANYONE, not even the President. This was his campaign, and his alone. Of course he had advisers, aides, staff people, secretaries, advance men, think tanks, speech writers, and the rest, in most cases highly competent men and women who were devoted to the cause and who did, exactly

556

as Blaik feared, work themselves into exhaustion. But not one of them was personally close to Nixon; not one of them had Nixon's unquestioned trust; not one of them could get through to the boss.

Every participant in the Nixon campaign urged him to slow down, to get some rest, to relax before major appearances, to leave some free time in his schedule, to abandon his foolish and self-defeating pledge to campaign in all fifty states. He would not listen, as he drove himself at a pace that was scarcely believable, even for the virtually inexhaustible Nixon. He paid a terrible price for the tremendous effort, not in terms of long-term physical health but in those terms Blaik had written about, the impression he projected on television. He was the opposite of "the relaxed, confident, fresh and unwearied candidate."

On the issues, Nixon had good reason to chart his own course, because—like all presidential candidates—he received conflicting advice on every issue. Some Republicans urged him to go after the Negro vote in the big cities; others wanted him to go easy on civil rights and concentrate on the southern states. Some wanted him to raise the religious issue, however obliquely; others said that would be disastrous. Some wanted him to be the old Nixon and conduct a "rock 'em, sock 'em" campaign; others felt that he should be the new Nixon, reasonable, persuasive, and responsible. In all cases, Nixon made his own decision.

Always surrounded by supporters and friends, Nixon in the 1960 campaign was one of the loneliest men in the United States. In his first two campaigns (1946 and 1950) he had consulted with and taken advice from Roy Day and Murray Chotiner, but beginning with the 1952 campaign, he had increasingly gone his own way, and by 1960 he kept all the details in his own hands. In some measure, this was a consequence of his growing maturity and self-confidence, and a positive development, but it also reflected a lack of trust in others. In many cases, Nixon's attitude toward even the most senior people in the Republican Party bordered on contempt. To some degree this was even true of his attitude toward Eisenhower.

It was in this area, not incidentally, that he differed most thoroughly from Eisenhower—the President had deep respect for the men around him, whether they be businessmen, professional men, politicians, military men, or even (at least in some cases) reporters. He wanted their opinions and sought them out. Nixon did not. There was hardly a subject, be it the pace of a campaign, or the kind of car to ride in for a motorcade, or the route to follow through a city, or the right position on civil rights or religion, or the proper makeup for a television appearance, on which Nixon went to experts for advice and help. After eight years in Eisenhower's shadow, after eight years of having to subordinate his own views to those of someone else, Nixon was finally on his own, the Republican candidate for the Presidency. He seized the opportunity and ran the campaign. Whatever mistakes that might be made would be his mistakes; whatever went right would be the result of his decisions.

THE PRESIDENT WAS EAGER TO HELP NIXON in any way he could, because of his fear of the big-spending Democrats. He gave his science adviser "a long discourse on how incompetent Kennedy is compared to Nixon, that even the more thoughtful Democrats are horrified by his selection, and that Johnson is the most tricky and unreliable politician in Congress." In 1956, Eisenhower had pronounced the Stevenson-Kefauver ticket "the sorriest" in the history of the Democratic Party. In 1960, he decided that Kennedy-Johnson was even worse.[2]

Kennedy's campaign, with its emphasis on the missile gap and other failures of the Eisenhower Administration to meet the challenges to freedom, made the President even more determined to stop him. He told his millionaire friends to start talking "optimistically, not pessimistically" about economic prospects, and urged them to accelerate the spending activities of their corporations, just as he was accelerating government spending. And, of course, he wanted them to make hefty contributions to Nixon.[3]

Eisenhower's behind-the-scenes activities were more or less helpful to Nixon, but what really mattered was the President's role in the public campaign. Immediately after the convention, Nixon met with the President to discuss that subject. According to his account, in *Six Crises*, Eisenhower "thought he should avoid taking so active a part early in the campaign as to overshadow my own appearances." The President therefore felt he should make a nonpolitical swing around the country in October, and save his partisan speeches until the first week in November.[4] According to Eisenhower, it was Nixon who suggested that he stay out of the active campaign until the last few days.[5] Eisenhower's friends thought that Nixon's decision to keep his distance from the President was a costly mistake, and Eisenhower himself complained that "Dick never asked me how I thought the campaign should be run." He nevertheless offered advice, only to have it spurned.[6]

At their postconvention meeting, the President advised Nixon to refuse to engage in a series of debates with Kennedy on television[7] (Congress had passed a bill making such debates possible, and Kennedy was eager for them). Eisenhower argued that

such debates were spurious, that they only tested a candidate's reaction time, not his real quality, and that in debate candidates tended to overstate their views. Further, he pointed out, as did many others, that Nixon was much better known than Kennedy, and that therefore a debate would only help the Democrats.

Nixon already knew all that. He also knew that Kennedy would have the advantage, as he could attack while Nixon would be forced to defend. But, as he also noted quite rightly, the pressure for debates was "irresistible."[8] Besides, Richard Nixon was not the man to turn down a debate—he had been debating since his grade-school days and was confident he could best the inexperienced Kennedy. After all, he had bested Khrushchev and in the process moved his popularity rating to an all-time high. On July 31, the day after his meeting with Eisenhower, Nixon sent telegrams to the heads of the three networks accepting their offer of prime evening time for a series of debates.[9]

When Eisenhower learned of Nixon's decision, he offered the Vice-President the services of television producer Robert Montgomery, who was an expert in lighting, makeup, and other aspects of television, and who had stage-managed Eisenhower's TV appearances. Nixon turned down the offer.[10]

Whether or not Nixon's rejections of Eisenhower's advice had a subconscious effect on the President can only be speculated upon, but what is certain is that in his press conferences in August, when he had innumerable opportunities to give Nixon a boost, Eisenhower did serious damage to Nixon's campaign. No matter what he was asked about Nixon, or what he intended to say, his answers could always be read two or more ways, and never constituted that clear-cut, total endorsement that Nixon so desperately needed. The most famous example occurred in a mid-August conference. Three times Eisenhower was asked about Nixon's role in the decision-making process. Nixon had been stressing his experience; as Charles Mohr of *Time* put it, "Nixon almost wants to claim that he has had a great deal of practice at being President." Each time the President replied that he alone made the decisions, although of course he listened to Nixon's advice. Mohr persisted. Could the President give an example of an idea of Nixon's that he had adopted?

"If you give me a week," the thoroughly exasperated Eisenhower replied, "I might think of one. I don't remember."

It was the worst possible thing he could have said, and he realized it at once. After the conference, he called Nixon to apologize and express his regret. But he also told Ann Whitman that it was all Nixon's fault—if he had accepted the job Eisenhower offered him in 1956, that of Secretary of Defense, he could have had all the decision-making experience he wanted, and "he would be in a lot better position today in his bid for the Presidency." [11]

THE POLLS WERE EXCEEDINGLY CLOSE, showing a slight Kennedy lead after the Democratic Convention, then a narrow Nixon margin after the Republican Convention. Nixon expected the election would be one of the closest in history, and therefore concluded, as he wrote in *Six Crises*, that "it would be decided by which candidate was able to put on the more intensive campaign." [12]

It was a significant choice of words. He did not say the "most imaginative campaign," or the "most thoughtful," or the "most innovative." It was almost as if he thought he could win by sheer hard work. He would beat Kennedy by shaking more hands, making more speeches, traveling to more places, appearing more often on television, organizing more people and groups, simply driving himself harder.

In planning the campaign, he insisted that he did not want to peak too soon, that the proper strategy was to build to a crescendo in the last week. But that was theory. In practice, he could not abide the thought of letting a single moment between his nomination and the election slip away unused. Thus, although he set September 12 as the opening date of his campaign, he went on his first swing on August 2. In four days he went to four states—Nevada, California, Hawaii, and Washington—for a series of speeches and rallies. Then he went south, to North Carolina, Alabama, and Georgia. Everywhere he drew big, enthusiastic crowds. While in the South, he did not back down from his advanced position on civil rights. (In Greensboro, North Carolina: "It is the responsibility of every American to do everything that he can to make this country a proud example of freedom and the recognition of human dignity in the world.") He tempered his remarks by claiming that the Republicans had become the true party of states' rights, telling southerners that Democrats who voted Republican would not be deserting their party because their party had already deserted them. [13]

Congress was in session in August, which required Nixon to spend some time in the capital. He used it to advantage, holding meetings and augmenting his staff. Bob Finch was campaign director, Herb Klein the press secretary, Jim Bassett in charge of scheduling. Other key staff people included Nixon's military aides, Don Hughes of the Air Force and Robert Cushman of the Marines, plus two young men who had worked on the fringes in 1956 and now began to move closer to the center, H. R. Haldeman and John

Ehrlichman. Haldeman had moved up to aide, while Ehrlichman took his place as advance man. Stanley McCaffrey was the Vice-President's executive assistant.

A new addition was former navy captain Louis P. ("Pat") Gray, who had been an assistant to General Nathan Twining, chairman of the JCS. E. Frederic Morrow, the first Negro to serve on the White House staff, took a leave of absence to join Nixon. Rose Mary Woods headed up the secretarial team that traveled with the boss; a Catholic herself, Woods found other Catholics to take positions on different committees and otherwise show their support for Nixon. She was fiercely loyal. When she overheard reporter Bill Lawrence make a crack about her boss, she angrily poured a drink over Lawrence's head.[14]

In 1952, Citizens for Eisenhower groups had run the presidential campaign, to the discomfort of the Republican regulars, who felt left out and ignored, and who resented all the Democrats who held top positions in the Citizens groups. Nevertheless, Nixon decided in 1960 to use Nixon-Lodge Volunteer Clubs instead of the party organization in the various states. However much it irritated party regulars, he felt it had to be done, because even if he won every Republican vote in the country he would still be ten points behind Kennedy. He had to attract Democratic and independent support, and Nixon-Lodge was more appealing to some voters than a ticket labeled Republican. In Southern California, Caspar Weinberger headed the Nixon-Lodge Volunteer Club.

There were other organizations. On August 13, Nixon attended the organizing meeting of Scholars for Nixon and Lodge at the Statler Hilton Hotel in Washington. He assured the assembled scholars—mainly university presidents and deans—that he would be receptive to ideas from the intellectual community and that his Administration would "encourage a greater flow of ideas." He hoped they would be able to set up a Scholars group on every campus of the nation, and wanted a personal letter sent to each of the approximately 100,000 professors around the country. He suggested that the letter include a position paper he had issued on Communism. Chairman Lon Fuller of the Harvard Law School convinced him that a paper on national goals would be more appropriate.[15]

Arthur Burns, professor of economics at Columbia University and former chairman of Eisenhower's Council of Economic Advisers, was a prominent member of the Scholars group. On August 19, Nixon wrote Burns, "Certainly you and your colleagues can make a real contribution, not only in the coming weeks, but should our campaign be successful, in the months and years ahead, as well."[16]

That was heady stuff for any professor, even one who had already served in the White House, and during the campaign Burns sent Nixon weekly letters full of sage advice. Nixon took almost none of it; he later wrote "that one of my major regrets was that I had not been able to make better use of the fine group of scholars. . . ." [17]

The real reason Nixon could not use the scholarly input was the insistence of the scholars on raising complex and controversial issues. Burns's suggestions, like those of his colleagues, tended to be esoteric even to an expert like Nixon, and hardly usable on the campaign trail. For another example, Dr. John Hannah, president of Michigan State University, urged Nixon to get behind a crash program on civil defense. Nixon gave the letter to Major Cushman for analysis. Cushman replied by memo that "Dept. of Defense is against this concept because Armed Forces are supposed to fight, and their primary missions take all and more money and people than they have now." Nixon agreed, and signed a reply to Hannah drafted by Cushman that promised only to look into the problem after the election. [18]

It was already clear, even before the active campaign began, that nuclear weapons would be a major issue, although not in the sense of building a defense against them, or in the sense of reducing the threat, but rather in the sense of who would build more to counter the threat. Kennedy was making the missile gap and defense spending his main thrusts, and Nixon more or less agreed with him, so he was not receptive to scholarly advice that he use the campaign to push for disarmament. Leo Szilard, the famous physicist who had played a key role in the Manhattan Project, suggested to Nixon that he come out in support of the Pugwash Conferences of Soviet and American scientists, organized by Cyrus Eaton in 1958 and dedicated to finding a way to nuclear disarmament. Szilard had exchanged letters with Khrushchev, who had— vaguely—endorsed the concept.

Nixon again turned to Cushman for advice. Cushman responded with a memo: "One cannot be against any such conference, out of which some good might come (if only from the intelligence point of view), but I should not think it necessary to publicly endorse it. To do so would alienate a large number of conservatives, give it the stamp of official approval, raise hopes, create an atmosphere of hoopla which would be counter-productive." Nixon decided to ignore Szilard's advice. [19]

He was comfortable with the Celebrities for Nixon Committee. They did not pester him with advice, but simply made speeches in his behalf. Helen Hayes and Mervyn LeRoy were cochairmen; charter members included John Wayne, Irene Dunne, Freeman Gosden, Jinx Falkenburg, Mary Pickford, Elizabeth Arden, Dina

Merrill, Jeanette MacDonald, and Gordon MacRae. Adela Rogers St. Johns suggested James Cagney and Jerry Wald. McCaffrey noted in a memo that "she also suggests Walt Disney's name, and that the right man might get Ronnie Reagan to come along."[20] Reagan, however, remained a registered Democrat, though he did make some speeches for Nixon.[21] Among the most prominent members of the Dick Nixon Sports Committee were Ted Williams of the Boston Red Sox and Frank Gifford of the New York Giants.

From businessmen, Nixon wanted money. His advantage over Kennedy was the general perception that Kennedy was antibusiness; his disadvantage was that Kennedy did not have to go after the fat cats, since his father could afford to pay for his campaign. A further Nixon problem was that, unlike Joe Kennedy, the Republican businessmen wanted something for their money and would not open up until certain promises had been made. Thus Roy Shaffer, one of the prominent oilmen in Fort Worth, informed Nixon (through Jack Porter of Gulf, who headed the Nixon-Lodge Volunteers in Texas) that "business people are greatly disturbed about the business persecution record that Attorney General Rogers has established." Shaffer recognized that unhappy businessmen could hardly threaten to go to Kennedy with their money, but he did warn that "there will be a great reluctance on their part to contribute campaign funds unless some assurance is given that this constant harassment of business will cease."[22]

The same mail brought a letter from Arthur Burns, illustrating one of almost innumerable possible ways a presidential candidate gets pushed and pulled and pressured in opposite directions. Burns suggested that Nixon have Rogers "look into the recent shady doings by the former head of Chrysler and the present head of the Prudential Insurance Company." Burns said that "the business world is much disturbed by these developments," and wanted Rogers to go after the guilty.[23]

BY THE END OF AUGUST, Nixon was eager to get started on the formal campaign, but on the twenty-ninth he suffered a grievous blow. He had bumped his knee while getting into a car in Greensboro a week earlier, and treated the injury with hot compresses while working on his speeches. But the pain became so intense that, on medical advice, he went to Walter Reed Hospital for a fluid tap to test for infection. On Monday morning, the twenty-ninth, Dr. Walter Tkach, the assistant White House physician, called him: "We want you to come out to the hospital right away." Nixon protested that he had no time. Dr. Tkach replied that "you had better get out to the hospital or you will be campaigning on one leg."

Nixon's knee was infected with hemolytic staphylococcus aureus, and Tkach insisted that he come to the hospital, get into bed, stay there for two weeks, and receive massive shots of penicillin and other antibiotics until the infection was cleared up. Nixon did as ordered; as he later noted, the pain in his knee was "bad enough . . . but the mental suffering was infinitely worse." As Kennedy toured the country, drawing big crowds, he was flat on his back.[24]

Eisenhower paid a visit. So did Nelson Rockefeller. Thousands of cards urged him to "get well." He got to see more of Tricia and Julie than he ever would have otherwise—they came to the hospital each evening with Pat. Still he felt trapped. He wrote Earl Blaik, "I am taking your advice about getting some rest but not by choice. Sitting here in bed for the last ten days has been rather exasperating," he confessed, but he was trying to look upon it as "a blessing in disguise. We don't really realize how much we are using up energy until we take a break from the battle."[25]

When Eisenhower returned from his visit to Nixon's bedside, he told Ann Whitman that "there was some lack of warmth." Whitman recorded in her diary, "He mentioned again, as he has several times, the fact that the Vice-President has very few personal friends." Eisenhower confessed to his secretary that he could not understand how a man could live without friends. Whitman wrote that in her opinion the difference between Eisenhower and Nixon "is obvious. The President is a man of integrity and sincere in his every action. . . . He radiates this, everybody knows it, everybody trusts and loves him. But the Vice-President sometimes seems like a man who is acting like a nice man rather than being one."[26]

Some of the friends Nixon did have were doing him no good. On September 8, he read in the papers that Dr. Norman Vincent Peale, "a long-time personal friend and supporter," had signed a public statement expressing concern over whether a Catholic President could dissociate himself from the influence of the Pope. Kennedy immediately charged that Peale had "loosed the floodgates of religious bigotry," and the outcry was so great that a number of newspapers canceled Peale's syndicated column. Many of Nixon's supporters urged him to denounce Peale by name. And Adlai Stevenson got off a quip: "Paul is appealing but Peale is appalling."[27]

Peale had put Nixon in a difficult position. There was nothing he could say on the religious issue that would help him. If there was an anti-Catholic vote (and there was; vicious pamphlets attacking Kennedy and the Pope and the Church were already being widely circulated), he was going to get it anyway, without saying a word. Nixon also knew that Kennedy's people had made a persuasive argument to his party's regulars that the religious issue would help the Democrats more than it hurt. Nixon was afraid that was true. What he needed to do was hold on to as many of the Republican Catholics as possible, while avoiding serious losses among Republican Protestants who would be tempted to vote for Kennedy just to prove that they were not prejudiced.

The effect of the religious issues was a hot topic for the politicians before the election, and for scholars afterward. Neither the politicians nor the scholars ever agreed, although one sample survey seemed to indicate that while Eisenhower carried 64 percent of the Protestant vote in 1956, Nixon got only 63 percent of that vote in 1960. Meanwhile, while Stevenson got about 50 percent of the Catholic vote in 1956, Kennedy won 80 percent of that vote in 1960.[28] But another investigation, by the Survey Research Center of the University of Michigan, concluded that Kennedy's faith resulted in a net loss to him of 1.5 million votes.[29]

Nixon figured the religion issue cost him votes, which only added to his distress over the advantages Kennedy had that he could do nothing about—which included Joe Kennedy's money and connections, the ten-point Democratic Party lead in votes, Kennedy's youthful good looks and his charisma, Jacqueline Kennedy's beauty, charm, and pregnancy, and Kennedy's freedom to attack rather than defend a record.

Nixon personally was distressed that religion had become an issue, apart from the help he thought it gave Kennedy. He was entirely free of anti-Catholic prejudice and wished that others would put it out of their minds. From his hospital bed, he dictated to Rose Mary Woods a letter to Clare Boothe Luce (herself a Catholic) on the subject, asking Luce's advice "as to what we can do to keep it out of the campaign." He had just seen a Joe Alsop column in which Alsop had pointed out, "with great indignation," that 25 percent of the people he interviewed in Akron were for Nixon because they were anti-Catholic. But, Nixon complained, Alsop "did not print out the number of people who were for Kennedy because he was Catholic!" For himself, Nixon said, "I could not be more distressed at the vicious anti-Catholic literature that is being circulated." One reason was "my strong moral convictions against raising religion as a political issue." Another was that "the effect may well be to drive the small percentage of Catholic voters who are still on our side to vote for Kennedy out of protest." He said he had received a number of reports indicating that heavy mailings of the anti-Catholic literature are "being made in neighborhoods with a high percentage of Catholic voters." He did not think that Kennedy himself would approve of such tactics, "but I wouldn't put this past the likes of [Walter] Reuther et al." It was, he sadly noted, "a predicament. Even the thought that choosing the man who is to lead the United States in the most critical period in our history might be affected by a completely extraneous issue is disheartening to a degree I find hard to describe." [30]

Nixon got all sorts of advice. Billy Graham told him that the Democrats had four objectives: to solidify the Catholic vote by arousing strong Protestant opposition, to split the Protestant vote, to present Kennedy as a persecuted martyr, and to obscure the real issues. Graham thought the Democrats were succeeding in all four areas. He recognized that Nixon himself could not say so publicly, but he did think "you should get the President to say it." Rockefeller, Dewey, and Javits "should make similar statements. No one could ever accuse them of religious bigotry or prejudice." [31]

Nixon refused to do any such thing. On September 11, two days after leaving the hospital, he appeared on *Meet the Press.* Herb Kaplow of NBC News asked him about the Peale statement concerning Kennedy's possible subservience to the Pope. "I have no doubt whatever about Senator Kennedy's loyalty to his country," Nixon replied, or about his ability to "put the Constitution of the United States above any other consideration." He said it would be "tragic" if the election were to be determined on religious grounds. He insisted he would keep religion out of the campaign, primarily "by not talking about it." He said he had ordered his people "not to discuss religion, not to raise it, not to allow anybody to participate in the campaign who does so on that ground." [32]

Kennedy partisans charged that each time Nixon deplored bigotry, he was actually making religion an issue—Tricky Dick at his worst. It is difficult, however, to see what more Nixon could have done to keep the issue out of the campaign, and impossible to see how he could have been more sincere about his abhorrence of bigotry.

Kennedy, meanwhile, used his religion adroitly. A week after the uproar over Peale's statement, Kennedy went to Texas for a highly publicized meeting with Protestant ministers of the Houston Ministerial Association. He gave one of his best performances ("I am not the Catholic candidate for President. I am the Democratic Party's candidate for President, who happens also to be a Catholic. If this election is decided on the basis that 40,000,000 Americans lost their chance of being President on the day they were baptized, then it is the whole nation that will be the loser in the eyes of history.") [33] He was a smashing success, and thereafter did not himself discuss the issue. Lyndon Johnson and other Democrats, however, did so throughout the campaign. Their favorite line was to point out that when Jack Kennedy was performing his heroics in the Pacific during the war, no one had asked about his religion. Kennedy himself, in his Houston speech, had pointed out that when his older brother died in Europe in World War II, no one had suggested that Catholics might have a divided loyalty in serving their country. The Houston speech, not incidentally, was played and replayed on television across the country.

So it went, day after day. Congressman Adam Clayton Powell said "the Klan is riding again . . . all bigots will vote for Nixon and all right-thinking Christians and Jews will vote for Kennedy rather than be found in the ranks of the Klan-minded." The AFL-CIO's Committee on Political Education put out a pamphlet that said the issue was not Kennedy vs. Nixon but "liberty vs. bigotry."[34] In spite of the provocation, Nixon did not speak about religion after his *Meet the Press* statement—although it was true that anti-Catholic pamphlets, some of them scurrilous, covered the country (*The New York Times* reported a rumor that H. L. Hunt of Texas was financing the campaign).[35]

FOLLOWING THE *Meet the Press* appearance, Nixon held a strategy meeting with Jim Bassett to go over the schedule. Bassett urged him to abandon the promise to campaign in all fifty states, "a backbreaking assignment," arguing that his stay in the hospital gave Nixon all the excuse he needed. There was no point, Bassett said, to going into states that were either hopelessly lost or relatively safe. But Nixon insisted on doing it his way, and all fifty states stayed on the schedule.[36]

The next morning, September 12, Nixon got started, flying from Baltimore's Friendship Airport to Indianapolis. Then on to Dallas and San Francisco. The next day it was Portland, Oregon; Vancouver, Washington; and Boise, Idaho. On the third day, Grand Forks, North Dakota; Peoria, Illinois; and St. Louis, Missouri.

He had pushed himself too hard. He woke at 3:30 A.M. with a 103-degree temperature and shaking with a chill. He had Don Hughes call the doctor traveling with him, John Lungren; when Lungren arrived, Nixon told him that if there was one meeting in the entire campaign he could not miss, it was the one scheduled for 8:15 that morning with the International Association of Machinists. He knew that the union was going to endorse Kennedy, but he wanted to speak over the heads of the union leaders to rank-and-file workers—or so he wrote in *Six Crises*, although he did not explain how he had hoped to find any rank-and-file workers at the union's national convention. If ever there was a scheduled speech he could safely drop, this was it. But he was obsessed with sticking to the schedule, and insisted that Dr. Lungren had to get him there. "I don't see how you can possibly do it," Lungren replied, "but let's try to get this fever under control." With heroic doses of aspirin and antibiotics, Lungren broke the fever. Nixon was up at seven and made the speech.[37]

Then he was off to Atlantic City, Roanoke, Virginia, and back cross-country to Omaha. After Omaha, Nixon and his party abandoned air travel for a motorcade through Iowa—it was advance man John Ehrlichman's idea—stopping at small towns across the way for short speeches. It was quickly obvious that Ehrlichman had made a blunder; the crowds were sparse, and the time it took to drive between them was wasting the better part of a campaign day. Haldeman was riding with Nixon in the backseat. Don Hughes was in the seat in front of Nixon. Haldeman reported that "Nixon seethed with anger." Probably still sick with the flu, no matter how masked it was with aspirin, and certainly dead tired, Nixon lost his temper. Haldeman described what happened: "Suddenly—incredibly—Nixon began to kick the back of Hughes' seat with both feet. And he wouldn't stop! Thump! Thump! Thump! The seat and the hapless Hughes jolted forward jaggedly as Nixon vented his rage." Finally the car stopped at a crossroads. Hughes jumped out and started walking away. "I believe he would have walked clear across the state," Haldeman wrote, "if I hadn't set out after him and apologized for Nixon and finally talked him into rejoining us."[38]

Nixon spoke that afternoon in Des Moines, the next day in Sioux City, Minneapolis, and St. Paul. He returned to Washington at 4:30 A.M. In his first week of campaigning, he had covered nine thousand miles and fourteen states.

In the second week of the campaign, he spoke in eleven more states. He defended the Republican farm program, and Agriculture Secretary Benson. He insisted that the Republican Party was not antilabor. He stood up for civil rights. He took the high ground, spurning advice that he attack Kennedy for his poor attendance record in the Senate, and refusing to bring Joe Kennedy into the campaign. He refused to hit out at Kennedy for his womanizing, or as a spoiled rich kid, although he did refer frequently to his own relatively impoverished youth, saying that he knew what it meant to be unemployed, or to have medical bills wipe out a family's savings. To reporter Theodore White, he appeared to be obsessed with proving that he was "just plain folks," a "regular fellow." White thought Nixon "was above all a friend seeker, almost pathetic in his eagerness to be liked."[39]

Aside from the usual warnings about Democratic fiscal irresponsibility, Nixon concentrated on foreign affairs and experience. He could maintain the peace without surrender, he claimed, because of his vastly superior experience. As always in his campaigns, he delighted in throwing out statistics. He had had 173 private meetings with Eisenhower, he said (in one slip that delighted the exhausted reporters following him around the country, he said, "I have sat with the President as he made those lonely decisions.")[40] He had been in 217 NSC meetings, and had presided over that group on twenty-six occasions. He had attended 163 Cabinet meetings, presiding over nineteen. He had visited fifty-four countries, talked to thirty-five presidents, nine prime ministers, two emperors, and the Shah of Iran. Meg Greenfield, in *The Reporter* magazine, described this as "leadership by association."[41]

He generally drew good crowds and a favorable response. However tired, or however sick he was, he appeared youthful and vigorous. He stood straight, spoke clearly and forcefully, his voice full of conviction. At the conclusion of his speeches, while the crowd cheered, he would throw his hands above his head, copying a symbol (V for Victory) that Eisenhower had made famous.

The content of his speeches, however, failed to impress Joe Alsop, who wrote privately to a friend: "I have not only liked and admired Nixon, I have also helped considerably to build him up as a man who has grown great with experience." But his campaign talks, Alsop said, are "a steady diet of pap and soothing syrup" with "the approximate content of a television commercial."[42]

UNCERTAINTY OVER THE CIA-SPONSORED INVASION of Cuba plagued Nixon throughout his campaign. He did not know if it would take place before the election, and as much as he yearned to make Cuba into a major issue, he dared not. He wanted, of course, to tell the public what he had been advocating in private, thereby demonstrating how much bolder than Eisenhower he would be if he became Commander in Chief, but he could not, because to do so would be to break with the President's policy. As it was, he went much further than the President, the State Department, or the CIA wanted him to go.

In the last week of August, speaking to the Veterans of Foreign Wars in Detroit, Nixon declared that there was "no question about our determination" to prevent "a foreign-controlled Communist dictatorship in Cuba. The United States has the power—and Mr. Castro knows this—to throw him out of office any day that we would choose." That sounded like a threat. Asked to clarify his position later that day, Nixon retreated to a safer position: "Now, if the United States wanted to use its full military and economic power, it could topple Mr. Castro. My point was that is simply out of the question."

In the first week of September, Castro was provocative. He blasted the OAS, literally ripped up a 1952 defense pact with the United States, recognized Communist China, and confiscated American-owned tire plants in Cuba. Several times during this period, Nixon invoked the possibility of an invasion, only to dismiss such a step as unworthy of the United States. In Omaha, on September 16, he insisted that it "wouldn't be the right thing" for the United States "to move in on Mr. Castro." On September 21, he asked rhetorically if Khrushchev had gained prestige from the Soviet invasion of Hungary in 1956 and whether Eisenhower was less attractive for refusing to use "our great power" in Cuba. "No," he concluded, "we gain; they don't."

Kennedy was making Cuba a part of his general campaign theme, a typical example of the Eisenhower Administration's tendency for "too little too late." He was free in his criticism of past Republican mistakes in Cuba, saying that Eisenhower should have forced Cuban dictator Fulgencio Batista to hold free elections. He recalled that when he had visited Cuba in 1957, "I was informed that the American Ambassador was the second most powerful man in Cuba. Today, the Soviet Ambassador is." He reminded voters that "in 1952 the Republicans ran on a program of rolling back the Iron Curtain in Eastern Europe. Today the Iron Curtain is 90 miles off the coast of the United States."

But in terms of future policy, Kennedy was moderate. He indicated his support of the partial embargo Eisenhower had declared, and on September 6 said that "any action which we take should be taken through the Organization of American States." [43]

Against this background of pious dissembling by both candidates, Castro came to New York for the United Nations session. From September 18 to 28 his antics competed with the presidential campaign for headlines. He publicly embraced Khrushchev, who was getting headlines of his own at the same session by pounding his shoe on a desk in protest at American perfidy in the U-2 incident.

THE FIRST NIXON-KENNEDY DEBATE was scheduled for Chicago on Monday night, September 26. Nixon spent the preceding Sunday in Washington, preparing his opening statement. At 10 P.M. he flew to Chicago, but instead of going straight to his hotel and bed, he went on a motorcade through Chicago, stopping for rallies in each of the city's wards. It was past 1 A.M. before he got to his hotel. That morning, Monday, he made a speech to the Carpenters Union convention; in the afternoon he studied the issues, cramming his mind with facts and figures. [44]

As a consequence of all this activity, plus that of the previous two weeks, when he arrived at the television studio he was physically exhausted, almost ten pounds underweight, his shirt collar loose around his neck (he ignored advice to get a new, smaller, and better-fitting shirt), his face wan. As he got out of his car, he cracked his knee again on the edge of the door. A reporter noted that his face went all "white and pasty," but he caught his breath, recovered, and walked in, mentally alert and eager to display his superiority over Kennedy before the largest television audience in history (estimated at 80 million).[45]

He had received all kinds of advice. Adela Rogers St. Johns sent a telegram: "God will go with you tonight when you walk before that camera. . . . Don't mention Kennedy by name. Call him my opponent. SMILE OH PLEASE PLEASE SMILE." She said she had just talked to the bookmakers in Las Vegas. "They say you can swing the odds back to yourself IF YOU ARE NIXON TONIGHT IF YOU TAKE CHARGE IF YOU ARE ON THE OFFENSIVE."[46] But Lodge urged him to use the occasion to erase the "assassin image."[47] Nixon's television consultant, Ted Rogers, urged makeup, but Nixon would allow Rogers to apply only some "beard stick" (a product called Lazy Shave, a pasty powder). Kennedy had spent the previous week in California, and the afternoon on the roof of his hotel, maintaining his suntan. "I had never seen him look more fit," Nixon remarked.[48]

Nixon had been, if possible, even more eager for this debate than Kennedy. It was not just that he was confident he could draw on his vast experience in debate and demolish his opponent. From the time of the Checkers speech onward, he had felt that television was his medium. It gave him an opportunity to bypass the reporters and pundits and speak directly to the people. What he did not seem to realize was just how bad he looked on television and how good Kennedy looked. The contrast between them was immediately apparent. As Teddy White saw it, Kennedy was "calm and nerveless," while Nixon was "tense, almost frightened, at turns glowering and, occasionally, haggard-looking to the point of sickness." By the end of the debate, Nixon "half slouched, his 'Lazy Shave' powder faintly streaked with sweat, his eyes exaggerated hollows of blackness, his jaw, jowls, and face drooping with strain."[49]

The strain was certainly there, and it was physical—Nixon's knee was in pain, but he had to stand throughout the program. The real problem, though, was what television did to Nixon's worst features, his heavy jowls and his dark beard, which gave him a five-o'clock shadow only minutes after he shaved. White caught this nicely once when he watched Nixon give a speech in San Francisco. He was only a few feet away, and could see Nixon both in person and on a television monitor. Nixon in person "was attractively slim, as lithe as . . . an athlete. His face . . . was a smiling one . . . broad [and] open . . . the heavy brows [and] the broad forehead give it a clean, masculine quality. Yet on television, the deep eye wells and the heavy brows cast shadow on the face and it glowered on the screen darkly . . . and showed ferocity." [50]

THE DEBATE HAD BEEN PRECEDED by a hoopla that was an unprecedented as the event itself. The most popular comparison was to the Lincoln-Douglas debates of 1858, which most reporters mistakenly thought Lincoln had won, and the anticipation was that like Lincoln and Douglas, the candidates would reveal new truths in memorable phrases that would ring through the ages. Nothing of the kind happened. One reason was the obvious fact that Nixon and Kennedy were not Lincoln and Douglas; another was that unlike their predecessors, they were in complete agreement about the basic issue—where Lincoln and Douglas had differed profoundly on the great issue facing the nation, the extension of slavery into the territories, Nixon and Kennedy had no difference at all on the perceived great issue of 1960, how to stop Communist expansion into the free world. But the major reason was the format of the "debate." It was not a debate at all, but rather a press conference, with each candidate responding to questions each had already answered a hundred times and more on the campaign trail. Neither candidate had anything at all new to say—virtually every line in this, and in the succeeding three debates, had been said already, ad nauseam.

Kennedy spoke first, in what amounted to a replay of his acceptance speech at the Democratic Convention and a restatement of the "Let's get America moving again" theme of his campaign talks. The question, he said, was "whether the world will exist half-slave or half-free. . . . If we do well here, if we meet our obligations, if we're moving ahead, then I think freedom will be secure around the world. If we fail, then freedom fails. . . . Are we doing as much as we can do? Are we as strong as we should be? . . . I do not think we're doing enough, I am not satisfied as an American with the progress that we're making." He wanted to get started on increasing steel production, hydroelectric power, teachers' salaries, civil rights, and farm income. [51]

Nixon's opening remarks were defensive, a reaction to Kennedy rather than a statement of Nixon's own agenda. "I subscribe completely to the spirit that Senator Kennedy has expressed tonight, the spirit that the United States should move ahead." Where did they disagree then? On their interpretations of the recent past. America had not been standing still, Nixon insisted, and he had the facts to prove it. He then launched into a series of historical comparisons between the Truman and Eisenhower Administrations. The Republicans had built more schools, generated more hydroelectric power, constructed more hospitals, built more highways. Overall, the Truman years had shown a total growth of 11 percent; the Eisenhower years had reached 19 percent. Average family income went up 15 percent in the Eisenhower years, as opposed to 2 percent in the Truman years. In short, the fifties were the best years of the century (which was more or less true) because of Republican policies (which was more debatable).

"Good as this record is," Nixon continued, "may I emphasize it isn't enough." He then used his favorite line from the campaign trail: "A record is never something to stand on. It's something to build on." He asserted that the Republicans had "the secret for progress," while the Democrats "do not seem to be [offering anything] new. They seem to be simply retreads of the programs of the Truman Administration." Republican programs would "stimulate the creative energies of 180 million free Americans," while Democratic programs "will have a tendency to stifle those creative energies." This was a far cry from his usual charge that Democratic policies would lead to socialism.

In his conclusion, Nixon responded to Kennedy's campaign speeches. "Senator Kennedy has suggested . . . that we lack compassion for the poor, for the old, and for others that are unfortunate. Let us understand throughout this campaign that his motives and mine are sincere. I know what it means to be poor. I know what it means to see people who are unemployed. . . . Our disagreement is not about the goals for America but only about the means to reach those goals." [52]

Stuart Novins of CBS News asked the first question of Nixon, and it was predictable: What about Nixon's experience? Was it as an observer or a participant or an initiator? Could he say specifically what major proposals he had made that had been adopted?

Nixon leaped on it. After each of his foreign trips, he said, he had made recommendations that had been adopted—for foreign exchange programs, for an inter-American lending agency, for admission of Hungarian refugees. As chairman of the President's Committee on Price Stability and Economic Growth, he had made recommendations that had helped hold inflation in check.

Kennedy, given the opportunity to respond, said: "Well, I would say in the latter that the—and that's what I found un— somewhat unsatisfactory about the figures uh—Mr. Nixon, that you used in your previous speech, when you talked about the Truman Administration. You—Mr. Truman came to office in nineteen uh—forty-four [*sic*] and at the end of the war, and uh—difficulties that were facing the United States during that period of transition—1946 when price controls were lifted—so it's rather difficult to . . . compare." It sounded better than it reads.[53]

Sander Vanocur of NBC News, in his first question for Nixon, quoted Eisenhower's press conference gaffe: "If you give me a week I might think of one." He asked Nixon to comment. "Well," Nixon replied, "I would suggest, Mr. Vanocur, that uh—if you know the President, that was probably a facetious remark. Uh—I would also suggest that insofar as his statement is concerned, that I think it would be improper for the President to disclose uh—the instances in which members of his official family had made recommendations, as I have made them through the years to him, which he has accepted or rejected." He went on to recite his extensive experience in the NSC, the Cabinet, and legislative leaders' meetings. "The President has asked for my advice. I have given it. Sometimes my advice has been taken. Sometimes it has not. I do not say that I have made the decisions."[54]

For the remainder of the debate, the candidates restated their positions on specific issues, such as federal support for teachers' salaries (Kennedy for, Nixon against), health care for the old folks (Kennedy for a federal program paid for through Social Security; Nixon for a voluntary program financed through private insurance), civil rights (both for), and so on. Toward the end, Nixon raised once again the sincerity factor: "And in that connection I again would say that while Senator Kennedy says we are for the status quo, I do believe that he uh—would agree that I am just as sincere in believing that my proposals . . . for education, my proposals for health care are just as sincerely held as his."[55]

Nixon's conclusion was a summary of Republican principles, and ended: "It is essential that a man who's president of this country certainly stand for every program that will mean for growth [*sic*]. And I stand for programs that will mean growth and progress. But it is also essential that he not allow a dollar spent that could be better spent by the people themselves."

Kennedy's conclusion was a restatement of his opening: "If we fail, if we fail to move ahead, if we fail to develop sufficient military and economic and social strength here in this country, then I think that uh—the tide could begin to run against us. And I don't want historians, ten years from now, to say, these were the years when the tide ran out for the United States. I want them to say these were the years when the tide came in; these were the years when the United States started to move again."[56]

As always after a major speech Nixon was keyed up, and wanted feedback. When he returned to his hotel, he had Don Hughes gather his staff for an appraisal. Before any of the members could arrive, he got the bad news from Rose Mary Woods. Her parents had called from Ohio and asked her if Nixon was feeling up to par. Hannah Nixon also had called Rose to ask if her son was "feeling all right." When the staff repeated these sentiments, Nixon realized that he had made a "basic mistake. . . . I had concentrated too much on substance and not enough on appearance." [57]

Telegrams and letters reinforced that conclusion. "Your make-up man betrayed you," Ralph Barstow wrote from California. "You are supposed to look mature but not old. Last night, you looked old, tired and pale while Kennedy looked tanned and fresh." [58] Jack Danciger wrote from Fort Worth that Nixon "looked tired and ill." He wanted Nixon to "slow down for a while" and regain his strength. [59] Jack Porter told Herb Klein, "The first order of the day is to fire the makeup man. Everybody in this part of the country thinks Nixon is sick. Three doctors agreed he looked as if he had just suffered a coronary." [60] Henry Cabot Lodge, watching from Texas, blurted out at the end of the debate, "That son-of-a-bitch just lost us the election!" [61]

THUS ENDED THE FIRST DEBATE. Nothing new had been said; there were no surprises. Nevertheless the Kennedy people were elated —the senator had shown that he could hold his own. Republicans generally were downcast—they had thought their man would slaughter the young upstart. The bulk of the people, and the press, were undecided in their initial reaction, although in the week that followed, the press concluded that Kennedy had "won." A majority of those who watched on television followed the lead of the press and came to the same conclusion.

What was most notable about these reactions was that a majority of those who listened on radio concluded that Nixon won. This pointed up his most serious problem, one that he had not anticipated—his appearance, especially in contrast to Kennedy.

The appearance factor could be corrected, and was. Thereafter Nixon used makeup when he went on television with satisfactory results. He started drinking milk shakes with every meal, plus one in midafternoon, and by the time of the second debate had put on five pounds, getting him back up to 165, still more than five below normal. [62]

Content was more difficult to correct. Eisenhower, over the telephone, advised Nixon to "once in a while . . . not appear to be quite so glib, to ponder and appear to think about something before answering a question." [63] That was a relatively easy criticism to deal with. Lodge's was harder. Robert Finch met with Lodge and his staff the morning after the first debate, and reported the consensus: "Nixon gave the appearance of allowing Kennedy to take the initiative. . . . Lodge wondered why RN did not articulate the constructive approach and take the affirmative instead of appearing to be somewhat apologetic. RN spent too much time defending the Eisenhower Administration. Simply take pride in it and move on to RN's own proposals."[64] Ralph Barstow was even more direct and brutal: "You are running for President, not Mr. Eisenhower. . . . It is fine to agree with Kennedy, but we are not interested in agreements. The differences are the real issue. . . . Last night was not a great debate. Dick Nixon wasn't the man who demolished Jerry Voorhees [sic] and smashed Helen Gahagan into oblivion. That's the man we want to vote enthusiastically for."[65]

IN THE INTERVAL BETWEEN THE DEBATES, Nixon campaigned in thirteen states, still drawing big and enthusiastic crowds. Pat was with him, giving her support and her own special touch at coffees, lunches, and other meetings of women's groups. What she lacked in glamour she made up for with pure energy. The pregnant Mrs. Kennedy was seldom seen on the campaign trail. Pat was seldom off it.

She got strong and favorable press coverage. Early in the campaign *The New York Times* did a feature story on her that began, "Anything the average woman can do, Pat Nixon can do better. She can cook a fine meal, chaperone a teenage party, keep a house in apple-pie order, type, mend, clip her husband's hair, shake a thousand hands with disarming enthusiasm and look fresh as a dewdrop at the end of a grueling day." It all seemed too good to be true, but there was more. "She can walk into a store and walk out ten minutes later in a size 10 dress that needs no alteration. She has pretty ankles and the knack of maneuvering the hills of San Francisco or the cobblestones of Sverdiovsky in high, needle-thin heels." With all that "she does not arouse jealousy or antagonism in the female heart." She accomplished this seeming miracle by being "very smart looking, but not a fashion plate," by "having her hair always in place, but not being stuffy." Unlike Mrs. Kennedy, she wore "American ready-to-wear clothes and saleswomen regard her as a customer of charm and swift decision."[66]

She was always smiling, always straight. Jackie Kennedy could make jokes; Pat could not. When *Women's Wear Daily* wrote that Mrs. Kennedy spent $30,000 a year just for her Parisian clothes, Jackie responded, "I couldn't spend that much unless I wore sable underwear." When Pat was asked if she would be willing to debate

Jackie on television about clothes, she soberly replied, "Clothes are not an' issue. I would be willing to debate on something of value, not clothes."

She was capable of saying the most improbable things. She insisted that when her husband came home, "he drops politics," and claimed that "he's the same gay young blade I knew when we were courting."[67] The woman who had challenged Khrushchev to his face, dined with the Queen of England, entertained Harold Macmillan in her home, and strolled the palace grounds with the Shah of Iran could tell a luncheon crowd of the Celebrities for Nixon Committee that she was awed by being in the presence of such famous people as Helen Hayes and Rosalind Russell.[68]

How many hands she shook during the campaign, no one could ever count. A reporter watched her in a receiving line in New York and noted that for the first hour "she shook the hands of eleven to thirteen women a minute, with a word for many and a smile for all." During the second hour, she stepped up the pace "to at least fifteen a minute," while Mrs. Nelson Rockefeller, standing beside her, dropped out after half an hour. Pat paid a price for her exertions: during the campaign, her weight fell from 115 to 103 pounds. But she never let up.[69]

THE SECOND DEBATE was scheduled for October 7, in Washington. Although his advisers told him it was essential that he get some rest, Nixon spent the day before the debate making speeches in Ohio, and did not get back to Washington until midnight. He was up at dawn and spent the day boning up for that evening's confrontation. Before leaving home for the television studio, he allowed an expert to apply makeup. At the studio, his aides persuaded the technicians to turn up the air conditioner, so much so that when the candidates arrived, the room temperature was down to 64 degrees. The technicians must have been Republicans, because they had also set up the floodlights in such a way that four bright lights shone directly into Kennedy's eyes, only one into Nixon's (Kennedy complained about both the cold and the lights, and adjustments were made to his satisfaction).[70]

The debate was sharper than the first one, in the questions as well as in the responses. Paul Niven of CBS led off by asking Nixon to compare Kennedy's recent statement that the Republicans had to take responsibility for the loss of Cuba, just as they had charged the Democrats with responsibility for the loss of China. Nixon would not agree that Cuba was lost. He reminded Kennedy that the United States had signed a treaty with the Organization of American States "which prohibits us from interfering in the internal affairs of any other state. . . . " That seemed clear enough, but Nixon went on to muddle his position. "Let me make one thing clear. There isn't any question but that the free people of Cuba— the people who want to be free—are going to be supported and that they will attain their freedom. No, Cuba is not lost, and I don't think this kind of defeatist talk by Senator Kennedy helps the situation one bit." [71]

That response set the tone, as again and again Nixon charged Kennedy with defeatist talk and downgrading the United States. When Kennedy defended his criticism of Eisenhower for not apologizing to Khrushchev over the U-2, Nixon declared that "when the President is doing something that's right, something that is for the purpose of defending the security of this country against surprise attack, he can never express regrets or apologize to anybody, including Mr. Khrushchev. . . . I don't intend ever to express regrets to Mr. Khrushchev or anybody else if I'm doing something that . . . is right. . . . "

Khrushchev's actions at the United Nations made him an ideal target. Indeed, at times one might have thought that the candidates were running against Khrushchev, not each other. Nixon even managed to get the Russian dictator into his answer on a civil rights question. He said one reason he spoke out on civil rights, even in the South, was that "when we have Khrushchev in this country—a man who has enslaved millions, a man who has slaughtered thousands—we cannot continue to have a situation where he can point the finger at the United States and say that we are denying rights to our citizens." [72]

Asked about Kennedy's charge that American prestige had fallen in the last eight years, Nixon replied, "I would suggest that after Premier Khrushchev's uh—performance in the United Nations, compared with President Eisenhower's eloquent speech, that at the present time Communist prestige in the world is at an all-time low and American prestige is at an all-time high." [73]

Paul Niven asked Kennedy why he never criticized Eisenhower while making "the decline of American power and prestige in the last eight years the main theme of your campaign. And in a speech last weekend you said you had no quarrel with the President. Now isn't Mr. Eisenhower and not Mr. Nixon responsible for any such decline?"

"Well," Kennedy replied, "I understood that this was the Eisenhower-Nixon Administration according to all the Republican uh —propaganda that I've read. . . . Mr. Nixon has been part of that Administration. He's had experience in it. . . . "

Nixon leaped on that one: "I think Senator Kennedy should

make up his mind with regard to my responsibility. He [has] indicated that I had not had experience or at least uh—had not participated significantly in the making of the decisions. I'm glad to hear tonight that he does suggest that I have had some experience."[74]

A high point of the debate was a clash over Quemoy and Matsu (surely by this time the two most famous small islands in the world). Kennedy took the position that they were militarily worthless and, "lying virtually in a harbor on the Chinese mainland, were indefensible." Nixon indignantly replied that "the question is not these two little pieces of real estate—they are unimportant. It isn't the few people who live on them—they are not too important. It's the principle involved. These two islands are in the area of freedom. We should not uh—force our Nationalist allies to get off of them and give them to the Communists. If we do that we start a chain reaction. . . . In my opinion this is the same kind of woolly thinking that led to disaster for America in Korea. I am against it. I would never tolerate it as president of the United States, and I will hope that Senator Kennedy will change his mind if he should be elected."[75]

Kennedy was not going to let Nixon out-tough him. He spoke at length on the need to strengthen America's defenses: "I'm talking about our willingness to bear any burdens in order to maintain our own freedom and in order to meet our freedom around the globe. . . . I would not want people to elect me because I promised them the easy, soft life."[76] Then he insisted that the Democrats were going to give the country better housing, better medical care, better education, better defense, all without raising taxes.

Nixon's reply was that Kennedy was wrong in saying that the Republicans "have no compassion for the poor, that we are against progress." Republican programs, he claimed, "will move America forward faster, and . . . more surely than in his program." Then he made another almost pathetic, and certainly awkward, appeal for Kennedy to at least give him credit for sincerity: "This is what I deeply believe. I'm sure he believes just as deeply that his will move that way. I suggest, however, that in the interest of fairness that he could give me the benefit of also believing as he believes."[77] Kennedy never did.

Nixon judged his own performance favorably. He felt—and the press agreed—that he had wiped out any advantage Kennedy had built in the first debate. His private polls showed that his stand on Quemoy-Matsu was highly popular. The only discouraging note was that the audience had fallen from 80 to 60 million.

On the campaign trail the following week, Nixon pounded away at Quemoy and Matsu. He added two paragraphs to his standard speech: "I think it is shocking for a candidate for the Presidency to say that he is willing to hand over a part of the Free World to the Communist World. The wooliness of foreign policy thinking of the opposition party has already cost America tragically in the loss of China to the Communists and in the Korean War.

"Let me say this to you: if you elect me President I assure you that I will not hand over one square foot of the Free World to the Communists." [78]

HIS MOMENTUM WAS BUILDING, but suffered a serious setback on October 12 when Lodge, speaking in Harlem, declared that "there should be a Negro in the Cabinet. . . . It is part of our program and it is offered as a pledge." Four days later on NBC television, Lodge repeated the remark, adding that "there should be greater use of Negroes in the Foreign Service from the rank of Ambassador on down." He also promised to end segregation in the public schools and in public facilities, and new legislation to guarantee Negroes the right to vote. "We offer this as a pledge," he declared. [79]

Lodge could hardly have done more to help Kennedy and hurt Nixon. Nixon had hoped to do as well in the South as Eisenhower had in 1956, when the Republicans carried Texas, Louisiana, Florida, Tennessee, Kentucky, and Virginia, but immediately after Lodge's pledge the polls showed a sharp decline in Nixon's southern support. Lodge had not cleared his statement with Nixon; why he made it—it was quite unprecedented, as presidential candidates never announce their Cabinet in advance—is a mystery. Nixon had to disavow it. Herb Klein issued a statement that said in choosing his Cabinet Nixon "would seek the best men possible," and that "a man's race or religion would not be a factor either for or against him." [80] That statement in turn alienated those Negroes and liberals who had not already concluded that Lodge's pledge was a cheap attempt to buy their votes, without pacifying southerners.

That Lodge was a drag on the ticket there can be little doubt. Of the four candidates, he was the least energetic, made the fewest speeches, and drew the smallest number of voters. Even in his home state, Massachusetts, he could not make a dent in Kennedy's huge lead in the polls. Johnson, meanwhile, added great strength to the Democratic ticket. If the oilmen in Texas and elsewhere much preferred Nixon to Kennedy, they also knew that if Nixon won, LBJ would stay on as majority leader in the Senate, where he could have a decisive influence on the oil depletion allowance that was so valuable to them—and they knew that Johnson was a vindictive man with a long memory. So they contributed almost as heavily to the Democratic as to the Repubican Party. Further, as a campaigner Johnson was nearly as active as Nixon himself. He concentrated on the South, where he told every audience—in his best southern drawl—about his grandpapa's service in the Confederate Army. But, as so often when things went wrong for him, Nixon had no one to blame but himself. Lodge's selection had been entirely his own.

FOR THE THIRD DEBATE, on October 13, the candidates were a full continent apart—Nixon spoke from a studio in Los Angeles; Kennedy, from New York. Quemoy and Matsu remained the hottest topic. During the preceding week, Kennedy had accused Nixon of being "trigger-happy." Nixon said he resented that comment, and reminded Kennedy of the facts of twentieth-century American history—"I would ask him to name one Republican President who led this nation into war. There were three Democratic Presidents who led us into war. I do not mean by that that one party is a war party and the other party is a peace party. But I do say that any statement to the effect that the Republican party is trigger-happy is belied by the record."[81]

Kennedy insisted that the treaty with the Nationalists on Formosa did not include Quemoy and Matsu. He was both right and wrong. The 1954 mutual defense treaty between the United States and Nationalist China had been restricted to Formosa and the Pescadores, but the Kennedy-Nixon debate was not over the treaty, rather over a congressional resolution. Adopted in 1955 at Eisenhower's request, it committed the United States to the defense of Formosa and "closely related localities." That seemed to mean Quemoy and Matsu. But Eisenhower deliberately never said that he meant those islands—he wanted to keep the commitment vague and the Communists guessing. Kennedy had supported an amendment to the resolution—introduced by Senator Herbert Lehman of New York—that drew a specific line back of Quemoy and Matsu. Eisenhower had strenuously opposed it and it was not adopted. Thus the Formosa Doctrine, as Eisenhower called it, confused more than it clarified, exactly as he intended. The trouble in 1960 was that the people most confused were the candidates, one of whom would succeed Eisenhower and have to uphold the doctrine. Kennedy said the doctrine excluded Quemoy and Matsu, which was incorrect; Nixon said it included Quemoy and Matsu, which was also incorrect.[82]

But of course the candidates were after votes and were uninterested in legal niceties. When Nixon recited his version of the "treaty," and pointed out that Johnson had voted against the Lehman amendment, Kennedy replied, "I don't think it's possible for Mr. Nixon to state the record in distortion of the facts with more precision than he just did." He continued, "I merely say that the treaty is quite precise and I sustain the treaty. Mr. Nixon would add a guarantee to islands five miles off the coast of the Republic of China when he's never really protested the Communists seizing Cuba, ninety miles off the coast of the United States." [83]

Later in the debate, Kennedy reinforced his counterattack to the point that he sounded more than a little like Nixon in 1952 on the subject of Truman, Acheson, and the millions of formerly free people who had been enslaved by Communism. Nixon, Kennedy said, was "indicating that we should fight for these islands come what may. . . . He didn't take that position on Tibet. He didn't take that position on Budapest. He doesn't take that position . . . in Laos. Guinea and Ghana have both moved within the Soviet sphere of influence in foreign policy; so has Cuba." [84]

On domestic policy, the chief disagreement was over health care for the aged. Kennedy made it sound as if it could be guaranteed practically for free: "The proposal that I have put forward . . . is for medical care financed under Social Security; which would be financed under Social Security taxes; which is less than three cents a day per person for medical care, doctors' bills, nurses, hospitals, when they retire." Nixon replied that Kennedy was indulging in a "mirror game of 'here-it-is-and-here-it-isn't.' . . . Social Security is a tax. The people pay it. It comes right out of your paycheck. This doesn't mean that the people aren't going to be paying the bill." [85]

Nixon's worst moment came when he indulged in a bit of gratuitous, sanctimonious preaching. Earlier that week, Harry Truman, who was campaigning actively against his old nemesis, had said that southerners who voted Republican could "go to hell." Although Nixon, after the first debate, had promised a "give 'em hell" campaign from then on (a phrase he lifted from Truman's own 1948 campaign), he jumped on Truman for his profanity.

"When a man's President of the United States, or a former President," Nixon preached, "he has an obligation not to lose his temper in public." Nixon said he had noticed large numbers of children in the crowds that came to hear the candidates—"I see mothers holding their babies up, so that they can see a man who might be President. . . . It makes you realize that whoever is President is going to be a man that all the children of America will either look up to, or will look down to. And I can only say that I'm very proud that President Eisenhower restored dignity and decency and, frankly, good language to the conduct of the Presidency of the United States." [86]

Commentators generally judged the third debate as about even, with possibly a slight edge for Nixon thanks to his tougher stand on Quemoy and Matsu. The pollsters, meanwhile, reported that after all the speeches, after three debates, after weeks of some of the most intense campaigning in American history, the race was too close to call, which only drove both candidates to try harder in the remaining twenty-five days.

CHAPTER TWENTY-SIX

THE SEVENTH CAMPAIGN
PART TWO
1960

EARLY IN THE CAMPAIGN, Eric Sevareid wrote a column on the candidates in which he argued that there were no real differences between them. "The 'managerial revolution' has come to politics and Nixon and Kennedy are its first completely packaged products." Both men, according to Sevareid, were sharp, ambitious, opportunistic, devoid of strong convictions and deep passions, whose only commitment was to personal advancement.[1]

Many voters agreed with Sevareid that no real differences separated these hot-blooded Cold Warriors so eager for power and so apparently short of principles. This attitude hurt Nixon more than it did Kennedy because there were so many more Democratic than Republican voters, which was why Nixon pleaded with the public to vote for the man rather than the party. But how could people vote for the man when they saw two peas in a pod? Still, although he was the beneficiary, the perception of no basic differences infuriated Kennedy as much as it did Nixon. Neither candidate could understand how anybody could feel that way; both men insisted that there were irreconcilable differences between them.

What *were* those differences? Some were quite obvious. Their backgrounds could hardly have been more unlike. Kennedy grew up on the East Coast; Nixon, on the West Coast. Kennedy was the son of a fabulously wealthy, politically powerful man; Nixon was the son of a struggling grocery-store owner. Each had lost a beloved and much-admired older brother, although in entirely different circumstances. As a young man, Kennedy had traveled extensively; Nixon, not at all. Kennedy studied at prestigious prep schools and

584

Harvard; Nixon, at Whittier High and Whittier College. Both had served as junior officers in the Navy, but Kennedy had come out as a hero. Both entered political life in 1946, although the rich kid went in as a Democrat, the poor kid as a Republican.

Both were astonishingly young men to be presidential candidates—Kennedy was forty-three; Nixon, forty-seven—but Kennedy projected a far more youthful appearance than Nixon did. Partly this was due to exposure—by 1960 Nixon had been a national figure for twelve years, ever since the Hiss case, while only about 50 percent of the public had even heard of Kennedy before he won the Democratic nomination—but mainly it was a consequence of looks. Kennedy could have passed for a man in his mid-thirties; Nixon, for a man in his mid-fifties. Kennedy had a young, pregnant wife and a small daughter. Nixon had a wife his own age and adolescent children. Kennedy was vigorous and athletic, a participant in sports—his love for touch football and softball games was widely publicized. Nixon had no athletic grace or ability—much as he loved sports, he was a spectator, not a participant.

Paradoxically, Nixon was in much better health than Kennedy, who had terribly painful back problems, suffered from Addison's disease, and took daily cortisone treatments.[2] Nixon had hardly lost a day in his life to illness—when he went into the hospital in August 1960, it was the first time in his career he had had to cancel a speaking engagement.

Kennedy was a notorious womanizer. He enjoyed an extremely active and varied sex life. Nixon was the opposite. It was not that women found him unattractive—many thought him quite sexy—but rather that he was simply uninterested in women, indeed uncomfortable around them. He had no gift for small talk, no ability to flirt, no interest in making sexual conquests. For nearly three full decades, he was the most controversial—and the most hated—politician in America. His opponents dug up and used every speck of dirt they could find. In all that time, no one ever accused him of being unfaithful to his wife. Finally, so desperate did his enemies become in their attempt to pin something on him that they circulated patently absurd whispers about his relationship with Bebe Rebozo. The truth was that Nixon was a monogamous heterosexual.

Another paradox. In public, Kennedy was solicitous about his wife. He held her hand, danced with her, kissed her, put his arm around her, and in many other ways showed how much he loved her. Nixon's public indifference toward Pat bordered on cruelty. He almost brutally ignored her as she trotted along behind him. They seldom danced (and were awkward when they did so), or held hands, or embraced. Only on the rarest occasions did she kiss him on the cheek, and he never kissed her. He had, in Fawn Brodie's apt phrase, "a problem with touching." [3]

Both men were extraordinarily intelligent and awesomely ambitious. Both loved politics and played the game with stunning intensity. But here too there were extreme differences. Kennedy was gregarious. He enjoyed the company of his fellow politicians, swapping stories with them, joking and laughing. Nixon was a loner. He spent time with his fellow politicians because he had to, not because he enjoyed it. Kennedy liked and trusted people; Nixon did not. With his charm, casual manner, and relaxed bearing, Kennedy was appealing to men as well as women; Nixon, with his awkwardness, his inability to relax, and his cold aloofness, was not.

Kennedy had a marvelous sense of humor; Nixon, almost none at all. Kennedy delighted in poking fun at himself, while Nixon took himself with the utmost seriousness. In the third debate, when asked about Truman's use of the word "hell," Nixon responded with a sermon, Kennedy with a quip ("I really don't think there's anything that I could say to President Truman that's going to cause him, at the age of seventy-six, to change his particular speaking manner. Perhaps Mrs. Truman can, but I don't think I can.").[4] "Do you realize," Kennedy told a liberal supporter, "the responsibility I carry? I'm the only person between Nixon and the White House." [5]

Kennedy could use his humor with devastating effectiveness. "The first living creatures to orbit the earth in space and return," he pointed out, "were dogs named Strelka and Belka, not Rover or Fido—or Checkers." [6]

When the two men appeared together at the annual Al Smith dinner in New York late in the campaign, Nixon gave a sober lecture on civic responsibility. Kennedy's opening remarks were: "Cardinal Spellman is the only man so widely respected in American politics that he could bring together amicably, at the same banquet table . . . two political leaders who are increasingly apprehensive about the November election—who have long eyed each other suspiciously and who have disagreed so strongly, both publicly and privately—Vice-President Nixon and Governor Rockefeller." [7]

When Kennedy got heckled by Nixon supporters, he turned them back with quips; Nixon responded to Kennedy supporters with snarls and threats. In Michigan, after a long day that included some eggs and tomatoes thrown at him, Nixon told a group of hecklers: "I would also suggest, while I am talking about manners, incidentally, that I have been heckled by experts. So don't try anything on me or we'll take care of you. All you do is to show your own bad manners when you do that." [8]

Kennedy joked about his wealth—his father, he said, had told him he would not pay for a landslide. Nixon seemed sometimes to wallow in self-pity. In Centralia, Illinois, he told the story of his brother Harold, who, when dying of tuberculosis, had wanted a pony in the worst way. His parents had wanted desperately to give one to him. "But, you know what happened? My mother and father had a little family council and they came in and they said, 'Now, look, if we buy this pony we're not going to have enough money . . . to get shoes for your younger brother.' It was an awfully hard decision for my mother and father but it was the right thing."[9]

Kennedy had never spent one day of his life at manual labor for pay, yet he managed to duplicate the FDR miracle of convincing millions that he was the real friend of the poor workingman. Nixon had worked at manual jobs every day of his life until he became a lawyer, but even his maudlin accounts of his youthful poverty failed to convince most people that he cared one fig for the common laborer. Thus Kennedy could get away with saying that "the basic issue that separates us" was the contest "between the comfortable and the concerned."[10]

Both men campaigned as if they were possessed, driving themselves to exhaustion. Nixon eventually went into all fifty states; Kennedy made it to forty-five. Toward the end of the campaign, Kennedy found it increasingly difficult to get up in the morning. But an aide knew exactly how to bring him charging out of bed. "What do you suppose Nixon's doing while you're lying there?" he would ask.[11] Kennedy masked his weariness effectively, almost always appearing fresh and bouncy, seldom making a slip in his speeches. Nixon often looked as haggard and worn as he felt, and made a number of slips in the final weeks. He spoke of his policy of "Peace and surrender" when he meant "Peace without surrender." He said, "We are going to make far more progress in education in the next four years than we did under the past administration." On another occasion he declared, "I will say this of my opponent, no man has done a better job of fighting Communism in the U.N. than Henry Cabot Lodge."[12] There were worse slips to come in the fourth debate.

There were, in short, vast differences between the two candidates, differences of background, experience, style, personality, and attitude. Nevertheless, Sevareid charged that none of them was really important because on the issues, on matters of principle, on their approach to America's problems, on their prescriptions for how to manage the Cold War, the candidates were alike.

IN FACT, they did disagree on a number of issues, although the natural tendency of candidates to move toward the center in the last weeks of the campaign blurred the distinctions. Housing, for example. Back in 1949, Nixon had opposed, and Kennedy had favored, the Housing Act of that year, which called for the construction of 810,000 low-rent public-housing units in six years, with the federal government committed to supplying up to $308 million in annual subsidies to local governments, plus $1.5 billion over five years for slum clearance. Nixon, and other Republicans, had denounced the bill as "socialistic," and although it passed, it was never fully put into effect. As a senator, Nixon had supported Republican attempts to cut public-housing construction to 5,000 units per year, and sponsored an amendment designed to end all public-housing programs in Los Angeles. The Korean War, followed two years later by Eisenhower's election, led to an economy-in-government drive that had reduced the number of units built annually from the promised 120,000 to 37,000. In 1958 Eisenhower vetoed a Democratic antirecession bill that called for a $2 billion housing program. In the campaign, Kennedy was advocating construction of 2 million public-housing homes a year. Nixon too indicated his willingness to spend more federal money on housing than Eisenhower had approved, although he did not indicate how much more.[13]

They also differed on federal aid to education. Kennedy advocated direct aid to the schools and federal support for teachers' salaries. Nixon proposed aid through construction loans to the states with no federal involvement in paying the teachers. On medical care for the retired, Kennedy proposed financing a program through Social Security, Nixon through federal support for private insurance plans. These were partisan issues, and the split was less between the two candidates than it was between the two parties. Nixon was insisting that the goals were in all cases the same; the differences were over means.

Their sharp exchanges on Quemoy and Matsu generated more heat and headlines than light and insight. Neither man could get the legal issue straight; both grossly exaggerated his opponent's position. Nixon continued to accuse Kennedy of appeasement; Kennedy accused Nixon of being trigger-happy. Nixon got the better of this one, as few voters were ready to "give away free territory" to the Communists, and late in the campaign Kennedy modified his position. He said he would fight to defend the islands if it appeared that an attack on them was but a prelude to an attack on Formosa itself.

SEVAREID WAS AWARE OF THESE DISAGREEMENTS, of course; what he had in mind in asserting that there were no differences between the candidates was in broader, deeper, and more important areas. There was, first of all, their common assumption that there were no limits to what America could achieve, if only given the proper leadership. Their goals were boundless. Both thought that it was possible to eliminate racial prejudice, end poverty, roll back Communism, and ensure freedom and prosperity to all the world, simultaneously. As noted earlier, in so thinking they reflected a national mood whose roots lay in the series of triumphs won in the candidates' lifetimes—victory over the Depression, over the Nazis, over the Japanese, over Communist aggression in Korea. A nation that could accomplish all that could accomplish anything.

People generally perceived Kennedy as the more optimistic of the candidates, which infuriated Nixon, because Kennedy's method of presenting his goals was to criticize what had *not* happened in the Eisenhower years (a favorite theme of all the incumbent's critics). Kennedy's speeches were about lost opportunities, how far short America had fallen of what could have been accomplished, and the self-imposed limits Eisenhower had put on the country's approach to racial injustice, poverty, and the Cold War.

Kennedy's argument was that we can do it if we try, whether "it" meant going to the moon, or building more missiles, or rolling back the Communists, or providing first-class health care for everyone. As Nixon said in the first debate, he fully agreed, so much so that by the end of the campaign he was trying to steal Kennedy's New Frontier slogan from him. In Marietta, Ohio, Nixon declared: "So I say, yes, there are new frontiers, new frontiers here in America, new frontiers all over the universe in which we live, but the way to cross those new frontiers is . . . to remember how we crossed the old frontiers and who did it. You remember? Pioneers, with individual spirit, with faith in themselves . . . thinking that they were the best in the world and that's what we are today. . . ." [14]

In his opening statement in the fourth debate, Nixon declared, "America must move forward in every area. . . . It is not enough for us simply to be the strongest nation militarily, the strongest economically. . . . We must have a great goal. And that is: not just to keep freedom for ourselves but to extend it to all the world." [15] He sometimes sounded more like Kennedy than Kennedy.

This shared sense of no limits, of impatience with Eisenhower conservatism, showed in their common positions on the big issues. Both men were committed to faster and more far-reaching progress in civil rights. Both wanted to cut taxes in order to stimulate the economy (although neither stressed the point, primarily because of Eisenhower's implacable opposition). Both were eager to spend more, much more, on the Department of Defense (although Nixon had to go easier on this point than Kennedy, because of Eisenhower's insistence that more than enough was already being spent). Both were prepared to accept large deficits (although neither said so publicly, in view of Eisenhower's horror of an unbalanced budget).

NEXT TO THEIR MAINLY RHETORICAL DIFFERENCES over Quemoy and Matsu, the issue on which they were the farthest apart in their public statements was what to do about Cuba. Paradoxically, this was the issue above all others that came closest to proving Sevareid's point, because in fact they were in perfect agreement. But Kennedy's adroit use of the Cuban question allowed him to turn the Quemoy and Matsu business on its head and to appear as the one who was tougher on the Communists.

Through the summer and into the fall, Nixon had pressed the CIA for action in Cuba, but the plans were not ready, the exiles had not been properly trained or equipped, and Eisenhower would not give his permission to act until the Cubans rallied behind a leader, so nothing had happened. Nixon still hoped for a CIA-sponsored invasion before the election. He talked it over with Herb Klein, who agreed with him that a successful Cuban operation would be "a major plus," indeed "a real trump card." [16] On October 5, Nixon sent a memo to Len Hall: "I would like you to go over and have a chat with the President about the Cuban situation." Hall did, but Eisenhower would not act until everything was ready, so again nothing was done.[17] Nixon then lowered his sights, and on October 13 presented the President with a proposal to ban all trade with Cuba. Again Eisenhower refused to act. He feared a hostile reaction from Mexico and the OAS, and explained "we must be concerned as to its political impact and the possibility it will get mixed up in the campaign." That was exactly what Nixon wanted to happen.

Nixon had hoped to make Cuba a major plus in his campaign, but it was becoming a definite minus as he caught it from both Castro and Kennedy. On October 14, Castro announced his government was nationalizing 382 American-owned firms in Cuba, including all banks, sugar mills, and other industrial operations. The following day, Kennedy suggested to Nixon that "the people of the United States would like to hear him discuss his views on an island not 4 miles off the coast of China [Quemoy], but 90 miles off the coast of the United States—Cuba."

Nixon judged that Castro and Kennedy had provoked Eisenhower to the point of action. On October 17, Eisenhower met with Under Secretary of State C. Douglas Dillon and Nixon. The Vice-

President told the President that "we ought to take some action with respect to Cuba at an early date." Eisenhower agreed. Nixon then said he would "like to be tied into the President's action in Cuba in some way." Eisenhower thought that could be arranged.

That same afternoon, Kennedy spoke to the American Legion Convention in Miami. He accused Nixon of "malicious distortion" in charging that he was advocating a policy of "surrender" with regard to Quemoy and Matsu, and said, "I do not want to get into any comparison of military experience." He added, "Let us come back from the mainland of China for a minute and worry about what is happening right off the mainland of the United States."[18]

The following day it was Nixon's turn before the Legion. He blasted Castro's government as "an intolerable cancer" and predicted that the United States would "very promptly take the strongest possible economic measures." The next day, October 19, the State Department announced an embargo on all trade with Cuba except for traffic in medicine and food. In addition, the American ambassador was recalled.[19]

Also on October 19, Castro predicted that the United States would launch "a large-scale invasion within the next few days." That possibility worried Kennedy. Cuban refugees in Miami had warned Kennedy's people that there was "an invasion fever" among Cuban exiles in Guatemala, who feared that they were being "rushed into it and that they are not yet equipped for it."[20]

The following morning, Kennedy put out a position paper. He ridiculed Eisenhower's embargo as "too little and too late, a dramatic but almost empty gesture." It would only increase Castro's dependence on the Soviets. As an alternative, he proposed stronger sanctions, an aid program for Latin America, and attempts "to strengthen the non-Batista democratic anti-Castro forces in exile and in Cuba itself, who offer eventual hope of overthrowing Castro. Thus far, these fighters for freedom have had virtually no support from the government."

Now, Kennedy knew that they *were* being sustained, even if he knew few details. Following Kennedy's nomination, Eisenhower had sent CIA Director Allen Dulles to brief Kennedy on intelligence operations. Whether or not Dulles had informed Kennedy of the planning for an invasion of Cuba later became a subject of intense controversy. Kennedy denied that he had been told of any specific plans, and Dulles was never forthright about the matter. If Dulles did tell Kennedy anything, it was vague at best, for the reason that no specific plan had yet been adopted. To Nixon's dismay and frequently expressed irritation, the Agency simply was not getting on with it. Thus there was little Dulles could tell the

Democratic nominee. Still, that little must have contained enough for Kennedy to know that training and material support were being given to Cuban exiles.

Nixon, indeed, was furious that Kennedy had been told anything. When Dulles reported to the NSC on his briefing of the Democratic nominee, Nixon "exploded." He "thundered" that under no circumstances should Kennedy be told anything more.[21]

The afternoon of October 20, Nixon read headlines that proclaimed: "KENNEDY ADVOCATES U.S. INTERVENTION IN CUBA: CALLS FOR AID TO REBEL FORCES IN CUBA."

"I could hardly believe my eyes," Nixon claimed in *Six Crises*. He had an aide, Fred Seaton, call the White House and ask if Kennedy had been briefed by Dulles on the invasion plans and preparations. He was told that Kennedy had been briefed. "For the first and only time in the campaign, I got mad at Kennedy—personally. . . . I thought that Kennedy, with full knowledge of the facts, was jeopardizing the security of a United States foreign policy operation. And my rage was greater because I could do nothing about it."[22] What made him even angrier was that Kennedy was advocating exactly the policy Nixon had been advocating in private, without success, all year. What made him maddest of all was that he felt he would have to reply, and in replying, disagree.[23]

His opportunity came the next day, as he responded to the opening question of the fourth debate. He did so brilliantly, presenting a devastating case against invasion. Kennedy's recommendations for handling Castro, he said, are "the most dangerously irresponsible recommendations that he's made during the course of this campaign." He cited the treaty with the Organization of American States, signed in Bogotá in 1948, which pledged America not to intervene in the internal affairs of her sister republics. He reminded the audience of the Charter of the U.N., which also forbade intervention in another nation's internal affairs. But it was not just the legal situation that made such an intervention dangerous and irresponsible. Were America to support an invasion of Cuba, "we would lose all of our friends in Latin America, we would probably be condemned in the United Nations, and we would not accomplish our objective. I know something else. It would be an open invitation for Mr. Khrushchev to come in, to come . . . into Latin America. . . ."[24]

In his long political career, Nixon made any number of predictions, some of them amazingly accurate, but never was he more exactly on the mark than in this case. The trouble was, he did not believe a word of what he said.

There remains a mystery about this whole strange affair. Why did Nixon feel impelled to respond publicly? He could have said that the Administration was studying the situation and that the topic was inappropriate for a political campaign. Eisenhower had refused to answer Stevenson's attacks on nuclear testing in the 1956 campaign on those grounds. Or why not approach Kennedy privately, telling him explicitly that plans were in motion for an invasion and that he was jeopardizing national security by bringing up the subject. Although it almost never happens, it is not against the law for presidential candidates to communicate with each other without using a podium or the press. Franklin Roosevelt did it in 1944, when he sent George Marshall to Tom Dewey to persuade Dewey not to use information that had come to the Republicans about Roosevelt's prior knowledge of Japanese movements before Pearl Harbor, because that information was based on the breaking of the Japanese code and Marshall did not want the Japanese to know that the Americans were reading their secret radio signals. Dewey did not raise the issue.

Perhaps Nixon responded as he did because of his combativeness. He never ignored his opponents' jabs; he always counterpunched. His debating background reinforced this tendency—like all great debaters, he knew both sides of any issue and could be eloquent in his defense of either one, whatever his true feelings.

THE OTHER HIGHLIGHT OF THE LAST DEBATE was a dispute over America's prestige. Walter Cronkite of CBS News asked Nixon about Kennedy's charge that the USIA was suppressing a report that showed a decline in America's standing in world public opinion. Nixon said the report was an old one that did not reflect current trends. Further, "when he [Kennedy] says as he did in January of this year that we have the worst slums, that we have the most crowded schools; when he says that seventeen million people go to bed hungry every night; when he makes statements like this, what does this do to American prestige? Well, it can only have the effect certainly of reducing it. Well let me make one thing clear. Senator Kennedy has a responsibility to criticize those things that are wrong, but he has also a responsibility to be right in his criticism. Every one of these items that I have mentioned he's been wrong—dead wrong. And for that reason he has contributed to any lack of prestige." He added that speaking up for America was the way to improve her prestige, "not running down America the way Senator Kennedy has been running her down."

Kennedy began his reply, "I really don't need uh—Mr. Nixon to tell me about what my responsibilities are as a citizen. I've served this country for fourteen years in the Congress and before that in the service. I've just as high a devotion, just as high an opinion. What I downgrade, Mr. Nixon, is the leadership the country is getting, not the country. . . . You yourself said to Khrushchev, 'You may be ahead of us in rocket thrust but we're ahead of you in color television' in your famous discussion in the kitchen. I think that color television is not as important as rocket thrust." [25]

In his summation statement, Nixon made an unfortunate word choice that delighted Democrats and appalled Republicans: "America . . . has not been standing still. But America cannot stand pat. We can't stand pat for the reason that we're in a race, as I've indicated. We can't stand pat because it is essential with the conflict that we have around the world that we not just hold our own, that we not keep just freedom for ourselves. It is essential that we extend freedom, extend to all the world." [26]

Thus ended the great debates. Their effect on the voters now became the subject of debate, among the candidates themselves, among pollsters and analysts, and among the public. Nixon's own conclusion was that "Kennedy had gained more from the debates than I." [27] Kennedy's speech writer Theodore Sorensen concluded that his man's "sincerity and vitality . . . appealed to millions of voters who would otherwise have dismissed him as too young. . . ." Sorensen estimated that four million voters made their final judgment on the basis of the debates, and that among that number Kennedy had a three-to-one advantage.[28] But Samuel Lubell, one of the most widely respected analysts, declared that "my own judgment is that the debates did not bring any basic change in the voting pattern of the nation." Still, he had "no doubt that the debates changed for the better the image of Kennedy that most voters held." [29]

The best that could be said from Nixon's perspective was that the debates did not hurt him. But insofar as he had ignored Eisenhower's and his aides' advice to refuse to debate because he believed that he would slaughter Kennedy in a face-to-face confrontation, Nixon was the clear loser.

IN THE WEEK FOLLOWING THE FOURTH DEBATE, the candidates competed with each other with conflicting statements on Cuba, in the process so badly confusing their positions that they left everyone thoroughly perplexed about what their policy would be if elected. On October 22, Nixon reiterated that it would be "immoral and dangerous" to aid the anti-Castro rebels. "We do not break our treaties," he proclaimed. "We do not work against the United Nations." He warned that any American involvement in Cuba would bring Soviet intervention, which would mean "a civil war in Cuba that could easily spread into a conflict, into a world war." The following day, he dared Kennedy to accept a fifth debate, limited to the topic "What should the U.S. government do about Cuba?"

That all seemed clear enough, and straightforward, but Nixon went on to defend the embargo in terms that suggested he had something else in mind. "We quarantined Mr. Arbenz," he said, referring to the Guatemalan president overthrown by a coup in 1954, a coup in which the CIA played a major role. "The result was that the Guatemalan people themselves eventually rose up and they threw him out." On October 26, he made an even more explicit threat, based on the Guatemalan coup: "We have quarantined Mr. Castro so that the Cuban people will see what kind of man he is, and in their own good time—and it will be a good time, and sooner, I think, than you think—they will get rid of him in their own way."

Nixon's heavy-handed references to the 1954 coup caused James Reston to reconsider his position. He had praised Nixon for his remarks in the fourth debate, and condemned Kennedy for his call to aid the rebels as "probably the worst blunder of the campaign." Now Reston described Nixon's version of the Guatemalan coup as "the joke of the weekend in the Latin American embassies." Walter Lippmann, dean of the columnists, characterized "Mr. Nixon's show of righteous indignation as false and insincere." Arthur Krock in *The New York Times* concluded that "Nixon promptly sacrificed his advantage" on Cuba by alluding to Guatemala.[30]

As Nixon tried, in his own way, to indicate that despite all his high-blow rhetoric about nonintervention, he was ready to send the CIA after Castro, Kennedy did his own backtracking. In declining Nixon's challenge to a fifth debate limited to Cuba, Kennedy denied that he had ever favored any action regarding the island that would violate existing treaties. He then explained that his Cuban policy advocated nothing more than a propaganda campaign "to let the forces of freedom in Cuba know that we believe that freedom will again rise in their country." On October 30, on *Face the Nation*, Kennedy was a model of restraint. Outdoing Nixon, he pledged cooperation with the OAS, and expressed his opposition to "naked force."

Nixon's critics have condemned him for his "incredible deception" in publicly denouncing the policy he was privately advocating, invasion of Cuba. Fawn Brodie called it "the baldest lie of his vice-presidency." Nixon's supporters have praised him for maintaining the cover story for the planned invasion, and Teddy White asserted that "Mr. Nixon would not play campaign politics" with

Cuba. Both views are wrong. Nixon did lie about Cuba, but so did Kennedy. Nixon also evaded, qualified, hinted, and fudged. His reference to Guatemala blew the cover story. And he played politics to the maximum with Cuba. But then, so did Kennedy.[31]

Nixon's later assertion that Cuba cost him votes cannot be tested, but given the conflicting statements both candidates made about Castro, it seems unlikely. What is clearly not true is Nixon's implication that he protected state secrets (the planned invasion) even when he knew it was costing him votes. In fact, he all but announced that the CIA was going to attempt in Cuba what it had achieved in Guatemala. It may have been too subtle an announcement for the average American voter, but Castro certainly understood what Nixon's references to Arbenz meant.

MANY UNEXPECTED THINGS HAPPENED in the last days of the campaign, when Nixon planned to peak, that ran against Nixon.

On October 19, Martin Luther King was arrested during a sit-in at Rich's department store in Atlanta. The civil rights workers with him were released on bail, but on October 25 the judge sentenced King to four months in prison on the ground that King had broken parole—he had been arrested earlier on the charge of driving without a valid license. There were widespread fears that he would never get out of a rural Georgia prison alive. Kennedy called Coretta King to reassure her, but the decisive call came from Robert Kennedy, who telephoned the judge in the case and secured King's release.

Herb Klein talked to Nixon about King's arrest. Nixon told him, "I think Dr. King is getting a bum rap. But despite my strong feelings in this respect, it would be completely improper for me or any other lawyer to call the judge. And Robert Kennedy should have known better than to do so." Nixon refused to make a public comment. He had, however, talked to Attorney General Rogers. Nixon asked Rogers if this was not a case of infringement of King's constitutional rights, which would give the federal government an opening to intervene. Rogers called Jim Hagerty, asking him to issue a statement to the effect that the Justice Department had been instructed by the President to look into the case. But Eisenhower would not get involved.[32]

Nixon had counted on a sizable vote from Negroes who were fundamentalists and because of his strong support of civil rights over the years. He had had good relations with King, better than Kennedy did; King had voted for the Republicans in 1956, and in 1960 King's father had endorsed Nixon. But Martin Luther King, Sr., angered by Nixon's silence and moved by the Kennedy intervention, said, "I've got a suitcase of votes, and I'm going to take them to Mr. Kennedy and dump them in his lap." The story was widely ignored by the white press, but it made headlines in the Negro newspapers. Two million pamphlets describing the incident and entitled " 'No comment' Nixon versus a Candidate with a Heart, Senator Kennedy" were distributed in Negro churches. The episode hurt Nixon badly. In 1956 Stevenson had won about 60 percent of the Negro vote; in 1960 Kennedy won about 80 percent.[33]

Simultaneously with the King affair, Drew Pearson wrote in his column that Nixon's younger brother Donald had received a $205,000 loan from Howard Hughes, the head of a far-flung empire that did extensive business with the government. The loan had been made in 1956, Pearson wrote, and since that time Hughes had received all sorts of favors from federal officials. Hughes's Trans-World Airlines had been authorized to fly a new route to Miami and another to Manila. Hughes Aircraft Company had received new defense contracts and some business from the Civil Aeronautics Board that it had been unable to get previously. In 1957 an antitrust suit against various Hughes's enterprises had been settled out of court by the Justice Department. Three months after Donald got the loan, the IRS had reversed a decision and granted the Howard Hughes Medical Institute a tax-exempt charitable organization status that reportedly was worth "tens of millions of dollars" to Hughes.[34]

Nixon had his campaign manager, Robert Finch, issue a statement charging Pearson with "an obvious political smear in the last two weeks of the campaign." Nixon said he was not involved in his brother's business activities and knew nothing about them. The next day Finch promised a full statement from Donald and asserted that the loan had not come from Hughes or his company but from Frank Waters, a California lawyer and friend of the Nixon family.[35] Democrats, meanwhile, demanded a full-scale congressional investigation.[36] The Justice Department put out its own statement. It said that the antitrust suit had been filed after the disputed loan was made, and that the consent decree on the case "had been approved by every interested lawyer in the department's antitrust division."[37]

But the story would not die. It dripped with sensationalism and intrigue—the elusive and mysterious Mr. Hughes buying off the Vice-President of the United States for a paltry $205,000 and receiving in return government favors worth "tens of millions of dollars." As the details emerged, the story became—if possible—even more lurid. As James Phelan of *The Reporter*, who wrote the seminal article on the affair, aptly put it, "From the beginning, the people involved [in the loan] followed a script that reads as if it had been written by an ardent Democrat with . . . a marked fondness for Rube Goldberg contraptions of enormous complexity and size for the performance of the simplest household chores."[38]

Donald Nixon was a small-business man on the make who had tried to cash in on his brother's fame. He had expanded the family grocery store into Nixon's Inc., an enterprise that included a drive-in restaurant featuring the Nixonburger, the original grocery store, a second restaurant, and a coffee shop in Whittier. But he was in deep financial difficulty. As Harry Schuyler of Whittier explained, "Somebody told him he was a big shot, and he believed it and went broke. He extended himself too fast."[39] In 1956 Donald tried to raise $300,000 through the sale of stock, but instead raised a storm when his broker sent a tender offer to some sixty-five leaders of the Young Republican clubs in Los Angeles. After the tender offer got into the newspapers, no stock was sold. Donald then turned to Hughes.

Hughes was willing to make the loan, but anxious to hide his own involvement. He had his attorney, Waters, a former Republican member of the California legislature, hand over the $205,000 (it came from the Hughes Tool Company) to Hannah Nixon, taking in return a trust deed from Mrs. Nixon for a Whittier lot as security. Hannah then gave the money to Donald.

Waters had anticipated the potentially disastrous political implications. When he brought the request for the loan to Noah Dietrich, executive vice-president of Hughes Tool, the two men had agreed to "talk to Howard" before making the loan. Dietrich did talk to Hughes, who reportedly said, "I want the Nixons to have the money." Still apprehensive, Dietrich flew to Washington to warn Nixon, "If this loan becomes public information, it could mean the end of your political career. And I don't believe that it can be kept quiet." Dietrich related later that Nixon replied. "Mr. Dietrich, I have to put my relatives ahead of my career."[40]

Hughes had Waters make the loan in his own name so that the legal papers involved showed Waters lending the money to Hannah in return for the trust deed on the lot. The value of the lot later became the subject of controversy; in 1956 the assessed value was only $13,000, and similar properties in the neighborhod were selling for around $50,000. But as Donald pointed out in a statement, he had a fifteen-year lease with the Union Oil Company for a filling station on the lot (Donald used $40,000 of the loan money to build the station), for which the company paid $800 minimum per month.[41]

Why did Donald Nixon go to Howard Hughes for the loan? He had earlier applied to a commercial lending institution for one on the basis of the Union Oil lease and been offered only $93,000. Why did Hughes make the loan? On the one hand, it was a trifling sum to him, and he was in the habit of making campaign contributions to both parties, more or less with no questions asked. But this was not a campaign contribution; it was a personal loan to the brother of one of the most prominent politicians in America. Even if Hughes himself had not seen the obvious dangers, his associates had and had warned him about them. Still he had gone ahead.

Waters transferrred the trust deed to an accountant; Donald went into bankruptcy; the accountant collected the $800 monthly fee from Union Oil; no one foreclosed on the lot. In November 1960, Hannah Nixon was still listed as the owner. The loan was never repaid.

The details of Donald Nixon's attempts to become an empire builder aside, the important question is, Did Nixon allow himself to be bought off by Howard Hughes? No one knows, although Nixon's enemies assumed that he did, and that the big payoff for Hughes was the consent decree in the antitrust suit and the favorable IRS ruling on the Hughes Medical Institute.[42] That assumption has never been tested in court, because influence peddling has never even been charged, for the good reason that no evidence has ever been produced. In all the thousands of memos from Nixon's staff to "RN" in Nixon's Vice-Presidential Papers, this author has found only one reference to Hughes. Dated January 23, 1959, from Nixon's military aide Don Hughes, it reads in full: "I spoke with Howard Hughes and relayed your message. He was most happy and enthusiastic over seeing you in California. He cannot come East at this time. I'll arrange an appointment when your California plans are firm."[43] That was two years after Donald had gone bankrupt and Hughes had received his favorable rulings on the Medical Institute and the antitrust suit.

It must also be pointed out that to believe Nixon secured government favors for Hughes is to believe that the Vice-President had a decisive influence in the Eisenhower Administration. At the time (1957) IRS and Justice ruled on the Hughes cases, George Humphrey was Secretary of Treasury and Herbert Brownell was Attorney General. They were Eisenhower men. They owed nothing to Nixon. Their overriding concern was to protect Eisenhower from any hint of scandal. In the absence of any conflicting evidence (when he became Attorney General in January 1961, Robert Kennedy looked into the case and decided there were no grounds for prosecution), and in view of the known character of Humphrey and

Brownell, not to mention their relationship with Eisenhower, this author has to conclude that the charge that Nixon was guilty of a conflict-of-interest violation in the case of the Hughes loan is false.

In 1960, the charge came too late in the campaign, and the case was too complex, to have a major effect.

UNTIL THE LAST FORTNIGHT of the 1960 campaign, Eisenhower was noticeable primarily for his absence. Harry Truman, however, was having great fun campaigning against Nixon. In Oakland, California, on October 28, he expressed "pity" for Nixon, who was too young to retire after the election and would be looking for a job. Truman suggested that he open an amusement park and name it "Nixonland." There Nixon could use "his considerable gifts of showmanship and his ability to create all kinds of illusions." Truman said that "one of the rules in Nixonland would be no cuss words because of the children there. Of course in Nixonland there would be nothing to cuss about because there our prestige would always be at an all-time high—and we would be morally, spiritually, economically and militarily stronger than anybody else anywhere. Nixonland would also be very neat. In fact, it would be as clean as a hound's tooth." [44]

Eisenhower finally began active campaigning in late October. Teddy White thought his speeches "crisp, fresh and dramatic." [45] Eisenhower had never thought much of either Kennedy or Johnson, and he was angered by Democratic charges that he had played golf while the country went to pot. He took off after Kennedy with gusto, and defended his own record skillfully and forcefully. From Nixon's point of view, however, the trouble was that he never talked about Nixon's superb preparation for the Presidency, and the point of the election was not how good a record Eisenhower had made in the fifties, but who was going to lead America in the sixties.

Nevertheless, the Eisenhower speeches were eliciting a strong response, so much so that they later became one of the biggest "what ifs" of the election. (What if Ike had come in earlier? What if Ike had spoken here or there in states lost by a razor-thin margin?) Eisenhower himself was eager to do more, and Nixon, who had earlier been hesitant about giving a leading role to the President, was all for it.

But on October 30, eight days before the election, Mamie Eisenhower called Pat Nixon to say that she was distraught at the thought of her man taking on additional burdens, and told Pat she feared that Eisenhower "was not up to the strain campaigning might put on his heart." She had tried to dissuade him, but could not, and therefore "begged" Pat to have her husband convince Eisenhower to change his mind, without letting Ike know that she had intervened. The following morning, Eisenhower's physician, Dr. Howard Snyder, added his opinion, telling Nixon to "either talk him out of it or just don't let him do it—for the sake of his health." [46]

That afternoon, Nixon went to see Eisenhower in the White House. "I had rarely seen Eisenhower more animated," Nixon wrote in his memoirs. He showed Nixon an expanded itinerary, one that included stops in downstate Illinois, upstate New York, and Michigan. Nixon began giving reasons why the President should not take on the extra burden. According to Nixon, "he was hurt and then he was angry." But Nixon insisted and Eisenhower "finally acquiesced. His pride prevented him from saying anything, but I knew that he was puzzled and frustrated by my conduct." [47]

IF NIXON WAS NOT READY to risk Eisenhower's health in his cause, he was ready to call into question Kennedy's physical condition. On November 5, Ann Whitman noted that an "air of desperation" had taken over the Nixon camp. Nixon had asked her on the fourth to ask Eisenhower to put out a statement that would refer to 1956, when the President had made public the results of a complete physical examination, and that would call on all the 1960 candidates to do the same. Nixon said that as soon as Eisenhower signed and issued the statement, he would immediately make his own physical records public.

Nixon's suggestion brought forth a distinctly negative reaction in the White House. Jim Hagerty called this attempt to make Kennedy's health an issue a "cheap, lousy, stinking political trick." Eisenhower agreed. When someone tried to explain to the President that rumors were flying around the country about Kennedy's case of Addison's disease, Eisenhower cut him off and said, "I am not making myself a party to anything that has to do with the health of the candidates." [48]

It is difficult to see what Hagerty found so cheap and dirty about the "trick." Certainly a candidate's health is a legitimate subject for concern, at any time in any election. But it is just as difficult to see why Nixon waited until so late in the day to make the request. Kennedy himself had raised the issue, even before the coventions, when his target was Lyndon Johnson (who, like Eisenhower, had suffered a heart attack). In the preconvention maneuvering, Truman had supported Johnson, and attacked Kennedy on the "age issue." Kennedy, in response, had called a press confer-

602 | THE SEVENTH CAMPAIGN, PART TWO

ence, where he asserted that youth had its advantages, and said that a presidential candidate's health was cause for concern: "The voters deserve to know that his strength and vigor will remain at the helm."[49] Johnson supporters had retaliated by circulating the rumors about Addison's disease. Kennedy had gotten two doctors to issue generalized statements declaring that he was in excellent health, and two aides—Sorensen and Robert Kennedy—to issue explicit denials that Kennedy was taking cortisone, steroids, or any other drugs. But no detailed physical examination results were released, as Eisenhower had done in 1956.[50]

On November 4, Rose Mary Woods made another call to Ann Whitman. Nixon wanted to say in a speech that night that if elected he would send Eisenhower on a goodwill tour to Eastern Europe. Whitman relayed the request to Eisenhower, who was "astonished, did not like the idea of 'auctioning off the Presidency' in this manner, spoke of the difficulty of his traveling once he is not President, and felt it was a last-ditch, hysterical action." He told Hagerty to call Nixon and tell him no. But two days later, Woods called Whitman again to ask her to make sure Eisenhower listened to Nixon's televised speech that night. Eisenhower did, and again was astonished as he heard Nixon make the promise to send him on a tour—with Truman and Herbert Hoover as traveling companions. Nixon said that he had consulted Eisenhower about the proposal and that the President "had indicated he would be willing to undertake such a trip." He added that Eisenhower had suggested bringing Hoover and Truman along.

Furious, Eisenhower told Hagerty to call Nixon and force him to retract the promise. Hagerty got the President to agree that such a course, twenty-four hours before the election, would be disastrous; Nixon's pledge had been the lead story in *The New York Times* that morning. Instead of demanding a retraction, Whitman reported, "The President dictated . . . a congratulatory telegram on the speech . . . to send to Nixon." Only in politics could such a thing happen. Whitman, no innocent herself in political maneuvering, confessed, "I do not understand."[51]

DESPERATE AS NIXON WAS —the polls were now predicting a narrow Kennedy victory—he refused to inject the religious issue into the campaign at the last minute. Billy Graham was ready to publish an article in *Life* magazine endorsing him, without explicitly mentioning Kennedy's religion, but Nixon vetoed the idea.[52] At a meeting that extended into the early-morning hours of November 3, the staff was unanimous in advising Nixon to make a speech denouncing the Democrats' use of "reverse bigotry"; the Democrats were urging Catholics to vote for Kennedy, the Republicans to do the same to prove that they were not prejudiced. Again Nixon refused, on the grounds that such a speech would "substantially set back" the cause of religious tolerance.[53]

Instead, in that last week, Nixon put the staff to work with a series of memorandums. To Bill Rogers on November 4: "I would like you to try your hand at an excerpt along the lines that the election of Kennedy would bring the economy to a standstill—risk jobs, recession, higher prices and higher taxes. . . . Indicate that he would be a very dangerous President, dangerous to the cause of peace and dangerous from the standpoint of surrender. Here we can put a fear into them."[54] He asked Arthur Flemming, Secretary of HEW, to issue a statement on Social Security—"use strong language—use the words 'lie,' 'despicable and vicious.' If Kennedy is elected, Social Security will be wrecked in this country—wrecked by inflation—millions will be driven to the wall."[55] He told Rogers to put out a statement citing the number of times Kennedy and Johnson had disagreed on issues and demanding a Kennedy-Johnson debate. "A real slugging deal on Johnson but not limited to civil rights."[56]

Nixon instructed Fred Seaton to have Secretary of Labor Mitchell put out a statement: "If Kennedy should win the election the political labor leaders will have access to the White House and will be calling the tune. . . . Also bringing out that RN would be free of this influence, that Kennedy is a captive of the radical labor people."[57] He also told Seaton to put someone to work on "the job of checking the morning paper—checking every hour on what Kennedy is saying and what his people are saying and then suggesting a way in which to counter attack."[58]

NIXON HAD PLANNED TO BRING HIS CAMPAIGN to a peak the day before the election, and despite the King affair, the Hughes loan, Eisenhower's limited appearances, and Eisenhower's refusal to be a party to raising the health issue, he was successful in doing so. He hardly slept as he made a final blitz of the West, speaking in Wyoming, Washington, and California. Republicans desperate to keep Kennedy out of the White House had responded generously to his fund-raising efforts; in the last week of the campaign $500,000 poured in, which put the total collected to nearly $2 million, some $290,000 over the projected budget.[59] That allowed Nixon to stage a number of national telecasts of rallies, including one with Eisenhower and Lodge from New York on November 2. The day before the election, Monday, November 7, Nixon had a four-hour telethon that, in Teddy White's view, "mixed schmaltz and substance in equal proportions, showing [him] at his best (talking of peace) and at his worst (discussing the high cost of living with Ginger Rogers, who said she too had to live on a salary)."[60]

He had driven himself as never before. He was so exhausted that he could no longer think clearly. He continued to reject all advice, no matter how patently correct. Every man around him insisted that he had to ignore his fifty-state pledge. Still he insisted, and on Sunday afternoon, November 6, he flew to Alaska. After an all-night flight back from the rally in Anchorage, he stopped in Madison, Wisconsin, for an 8 A.M. airport rally in five-degree weather. Then on to Detroit for a speech and then the telethon. "I was tired physically," Nixon wrote in *Six Crises,* "but despite lack of sleep, I had never felt more alert mentally."[61] Then it was on to Detroit and Chicago for the television rally and a final election-eve broadcast. Late Monday night, he, Pat, the girls, and his aides got on a plane for Los Angeles. Pat and the girls immediately fell into an exhausted sleep, but he was too keyed up to drop off. In Los Angeles, there was one last airport rally. At 4 A.M. on November 8, Election Day, he finally reached his hotel. He had put on a campaign that displayed an awesome mixture of energy, determination, ambition, and stubbornness.

"IT IS THE ALMOST UNANIMOUS OPINION of all those concerned with the election of 1960," Teddy White wrote, "that the last ten days of the 1960 campaign produced a surge for Nixon. . . ."[62] Had the campaign gone on two days longer—and had Nixon been physically capable of maintaining the pace—he might well have forged into the lead. As it was, he had reduced Kennedy's margin in the polls to zero. On election morning, the pollsters threw up their hands.

TWO HOURS AFTER GOING TO BED, Nixon was up. He and Pat drove to Whittier to vote. Back at the hotel, Nixon received a handwritten letter from Tom Dewey. "In another 12 hours," Dewey said, "you will be elected to the most awesome responsibility in the World or you will be liberated. If elected, you . . . will have earned it in heart-ache and labor far above and beyond the call of duty. . . . If you are defeated, pay no attention to the Monday morning quarterbacks. Everybody knows how to conduct a campaign better after the event."[63]

Pat went off with the girls to get their hair done. Nixon, Don Hughes, and Jack Sherwood slipped away from the press and drove in an open convertible to San Diego, then on to Tijuana for lunch. On the way home—with Nixon driving—they stopped off at San Juan Capistrano to sight-see at the mission. About 5 P.M. they were back at the Ambassador Hotel, and the early returns from the East were coming in.[64]

It was the beginning of the longest night of Nixon's life. He described the tension, the strain, the ups and downs, in fifteen pages of painful detail in *Six Crises*. The American people, finally given the opportunity to make their judgment after one of the longest and bitterest campaigns of the century, split almost fifty–fifty. Kennedy established an early lead in the East, but all night long Western votes chipped away at it. Early projections of a Kennedy victory faded, and by midnight in the East the race was too close to call. But Nixon, who knew electoral votes per state, trends, who was doing the counting, and all the other details of politics better than any other man in the country, calculated that he could not win. He knew the computers were wrong early in the evening when predicting a Kennedy sweep; he thought them wrong now in calling the outcome uncertain.

Pat and the girls had a suite above Nixon's in the hotel; at 11:30 P.M. they came downstairs. "Hi, Daddy," Tricia called out. "How is the election coming?" Nixon said he was afraid he had lost. Tricia broke into tears. "I'm not crying because of myself," she explained between sobs, "but for you and Mommy. You have worked so hard and so long." Nixon told Pat that he felt he should make a statement to the effect that if the present trends continued, Kennedy would be elected. Pat was opposed. She said, "[I] simply cannot bring myself to stand there with you while you concede the election to Kennedy." She went back to her suite while Nixon wrote out his statement. A few minutes later she returned. "I have been thinking of all those people in the ballroom who have given so much of themselves to all our campaigns. I think we should go down together and tell them how much we appreciate what they have done."

Nixon's statement was not a concession, with good reason. If he carried California, as he expected to do when the absentee vote was counted, along with two out of three other undecided states— Illinois, Minnesota, and Michigan—he could still win. As he began speaking, Pat began crying. He put his arm around her—unusual for him—and went on. "While . . . there are still some results to come in," he said, "if the present trend continues, Senator Kennedy will be the next President of the United States." His supporters began yelling, "No, no, don't concede," but he continued. "Certainly if this trend continues, and if he does become our next President, he will have my wholehearted support."

Back in his suite, he continued to listen to returns until 4 A.M. There was still a slim chance—if he could carry California, get enough votes downstate to take Illinois, and win in Minnesota, he would be the victor.

He woke two hours later, to find that he had narrowly lost Illinois and Minnesota, and with them the election. He had carried twenty-six states to Kennedy's twenty-three, but Kennedy had a 303 to 219 lead in the electoral college. He had won 49.6 percent of the total vote, running nearly five full points ahead of the Republican ticket (the Republicans did manage to gain twenty-two seats in the House and two in the Senate). He sent a telegram of congratulations to Kennedy, and it was over.

A shift of a few hundred votes here, a thousand or so there, out of 68.8 million cast, would have reversed the outcome. In so close an election, everyone supporting Nixon tortured himself with "what ifs" and "might have beens." No one can know with certainty whether or not, for example, if he had spent the Sunday before the election in Illinois instead of Alaska it would have made the difference. Perhaps the most despondent was Don Nixon, who told his brother as he left the Ambassador, "I hope I haven't been responsible for your losing the election." Nixon replied, "The only place the charge [about the Hughes loan] meant anything was here in California, and we are going to carry California anyway." [65]

No ONE CAN KNOW, either, which of the two candidates the American people chose in 1960. Charges of fraud in Texas and Illinois were too widespread, and too persistent, to be entirely without foundation. Nixon's daughters, his friends, and many of his supporters urged him to demand a recount in those states; so did the President. On November 30, Eisenhower called Attorney General Rogers. The President "admitted that the election was a closed issue, but he felt we owed it to the people to assure them . . . that the federal government did not shirk its duty." But Rogers said he had talked to Nixon about an investigation, and Nixon was against it. Eisenhower let it drop. [66]

A recount was never a possibility. It would have taken at least a year and a half in Cook County, Illinois, where Mayor Richard Daley had turned in an overwhelming Kennedy vote, and there were no provisions whatever for a recount in Texas. Had Nixon demanded a recount, he might have thrown the government into chaos, and certainly would have prevented an orderly transfer of power. Besides, as he himself put it, "I could think of no worse example for nations abroad, who for the first time were trying to put free electoral procedures into effect, than that of the United States wrangling over the results of our presidential election, and even suggesting that the presidency itself could be stolen by thievery at the ballot box." [67]

But whether circumstances forced Nixon's hand or not, there is no question that he was statesmanlike in defeat. Nor is there any question that this was his finest campaign. If he was on occasion extreme, and even irresponsible on the Cold War, if he was guilty of pitching his campaign on the issue of who would be tougher on the Communists instead of who would be most capable of finding a way to live with them in peace without surrender, he was no more so than Kennedy. Kennedy also exaggerated the so-called "missile gap."

On such issues as race, religion, or bringing Joe Kennedy's or Jack's girl friends into the campaign, Nixon was a model of propriety and statesmanship.

IF NIXON HAD BEEN declared the winner, our view today of the 1960 campaign would be wholly different. Instead of what might be called the Teddy White thesis—that Kennedy ran a brilliant campaign while Nixon committed blunder after blunder—we would have an interpretation that would stress what Nixon did right and Kennedy did wrong. With a shift of one-tenth of 1 percent of the national vote, we would be writing about a campaign in which Nixon peaked at exactly the right moment, while Kennedy peaked too soon. We would be praising Nixon for his shrewdness in accepting Kennedy's challenge to debate, congratulating him on his wisdom in staying away from the religious issue, admiring his good political sense in saving Ike until the last minute, blessing him for his insistence on a balanced budget, showering him with kudos for his determination to defend Quemoy and Matsu while criticizing Kennedy for calling for an invasion of Cuba. With a shift of a few thousand votes, Kennedy would have been the one torturing himself with thoughts of "What if . . . ?" What if I'd spent more time in California? Been even more strident in asking "Who lost Cuba?" Taken a stronger stand on Quemoy and Matsu? Not pushed quite so hard on Medicare?

The point being that Nixon did do many things right. In spite of the great disparity in the numbers of registered Democrats and Republicans, he got half the votes. In direct competition with an opponent who was younger than he was, far more appealing physically, more dynamic, and richer, Nixon got half the votes. In spite of the vast gulf between the vote-getting abilities of Lyndon Johnson and Henry Cabot Lodge, Nixon got half the votes. In spite of a series of bad breaks, ranging from the President's refusal to act against Castro through Ike's "give me a week" gaffe to King's arrest, Nixon got half the votes. He had to defend a record he had not made and did not endorse, a conservative record in a day of liberal expectations, and he still got half the votes.

It was a crucial election for the nation, and for Nixon. He had spent eight years preparing himself for it, and for the leadership role that victory would have given him. He could not be faulted for thinking that he deserved to win, nor for being bitter about his failure to do so, especially in view of the nature of the vote count in Illinois and Texas.

TOM DEWEY HAD TOLD HIM that if he lost, he would be "liberated." But liberation from politics was the last thing Nixon wanted. He could not imagine life without action in the center of the arena. After a brief vacation with Bebe Rebozo and Bill Rogers in Florida, he was back in Washington, back at work. His staff typed up, and he signed, 160,000 letters to campaign workers. He dictated replies to condolence letters from hundreds of friends and VIPs. On January 6, he presided with Sam Rayburn over a joint session of Congress for the counting of the electoral votes; when it was concluded, he made a gracious speech wishing Kennedy and Johnson well.

THE MORNING AFTER THE ELECTION, Julie had asked him, "What are we going to do? Where are we going to live? What kind of a job are you going to be able to get? Where are we going to school?"[68]

He decided to return to California, where Pat wanted to be, and where his supporters were already urging him to prepare to challenge Kennedy again in 1964. On Christmas Day, Peter Braestrup reported in *The New York Times:* "Speculation here has centered on a possible effort by Mr. Nixon to build a 'political base' by running for the governorship of California in 1962, when the term of the incumbent Democrat, Edmund G. Brown, expires."[69]

On January 20, 1961, the Eisenhower Administration handed over the office of the Presidency to the Kennedy Administration. After the inaugural ceremonies, the Nixons attended a farewell lunch for Ike and Mamie. Nixon had the use of his official car and chauffeur until midnight. During that evening, he had his driver take him around the city, glittering in the cold and snow and alive with the festivities. No one noticed as he drove past the White House. He went on to the Capitol, where he got out and walked past the entrance to the Senate Chamber and down the corridor to the Rotunda. On a balcony, he looked out over Washington. The Democrats, dancing at their various balls all over town, may have thought that they had finally and forever rid themselves of Dick Nixon, but he thought that someday he would be back.[70]

CHAPTER TWENTY-SEVEN

NIXON AS VICE-PRESIDENT:
AN ASSESSMENT
1953–1961

THE DIFFICULTY IN JUDGING any particular Vice-Presidency is the nature of the office itself. The Vice-President's only constitutional duties are to preside over the Senate and cast the occasional tie-breaking vote. Otherwise, he has nothing to do except to be ready to assume the Presidency.

As presiding officer in the Senate, Nixon did a creditable job at a task that almost never gave him an opportunity to do anything newsworthy or important. There were only two exceptions. In 1957 and again in 1959 he got into battle with the southern Democrats over the controversy surrounding the filibuster, cloture, and the Senate rules. At the opening of the 1957 session, Nixon ruled that a simple majority of senators could adopt new rules at the beginning of each session. A simple majority could, in other words, eliminate a filibuster. Nixon made the ruling as a part of his attempt to push through the 1957 Civil Rights Act, and he made it in defiance of the senior Republicans in the Senate. The day after his ruling, the Senate overturned it by a vote of 55 to 38. In 1959, on a similar issue, Nixon again lost to the senators intent on preserving their traditions. His biographer Earl Mazo claimed that Nixon's "threat" against the filibuster was a major factor in persuading southerners not to abuse the filibuster in opposing the 1957 civil rights bill, and thus thanks to Nixon it became law.[1] It is not much of a claim, insofar as the southern senators had so watered down the bill that roughly half the Negro community denounced it, but it is the only one that can be made about Nixon's achievement as presiding officer in the Senate.

609

The first tie-breaking vote he cast came in January 1953, when the Senate was split 48 to 48. It was Nixon's vote that made the Republicans the majority party and thus able to organize the Senate. Otherwise, the vast majority of what he did in the Senate as Vice-President was dull and routine (and he delegated much of it to others).

Still, he was not wasting his time in the Senate. Although he made no intimate friends, he had good relations with nearly all the Republicans and most of the southerners. In the Senate, he plied his trade, which was politics, in a never-ending stream of conversation. The Senate floor and cloakroom and offices were ideal places for picking up information. One of Nixon's outstanding characteristics was his ability to absorb knowledge, facts, and details, and he did so in the Senate as well as any man ever has. There was not a political subject in the country that escaped him. He knew the issues, and the senators themselves, their strengths and their vulnerabilities, how to pick up a vote here, how to stave off an unwelcome measure there. In this, he was very like his contemporary, Lyndon Johnson.

The touchstones for great senators are Daniel Webster and Henry Clay. Nixon was in the Senate only two years, and as presiding officer for eight years he could not participate in Senate debates, so he never established anything like Webster's and Clay's records. The touchstone for the best-informed politician in the Senate's history is Lyndon Johnson. But Nixon was at least as good. If one could have given a trivia test on politics to Johnson and Nixon in 1960, with questions like the vote in this or that district three elections ago, the name of the county chairman, the money behind that senator, the results of the latest poll in Santa Fe, and so on, well then, this author would have bet on Nixon. In politics, knowledge is power, a truism that is nowhere more perfectly illustrated than in the careers of these two master politicians.

LEARNING IS CRITICAL TO THE VICE-PRESIDENT because he has to be in a constant state of readiness to replace the President. Nevertheless, none of Nixon's predecessors were ever really ready to take over if necessary. The most recent case was also the most dramatic —Harry Truman became President just as the Manhattan Project was coming to completion, and Truman had never heard of it. Neither did Truman know much about FDR's thinking concerning the Russians, not to mention a host of lesser problems. Eisenhower thought Truman's ignorance was both shameful and dangerous, and he had promised that Nixon would become the best-informed and most-involved Vice-President in history.

That was accomplished. Nixon's attendance at NSC, Cabinet, and congressional leaders' meetings gave him information and insight and a chance for input unique in the annals of the Vice-Presidency to that time. He was by no means privy to all of Eisenhower's secrets, but he knew more of them than anyone else. This is not to say that he was the closest to Eisenhower, because he was not—Andrew Goodpaster, Foster Dulles, George Humphrey, Jim Hagerty, and some others were closer, and each of them knew something that Nixon did not. But it was also true that he knew things they did not.

To be more specific: Humphrey and Hagerty knew more about the President's thinking on the budget and other domestic problems than Nixon did, but not much, because it was in this area that Eisenhower came closest to achieving his aim of making Nixon the best-informed Vice-President ever. But Goodpaster (and AEC Chairman Lewis Strauss) knew a great deal more about the President's thinking on nuclear testing and defense spending than Nixon did, and Dulles knew more about foreign policy (although Dulles tended to share what he knew with Nixon, something Goodpaster never did). Nixon had no involvement in the U-2 decisions. Allen Dulles did not volunteer information on CIA covert activities to Nixon, although he would actually give the Vice-President an outline if asked directly.

But although there were government operations going on that Nixon did not know about, aspects of nuclear policy that were a blank to him, nuances in foreign policy he was not aware of, given Nixon's intelligence and his ability to do a quick study, plus his prior accumulation of knowledge, he was quite prepared to step into the Presidency, as well prepared as he possibly could have been. At the time of Eisenhower's heart attack in 1955, and again after Eisenhower's stroke in 1957, he conducted himself in an exemplary fashion, diffident about seizing power (even when encouraged by the Secretary of State), careful not to claim "I'm in charge" even when he presided over NSC and Cabinet meetings, meanwhile preparing himself to take over if he had to. For eight years, he kept himself ready.

BUT HE WAS NOT CALLED UPON, so being prepared was an unknown accomplishment. His second most important nonofficial task, however, was highly publicized, while his success at it was highly debatable.

The task was to serve for eight years as the Republican Party spokesman. Not as party leader—that job could only belong to the President, who controlled the patronage and the policies—but as spokesman. It came to him by default. Taft's death, Dewey's removal of himself from national politics, and Eisenhower's refusal —unique among all Presidents, save only Washington—to be party spokesman combined to thrust the task upon Nixon. Not that he took it up reluctantly. Despite his later protests about self-sacrifice, he relished pounding the Democrats and did so with gusto. In Lyndon Johnson's characterization, he was a "chronic campaigner." Indeed, the only man who enjoyed campaigning as much as Nixon did was Johnson himself. Nor was Nixon unaware of the credits he collected in all parts of the country from his willingness to speak at party fund raisers; nor was he ever more at home than when speaking to a Republican gathering.

How successful he was as party spokesman, from the party's point of view, is another matter. In the eight years he served in that capacity, the Republican percentage of the vote slipped badly. Not even in '56, with Eisenhower sweeping the country, could the Republicans take control of the Congress, lost in '54 and then put out of sight for more than a decade by the debacle of '58. Nixon was widely blamed for the '54 and '58 outcomes. Critics charged that his slashing campaign style repelled Democrats and independents. Defenders claimed that Republican losses would have been much worse without Nixon's active role. As he himself was not on the ballot, it is impossible to judge.

But it is clear that the dismal decline in Republican voters in the fifties was not altogether Nixon's fault. There was little or nothing he could do about the basic cause of that decline, which was Republican policies. Eisenhower was popular, but his policies were not. Nearly every organized group in the country, and nearly every elected politician, including Nixon, thought more should be spent on defense. A majority of the people, including Nixon, wanted a more active and more aggressive foreign policy. Only a small minority supported the President in his insistence on balancing the budget at the price of high taxes and low defense and social spending. On these basic issues, the President was as unmovable as the tide he was resisting was irreversible. The country wanted more defense and lower taxes and was more than willing to pass the cost along to the next generation. In the 1980s it was the Republicans under Ronald Reagan who best expressed the majority mood—that anything was possible, at home and abroad, and that there was nothing to fear from massive deficits because the economy was on a permanent boom. But in the 1950s, it was the Democrats who managed to identify themselves with that mood, to their great profit.

But not until the 1960 campaign was Nixon free to indicate his support for lower taxes, a more action-oriented foreign policy, more social spending, more defense spending, and a willingness to live with deficits. Even then, he had to mute his public disagreements with Eisenhower's policies. It was not his fault that a majority rejected the Republican Party, as he was only its spokesman, not its leader.

IF NIXON'S ROLE OF PARTY SPOKESMAN put him in the unhappy position of having to defend policies that were not his, it also gave him the welcome task of taking the point in the never-ending battle with the Democrats. He did so every other year. With each campaign, he changed his style, leading to biannual stories about the new Nixon. He gradually became a bit less strident, softer in his words. But from 1952 through 1960, the basic message never changed. It was that a Democratic victory would lead to socialism at home and surrender to Communism abroad. In 1952 he called Stevenson a graduate of Dean Acheson's Cowardly College of Communist Containment. In 1960 he called Kennedy an advocate of "retreat and surrender." Always, he charged that the left-wing Democrats were going to take the country down the road to socialism.

As a campaigner, in other words, he was guilty of the grossest exaggerations. This infuriated his opponents and delighted his supporters. His sly use of innuendo, his denials that he had just said what everyone had just heard him say, his overpowering self-righteousness, his trickiness with figures, his flights of hyperbole, his shameless hypocrisy—all these combined to make him hated, and admired. He polarized the public more than any other man of his era. It is remarkable but probably true that in 1960, when he was only forty-seven years old, he was the most hated and feared man in America—and next to Eisenhower himself, the most admired and wanted. That the split was almost exactly 50–50 was demonstrated in the election of 1960.

This was a direct consequence of his campaigning style and prominence—he was far better known than any of his predecessors as Vice-President, save Teddy Roosevelt—as well as his role of spokesman. But there were other causes, of which partisanship was the most important (although not all Democrats were Nixon haters, nor all Republicans his admirers). But beyond political divisions, which all politicians have to deal with, the central question in discussing the problem of the response to Nixon remains, Why did so many people hate him so much?

No definitive answer is possible, but any attempt to begin must consider Nixon's personality. To millions of Americans, including at that time this author, the man seemed utterly insincere. We believed that everything he did was coldly calculated, the opposite of spontaneous, unrelated to any interest other than Richard Nixon's own. His motives were always the lowest. Everything he did was a put-on. We could see nothing good in him whatsoever. His face on the television screen filled us with fear and loathing.

These were extraordinarily extreme reactions, but nevertheless widely shared. They were best summed up in Herblock's cartoons of the era, when Nixon—the Nixon of the liberals' nightmares—was Herblock's favorite target, climbing up out of the sewer, club in hand, to bash in all the liberals, take power, and institute the dark ages.

His supporters' response was equally extreme. To the vast majority of conservative Republicans, he was a natural leader, born to command, a man of integrity, intelligence, and virtue, who was full of common sense and could be trusted and should be President. In their view, he always put the interest of his country first, he proved his courage in South America, he stood up to Khrushchev, and thank God he stands up to the Democrats.

These wildly different if similarly extreme reactions to the same man's personality were the price he paid for his polarization of the electorate. He drove people apart. Not with his policy positions, not on specific issues, where he usually was a uniter rather than a divider, but with his campaign speeches, where his mannerisms and his strategy and what he said were all directed toward deepening the political split rather than narrowing it. People responded to the power of Nixon's personality. He wanted to divide the community into "us" and "them," and he succeeded. His gross exaggerations on the campaign trail cost him dearly, as he created new Nixon haters with every speech, but they also paid him off handsomely, as he created new Nixon admirers with every speech. His politics were the politics of division.

HE DIVIDED PEOPLE ALONG PARTY LINES, but he refused to use race, class, or religion as his issues. In these areas, where the American people were already sharply divided, Nixon tried to bring them together. His record as Vice-President on racial relations was excellent. He called on the North to show a little understanding toward the South, to realize that a revolution in race relations in Dixie was going to take time. He called upon the South to strive for progress, especially in regard to voting rights, economic opportunity, access to public facilities, and better schools for Negroes.

He was consistent in his denunciaton of Jim Crow, as much so as any of his rivals for national leadership and much more so than most. He made strenuous efforts to appeal to the working-class vote, by speaking at union conventions, by refusing to endorse right-to-work, by insisting that there were no class divisions in America. What eventually became a love affair between Nixon and the hard hats began in the fifties.

On religion, he not only refused to raise the issue in the 1960 campaign, he forbade the use of it by the people around him and he decried the anti-Catholic hate literature that popped up independently.

Racial, religious, and class divisions are the oldest and deepest in any society, which is why they have been the classic issue for demagogues everywhere. Nixon was no demagogue. He attacked philosophical and political enemies, not Negroes, union men, or Catholics.

ALTHOUGH NIXON HAD WON HIS NATIONAL FAME as the man who found and exposed Alger Hiss, as Vice-President he was not about to admit that Eisenhower had Communists in his Administration. Joe McCarthy was sure there were Reds hiding out, and he went after them—most of all in the Army—and in the process he divided the nation and the Republican Party. Further, he gave anti-Communism a bad name.

Nixon exerted all his considerable powers of persuasion on McCarthy to get him to back off, alas for the senator to no avail. Nixon also used his talents to persuade Republicans who opposed McCarthy to put party ahead of conscience. McCarthy helped Nixon in the sense that he made him appear moderate or even liberal on civil liberties cases. Nixon's broader role—to serve as the bridge between the two wings of his party, on McCarthy and all the other divisive issues—he carried out with aplomb. Brokering between wings came naturally to him and he excelled at it. In Cabinet meetings, he explained political realities to the department heads; in congressional leaders' meetings, he explained administrative realities to the lawmakers.

As VICE-PRESIDENT, Nixon stayed away from domestic anti-Communism as an issue, but he made international Communism his number-one issue, a special area of expertise and experience. From his first trip to Asia in 1953 to his last to Russia in 1959, he toured the outposts of freedom around the world. The Iron Curtain virtually encircles the globe. Nixon studied it with binoculars, figuratively if not literally, from every angle. From Hanoi, the Philippines, and Japan; from India and Pakistan; from Formosa and Korea; from Iran and Turkey; from Greece and Austria and West

Germany. In the New World, he had gone to every country in South America save Chile and nearly every one in Central America. He had been all over Africa and the Middle East. He had actually penetrated the Iron Curtain, the first American Vice-President to do so, visiting Poland and Russia itself. Small wonder that Khrushchev and his pals had the terrible feeling that wherever they looked, there was Nixon. He had indeed encircled them.

He had also provoked them. Wherever he went he made the Communist threat into the central issue. He became the world's best-known anti-Communist. One result was rocks and spittle in Caracas. Another was a shower of roses in Warsaw. To millions around the world he represented the forces of reactionary capitalism. To other millions, he represented the forces of freedom. He divided the people of the world much as he did the people of America.

He believed that Communism was a terrible evil, that it was aggressive, and that it had designs, whether hidden or open, against every non-Communist nation in the world. If he never really believed that the Democrats were leading the United States to socialism and surrender, he certainly did believe that the Communists were leading the world to slavery. He saw a Cold War battleground wherever he visited, even in India and Pakistan and Africa and most of all in the Middle East, areas where ancient rivalries divided the people, not Communism.

But to the north, around the Iron Curtain, he was correct in considering aggressive Communism as the great historical and political problem of his time. Wherever he went, he went as a prophet, warning the people of what would happen to them if they let their guard down and the Communists took power. He spoke for freedom. Freedom of speech, of the press, of the economy, of political action. On the Communist side of the Iron Curtain, this had about as much effect as throwing rocks against the Berlin Wall, but on the free-world side he was applauded and admired. It cannot be said that his confrontational style in his goodwill visits did anything to ease the tensions of the Cold War, but as Nixon himself wrote in his eulogy to John Foster Dulles, in reference to Dulles' holding out the hope of liberation to the captive peoples, so widely criticized as provocative, "What other tenable position can self-respecting free peoples take?" His advice to those on the free side of the Iron Curtain was to never retreat and never negotiate. And he promised that if he had anything to do about it, the United States would be standing beside them in the deadly struggle.

Within the United States too he was a leading advocate and one of the most important supporters of the Marshall Plan and the

Mutual Security program. He did his best to educate recalcitrant senators and an isolationist public about America's position and responsibility in the world.

As Vice-President, Richard Nixon the campaigner often did grave disservice, but in his nonpartisan actions, both at home and abroad, he did good service for his country and mankind.

IN THE 1960 CAMPAIGN his claim that he was the man best suited for the Presidency, because of his knowledge and experience and proved capacity, was based on a solid record. But his further claim, that he had been one of Eisenhower's closest advisers, a man intimately involved with the great decisions and crises of the fifties, a man Eisenhower looked to for help on policy decisions, was not.

Eisenhower's "give me a week . . ." was a shattering statement, but almost as bad was something the President had said two weeks earlier. A reporter asked if there were any differences between Nixon and the President on the question of nuclear testing. "Well," Eisenhower responded, "I can't recall what he has ever said specifically about nuclear underground testing."[2] Insofar as it was the number-one issue in the world that summer, Eisenhower's confession that he did not even remember what Nixon's advice on testing might have been was a devastating revelation.

Although Eisenhower never knew it, Nixon disagreed with him on some of the most basic decisions of the decade. In 1953 Nixon did not want to accept the armistice in Korea; rather he wanted to take the offensive and drive to the Yalu River. In 1954 Nixon wanted to support the French at Dien Bien Phu, using atomic weapons if necessary. He opposed accepting the Geneva Accords. In 1959 he wanted to spend more money on defense, not less; he wanted to lower taxes and was willing to accept an unbalanced budget. In 1960 he wanted to invade Cuba. But in all his many meetings with the President, whether in private in the Oval Office or in the Cabinet Room or with the congressional leaders, Nixon never spoke directly about his disagreements.

As Vice-President, Nixon had no important influence on policy decisions. Nor could he, nor can any Vice-President. The point would not even be worth making, except that Nixon himself so persistently claimed the contrary.

NIXON'S PRIVATE LIFE, like his public life, was full of contradictions. He knew an enormous number of people at home and abroad, and was on good terms with most of them, excellent terms with many. He had friends in the political world, and among the press, businessmen large and small, sports heroes, college presidents, all successful men. But of intimate friends he had almost none, except for Robert Abplanalp and Bebe Rebozo, and they were more often together for long periods of silence than for hours of conversation and sharing. Pat Nixon once said, "Bebe is like a sponge; he soaks up whatever Dick says and never makes any comments. Dick loves that."[3] Eisenhower was only the most prominent man who knew Nixon well to comment on how odd it was that Nixon was so lonely in a profession filled with so many gregarious personalities.

Nixon himself spoke to this point in some detail. "The more you stay in this kind of job," he said in 1959, "the more you realize that a public figure, a major public figure, is a lonely man—the President very much more so, of course." His perception of Eisenhower could not have been wider of the mark; few public men have ever managed to be so *un*lonely as Ike. This was because he opened up with people and shared his feelings with them and enjoyed their company. None of this existed with Nixon, who pointed it out specifically to Stewart Alsop: "In my job you can't enjoy the luxury of intimate personal friendships. You can't confide absolutely in anyone. You can't talk too much about your personal plans, your personal feelings."[4]

Nixon did not tell Alsop why he felt that way; he avoided dealing with that difficult question by shrugging that this was the way it was, for all politicians. But of course it was *not* that way for such men as Eisenhower, Johnson, Kennedy, or Reagan, each of whom had a tight group of people they admired and trusted who were intimate friends, men with whom they could share something of themselves, indulge in prejudices and peeves, do some philosophizing about the nature of man and of the state, make jokes, relax, be themselves in a flow of rapport and exchange. Friendships free of cant, of rivalries, of double meanings, of manipulation, of suspicion have been as precious as they were essential to many great men. But not for Nixon, who claimed to be trapped in a situation in which he could not be himself, not ever. He disqualified himself for love by refusing to ever open himself and become vulnerable.

The effect of his holding back his emotions even from close friends was off-putting. Bill Rogers, who was his closest political friend, said in 1959, "His personality is more outgoing in his public appearances than in his private appearances. Most people are very outgoing and very much at ease when it is two or three people but you get a crowd and they become introverts. He is the opposite, a lot shyer on a man to man basis. Has a little difficulty making that person he's talking to realize he likes him a lot."[5]

As Nixon never gave fully of himself, so he never fully trusted anyone, and of those around him only Rebozo and Abplanalp ever fully trusted him. In the 1960 campaign, his advisers could not get through to him; thus the Alaska trip. Nor could he hear them; thus the absence of makeup in the first debate. He paid not only the personal price of loneliness, but the political price of a difficulty in communication.

That he was a cynic was obvious to reporters and associates alike. He had plenty to be cynical about. His introduction to big-time politics came with the Hiss case, a case marked by the use of executive power by Harry Truman to cover up for Alger Hiss, a cover-up involving the FBI and the State Department among others. He had seen so-called "friends" bail out on him when the fund crisis arose. He had watched Joe McCarthy's friends bail out on him. The cynicism they displayed in first using McCarthy, then jumping, was absolute. Nixon had seen other examples: Harold Stassen, who had endorsed him in 1946, 1948, and 1952, turned on him in 1956. Nixon had played an important role in the drama of the forced resignation of Sherman Adams, a play in which the hypocrisy of the characters challenged believability.

Finally, there was Eisenhower himself, a man who was world-renowned for his honesty, sincerity, and straightforwardness, but who had nevertheless used Nixon in the most cynical fashion. After ordering Nixon to take the low road while he stayed on the high road, Eisenhower would admonish Nixon that he had gone too far —and then once again order Nixon to go after the Democrats. This happened in every election year. Then there was Eisenhower's indecision during the fund crisis, his excessive coyness about the vice-presidential nomination in 1956, and his hesitancy in endorsing Nixon in 1960. And despite all that Nixon did for Eisenhower —on the campaign trail, on goodwill visits around the world, on the occasions of Eisenhower's illnesses, on McCarthy and Adams, on Republican Party fund raisers, on serving as liaison between the White House and Congress and between the two wings of the Republican Party—despite all this, and more, Eisenhower hardly ever had bothered to say "thank you."

It is a mark of the ambiguousness of Nixon's feelings about Eisenhower that he never complained that he had been used. It was also a mark of his realism—to be used is what a Vice-President is for, from the President's perspective. The closest Nixon ever came to criticizing Eisenhower was in his memoirs, written in 1977, when he quoted Eisenhower's wartime chief of staff, Walter B. Smith, at a time when Smith was tired and had been doing some drinking. According to Nixon, Smith had tears streaming down his face as he said, "I was just Ike's prat boy. Ike always had to have a prat boy, someone who'd do the dirty work for him."[6] Nixon did not identify himself with Smith's remark, but he did quote it.

Despite his frequent policy disagreements with Eisenhower,

Nixon—like almost everyone else who was close to the President
—stood in awe of him, while simultaneously responding to Eisenhower's warm and generous personality. Although Eisenhower and
Nixon were not friends, Nixon had genuine respect for the President, and enjoyed being with him. In addition, he used Eisenhower just as Eisenhower used him. Nixon's great claim to fame,
other than the Hiss case, was that he had served next to a great man
("I have sat with him as he made those lonely decisions") for eight
years. That was why 1956 was his greatest personal crisis. Stassen
threatened to separate him from Ike, which could have led to the
fate of John Nance Garner or Charles Dawes or Henry Wallace. No
wonder Nixon was ambiguous about Eisenhower—he had to stay
as close to Eisenhower as he possibly could, and give him his
unquestioning support on every issue, while realizing that Eisenhower could get along quite well without him, and knowing that
he never had Eisenhower's unqualified respect.

Eisenhower's feelings about the relationship were also complex. Sometimes he liked Nixon, sometimes he didn't. On occasion
he would have feelings close to those of a father for a son. At other
times he would tell his confidants that he just did not think Nixon
was mature enough to take command. Almost everything he said in
public about Nixon was convoluted and could be read two ways.
But it was also true that by keeping Nixon on the ticket in 1956,
Eisenhower was indicating that he would be willing to turn the
country over to Nixon in the event that his own health failed, an
event that seemed so possible that this must be viewed as the
ultimate endorsement.

What Eisenhower most regretted about Nixon was his partisanship and cynicism and lack of personal friends. Eisenhower too
lived in the political world, where cynicism is endemic. So did
John Kennedy, and Harry Truman, and later Ronald Reagen, and
all these men had their fair share of cynicism. But what they had,
that Nixon did not have, was that small inner group where they
could leave the cynicism behind them and open up their hearts.
Nixon paid a terrible price for the absence of such intimacy.

THE PLACE WHERE NIXON DID HAVE an intimate relationship was
with his family. That his daughters had quite stolen his heart there
can be no doubt; nor can there by any doubt about the genuine
pleasure he took in being their father, or in the love and adulation
they had for him. When he came in the door of his home, there
were kisses and hugs, and romps with Checkers, and show and tell,
and breathless accounts of what happened at school that day. The
girls were happy to be with their father, and proud of him, and only
wished they could have more of his time.

With Pat, things were more complicated. Physical signs of affection were nonexistent in public. Hugging, kissing, a protective arm around her shoulder, seldom occurred. Even in Caracas, in that shower of spittle, he did not put his arm around her. When he spoke of her, it was with pride and admiration and appreciation, not affection. Nor could he say "I love you" in public. He explained it himself by saying he just wasn't that way.

Nevertheless, they had a solid marriage, major reasons for which were Pat's forbearance and patience. She understood that her husband had to do what he had to do, that he was a great man, a man of destiny, and it was her fate—and glory—to be his helpmate. She had long ago put behind her her dreams and hopes for a quiet life in Whittier, and she never looked back. She threw herself into political life, where she was a tireless campaigner and a great asset.

In 1976, Julie wrote of her mother that "people who have labeled her 'superhuman' or 'Plastic Pat' underestimate her. She is a woman of tremendous self-control because all her life self-control has been necessary simply to survive. She is a woman of dignity who does not seek pity from others or feed on pity herself. But she has grieved, she has wept."[7]

Had she been a woman who indulged herself in complaints, her chief complaint would have been the small amount of time she got to spend with her husband. She often got to see more of him when they were together on the campaign trail than when they were living in Washington. He was home for dinner only one or two nights a week, more often arriving at midnight with work still to do, then leaving immediately after breakfast.

Pat endured. And of course got her rewards, fame and travel, most of all. She had not really wanted fame, but it had its advantages, not least of which was that she got to spend much of her time with famous people in elegant surroundings. She would have had to have been plastic indeed to have lunch across from Nikita Khrushchev in his dacha, or dinner with the Queen in Buckingham Palace, and not be excited by the occasion. As for traveling, she never could get enough of it. Her curiosity was never jaded, her feet were never tired, her instinct to reach out to the children of the world never failed. Around the world, in every country she visited, she was a credit to the United States. She, not her husband, was the real goodwill ambassador.

She shared his work with him. It was their bond. It was strong enough to hold together through countless ups and downs. Together, they raised two healthy, happy kids. These are not small accomplishments.

In short, Nixon was head of a warm, loving, happy family. Pat had insisted on giving their children a normal upbringing. When she first agreed to enter politics in 1946, she made Dick promise that he would not bring his work home with him. To a very large degree, she succeeded in holding him to it. To the extent that she was unsuccessful, it was because of the time factor. Nixon's home was a sanctuary to him, but he hated not being in the arena. He did not bring his work home with him, but then he hardly ever left his work. He gave his family everything of himself, except his time. He enjoyed himself more at home than anywhere else, but he was not a man altogether free of a guilty conscience about enjoying himself. Besides, he hated being out of the arena when something might be going on—and something always was.

THE CLOSENESS OF THE 1960 ELECTION prompts a question. What if Nixon had won? What kind of a President would he have made if he had taken office in January 1961 instead of January 1969?

Two of his early biographers, Mazo and Costello, made their own predictions. Mazo, writing in 1959, thought Nixon as President "would be perhaps the hardest-driving chief executive and the most controversial since Theodore Roosevelt. There would be nothing haphazard, nothing bland about his administration, nor any doubt about its political identity." That was certainly accurate, as was Mazo's further comment, that a Nixon Administration would be "conservative on domestic matters and internationalist in foreign affairs." Mazo did not go into particulars, but one of his generalizations was prescient: "To uphold executive immunity in his administration after having demanded, as a congressman, that President Truman's people testify before Congress . . . Nixon would need the best of his political skills."[8]

Costello, also writing in 1959, had a darker vision. He thought that Nixon would be "indestructible in the sense of being proof against slights that would destroy a thin-skinned man." What frightened Costello about Nixon was that "he understands the use of power but not the unwritten restraints on its use." Costello even used the words "fascist tendencies," and warned that "[in Nixon's] administration, anyone running afoul of policy, even inadvertently, could expect only the swiftest and most merciless reprisals."[9]

Nearly everything Mazo and Costello foresaw, from their different perspectives, came to pass when Nixon did become President. But their predictions were generalizations, and thus avoided the problem of speculation on how Nixon would have handled the specific crises of the early sixties. In many cases, we know what he said he would do if he had been in power, as for example at the Bay of Pigs (he said he would have reinforced the invasion and provided air cover). When Khrushchev built the Berlin Wall, Eisenhower urged President Kennedy to send in the bulldozers that afternoon and tear the damn thing down. Kennedy did not act, but such a response would certainly have appealed to the bold, the imaginative, and the tough-guy side of Nixon. Had the counterrevolution triumphed in Cuba, and had the Wall been torn down, everything that happened afterward would have been different. There would have been no Cuban missile crisis, on the one hand; but on the other, the overthrown Castro would have been a supreme symbol to Communists not only in Cuba but throughout Latin America. There would have been no brutal cutting off of the people of Berlin from one another, but there would have been a massive flight of refugees out of East Germany, one of such proportions as to force a crisis of great potential danger in Central Europe. In short, there is no way of knowing whether tougher responses in these cases, as in others, would have led to better or worse end results.

But suppose that in November 1964, riding a wave of prosperity at home and triumphs abroad, Nixon were re-elected. He then would have had to face the problem in Vietnam. Like President Johnson, he would have seen Communist aggression in Indochina as both a test of America's will and a threat to America's vital interests. Unlike Johnson, he probably would have carried the war to the North Vietnamese, sooner and with greater firepower. Whether that would have worked or not we will never know. We do know that what was tried did not work.

There is a more generalized speculative question that requires some attempt at an answer. Would a Nixon Administration born in 1961 rather than in 1969 have produced a Watergate?

Consider, to begin with, how utterly different the two situations were. In 1961 the economy was strong, the budget was balanced, inflation was less than 2 percent, the nation was at peace, people were happy. By 1969, the economy was racked by stagflation, the nation was in a war that divided the American people more decisively than any event since the Civil War, race riots were tearing apart the big cities, political assassinations shocked everyone, students were demonstrating on their campuses, drugs and crime had become major problems, and other bad things had happened. The point is, no President since the twenties had handed the country over to his successor in better shape than Eisenhower did in 1961, and no President since Hoover had handed the country over to his successor in worse shape than Johnson did in 1969. Put another way, by the time Nixon finally got to the White House, there was a great deal for the President to be paranoid about. The body politic was crumbling all around him. Strong, tough measures were required. They were not in 1961.

Consider, further, that by 1969 Nixon had much to be bitter about. He had lost the Presidency in 1960 in an election marked by fraud, and could hardly be blamed for feeling that the Presidency had been stolen from him. He had then been crucified by the press for a disastrous campaign climax to the race for governor in California (before that campaign, his relations with the press were as good as those of most politicians, and better than many).

Another point. In 1969, his White House predecessor was Lyndon Johnson, of whom it can be fairly said that he did not set a good example. Johnson had greatly increased the powers and preeminence of the Presidency. He spied on people, kept secret tape recordings of their conversations, used the FBI for partisan purposes, treated men around him with contempt, bullied the legislative branch, exploited his access to television to the maximum, manipulated his fellow politicians, and otherwise used every bit of power available to him to achieve his ends.

When Nixon got to the White House, he followed Johnson's lead. But had he become President in 1961, he would have succeeded a man whose honesty and integrity were bywords. In eight years under Eisenhower's direction the government was so free of scandal that the best the Democrats ever came up with was that Sherman Adams had accepted a coat from Bernard Goldfine, and President Eisenhower was so far from abusing the power of his office that the chief Democratic complaint was that he did not do enough. Had he won in 1961, Nixon would have had Eisenhower looking over his shoulder, offering a bit of advice here, a comment or two there. And Nixon would have been surrounded by Eisenhower men, officeholders appointed by Eisenhower and congressmen and party officials loyal to him.

A Nixon Presidency following Eisenhower would have been different than the Nixon Presidency that followed Johnson, and almost certainly much better. For one reason, the men around Nixon in 1961 were not the men around him in Watergate. Nixon had no lifelong political friendships. The people close to him in 1961 were such Establishment types as Dewey, Brownell, Bill Rogers, and Fred Seaton on the administrative side, and Halleck, Dirksen, and Lodge on the political side. Haldeman and Ehrlichman had minor jobs in Nixon's 1960 campaign, and few of the other major characters in Watergate were even known to him in 1961—not Chuck Colson, not John Mitchell, not Howard Hunt, not John Dean, not Spiro Agnew.

Nixon himself mused on this point in 1972, when he reflected in his diary on what might have happened to him if he had won in 1960. He would have been tougher in Cuba and Vietnam, he wrote, but he expressed the fear that "we would have continued the establishment types in office too long and would not have done the job we should have done as far as the country was concerned." [10]

It was his impatience with Eisenhower conservatism, with the self-imposed restraints Eisenhower put on the Presidency and his Administration, with the compromises with the enemy, whether in the halls of Congress or on dividing Korea and Vietnam with the Communists, that led him to actively seek out such men as Haldeman, Ehrlichman, Mitchell, Colson, and Agnew. If he had succeeded in finding them during his first term, and elevating their influence at the expense of the Eisenhower types, he might well have had a Watergate in 1965.

ENOUGH SPECULATION. What is solid is that as Vice-President, Nixon had his low spots, most of all on the campaign trail, but he also had his grander moments. In the process he became the most visible Vice-President of the twentieth century, and the most successful.

CHAPTER TWENTY-EIGHT

"IT WAS NOT AN EASY TIME"
1961

On January 21, 1961, Nixon gave up his office, his title, his staff, his Secret Service protection, his chauffeur and car, and his salary. When he had started his political career, fifteen years earlier, he had assets of about $10,000; when he finished, in 1961, he had a $48,000 equity in his house in Washington. He had not made money in politics, in fact had never been interested in money, but with college expenses for the girls just a few years away, and with his fiftieth birthday coming in two years, he felt the need to build an estate.

He had many rich and powerful friends, and as the man who had received virtually half the votes cast in the 1960 election, he had an obvious political future, which meant that his job prospects were excellent. Robert Abplanalp, developer of the aerosol spray can, told him that if he joined a law firm, the Precision Valve Corporation would like to hire him as a consultant, paying him a retainer fee.[1] Walter Annenberg, publisher of the Philadelphia *Inquirer*, made a similar offer, as did many others.[2] This was not giveaway money—the men who offered to retain Nixon expected in return the benefit of his advice and wisdom on their governmental and foreign operations, areas where he had much to contribute. Nixon was also offered memberships on various boards of directors, such as American Export Lines, but these he turned down on principle ("my public responsibilities," as he put it).[3]

A law firm was the obvious place for him to go; he had been trained as a lawyer, the only non-public-service job he had ever held was as a lawyer, and as a lawyer in a major firm he could pick and choose his cases, set his own schedule, stay active in politics at a national level, maintain and profit from his contacts, and make a lot of money. The question was where to settle. Tom Dewey offered him a position with his firm in New York City, where the fees were the highest in the world, and the young lawyer who in 1937 could not find a job in New York now could pick and choose from among the top firms. In Washington too he was eagerly sought after.

Instead, he chose California. Pat wanted to return there—she had always wanted to go home—and it had attractions for Nixon beyond familiarity and the climate. California was his base. He was registered there. Only in California could he run for office before 1964. And as he repeatedly said in the years that followed, no Republican could ever win the Presidency without carrying California. He was not necessarily thinking of running against Kennedy again in '64, but neither was he ready to abandon the national political scene. While it was true that California was isolated and that the press tended to ignore anyone not living in Washington or New York, it was also true that California was the heart of the Republican West, which in turn was rapidly becoming the heart of the Republican Party.

Way back in 1946, when Nixon first ran for office, Earl Adams of the Committee of 100 had told him that if he lost to Voorhis he could count on a job with Adams' law firm. Fifteen years later, having finally lost an election, Nixon took Adams up on the offer. He joined the Los Angeles firm of Adams, Duque, and Hazeltine, not as a partner but as a consultant. He brought lucrative accounts with him; in return, he got the free time he needed to stay active in politics.[4]

It was a month after Kennedy's inaugural before he got out of Washington. He had a huge stack of mail to go through, campaign contributors and workers to thank, political chores to do. In December and the first part of January he had worked his staff twelve hours a day at these tasks, but still failed to get everything done. No wonder, as it was a task of monstrous proportions.

In April 1961, Eisenhower wrote Nixon. The former President said he did not want to meddle, and that he was embarrassed to bring up the subject, but "a number of substantial contributors to your campaign have told me that they have received no word of thanks from you." Eisenhower admitted that such contributions should be regarded as support for a cause rather than as a gift to an individual, but pointedly added, "Frankly, I have written hundreds of such letters myself even though in principle I realize that this should not be necessary."[5] Over the next few months,

Nixon got out dozens of such letters, but it was a full year after the election before he completed the job.[6]

Then there were farewells to write, to every Republican congressman, to the members of the Administration, to prominent Republicans out of Washington, and to personal friends and advisers. One went to Douglas MacArthur ("Of all the speeches I made in the House and the Senate, there is none of which I am more proud or which I believe will better stand the test of time than the one I made castigating Mr. Truman for his action in recalling you from Korea.").[7] Another went to Tom Dewey, thanking him for his "wise counsel and loyal friendship."[8] After thanking William Randolph Hearst, Jr., for the support of his newspaper chain through the years, Nixon expressed the hope that "we will be fighting together in some more good causes in the future."[9]

To Eisenhower himself, Nixon said he was confident that "the verdict of history will be that the country has never had an administration which set a higher standard for honesty, efficiency and dedication. . . . The American people, because of your leadership, have enjoyed the best eight years in their history." For himself, Nixon said, "never in this nation's history has one man in public owed so much to another as I owe to you."[10]

It was not just the big shots who got warm, personal letters. Nixon wrote one to Ann Whitman, Eisenhower's personal secretary. Whitman had agreed to stay with General Eisenhower in his retirement, just as that other paragon of loyalty and efficiency, Rose Mary Woods, had agreed to stay with Nixon. In his letter to Whitman, Nixon praised her virtues as a secretary, quite rightly, and said he knew what he was talking about, because he too had an outstanding secretary (as Whitman knew; she and Woods were close friends). Best of all, Nixon said, "I can never recall an instance, no matter how grim the problem or the crisis, that the day didn't become brighter after I had the opportunity to talk to you."[11]

In return, Nixon received hundreds of letters of thanks and appreciation for all that he had done. The one that pleased him most came from Eisenhower. The high spots of a long and friendly letter were: "I have always felt a complete confidence in your ability and capacity for taking on the Presidency at any instant," and "The future can still bring to you a real culmination in your service to the country."[12]

NIXON CERTAINLY HOPED THAT the last was true, but meanwhile he had to establish a new home and make a living. In early February, he and Pat flew to Los Angeles to find a house. They wanted one close to the airport, close to Nixon's office in the Pacific Mutual Building in downtown Los Angeles, and with a view of the ocean.

Pat thought she could find a suitable home in a week, but for the next three months she was a cross-continent commuter as she searched and searched (the girls stayed in Washington to finish the school year). Eventually, the Nixons threw up their hands and decided they would have to build. They purchased 410 Martin Lane, in a new development, the Trousdale Estates, near the exclusive Bel Air section of Los Angeles, overlooking Beverly Hills. The house they planned was long, low, ranch-style, with seven baths and four bedrooms, three fireplaces, a huge living room, and a swimming pool. It would cost about $100,000. Nixon sold his Wesley Heights home in Washington for $101,000.

Nixon could not even buy a lot without stirring up controversy. In this case, the Los Angeles *Times* reported that he had been given a "celebrity discount," paying $35,000 for a lot worth $42,000, and that the generous seller was none other than Teamster boss Jimmy Hoffa. It was also rumored that subcontractors were asked to "donate" some of their work.

An angry Nixon called editor Frank McCulloch of the *Times*. "What's wrong with what I did?" he demanded.

"You're not entirely a private citizen, Dick," McCulloch replied. "You've been Vice-President . . . and you may well have a political future."

"I don't see what's wrong," Nixon responded. He merely paid the asking price. Later, when the question came up at a press conference, Nixon pointed out that "builders all over the state and county offered me lots free, which I did not take because I did not think that was appropriate." Nixon's Vice-Presidential Papers in the Federal Archives confirm this claim, and Nixon might well have let it go at that, but he was so angry that he could not, and made a threat of his own. He called the charges a "smear," and said, "I intend no longer to take it lying down. . . . I so serve warning, here and now . . . that anybody that makes charges of this type will have to answer for them, and they will be in for the fight of their lives on the charges."[13]

Despite his lack of any substantial savings, Nixon had no money problems. Adams' firm paid him a $60,000 salary, plus one-quarter of the fees from the business he brought with him, which gave Nixon an additional $40,000 per year. In May, he began writing a syndicated newspaper column, for another $40,000. Later, Nixon said that he had earned more money in his first fourteen months in Los Angeles than he had in his fourteen years in Washington.[14]

FROM FEBRUARY TO JUNE, Nixon lived alone in a bachelor apartment on Wilshire Boulevard. "It was not an easy time," he confessed in his memoirs. "I preferred to be alone." He ate TV dinners. He found it difficult to settle down to work in the law firm. Everything he did seemed "unexciting and unimportant." Fortunately, Pat and the girls flew out for Easter vacation, which the family spent on the beach in Santa Monica. Tricia and Julie "loved the beach and the warm weather," Nixon recorded, "and their enthusiasm about California began to rub off on me." [15]

His spirits also revived as the "honeymoon" period passed. For the first three months of the Kennedy Administration, Nixon kept quiet, but by mid-April he felt free to take up his responsibilities as leader of the opposition. The role, however, was ill-defined and not easy to fill. In the American system, unlike a parliamentary system, no formal place exists for the losing party leader in a national election. Half the American people had voted for Nixon as head of government, but as a loser he had no spot in government at all. In the United Kingdom, he would have been in Commons, leading the opposition, with both the opportunity and the responsibility to question and challenge the government on a daily basis and on every issue. But in America he was only the "titular" leader of his party, with no enforcement powers, no chance to establish a Republican position on issues (he could only assert his own positions), no chance to demand that the Kennedy Administration answer this or that barbed question.

Nixon had friends in the legislative branch who could ask questions for him, but in the case he most cared about they let him down. Back in January 1953, Eisenhower had made Charlie Wilson sell his stock in General Motors, at a considerable financial sacrifice, before appointing him the Secretary of Defense. In January 1961, two Kennedy Cabinet appointees also divested themselves of their holdings, Labor Secretary Arthur Goldberg and Secretary of Defense Robert McNamara. As Charlie McWhorter pointed out to Nixon, their actions gave the Republicans a golden opportunity to embarrass Kennedy. McWhorter suggested that Nixon prod Senator Everett Dirksen to use the Senate Judiciary hearings on the confirmation of Bobby Kennedy for Attorney General as an opportunity to put on the record the entire Kennedy financial empire. If McNamara and Goldberg had to divest themselves of their holdings, McWhorter said, "then Bobby should be required to make a complete disclosure of the various interests and arrangements of the Kennedy fortune." [16] Nixon thought it a good idea, and talked to Dirksen, who was vague but hopeful. In the confirmation hearings, however, not one Republican asked one embarrassing question. Nixon expressed "amazement" at the "lousy job [the Republicans] did questioning Bobby Kennedy." [17]

As he could not ask questions himself, and his friends would not do it for him, Nixon had to make his critique in public speeches. He wrote Arthur Flemming in April, "I believe the country needs to hear some responsible, constructive criticisms of the new Administration," but said he was also "keenly aware that almost anything I say will be examined with a microscope by the press with the purpose of trying to point to a phrase which would enable them to charge me with being a poor loser and a carping critic." [18]

But there was another side to Nixon's "Poor Richard" situation. If he had to watch helplessly while questions went unasked, and if he felt constrained in what he himself could say, he did have the advantage that he could pick the time and choose the place for his battleground. Not since the 1952 campaign had he enjoyed that advantage—in the last eight years he had been on the defensive, forced to react no matter where the Democrats attacked.

IN MID-APRIL, Nixon began to seize his opportunity. For help, he turned to the Republican leadership. Not being in Washington, he consulted through a form letter that went out to a couple of dozen men, including Tom Dewey, Arthur Flemming, and Robert Anderson. Nixon announced that he was going on a speaking tour, beginning May 2, and asked for suggestions "as to what I might say that would be constructive from the standpoint of the country as well as the party." [19]

The answers were almost unanimous—hit Kennedy on foreign policy. The immediate issue was Laos, where Kennedy had accepted a neutral government that Republicans warned was proCommunist. Kennedy's foreign policy was Nixon's natural target anyway, but events as well as advice made Nixon's topic inevitable.

On April 17, a week after Nixon sent off his request and even as the first responses were coming in, Cuban exiles landed at the Bay of Pigs. For Nixon this should have been a happy moment. He had been the strongest and earliest supporter of the CIA plan to overthrow Castro, and six months earlier had done all he could to persuade Eisenhower to put the plan into action. Despite his devastating critique of an American-sponsored invasion of Cuba in the 1960 campaign, Nixon believed in the plan.

Because he had already decided to make foreign policy the subject of his speeches on his tour, Nixon had requested and been granted a briefing by Allen Dulles. On April 19, the two men met in Nixon's Washington home. Press reports on the progress of the invasion were pessimistic but inconclusive. Nixon was eager to get the inside story. When he asked Dulles if he wanted a drink, Dulles replied, "I certainly would—I really need one. This is the worst day of my life!" He explained that the invasion had failed, and said the reason was Kennedy's last-minute cancellation of the air strikes that the CIA had counted on to knock out Castro's air forces. "I should have told him that we must not fail," Dulles said, staring at the floor. "And I came very close to doing so, but I didn't. It was the greatest mistake of my life." [20]

The next morning, Nixon conferred with Republican leaders on Capitol Hill. They agreed to withhold their criticism of the President until the crisis was over. When Nixon got home, he found a triumphant note from Tricia: "JFK called. I knew it! It wouldn't be long before he would get into trouble and have to call on you for help."

Nixon returned the President's call; Kennedy was angry and frustrated, cursing all his advisers. "I was assured by every son of a bitch I checked with—all the military experts and the CIA—that the plan would succeed." Nixon thought that Kennedy felt himself to be "the innocent victim."

Kennedy stopped pacing, turned to Nixon, and asked directly, "What would you do now in Cuba?"

With no hesitation, Nixon replied, "I would find a proper legal cover and I would go in." He continued, "There are several justifications that could be used, like protecting American citizens living in Cuba and defending our base at Guantánamo. I believe that the most important thing at this point is that we do whatever is necessary to get Castro and communism out of Cuba."

Kennedy protested that if he did "go in," Khrushchev would move on Berlin. Nixon dismissed the risk. Khrushchev, Nixon said, would "probe and prod" to find weak spots, but if resisted he would back down. Therefore, "we should take some action in both Cuba and Laos, including if necessary a commitment of American air power." But Kennedy had lost his desire for adventure. He said America could not go into Laos; we would find our troops fighting "millions of Chinese." [21]

Both men were reversing their previous positions. Six months earlier, Kennedy had called for full American support of the Cuban exiles, while Nixon had insisted, albeit insincerely, that for the United States to be involved in an invasion of Cuba would damage relations with the Organization of American States, violate international law and treaty commitments, and invite the Soviet Union into Cuba on a large scale. A month earlier, Kennedy had made a bellicose speech on Laos. That very afternoon, he had told the American Society of Newspaper Editors that American restraint toward Cuba was "not inexhaustible" and that he had no intention of "abandoning the country to communism."[22]

In the 1960 campaign, Kennedy had tried, with considerable success, to project the image of a leader who would be tougher on the Communists. A centerpiece of his campaign had been criticism of the Republicans for not spending more on defense and not engaging in a more active foreign policy. Nixon had agreed with him on both points.

Now, as President, Kennedy had reacted to his first crisis by adopting a policy of restraint. True, he had sharply increased the defense budget, but Nixon was unimpressed. Nixon explained to Professor Don Pearlberg of Purdue University that Kennedy's failure was "due not to a lack of military power, but to a lack of will to use that power if it involves great risks. A few billion dollar increase in our ability to wage conventional warfare is not going to frighten Mr. Khrushchev very much."[23] Nixon felt, as he told another correspondent, that "once begun, it was near-criminal to have permitted the Cuban operation to fail—least of all for want of courage and determination on our part."[24]

But in April 1961, Kennedy was governing, not campaigning, an experience Nixon had never had. Giving tough advice was different from having to carry it out. Kennedy took care not to say this directly to Nixon, but Nixon had long experience in giving Oval Office advice to "go in" and getting rebuffed. In North Korea, in Vietnam, in the Formosa Straits, in Hungary, in Cuba, and at other places, Nixon had urged Eisenhower to go for victory, only to experience the frustration of seeing Eisenhower adopt a policy of restraint.

Nixon believed deeply in the policy he was recommending, so much so that he made Kennedy a promise: "I will publicly support you to the hilt if you make such a decision [to go in] in regard to either Laos or Cuba." Actually, it was more a convoluted threat than a promise. Nixon was saying that if Kennedy adopted his policies, he would not criticize Kennedy for doing so. Still, Nixon repeated his pledge: if Kennedy found it necessary to send American troops into Laos and Cuba, "I am one who will never make that a political issue. . . ."[25]

In early May, Nixon began his speaking tour. His most important talk was on May 5 to the Executives Club of Chicago. He began with a standard Nixon ploy—to claim that the "more popular course" would be for him to refrain from speaking at all on Cuba and Kennedy, that such would be the "easy choice." But no matter what the cost to himself, he said he was determined to speak out, because "our existence is threatened and in recent weeks the threat has manifestly increased." With such stakes, who could remain silent?

Nixon went on to warn that "the worst thing that can flow from our failure in Cuba is . . . that this failure may discourage American policymakers from taking decisive steps in the future because there is a risk of failure." He pledged that "I will support him [Kennedy] to the hilt in backing whatever positive action he may decide is necessary to resist Communist aggression," and got sustained applause when he asserted "whenever American prestige is to be committed . . . we must be willing to commit enough power to obtain our objective. . . . Putting it bluntly, we should not start things in the world unless we are prepared to finish them." [26]

In Detroit, on May 9, he declared that the United States had to convince Khrushchev that "it is prepared to risk the possibility of war on a small scale if it is to avoid the eventual certainty of war on a large scale." In discussing Cuba, Nixon said that "some Americans" were urging an open intervention or a naval blockade (for "some Americans," read Nixon, who had just given precisely that advice to Kennedy in the Oval Office). But in Detroit, Nixon was emphatic in his opposition to such intervention without specific provocation. [27] He did say, in response to a question, that the United States "might well" stop Soviet shipments of arms to Cuba after a due warning that they were a threat to the United States.

Although Nixon said that he was making his tour as a private citizen, inevitably there were strong political overtones to it. Everywhere he went the local Republican leaders and contributors flocked to him, at lunches, breakfasts, coffees, afternoon meetings, and following his public speeches. Although he insisted that he was not a candidate for the 1964 Republican nomination, no one believed him. His private actions indicated otherwise.

In mid-May, for example, he told Bill Sprague, a Republican leader from Chevy Chase, Maryland, that he wanted to organize a letter-writing campaign to *Look* magazine. In its May 9 issue, *Look* had carried an article by James Michener on the 1960 election. Nixon protested that the article was "designed to continue to build up the myth that our campaign in '60 was ineffective, to knock me down as a potential candidate for '64 and to build Rockefeller up as the man to nominate." He feared that there was some "Rockefeller influence" behind Michener's article, and wanted Sprague and his friends to write letters of protest. He realized that Sprague, like others supporting him, were working on a "volunteer basis," which he said made him even more appreciative of efforts in his behalf. [28]

There were other volunteers. Bob Haldeman gave Nixon help when and where he could, and offered to do more. John Ehrlichman, back in Seattle practicing law, and who was by now on a "Dick" and "John" basis, wrote a long, chatty letter that concluded: "If occasions arise during the next months when I can be of help to you . . . please call upon me." [29]

IN JUNE, Nixon flew back to Washington to help Pat with the packing for the move. "Now I've got something in common with President Kennedy," Nixon told reporters, "a sore back." As the family walked out the door together for the last time, the press reported that Nixon looked "wistful," while Pat and the girls wept. Tricia had lived almost all of her life in Washington, and Julie had been born there. Much as the girls looked forward to California, they hated leaving their friends. Pat too was leaving friends behind; as Nixon said, "We don't like to leave this house." Checkers and the cats came along in air-freight carrying cases. [30]

The new home in the Trousdale Estates was not yet finished; while the construction went on, the Nixons lived in movie director Walter Lang's old house in the Brentwood section of Los Angeles. A fine English Tudor home on North Bundy Avenue, it included a swimming pool, a fruit grove, and an avocado ranch. Nixon soon discovered that his girls, now fifteen and thirteen years of age, were growing up fast. He was astonished when they beat him in a swimming race. Tricia was showing an interest in boys, and they in her. "Isn't she too young?" Nixon asked Pat.

"Oh, Dick," she replied, "you've got a lot to learn."

After they settled in, Nixon was off again, this time for the Bohemian Grove encampment above San Francisco. He reportedly stole the show on stunt night when he did a comic re-enactment of his "kitchen debate" with Khrushchev. [31]

There were other pleasant moments. Eisenhower spent the winter in Palm Desert, California, and had Nixon join him for a golf game. In September, playing at Bel Air with Randolph Scott and Bebe Rebozo, Nixon shot a hole in one. "The greatest thrill of my life," he told reporters. [32] Eisenhower wrote to congratulate him and say that he, Eisenhower, was taking all the credit. Nixon confessed in his reply that despite the hole in one, he had shot a 91 and ended up losing three dollars. [33]

The Nixons had lots of guests, especially young ones, as many of the girls' Washington friends flew out for a visit. "I've really been running a small hotel," Pat said when schools finally reopened and the last visiting child had departed. [34] The Nixons had their own friends in Southern California, of course; when they arrived, the Greater Los Angeles Press Club held a welcome-home party with sixteen hundred guests. The University of Southern California awarded Pat an honorary doctor's degree.[35]

Nixon himself was offered such a degree from Duke University. President Deryl Hart of Duke informed him that he had always regretted the 1954 "episode," when Duke offered an honorary degree only to have the faculty veto it. Hart said that this time he had the prior approval of both the faculty and the trustees, and one of those trustees wrote Nixon that "I know you are much too big a man to let that 1954 incident influence your judgment now."[36] Nixon nevertheless declined, on the grounds that to accept would "reopen a controversy over an incident which the great majority of people, except for those directly connected with it, have now forgotten."[37]

PAST TRIUMPHS AND DEFEATS were very much on Nixon's mind in the summer and fall of 1961, because he was hard at work on a sort of autobiography. Although he said later that writing a book was "the last thing I ever intended or expected to do after the 1960 election,"[38] it was such a natural thing to do that it was almost inevitable. As with any memoir, it would give him an opportunity to put forward his own point of view on his political career and, in some measure, achieve vindication. It promised to be profitable—although one never knows with a book—and despite his six-figure-plus income, Nixon needed money. Speaking tours were costly, and he had to pay his own way—the Republican Party could not pay his expenses, and contributors were reluctant to give money to a man who was not a candidate for any office. Most of all, writing a book about his career would let him relive great moments at a time in his life when he found everything dull and unexciting.

Adela Rogers St. Johns had been after him for some time to do a book. In January 1961, she called Rose Mary Woods to leave a message for the boss. "Don't let him lose sight of the book," St. Johns said. "I know how he feels because I have to nag a little bit. But if he is to have a best seller on the 1962 list he has to get at it right now." She reminded Nixon of how much good Kennedy had done himself with *Profiles in Courage*.[39]

Nixon, busy with a million other things, put it off. In April, St. Johns took action. She told Nixon that Ken McCormick of Doubleday and Company was flying to California to talk to him about a memoir. McCormick had strong Republican connections—he had been one of Eisenhower's editors for *Crusade in Europe*, and had persuaded Eisenhower to sign a contract with Doubleday for his White House memoirs (once again serving as one of the editors).

The night before McCormick arrived, Nixon jotted down some ideas. Mamie Eisenhower had earlier suggested to him that he write about his trips, especially the South American and Russian ones. He put those down. Then his mind turned to the crises he had been through. Always crisis-oriented, often depressed when there was not a crisis going on, he had been through enough of them to make a book. There was the Hiss case, the fund crisis of 1952, Eisenhower's 1955 heart attack, and the 1960 election. Altogether, six crises. It had a nice ring to it, reminiscent of Walter B. Smith's tremendously popular work, *Eisenhower's Six Great Decisions*. McCormick was enthusiastic. He told Nixon that writing was "easy and enjoyable" and a deal was struck.[40]

Shortly thereafter, Nixon met with Kennedy in the White House for their Bay of Pigs discussion. Nixon mentioned that he was thinking of doing a book. Kennedy urged him on, saying that "every public man should write a book at some time in his life, both for the mental discipline and because it tends to elevate him in popular esteem to the respected status of an 'intellectual.' "[41] That was certainly gratuitous advice from Kennedy, who, as his biographer Herbert Parmet has shown, accepted the Pulitzer Prize for *Profiles in Courage* after his ghostwriter, Ted Sorensen, did the work, and after his father, Joe, intervened with the Pulitzer Committee.[42]

"WRITING EASILY AND FLUENTLY is something I have never been able to do," Nixon had told a cousin, novelist Jessamyn West, back in 1955.[43] He had begun a syndicated newspaper column in the spring of 1961, but the writing was done by Stephen Hess, a young, prolific intellectual who had his own writing and research firm in Washington.[44] Alvin Moscow also helped on the columns, and both Moscow and Hess helped on *Six Crises*. But it was such an intensely personal book that Nixon necessarily had to do most of the writing himself. He told Eisenhower he found it "the hardest work I have ever done from the standpoint of concentration and discipline required,"[45] and informed St. Johns that writing the book was "crisis number seven."[46]

Besides Moscow and Hess, Earl Mazo came out to California to help out. But Nixon did much of the research himself. He wrote David Sarnoff of RCA, for example, asking for the transcripts of NBC's election-night coverage in 1960.[47] He asked Bill Rogers, Herb Brownell, Sherman Adams, and other members of the Eisenhower Administration for their recollections of various events.[48] He asked Billy Graham for his account "of what happened on the story which you prepared for *Life* Magazine during the campaign," an article that endorsed Nixon but was not printed.[49] In his reply, Graham said that after due consideration and considerable prayer, he had decided to pull the article, but in *Six Crises* Nixon wrote that he personally vetoed the article for fear of stirring up religious bigotry. The discrepancy was not reconciled, but the friendship continued.[50]

Mazo described Nixon's method of writing: "He never goes near a typewriter, but with the facts and data gathered for him by his researchers, he scribbles notes and phrases on a large, yellow lawyer's pad, then dictates the finished product into a machine." Woods did the typing. Often he went off alone, to Apple Valley, near Palm Springs, or to Trancus Beach, to spend a week or so dictating. Like many writers, he would take long walks to collect his thoughts, becoming oblivious to everything around him. He would forget his front-door key and have to climb over a fence to get back in. He took Checkers along for company, and once when walking along Trancus Beach he almost lost her. She was chasing gulls and dashing into the surf; he was deep in thought; suddenly he realized she was nowhere to be seen. He ran down the beach for almost a full mile and finally found her still happily chasing the gulls. "I don't remember ever being happier to see that dog," he said.[51]

He needed to get away from everything to write, because his regular daily routine was hectic, sometimes even more hectic than when he had been in office. He wrote Father Cronin in August, "My schedule is about the heaviest I have ever experienced. When you add writing a book and a column to a law practice, family responsibilities, and an obligation to give leadership to the Party here in the State, you end up, as you might imagine, with some pretty full days."[52]

"As usual," Nixon admitted in his memoirs, "the ones who suffered most, and most silently, were my family." Although he had said, when moving to California, that one of his reasons was to have more time with his girls and Pat, "I saw them even less that year [1961] than I had when we were in Washington."[53]

From early October to Christmas, he had to sacrifice not only his family life but his business and political life as well, as he worked full time on the final draft. Doubleday repaid him for his diligence by having bound copies of the book available in ten weeks, and in the book stores by April 1, 1962, a remarkable accomplishment.

IN HIS INTRODUCTION to *Six Crises*, Nixon wrote that "this book is an account not of great men but rather of great events—and how one man responded to them."[54] That was only partly true. Certainly the Hiss case fit the description, as did the long and painfully detailed account of the 1960 election, but he stretched things a bit in calling the Checkers speech a great event. Eisenhower's heart attack had the potential of being a great event, but his rapid recovery meant that it was not. So too for Caracas—had Nixon or his wife been killed or even harmed, it would have qualified, but as things turned out it was a personal challenge only. The "kitchen debate" was little more than a publicity stunt by both principals. In part then, *Six Crises* was a book written by a great man about small events.

The book was as complex as the author himself. On one level, it was a campaign document, aimed at a possible bid for the 1962 California governorship or a 1964 bid for the Presidency. Nixon sent out hundreds of autographed advance copies to prominent Republicans in California and throughout the country.[55] As such, it was highly effective. Nixon had carefully selected the six incidents in his career that showed him at his best—exposing Hiss, beating off attackers in the '52 campaign, conducting himself superbly after Eisenhower's heart attack, standing tall for the United States at the airport in Caracas and in the kitchen in Moscow, and running far ahead of the Republican Party in 1960. Overall, it reminded voters that he had been Vice-President for eight years, that he had vast experience in government, and that he could be a good loser.

On another level, the book was a political memoir, no more or less self-serving than most works of the genre. Throughout, he made the best case for himself as he could, the worst for his opponents. He told some fibs, was guilty of some exaggerations, but overall wrote an accurate, if partisan and one-sided, record of the events he described. It was a valuable addition to the political literature of the fifties.

At a third level, writing the book was therapy for Nixon, as autobiographies written in middle age often are, and in that sense it was self-revealing. Nixon wrote long passages on his feelings and emotions and thinking as he went through his crises. Far too often he generalized, claiming that his reactions were universal. But few men regard a crisis as "exquisite agony," and few leaders felt as much anxiety, elation, and depression in their crises as Nixon did in his.

Nixon was as highly selective in the events he chose to write about as he was in his descriptions of his emotions. There is scarcely a word, for example, on his feelings toward Eisenhower, and not one word on how he felt at the Caracas airport when the spittle dripped down his wife's face. Readers learned what he re-

sented and hated, but not what he loved and cherished. Throughout his career, one of the most persistent complaints about him had
been that no one knew the "real Nixon." Tom Wicker, in his *New
York Times* review, wrote: "The book's great lack . . . is any significant disclosers about Nixon the man—what he really felt, thought,
believed, what he really was."[56]

Insofar as Nixon had long passages on how he had to force
himself to get up for a crisis, and watch for a letdown afterward,
and how and why and where he lost his temper or made a misjudgment, Wicker's complaint was surprising, and few reviewers
agreed with him. Fawn Brodie found the book "astonishing as revealing a veritable passion for self-analysis. *Six Crises* showed an
introspective, troubled man, the epitome of moral virtue, but also
a man subject to mortal fears of indecision and failure." She de-
tected a "kind of terror" in his "fear of loss of control."[57] Templeton
Peck in the San Francisco *Chronicle* thought that "a sincere effort
has been made to be fair, precise and relentlessly self-analytical."[58]
Roscoe Drummond, in the New York *Herald Tribune*, called the
book "vivid, candid and self-revealing." Like other reviewers,
Drummond expressed surprise that Nixon, always before so protective of his privacy, quoted so extensively from his wife and daughters in intimate family conversations.[59] C. R. Foster thought the
book showed Nixon to be "sensitive and intelligent rather than
cynical."[60] William Costello, writing in the *New Republic* (which
had serialized his critical biography of Nixon), disagreed. He said
Six Crises revealed a man who "is never unaware of nameless,
faceless enemies waiting to pounce," and that the book was "devoid of eloquence or elegance, surcharged with banalities, intellectual clichés, and tasteless bravado, until at last the reader averts his
mind's eye in embarrassment."[61]

THE BOOK DID MAKE THE BEST-SELLER LIST, and stayed there for half
a year. It sold more than a quarter of a million copies, earning
royalties in excess of $200,000. Nixon was proud of his first book.
Decades later, he was still proud of it. *Six Crises* took on a life of
its own, until Nixon began referring to it almost in the third person,
as if he had nothing to do with its creation. During Watergate, he
would constantly urge his aides to read *Six Crises* for inspiration
and insight. "Read that book again," he would tell Bob Haldeman,
"really, a hell of a book, great stuff in there, everything you need
to know is in it."[62] Charles Colson claimed to have read the book
fourteen times.[63]

The publication of *Six Crises* produced a minor political flap.
Nixon asserted that Kennedy had been briefed by Allen Dulles on

the CIA's plans and preparations for what became the Bay of Pigs invasion, but had nevertheless called for American support for Cuban exiles, thereby endangering "the security of a United States foreign policy operation."[64] The White House immediately issued a statement denying that the Dulles briefing had included any information on the CIA and the Cubans.[65]

Nixon called Eisenhower, who referred him to Robert Donovan, a reporter with an inside track in Washington. Eisenhower suggested that Donovan interview Dulles and get at the truth. Donovan tried, but as Nixon reported to Eisenhower on the telephone, Dulles would not cooperate. "Dulles insists that it was not his job to brief the candidates on 'plans and policies' of your Administration, but simply to report intelligence in the countries that were trouble spots." Nixon then called John McCone, head of the AEC under Eisenhower, now Dulles' replacement as head of the CIA. Nixon reported to Eisenhower: "John McCone told me . . . that Kennedy had been briefed that we were supporting underground and guerrilla activities in Cuba including the training of exiles." Nixon also quoted Henry Luce, who told him that Dulles had told *Life* that he had told Kennedy everything.

Dulles issued his own statement: "My briefings were intelligence briefings on the world situation; they did not cover our own government's plans or programs for action overt or covert." Nixon called Eisenhower again. "McCone says categorically that Dulles told him that he had told Kennedy about the covert operation," and suggested that somehow Kennedy must have gotten to Dulles.[66]

The truth is elusive. No record of the Dulles briefing of Kennedy has emerged. Motivation for dissembling was high on all sides. That Kennedy was as totally ignorant of the CIA's Cuban program as he claimed is difficult to believe. It is impossible to believe the defense of his supporters—that the key press release ("We must attempt to strengthen the non-Batista Democratic anti-Castro forces. . . . Thus far these fighters for freedom have had virtually no support from our Government.") was the single press release in the entire campaign not personally approved by Kennedy. He had been making the point regularly, especially when in Miami.[67]

Nixon's implication, that he had protected state secrets even at the cost of the Presidency itself, was as brazen as his charge in the 1946 campaign that Jerry Voorhis had a CIO endorsement. In the last days of the 1960 campaign, Nixon had all but announced that the CIA was planning to do to Castro in Cuba what it had done to Arbenz in Guatemala. He was no more a defender of the national security at his own expense than Kennedy was. What really bothered him was not jeopardizing national security. It was that Kennedy got the better of the dispute, both in 1960 and again when *Six Crises* was published and Allen Dulles dismissed the whole thing as an "honest misunderstanding" between two honest men. The truth, sad to say, was the opposite in both cases.

NIXON DEDICATED *Six Crises* "To Pat/she also ran." Friends and admirers winced at this unhappy phrase. Many wished that he had made more reference to her absolutely critical support in his crises. In 1946, a large portion of the $10,000 he gambled on his first campaign had been hers. In 1948, in the Hiss case, she had provided him with encouragement when he most needed it. In 1952, at the time of the fund crisis, it had been Pat who was tough at the crucial moments, telling Dick that he just had to go on—most dramatically two minutes before the Checkers speech began, when he would have walked out of the studio and out of history had Pat not insisted that he fight back. In 1954 and again in '56 and '58, she had campaigned at his side, listened attentively to every speech, always telling him how good he had been, thereby providing an indispensable boost at the precise moment every speaker wants to be told by someone he trusts that he has done well. He always looked to Pat first for approval of his efforts.

There was much more to her central role in his various crises. In 1958, in Caracas, her courage, her dignity, her poise, her composure, and her beauty impressed almost all observers. At that awful moment at the airport, she stood straight and at her husband's side. In 1959, when her husband had shown signs of flagging in his running debate with Khrushchev, she had helped him along with some biting remarks of her own to Khrushchev. In 1960, she had worked for him as never before, throwing all of herself into the effort and thereby adding greatly to it. But all this, and more, was lightly passed over—at best—in *Six Crises*.

Still, the truth was that Dick could never get through a crisis without Pat. She was his partner, from the first campaign to the last. The popular image of Pat, which might be roughly described as weak, subservient, with no mind of her own—"Plastic Pat," infinitely malleable to whatever mold her husband wanted to put her into—was reinforced by Nixon's unfortunate "she also ran" dedication. But in fact, she was a woman of great depth, high intelligence, strong willpower, and a hot temper. The reason she never succeeded in holding Dick to his promises that he was quitting politics was not that she was weak, but rather that his willpower was stronger than hers. But of course it was also stronger than that of almost every politician and person in the country.

SIX CRISES WAS NOT A FAREWELL TO POLITICS. "The best and most productive years of my life are still ahead," Nixon told friends who wanted to commiserate with him when he returned to California.[68] Eisenhower had told him so, and in February, Whittaker Chambers had written to express similar sentiments. Chambers, who was in the last stages of his final illness (he died July 9, 1961), had drifted away from Nixon since the Hiss case. Their last meeting had been in March 1960. "I came away with a most unhappy feeling," Chambers wrote columnist William F. Buckley. "I suppose the sum of it was: we have really nothing to say to each other."[69] But lost friendship or not, Chambers remained a staunch Nixon supporter. In his February 1961 letter, he said that he had sensed in Nixon "some quality, deep-going, difficult to identify in the world's glib way, but good, and meaningful for you and multitudes of others. . . . You have years in which to serve. Service is your life. You must serve. You must, therefore, have a base from which to serve." Chambers then recommended that Nixon run for governor of California.[70]

He was hardly alone. Republicans in California and around the country were urging him to run almost from the moment he arrived in Los Angeles. The press speculated on it incessantly. His own instinct was that "it would be a case of running for the wrong office at the wrong time," but still the pressure mounted.[71]

His instinct was sound. Although he had carried California against Kennedy by thirty-five thousand votes, and although polls indicated he could beat incumbent Pat Brown 5 to 3, he knew it would be a tough race. Brown was affable, generally popular, had made no major mistakes, was untouched by scandal. California was prosperous and booming. Nixon knew little about California's problems—water, roads, schools—and had no particular desire to be governor of the state. The Republican Party was badly split between ultraconservatives, who had joined the John Birch Society, and moderates, who denounced the society. The big wheels in the party, Bill Knowland and Goodwin Knight, had each lost his last election—Knowland for the governorship and Knight for the Senate—and each blamed Nixon in some measure for his defeat. Democratic registration was a full one million ahead of Republican registration. Further, Nixon would inevitably be stuck with the charge that he was using the state's highest office merely as a stepping-stone to the Republican nomination for the Presidency in 1964. By no means could Nixon consider himself the shoo-in that his supporters insisted he would be in a race against Brown.

Actually, with regard to the "stepping-stone" charge, which Brown was already using in the spring of 1961, long before Nixon had announced his decision, the truth was the other way around.

Nixon viewed the governorship as a way to avoid the 1964 Republican nomination. His own judgment was that "Kennedy would be almost unbeatable in 1964." If he were in Sacramento at that time, it "would leave someone else to square off in 1964 against Kennedy, his money, and his tactics." [72] This did not mean that he had set his sights on 1968, when he would be fifty-five years old—he was far too realistic a politician for that. There would be too many accidents and unexpected events in those seven years to believe that he could chart a course in 1961 that would carry him through to 1968. But the governorship of the most populous state in the nation would give him a solid base from which to take advantage of whatever popped up.

Pat and the girls had to be taken into consideration. Adela Rogers St. Johns, while consulting with Nixon on *Six Crises* in the Lang home on Bundy Avenue, overheard Dick and Pat quarreling. "If you ever run for office again," Pat told her husband, "I'll kill myself." [73] Tricia, however, was eager to get back into the arena and seek vindication. She gave her Christmas money gifts—more than $50—to a "recount committee" that was seeking to recheck the vote in Chicago. So did Julie, but she was torn between her mother's desire to get out altogether and forever, and her father's and sister's desires to launch yet another campaign. "All I want," Julie said, "is for everyone to love everyone and be happy. I can't study or do anything when one of us is not happy." [74]

The Republican Party split was as deep as that in the Nixon family. The John Birch Society had made considerable inroads into Republican organizations. Two Republican congressmen were Birchers. Joe Shell, the Republican leader in the state assembly and already campaigning for the nomination for governor, was also on the far right. The Birchers were as aggressive as their leader was irresponsible. Robert Welch had called Eisenhower "a dedicated, conscious agent of the Communist conspiracy," and charged that John Foster Dulles was "a Communist agent." Nixon obviously could not join or support such an organization. His stand on the issues was also hurting him with the right wing of the party. In his speeches, and in his replies to reporters' questions, he was advocating a more liberal trade program than the Kennedy Administration. He remained an enthusiastic supporter of foreign aid, and a reluctant one of the United Nations. As James Reston noted, "The big money in California is most easily available to candidates who will come out against foreign aid, the United Nations, and a liberal trade policy."

Reston, who was in Seattle to hear both Kennedy and Nixon speak, contrasted their arrivals in that city. Kennedy came in "right on the minute in his gleaming jet, surrounded by all the excitement and trappings of power." Nixon "arrived late and tired after sitting around the airport in Chicago for three hours because his flight was cancelled and nobody bothered to let him know." The juxtaposition inspired Reston to comment: "To find Nixon out of office picking up his own baggage and missing planes, condemning the very people who helped start him on his political career [the California Birchers], and pleading with Republican audiences not to take extreme positions against Kennedy's foreign policy—all this just a year after his narrow defeat—is merely another of the odd political ironies of the time." [75]

A DIVIDED FAMILY, a divided party, access to the big money apparently closed off, a popular incumbent to run against, a million-vote Democratic advantage in registration, the lack of any desire to hold the job, the impossibility of dealing effectively with the steppingstone charge—all these were powerful arguments against Nixon's entering the race for governor in 1962.

But that was the only campaign available to him until 1964, and Nixon was hooked on campaigning. (He did consider running for Congress, but decided against it because, as he told a friend, his district was "Jimmy Roosevelt's and one which is overwhelmingly Democratic as far as registration is concerned." [76]) Either he ran for governor or he sat on the sidelines.

Further, he was under very great pressure from the moderates in the Republican Party, from Eisenhower on down, to make the race. They feared that if he did not, the California Republican Party would become a branch of the John Birch Society. State chairman John Krehbiel had recently suggested Ronald Reagan as a gubernatorial possibility, which caused moderates to wince, as they considered Reagan to be "an unelectable two degrees to the right of Barry Goldwater." [77]

By the summer of 1961, Nixon had become obsessed with the decision he had to make. It was virtually the only subject of his conversation or correspondence. He made up interminable lists of the pros and cons, and sent form letters to every one of his friends around the country, asking advice. He was forthright in stating his preference: "I still lean strongly against the idea primarily because my entire experience is national and international affairs and the idea of concentrating almost exclusively on state issues for four years simply has no appeal to me." [78]

On July 25, he sent his pro-and-con list to Eisenhower, asking his advice. Arguments for running included: he could win, according to the polls; any other Republican candidate would lose, and

Nixon would be blamed; as governor, he would have an office and a staff; he could develop a reputation for handling administrative problems (Eisenhower smiled as he read that one, thinking back to 1956 and his suggestion that Nixon become Secretary of Defense).

Arguments against running included: there was always the risk of defeat, and "if I were to lose, I would be virtually finished as far as public influence is concerned"; if he won, he would have to deal with a Democratic legislature; as governor, "I would not be able to speak at all constructively on national and international issues." Finally, "I think the problems which governors have to handle are immensely important but my interests simply are in other fields."

Overall, Nixon said his intuition was "to continue to write and speak on national and international issues" and stay out of the gubernatorial race.[79] In his form letter to friends in the Republican Party, Nixon said he was going to devote his energies to finding a suitable Republican candidate, so that the argument that he had to run for the good of the party would be invalid. But the adding up of all the points, almost as if he were a debating judge, obscured rather than illuminated his intentions. There is not one scintilla of evidence that he did anything at all in the summer of 1961 to find a suitable Republican candidate to run against Pat Brown. All his hundreds of letters asking for advice were really letters asking for sympathy for his tough situation, and support for his candidacy once he made the agonizing decision. He was pretending to consult when he had already made up his mind, a Nixon trait that Jerry Ford had noted in the discussions over the 1960 Republican vice-presidential nominee.

The advice that came back was predictably mixed. Herb Klein said he had checked with newspaper editors and publishers around the country and they were virtually unanimous in saying that he should *not* run.[80] Arthur Burns thought he should, as did Ralph de Toledano—although both added the caveat "if you can win." Tom Dewey and J. Edgar Hoover thought he should run; Herbert Hoover and Douglas MacArthur wished he would run for Congress instead.[81]

Eisenhower initially refused to commit himself. "I shall not venture any opinion of my own," he wrote on August 8, although he did promise that "I am behind you one hundred percent, no matter what you decide to do."[82] But in early September, after Nixon had been to Gettysburg for a talk with Eisenhower, the former President changed his mind. He said there was "no alternative to an affirmative decision." It was Nixon's "duty." He owed it to the party. Besides, "I can see no reason why, if you are elected Governor, you cannot make the 1964 Presidential race—and in a far more powerful position as Governor than otherwise."[83]

"I DREADED BRINGING UP THE SUBJECT with Pat and Tricia and Julie," Nixon confessed in his memoirs, "so I left it until the last possible moment." He had scheduled a press conference for September 27 to announce his decision. Two days before, sitting around the family table after dinner, he presented his list of pros and cons, recounted the conflicting advice he had been getting, and said that he was thinking of running but wanted to know Pat's and the girls' feelings before making up his mind. According to widespread rumors in California Republican circles, there was an uproar. Pat was described as "visibly shaken."[84] Nixon merely recorded that Pat "took a strong stand" against running. He did mention a threat Pat made: "If you run this time, I'm not going to be out campaigning with you as I have in the past." Julie said she would support her father whatever he decided, while Tricia was ready to go. "I am not sure whether you should run," she said, "but I kind of have the feeling that you should just to show them you aren't finished because of the election that was stolen from us in 1960!"

Nixon went up to his study. There, he claimed, he began making notes for an announcement that he would not run. After half an hour, Pat came in. "I have thought about it some more," she said, "and I am more convinced than ever that if you run it will be a terrible mistake. But if you weigh everything and still decide to run, I will support your decision. I'll be there campaigning with you just as I always have."

Nixon told her he was making notes to announce that he would not be running. "No," Pat replied, "you must do whatever you think is right. If you think this is right for you, then you must do it." She kissed him and left. He tore the top sheet off his legal pad and threw it in the wastebasket, then began making notes for his announcement of his candidacy.[85]

IN HIS ANNOUNCEMENT, Nixon tried to undercut Brown's best issue. He renounced any intention of being the Republican candidate for the Presidency in 1964, and insisted that he wanted to be governor of California for four years. Hearkening back to the proved formula from the 1952 campaign, he said he would "clean up the mess in Sacramento. We find today that our government expenditures in this state are the highest in the nation and the efficiency of state government is among the lowest." Law enforcement was below the national average, and education had been shortchanged by the Democrats. He accused Brown of running for President from the Governor's Mansion in Sacramento. As for himself, he was running out of a sense of public duty. "I often hear it said that it is a sacrifice for men and women to serve in public life," he declared, without citing a specific source, but admitted that for him it was different. "On my return to private life I have found that from a salary standpoint the income has been beyond anything I could ever have dreamed . . . but I find that my heart is in public service." [86]

After making the announcement, Nixon went to Apple Valley to work on *Six Crises*. He would do no active campaigning until January 1962. His potential opponents, however, went after him immediately. Brown said that whatever Nixon might pledge, everyone knew that "he sees the governorship of this state only as a stepping-stone for his own presidential ambitions." That was predicted and expected; what hurt was the way Goodwin Knight joined in the chorus. Knight had already announced that he would again seek the governorship, as a liberal Republican candidate, and he tore into Nixon with gusto. Nixon knew nothing about California, Knight charged, despite a series of crash briefings from Caspar Weinberger, currently the vice-chairman of the Republican Party in California. Knight said that in his previous primary campaigns, Nixon had "pressured or beat or clubbed the other guy out of the race," but insisted that he would stay in to fight the "Republican machine." Nixon ignored Knight, although he did privately spread a rumor that there was Rockefeller money behind Knight (knowing full well that Knight was immensely wealthy himself). Shortly thereafter, Knight withdrew from the race, citing health reasons. Nixon's remaining opponent was to his right, Joe Shell and the Birchers. [87]

In November, Nixon took some time off from *Six Crises* to get organized. For all his disadvantages, he had the great assets of instant name recognition and a statewide organization. On November 16, in a form letter, he wrote to all those who had worked for him in 1960. "I am looking forward to getting started in what I intend to make the most intensive campaign in California's history," he said, and asked for advice, financial contributions, and volunteer help. [88] On November 13, he held a fund-raising lunch at the Bohemian Club. The guest list made quite a contrast to the Committee of 100 from the 1946 campaign—instead of insurance salesmen and car dealers, the list was dotted with names of the presidents or chairmen of the boards of the Bechtel Corporation, the Bank of America, the Crocker-Anglo National Bank, Wells Fargo, Pacific Gas & Electric, Levi Strauss & Company, Standard Oil of California, Kaiser Industries, and so forth. It was a good start. [89]

BY THE END OF THE YEAR, when Nixon had finished *Six Crises*, he was eager for another campaign. He had shaken off the depression that had followed his loss to Kennedy. Although he described himself as "more tired than I had been at the end of the 1960 campaign," ten pounds underweight, and short-tempered, observers thought he never looked better.[90]

Forty-eight years old, trim and fit, he had gotten through a year that most defeated presidential candidates find a difficult one. In the process, he had made lots of money, learned to smile a bit more, even make a joke or two at his own expense. He had provided constructive and responsible criticism of the Kennedy Administration and generally conducted himself with dignity and poise. He had written what was going to be a best-selling book. Altogether, 1961 had not been such a bad year after all. If the polls were right, 1962 promised to be an even better one. In any case, there was another campaign coming up, which always made Nixon happy.

CHAPTER TWENTY-NINE

THE EIGHTH CAMPAIGN
1962

EARLY IN 1962, on his first political swing through California, Nixon went to the reporters' section of his campaign bus and announced that he would hold a "background" conference, a standard Washington technique that meant he could not be quoted by name.

Dick Bergholz, a Los Angeles *Times* reporter, fixed the former presidential candidate with a cold eye. "Nixon," he said, "you're a candidate for Governor of California. Out here, candidates say it on the record or not at all." [1]

The incident set the tone for the campaign. Bergholz may have been unduly blunt, but many Californians wanted Nixon to know that just because he had been Vice-President for eight years and had almost beat Jack Kennedy did not mean that he was entitled to be their governor. He would have to earn his way, in the process overcoming widespread press hostility and deep public suspicion of his real intentions.

Nixon tried to revive the aura of his 1960 campaign, and earlier ones, when he had been accustomed to respect and deferential treatment as a national figure who for five years had been only a damaged heartbeat away from the White House. In his announcement he had promised to clean up "the mess in Sacramento," and to campaign in every one of California's counties. He reinforced these reminders of who he was at coffees, fund raisers, and other gatherings during the primary.

"I was in the Navy in the South Pacific," he would declare, "but I wasn't on a PT boat. That's why I'm here and not in Washington." He never said directly that the Democrats had stolen the

Presidency from him, but he would point out that "my little [sic] daughter, Tricia, says she doesn't blame the people who voted for Kennedy, she blames the ones who counted the votes in Chicago." [2]

The attempted revival failed. The '62 campaign for governor was much different from the '60 campaign for the Presidency. He had to drop the "mess in Sacramento" line because no one could see any mess. He had to drop his barbed references to Kennedy because Kennedy, in part thanks to an infatuated press, was immensely popular, especially with the younger voters, who made up such a large percentage of California's electorate. Pat was not in the first row for all his speeches, staring at him respectfully and afterward shaking hands interminably. His attempt to pin a "soft on Communism" label on Governor Brown hurt him more than it did Brown, as did his use of Chotiner-inspired campaign literature reminiscent of the pink sheet of 1950. He tried to take the offensive, as he had in all his previous campaigns, but even more than in 1960 he found himself thrown on the defensive, forced to defend his record rather than attacking his opponent's record. To his dismay and at his expense, voters' attention centered on two issues that were not political, but personal—the Hughes loan to his brother Don and Brown's stepping-stone charge.

He never could provide a satisfactory answer on either one. However innocent he was of any involvement in the Hughes loan, however much he protested that he had never done anything for Hughes, the essential facts were damning—his brother had gotten more than $200,000 from Howard Hughes, who never demanded repayment. However sincerely he meant it when he said he intended to serve four years as governor and would not be a candidate for the Presidency in 1964, however much he yearned for a political sanctuary to escape having to run against Kennedy again, he could not convince the voters. They were right to be suspicious, as Nixon confessed in his memoirs, because although he meant it when he said he was not seeking the '64 nomination, "I was really not all that eager to be governor of California." [3]

In the primary, against Joe Shell, Nixon found out just how different things were going to be. Money was hard to raise. His opponent was to his right, a new experience for Nixon. Bergholz' remark was another indication. In every previous campaign, the Los Angeles *Times* had been an enthusiastic supporter, but in 1962, although it eventually endorsed Nixon, it did not give him the kind of favorable coverage, or ignore his opponent, as it had in the past. Kyle Palmer, the former political editor of the *Times*, was dying of leukemia, but he would call the office demanding more sympathetic treatment of Nixon.[4] He got no response, because the *Times* was in new hands—Norman Chandler had given over the paper to his son Otis, who set out to turn the paper from a local Republican organ into a national rival of *The New York Times*. Otis Chandler hired two new reporters, Richard Bergholz and Carl Greenberg, to cover the campaign, and the *Time's* editor, Frank McCulloch, said he would "measure the length of Nixon and Brown stories" to insure equality.[5]

Most of all, '62 was different from '60 because Nixon had an almost totally new staff. This was not unusual for him—few people managed to stay on his staff for very long. Herb Klein noted in his memoirs that "one consistent characteristic" of Nixon was the "great number of loyal people [who] rose quickly in his favor and fell out of favor just as rapidly." Some were too weak; some were not good enough; some argued with him too often.

First in and first out was Bill Arnold, his administrative assistant in Congress. Then there was Bob King, and after him Jim Bassett, who stayed from 1952 to 1960, although he fell from press secretary to assistant campaign manager. Bassett left after that campaign, taking a job as a reporter with the Los Angeles *Times*. Don Hughes was gone in 1962, as were Major Cushman and Charlie McWhorter. Bill Rogers was not at his side, nor was Len Hall (although Hall did write frequently, giving advice).

In their place, Nixon's inner circle consisted of Bob Haldeman, the thirty-six-year-old campaign manager who had been an advance man in '56 and an aide in '60; Herb Klein, the forty-four-year-old press secretary and special assistant; Herbert Kalmbach, the forty-year-old Southern California campaign director, a former lawyer who had joined Nixon in November 1961; Alvin Moscow, a thirty-six-year-old special assistant who had ghostwritten Nixon's newspaper columns and helped with *Six Crises*; Richard Quinn, a twenty-seven-year-old press assistant; Jerry Reynolds, the thirty-three-year-old research assistant; Ronald Ziegler, the twenty-two-year-old press aide; Maurice Stans, the financial chairman; Sammy Sammelman, the administrative director; and Rose Mary Woods, personal secretary. Field men included Dwight Chapin, Bob Finch, Nick Ruwe, and John Ehrlichman. Finch had been the 1960 campaign director, and Ehrlichman an advance man—the others were new.

The group as a whole was young, eager, tough, and partisan. Most thought of politics as campaigning; few had had any experience in the politics of governing, of trade-off and compromise, of responsibility, of fashioning and carrying through a program or a policy. Few had known Nixon as a congressman (only Klein went back to '46—he had covered the Voorhis campaign) or even as Vice-President, and most were awed by him, and not a little afraid of his outbursts of temper.

Consequently, few would stand up to him, even when they thought he was wrong—Finch and Woods were notable exceptions. One of Nixon's old friends told Tom Wicker, "In 1960, people said no and Dick wouldn't listen. Now there's no one who dares say no."[6] Jim Bassett told Fawn Brodie, "After 1960 I didn't know a single 'No' man. Tough men, yes. Men who said 'Screw You!' to everyone else."[7]

Most of these people stayed with Nixon when he became President, and many became household names during the Watergate investigation, most notably Haldeman and Ehrlichman. It is therefore tempting to see them as the bad guys, the ones who led Nixon to his downfall. In this view, they brought out the "bad Nixon" by encouraging his paranoia and his dark side. They were conspirators by temperament, intensely loyal to Nixon, or at least to his cause, and concerned only with how many votes he could get.

But in truth, Richard Nixon was hardly the man to be pushed and pulled by these young innocents. Tom Wicker saw this immediately, when he covered the primary for *The New York Times*. "To an astonishing extent," Wicker wrote, "the candidate is his own strategist, campaign manager, speechwriter and fund-raiser."[8] As in 1960, he was so completely in charge that in practice he ran alone. His team did as he ordered; it was made up of aides, not advisers.

As in every campaign since 1954, the press speculated about a "new" Nixon. Wicker would have none of it. After traveling through the state listening to Nixon on the stump, Wicker saw only an intensification of the basic traits of the old Nixon. "He is, if anything, more reserved and inward, as difficult as ever to know, driven still by deep inner compulsions toward power and personal vindication, painfully conscious of slights and failures, a man who has imposed upon himself a self-control so rigid as to be all but visible."[9]

HE DID HAVE A NEW HOUSE TO LIVE IN. Completion date, originally scheduled for early December, kept getting put back, but eventually, in early April 1962, the Nixons moved in. Most of the furnishings were gifts; all were expensive.[10] On May 8, Pat took reporters on a guided tour of the home (Nixon insisted, after seeing the reaction to a television show featuring Mrs. Kennedy conducting a tour of the White House). Gladwyn Hill covered the event for *The New York Times* and declared, "Its decor and appurtenances are so austerely elegant and formal as to evoke the appellation: 'Georgetown-on-the-Pacific.' " It was a ranch-style home, spreading over almost the entire lot. Hill thought it "neutral in architecture and conventional in layout," [11] but Pat loved it, and Stephen Hess said that Nixon "became inordinately proud of it." [12]

But he was hardly ever there—more often than not, his clothes came out of a suitcase instead of out of his closet. In '62, however, Pat was seldom in the hotel to do the packing and unpacking. Nixon had written that she promised she would campaign at his side, as always, but except for an occasional Saturday or Sunday appearance, she stayed home. Nixon felt it necessary to explain her absence. "Our oldest daughter is 16 and won't be at home but two more years," he would say, "so this year we decided Pat ought to stay with her and only go out with me on weekends." When she did appear, Wicker noted, she did "her share of the handshaking." Nixon later claimed that she shook forty-three thousand hands. "She is told by gushing ladies," Wicker wrote, "with what must be maddening frequency, how wonderful she would have been as First Lady." [13]

Nixon's promises to spend more time with the girls were as worthless as ever. In August, Pat convinced him to take a family vacation to Seattle and Victoria, to see the sights and get to know the girls. She insisted that no aides come along; as Rose Woods wrote one volunteer, "I hope we can really leave them alone so they can have a good time away from all of us for a change!" [14] But in Seattle, while sight-seeing, Nixon stopped into a department store and spent the afternoon autographing copies of *Six Crises*. When they took a cruise through the San Juan Islands to Vancouver Island, Nixon invited John Ehrlichman and his wife to join the family. Ehrlichman's legal practice had made him into something of an expert on planning and zoning, highways, and environmental litigation—the veritable heart's blood of local politics—so while the ladies admired the surrounding scenery, the men "talked for hours" about urban blight, land-use planning, school finances, and related issues. When the group rode around Victoria in a horse-drawn surrey, Ehrlichman reported, Nixon "quizzed me intensively about what we were seeing—restored neighborhoods, huge parks, a thriving business district. . . . But it was evident they interested him only as campaign issues." [15]

HE WAS ALWAYS TALKING POLITICS. In February, Nixon spent a day at Palm Springs with Eisenhower; the day after he left, Eisenhower wrote him a letter: "There seems to be a great residue of political fever left in me, and I must admit that the discussions with you left me far better informed than I have been in some time about the situation in California and throughout the country."[16]

Nixon wanted Eisenhower's endorsement in the primary, but bowed to the former President's insistence that he could not make an endorsement until the party had nominated its candidate. Nixon was able, however, to improve the strained relationship that had prevailed between them since the 1960 campaign. John Eisenhower helped with a long letter explaining why his father had not done more in the campaign: "He was beginning to develop physical symptoms, such as heart flutters and the like, and we were all worried about him." John added that the reason the President did not come to the airport to meet Nixon the night after the election was because he, John, had "practically shoved him [the President] on the airplane" that morning to go to Augusta for some rest. Eisenhower was "more tired and more discouraged than any of us had seen him in his career," John wrote. "The one remark he made to me was, 'The whole thing has been useless; I might as well have been having fun these last eight years.' "[17] Eisenhower himself helped improve the relationship by inviting Nixon to Palm Desert on three occasions that winter of 1961–1962, and by writing chatty letters and giving advice on raising funds.

Nixon also kept up his contacts with other prominent Republicans, maintaining a correspondence that was staggering in its proportions, and that detracted from his campaign for governor. Still, he had no inclination to give up his status as a national figure, so when Republican leaders came to California, he usually found time to meet with them. Typical was an August letter from George Fuller of Washington to Rose Woods. "The Boss' good friend Judge John Sirica will be in San Francisco," Fuller wrote, and he hoped Nixon could manage to see him. Sirica, Fuller said, had been one of the "strong Republicans" in the District of Columbia before Eisenhower appointed him to his judgeship and "has always been a real admirer of Dick."[18] On this occasion, unfortunately, Nixon was unable to arrange a meeting.

DESPITE NIXON'S STATUS, money was hard to raise. The big-money boys who were eager to whip out the checkbook for a potential President were reluctant to do so for a mere gubernatorial possibility. Justin Dart, who had owned the Rexall Drug Company, and whom both Eisenhower and Len Hall regarded as the best fund raiser in the country, did agree to serve on Nixon's Southern California Finance Committee, but still the money came only in a trickle.[19] This was especially true during the primary, where Joe Shell attracted the right-wing money in the state. Nixon, who thought that the four-hour telethon he did from Detroit on election eve, 1960, was the most effective program in his campaign, wanted to do some repeat performances in California, but as he told Alger Chapman, head of Beech-Nut Life Savers, Inc., "at the present time [February 19], we simply haven't the funds for paid programs of any consequence." Nixon was therefore reduced to "person-to-person" campaigning, traveling the state to deliver speeches and appear at rallies, receptions, coffees, and so forth, much as he had done back in '46 and '50.[20]

Eisenhower told him the problem was his own fault—if he had sent out more thank-you letters after the '60 campaign, he would have more money coming in in '62. Eisenhower advised Nixon to have rich Californians over for dinner and "a nice little social evening," the point being that they wanted some special attention before they would hand over the money.[21]

Some of Nixon's old supporters did come across. Jack Drown, for example, and Abplanalp and Rebozo helped, as did Charlie Daniel of South Carolina and Leonard Firestone.[22] But overall, Nixon ran his primary campaign on a relatively tight budget.

DEFENDING HIMSELF FROM ATTACKS from the right was a new experience for Nixon. Generally, he handled it well. The fervent John Birchers were never going to support him anyway, and he managed to get through the primary without alienating too badly those right-wingers who were not on the lunatic fringe. He had some luck here —the right wing was more interested in the race for the Republican nomination for the Senate than in the governor's nomination. Two right-wingers, Howard Jarvis and Lloyd Wright, were challenging incumbent Republican Senator Thomas Kuchel.

Nixon tried to stay on good terms with all three candidates. He wrote a long, sympathetic letter to Jarvis when Jarvis announced, although he did say that he personally was going to vote for Kuchel, who "seems to me to have a broader appeal." [23] Nixon had a friend on the inside of the Wright campaign—Murray Chotiner was Wright's campaign manager. Another friend, Ronald Reagan, was making speeches for Wright.

In April, Jarvis launched an attack on Wright and Reagan. Both men were former Democrats who only recently had registered as Republicans. Jarvis said he doubted the sincerity of their conversion. He blasted Reagan as a member of the United World Federalists (which Reagan had been but was no longer) and said that he was "concerned that Mr. Reagan uses so many pro-communist people on his General Electric show." Jarvis wondered if Hollywood did not have "enough identified real Americans for the show."

Nixon learned of all this through his informant, Chotiner, who regularly called in reports from the Wright camp to Rose Mary Woods. When she passed it along to Nixon, he prepared a statement defending Reagan, but before issuing it he had Al Moscow check with Reagan.[24]

Moscow did, and Reagan said he thought Nixon's statement would create even more of a fuss, so he asked Nixon to withhold it. Reagan told Moscow he was "staying out of the primary fight between Nixon and Shell" so that he could be "more effective in the final campaign in Nixon's behalf." In a way, Reagan was assuming the old Nixon role of liaison between the moderates and the right wing of the Republican Party. "He believes," Moscow wrote in a memo to Nixon, "he has quite a following among the conservative element; he has been talking generally on the factional fight in the Republican Party—and he feels he can go a long way in leading his conservatives back after the primary." To Nixon's delight, Reagan said he was going to pin Shell down to a promise to "unite to beat Brown" when the primary was over.[25]

The right wing did not completely ignore the Nixon-Shell race. One rumor that it circulated, for example, was that Nixon was a secret member of the NAACP. Dozens of letters came in asking Nixon if this could possibly be true. His reply was that he had accepted an honorary membership in the Monrovia, California, branch of the NAACP back in the late forties, but was not a member of the organization.[26]

Much more difficult to deal with was the John Birch Society. The society had made serious inroads in the California Republican Party. Two congressmen, John Rousselot and Edgar Hiestand, were members, as were many Republican members of the California legislature. The Birchers were at the peak of their strength in California in the early sixties. Their principal targets were a dead man (John Foster Dulles), a retired politician (Eisenhower), and the Chief Justice of the United States. They had plastered California with billboards saying "IMPEACH EARL WARREN!" Nixon defended the reputations of Dulles and Eisenhower, but said nothing about Warren. Reporters, meanwhile, pressed him to take a stand on the society itself.

Nixon had no choice but to denounce it, even though Rousselot and Hiestand were friends, many of his supporters were also members, and he agreed with the Birchers' position on a number of issues. Nixon took his stand in the heart of the arena, at an early March meeting of the thirteen-thousand-member California Republican Assembly. His denunciation was forthright; nevertheless, with help from Chotiner, he brought about an outcome that pleased liberals and moderates without completely alienating the Birchers.

In a speech to the assembly (later distributed in leaflet form),

Nixon said that "one of the major issues" in the campaign would be "fighting Communism within California." He reminded the audience of his own record and experience in the field, and said he had learned "how to fight Communism and how not to fight it." According to Nixon, "no greater disservice can be done to the effort of combating Communism than to demagogue and overstate the case," and he cited J. Edgar Hoover in support of that point.

He then outlined his own program for saving California from the Communists. Support for HUAC was the starter—the Young Democrats had just passed a resolution calling for its abolition. Support the FBI. Keep the loyalty oath—which the Young Democrats also wanted to abolish. Teach Communism in the schools, so that students could learn about its "true nature."

He then cited Robert Welch, who had called Eisenhower a Communist and had said that "treason" was the only word to describe Eisenhower's "purposes and his actions" as President. "No responsible candidate can traffic with this viewpoint," Nixon retorted, adding that "responsible Republicanism abhors demagoguery and totalitarianism wherever and however it appears." He noted that in the Blue Book of the society, Welch insisted that members had to either support his views or get out. He then asked that the assembly "repudiate, once and for all, Robert Welch and those who accept his leadership and viewpoints." [27]

This amounted to a call on the assembly to expel the Birchers, which, given the number of officeholding Birchers, not to mention their supporters, would have caused severe problems for the Republicans in November. Chotiner came to the rescue. He substituted a simple resolution of condemnation of Robert Welch for Nixon's demand for expulsion. That passed without causing a split. [28]

Nixon had maneuvered his way through a delicate maze without a collision. As he wrote Eisenhower, in a letter that included a copy of his speech, "This statement of mine will undoubtedly cost some financial support and probably a few votes as well but in the end I think it is vitally important that the Republican Party not carry the anchor of the reactionary right into our campaigns this Fall." [29] Besides, thanks to the Chotiner compromise, the Birchers were not all that mad at him. Some privately told Nixon that they too disagreed with Welch's wilder charges. He had managed to turn attention away from the question of Bircher influence in the Republican Party to the issue of Communism in California, at least within the Republican Assembly. He had, in short, made the Birchers' issue into his issue, thrown Brown on the defensive, and recalled to mind his own greatest triumph, the Hiss case.

Unfortunately for Nixon, as it turned out, '62 wasn't '46 or '50, and this time he just could not get anti-Communism to the center stage of his campaign.

In the spring, he still had high hopes. Pat Hillings wrote him that his denunciation of the Birchers "has caused concern in the Brown camp. They fear now that you may open up big on the left-wing extremists" in the Democratic Party.[30] Nixon intended to do just that. In May, he wrote Jim Hagerty: "At the present time I face the dilemma of having to take brickbats from both the far left and the far right. After June, at least, the far right front will have been contained and I can concentrate my fare on the far left which Brown now pretty conclusively represents."[31]

In June, Nixon won the primary, two to one over Shell. Now he prepared to do battle with Brown. He badly underestimated his opponent—interoffice memos referred to the governor as "Patsy Brown." But he was eager to go, and had planned a strategy that would bring his campaign to a peak on the very eve of the election.

NIXON'S FIRST MOVE was to get the right-wing press on his team. Ralph de Toledano had gone "sour" on Nixon, but at Al Moscow's urging Nixon wrote him a warm letter, which ended with a warning that the "radicals" had taken over Brown's campaign.[32] De Toledano came around. Fulton Lewis had supported Shell in the primary. Nixon wrote one of Lewis' radio advertisers that he knew Lewis would take "the most conservative line, but now when the chips are down, he should be the first to recognize that the left wing gang is out to erase me from public life this November." Nixon hoped that his friend Richard Guylay of Thomas Deegan Company would call on Lewis "and give him some therapy."[33] Lewis came around. Nixon asked Herb Brownell to talk to Bill Hearst, who had leaned toward Shell—Brownell did, and Hearst came around.[34]

Nixon needed all the right-wing support he could gather, because liberals in the Republican Party in California were deserting him. Goodwin Knight endorsed Brown. Norris Poulson, former Republican mayor of Los Angeles, and Earl Warren, Jr., son of the Chief Justice, also endorsed Brown. Former Republican Lieutenant Governor Harold J. Powers called Nixon "a discard from the rubble heap of national politics."[35]

The Democrats had defectors too, the most notable being Ronald Reagan, now registered as a Republican and spending almost full time on the chicken-and-peas circuit. At the California Real Estate Association convention in San Francisco, Brown got polite applause from the twenty-five hundred realtors when he bragged about his water program, but otherwise a cool reception. Reagan, by contrast, got "a wild ovation" from the realtors. He told them that middle-of-the-road liberals were "more dangerous than the outright Communists." He urged a vote for Nixon.[36]

The Democrats had their own big guns, including the biggest of them all, the President of the United States. Kennedy campaigned in California for Brown, as did six of his Cabinet members, plus Vice-President Johnson. They ignored Nixon's complaints about an "invasion of carpetbaggers." Nixon responded by bringing in Eisenhower, who spoke in his behalf at a $100-a-plate dinner that was broadcast over closed-circuit television. "Everything he has done has increased my respect for him," Eisenhower said of Nixon. "I can personally vouch for his ability, his sense of duty, his sharpness of mind, his wealth in wisdom." Nixon replied, "All the work I've done has been worth it just to hear these words from the greatest living American," but as one of his aides remarked about Eisenhower's warm endorsement, "If he'd only given that speech two years ago, Dick Nixon would be President."[37] The program was best remembered, however, not for what Eisenhower said, but for a remark by master of ceremonies Arch Monson, Jr.: "Too many people are saying, 'I don't like Nixon, but I don't know why.' "[38]

One of Nixon's problems was that his stars were out of office, while Brown's were very much in charge. In August, Nixon complained to Bryce Harlow, Robert Humphreys, and other prominent Republicans, "The Administration is really loading the defense contracts into this area and getting maximum publicity every time such an allocation is made. With all of their faults we will have to agree that they play their politics to the hilt!"[39] To Arthur Burns, Nixon added a heartfelt, "If only we had done likewise in 1960 as you so strongly urged!" He also complained about the Kennedy Administration's "hanky-panky with regard to the unemployment figures."[40]

DESPITE NEW CAMPAIGN LAWS IN CALIFORNIA, and despite a Code of Fair Campaign Practices that both Nixon and Brown signed, the campaign was full of dirty tricks. One of the reasons was that that was the way things were done in California politics; another was that Chotiner, out of work after his candidate lost in the primary to Senator Kuchel, was free to spend his time advising Haldeman. Returning to what had worked in 1950, Chotiner concentrated on leaflets, posters, bumper stickers, and slogans. One bumper sticker read, "Is Brown Pink?" He circulated a warning from the "Committee for the Preservation of the Democratic Party" that said Brown was controlled by left-wing extremists. Another pamphlet

called Brown a "Red appeaser" and included a doctored photograph showing him bowing to Khrushchev.[41] Chotiner organized
an intelligence operation that relied on sympathetic newsmen and
paid informants.[42] Nixon in turn was convinced that Dick Bergholz,
whom he disliked intensely (Bergholz kept asking him about the
Hughes loan), was a paid informant for the Brown camp.[43]

The Democrats had their own tricksters and informants, led by
Dick Tuck, who—according to Herb Klein—was a perpetual Kennedy spy, a pixie and a prankster who followed Nixon wherever he
went. When Tuck called in his daily reports to the White House,
Klein usually managed to get one of his men to listen in. All this
went under the name of intelligence and counterintelligence, and
was about as meaningless as it sounds.[44]

More serious were Democratic leaflets. One, supposedly distributed by the "Independent Voters of California," came out of
Brown's headquarters in Los Angeles. It featured a section of the
deed Nixon signed in 1951 when he bought a house in Washington,
a restrictive covenant whereby Nixon pledged not to sell to a Negro
or a Jew. Ehrlichman, who was called in for advice by Bob Finch
because he was an expert in real-estate transactions, thought that
Nixon should say he had signed without reading the small print.
Instead, Nixon did not respond, according to Ehrlichman "upon
the premise that deep in their hearts most of the people who would
vote for him approved of such covenants. . . ."[45]

In two years, Nixon had fallen from debating with John Kennedy over the fate of the world in front of the largest audience in
history to arguing with Pat Brown over a house deed he had signed
eleven years ago. No wonder his heart really wasn't in it. It is to
his credit, however, that even after the campaign turned against
him, he never said, "I wish I hadn't done this."[46]

INSTEAD, he put more of himself into the campaign. He especially
wanted to go after Brown, head to head, demanding a series of
debates. When Brown hesitated, Nixon pressed. He offered to debate in front of newsmen asking questions, or in a direct confrontation in a classic debate style. Brown refused. Nixon then invited
Brown to appear on "any or all" of his scheduled telethons to ask
and answer questions. Brown turned down this remarkable offer.
Finally, Brown agreed to a joint press conference, before editors
and reporters at a United Press International Conference in San
Francisco on October 1.[47] Klein, who negotiated for Nixon, imposed a condition—questions would be on issues and would include none of a personal nature.

The high point in the confrontation came when Tom Braden,

a California publisher and a Brown appointee as chairman of the California Board of Education, ignored Klein's condition and challenged Nixon. "I want to ask you," Braden said, "whether you as Vice President, or as a candidate for governor, think it proper for a candidate for governor, morally and ethically, to permit his family to receive a secret loan from a major defense contractor in the United States."

The moderator immediately declared that Nixon did not have to answer the question, as it was "outside the issues of this campaign." Nixon, however, seized what he saw as an opportunity. "I insist on answering it," he replied. "I welcome the opportunity of answering it." (This was a bit better than his usual reply to embarrassing questions—"I am glad you asked me that"—which Pat Hillings had warned him always alerted reporters, who "all watch for it and know when you say it that you are on the defensive.")[48]

Nixon then gave some of the details of the Hughes loan of $205,000 to Donald Nixon. He pointed out that his mother had put up "practically everything she had—a piece of property, which, to her, was fabulously wealthy," as security. When Donald's restaurant chain went bankrupt, Hannah Nixon turned over the property to Hughes, he claimed (actually, Hughes had not taken ownership, evidently to hide his involvement in the loan, and the income from the property was going into an escrow fund). In 1960, Nixon said, Kennedy knew the details of the loan, but refused to "make a political issue out of . . . my mother's problems, just as I refused to make a political issue out of any of the charges made against the members of his family."

Having established his position as a paragon of campaign virtue, and not incidentally as a defender of his mother's honor, Nixon went into a monologue that was reminiscent of the two great moments of his early political career, his challenge to Voorhis on the CIO "endorsement" and the Checkers speech. He said that although he had nothing to do with Don's business, and had never done anything for the Hughes Tool Company, "Mr. Brown, privately, in talking to some of the newsmen here in this audience, and his hatchetmen have been constantly saying that I must have gotten some of the money—that I did something wrong."

"Now it is time to have this out," he continued. "I was in government for fourteen years. . . . I went to Washington with a car and a house and a mortgage. I came back with a car and a house and a bigger mortgage. I have made mistakes, but I am an honest man."

Then he launched his counterattack. "If the Governor of this state has any evidence pointing up that I did anything wrong in this case," he said, "then instead of doing it privately, doing it slyly, the way he has—and he cannot deny it, because newsmen in this audience have told me that he has said, 'We are going to make a big issue out of the Hughes Tool Company loan'—now, he has a chance."

In 1946 Nixon had strode defiantly across the stage to thrust his "proof" of a CIO endorsement into the face of the startled Jerry Voorhis. In 1962, he turned aggressively to Brown and declared, "All the people of California are listening on television. The people of this audience are listening. Governor Brown has a chance to stand up as a man and charge me with misconduct. Do it, sir!"

Brown replied that he had not raised the question, except to "ask some people" about Bob Finch's statement, when the loan first came up in 1960, that Howard Hughes was not involved. Otherwise, he maintained, he had never said anything about the loan "other than in casual conversation from time to time."[49]

Nixon got much the better of the exchange, at least for the moment. Brown refused any further joint appearances; Nixon later told the Los Angeles *Times* that the governor "cringed and went away like a whipped dog."[50] But Brown was not Voorhis, and this was a race for governor of the nation's most populous state, covered by reporters with national reputations, not a race for a congressional seat in a district in which the newspapers were nearly all partisan Republican. The story, in short, would not die.

Brown himself, after recovering his composure, helped keep it alive. On October 5, he challenged Nixon to answer reporters' questions about the loan. Noting that Nixon had insisted that Brown himself ask the questions, Brown did just that: "Mr. Nixon," he declared, "why don't you answer the specific inquiries of the press and attempt to satisfy them that there was nothing wrong with the Hughes loan?" In lieu of an answer from Nixon, Klein issued a statement: "This smear is an obvious admission by Mr. Brown that he failed and fell on his face at the UPI meeting. I can only draw the conclusion that with this descent to the depths, Mr. Brown is now acting in desperation." Klein then asserted that Nixon had already answered fully, before the UPI meeting. Nixon himself told the Los Angeles press club that he would discuss the matter further only if Brown had "the guts to stand up and ask me" in a debate.[51]

Nixon's attempt to thus dismiss the Hughes loan failed miserably. Every time he faced reporters thereafter, they asked him about it—usually led by Dick Bergholz. In his memoirs Nixon wrote that "I must have answered the question about the Hughes loan at least a hundred times,"[52] but in fact he never answered, instead insisting that he would do so only if Brown asked him in a debate. In the end, Nixon's handling of this delicate issue cost him badly.

FROM THAT LOW POINT ON, the campaign went steadily downhill. It was characterized by smear, innuendo, charge, and countercharge of an extreme and often ridiculous nature—on both sides. When it was over, Nixon claimed that he had been ill treated by a hostile press. He did so bluntly and with great emotion, which makes some examination of the role of the press in the campaign necessary.

In the judgment of this author, the reporters and their publishers were highly professional. The major newspapers in the state assigned their top political reporters to the campaign, gave equal space to the candidates (in almost all cases, running the accounts of Nixon's speeches side by side with the accounts of Brown's press conferences, or whatever), and recorded accurately what they said. The biggest newspaper in the state's largest city, the Los Angeles *Times*, certainly made every effort to be scrupulously fair. Bergholz covered Nixon during the first half of the campaign, while Greenberg covered Brown. For the last three weeks, they switched. Reading their stories twenty-five years later, one would be hard pressed to find any favoritism.

Nixon's press secretary, Herb Klein, provided the authoritative judgment. Klein wrote, " . . . the election was not decided by press coverage. The press mainly reported what was said by the two candidates—and, with exception, little more." [53]

APART FROM THE SUITS AND COUNTERSUITS the two sides filed, charging unfair campaign practices in the scurrilous literature that was widely distributed under the names of dummy organizations, it was the candidates themselves who brought the campaign down into the gutter. The headlines tell the story. Los Angeles *Herald Examiner*, October 7: "RECORD SLUSH FUND CHARGED BY NIXON." Nixon said "outside money" was pouring into Brown's campaign, implying but not actually saying that it was Kennedy money. The same paper, October 10: "NIXON SET TO 'SEIZE POWER' SAYS BROWN." At issue was whether or not Communists would be allowed to speak on state college and university campuses; Brown had said that Nixon was placing himself "above the courts, above the legislature and above our traditions of home rule." "BROWN RESORTS TO 'SMEARS,' SAYS NIXON" was the headline the next day. Greenberg's headline, in the October 10 *Times*, was "NIXON WANTS TO BECOME DICTATOR, BROWN CHARGES IN TOUGH SPEECH."

On October 8, the headline on Earl Behrens' story in the San

Francisco *Chronicle* was " 'SMEAR' ON NIXON CHARGED." The story concerned the Hughes loan. On October 12, the side-by-side headlines in the *Chronicle* were "NIXON BLASTS BROWN" and "BROWN SAYS NIXON USING BIRCH TACTICS." On November 1, they were "NIXON CLAIMS FOES PLAN 'BIG SMEAR' " and "BROWN BLASTS NIXON 'FOR USE OF FEAR.' " In the *Times*, on October 8, the side-by-side headlines were "NIXON AGAIN DISAVOWS PRESIDENTIAL AMBITIONS" and "NIXON HAS EYES ON 1964, SAYS WARREN'S SON." On October 11, "QUESTION ABOUT CRUISE ON YACHT ANGERS BROWN" (the Republicans had charged that Brown took free luxury cruises on an oilman's yacht) and "NIXON ACCUSES GOV. BROWN OF VILIFYING HIM."

Things got worse. On November 1, a *Times* headline read, "BETTER AMERICAN THAN NIXON, BROWN DECLARES." And three days later, "BROWN SAYS NIXON HAS NO HEART." "NIXON PREDICTS FINAL DEMO SMEAR ATTACK" was one counter; another was "NIXON ATTACKS SLUSH FUND: SAYS BROWN TRIES VOTE BUY."

Perhaps the most irritating story to Nixon was one filed by Bergholz on October 28, not because Bergholz reported a Democratic smear, but because he reported a Republican Party charge against Nixon. "GOP CANDIDATES CLAIM NIXON GRABBED FUNDS" read the headline; the story was that the Republican congressional candidates were furious at Nixon for taking all the funds from a $100-a-plate dinner in Hollywood on October 8. According to Nixon's accusers, the money was supposed to have been divided up among Republican candidates. Nixon denied that he had taken all the money.

THROUGH THE MASS OF SUPERCHARGED SILLINESS about smears and dictators and who had the most heart and who was a better American, Nixon tried to present a positive program for California. He proposed raising teachers' salaries, more freeway construction, more water projects, a tougher and bigger police force, an immediate budget reduction of $50 million, anti-Communist courses in the classrooms, no Communists on the speaker's podium, a death penalty for thrice-convicted dope peddlers, and so forth. But little of this got through to the voters, who saw the campaign not as a referendum on Brown's policies and actions, but rather as a vote on Richard Nixon. This was his great strength, and his great weakness. Right up to Election Day, the polls called for a close contest —Nixon's admirers were staying with him. But the Nixon denouncers were determined to humiliate him, and they worked even harder than they had in 1960, getting many more Democrats registered in 1962 and on Election Day getting out a much larger percentage of the Democratic vote than in 1960. Samuel Lubell, the professional pollster who pioneered the techniques of discovering why people voted the way they did, came to California and was amazed to find an "almost unbelievable personal bitterness toward Nixon among many California voters." [54]

NIXON PLANNED TO BRING HIS CAMPAIGN to its peak on election eve. To that end, in the last third of October he stepped up his already frenetic traveling and speechmaking, and Pat finally hit the trail with him. She even broke her sixteen-year rule and made some speeches. On the Sunday before the election, she went to five cities, ending up in Whittier, to speak out for her husband. "The smears are flying fast and furiously," she told her audiences. "Dick has always attempted to carry on his campaign on a high plane. These smears are hard on our family and particularly on our teen-age daughters. I am sure you will be glad at last that Dick is taking off the gloves and is going to nail the smears." [55] As always, she had a positive effect, and along with his final blitz, Nixon could anticipate a last-minute surge, as in 1960, only this time strong enough to carry him to victory.

Events intruded and, at least in Nixon's view, cost him the election. The Cuban missile crisis, in the last week of October, did not drive Brown and Nixon and their statements off the front pages, but it did drive their race out of the forefront of voters' minds. Brown surely benefited from the outpouring of support for Kennedy, helped considerably by a dramatic flight to Washington to chair a Governors' Conference on Civil Defense, followed by a Kennedy letter to Brown praising the governor for his calm and decisive leadership. Nixon, meanwhile, was trapped. In the national emergency, he had to rally behind the President and praise his blockade of Cuba (which Nixon himself had called for a month earlier, and many times before that).

Nixon tried to take the civil-defense issue away from Brown, prodded by a near-riot in Los Angeles. On October 24, Los Angeles Civil Defense Director Joseph Quinn said that "in the event of hostilities, President Kennedy likely would sign an order closing all retail outlets for five days." Panic swept through Los Angeles, Orange County, and other areas. Lines at supermarkets were twenty-five deep. Shelves were stripped. Some fighting was reported. [56] In a speech the next day, in San Mateo, Nixon urged people to remain calm, to avoid panic runs on food stores and gasoline stocks, and to support their President. [57] A couple of days later, however, he went after Brown, charging that the governor was guilty of "gross negligence that potentially endangers the lives of 17 million Californians." Brown, Nixon said, had ignored fallout shelters; as a consequence, the state was "completely naked" in the event of enemy attack.[58] Brown replied that California and New York were rated tops in civil-defense readiness, that Nixon "doesn't know anything about civil defense," and that "we never heard a word of complaint from him about civil defense until the last 48 hours of the campaign."[59]

The night before the election, Nixon held a four-hour telethon. It was televised from his living room, with Pat and the girls at his side on the sofa. It reminded many voters of the Checkers speech (even though Checkers did not appear on the screen).

The show went badly. The worst point came when Nixon, answering a question, began, "When I become Pres . . ." then caught himself and started over: "When I become Governor of the United States." Brown jumped all over that one, telling his supporters at his final rally it proved what he had been saying all along about the stepping-stone. Then Brown slipped himself, calling on the party faithful to "elect good Democrats like Tommy Kuchel." He corrected himself, saying he meant Richard Richards, Kuchel's Democratic opponent.

Both incidents were reported in the leading newspapers, although in both cases buried deep in the Election Day coverage. There were no headlines about either blunder. But, in a lapse, the *Times* failed to carry the Brown blooper, only Nixon's.[60]

ON ELECTION DAY, Nixon and Pat were up at six-thirty. They were numbers six and seven to vote at their local polling place, having their picture taken in the ritual exercise. Pat then went home, while Nixon went to his office to call friends.

One of the calls was to Stephen Hess. Nixon thanked him for his help with the speech writing during the campaign.

"You still think you're going to lose?" Hess asked him.

"Yes," Nixon answered—he had come to that conclusion when the missile crisis broke.

"You may be wrong," Hess said.

"I'm not wrong," replied Nixon the realist.[61]

He had Chinese food sent up for lunch, then made more calls. He jotted comments on a legal pad, including "no prediction" and "Only God & people know who is winning." Later, he did make a prediction: "This race will be 50½–49½ [and] somebody will win by a noze—only hope my noze is longer."

Toward evening he wrote "was going to house but called and found family had already eaten." He had a pineapple milk shake and coffee sent to his office.

When the counting began he noted, "Last results showed we

are 10,000 votes ahead. No trend as yet however." But Brown was getting big margins in Los Angeles, which Nixon would have to overcome in Orange County and San Diego. His aides tried to remain cheerful, but nobody in politics could see a trend quicker than he could, and toward midnight he made a one-word notation that summed it up: "Never."[62]

He lost by 297,000 votes out of 6,000,000 cast. The outcome was even more painful for Nixon because Kuchel won his senatorial contest by more than 100,000 votes.

THROUGH MOST OF ELECTION NIGHT Nixon sat alone, immobile and brooding. Klein saw him about midnight. He had written out a concession telegram to Brown. Klein persuaded him to hold it until morning and he went to bed. Klein told reporters that there would be no statement that night, but that there would be a 10 A.M. press conference.

The following morning, around 8 A.M., Nixon was stirring and looking for coffee. Finch, Haldeman, and Klein went into his suite. He was haggard. His eyes showed that he had gotten little sleep. "He looked bad," Klein recalled, "but his spirits did not seem as low as I had anticipated." Indeed, his first words were defiant: "Herb," Nixon said, "don't try to talk me into going down and facing the press. Damn it, I am not going to do it." Klein endorsed that decision. He said he would meet the press, read Nixon's telegram of congratulations to Brown, and answer questions. They talked about the campaign. Nixon, Klein remembered, "was philosophical about it." He felt he might have won had it not been for the missile crisis. Nixon knew how much of a factor luck is in any campaign; he put his own bad luck into perspective when he wrote in his memoirs, "Now I knew how Stevenson must have felt when Suez and the Hungarian rebellion flared up in the last days before the election in 1956."[63]

That would have made a nice line for the press, but Nixon continued to insist that he was not going to face the reporters. Instead, he said he would leave the hotel for home while Klein held the press conference.

While Klein went down to see the reporters, Nixon came out of his suite to thank members of his staff for their help. A number of the secretaries began crying. So did one of the television assistants, who embraced Nixon as the tears rolled down his cheeks. Emotion was high, self-restraint low.

What happened next is not clear. According to Nixon, he glanced at a television screen just as he was leaving for home and heard reporters, using an "insulting tone," ask "Where's Nixon?"

At that, Nixon wrote, he snapped, "I'm going down there."[64] But according to Klein, what happened was that just as Nixon was leaving, Ray Arbuthnot and Jack Drown showed up to take Nixon home. When they heard his plans, one of them declared indignantly, "You can't let the press chase you out the back door. You ought to face them or at least go out in your own style!"[65] A third version has it that when Klein told the press "the boss won't be down," Haldeman was watching on television. Several of the reporters snickered, which made Haldeman furious. He burst into a diatribe against "the liberal press," blaming it for the defeat. "They should be told just where the hell to get off."[66] Nixon then decided to do just that.

HALDEMAN, FINCH, AND FOUR OTHERS were with him on the elevator as he rode down to the ballroom for the press conference. "Oh, hell," Nixon sighed. "It was a pretty good fight. We fought hard. We fought clean." As the elevator door opened, he remarked, "Losing California after losing the Presidency—well, it's like being bitten by a mosquito after being bitten by a rattlesnake."[67]

He strode up to the microphones just as Klein announced that he was on his way home. Hands in his pockets, head thrust forward, he began, "Now that Mr. Klein has made a statement, now that all the members of the press are so delighted that I lost, I would just like to make a statement of my own." Reporters exchanged startled glances as they scribbled down what was obviously going to be a big story.

Nixon's next words, however, were conciliatory. "I appreciate the press coverage in this campaign," he said. "I think each of you covered it the way you saw it." He asserted his belief in a free press and declared, "I have no complaints about the press coverage." Next he congratulated Brown and wished him well, saying he had never had any personal feelings of hostility toward the governor.

But clearly Brown had got to him with some of his remarks, and Nixon let a bit of his anger show. "I believe Governor Brown has a heart, even though he believes I do not. I believe he is a good American, even though he feels I am not." At this point he appeared to be angrier at Brown than at the press. He said he had defended Brown's patriotism. Then he turned on the press, his left hand clenched tightly into a fist that he thrust at the reporters. "You gentlemen didn't report it," he claimed, "but I am proud that I did that. I am proud also that I defended the fact that he was a man of good motive, a man that I disagreed with very strongly, but a man of good motives." (Actually, all the California papers had reported

Nixon's statement on Brown and Communism to the effect that Brown was just as anti-Communist as Nixon, but did not know how to work effectively against the conspiracy.)

"I want that . . ." he continued, then broke off and started again. "For once, gentlemen, I would appreciate it if you would write what I say, in that respect. I think it's very important that you write it—in the lead—in the lead."

Then he spotted Carl Greenberg, and immediately added that he did not mean to indict all the reporters. He said that Greenberg was "the only reporter on the *Times* who wrote every word that I said. He wrote it fairly. He wrote it objectively. I don't mean that others didn't have a right to do it differently. But Carl, despite whatever feelings he had, felt that he had an obligation to report the facts."

He gave an obligatory "thank you" to his staff and volunteers, said they had been wonderful and that it was not their fault that the Democrats outspent the Republicans by two to one (a complaint he had made frequently during the campaign—always faithfully reported in the press—although a month later the two parties admitted to spending about the same, $1,421,000 for the Republicans, $1,482,000 for the Democrats).

He commented on the national election, giving as his judgment that "the most significant result of this election" was the Republican victory in four major states—Rockefeller in New York, William Scranton in Pennsylvania, Jim Rhodes in Ohio, and George Romney in Michigan. Taken together, this meant a "revitalization" of the Republican Party. That brought him around to the '64 presidential race. He said he realized that Kennedy had increased his popularity by his handling of the missile crisis, but asked if Kennedy had made a deal that was going to allow Khrushchev to "ring an Iron Curtain down around Cuba." He hoped Kennedy would get rid of "all the woolly heads around him" and be tough.

He started to comment on the domestic economy—"it needs to get going again"—but got sidetracked. "A lot of defense contracts have come into California," he complained, then immediately added, "I'm not complaining about it. That's the way the political game is played." Returning to his theme, he said, "America has got to move. It's got to move forward economically. It's got to move forward. It's got to move forward relying on individual enterprise and individual opportunity."

Having thus (unconsciously?) used one of Kennedy's favorite lines from the 1960 campaign, Nixon went on. "One last thing," he said. "What are my plans?" He was going home "to get acquainted with my family again." He would take a holiday. Switching subjects, he repeated his praise for his staff. "We fought a good fight. We didn't win. And I take the responsibility for any mistakes."

Then there was another "One last thing." It was back to Brown. "I can only hope that his leadership will now become more decisive, that it will move California ahead so that America can move ahead."

A third "One last thing." He said he had noted looks of irritation at his opening paragraph. "And my philosophy with regard to the press has really never gotten through. And I want to get it through." He claimed that he was unique among American politicians in that he had in his sixteen years in politics "never complained to a publisher, to an editor, about the coverage of a reporter. . . . And as I leave the press, all I can say is this: For 16 years, even since the Hiss Case, you've had a lot of fun—a lot of fun—that you've had an opportunity to attack me and I think I've given as good as I've taken." He complained, bitterly, however, about the *Times*'s coverage of his election-eve flub ("Governor of the United States") while it left out Brown's gaffe on Kuchel. "And I can only say thank God for television and radio for keeping the newspapers a little more honest." He lectured on the responsibility of editors "to put a few Greenbergs on the candidate they happen to be against," and to keep their opinions on the editorial page (a majority of the big papers in California had endorsed Nixon).

A final "One last thing." Glaring at the reporters, he spoke with tight lips and a fearsome scowl. "I leave you gentlemen now and you will now write it. You will interpret it. That's your right. But as I leave you I want you to know—just think how much you're going to be missing." Now he brightened up, extended an open hand, and tried to smile. "You won't have Nixon to kick around anymore, because, gentlemen, this is my last press conference and it will be one in which I have welcomed the opportunity to test wits with you." Actually, he had given the press no opportunity to ask questions. Instead, he said, "I hope that what I have said today will at least make television, radio, the press . . . recognize that they have a right and a responsibility, if they're against a candidate, give him the shaft, but also recognize if they give him the shaft put one lonely reporter on the campaign who will report what the candidate says now and then."

Finally it was over. He gave an awkward wave, attempted another smile, and stalked out.[68] Mary McGrory of the Washington *Star* called it "exit snarling."

WHETHER THE OUTBURST WAS SPONTANEOUS OR CALCULATED, only Nixon ever knew. Most of those present thought he looked pale and exhausted, and he wrote in his memoirs that he had not had time to shave, but the photographs and newsreels of the event show that he was freshly shaven, was wearing a well-pressed business suit, and stood erect before the microphones. Reporters wrote that he babbled, stumbled, and wandered, but a close reading of the text of his statement shows that although he did switch from subject to subject, he stuck to the general point. The *Herald Examiner* headline asserted that "NIXON SAYS BIAS COST HIM ELECTION," an interpretation that was repeated, one way or another, across the state and the nation. But in fact he never blamed the press for his defeat; he blamed the missile crisis.

Democrats assumed that it was his swan song to politics, a thought that made them joyful. For years afterward, whenever Nixon's name popped up as a possible presidential candidate, Democrats assured one another that he would never, ever live down that last press conference. All they had to do to kill a Nixon candidacy, Democrats said, was to show film clips of the event. But in 1968, when they studied those clips carefully, they found there was nothing on the tape that was usable. Nixon had eluded them again.[69]

NEARLY EVERYONE ASSUMED that he was walking out of history. That "last press conference" phrase seemed definitive. The next day James Reston, calling it "A Tragic Story," wrote Nixon's political obituary. "It was the system that produced Nixon in the beginning and destroyed him in the end," Reston wrote. "He came to power too early and retired too soon." Reston defended his fellow reporters, saying they only wrote what was obvious. Nixon's great weakness was his preoccupation with the machinery of politics. "Everything seemed to be contrived, even the appearance of naturalness. He attacked planning but planned everything. He seemed bold and elaborately objective in public but in private seemed less composed, even uneasy and disturbingly introspective." Nevertheless, he had great gifts, now lost to the nation. Anyway, Nixon was "beyond journalism now and will have to be left to the historians and the psychological novelists."[70]

The California press was, naturally enough, furious. Every paper defended its coverage, citing chapter and verse. Greenberg was embarrassed. So were many of Nixon's friends. Billy Graham wrote him on November 11 to urge him to call another press conference and apologize. "Dick," Graham wrote, "I have thousands of friends but very few close, intimate friends. There are few men whom I have loved as I love you. . . . It would be the greatest tragedy I can think of for you to turn to drink or any of these other escapisms. Millions of Americans admire you as no other man of our time. You have a tremendous responsibility to live up to the confidence they have placed in you."[71]

Graham need not have worried—Nixon was not about to become a drunk. But he need not have hoped, either—Nixon was not about to apologize to the press. Indeed, he never did, and fifteen years later wrote in his memoirs, "I have never regretted what I said at the 'last press conference.' . . . It was worth it."[72]

Graham also need not have worried about Nixon ignoring his responsibility and retiring from political life. In the first week after the conference, only a few people saw this—one of them was Pat Brown, another Harry Truman, both of whom were sure the Democrats would have to face Nixon again. So was Republican State Chairman Caspar Weinberger, who said, "I don't think anybody with the record, the accomplishments and the experience Nixon has had can ever be washed up."[73]

What Weinberger saw, and Brown and Truman realized, was that millions of Republicans agreed wholeheartedly with Nixon. Ever since the thirties they had felt that the press gave the shaft to their candidates, and they were damned glad somebody had finally had the guts to stand up to the reporters and tell them off. They were especially delighted that it was the man who had been their spokesman for the past decade who was the one who did it. Nixon got thousands of letters of approval.

MUCH OF WHAT HAPPENS IN POLITICS IS LUCK, chance, happenstance —the missile crisis, for instance. The professional politician has to adopt the position of the professional athlete—that the bad calls will be balanced by ones that go his way. Never in his life had Nixon had a victory that did not bring some pain with it; now, in defeat, he found that luck could run with him as well as against.

Five nights after the election, Howard K. Smith hosted a half-hour special on ABC television called "The Political Obituary of Richard Nixon." His guests included Murray Chotiner and Jerry Ford, who regretted Nixon's defeat and apparent retirement from politics. They were balanced by Jerry Voorhis, who had complaints about the 1946 campaign, and Alger Hiss, who said he was bitter about the way Nixon had used him to advance his own career at the expense of the truth.

The uproar was immediate. Even before the program concluded, the ABC switchboard was jammed with furious callers who wanted to protest this putting of a convicted perjurer on television to comment on Nixon. Some eighty thousand letters and telegrams poured into ABC, virtually all critical and most intensely so. Tom Dewey wrote Nixon: "It seems to me that Howard K. Smith has been quite helpful, unwittingly. . . . Decent people are outraged. Smith has proved you were right in your comments about the press."[74]

Nixon was of course pleased and touched that so many people rallied to him. ("What does an attack by one convicted perjurer mean when weighed on the scales against thousands of wires and letters from patriotic Americans?" he said.[75]) It gave him a real boost. But he did not need one, just as he did not need Graham to tell him to not give up. As he drove home from his last press conference, he was already discussing his future.[76]

NOTES

The key to abbreviations in these citations will be found on pages 720–22.

CHAPTER ONE

1. Kornitzer, *The Real Nixon*, 25–30; de Toledano, *One Man Alone*, 14–17; Mazo and Hess, *Nixon: A Political Portrait*, 14; Gardner, "Richard Nixon," 9–12; Spaulding, *The Nixon Nobody Knows*, 10–15.
2. Kornitzer, *The Real Nixon*, 39–40.
3. Mazo, *Nixon*, 19.
4. Kornitzer, *The Real Nixon*, 40–41.
5. Abrahamsen, *Nixon vs. Nixon*, 12.
6. Brodie, *Nixon*, 54.
7. Abrahamsen, *Nixon vs. Nixon*, 22.
8. *Ibid.*, 18.
9. de Toledano, *One Man Alone*, 16.
10. Abrahamsen, *Nixon vs. Nixon*, 4; Gardner, "Richard Nixon," 3–4.
11. Kornitzer, *The Real Nixon*, 71.
12. Abrahamsen, *Nixon vs. Nixon*, 6.
13. *Ibid.*, 7; Kornitzer, *The Real Nixon*, 71.
14. Gardner, "Richard Nixon," 5.
15. *Ibid.*, 6–7.
16. *Ibid.*, 8.
17. Kornitzer, *The Real Nixon*, 73.
18. Brodie, *Nixon*, 38.
19. West, *Hide and Seek*, 238–239.
20. Hadley Marshburn interview, CSF.
21. Brodie, *Nixon*, 38.
22. Jane Milhous Beeson interview, CSF.
23. West, *Hide and Seek*, 239.
24. Gardner, "Richard Nixon," 9.
25. West, *Hide and Seek*, 239–240.
26. Cecil Pickering interview, CSF.
27. Mary Skidmore and Ellen Cochran interviews, CSF.

675

28. Cecil Pickering interview, CSF.
29. Schreiber, "A Mother's Story," 212.
30. Ollie Burdge and Lucille Parsons interviews, CSF.
31. William Barton interview, CSF.

CHAPTER TWO

1. Ella Furnas and Lucille Parsons interviews, CSF.
2. Edith Timberlake interview, CSF.
3. Lucille Parsons interview, CSF.
4. Ollie Burdge interview, CSF.
5. *Ibid.*
6. Elizabeth Guptill Rez interview, CSF.
7. Brodie, *Nixon*, 70.
8. *Ibid.*, 40; Merle West interview, CSF.
9. Kornitzer, *The Real Nixon*, 62–64.
10. Floyd Wildermuth interview, CSF.
11. "Richard Nixon, A Self-Portrait," 1968 campaign film, VPP.
12. Gardner, "Richard Nixon," 18; Ella Furnas interview, CSF.
13. William Barton interview, CSF.
14. Alsop, *Nixon and Rockefeller*, 185–186.
15. Hoyt, *The Nixons*, 188.
16. Merle West interview, CSF.
17. Hoyt, *The Nixons*, 188; Nixon, *Memoirs*, 6.
18. Kornitzer, *The Real Nixon*, 79.
19. Nixon, *Memoirs*, 6.
20. Kornitzer, *The Real Nixon*, 46.
21. Floyd Wildermuth interview, CSF.
22. Nixon, *Memoirs*, 3.
23. Brodie, *Nixon*, 74.
24. Nixon, *Memoirs*, 4.
25. Gardner, "Richard Nixon," 20.
26. Schreiber, "A Mother's Story," 208.
27. Kornitzer, *The Real Nixon*, 45–46.
28. Schreiber, "A Mother's Story," 208; Jackson, "The Young Nixon," 54.
29. Virginia Shaw Critchfield interview, CSF.
30. Mary Skidmore interview, CSF.
31. Virginia Shaw Critchfield interview, CSF.
32. Mazo, *Nixon*, 21.
33. West, *Hide and Seek*, 239.
34. Raymond Burbank interview, CSF.
35. Nixon, *Memoirs*, 6–7.
36. West, *Hide and Seek*, 240.
37. de Toledano, *One Man Alone*, 26.
38. Gardner, "Richard Nixon," 21; Brodie, *Nixon*, 31.
39. Schreiber, "A Mother's Story," 212; Nixon, *Memoirs*, 1088.
40. Nixon, *Memoirs*, 7.
41. Hoyt Corbit interview, CSF; Abrahamsen, *Nixon vs. Nixon*, 50.
42. Alsop, *Nixon and Rockefeller*, 185–186.
43. Abrahamsen, *Nixon vs. Nixon*, 50.

44. *Ibid.*, 52.
45. Alsop, *Nixon and Rockefeller*, 195.

CHAPTER THREE

1. Nixon, *Memoirs*, 6.
2. Brodie, *Nixon*, 44; Gardner, "Richard Nixon," 25.
3. Helen Letts interview, CSF.
4. Wilma Funk interview, CSF.
5. Lucille Parsons interview, CSF.
6. Brodie, *Nixon*, 46.
7. Alsop, *Nixon and Rockefeller*, 185.
8. Floyd Wildermuth interview, CSF.
9. Clemens, "Mark Twain and Richard M. Nixon," 142–143.
10. Kornitzer, *The Real Nixon*, 57.
11. *Ibid.*
12. Raymond Burbank interview, CSF; Jackson, "The Young Nixon," 55.
13. Kornitzer, *The Real Nixon*, 52.
14. Merle West interview, CSF.
15. Kornitzer, *The Real Nixon*, 54.
16. Gardner, "Richard Nixon," 26.
17. Clawson, "A Loyalist's Memoir."
18. Jane Milhous Beeson interview, CSF.
19. *Ibid.*
20. Nixon, *Memoirs*, 9.
21. Jane Milhous Beeson interview, CSF.
22. *Ibid.*
23. Kornitzer, *The Real Nixon*, 61–64.
24. *Ibid.*, 65; Nixon, *Memoirs*, 9.
25. Schreiber, "A Mother's Story," 212, Nixon, *Memoirs*, 10.
26. Helen Letts and Harry Schuyler interviews, CSF.
27. Ollie Burdge interview, CSF; Brodie, *Nixon*, 91.
28. Kornitzer, *The Real Nixon*, 65–66.
29. *Ibid.*, 47–49.
30. Merle West interview, CSF.
31. Gardner, "Richard Nixon," 47.
32. Floyd Wildermuth interview, CSF.
33. *Ibid.*
34. Gardner, "Richard Nixon," 29.
35. *Ibid.*, 45.
36. James Grieves interview, CSF.
37. Kyle Palmer interview, CSF.
38. Gardner, "Richard Nixon," 44.
39. Kornitzer, *The Real Nixon*, 46.
40. Richard Heffern interview, CSF
41. Schreiber, "A Mother's Story," 208.
42. Francis Stanley and Merle West interviews, CSF.
43. Richard Heffern interview, CSF.
44. Winifred Wingert and Merton Wray interviews, CSF.
45. Costello, *The Facts About Nixon*, 23; Alsop, *Nixon and Rockefeller*, 134.

46. Merton Wray interview, CSF.
47. The speech is reprinted in Gardner, "Richard Nixon," 39–43.
48. Mazo, *Nixon*, 21.
49. The speech is reprinted in the Whittier High School annual for 1930; Gardner, "Richard Nixon," 43.
50. Jackson, "The Young Nixon," 55.
51. Gardner, "Richard Nixon," 55.
52. Kornitzer, *The Real Nixon*, 56; Brodie, *Nixon*, 123.
53. Helen Letts interview, CSF.
54. Alma Chapman interview, CSF.
55. Brodie, *Nixon*, 80.
56. Nixon, *Memoirs*, 14–15.
57. *Ibid.*, 7.
58. Harry Schuyler interview, CSF.
59. Merle West interview, CSF.
60. "Richard Nixon, a Self-Portrait," 1968 campaign film, VPP.
61. Brodie, *Nixon*, 93.
62. Gardner, "Richard Nixon," 48.

CHAPTER FOUR

1. *Whittier College Bulletin*, 1931.
2. Morgan, "Whittier '34," 34.
3. Paul Smith interview, CSF.
4. Morgan, "Whittier '34," 36.
5. Paul Smith interview, CSF.
6. Nixon, *Memoirs*, 15.
7. *Ibid.*, 12.
8. Abrahamsen, *Nixon vs. Nixon*, 89; Brodie, *Nixon*, 99.
9. Floyd Wildermuth interview, CSF.
10. Nixon, *Memoirs*, 12.
11. Schreiber, "A Mother's Story," 212.
12. Nixon, *Memoirs*, 16.
13. Kornitzer, *The Real Nixon*, 104; Paul Smith interview, CSF.
14. Merton Wray interview, CSF.
15. William Hornaday interview, CSF.
16. Nixon, *Memoirs*, 15; Paul Smith interview, CSF.
17. Kornitzer, *The Real Nixon*, 101.
18. Paul Smith interview, CSF.
19. Gardner, "Richard Nixon," 54.
20. Morgan, "Whittier '34," 34, 36.
21. Charles Kendle interview, CSF.
22. *Quaker Campus*, 3/16/34 and 2/9/34.
23. *Ibid.*, 10/20/33.
24. Abrahamsen, *Nixon vs. Nixon*, 97.
25. *Quaker Campus*, 4/30/32 and 5/6/32.
26. Ralph Rupard interview, CSF.
27. Charles Kendle and Paul Smith interviews, CSF.
28. Gardner, "Richard Nixon," 59.
29. *Quaker Campus*, 9/24/32.
30. *Ibid.*, 10/9/32.
31. *Ibid.*, 5/5/33.

32. Morgan, "Whittier '34," 37.
33. Merton Wray and William Hornaday interviews, CSF.
34. *Quaker Campus,* 9/22/33.
35. *Ibid.,* 11/3/33.
36. Gardner, "Richard Nixon," 73.
37. Alsop, *Nixon and Rockefeller,* 218.
38. *Ibid.,* 135, 222; Kornitzer, *The Real Nixon,* 100.
39. Alsop, *Nixon and Rockefeller,* 225.
40. *Quaker Campus,* 3/2/34.
41. *Ibid.,* 10/23/33.
42. Ralph Rupard interview, CSF.
43. Alsop, *Nixon and Rockefeller,* 222.
44. Gardner, "Richard Nixon," 75.
45. *Acropolis,* 1934.
46. William Soeberg interview, CSF.
47. Mazo, *Nixon,* 22.
48. Costello, *The Facts About Nixon,* 24.
49. William Soeberg interview, CSF; Morgan, "Whittier '34," 35; Kornitzer, *The Real Nixon,* 110.
50. Charles Kendle and Hubert Perry interviews, CSF.
51. Nixon, *Memoirs,* 19.
52. Charles Kendle interview, CSF; Nixon, *Memoirs,* 20; Abrahamsen, *Nixon vs. Nixon,* 96.
53. Alsop, *Nixon and Rockefeller,* 227.
54. Charles Kendle interview, CSF.
55. Brodie, *Nixon,* 122.
56. Morgan, "Whittier '34," 34.
57. Brodie, *Nixon,* 123.
58. *Ibid.,* 124.
59. Washington *Post,* 7/13/70.
60. Abrahamsen, *Nixon vs. Nixon,* 103.
61. *Ibid.,* 102.
62. Brodie, *Nixon,* 124.
63. Washington *Post,* 7/13/70.
64. Nixon, *Memoirs,* 17.
65. *Quaker Campus,* 2/26/32.
66. Gardner, "Richard Nixon," 56; William Hornaday interview, CSF.
67. Kornitzer, *The Real Nixon,* 112.
68. Washington *Post,* 7/13/70.
69. Brodie, *Nixon,* 111.
70. Gardner, "Richard Nixon," 60.
71. *Quaker Campus,* 11/18/32.
72. Kornitzer, *The Real Nixon,* 106–107, Alsop, *Nixon and Rockefeller,* 133.
73. Brodie, *Nixon,* 116.
74. Gardner, "Richard Nixon," 75–76.
75. Jackson, "The Young Nixon," 56.
76. *Ibid.*
77. Ralph Rupard interview, CSF.
78. Earl Chapman interview, and many others, CSF.
79. Nixon, *Six Crises,* 295.
80. William Hornaday interview, CSF.
81. Gardner, "Richard Nixon," 78.

CHAPTER FIVE

1. Kornitzer, *The Real Nixon*, 116.
2. Schreiber, "A Mother's Story," 213.
3. Nixon, *Memoirs*, 20.
4. Mazo, *Nixon*, 25.
5. Abrahamsen, *Nixon vs. Nixon*, 115.
6. Jackson, "The Young Nixon," 56.
7. Alsop, *Nixon and Rockefeller*, 137.
8. Mazo, *Nixon*, 26.
9. Jackson, "The Young Nixon," 56.
10. Alsop, *Nixon and Rockefeller*, 237–238.
11. Schreiber, "A Mother's Story," 213.
12. Brodie, *Nixon*, 125.
13. *Ibid.*, 127.
14. Nixon, *Memoirs*, 21.
15. Jackson, "The Young Nixon," 56.
16. Kornitzer, *The Real Nixon*, 117.
17. Morgan, "Whittier '34," 35.
18. Brodie, *Nixon*, 127–128.
19. Kornitzer, *The Real Nixon*, 118–119.
20. *Ibid.*, 120.
21. Brodie, *Nixon*, 131; Abrahamsen, *Nixon vs. Nixon*, 116–119.
22. Jackson, "The Young Nixon," 57.
23. See the William Brock folder on VPP.
24. Brodie, *Nixon*, 126.
25. Nixon, *Memoirs*, 21.
26. Alsop, *Nixon and Rockefeller*, 230, 234–235.
27. Gardner, "Richard Nixon," 80.
28. Kornitzer, *The Real Nixon*, 122.
29. Gardner, "Richard Nixon," 11.
30. Mazo, *Nixon*, 26.
31. Brodie, *Nixon*, 130.
32. Mazo, *Nixon*, 25.
33. Abrahamsen, *Nixon vs. Nixon*, 121.
34. Nixon, *Memoirs*, 21.
35. Jackson, "The Young Nixon," 57.
36. Mazo, *Nixon*, 26.
37. Gardner, "Richard Nixon," 85.
38. Alsop, *Nixon and Rockefeller*, 200–201.
39. *Ibid.*
40. Gardner, "Richard Nixon," 85–86.
41. See Perdue file, VPP.

CHAPTER SIX

1. Kornitzer, *The Real Nixon*, 127.
2. Gardner, "Richard Nixon," 87; Mazo, *Nixon*, 28.
3. Brodie, *Nixon*, 135–136; Abrahamsen, *Nixon vs. Nixon*, 126–127; Kornitzer, *The Real Nixon*, 128.
4. Alsop, *Nixon and Rockefeller*, 195.

5. Gardner, "Richard Nixon," 89.
6. *Ibid.*, 91.
7. Kornitzer, *The Real Nixon*, 130.
8. Brodie, *Nixon*, 154.
9. Wallace Black interview, CSF.
10. Gardner, "Richard Nixon," 87–88; Costello, *The Facts About Nixon*, 27; Kornitzer, *The Real Nixon*, 128.
11. Nixon, *Memoirs*, 22.
12. According to Wingert's daughter, Mrs. W. Loubet interview, CSF.
13. Nixon, *Memoirs*, 22.
14. Mazo, *Nixon*, 14.
15. Wallace Black interview, CSF.
16. Nixon, *Memoirs*, 23.
17. Harry Schuyler interview, CSF.
18. Harold Stone interview, CSF.
19. Mrs. W. Loubet interview, CSF.
20. Mrs. W. Loubet and Wallace Black interviews, and Harold McCabe interview, CSF.
21. Meredith, "Richard the Actor," 52.
22. Wallace Black interview, CSF.
23. Gardner, "Richard Nixon," 92.
24. Hortense Behrens interview, CSF.
25. Mazo, *Nixon*, 30–31.
26. Eloise Hilberg and William Barton interviews, CSF.
27. Elizabeth Cloes interview, CSF.
28. Nixon, *Memoirs*, 23.
29. David, *Lonely Lady*, 24–28.
30. Mazo, *Nixon*, 31–32.
31. David, *Lonely Lady*, 34.
32. *Ibid.*, 36–37.
33. *Ibid.*, 32; Jackson, "The Young Nixon," 57.
34. Brodie, *Nixon*, 151.
35. West, "The Real Pat Nixon," 124.
36. *Ibid.*, 126.
37. *Ibid.*
38. Mazo, *Nixon*, 33.
39. David, *Lonely Lady*, 42.
40. *Ibid.*, 61; Mazo, *Nixon*, 33.
41. Ellen Waer interview, CSF.
42. David, *Lonely Lady*, 46.
43. *Ibid.*, 46–47.
44. *Ibid.*, 47.
45. Mrs. W. Loubet interview, CSF.
46. David, *Lonely Lady*, 55–56.
47. Schreiber, "A Mother's Story," 213.
48. David, *Lonely Lady*, 59–60.
49. Mazo, *Nixon*, 33–34.
50. *Ibid.*, 31.
51. David, *Lonely Lady*, 60.
52. Schreiber, "A Mother's Story," 213.
53. David, *Lonely Lady*, 61.
54. Gardner, "Richard Nixon," 98.
55. David, *Lonely Lady*, 62.

56. *Ibid.*, 63.
57. Mazo, *Nixon*, 34.
58. Brodie, *Nixon*, 155–156.
59. Schreiber, "A Mother's Story," 214; Jackson, "The Young Nixon," 58.
60. Wallace Black interview, CSF; see also Nixon, *Memoirs*, 25.
61. Nixon, *Memoirs*, 25.
62. Viorst, "Nixon of the O.P.A.," 72.
63. *Ibid.*, 72; de Toledano, *One Man Alone*, 36–37.
64. Mazo, *Nixon*, 36.
65. Viorst, "Nixon of the O.P.A.," 72.
66. Mazo, *Nixon*, 36.
67. Kornitzer, The Real Nixon, 143.
68. Nixon, *Memoirs*, 26.
69. Mazo, *Nixon*, 36.
70. Viorst, "Nixon of the O.P.A.," 74.
71. Nixon, *Memoirs*, 26.
72. Viorst, "Nixon of the O.P.A.," 76.
73. Gardner, "Richard Nixon," 101.
74. Nixon, *Memoirs*, 26.
75. Kornitzer, *The Real Nixon*, 139–140.
76. National Personnel Records Center, St. Louis, "Employment Record of Patricia R. Nixon," compiled January 30, 1970.

Chapter Seven

1. Brodie, *Nixon*, 166.
2. David, *Lonely Lady*, 68–69.
3. Nixon, *Memoirs*, 27.
4. General Services Administration, "Employment Record of Patricia Nixon."
5. Jackson, "The Young Nixon," 59.
6. Kornitzer, *The Real Nixon*, 147.
7. Nixon, *Memoirs*, 28.
8. Gardner, "Richard Nixon," 103; Jackson, "The Young Nixon," 59.
9. Gardner, "Richard Nixon," 104–105.
10. Conn, "Nixon—the Naval Officer," 20–21.
11. Jackson, "The Young Nixon," 60.
12. de Toledano, *One Man Alone*, 28.
13. Nixon, *Memoirs*, 28.
14. *Ibid.*, 29.
15. Spaulding, *The Nixon Nobody Knows*, 137, 140.
16. de Toledano, *One Man Alone*, 39.
17. Gardner, "Richard Nixon," 106.
18. Conn, "Nixon—the Naval Officer," 21; Kornitzer, *The Real Nixon*, 149.
19. Office of Naval Information, "Commander Richard M. Nixon," Nixon's official record.
20. Nixon, *Memoirs*, 29.
21. Kornitzer, *The Real Nixon*, 144–145; Brodie, *Nixon*, 167.
22. Kornitzer, *The Real Nixon*, 144–145.
23. Nixon, *Six Crises*, xv–xvi.

24. Edward McCaffrey to RN, 2/24/50, VPP; Jackson, "The Young Nixon," 59.

25. Gardner, "Richard Nixon," 106.

26. Abrahamsen, *Nixon vs. Nixon,* 145.

27. Or so Nixon told Black. Wallace Black interview, CSF.

28. Gardner, "Richard Nixon," 107.

29. *Ibid.,* 108.

30. Conn, "Nixon—the Naval Officer," 22.

CHAPTER EIGHT

1. Wallace Black interview, CSF.

2. Nixon, *Memoirs,* 34.

3. Harry Schuyler interview, CSF.

4. David, *Lonely Lady,* 72; Mazo, *Nixon,* 41.

5. Nixon, *Memoirs,* 35.

6. Frank Jorgensen interview, UCB.

7. Roy Day interview, UCB.

8. Nixon, *Memoirs,* 35.

9. Roy Day interview, UCB.

10. *Ibid.;* Nixon, *Memoirs,* 35.

11. Joseph Martin to RN, 12/5/45, VPP.

12. Nixon, *Memoirs,* 35–36.

13. Mazo, *Nixon,* 44.

14. David, *Lonely Lady,* 73–74.

15. The quote comes from Whittier *News,* 1/15/46; for other examples, see the *News* for the entire month.

16. Frank Jorgensen interview, UCB.

17. Roy Day interview, UCB.

18. David, *Lonely Lady,* 75.

19. Roy Day interview, UCB.

20. Los Angeles *Times,* 2/13/46.

21. David, *Lonely Lady,* 76.

22. Whittier *News,* 3/6/46.

23. Kornitzer, *The Real Nixon,* 159–161.

24. Roy Day interview, UCB.

25. Brodie, *Nixon,* 175.

26. William Kepple interview, CSF.

27. Roy Day interview, CSF.

28. Voorhis, *Richard Milhous Nixon,* 9.

29. Nixon, Patricia, "Wonderful Guy," 17–19; David, *Lonely Lady,* 73–75.

30. Brodie, *Nixon,* 179.

31. *Ibid.,* 177–178.

32. David, *Lonely Lady,* 74.

33. Frank Jorgensen interview, UCB.

34. Nixon, Patricia, "Wonderful Guy," 7.

35. Kornitzer, *The Real Nixon,* 157.

36. Voorhis, *Confessions,* 331.

37. Paull Marshall to RN, 2/20/46, VPP.

38. Marshall to RN, 4/23/46, VPP.

39. Whittier *News*, 5/14/46.
40. *Ibid.*, 4/18/46.
41. *Ibid.*, 5/9/46.
42. *Ibid.*, 4/24/46.
43. For a detailed discussion of this whole issue, see Bullock, *Voorhis*, Chapter 13.
44. *Ibid.*, 250, 260.
45. Bullock, "Rabbits and Radicals," 324; Roy Day interview, UCB.
46. Los Angeles *Times*, 8/16/46.
47. Whittier *News*, 8/30/46.
48. Voorhis, *Confessions*, 335–336.
49. Bullock, *Voorhis*, 253–254.
50. Jerry Voorhis to RN, 9/16/46, VPP.
51. This account of the debate is taken from Whittier *News*, 9/14/46; Los Angeles *Times*, 9/14/46; and Bullock, *Voorhis*, 259–261.
52. Bullock, *Voorhis*, 262.
53. *Ibid.*, 264.
54. Nixon, *Memoirs*, 39.
55. Whittier *News*, 9/21/46.
56. *Ibid.*, 9/23/46.
57. *Ibid.*, 10/24/46.
58. Bullock, *Voorhis*, 266–268; Voorhis, *Confessions*, 340.
59. Bullock, *Voorhis*, 264–265.
60. Alsop, *Nixon and Rockefeller*, 187–188.
61. Bullock, *Voorhis*, 269–270.
62. Whittier *News*, 10/24/46.
63. Bullock, *Voorhis*, 271.
64. Mazo, *Nixon*, 271.
65. Bullock, *Voorhis*, 266.
66. Brodie, *Nixon*, 180–181.
67. Bullock, *Voorhis*, 273.
68. *Ibid.*, 263.
69. Whittier *News*, 10/8/46.
70. *Ibid.*, 11/4/46.
71. Bullock, *Voorhis*, 274.
72. *Ibid.*, 276.
73. Mazo, *Nixon*, 39–40.
74. See Voorhis clipping file, VPP, for numerous examples.
75. de Toledano, *One Man Alone*, 44.
76. Bullock, *Voorhis*, 280.
77. Voorhis, *Confessions*, 347–349; Brodie, *Nixon*, 183.
78. Nixon, *Memoirs*, 40.

Chapter Nine

1. Reinhard, *The Republican Right*, 15.
2. RN to Marshall, 11/13/46, VPP.
3. Kornitzer, *The Real Nixon*, 163.
4. Costello, *The Facts About Nixon*, 179.
5. Nixon, *Memoirs*, 44; Keogh, *This Is Nixon*, 39.
6. Arnold, *Back When It All Began*, 27.
7. Brodie, *Nixon*, 189; Kornitzer, *The Real Nixon*, 163.

8. Costello, *The Facts About Nixon*, 180.

9. Arnold, *Back When It All Began*, 7.

10. Nixon, *Memoirs*, 43.

11. Weinstein, *Perjury*, 361.

12. The best sources on Father John Cronin are the three thick folders under his name in VPP. See also Weinstein, *Perjury*, 7–8; Abrahamsen, *Nixon vs. Nixon*, 153–155; and Wills, *Nixon Agonistes*, 36–37.

13. HUAC Hearings, 2/6/47, 1–3, 53–55.

14. de Toledano, *One Man Alone*, 64–65.

15. *Congressional Record, House*, Vol. 93, Pt. 1 (2/18/47), 1129–1130; de Toledano, *One Man Alone*, 66; Brodie, *Nixon*, 189.

16. *New York Times*, 3/22/68.

17. Quoted in Ambrose, *Rise to Globalism*, 151.

18. Nixon, *Memoirs*, 43–44.

19. HUAC Hearings, 3/5 and 3/21/47, 1–28; Goodman, *The Committee*, 196.

20. Los Angeles *Times*, 3/13/57.

21. HUAC Hearings, 3/24/47, 11.

22. *Ibid.*, 62.

23. *Ibid.*, 292–293.

24. HUAC Hearings, 3/26/47, 47.

25. Nixon, *Memoirs*, 47.

26. RN to Jack Anderson, 3/28/47, VPP.

27. *Congressional Record, House*, Vol. 93, Pt. 3 (4/16/47), 3544–3545.

28. RN to Anderson, 3/28/47, VPP; Costello, *The Facts About Nixon*, 185.

29. See News Letter file, VPP.

30. Los Angeles *Times*, 5/29/47.

31. RN to Irving Raab, 3/11/47, VPP.

32. Nixon, *Memoirs*, 48–49.

33. Ambrose, *Rise to Globalism*, 161.

34. Nixon, *Memoirs*, 49–51.

35. *Ibid.*, 51; see Form Letters file, VPP.

36. Los Angeles *Times*, 10/26/47.

37. Fred Thompson to RN, 12/4/47, and RN to Thompson, 12/12/47, VPP.

38. RN to James Stewart, 6/13/47, VPP.

39. RN to Roger Thorpe, 12/9/47; to John McCoy, 12/3/47; and to Frank Vanderwall, 12/3/47, VPP.

40. HUAC Hearings, 10/20/47, 21–49.

41. *Congressional Record, House*, Vol. 93, Pt. 9 (11/24/47), 10792.

42. *Appendix to Congressional Record, House*, Vol. 94, Pt. 9 (2/3/48), A643–645.

43. HUAC Hearings, 2/5, 6, 9–11, 1948, 34.

44. Goodman, *The Committee*, 228.

45. HUAC Hearings, 2/5, 6, 9–11, 1948, 232.

46. *Congressional Record, House*, Vol. 94, Pt. 5 (May 1948), *passim*.

47. *Ibid.*, 5888–5889.

48. *Ibid.*, 6104, 6146.

49. Smith, *Dewey*, 493.

50. RN to Paul Smith, 7/6/48, VPP.

51. RN to Daisy Sherwood, 7/6/48, VPP.

52. RN to Smith, 7/6/48, VPP.

53. RN to C. Brennan, 7/15/48, VPP.
54. RN to Smith, 7/6/48, VPP.

CHAPTER TEN

1. See Wills, "The Hiss Connection," 8/25/74.
2. HUAC Hearings "Regarding Communist Espionage in the U.S. Government," July, August, September, 1948, 556. Every account of Stripling's decision to call Chambers before HUAC that I have read is extremely vague, and usually written in the passive voice—"It was decided," etc. For reasons that escape this author, Nixon never admitted in public his prior knowledge about Chambers that came from Father John Cronin. But Earl Mazo, who had Nixon's active cooperation on his 1960 campaign biography, records that "although Chambers had shown no inclination to cooperate with the committee, *its members felt* [my italics] he might corroborate some of the Bentley testimony." Mazo, *Nixon,* 52. See also Goodman, *The Committee,* 247, and Weinstein, *Perjury,* 5. Weinstein writes that the decision to call Chambers "seems to have been Karl Mundt's idea," but he does not explore the possibility that Mundt got it from Nixon, instead attributing it to a reporter. Stripling, *Red Plot,* 96, discusses Chambers' reluctance to appear.
3. Nixon, *Six Crises,* 2.
4. Weinstein, *Perjury,* 6; Goodman, *The Committee,* 248.
5. HUAC Espionage Hearings, 580–581.
6. Goodman, *The Committee,* 250–251.
7. Weinstein, *Perjury,* 10.
8. Nixon, *Six Crises,* 6.
9. *Ibid.,* 7.
10. Kornitzer, *The Real Nixon,* 173.
11. Nixon, *Six Crises,* 8.
12. *Ibid.,* 9. Weinstein, *Perjury,* 15.
13. Nixon, *Six Crises,* 10, Weinstein, *Perjury,* 15.
14. Nixon, *Six Crises,* 10–11. On this and all other incidents in the Hiss case, consult in addition to *Six Crises,* Weinstein, *Perjury;* Goodman, *The Committee;* Levitt and Levitt, *A Tissue of Lies;* Stripling, *Red Plot;* Brodie, *Nixon;* Mazo, *Nixon;* Tiger, *Alger Hiss;* Chambers, *Witness;* Andrews and Andrews, *Tragedy;* and indeed all the other books on the Hiss case. There are differences in details in the literature that are beyond the scope of this biography; the narrative given here is the author's best judgment on what happened. But none of this is set in stone, and the author urges the interested reader to plunge into the case on his or her own.
15. *Ibid.,* 14–15.
16. Mazo, *Nixon,* 54.
17. HUAC Espionage Hearings, 666–667.
18. *Ibid.,* 671.
19. Mazo, *Nixon,* 56.
20. *Ibid.,* 56–57; Nixon, *Six Crises,* 22–23.
21. Schreiber, "A Mother's Story," 214.
22. Nixon, *Six Crises,* 19, xv–xvi.
23. Kornitzer, *The Real Nixon,* 170–171; Weinstein, *Perjury,* 25–26; Mazo, *Nixon,* 57.
24. Nixon, *Six Crises,* 20.
25. Mazo, *Nixon,* 58.

26. Nixon, *Six Crises*, 21.
27. Chambers, *Witness*, 792–793.
28. Andrews and Andrews, *Tragedy*, 73–75.
29. Nixon, *Six Crises*, 23.
30. HUAC Espionage Hearings, 942, 945.
31. Nixon, *Six Crises*, 23–24.
32. HUAC Espionage Hearings, 950–951.
33. *Ibid.*, 955.
34. *Ibid.*, 957.
35. *Ibid.*, 961–962.
36. *Ibid.*, 978–979.
37. *Ibid.*, 986–987.
38. *Ibid.*, 988–989.
39. Mazo, *Nixon*, 60–61.
40. HUAC Espionage Hearings, 1001.
41. *New York Times*, 8/18/48; Weinstein, *Perjury*, 38.
42. Weinstein, *Perjury*, 39.
43. HUAC Espionage Hearings, 1011–1013.
44. Nixon, *Six Crises*, 37–38.
45. *Ibid.*, 39–41.
46. HUAC Espionage Hearings, 1180–1191.
47. See the newspapers listed for 8/28/48.
48. Andrews and Andrews, *Tragedy*, 81.
49. Smith, *Dewey*, 507.
50. Weinstein, *Perjury*, 58; Nixon, *Six Crises*, 45.
51. Nixon, *Six Crises*, 46.
52. This account is based on all the usual sources on the case, but relies most heavily on Weinstein, *Perjury*, 186–189. There are serious contradictions in the various sources; according to Nixon, *Six Crises*, 46–47, he never lost his temper and it was he who suggested to Stripling that they go to Westminster to see Chambers. Stripling, *Red Plot*, 141–144, told a somewhat different story. I follow Weinstein because he is the most reliable.
53. Weinstein, *Perjury*, 189.
54. *Ibid.*, 54.
55. Nixon, *Six Crises*, 48; Weinstein, *Perjury*, 190.
56. Weinstein, *Perjury*, 193; Andrews and Andrews, *Tragedy*, 179.
57. Nixon, *Six Crises*, 48–49; Weinstein, *Perjury*, 190.
58. Weinstein, *Perjury*, 272–273; Nixon, *Six Crises*, 54–55; Stripling, *Red Plot*, 148–150.
59. Nixon, *Six Crises*, 56.
60. HUAC Espionage Hearings, December 7–8, 1948.
61. Weinstein, *Perjury*, 275–276.
62. *New York Times*, 12/9/58.
63. *Ibid.*
64. Washington *Post*, 12/10/48.
65. Weinstein, *Perjury*, 282.
66. Nixon, *Six Crises*, 60.

Chapter Eleven

1. RN to Perry, 1/3/49, VPP.
2. HUAC *Hearings Regarding Shipment of Atomic Material*, 12/5/49.

3. *New York Times,* 6/21/49.

4. *Congressional Record, House,* Vol. 95, Pt. 3 (3/25/49), 322.

5. *Ibid.,* Pt. 4, (4/27/49), 5173, 5267.

6. RN to Hillings, 6/8/49, VPP.

7. RN to Jorgensen, 8/11/49, VPP.

8. Roy Day interview, UCB.

9. Frank Jorgensen interview, UCB.

10. Roy Day interview, UCB; Frank Jorgensen interview, UCB.

11. Frank Jorgensen interview, UCB; Mazo, *Nixon,* 72.

12. Weinstein, *Perjury,* 469; Levitt and Levitt, *A Tissue of Lies,* 135.

13. Weinstein, *Perjury,* 469; Levitt and Levitt, *A Tissue of Lies,* 116.

14. Weinstein, *Perjury,* 469; Mazo, *Nixon,* 65; *New York Times,* 7/12/49, 7/15/49.

15. Weinstein, *Perjury,* 469; Mazo, *Nixon,* 66; *New York Times,* 7/13/49.

16. *New York Times,* 7/13/49.

17. RN to Hillings, 7/20/49, VPP.

18. Frank Jorgensen to RN, 2/1/49.

19. Frank Jorgensen interview, UCB.

20. *Ibid.*

21. Los Angeles *Times,* 11/4/49; *New York Times,* 11/4/49.

22. Weinstein, *Perjury,* 470, 485–488.

23. San Francisco *Chronicle,* 1/22/50; quoted in Mazo, *Nixon,* 66.

24. *New York Times,* 1/28 to 1/30/49; Levitt and Levitt, *A Tissue of Lies,* 294.

25. *New York Times,* 1/28/49; San Francisco *Chronicle,* 1/22/50.

26. *Congressional Record, House,* Vol. 96, Pt. 1 (1/26/50), 999–1007.

27. See newspaper file, 2/4/50, VPP.

28. Kornitzer, *The Real Nixon,* 176.

29. RN to Ralph Turner, 1/31/49, VPP.

30. Frank Jorgensen interview, UCB.

31. Quoted in Costello, *The Facts About Nixon,* 61.

32. Frank Jorgensen interview, UCB.

33. Brodie, *Nixon,* 239.

34. Mazo, *Nixon,* 74.

35. Quoted in Costello, *The Facts About Nixon,* 62.

36. Los Angeles *Times,* 5/23/49.

37. Mazo, *Nixon,* 75.

38. *Ibid.,* 81.

39. Nixon, *Memoirs,* 75.

40. Mazo, *Nixon,* 76.

41. Quoted in Costello, *The Facts About Nixon,* 62.

42. *Ibid.,* 63.

43. San Francisco *Chronicle,* 4/16/50.

44. *Ibid.,* 3/22/50.

45. *New York Times,* 5/11/50.

46. San Francisco *Chronicle,* 6/5/50.

47. *Ibid.,* 5/18/50.

48. *Ibid.,* 5/14/50.

49. Los Angeles *Times,* 2/1/50; San Francisco *Chronicle,* 3/1/50.

50. Roy Croker and Frank Jorgensen interviews, UCB.

51. San Francisco *Chronicle,* 4/22/50.

52. *New York Times,* 11/1/50; Costello, *The Facts About Nixon,* 80.

53. Quoted in Costello, *The Facts About Nixon*, 73.
54. *New York Times*, 11/1/50.
55. *Ibid.*, Nixon, *Memoirs*, 76–77.
56. Los Angeles *Times*, 9/1/50; San Francisco *Chronicle*, 8/31/50, 9/1/50.
57. Los Angeles *Times*, 9/7/50.
58. Quoted in Costello, *The Facts About Nixon*, 69.
59. Los Angeles *Times*, 10/30/50 and 11/2/50.
60. *The Independent Review* first used the phrase; Douglas picked it up and used it frequently thereafter.
61. Kornitzer, *The Real Nixon*, 187.
62. Mazo, *Nixon*, 81.
63. There is a copy of the pink sheet—and other broadsides—in VPP.
64. Brodie, *Nixon*, 241–242; Nixon, *Memoirs*, 77.
65. Quoted in Costello, *The Facts About Nixon*, 69.
66. San Francisco *Chronicle*, 9/19/50.
67. Los Angeles *Times*, 10/30/50.
68. Quoted in Costello, *The Facts About Nixon*, 70–71.
69. San Francisco *Chronicle*, 9/7/50.
70. *Ibid.*, 10/22/50 and 10/30/50.
71. Quoted in Costello, *The Facts About Nixon*, 70.
72. San Francisco *Chronicle*, 11/5/50.
73. Mazo, *Nixon*, 82–83.
74. San Francisco *Chronicle*, 10/31/50.
75. *Ibid.*, 11/4/50.
76. Mazo, *Nixon*, 71.
77. *New Republic*, 5/5/58.
78. See the *New Republic* file in VPP.
79. Brodie, *Nixon*, 232, 239–240.
80. Los Angeles *Times*, 11/8/50.
81. Brodie, *Nixon*, 244.
82. San Francisco *Chronicle*, 11/21/50.

Chapter Twelve

1. Mazo, *Nixon*, 84.
2. *Ibid.*, 85.
3. RN to Palmer, 2/17/51, VPP.
4. Nixon, *Memoirs*, 78.
5. Speech file, VPP; Mazo, *Nixon*, 85–87; Costello, *The Facts About Nixon*, 77–78.
6. *New York Times*, 11/4/50.
7. Reinhard, *The Republican Right*, 73.
8. *Ibid.*
9. Quoted in *ibid.*, 74.
10. RN to Palmer, 6/20/52, VPP.
11. *Ibid.*, 2/17/51.
12. Nixon, *Memoirs*, 80–81.
13. *Ibid.*, 81–82.
14. *Ibid.*, 83.
15. RN to Elwood Robinson, 4/4/51, VPP.
16. RN to Herbert Klein, 7/24/51, VPP.

17. Mazo, *Nixon*, 88–89.
18. *Ibid.*, 89.
19. See the files in VPP for all those listed.
20. de Toledano, *One Man Alone*, 128.
21. RN to Palmer, 2/17/51,VPP.
22. Griffith, *The Politics of Fear*, 90–93.
23. Rough draft, speech file, 10/8/51, VPP.
24. Press release file, 3/12/51, VPP.
25. RN to Austin Canfield, 4/4/51, VPP.
26. RN to George MacKinnon, 8/30/51, VPP.
27. RN to John Foster Dulles, 1/14/52, and Dulles to RN, 1/16/52, VPP.
28. The draft of this review is in VPP; it was printed on 5/24/52.
29. *Saturday Review*, 5/24/52.
30. Nixon, *Memoirs*, 873, 937.
31. Reeves, *McCarthy*, 245, 249.
32. For example, he was the only Republican who stayed on good terms with the Taft-Goldwater-Reagan wing of the party on the one hand, and with the Dewey-Eisenhower-Rockefeller wing on the other.
33. This about a role that eventually got him the vice-presidential nomination and ultimately the Presidency itself!
34. Nixon, *Memoirs*, 139.
35. Reeves, *McCarthy*, 348–349; Nixon, *Memoirs*, 138–139.
36. Press release, 4/11/51, Douglas MacArthur file, VPP.
37. Press release, 4/12/51, MacArthur file, VPP.
38. *Congressional Record, Senate* (4/11/51), 3653.
39. *Ibid.*, 4/27/51, 4468.
40. *Ibid.*, 4/11/51, 3651–3653.
41. *Ibid.*, 4/15/51, 4245.
42. *Ibid.*, 4/11/51, 3655–3657.
43. Form letter file, April '51, VPP.
44. Los Angeles *Examiner*, 4/23/51.
45. Quoted in Costello, *The Facts About Nixon*, 212.
46. KFT Radio Talk, 3/4/51, VPP.
47. RN to Averell Harriman, 4/28/52, and Harriman to RN, 5/21/52, VPP.
48. *Congressional Record, Senate* (8/24/51), 10646; RN to Victor Lasky, 8/30/51, VPP.
49. RN to David Lloyd, 3/22/52, Lloyd Papers, Harry S. Truman Library.
50. David, *Lonely Lady*, 89–90.
51. Reeves, *McCarthy*, 319.
52. Brodie, *Nixon*, 233–235.
53. David, *Lonely Lady*, 88.
54. RN to Arthur Paik, 10/30/51, VPP.
55. Earl Chapman interview, CSF.
56. Nixon, Patricia, "Wonderful Guy," 19.
57. *Ibid.*, 93.
58. See the form letter files and staff files, VPP.
59. Woods, "Nixon's My Boss," 77.
60. *Ibid.*, 78.
61. Brodie, *Nixon*, 238.
62. Woods, "Nixon's My Boss," 77–78.
63. *Ibid.*, 77.

CHAPTER THIRTEEN

1. Mazo, *Nixon*, 89.
2. *Ibid.*
3. Smith, *Dewey*, 584.
4. Mazo, *Nixon*, 89.
5. Costello, *The Facts About Nixon*, 82.
6. *Ibid.*, 79–81.
7. Costello, *The Facts About Nixon*, 80; Smith, *Dewey*, 584; Nixon, *Memoirs*, 84.
8. Mazo, *Nixon*, 90.
9. *Ibid.*
10. Smith, *Dewey*, 584.
11. Nixon, *Memoirs*, 84.
12. *Ibid.*, 84–85.
13. Mazo, *Nixon*, 91.
14. John Walton Dinkelspiel interview, UCB.
15. Costello, *The Facts About Nixon*, 85.
16. See Nixon's form letter, 5/31/52, Murray Chotiner file, VPP.
17. Smith, *Dewey*, 595.
18. Costello, *The Facts About Nixon*, 85; Mazo, *Nixon*, 91.
19. All the basic documents about the fund were reprinted in *U.S. News & World Report*, 10/3/52; Dana Smith's form letter, dated 9/25/51, is in VPP. See also Mazo, *Nixon*, 104; Costello, *The Facts About Nixon*, 100.
20. RN to Smith, 6/9/52, VPP, reprinted in Mazo, *Nixon*, 105; Smith to RN, 6/11/52, VPP, also reprinted in Mazo, *Nixon*, 105–106.
21. Mazo, *Nixon*, 102.
22. See the legal opinion issued by Gibson, Dunn and Crutcher on 9/23/52, reprinted in *U.S. News & World Report*, 10/3/52, and Costello, *The Facts About Nixon*, 112.
23. Mazo, *Nixon*, 91.
24. *Ibid.*, 92.
25. Roy Day interview, UCB.
26. Frank Jorgensen interview, UCB.
27. Chicago *Daily News*, 7/9/52; Kornitzer, *The Real Nixon*, 211–212.
28. Mazo, *Nixon*, 94; Nixon, *Memoirs*, 85.
29. Mazo, *Nixon*, 94–95.
30. Roy Day, Frank Jorgensen, and John Walton Dinkelspiel interviews, UCB; *New York Times*, 7/10 to 7/12/52; Mazo, *Nixon*, 93; Costello, *The Facts About Nixon*, 87–88.
31. Smith, *Dewey*, 596.
32. Mazo, *Nixon*, 95.
33. Nixon, *Memoirs*, 86; David, *Lonely Lady*, 94.
34. Mazo, *Nixon*, 96.
35. Costello, *The Facts About Nixon*, 90.
36. Ambrose, *Eisenhower*, Vol. I, 541–542.
37. Nixon, *Memoirs*, 86–88.
38. Smith, *Dewey*, 597.
39. Patricia Nixon, "Wonderful Guy," 94.
40. *New York Times*, 7/12/52.
41. Nixon, *Memoirs*, 89.
42. *New York Times*, 7/12/52; photographs of the event are in Patricia Nixon, "Wonderful Guy," 18.

43. *New York Times*, 1/12/52.
44. Mazo, *Nixon*, 98.
45. Nixon, *Memoirs*, 89.
46. *New York Times*, 7/12/52; Nixon, *Memoirs*, 90.
47. Nixon, *Memoirs*, 90.
48. David, *Lonely Lady*, 95.
49. Nixon, Patricia, "Wonderful Guy," 96.
50. Mazo, *Nixon*, 109.
51. *Ibid.*, 99.
52. Paul Hoffman to RN, 8/20/52, Hoffman file, Harry S. Truman Library.
53. Chotiner to Hoffman, 8/26/52, *ibid.*
54. "Quizzing Nixon," *U.S. News & World Report*, 8/29/52.

Chapter Fourteen

1. Costello, *The Facts About Nixon*, 95–96.
2. *New York Times*, 7/12/52.
3. Nixon statement, 10/8/51, VPP.
4. Brashear, "Who Is Richard Nixon?"
5. Costello, *The Facts About Nixon*, 96–97.
6. Mazo, *Nixon*, 102.
7. Nixon, *Six Crises*, 73–74; Mazo, *Nixon*, 106–107.
8. San Francisco *Chronicle*, 9/19/52; Costello, *The Facts About Nixon*, 99–100.
9. Patricia Nixon, "Wonderful Guy," 93.
10. Mazo, *Nixon*, 108.
11. *Ibid.*, Nixon, *Six Crises*, 81–82.
12. New York *Post*, 9/18/52.
13. Nixon, *Six Crises*, 80.
14. *New York Times*, 9/19/52.
15. Ambrose, *Eisenhower*, Vol. I, 554.
16. *New York Times*, 9/19/52.
17. Los Angeles *Examiner*, 9/20/52; Costello, *The Facts About Nixon*, 102–103.
18. Nixon, *Six Crises*, 84.
19. *Ibid.*, 85.
20. *New York Times*, 9/20/52.
21. Mazo, *Nixon*, 112.
22. *New York Times*, 9/24/52.
23. Washington *Post*, 9/20/52.
24. New York *Herald Tribune*, 9/20/52.
25. DE to Bill Robinson, 9/20/52, EL.
26. Robinson to DE, 9/21/52, EL.
27. Harold Stassen to RN, 9/21/52, VPP.
28. Mazo, *Nixon*, 115.
29. DE to RN, 9/19/52, draft, EL.
30. Ambrose, *Eisenhower*, Vol. I, 556.
31. *Ibid.*, 557.
32. Nixon, *Memoirs*, 95.
33. Mazo, *Nixon*, 117.
34. Nixon, *Memoirs*, 97.

35. Mazo, *Nixon*, 120–121.
36. Nixon, *Memoirs*, 97–98
37. *Ibid.*, 99.
38. Mazo, *Nixon*, 122.
39. Nixon, *Memoirs*, 101.
40. Mazo, *Nixon*, 124–125.
41. *Ibid.*, 126–128; Nixon, *Memoirs*, 102–103.
42. *New York Times*, 9/24/52; Ambrose, *Eisenhower*, Vol. I, 559; Mazo, *Nixon*, 129–131.
43. Mazo, *Nixon*, 131; Nixon, *Memoirs*, 104.
44. Costello, *The Facts About Nixon*, 109.
45. Ambrose, *Eisenhower*, Vol. I, 559.
46. Costello, *The Facts About Nixon*, 109.
47. DE to RN, 9/23/52, EL.
48. Nixon, *Memoirs*, 105–106.
49. Mazo, *Nixon*, 133.
50. Nixon, *Memoirs*, 106.
51. Woods, "Nixon's My Boss," 77.
52. Mazo, *Nixon*, 133–135.
53. Nixon, *Memoirs*, 106.
54. Nixon, *Six Crises*, 126.
55. *New York Times*, 9/25/52.
56. Brodie, *Nixon*, 116.
57. Mazo, *Nixon*, 137; Nixon, *Memoirs*, 110.
58. Weinstein, *Perjury*, 511.
59. See "Nixon's Employment at O.P.A.," Lloyd Papers, Truman Library.
60. Costello, *The Facts About Nixon*, 114.
61. St. Louis *Post Dispatch*, 10/20/52.
62. Nixon, *Memoirs*, 108–109; Costello, *The Facts About Nixon*, 114.
63. Nixon, *Memoirs*, 109; see also Wilson, "Is Nixon Fit to Be President?"
64. RN to Adela Rogers St. Johns, 11/28/52, VPP.
65. Nixon, *Memoirs*, 108–109.
66. *Ibid.*, 110.
67. *Ibid.*, 111.
68. Quoted in Brodie, *Nixon*, 306.
69. Quoted in Costello, *The Facts About Nixon*, 117.
70. Nixon, *Memoirs*, 112; Miller, *Plain Speaking*, 135, 178.
71. Los Angeles *Times*, 10/31/52.
72. Quoted in Costello, *The Facts About Nixon*, 116.
73. Ambrose, *Eisenhower*, Vol. I, 569.

CHAPTER FIFTEEN

1. For background on Bebe Rebozo, see Leinster, "Nixon's Friend Bebe," 19–24, and Brodie, *Nixon*, 340–344.
2. Brodie, *Nixon*, 340; Leinster, "Nixon's Friend Bebe," 24–25.
3. Leinster, "Nixon's Friend Bebe," 18.
4. *New York Times*, 11/16 and 11/17, 1952.
5. RN to Rebozo, 11/28/52, VPP.
6. Rebozo to Rose Mary Woods, 12/5/52, VPP.

7. Nixon memo, 1/6/53, Staff File, VPP.
8. John Oakley letter, 1/15/53, VPP.
9. *New York Times*, 1/21/53.
10. Minnich, Cabinet, 1/30/53.
11. This section on Pat is based on David, *Lonely Lady*, 110–113.
12. Costello, *The Facts About Nixon*, 233, 237.
13. *Ibid.*, 242; DE to RN, 8/8/53 and 9/4/53, EL.
14. Minnich, LLM, 4/30/53.
15. Minnich, Cabinet, 7/10/53.
16. *Ibid.*, 4/3/53.
17. *Ibid.*, 5/22/53.
18. Minnich, LLM, 5/12/53 and 5/25/53.
19. Minnich, Cabinet, 5/8/53.
20. Nixon to Eisenhower, 1/25/53, EL.
21. Minnich, Cabinet, 1/30,53 and 2/12/53.
22. Minnich, LLM, 5/12/53.
23. Ambrose, *Eisenhower*, Vol. II, 57–58.
24. *Ibid.*, 56, 59.
25. Minnich, Cabinet, 2/6/53.
26. Hughes, *The Ordeal of Power*, 94; Ambrose, *Eisenhower*, Vol II, 59–60.
27. Reeves, *McCarthy*, 464.
28. Mazo, *Nixon*, 144–145.
29. Reeves, *McCarthy*, 486; Nixon, *Memoirs*, 139.
30. Mazo, *Nixon*, 145–146; Ambrose, *Eisenhower*, Vol. II, 63.
31. Joseph McCarthy to DE, 5/20/53, VPP; Mazo, *Nixon*, 146.
32. Nixon, *Memoirs*, 139–140.
33. Reeves, *McCarthy*, 505.
34. Walter Trohan to RN, 2/10/53, VPP.
35. RN to St. Johns, 3/7/53, VPP.
36. *New York Times*, 3/31/53.
37. Minnich, Cabinet, 8/27/53.
38. *Ibid.*, 12/15/53.
39. *Ibid.*, 10/2/53.
40. *Ibid.*, 12/15/53.
41. Ambrose, *Eisenhower*, Vol. II, 136.
42. Brock to RN, 3/26/53, VPP.
43. Nixon memo, 2/2/54, VPP.
44. Reeves, *McCarthy*, 512–513.
45. Costello, *The Facts About Nixon*, 247.
46. Nixon interview, Dulles Oral History Project, Princeton; Mazo, *Nixon*, 203.
47. *New York Times*, 7/8/53.
48. Nixon, *Memoirs*, 120.
49. *Ibid.*, 119.
50. *Ibid.*, 121.
51. Cloake, *Templer*, 296–297; Nixon, *Memoirs*, 121–122.
52. Nixon, *Memoirs*, 122–125.
53. *Ibid.*, 126.
54. Thomas Dewey to RN, 11/9/53, and RN to Dewey, 12/1/53, VPP; New York *Herald Tribune*, 11/9/53.
55. Nixon, *Memoirs*, 127–129.
56. *Ibid.*, 129–130.

57. *Ibid.*, 130–131.
58. *Ibid.*, 131–133; Costello, *The Facts About Nixon*, 250.
59. Nixon, *Memoirs*, 133.
60. *U.S. News & World Report*, 12/4/53, 37–40.
61. *New York Times*, 12/14/53.
62. *New Republic*, 12/14/53, 22.
63. *U.S. News & World Report*, 12/4/53, 40.
64. *New York Times*, 12/15/53.
65. DE to Syngman Rhee, 1/2/54, EL.
66. *U.S. News & World Report*, 1/1/54, 68.
67. RN to Dewey, 12/1/53, VPP.
68. ACWD, 11/27/53; *New York Times*, 11/26/53.
69. HD, 4/10/54.
70. *Ibid.*, 4/9/54.
71. Mazo, *Nixon*, 147.
72. *Ibid.*, 147–148; *New York Times*, 12/31/53; Nixon, *Memoirs*, 140–141.

CHAPTER SIXTEEN

1. *New York Times*, 12/31/53 and 1/1/54.
2. Reeves, *McCarthy*, 534.
3. Ambrose, *Eisenhower*, Vol. II, 161.
4. Nixon, *Memoirs*, 141–142; Reeves, *McCarthy*, 551–552.
5. Greenstein, *Hidden-Hand Presidency*, 184–185.
6. Ambrose, *Eisenhower*, Vol. II, 162.
7. HD, 2/25/54.
8. *New York Times*, 2/25/54.
9. Nixon, *Memoirs*, 142–143.
10. *Ibid.*, 143–144.
11. Mazo, *Nixon*, 148.
12. Quoted in Brodie, *Nixon*, 297.
13. *New York Times*, 3/7/54.
14. Nixon, *Memoirs*, 144.
15. Quoted in Brodie, *Nixon*, 300.
16. HD, 7/16/54.
17. Minnich, LLM, 3/12/54.
18. Nixon, *Memoirs*, 145–146.
19. Ambrose, *Eisenhower*, Vol. II, 172.
20. Nixon's speech is reprinted in *New York Times*, 3/14/54.
21. See Minnich notes for various meetings in the spring of 1954, LLM.
22. Reeves, *McCarthy*, 578.
23. Greenstein, *Hidden-Hand Presidency*, and Ewald, *Who Killed Joe McCarthy?*
24. Mazo, *Nixon*, 150.
25. HD, 4/26/54.
26. *Ibid.*, 5/14/54.
27. Minnich, LLM, 5/17/54.
28. Reeves, *McCarthy*, 673.
29. Nixon, *Memoirs*, 149–150.
30. See phone conversation of 3/19/54, JFD Papers.

31. *Ibid.*, 3/29/54.
32. *Ibid.*, 8/3/54.
33. *Ibid.*, 10/5/54.
34. See Woods to Hillings, 3/6/54, VPP.
35. Minnich, LLM, 5/10/54.
36. C. D. Jackson to RN, 1/4/54 (misdated 1953), CDJ Records.
37. HD, 4/16/54.
38. Ambrose, *Eisenhower*, Vol. II, 178.
39. Dulles to DE, 4/23/54, EL.
40. DE-Dulles telephone conversation, 4/5/54, EL.
41. Nixon, *Memoirs*, 151.
42. New York *Herald Tribune*, 4/22/54.
43. Nixon, *Memoirs*, 152–153.
44. HD, 4/16/54.
45. *Ibid.*, 4/17/54.
46. Nixon, *Memoirs*, 153.
47. NSC Minutes, 4/29/54.
48. Nixon, *Memoirs*, 154.
49 *Ibid.*, 155.
50. *New York Times*, 4/6/54.
51. Mazo, *Nixon*, 139.
52. *Ibid.*, 152.
53. Jackson to RN, 3/9/54, CDJ Papers.
54. Minnich, Cabinet, 4/17/54.
55. *Ibid.*
56. *Ibid.*, 4/30/54.
57. Costello, *The Facts About Nixon*, 122.
58. ACWD, 6/29/54.
59. Brodie, *Nixon*, 336.
60. *Ibid.*
61. *New Republic*, 10/25/54.
62. Erskine, "Dick and Pat Nixon," 33.
63. Brodie, *Nixon*, 338.
64. *New York Times*, 1/10/54.
65. Mazo, *Nixon*, 139.
66. Quoted in Brodie, *Nixon*, 331. Brodie's Chapter XXIII, "Hidden Problems: The Early Surfacing," explores Nixon's relationship with Hutschnecker with some interesting speculations; a good corrective to laying too much stress on Hutschnecker is Mazlish, *In Search of Nixon*, Chapter 1.
67. Mazo, *Nixon*, 153; Costello, *The Facts About Nixon*, 123.
68. Costello, *The Facts About Nixon*, 124; Mazo, *Nixon*, 152.
69. Nixon, *Memoirs*, 159.
70. DE interview.
71. RN to Dan Thornton, 7/17/54, VPP.
72. Nixon, *Memoirs*, 160.
73. Mazo, *Nixon*, 156–157.
74. RN to Arthur Summerfield, 10/7/54, Summerfield Papers.
75. *New York Times*, 10/30/54.
76. Washington *Post*, 10/18/54.
77. Costello, *The Facts About Nixon*, 126.
78. *Ibid.*
79. *Ibid.*, 126–127.

80. *Ibid.*, 128.
81. *Ibid.*, 129.
82. *New York Times*, 10/30/54 and 11/27/54.
83. Mazo, *Nixon*, 154.
84. DE to RN, 9/29/54, EL.
85. Mazo, *Nixon*, 154–155.
86. Ambrose, *Eisenhower*, Vol. II, 218.
87. *New York Times*, 11/2/54.
88. Nixon, *Memoirs*, 163.
89. ACWD, 11/4/54.
90. RN to Roscoe Drummond, 11/9/54, VPP; see also RN to Robinson, 12/8/54, and Ralph de Toledano, 12/7/54, VPP.
91. RN to Lasky, 11/18/54, VPP.
92. Minnich, Cabinet, 11/5/54.
93. RN to Lasky, 11/18/54, VPP.
94. RN to Harvey Hancock, 12/28/54, VPP.
95. RN to Whittaker Chambers, 12/28/54, VPP.
96. Mazo, *Nixon*, 157.

Chapter Seventeen

1. Erskine, "Dick and Pat Nixon," 35.
2. Clements to RN, 1/6/55, VPP.
3. Nixon, *Six Crises*, 131.
4. Minnich, LLM, 1/11/55.
5. Minnich, Cabinet, 1/18/55; HD, 1/18/55.
6. Minnich, Cabinet, 2/4/55.
7. *Ibid.*, 4/22/55.
8. RN to Hillings—and scores of others—6/20/55, VPP
9. Bob Finch memo to RN, 6/4/55, VPP.
10. Chotiner to RN, 7/9/55, VPP.
11. Minnich, LLM, 1/25/55.
12. Schwartz, "Urban Freeways."
13. HD, 1/14/55.
14. See *New York Times* for February 1955 for coverage of the trip.
15. Minnich, Cabinet, 3/11/55.
16. *Ibid.*, 3/25/55; Minnich, LLM, 3/29/55; *New York Times*, 2/5/55, 2/25/55, and 2/27,55; RN to Henry Holland, 5/19/55, VPP.
17. *New York Times*, 3/6/55.
18. RN memo, 7/15/55, and DE to RN, 7/15/55, EL.
19. Minnich, Cabinet, 7/22/55.
20. ACWD, 11/18/54.
21. *Ibid.*, 12/1/54.
22. *Ibid.*, 5/25/55.
23. RN to Robert Cutler, 9/6/55, VPP.
24. Nixon, *Six Crises*, 131–133.
25. *Ibid.*, 133–135.
26. *Ibid.*, 138–140.
27. Nixon, *Memoirs*, 164–165.
28. Nixon, *Six Crises*, 143–144.
29. *New York Times*, 9/25/55.
30. Nixon, *Six Crises*, 144–145.

31. *New York Times*, 9/26/55.
32. Rovere, "Letter from Washington."
33. Ambrose, *Eisenhower*, Vol. II, 273.
34. C. D. Jackson to RN, 9/28/55, C. D. Jackson Papers.
35. Ambrose, *Eisenhower*, Vol II, 272.
36. *New York Times*, 9/29 and 9/30/55.
37. Minnich, Cabinet, 9/30/55.
38. Dulles-RN telephone conversation, 9/30/55, JFD Papers.
39. *New York Times*, 10/3/55.
40. Nixon, *Six Crises*, 155.
41. Hughes, *The Ordeal of Power*, 317.
42. Nixon, *Six Crises*, 150.
43. Beschloss, *Mayday*, Chapter 4.
44. Ambrose, *Eisenhower*, Vol. II, 275.
45. HD, 10/10/55.
46. Dulles memo of conversation, 10/11/55, JFD Papers.
47. Dulles-RN conversation, 10/17/55, JFD Papers.
48. Nixon, *Six Crises*, 152.
49. *Ibid.*
50. DE to RN, 10/18/55, EL.
51. HD, 12/13/55.
52. *Ibid.*, 12/14/55.
53. Ambrose, *Eisenhower*, Vol. II, 285; Nixon, *Six Crises*, 159.
54. Nixon, *Six Crises*, 154.
55. *Ibid.*, 160–162.
56. *Ibid.*, 161.
57. Quoted in Brodie, *Nixon*, 350.
58. Mazo, *Nixon*, 164.
59. Nixon, *Six Crises*, 161.

Chapter Eighteen

1. Milton S. Eisenhower interview.
2. Nixon, *Six Crises*, 161.
3. Costello, *The Facts About Nixon*, 152.
4. ACWD, 2/7/56; telephone calls, 2/10/56, ACWD; Ambrose, *Eisenhower*, Vol. II, 294.
5. Pre–press conference briefing, 1/25/56, EL.
6. Dulles memo, 2/9/56, JFD Papers.
7. ACWD, 2/9/56.
8. *Ibid.*, 2/13/56.
9. Quoted in Brodie, *Nixon*, 350.
10. Woods memo, 2/28/56, VPP.
11. *New York Times*, 2/4/56 and 2/18/56.
12. *Ibid.*, 1/18/56 and 2/14/56.
13. See RN to Gerald Ford, 1/12/56, VPP, and Costello, *The Facts About Nixon*, 148.
14. de Toledano to RN, 11/20/55, and RN to Soderstrom, 8/11/56, VPP.
15. Preinaugural Papers (1956), 266–267.
16. Mazo, *Nixon*, 164.
17. de Toledano to RN, 3/2/56, VPP.
18. PP (1956), 287, 289.

19. Mazo, *Nixon*, 165; Nixon, *Memoirs*, 170–171.
20. Nixon, *Memoirs*, 170–171.
21. George Whitney to DE, 3/9/56, EL.
22. DE to Whitney, 3/12/56, EL.
23. ACWD, 3/13/56.
24. *New York Times*, 3/11/56.
25. ACWD, 3/13/56.
26. Costello, *The Facts About Nixon*, 146; *New York Times*, 3/14/56.
27. Quoted in Nixon, *Memoirs*, 171–172.
28. Chotiner to RN, 1/24/56, VPP.
29. ACWD, 3/19/56.
30. *Ibid.*, 4/9/56.
31. Eisenhower, *Waging Peace*, 9.
32. Costello, *The Facts About Nixon*, 147.
33. Nixon, *Memoirs*, 172.
34. ACWD, 4/26/56.
35. Press conference, 4/26/56, VPP.
36. Quoted in Costello, *The Facts About Nixon*, 147–148.
37. "Mr. Chotiner's Clients," *The New Republic*, 5/21/56.
38. de Toledano phone call, 6/7/56, VPP.
39. H. R. Haldeman to RN, 5/22/56, VPP.
40. Loie Gaunt to Ray Arbuthnot, 5/26/56, VPP.
41. Sidney Weinberg phone call, 5/14/56, VPP; Costello, *The Facts About Nixon*, 148–149.
42. Nixon, *Memoirs*, 173.
43. See Dewey to Tom Ettinger, 6/27/56; John J. McCloy to George Humphrey, 7/3/56; Humphrey to RN, 7/9/56, VPP.
44. Mazo, *Nixon*, 168; Costello, *The Facts About Nixon*, 149.
45. Minnich, Cabinet, 4/27/56.
46. *New York Times*, 7/4/56.
47. *Ibid.*, 7/12/56.
48. *Ibid.*, 7/10/56.
49. *Ibid.*, 7/7/56.
50. Quoted in Mazo, *Nixon*, 187.
51. Quoted in Costello, *The Facts About Nixon*, 151.
52. Eisenhower, *Waging Peace*, 10.
53. Larson, *Eisenhower*, 9.
54. Mazo, *Nixon*, 173.
55. Stassen to RN, 7/23/56, VPP.
56. Mazo, *Nixon*, 173.
57. Nixon, *Memoirs*, 174.
58. Mazo, *Nixon*, 174.
59. *New York Times*, 7/24/56.
60. Eisenhower, *Waging Peace*, 10.
61. Costello, *The Facts About Nixon*, 150.
62. Mazo, *Nixon*, 176.
63. Adams, *Firsthand Report*, 240–241.
64. Phone calls, 7/27/56, EL.
65. Preinaugural Papers (1956), 625, 633.
66. Milton Eisenhower to RN, 8/6/56, VPP.
67. RN to Eisenhower, 8/17/56, VPP.
68. Stassen to RN, 8/16/56, VPP.
69. RN to Billy Graham, 8/16/56, VPP; *New York Times*, 10/3/56.

70. Ambrose, *Eisenhower*, Vol. II, 335.
71. *New York Times*, 8/21/56.
72. *Ibid.*, 8/23/56; Nixon, *Memoirs*, 175–176.
73. *New York Times*, 9/8/56.

CHAPTER NINETEEN

1. Nixon, *Memoirs*, 176–177.
2. Costello, *The Facts About Nixon*, 156.
3. *Ibid.*, 230; Merriman Smith interview, EL.
4. Phone calls, 9/25/56, EL.
5. Nixon, *Memoirs*, 177; Costello, *The Facts About Nixon*, 157.
6. Costello, *The Facts About Nixon*, 159.
7. *Ibid.*, 160.
8. *Ibid.*, 161.
9. *Ibid.*
10. Nixon, *Memoirs*, 179.
11. David Brinkley to Len Hall, 10/19/56, VPP.
12. Race Problem notes, 9/17/56, VPP.
13. Washington *Evening Star*, 9/26/56.
14. RN-Cronin conversation, 10/6/56, Cronin file, VPP.
15. *New York Times*, 10/19/56.
16. *Ibid.*
17. Quoted in Brodie, *Nixon*, 357.
18. RN to Bertha Rourke, 9/17/56, VPP.
19. Los Angeles *Times*, 11/3/56.
20. Costello, *The Facts About Nixon*, 161.
21. Nixon, *Memoirs*, 178.
22. Costello, *The Facts About Nixon*, 163.
23. *New York Times*, 10/5/56.
24. Quoted in Brodie, *Nixon*, 425.
25. *New York Times*, 10/5/56.
26. Divine, *Blowing on the Wind*, 93–95.
27. Ambrose, *Eisenhower*, Vol. II, 348.
28. *New York Times*, 10/4/56.
29. Divine, *Blowing on the Wind*, 100.
30. Telephone calls, 8/11/56, JFD Papers.
31. John Eisenhower, *Strictly Personal*, 189.
32. Telephone calls, 10/29/56, JFD Papers.
33. *Ibid.*, 10/31/56.
34. Nixon, *Memoirs*, 179.
35. *Ibid.*, 178.
36. Quoted in *ibid.*, 180.
37. Brodie, *Nixon*, 357.
38. Nixon, *Memoirs*, 180–181.
39. *New York Times*, 11/14/56 and 11/23/56.
40. RN to Arbuthnot, 12/15/56, VPP.
41. Carl Greenberg to RN, 11/12/56, VPP.
42. Telephone calls, 12/7/56, JFD Papers.
43. Nixon, *Memoirs*, 182.
44. *Ibid.*, 183.
45. Kornitzer interview with Julius Raab, VPP.

46. ACWD, 12/26/56.
47. *New York Times*, 1/2/57.
48. Minnich, LLM, 1/1/57.
49. RN to Cutler, 1/17/57, and Cutler to RN, 1/25/57, VPP.

CHAPTER TWENTY

1. *New York Times*, 1/27/57.
2. *Ibid.*, 6/4/57.
3. RN to Jack Drown, 4/3/57, VPP.
4. Ann Whitman call, 8/7/57; Pat to Dan Hendrickson, 11/25/57—both in Hendrickson file, VPP.
5. RN to Arthur Godfrey, 12/17/57, VPP.
6. Lewis Strauss to RN, 7/29/57; RN to Strauss, 8/3/57, VPP.
7. DE to RN, 10/2/57, VPP.
8. RN to Claude Dixon, 12/6/57, VPP.
9. *New York Times*, 12/9/57.
10. See Haldeman and Charles McWhorter files, VPP.
11. See for example Klein to RN, 12/12/57, VPP.
12. Jack Hughes to RN, 4/13/57, VPP.
13. Memos in Leland Kaiser file, VPP.
14. McWhorter to RN, 12/18/57, VPP.
15. Memo: "Favorites," 4/6/57, VPP.
16. RN to Staff, 12/4/57, VPP.
17. See the files on each man in VPP.
18. Dulles memcon, 2/2/57, JFD Papers.
19. *New York Times*, March 1957.
20. New York *Herald Tribune*, 3/6/57.
21. *Ibid.*
22. *New York Times*, 4/7/57.
23. Minnich, LLM, 7/2/57.
24. Martin Luther King to RN, 8/30/57, William Rogers Papers.
25. RN to Jacob Javits, 7/22/57, VPP.
26. Minnich, LLM, 8/6/57
27. *Ibid.*, 8/13/57.
28. RN to Clarence Mitchell, 9/19/57, VPP.
29. Minnich, LLM, 7/23/57.
30. *Ibid.*
31. New York *Herald Tribune*, 9/19/57; McWhorter to RN, 9/18/57, VPP.
32. RN to Bayard Ewing, 10/31/57, VPP.
33. RN to Robert LaVergne, 12/26/57, VPP.
34. DE to Meade Alcorn, 8/30/57, EL.
35. See RN to Steve Johnson, 5/1/57, VPP, for an example.
36. Dulles memcon, 2/2/57, JFD Papers.
37. See Sherman Adams to RN, 2/25/57, and RN to William Randolph Hearst, 4/3/57, VPP.
38. Dulles memcon, 9/2/57, JFD Papers.
39. Telephone calls, 9/3/57, JFD Papers.
40. Dulles memcon, 9/3/57, JFD Papers.
41. DE to RN, 9/3/57, EL.
42. Dulles memcon, 9/30/57, JFD Papers.

43. Ambrose, *Eisenhower*, Vol. II, 246.
44. RN to Strauss, 5/20/57, VPP.
45. Memo, 10/6/57, VPP.
46. Dulles memcon, 10/9/57, JFD Papers.
47. Telephone conversation, 10/15/57, JFD Papers.
48. *Ibid.*
49. Telephone calls, 11/15/57, JFD Papers.
50. Minnich, Cabinet, 10/11/57.
51. Memos, 10/14/57 and 10/23/57, between Jack Hughes and RN, VPP.
52. RN to Stanley Holt, 10/23/57, VPP.
53. Ambrose, *Eisenhower*, Vol II, 435.
54. RN to Arthur Larson, 11/6/57, VPP.
55. Ambrose, *Eisenhower*, Vol. II, 433.
56. For example, see Steve Dunn phone call, 10/21/57, VPP.
57. Telephone call from Finch, 4/26/57, VPP.
58. RN to Jorgensen, 8/20/57, VPP.
59. Call to Jorgensen, 8/30/57, VPP.
60. RN to Ray Moley, 9/19/57, VPP.
61. See RN to John Longionotti, 9/26/57, and to Lou Aragon, 10/2/57, VPP.
62. RN to Jack Warner, 10/29/57, VPP.
63. Minnich, Cabinet, 2/8/57.
64. Nixon, *Memoirs*, 184.
65. John Eisenhower, *Strictly Personal*, 196; Adams, *Firsthand Report*, 196–197.
66. *New York Times*, 11/28/57.
67. Telephone calls, 12/1/57, JFD Papers.
68. Telephone calls, 12/1/57, JFD Papers.
69. Dulles memo, 12/2/57, JFD Papers.
70. Bill Rogers to RN, 12/3/57, copy 2 of 2, William Rogers Papers.
71. Nixon, *Six Crises*, 177.
72. ACWD, 1/3/58.
73. DE to RN, 2/5/58, EL.
74. *U.S. News & World Report*, 3/7/58, part of a series on presidential disability.
75. Dulles memcon of conversation with RN, 2/8/58, JFD Papers.
76. *U.S. News & World Report*, 3/14/58.
77. PP (1958), 198.
78. DE to RN, 2/5/58, EL.

Chapter Twenty-One

1. RN to Rebozo, 1/22/58, VPP.
2. Memo, McWhorter to RN, 3/25/58, VPP.
3. RN to Bob Addie, 6/26/59, VPP.
4. Pete Howard to RN, 2/1/58, and RN to Howard, 2/5/58, VPP.
5. RN memo, 3/12/59, Kornitzer file, VPP.
6. RN to Earl Mazo, 1/2/59, VPP.
7. Telephone calls, Nora de Toledano, 12/23/59, VPP.
8. Pasadena *Star News*, 1/3/58.
9. RN to St. Johns, 1/31/58, VPP.

10. RN to Pegler, 1/2/58, VPP.
11. Memo, 8/18/58, VPP.
12. Telephone calls, 1/21/58, JFD Papers.
13. Minnich, LLM, 7/16/58.
14. Minnich, Cabinet, 3/21/58.
15. RN to John Dewicki, 3/12/58, VPP.
16. RN to Cutler, 4/23/58, VPP.
17. Dulles memcon, 2/8/58, JFD Papers.
18. Nixon, *Six Crises*, 186.
19. RN to Strauss, 4/8/58, VPP.
20. Los Angeles *Times*, 4/28/58.
21. *Ibid.*, 4/29/58; *New York Times*, 4/29/58.
22. Nixon, *Six Crises*, 188.
23. Los Angeles *Times*, 4/29/58.
24. *Ibid.*, 4/30/58.
25. *Ibid.*, 5/1/58.
26. *Ibid.*, 5/2/58.
27. Nixon, *Six Crises*, 191.
28. Los Angeles *Times*, 5/4/58.
29. *Ibid.*, 5/6/58.
30. *Ibid.*, 5/7/58.
31. Nixon, *Six Crises*, 194–198; New York *Herald Tribune*, 5/8/58.
32. Nixon, *Six Crises*, 199.
33. *Ibid.*, 201.
34. *New York Times*, 5/9/58.
35. Los Angeles *Times*, 5/8/58.
36. Brodie, *Nixon*, 366.
37. Los Angeles *Times*, 5/8/58.
38. Walters, *Silent Missions*, 323.
39. Mazo, *Nixon*, 214.
40. Los Angeles *Times*, 5/8/58.
41. Nixon, *Six Crises*, 204.
42. Los Angeles *Times*, 5/8/58.
43. *New York Times*, 5/9/58; Los Angeles *Times*, 5/8/58.
44. Nixon, *Six Crises*, 207.
45. Nixon, *Six Crises*, 209; Los Angeles *Times*, 5/9/68.
46. Los Angeles *Times*, 5/9/58.
47. *Ibid.*
48. Nixon, *Six Crises*, 210.
49. Mazo, *Nixon*, 216–217.
50. Los Angeles *Times*, 5/12/58.
51. *Ibid.*
52. *Ibid.*, 5/28/58.
53. Mazo, *Nixon*, 218.
54. Los Angeles *Times*, 5/15/58.
55. Nixon, *Six Crises*, 215.
56. Mazo, *Nixon*, 227.
57. *Ibid.*
58. *Ibid.*, 231.
59. Los Angeles *Times*, 5/25/58.
60. Mazo, *Nixon*, 231.
61. Los Angeles *Times*, 5/25/58.
62. Nixon, *Six Crises*, 218.

63. Walters, *Silent Missions*, 331–332.
64. Nixon, *Six Crises*, 219.
65. Walters, *Silent Missions*, 331.
66. Mazo, *Nixon*, 234.
67. Nixon, *Six Crises*, 220.
68. Walters, *Silent Missions*, 333.
69. Los Angeles *Times*, 5/25/58.
70. Mazo, *Nixon*, 238.
71. Los Angeles *Times*, 5/13/58.
72. *New York Times*, 5/14/58.
73. Mazo, *Nixon*, 242–243.
74. Washington *Post*, 5/16/58.
75. Los Angeles *Times*, 5/15/58.
76. Brodie, *Nixon*, 373.
77. Chotiner to RN, 5/15/58, VPP.
78. RN to Chotiner, 6/23/58, VPP.
79. Los Angeles *Times*, 5/21/58.
80. Quoted in Brodie, *Nixon*, 372.
81. *New York Times*, 5/18/58.

Chapter Twenty-Two

1. Mazo, *Nixon*, 273.
2. *Ibid.*, 267, 277.
3. *Ibid.*, 285–286.
4. Ambrose, *Eisenhower*, Vol. II, 488.
5. Joe Alsop to Berlin, 4/30/58, Alsop Papers, Library of Congress, with thanks to Michael Beschloss for bringing this to my attention.
6. McWhorter to RN, 3/4/58, VPP.
7. RN to Cronin, 8/21/58, VPP.
8. Mazo, *Nixon*, 284.
9. "Charlie from RN," 9/5/58, Anderson file, VPP.
10. RN to Cronin, 8/21/58, VPP.
11. Harvard speech, 9/6/58, VPP.
12. *Ibid.*
13. See RN to Bill Henry, 9/22/58, VPP.
14. RN to Henry Luce, 9/23/58, VPP.
15. Chotiner to RN, 9/22/58, VPP.
16. RN memo, 9/26/58, Palmer file, VPP.
17. Chotiner to RN, 9/18/58, VPP.
18. RN to Cronin, 8/21/58, VPP.
19. Ambrose, *Eisenhower*, Vol. II, 467.
20. Mazo, *Nixon*, 273.
21. See Bill Key file for the last two weeks in June 1958, VPP.
22. Costello, *The Facts About Nixon*, 278; Mazo, *Nixon*, 198.
23. RN notes, 7/15/58, ACWD.
24. Nixon, *Memoirs*, 195.
25. Telephone calls, 8/25/58, ACWD.
26. ACWD, 9/1/58.
27. Nixon, *Memoirs*, 196.
28. Telephone calls, 9/4/58, ACWD.
29. ACWD, 9/17/58.

30. MacArthur to RN, 3/27/58, VPP.
31. Nixon, *Memoirs*, 199.
32. *Ibid.*
33. Telephone calls, 8/22/58, JFD Papers.
34. "Radical Democrats," 10/19/58, Cronin file, VPP.
35. Memo, 10/20/58, Rebozo file, VPP.
36. RN to McWhorter, 8/20/58, VPP.
37. Mazo, *Nixon*, 280.
38. *Ibid.*, 281.
39. Nixon, *Memoirs*, 199.
40. Costello, *The Facts About Nixon*, 173.
41. *Ibid.*, 173–174.
42. *Ibid.*, 166–167.
43. Phillips, "Nixon in '58."
44. Statement, 9/27/58, VPP.
45. Costello, *The Facts About Nixon*, 290.
46. Telephone calls, 9/29/58, JFD Papers.
47. Mazo, *Nixon*, 200–201.
48. RN to Ernest Klein, 10/11/58; to Serge Korff, 10/13/58, VPP.
49. Mazo, *Nixon*, 201.
50. Costello, *The Facts About Nixon*, 169–170.
51. *Ibid.*, 170.
52. DE to RN, 10/16/58, EL.
53. *Ibid.*, 10/15/58.
54. Costello, *The Facts About Nixon*, 171–172.
55. *New York Times*, 10/26/58 and 10/29/58.
56. Dewey to RN, 10/24/58, VPP; *New York Times*, 10/25/58.
57. Quoted in Mazo, *Nixon*, 266.
58. Telephone callls, 11/5/58, JFD Papers.
59. Nixon, *Memoirs*, 200.
60. RN to Paul Dague, 11/7/58 VPP.
61. RN to Bayard Ewing, 11/7/58, VPP.
62. RN to Brooks Hays, 11/18/58, VPP.
63. McWhorter to RN memo, 12/2/58, VPP.
64. RN to McWhorter, 12/3/58, VPP.
65. Telephone calls, 11/13/58, EL.
66. *New York Times*, 11/13/58.
67. McWhorter to RN, 11/13/58, VPP.
68. RN to Charles Wilson, 12/29/58, VPP.
69. Barry Goldwater to RN, 12/16/58, VPP.
70. RN to Goldwater, 12/30/58, VPP.
71. See McWhorter memo to RN, 12/6/58, VPP.
72. New York *Herald Tribune*, 11/27/58.
73. New York *Times*, 11/28/58.
74. *Ibid.*, 11/30/58.
75. RN to Hillings, 12/9/58, VPP.
76. RN to Herb Klein, 12/10/58, VPP.

Chapter Twenty-Three

1. Sevareid, ed., *Candidates 1960*, 102.
2. ACWD, 6/11/59.

3. Minnich, LLM, 3/3/59.
4. Telephone calls, 1/24/59, JFD Papers.
5. Telephone calls, 3/4/59, CAHP.
6. See Willard Garvey file, VPP.
7. Minnich, Cabinet, 4/22/59.
8. Nixon, *Memoirs*, 201–202.
9. RN to Bill Baggs, 5/18/59, VPP.
10. Nixon, *Memoirs*, 202.
11. *New York Times*, 3/22/59.
12. RN to McWhorter memo, 3/23/59, VPP.
13. Phone calls, 1/15/59, JFD Papers.
14. Eisenhower, *Waging Peace*, 339.
15. Phone calls, 1/27/59, JFD Papers.
16. RN to Henry Luce, 2/13/59, VPP.
17. Nixon, *Memoirs*, 204.
18. Nixon, *Six Crises*, 240.
19. Nixon, *Memoirs*, 205.
20. *Life*, 6/8/59.
21. Brodie, *Nixon*, 379.
22. Nixon, *Six Crises*, 241.
23. Memcon, 7/22/59, EL.
24. RN to Robert E. Cushman, 7/17/59, VPP.
25. Haldeman to Finch, undated, VPP.
26. *New York Times*, 7/24/59.
27. Nixon, *Six Crises*, 245.
28. *New York Times*, 7/25/59.
29. Nixon, *Memoirs*, 206–207.
30. *New York Times*, 7/25/59.
31. de Toledano, "Notes," Toledano file, VPP.
32. *New York Times*, 7/25/59.
33. de Toledano, "Notes," VPP.
34. RN, "Remarks," 7/24/59, VPP.
35. Nixon, *Six Crises*, 261.
36. Nixon, *Memoirs*, 210.
37. Milton Eisenhower interview.
38. Nixon, *Six Crises*, 268, 271.
39. *Ibid.*, 272.
40. RN to DE, 7/26/59, EL.
41. *London Telegraph*, 9/20/59.
42. Ambrose, *Eisenhower*, Vol. II, 535–536.
43. RN to DE, 7/31/59, EL.
44. *New York Times*, 7/27/59; *Time*, 8/10/59; *Newsweek*, 8/3/59.
45. *New York Times*, 7/27/59 and 8/1/59.
46. Nixon, *Memoirs*, 211.
47. Herb Klein to Kornitzer, 12/7/59, VPP.
48. Nixon, *Six Crises*, 279.
49. There is a copy of the speech in VPP.
50. *New York Times*, 8/2/59.
51. *Ibid.*, 8/5/59.
52. Nixon, *Six Crises*, 281.
53. *Ibid.*, 283–285.
54. RN to DE, 8/4/59, EL.
55. Nixon, *Memoirs*, 213.

56. Ronald Reagan to RN, 9/7/59, VPP.
57. Nixon, *Memoirs*, 214.
58. *New York Times*, 8/6/59.
59. Memcon, 8/5/59, EL.

CHAPTER TWENTY-FOUR

1. Minnich, Cabinet, 11/27/59.
2. *Ibid.*, 6/22/59.
3. Minnich, LLM, 6/2/60.
4. *Ibid.*, 3/10/59.
5. *Ibid.*, 6/9/60.
6. McWhorter to RN, 3/29/60, VPP.
7. RN to Eugene Pulliam, 5/24/60, VPP.
8. RN to Ford, Melvin Laird, et al., 5/19/60, VPP.
9. RN to Greenberg, 5/11/59, VPP.
10. RN to Elliott, 1/2/59, VPP.
11. RN to Jackie Robinson, 6/3/60, VPP.
12. McWhorter to RN, 3/28/59, VPP.
13. J. Don Hughes to RN, 1/10/59, VPP.
14. Alcorn to RN, 2/20/59, VPP.
15. Finch to RN, 2/28/59, VPP.
16. McWhorter to RN, 2/4/59, VPP.
17. *Ibid.*, 6/6/59, VPP.
18. *Ibid.*, 8/17/59, VPP.
19. *Ibid.*, 8/27/59, VPP.
20. See the various files in VPP.
21. McWhorter to RN, 6/3/59, VPP.
22. "Notes on Rockefeller's North Dakota Trip," 6/4/60, VPP.
23. DE to RN, 8/18/59, EL.
24. Telephone calls, 6/11/60, ACWD.
25. DE to Oveta Hobby, 5/9/60, VPP.
26. Nixon Club Newsletter, number 2, April 1960, VPP.
27. See C. H. Duell—of Duell, Sloan & Pearce, publishers—to Finch, 3/5/60, VPP.
28. RN to Finch, 7/14/60, VPP.
29. RN to Reagan, 6/18/59, VPP.
30. Reagan to RN, 6/27/59, VPP.
31. RN to Reagan, 7/6/59, VPP.
32. See RN to Thomas Buckley, 9/29/59, VPP.
33. RN to Drown, 6/26/59, VPP.
34. Montgomery, "Christmas at the Nixons'," 46.
35. *Ibid.*, 46–51.
36. Robert Spindell to RN, 8/17/59, VPP.
37. RN to James Stahlman, 2/19/59, VPP.
38. *New York Times*, 2/6/59.
39. Guest List, 9/25/59, VPP.
40. RN to Corrin Strong, 12/30/59, VPP.
41. RN to John Bricker, 4/18/60, VPP.
42. Minnich, LLM, 4/5/60.
43. RN to John Irwin, 5/19/60, VPP.
44. RN to Milton Eisenhower, 7/13/60, VPP.

45. RN to George Sokolsky, 7/13/60, VPP.
46. RN to Dillon Anderson, 7/60, VPP.
47. Reagan to RN, 7/15/60, VPP.
48. ACWD, 7/29/59.
49. Graham to RN, 6/21/60, VPP.
50. Telephone calls, 7/19/60, ACWD.
51. Ambrose, *Eisenhower*, Vol. II, 596–597.
52. RN to Sokolsky, 7/13/60, VPP.
53. Minnich, LLM, 5/10/60.
54. Nixon, "Cuba, Castro and John F. Kennedy," 288.
55. Ambrose, *Eisenhower*, Vol. II, 557.
56. RN to Cushman, 4/10/60, VPP.
57. Wyden, *Bay of Pigs*, 29–30.
58. Ambrose, *Eisenhower*, Vol. II, 557–558.
59. Nixon, *Six Crises*, 314.
60. Eisenhower, *Waging Peace*, 595.
61. William Robinson Diary, 7/18 to 7/25/60, WRP.
62. Telephone calls, 7/24/60, ACWD.
63. Eisenhower, *Waging Peace*, 596.
64. Woods to RN, 7/22/60, VPP.
65. Ford, *A Time to Heal*, 73; White, *The Making of the President*, 206.
66. RN to Clare Boothe Luce, 9/2/60, VPP.
67. Goldwater, *With No Apologies*, 119.
68. *New York Times*, 7/29/60.
69. Quoted in Brodie, *Nixon*, 423.

Chapter Twenty-Five

1. Earl Blaik to RN, 7/31/60, VPP.
2. Ambrose, *Eisenhower*, Vol. II, 597.
3. *Ibid.*, 599.
4. Nixon, *Six Crises*, 321.
5. See DE to Robinson, 9/21/66, WRP.
6. Slater, *The Ike I Knew*, 230–231.
7. Eisenhower, *Waging Peace*, 598–599.
8. Nixon, *Six Crises*, 323.
9. The telegrams are in VPP.
10. Ambrose, *Eisenhower*, Vol. II, 604.
11. *Ibid.*, 600–601.
12. Nixon, *Six Crises*, 320.
13. *Ibid.*, 325.
14. Woods to Irwin, 8/25/60, VPP; Klein, *Making It Perfectly Clear*, 98.
15. Minutes of meeting, 8/13/60, VPP.
16. RN to Arthur Burns, 8/19/60, VPP.
17. Nixon, *Six Crises*, 408.
18. Cushman to RN, 9/1/60, and RN to Hannah, 9/6/60, VPP.
19. William Foster to RN, 9/15/60, and Cushman to RN, 9/17/60, VPP.
20. Stanley McCaffrey memo, 9/2/60, VPP.
21. Cannon, *Reagan*, 96.
22. Roy Shaffer to Jack Porter, 8/6/60, VPP.

23. Burns to RN, 8/6/60, VPP.
24. Nixon, *Six Crises*, 326.
25. RN to Blaik, 9/8/60, VPP.
26. ACWD, 8/30/60.
27. Nixon, *Six Crises*, 327–328.
28. Campbell, et al., *Elections*, 84.
29. Cited in Parmet, *JFK*, 40.
30. RN to Clare Boothe Luce, 9/7/60, VPP.
31. Graham to RN, 9/24/60, VPP.
32. *New York Times*, 9/12/60.
33. Parmet, *JFK*, 42–43.
34. Nixon, *Six Crises*, 366.
35. *New York Times*, 10/22/60.
36. Nixon, *Six Crises*, 329.
37. *Ibid.*, 331–332.
38. Haldeman, *The Ends of Power*, 75.
39. White, *Making of the President*, 300.
40. *Ibid.*, 303.
41. Quoted in Brodie, *Nixon*, 421.
42. Alsop to Paul Miller, 10/6/60, Alsop Papers.
43. Beck, "Necessary Lies, Hidden Truths," 39–43.
44. Nixon, *Six Crises*, 336–337.
45. White, *Making of the President*, 286.
46. St. Johns to RN, 9/26/60, VPP.
47. White, *Making of the President*, 285.
48. Nixon, *Six Crises*, 337.
49. White, *Making of the President*, 289.
50. *Ibid.*, 275–276.
51. Kraus, ed., *The Great Debates*, 348–349.
52. *Ibid.*, 351–353.
53. *Ibid.*, 354.
54. *Ibid.*, 357.
55. *Ibid.*, 364–365.
56. *Ibid.*, 367–368.
57. Nixon, *Six Crises*, 340–341.
58. Ralph Barstow to RN, 9/27/60, VPP.
59. Jack Danciger to RN, 9/27/60, VPP.
60. Porter to Klein, 9/28/60, VPP.
61. Brodie, *Nixon*, 427.
62. Nixon, *Six Crises*, 341.
63. ACWD, 10/14/60.
64. Finch to RN, 9/27/60, VPP.
65. Barstow to RN, 9/27/60, VPP.
66. *New York Times*, 7/31/60.
67. *Ibid.*, 9/29/60.
68. *Ibid.*, 10/22/60.
69. *Ibid.*, 10/10/60.
70. *Ibid.*, 10/8/60.
71. Kraus, ed., *The Great Debates*, 370.
72. *Ibid.*, 372–373.
73. *Ibid.*, 376.
74. *Ibid.*, 380–381.
75. *Ibid.*, 387–388.

76. *Ibid.*, 384.
77. *Ibid.*, 388–389.
78. Notes, F. A. Seaton Papers.
79. Transcript of Lodge's TV remarks, 10/16/60, Seaton Papers.
80. Statement, 10/18/60, Seaton Papers.
81. Kraus, ed., *The Great Debates*, 391.
82. Ambrose, *Eisenhower*, Vol. II, Chapter Ten.
83. Kraus, ed., *The Great Debates*, 396.
84. *Ibid.*, 399.
85. *Ibid.*, 402–403.
86. *Ibid.*, 397.

Chapter Twenty-Six

1. Quoted in Schlesinger, *A Thousand Days*, 64.
2. Parmet, *JFK*, 18.
3. Brodie, *Nixon*, Chapter XI.
4. Kraus, ed., *The Great Debates*, 397.
5. Sorensen, *Kennedy*, 180.
6. *Ibid.*, 182.
7. White, *Making of the President*, 298.
8. *Ibid.*, 301.
9. *Ibid.*, 302.
10. Sorensen, *Kennedy*, 184.
11. *Ibid.*, 179.
12. White, *Making of the President*, 302.
13. *New York Times*, 9/29/60.
14. White, *Making of the President*, 304.
15. Kraus, ed., *The Great Debates*, 413.
16. Wyden, *Bay of Pigs*, 68.
17. RN to Hall, 10/5/60, VPP.
18. Beck, "Necessary Lies, Hidden Truths," 49.
19. Wyden, *Bay of Pigs*, 67; Beck, "Necessary Lies, Hidden Truths," 54.
20. Beck, "Necessary Lies, Hidden Truths," 52–54.
21. *Ibid.*; *New York Times*, 10/19/60.
22. Nixon, *Six Crises*, 353–354.
23. Beck, "Necessary Lies, Hidden Truths," 50.
24. Kraus, ed., *The Great Debates*, 417.
25. *Ibid.*, 420–421.
26. *Ibid.*, 429.
27. Nixon, *Six Crises*, 357.
28. Sorensen, *Kennedy*, 213.
29. Kraus, ed., *The Great Debates*, 157–160.
30. Beck, "Necessary Lies, Hidden Truths," 50–53.
31. *Ibid.*
32. Nixon, *Six Crises*, 362–363.
33. Brodie, *Nixon*, 431; Parmet, *JFK*, 55.
34. *New York Times*, 10/27/60; Brodie, *Nixon*, 436–437.
35. *New York Times*, 10/28/60.
36. *Ibid.*, 11/4/60.
37. *Ibid.*
38. Phelan, "The Nixon Family and the Hughes Loan," 21.

39. Schuyler interview, CSF.
40. Dietrich and Thomas, *Howard*, 283–284.
41. Phelan, "The Nixon Family and the Hughes Loan," 22; Donald's six-page statement is in F. A. Seaton Papers.
42. Brodie, *Nixon*, 437.
43. J. Don Hughes to RN, 1/23/59, VPP.
44. *New York Times*, 10/29/60.
45. White, *Making of the President*, 309.
46. Nixon, *Memoirs*, 222.
47. *Ibid.*
48. ACWD, 11/5/60.
49. Parmet, *JFK*, 17.
50. *Ibid.*, 18.
51. ACWD, 11/8/60; *New York Times*, 11/7/60.
52. Nixon, *Six Crises*, 365.
53. *Ibid.*, 367–368.
54. RN to Rogers, 11/4/60, VPP.
55. RN to Arthur Flemming, 11/3/60, F. A. Seaton Papers.
56. RN to Rogers, 11/1/60, F. A. Seaton Papers.
57. RN to Seaton, 11/1/60, F. A. Seaton Papers.
58. *Ibid.*
59. Walter Thayer to Finance Committee, Volunteers for Nixon-Lodge, 11/5/60, VPP.
60. White, *Making of the President*, 311.
61. Nixon, *Six Crises*, 372.
62. White, *Making of the President*, 307.
63. Dewey to RN, 11/8/60, VPP.
64. Nixon, *Six Crises*, 377–379.
65. *Ibid.*, 398.
66. Ambrose, *Eisenhower*, Vol. II, 604.
67. Nixon, *Six Crises*, 413.
68. *Ibid.*, 392.
69. *New York Times*, 12/25/60.
70. Nixon, *Memoirs*, 227–228.

Chapter Twenty-Seven

1. Costello, *The Facts About Nixon*, 237–239.
2. Quoted in Ambrose, *Eisenhower*, Vol. II, 600.
3. Quoted in Brodie, *Nixon*, 473.
4. Alsop, *Nixon and Rockefeller*, 195.
5. Kornitzer interview with Rogers, 3/27/59, VPP.
6. Nixon, *Memoirs*, 198.
7. Eisenhower, Julie Nixon, "My Mother," 13.
8. Mazo, *Nixon*, 288.
9. Costello, *The Facts About Nixon*, 283, 290.
10. Nixon, *Memoirs*, 226.

Chapter Twenty-Eight

1. Robert Abplanalp to RN, 1/13/61, VPP.
2. RN to Walter Annenberg, 6/2/61, VPP.

3. RN to James Stewart, 4/26/61, VPP.
4. Nixon, *Memoirs*, 231.
5. DE to RN, 4/25/61, EL.
6. See, for example, RN to Bruce Barton, 9/15/61, VPP.
7. RN to MacArthur, 1/15/61, VPP.
8. RN to Dewey, 1/15/61, VPP.
9. RN to Hearst, 1/3/61, VPP.
10. RN to DE, 1/15/61, VPP.
11. RN to Whitman, 1/15/61, VPP.
12. DE to RN, 1/19/61, EL.
13. Brodie, *Nixon*, 448–449; Los Angeles *Times*, 9/28/61.
14. Mazo, "The Nixons Now," 71.
15. Nixon, *Memoirs*, 232.
16. McWhorter to RN, 1/3/61, VPP.
17. RN to McWhorter, 1/14/61, VPP.
18. RN to Flemming, 4/28/61, VPP.
19. These letters, all dated 4/11/61, are in the appropriate folders in VPP.
20. Nixon, *Memoirs*, 233.
21. *Ibid.*, 233–235.
22. Parmet, *JFK*, 177.
23. RN to Don Pearlberg, 8/17/61, VPP.
24. RN to S. Romualdi, 7/31/61, VPP.
25. Nixon, *Memoirs*, 235.
26. *New York Times*, 5/6/61.
27. *Ibid.*, 5/10/61.
28. RN to Bill Sprague, 5/15/61, VPP.
29. John Ehrlichman to RN, 4/6/61, VPP.
30. *New York Times*, 6/16/61.
31. Mazo, "The Nixons Now," 164.
32. *New York Times*, 9/5/61.
33. DE to RN, 9/5/61, and RN to DE, 9/6/61, EL.
34. Mazo, "The Nixons Now," 164.
35. Brodie, *Nixon*, 451.
36. Deryl Hart to RN, 3/22/61, and T. L. Perkins to RN, 3/9/61, VPP.
37. RN to Perkins, 3/22/61, VPP; Greensboro *Daily News*, 6/15/61.
38. Nixon, *Six Crises*, xi.
39. Telephone call, 1/9/61, VPP.
40. Nixon, *Six Crises*, xi–xii.
41. *Ibid.*
42. Parmet, *Jack*, 330–333.
43. RN to Jessamyn West, 5/19/55, VPP.
44. See the Hess file in VPP.
45. RN to DE, 2/20/62, EL.
46. RN to St. Johns, 8/16/61, VPP.
47. RN to David Sarnoff, 8/10/61, VPP.
48. See the appropriate files in VPP.
49. RN to Graham, 5/31/61, VPP.
50. See Graham file in VPP; Nixon, *Six Crises*, 365.
51. Mazo, "The Nixons Now," 164.
52. RN to Cronin, 8/26/61, VPP.
53. Nixon, *Memoirs*, 236.
54. Nixon, *Six Crises*, xiv.

55. There is a copy of his cover letter, dated 3/13/62, in almost every file in VPP.

56. *New York Times*, 4/1/62.

57. Brodie, *Nixon*, 445.

58. San Francisco, *Chronicle*, 4/1/62.

59. New York *Herald Tribune*, 4/1/62.

60 *Christian Century*, 6/6/62.

61. *New Republic*, 4/9/62.

62. Haldeman, *The Ends of Power*, 49.

63. Weinstein, *Perjury*, 554.

64. Nixon, *Six Crises*, 354.

65. *New York Times*, 3/21/62.

66. These telephone conversations, 3/20/62, are in EL.

67. Parmet, *JFK*, 46–50.

68. Mazo, "The Nixons Now," 164.

69. Weinstein, *Perjury*, 538.

70. Chambers to RN, 2/2/61, VPP.

71. Nixon, *Memoirs*, 237.

72. *Ibid.*, 239.

73. Brodie, *Nixon*, 451.

74. Mazo, "The Nixons Now," 166.

75. *New York Times*, 11/17/61.

76. RN to H. A. Andresen, 7/18/61, VPP.

77. *New York Times*, 2/26/61.

78. RN to MacKinnon, 7/18/61, VPP.

79. RN to DE, 7/25/61, EL.

80. Klein to RN, 8/7/61, VPP.

81. Nixon, *Memoirs*, 238.

82. DE to RN, 8/8/61, VPP.

83. DE to RN, 9/11/61, EL.

84. Brodie, *Nixon*, 454.

85. Nixon, *Memoirs*, 240.

86. *New York Times*, 9/28/61.

87. See RN to John Denson, 10/10/71, and St. Johns to RN, 10/12/61, VPP.

88. RN to Peter Andre, 11/16/61, VPP.

89. The Guest List is in VPP.

90. Nixon, *Memoirs*, 237.

Chapter Twenty-Nine

1. Wicker, "Nixon Starts Over," 106.

2. *Ibid.*, 108.

3. Nixon, *Memoirs*, 243.

4. Brodie, *Nixon*, 459.

5. *Ibid.*, 454.

6. Wicker, "Nixon Starts Over," 106.

7. Brodie, *Nixon*, 459.

8. Wicker, "Nixon Starts Over," 106.

9. *Ibid.*, 17.

10. See RN to Frank Jameson, 4/2/62, and to Abplanalp, 4/2/62, VPP.

11. *New York Times*, 5/9/62.

12. Quoted in Brodie, *Nixon*, 448.
13. Wicker, "Nixon Starts Over," 108.
14. Woods to George Fuller, 8/10/62, VPP.
15. Ehrlichman, *Witness to Power*, 29.
16. DE to RN, 2/20/62, EL.
17. John Eisenhower to RN, 6/14/62, VPP.
18. Fuller to Woods, 8/6/62, VPP.
19. RN to Justin Dart, 2/13/62, VPP.
20. RN to Alger Chapman, 2/19/62, VPP.
21. DE to RN, 3/24/62, EL.
22. See the appropriate files in VPP.
23. RN to Howard Jarvis, 7/24/61, VPP.
24. See Chotiner fiile, VPP, for April 1962.
25. Al Moscow to RN, 4/18/62, VPP.
26. See NAACP file, VPP.
27. Statement, 3/62, in Robert Welch file, VPP.
28. Fresno *Bee*, 3/7/62.
29. RN to DE, 3/5/62, VPP.
30. Hillings to RN, 3/5/62, VPP.
31. RN to Hagerty, 5/7/62, VPP.
32. Moscow to RN, 7/18/62, VPP.
33. RN to Richard Guylay, 8/15/62, VPP.
34. RN to Herb Brownell, 8/15/62, VPP.
35. Brodie, *Nixon*, 452.
36. San Francisco *Chronicle*, 10/10/62.
37. Los Angeles *Times*, 10/9/62; Brodie, *Nixon*, 460.
38. *Newsweek*, 10/29/62.
39. RN to Bryce Harlow and Robert Humphreys, 8/23/62, VPP.
40. RN to Burns, 8/27/62, VPP.
41. Brodie, *Nixon*, 457–458.
42. Klein, *Making It Perfectly Clear*, 139.
43. *Ibid.*, 59.
44. *Ibid.*, 144.
45. Haldeman telegram to Fair Campaign Practices Committee, 8/10/62, VPP; Ehrlichman, *Witness to Power*, 31.
46. Witcover, *Resurrection of Richard Nixon*, 29.
47. See Klein statement enclosed in a RN to Humphreys letter of 9/17/62, VPP.
48. Hillings to RN, 10/6/61, VPP.
49. San Francisco *Chronicle*, 10/2/62; Los Angeles *Times*, 10/2/62; Los Angeles *Herald Examiner*, 10/2/62; Nixon, *Memoirs*, 242–243.
50. Los Angeles *Times*, 11/6/62.
51. *Ibid.*, 10/6/62; *New York Times*, 10/5/62.
52. Nixon, *Memoirs*, 243.
53. Klein, *Making It Perfectly Clear*, 63.
54. Los Angeles *Times*, 10/3/62.
55. Los Angeles *Herald Examiner*, 11/5/62.
56. San Francisco *Chronicle*, 10/25/62.
57. Los Angeles *Times*, 10/26/62.
58. *Ibid.*, 10/31/62
59. Los Angeles *Herald Examiner*, 11/3/62.
60. See Los Angeles *Herald Examiner*, Los Angeles *Times*, and San Francisco *Chronicle* for 11/6/62.

61. Witcover, *Resurrection of Richard Nixon*, 31.
62. Klein, *Making It Perfectly Clear*, 53.
63. *Ibid.*, 56; Nixon, *Memoirs*, 244.
64. Nixon, *Memoirs*, 244–245.
65. Klein, *Making It Perfectly Clear*, 56.
66. Brodie, *Nixon*, 461–462.
67. Los Angeles *Times*, 11/8/82.
68. There are a number of "complete texts" of the conference; there are some variations in them; I used *The New York Times* version of 11/8/62.
69. Wills, *Nixon Agonistes*, 416.
70. *New York Times*, 11/9/62.
71. Graham to RN, 11/11/62, VPP.
72. Nixon, *Memoirs*, 246.
73. *New York Times*, 11/8/62.
74. Dewey to RN, 11/15/62, VPP.
75. Los Angeles *Times*, 11/15/62.
76. Witcover, *Resurrection of Richard Nixon*, 32.

BIBLIOGRAPHY

Abrahamsen, David. *Nixon vs. Nixon: An Emotional Tragedy.* New York: Farrar, Straus and Giroux, 1977.

Adams, Sherman. *Firsthand Report: The Story of the Eisenhower Administration.* New York: Harper & Brothers, 1961.

Alsop, Stewart. *Nixon and Rockefeller: A Double Portrait.* Garden City, N.Y.: Doubleday, 1960.

Ambrose, Stephen E. *Eisenhower: Soldier, General of the Army, President-Elect,* Vol. I. New York: Simon and Schuster, 1983.

———. *Eisenhower: The President,* Vol. II. New York: Simon & Schuster, 1984.

———. *Rise to Globalism: American Foreign Policy Since 1938.* New York: Penguin Books, 1985.

Andrews, Bert, and Peter Andrews. *A Tragedy of History.* Washington, D.C.: Luce, 1962.

Arnold, William A. *Back When It All Began: The Early Years.* New York: Vantage Press, 1975.

Beck, Kent M. "Necessary Lies, Hidden Truths: Cuba in the 1960 Campaign." *Diplomatic History,* Vol. 8, Winter 1984, pp. 37–59.

Beschloss, Michael. *Mayday.* New York: Harper & Row, 1986.

Brashear, Ernest. "Who Is Richard Nixon?" *New Republic,* September 1, 1952; September 8, 1952.

Brodie, Fawn M. *Richard Nixon: The Shaping of His Character.* Cambridge: Harvard University Press, 1983.

Bullock, Paul. *Jerry Voorhis: The Idealist as Politician.* New York: Vantage Press, 1978.

———. "Rabbits and Radicals, Richard Nixon's 1946 Campaign Against Jerry Voorhis." *Southern California Quarterly,* Fall 1973.

Campbell, Angus, et al. *Elections and the Political Order.* New York: John Wiley & Sons, 1966.

Cannon, Lou. *Reagan.* New York: G. P. Putnam's Sons, 1982.

Chambers, Whittaker. *Witness.* New York: Random House, 1952

Clawson, Kenneth. "A Loyalist's Memoir." Washington *Post*, October 9, 1979.

Clemens, Cyril. "Mark Twain and Richard M. Nixon." *Hobbies*, November 1970.

Cloake, John. *Templer: Tiger of Malaya*. London: Harrap, 1985.

Conn, Virginia. "Nixon—the Naval Officer." *Navy Magazine*, January 1969.

Costello, William. *The Facts About Nixon: An Unauthorized Biography*. New York: Viking Press, 1960.

David, Lester. *The Lonely Lady of San Clemente: The Story of Pat Nixon*. New York: Berkley Publishing Corp. edition, 1978.

de Toledano, Ralph. *One Man Alone: Richard Nixon*. New York: Funk & Wagnalls, 1969.

Dietrich, Noah, and Bob Thomas. *Howard: The Amazing Mr. Hughes*. Greenwich, Conn.: Fawcett, 1977.

Divine, Robert A. *Blowing on the Wind: The Nuclear Test Ban Debate*. New York: Oxford University Press, 1978.

Ehrlichman, John. *Witness to Power: The Nixon Years*. New York: Simon & Schuster, 1982.

Eisenhower, Dwight D. *Mandate for Change*. Garden City, N.Y.: Doubleday, 1963.

———. *Waging Peace*. Garden City, N.Y.: Doubleday, 1965.

Eisenhower, John S. D. *Strictly Personal*. Garden City, N.Y.: Doubleday, 1974.

Eisenhower, Julie Nixon. "My Mother." *Newsweek*, May 24, 1976.

Erskine, Helen. "Dick and Pat Nixon: The Team on Ike's Team." *Collier's*, July 9, 1954.

Ewald, William B. *Who Killed Joe McCarthy?* New York: Simon & Schuster, 1984.

Ford, Gerald. *A Time to Heal*. New York: Harper & Row, 1979.

Gardner, Richard. "Richard Nixon, The Story of a Fighting Quaker." Unpublished manuscript, Whittier College Library.

Goldwater, Barry. *With No Apologies*. New York: William Morrow, 1979.

Goodman, Walter. *The Committee*. New York: Farrar, Straus and Giroux, 1968.

Greenstein, Fred I. *The Hidden-Hand Presidency: Eisenhower as Leader*. New York: Basic Books, 1982.

Griffith, Robert. *The Politics of Fear: Joseph R. McCarthy and the Senate*. Lexington: University Press of Kentucky, 1970.

Haldeman, H. R., with Joseph DiMona. *The Ends of Power*. New York: Times Books, 1978.

Hoyt, Edwin P. *The Nixons: An American Family*. New York: Random House, 1972.

Hughes, Emmet John. *The Ordeal of Power: A Political Memoir of the Eisenhower Years*. New York: Atheneum, 1963.

Jackson, Donald. "The Young Nixon." *Life*, November 6, 1970.

Keogh, James. *This Is Nixon*. New York: G. P. Putnam's Sons, 1956.

Klein, Herbert G. *Making It Perfectly Clear*. Garden City, N.Y.: Doubleday, 1980.

Kornitzer, Bela. *The Real Nixon: An Intimate Biography*. Chicago: Rand McNally, 1960.

Kraus, Sidney, ed. *The Great Debates: Kennedy vs. Nixon, 1960*. Bloomington: Indiana University Press, 1962.

Larson, Arthur. *Eisenhower: The President Nobody Knew.* New York: Charles Scribner's Sons, 1968.

Leinster, Colin. "Nixon's Friend Bebe." *Life,* July 31, 1970.

Levitt, Morton, and Michael Levitt. *A Tissue of Lies: Nixon vs. Hiss.* New York: McGraw-Hill, 1979.

Mazlish, Bruce. *In Search of Nixon: A Psychohistorical Inquiry.* Baltimore: Penguin Books, 1972.

Mazo, Earl. "A Family's Comeback from Defeat: The Nixons Now." *Good Housekeeping,* March 1962.

———. *Richard Nixon: A Political and Personal Portrait.* New York: Harper & Brothers, 1959.

———, and Stephen Hess. *Nixon: A Political Portrait.* New York: Harper & Row, 1968.

Meredith, Scott. "Richard the Actor." *Ladies Home Journal,* September 1975.

Miller, Merle. *Plain Speaking: An Oral Biography of Harry S. Truman.* New York: Putnam, 1974.

Montgomery, Ruth. "Christmas at the Nixons'." *Cosmopolitan,* December 1959.

Morgan, Lael. "Whittier '34: Most Likely to Succeed." Los Angeles *Times,* May 10, 1970.

Nixon, Patricia Ryan (as told to Joe Alex Morris). "I Say He's a Wonderful Guy." *Saturday Evening Post,* September 6, 1952.

Nixon, Richard. "Cuba, Castro and John F. Kennedy." *Reader's Digest,* November 1964.

———. *The Memoirs of Richard Nixon.* New York: Grosset & Dunlap, 1978.

———. *Six Crises.* Garden City, N.Y.: Doubleday, 1962.

Parmet, Herbert S. *Jack: The Struggles of John F. Kennedy.* New York: Dial Press, 1980.

———. *JFK: The Presidency of John F. Kennedy.* New York: Dial Press, 1983.

Phelan, James R. "The Nixon Family and the Hughes Loan." *The Reporter,* August 16, 1962.

Phillips, Cabell. "Nixon in '58." *New York Times Magazine,* October 26, 1958.

Reeves, Thomas C. *The Life and Times of Joe McCarthy.* New York: Stein and Day, 1982.

Reinhard, David W. *The Republican Right Since 1945.* Lexington: University of Kentucky Press, 1985.

Rovere, Richard. "Letter from Washington." *The New Yorker,* September 29, 1955.

Schlesinger, Arthur M., Jr. *A Thousand Days: John F. Kennedy in the White House.* New York: Crown Publishers, 1983.

Schreiber, R. "Richard Nixon: A Mother's Story." *Good Housekeeping,* June 1960.

Schwartz, Gary T. "Urban Freeways and the Interstate System." *Southern California Law Review,* Vol. 49, March 1976.

Sevareid, Eric, ed. *Candidates 1960.* New York: Basic Books, 1959.

Slater, Ellis. *The Ike I Knew.* Privately printed, 1980.

Smith, Richard N. *Thomas E. Dewey and His Times.* New York: Simon & Schuster, 1982.

Sorenson, Theodore. *Kennedy.* New York: Harper & Row, 1965.

Spalding, Henry D. *The Nixon Nobody Knows*. Middle Village, N.Y.: Jonathan David, 1972.

Stripling, Robert E. *The Red Plot Against America*. Drexel Hill, Pa.: Bell, 1949.

Tiger, Edith, ed. *In Re Alger Hiss*. New York: Hill & Wang, 1979.

Viorst, Milton. "Nixon of the O.P.A." *New York Times Magazine*, October 3, 1971.

Voorhis, Jerry. *Confessions of a Congressman*. Garden City, N.Y.: Doubleday, 1947.

————. *The Strange Case of Richard Milhous Nixon*. New York: Popular Library, 1972.

Walters, Vernon. *Silent Missions*. Garden City, N.Y.: Doubleday, 1978.

Weinstein, Allen. *Perjury: The Hiss-Chambers Case*. New York: Knopf, 1978.

West, Jessamyn. *Hide and Seek: A Continuing Journey*. New York: Harcourt Brace Jovanovich, 1973.

————. "The Real Pat Nixon." *Good Housekeeping*, February 1971.

White, Theodore H. *The Making of the President 1960*. New York: Atheneum, 1962.

Wicker, Tom. "Nixon Starts Over—Alone." *New York Times Magazine*, May 13, 1962.

Wills, Garry. "The Hiss Connection Through Nixon's Life." *New York Times Magazine*, August 25, 1974.

————. *Nixon Agonistes: The Crisis of the Self-Made Man*. New York: Signet edition, New American Library, 1970.

Wilson, Richard. "Is Nixon Fit to Be President?" *Look*, February 24, 1953.

Witcover, Jules. *The Resurrection of Richard Nixon*. New York: G. P. Putnam's Sons, 1970.

Woods, Rose Mary. "Nixon's My Boss." *Saturday Evening Post*, December 28, 1957.

Wyden, Peter. *Bay of Pigs: The Untold Story*. London: Jonathan Cape, 1979.

INTERVIEWS

By author
Dwight D. Eisenhower
Milton S. Eisenhower

By California State University, Fullerton (CSF)
William Barton
Jane Milhous Beeson
Hortense Behrens
Wallace Black
Raymond Burbank
Ollie Burdg
Alma Chapman
Earl Chapman
Elizabeth Cloes
Ellen Cochran
Hoyt Corbit

Virginia Shaw Critchfield
Roy Day
Wilma Funk
Ella Furnas
James Grieves
Richard Heffern
Eloise Hilberg
William Hornaday
Charles Kendle
William Kepple
Helen Letts
Mrs. W. Loubet
Harold McCabe
Hadley Marshburn
Kyle Palmer
Lucille Parsons
Hubert Perry

Cecil Pickering
Elizabeth Guptill Rez
Ralph Rupard
Harry Schuyler
Mary Skidmore
Paul Smith
William Soeberg
Francis Stanley
Harold Stone
Edith Timberlake
Ellen Waer
Merle West
Floyd Wildermuth
Winifred Wingert
Merton Wray

*By Dulles Oral History Project,
Princeton*
Richard Nixon

*By Earl Warren Oral History
Project, University of
California, Berkeley (UCB)*
Roy Crocker
Roy Day
John Walton Dinkelspiel
Frank Jorgensen

By Eisenhower Library (EL)
Merriman Smith

MANUSCRIPTS

*EL (Eisenhower Library,
Abilene, Kansas)*
ACWD (Ann C. Whitman Diary)
CAHP (Christian A. Herter Papers)
C. D. Jackson Papers
C. D. Jackson Records
F. A. Seaton Papers
HD (Hagerty Diary)
JFD Papers (John Foster Dulles)
Minnich, Cabinet notes
Minnich, LLM (Legislative
Leaders Meeting)
NSC Minutes
William Rogers Papers
Summerfield Papers
WRP (William Robinson Papers)

Others
Alsop Papers, Library of Congress
Hoffman file, Harry S. Truman
Library
Lloyd Papers, Harry S. Truman
Library
Carl Mundt Papers, University
of South Dakota

VPP
(Richard M. Nixon Vice-President-
ial Papers, Laguna Niguel,
California)

Newspapers
Chicago *Daily News*
Chicago *Tribune*
Fresno *Bee*
Greensboro *Daily News*
London *Telegraph*
Los Angeles *Examiner*
Los Angeles *Herald Examiner*
Los Angeles *Times*
New York *Herald Tribune*
New York Times
Pasadena *Star News*
Quaker Campus
San Francisco *Chronicle*
Washington *Post*
Whittier *News*

ACKNOWLEDGMENTS

In the summer of 1983, when I was at my cabin in the wilds of northernmost Wisconsin writing the last chapter of my Eisenhower biography, my editor at Simon and Schuster, Alice Mayhew, called. She said she wanted me to write a biography of Richard Nixon. I protested, saying that I had never admired the man and did not want to write about him. She kept at me, and finally prevailed, primarily because she pointed out that nowhere else could I find so challenging or fascinating a subject. In her editing of the manuscript, she was tough, insightful, demanding, and enormously helpful. Her assistant, Ann Godoff, provided not only her wisdom and skill but also encouragement and support at a time I badly needed both.

It is a privilege to be able to work with such outstanding editors as Alice Mayhew and Ann Godoff. I would not have thought it possible that I could learn so much about writing as I have from their editing of this manuscript.

The copy editor, Patricia Miller, performed her crucial role in an insightful, imaginative, and thorough manner, saving me more embarrassing errors than I would want to count. I am very lucky to have her as copy-editor, and very grateful. Henry Ferris, of Simon and Schuster, oversaw the production of the volume, a daunting task with a manuscript of this size, but one that he carried through admirably and always in good humor.

It smacks of self-serving for an author to praise his publisher, but I have written enough books with enough publishers by now to feel confident that I can recognize quality, and I should like to

record that Simon and Schuster, from top to bottom, is a quality house.

Every historian depends absolutely on the archivists. In my case, I was fortunate to have archivists with the highest professional standards who were, as a bonus, consistently courteous and friendly. At the Eisenhower Library in Abilene, Kansas, Dr. John Wickman and his staff are the very model of what the archivists at a presidential library ought to be. The Nixon Papers have not yet found such a splendid home, but those that are available (covering 1946 to 1963, called his Vice-Presidential Papers) are at the Federal Archives at Laguna Niguel, California. Diane S. Nixon, the director of the Los Angeles Branch of the National Archives, Ken Rossman, in charge of the Vice-Presidential Papers, and Fred Klose, a member of the staff, were as helpful as they possibly could be.

A very special word of thanks is due Rose Mary Woods. As Nixon's personal secretary through most of the years covered in the Vice-Presidential Papers, she was the person responsible for maintaining his files. She did an outstanding job, as good as Ann Whitman did with Eisenhower's files, which is the highest praise I can give.

The staffs at Whittier College Library and at the Whittier Public Library were generous with their time, support, and encouragement. Shirley E. Stephenson, of the California State University (Fullerton) Oral History Program, was my guide through the hundreds of invaluable interviews with Nixon's childhood friends. I need also to thank the librarians at the Library of Congress, the Wisconsin State Historical Society, and North Dakota State for their help. At my own school, the University of New Orleans, Dr. Donald Hendricks, the director of the library, and his staff were, as always, indispensable. Without a modern, comprehensive university library across the campus from my office, I could not possibly undertake any major research tasks.

As 1986 is the twenty-fifty anniversary of the publication of my first book, I would like to pause and take note of how much more efficiently one can research and write history today as opposed to a quarter of a century ago, all thanks to the archivists and librarians of the nation. When I began, working in a manuscript collection meant taking notes from the documents by hand or on a typewriter. It was terribly time-consuming. One used what shortcuts one could —paraphrasing from a letter, summarizing, shorthand—but at the risk of serious error or overlooking a key phrase. Today, I can skim a letter, decide I want it, and for a pittance purchase a copy that is full, complete, and exact. By a rough estimate, the copying machines—and the staffs that so carefully make the copies for me—

have reduced my research time by a factor of twenty. Put another way, I can now do in one week what formerly took five months.

Cooperation between libraries is now much better than it was in the fifties, to the great benefit of researchers. Obscure books used to require long searches; today the interlibrary loan system can deliver virtually any book within a matter of days to your own library. So too with articles from scholarly magazines and journals. In addition, libraries today are much more willing to send microfilm copies of their manuscript holdings to other libraries, which saves a great deal of time and travel. In short, librarians and archivists are my favorite people. The improvements they have brought about in the last twenty-five years are invaluable to me. The copying machine and microfilm I regard as the most important products of the technological revolution in my lifetime—although the electric typewriter is also high on my list.

The final copy of the manuscript was typed by Mrs. Elizabeth Smith. Betty and I have been working together since 1965. We have been close friends all those years. It is impossible for me to imagine how I could do a book without her.

The Notes show my debt to previous biographers, but I would like to especially thank Bela Kornitzer, Earl Mazo, William Costello, and Fawn Brodie for their pathbreaking labors.

Many friends have spent many hours talking with me about Nixon, giving me the benefit of their insights and information. I want to thank them all, especially Joe Logsdon, Ollie Brown, Michael Beschloss, Tom Reeves, Michael Foot, the late Ronald Lewin, Kent Beck, Julian Pleasants, Ted Wilson, Jim Wimmer, and Dick Lamm. My agent, John Ware, was a source of support throughout.

My daughter and my wife worked full time as research assistants. Stephenie Ambrose Tubbs, who has an M.A. in history from the University of Montana, went through sixteen years of *The New York Times*, the Los Angeles *Times*, and the San Francisco *Chronicle*, as well as selected years of other California newspapers, copying the Nixon items for me. She also found and copied the Nixon speeches and remarks in the *Congressional Record* for the period from 1947 to 1953. Moira Buckley Ambrose helped me go through and select items in the Eisenhower Library, concentrating on the handwritten minutes of Cabinet and Legislative Leaders' meetings. At Laguna Niguel, she spent months with me going through the Nixon Vice-Presidential Papers, one by one, making selections. On the average, one out of one hundred documents was worth copying (and about one out of every twenty copied were used in the final manuscript). This makes for long, dull hours of reading form letters, memos on trivial subjects, innumerable bread-and-butter notes, countless letters regretfully turning down invitations to make a speech, and so forth. But Moira never complained—although she did insist on taking an apartment overlooking the surf at Laguna Beach—and indeed would become as pleased as could be on finding a revealing document. Back home, she put the documents we had collected into chronological order for me.

Without Stephenie and Moira, I would be today still stuck in the research phase of Nixon's first fifty years, instead of looking forward to beginning the research on his resurrection, triumph, and fall.

Stephen E. Ambrose
The Cabin
Dunbar, Wisconsin
Memorial Day, 1986

INDEX

Humphreys, Robert, 404, 660
Hungary:
  refugees from, 423–26
  Soviet invasion of (1956), 419, 420–421, 422–23
Hunt, H. L., 244
Hunt, Howard, 624
Hunter, Ethel Farley, 78
Hutschnecker, Arnold, 351

Indochina, French, Nixon's visit to, 320–22
information, freedom of, 537
integration, 395–96, 407
  as issue in 1956 elections, 409, 413–414, 417
Inter-American Highway, 367–68
Internal Revenue Service (IRS), 597, 599
International Association of Machinists, 567
Interstate Highway System, 364–65, 485
Irwin, Jack, 246, 545
Ives, Irving, 251
Izvestia, 525

Jackson, Andrew, 15, 204, 415
Jackson, C. D., 312, 316–17, 327, 347–348, 363, 374
  Nixon's Southeast Asian initiatives and, 342–43
Jackson, Donald, 143
Jackson, Thomas "Stonewall," 80
James, Hubert E., 200
Jameson, Frank, 444–45
Jarvis, Howard, 656
Javits, Jacob, 434, 566
Jefferson, Thomas, 15, 40, 204, 415
Jenner, William, 141, 298
  on foreign policy, 240–41, 243
  Nixon on investigations by, 310–11
Jessup, Philip, 227, 239–40
Jesus Christ, 58, 468–69
Jobe, Gail, 65, 67, 78
Jobe, Ola Florence Welsh, 49, 55, 66–69, 70–71, 74, 78, 85, 99
Johansson, Ingemar, 543
John Birch Society, 643–45, 648, 656–658
Johnson, Joseph, 80
Johnson, Lady Bird, 302
Johnson, Lyndon, 302, 309, 539
  civil rights record of, 546
  Eisenhower's opinion of, 547, 600
  foreign aid and, 459–60
  1958 election and, 494, 503
  1960 presidential nomination and, 514, 601–2
  Nixon characterized by, 612
  Nixon compared with, 610, 618, 623

Nixon-Kennedy debate and, 581–582
Nixon's gubernatorial campaign and, 660
Nixon's Latin American trips and, 481
vice-presidential campaign of, 566, 580–81, 603, 607–8
vice-presidential nomination of, 545–46, 547, 549, 558
Johnston, Eric, 150
Johnston, Vic, 391
Joint Chiefs of Staff (JCS), 441, 519, 544, 561
Jones, Charles, 391
Jorgensen, Frank, 254
  California politics and, 446–47
  Nixon's campaign for House and, 120–22, 126
  Nixon's campaign for Senate and, 198, 201, 203, 209, 213
Judd, Walter, 259, 547, 553
Justice Department, U.S., 258, 435
  on Donald Nixon-Hughes loan, 597, 599
  Hiss case and, 173–74, 188–90, 192–195, 206, 226
  King's arrest and, 596
  Nixon investigated by, 295

Kaiser, Leland, 430
Kalmbach, Herbert, 652
Kansas City Star, 271, 418
Kaplow, Herb, 463, 477–78, 566
Katcher, Leo, 275, 276
Kaufman, Samuel, 200
Keating, Kenneth, 144, 502
Kefauver, Estes, 407, 558
Kendle, Charles, 61, 65–66
Kennedy, Jacqueline, 565
  husband as solicitous of, 585
  husband's 1960 presidential campaign and, 576–77
Kennedy, John F., 32, 104, 111, 304, 318, 407, 435, 627, 650
  administration of, Nixon's criticisms of, 630–34, 644
  age issue and, 601–2
  on aid to education, 588
  on Algerian independence, 433
  Allen Dulles's briefing of, 591–92, 640–42
  background of, 584–87
  on Cuba issue, 570, 590–92, 594–596, 632–34, 637, 640–41
  on defense, 549, 562
  Eisenhower's opinion of, 547, 558, 578, 600
  gregariousness of, 586
  health problems of, 485, 601–2
  Houston speech of, 566–67
  interviews given by, 595